D1453072

HISTORICAL DICTIONARIES OF
RELIGIONS, PHILOSOPHIES, AND MOVEMENTS
Edited by Jon Woronoff

1. *Buddhism*, by Charles S. Prebish, 1993
2. *Mormonism*, by Davis Bitton, 1994
3. *Ecumenical Christianity*, by Ans Joachim van der Bent, 1994
4. *Terrorism*, by Sean Anderson and Stephen Sloan, 1995
5. *Sikhism*, by W. H. McLeod, 1995
6. *Feminism*, by Janet K. Boles and Diane Long Hoeveler, 1995
7. *Olympic Movement*, by Ian Buchanan and Bill Mallon, 1995
8. *Methodism*, by Charles Yrigoyen Jr. and Susan E. Warrick, 1996
9. *Orthodox Church*, by Michael Prokurat, Alexander Golitzin, and Michael D. Peterson, 1996
10. *Organized Labor*, by James C. Docherty, 1996
11. *Civil Rights Movement*, by Ralph E. Luker, 1997
12. *Catholicism*, by William J. Collinge, 1997
13. *Hinduism*, by Bruce M. Sullivan, 1997
14. *North American Environmentalism*, by Edward R. Wells and Alan M. Schwartz, 1997
15. *Welfare State*, by Bent Greve, 1998
16. *Socialism*, by James C. Docherty, 1997
17. *Bahá'í Faith*, by High C. Adamson and Philip Hainsworth, 1998
18. *Taoism*, by Julian F. Pas in cooperation with Man Kam Leung, 1998
19. *Judaism*, by Norman Solomon, 1998
20. *Green Movement*, by Elim Papadakis, 1998
21. *Nietzscheanism*, by Carol Diethe, 1999
22. *Gay Liberation Movement*, by Ronald J. Hunt, 1999
23. *Islamic Fundamentalist Movements in the Arab World, Iran, and Turkey*, by Ahmad S. Moussalli, 1999
24. *Reformed Churches*, by Robert Benedetto, Darrell L. Guder, and Donald K. McKim, 1999
25. *Baptists*, by William H. Brackney, 1999
26. *Cooperative Movement*, by Jack Shaffer, 1999
27. *Reformation and Counter-Reformation*, by Hans J. Hillerbrand, 1999
28. *Shakers*, by Holley Gene Duffield, 1999

Historical Dictionary of the Cooperative Movement

Jack Shaffer

Historical Dictionaries of
Religions, Philosophies, and Movements, No. 26

The Scarecrow Press, Inc.
Lanham, Md., & London
1999

SCARECROW PRESS, INC.

Published in the United States of America
by Scarecrow Press, Inc.
4720 Boston Way, Lanham, Maryland 20706
http://www.scarecrowpress.com

4 Pleydell Gardens, Folkestone
Kent CT20 2DN, England

British Library Cataloguing in Publication Information Available

Library of Congress Cataloging-in-Publication Data

Shaffer, Jack, 1925–
    Historical dictionary of the cooperative movement / Jack Shaffer.
        p.   cm.—(Historical dictionaries of religions, philosophies, and
    movements ; no. 26)
    Includes bibliographical references (p.   ).
    ISBN 0-8108-3666-1 (cloth : alk. paper)
    1. Cooperation—History Dictionaries.   I. Title.   II. Series.
HD2956.S43   1999
334'.09—dc21   99-22973
                                                            CIP

⊗™ The paper used in this publication meets the minimum requirements of
American National Standard for Information Sciences—Permanence of Paper for
Printed Library Materials, ANSI/NISO Z39.48–1992. Manufactured in the United
States of America.

Contents

Editor's Foreword	vii
Preface	ix
Acronyms and Abbreviations	xiii
Chronology	1
Introduction	39
The Dictionary	141
Appendixes	
1. Year First Cooperatives Established	419
2. Types of Cooperatives by Country	427
3. Basic Data on Cooperatives by Country	437
Bibliography	445
About the Author	609

Editor's Foreword

The cooperative movement has attracted much less attention than more aggressive movements such as capitalism, socialism and communism. And its philosophy, while optimistic, is positively dull compared to their highly articulate ideologies. So much the better, one might remark. For this has allowed cooperatives to develop, assuming many different forms, and to grow in membership. They could also spread more widely, being accepted in capitalist countries, often promoted in democratic socialist ones, and even tolerated and used by communist regimes. While the cooperative movement has waxed less dramatically, it has, once established, rarely waned. Indeed, today there are more cooperatives than ever with more members than ever in more places than ever.

Unlike many other volumes in this series, the *Historical Dictionary of the Cooperative Movement* is virtually the sole reference work of its kind. It is the only single source one can consult to find information on different kinds of cooperatives; significant figures, including philosophers, pioneers, officials and leaders; and the cooperative situation in a large number of countries. It also has a handy list of acronyms, an extensive chronology of the international development of cooperatives, several useful appendixes and an exceptionally comprehensive bibliography. The introduction is a particularly enlightening summary of the movement.

To write this volume took some doing. Much of the material was available somewhere, but often in many different, occasionally inaccessible places. But part of the information had never been written down and could be supplied only by an author with broad experience and an intimate knowledge of the movement, a person like Jack Shaffer. Part of this knowledge was gained as an insider participating in coop buying clubs, consumer cooperatives, credit unions, a student housing cooperative and farming cooperatives. It also came partly as an outsider, a student of cooperation and coordinator of cooperative development for the United States Agency for International Development, where he managed USAID's relationships with American cooperatives. He gained worldwide perspective on the cooperative movement through his work as executive secretary of the Committee for the Promotion and Advancement of Cooperatives and as a consultant to the International Cooperative Alliance and the World Council of Credit Unions. Jack's deep understanding and strong belief in the cooperative movement has allowed him to write a unique work.

Jon Woronoff
Series Editor

Preface

Cooperatives are found everywhere, doing all kinds of things. Identify almost any human activity involving a group of people, and among some of them you will find a cooperative. They are crucial elements in the economies of more than half the countries of the world, large and small. Among the other countries they are still a fledgling movement or, as in a number of nations, their memberships have not yet developed the "evangelistic" enthusiasm and zeal necessary for a group activity to become a popular movement. Cooperatives carry on their affairs in virtually all the languages of the world, located as they are in all populated parts of the planet. Their affairs are carried out by elected leadership that runs the gamut from the illiterate to the scholarly. They are made up of rich and poor, though nearly all their members aspire to be more the former than the latter and hope that their cooperative can help in that regard.

An American politician (nameless in my memory) once commented that "all politics are local." In a sense, that is true of cooperatives as well. They rise or fall largely determined by how they serve their local members. But cooperatives as a popular movement will also be judged in other ways. A judgment will be made on the totality of their impact—local, national and international. People will ask about how they helped ameliorate the economic and social problems of the dispossessed. But they will also inquire about their influence on economic systems, whether these were made more humane, egalitarian and inclusive in their benefits because of cooperative principles and practices. Their impact upon the international order will be judged collectively by how they contributed more than just resolutions to peace, but to justice and human inclusiveness.

This book provides readers with only snapshot views of the cooperative movement in all its diversity. The brevity of many entries is acknowledged, and many readers will be disturbed to find the history and present complexity of their national movements reduced to a few paragraphs. I apologize in advance to those I may have offended by such necessary brevity.

This handbook to the cooperative movement is a distillation of the works of a host of anonymous people. I have tried to identify many of them in the bibliography and thereby make them accessible to a wider audience. Because of the sheer volume of sources, however, I have almost exclusively restricted citations to published books. The vast literature to be found in periodicals and journals, much of equal insight, remains to be collected, reviewed and properly catalogued.

Several sources referred to extensively require special acknowledgment. For information on the ongoing historical development of the cooperative movement in all its complexity, the *Review of International Cooperation* of the International Cooperative Alliance, the *Year Book of Agricultural Cooperation* of the Plunkett Foundation, and *Cooperative Information* published for many years by the International Labour Office were invaluable resources. Two special supplements to *Cooperative Information* were of great help and are recommended to anyone trying to further document and understand the evolution of the cooperative movement: *Supplement No. 1, Bibliography*, published in September 1973 as *Survey of Cooperative Literature from 1813 to 1973*, and *Supplement No. 2, Cooperative Chronology*, also published in 1973, which chronicle year-by-year, country-by-country, and event-by-event much of the complex history of cooperation to that date.

For the accumulation of statistical data, several sources should be acknowledged for their usefulness. The several statistical reports prepared on a current basis by the headquarters and regional offices of the International Cooperative Alliance were particularly important and useful. The annual reports and statistical reports of the World Council of Credit Unions were unique and invaluable in portraying the status of their sector of the cooperative movement. The *International Directory of Cooperative Organizations, Thirteenth Edition*, published in 1988 by the International Labour Office, was a valuable resource for a number of countries where data remains sketchy. *The Cooperative Network in Developing Countries—A Statistical Profile*, published by the Committee for the Promotion and Advancement of Cooperatives in February 1987, was useful in providing data on a number of developing-country cooperative movements. The statistical tables of the annual World Bank *World Development Report* were used as a common basis for national data.

Special thanks go to some people who have been particularly helpful in making this book a reality, including the staff of the International Cooperative Alliance, particularly Alina Pawlowska, MariaElena Chavez, and Mary Treacy, and Gabriella Ulrich, then of the Cooperative Branch of the International Labour Office. The library resources of the International Cooperative Alliance, the International Labour Office, the Committee for the

Promotion and Advancement of Cooperatives, and the United States Library of Congress proved to be particularly valuable.

Thanks are also due to a number of people whose interest and volunteer efforts helped bring this volume into existence. Two family members were particularly helpful. My wife, Judy Shaffer, not only tolerated the spread of cooperative documents and papers throughout our home but edited the manuscript at various points, including the French citations in the bibliography. My daughter, Kimberly Shaffer, not only organized and made corrections in the computer version of the text at a number of points but literally saved the project by completing essential research at the International Cooperative Alliance in Geneva at a crucial point when I was unable to undertake it myself. Thanks to Mariana Griff, who edited the Spanish citations, and to Edu von Keber, who handled the German. Jon Woronoff has been a most patient and helpful editor.

Finally, I want to dedicate this book to two people who many years ago played an important role in my intellectual and ethical development—my most important "gurus," if you will. Dr. Harvey Seifert, professor of social ethics at the Claremont School of Theology, introduced me in a systematic way to cooperation and the cooperative movement. His view that organized cooperation represented the most ethical of contemporary economic alternatives still resonates with my reality. Dr. Paul Irwin, professor of religious education at Claremont, blazoned democracy as the guiding precept of sound learning and of group action, both principles that guide the cooperative movement at its best. To these men I say thanks for these and other helpful guideposts that they pointed out and that have given direction to my life and work. Harvey and Paul, this book's for you!

Acronyms and Abbreviations

ACCOSCA	African Confederation of Cooperative Savings and Credit Associations
ACCU	Asian Confederation of Credit Unions
ACDI	Agricultural Cooperative Development International
ACI	Alliance coopérative internationale; Alianza Cooperativa Internacional (French and Spanish titles for ICA)
AIC	American Institute of Cooperation
BIT	Bureau international de travail (French title of ILO)
CBI	Cooperative Business International
CCA	Canadian Cooperative Association
CCC-CA	Confederación de Cooperativas del Caribe y Centro América
CCCU	Caribbean Confederation of Credit Unions
CEMAS	Cooperative Educational Materials Advisory Service
CENTROSOYUS	Apex cooperative in Russia
CHF	Cooperative Housing Foundation
CICOPA	International Organization of Industrial, Artisanal and Service Producers Cooperatives
CIRCOM	International Research Center for Rural Cooperative Communities, Israel
CIRIEC	International Center of Research and Information Center on the Public, Social and Cooperative Economy
CLEAR UNIT	Cooperative Liaison, Education, and Research Unit, Cooperative College, Loughborough

CLICEC	International Liaison Committee on Cooperative Thrift and Credit
CLUSA	Cooperative League of the U.S.A.
COADY	Coady International Institute, St. Francis Xavier University, Canada
COGECA	Comité général de la coopération agricole of the European Union cooperatives
COLAC	Confederación Latinoamericana de Cooperativas de Ahorro y Crédito
COOP UNION	The Cooperative Union Ltd., United Kingdom
COPAC	Committee for the Promotion and Advancement of Cooperatives
CUC	Cooperative Union of Canada
CUCC	Credit Union Central of Canada
CUNA	Credit Union National Association
CUNA MUTUAL	CUNA Mutual Insurance Society, U.S.A.
CWS	Cooperative Wholesale Society
DESWOS	Development Assistance Association for Social Housing, Germany
DG BANK	Deutsche Genossenschaftskasse
ECOSOC	United Nations Economic and Social Council
FAO	Food and Agriculture Organization
FCA	Farm Credit Administration, U.S. Government
FCH	Foundation for Cooperative Housing (Renamed Cooperative Housing Foundation)
FCS	Farmer Cooperative Service, U.S. Department of Agriculture
FECOLAC	Fundación Educativa de la COLAC
FNCC	Fédération nationale des coopératives de consommation, France

GPO	Government Printing Office, U.S.A.
Grange	National Grange of the Patrons of Husbandry
HMO	Health Maintenance Organization
ICA	International Cooperative Alliance
ICHDA	International Cooperative Housing Development Association
ICMIF	International Cooperative and Mutual Insurance Federation
ICPA	International Cooperative Petroleum Association
ICWS	International Cooperative Wholesale Society
IDACA	Institute for the Development of Agricultural Cooperatives in Asia
IFAP	International Federation of Agricultural Producers
IFPAAW	International Federation of Plantation, Agricultural and Allied Workers
IHEC	Institut des hautes études coopératives
ILO	International Labour Office (Secretariat for the International Labour Organisation)
ILO	International Labour Organisation
ILO DIRECTORY (1988)	International Directory of Cooperative Organizations, Thirteenth Edition (1988)
INTERCOOP	Intercoop Editora Cooperativa Limitada, Argentina
INTER-COOP	International Organization for Consumer Cooperative Distributive Trade
IRU	International Raiffeisen Union
IUF	International Union of Food, Agricultural, Hotel, Restaurant, Catering, Tobacco and Allied Workers' Associations
KF	Kooperativa Förbundet, Sweden
MATCOM	Materials and Techniques for Cooperative Management

MEHTA	Vaikunth Mehta National Institute of Cooperative Management, India
NAF	Nordisk Andelsförbund (Scandinavian Cooperative Wholesale Society)
NASCO	North American Students of Cooperation
NCBA	National Cooperative Business Association
NCFC	National Council of Farmer Cooperatives
NCUI	National Cooperative Union of India
[n.d.]	Date of publication not identified
[n.l.]	Location of publisher not identified
NGO	Non-Governmental Organization
[n.p.]	Name of publisher not identified
NRECA	National Rural Electric Cooperative Association
OAS	Organization of American States
OCA	Organización de las Cooperativas de América
OCDC	Overseas Cooperative Development Committee, U.S.
ODA	Overseas Development Administration, U.K.
OIT	Oficina Internacional de Trabajo (Spanish title of the International Labour Office)
OK	Sveriges Olijekonsumenternas Riksförbund (Swedish Oil Consumers' Cooperatives Federation)
ORCC	ACI, Oficina Regional para Centroamérica y el Caribe
PAU	Pan American Union
PCPI	Parent Cooperative Preschools International
Plunkett	Plunkett Foundation for Cooperative Studies
PUF	Presses universitaires de France
RABOBANK	Coöperatieve Raiffeisen-Boerenleenbank
ROAM	ICA Regional Office for the Americas

ROAP	ICA Regional Office for Asia and the Pacific
ROECSA	ICA Regional Office for East, Central and Southern Africa
ROECSEA	ICA Regional Office and Education Center for South-East Asia (Renamed ROAP)
ROWA	ICA Regional Office for West Africa
SCC	Swedish Cooperative Center
SDID	Société de développement international Desjardins, Canada
SIDA	Swedish International Development Authority
SIDEFCOOP	Sociedad Interamericana de Desarrollo y Financiamiento Cooperativo
SOCODEVI	Société coopérative de développement international, Canada
UN	United Nations
UNCTAD	United Nations Conference on Trade and Development
UNDP	United Nations Development Program
UNESCO	United Nations Educational, Scientific and Cultural Organization
UN Habitat	United Nations Center for Human Settlements
UNIDO	United Nations Industrial Development Organization
UNIFEM	United Nations Development Fund for Women
UNRISID	United Nations Research Institute for Social Development
USAID	U.S. Agency for International Development
USC	Union Suisse des Coopératives (Swiss Union of Co-operatives; see also VSK)
USDA	U.S. Department of Agriculture

VSK	Verband Schweizerische Konsumvereine (Swiss Union of Cooperatives; see also USC)
WFP	World Food Program
WOCCU	World Council of Credit Unions
WORLD BANK	International Bank for Reconstruction and Development
WPA	Works Progress Administration, U.S. Government

Chronology

A chronology of the evolution of the whole cooperative movement in all its national manifestations would be a massive undertaking, too large for this book. Instead, this selected chronology acknowledges national movements as they emerge at particular points in time, but gives major attention to the events that were manifestations of a growing international movement.

1750s Cheesemakers' cooperatives established in Franche-Comté in France; they were the world's first producer cooperatives and the first cooperatives in France.

A mutual fire insurance society established in London; it was the first cooperative in the United Kingdom (U.K.).

Benjamin Franklin and others established a fire protection company in Philadelphia; it soon became the Philadelphia Contributionship for the Insurance of Houses from Loss by Fire (still in existence today). This is regarded as the first cooperative in the United States of America (U.S.).

1780 The first cooperative in Greece, the Red Yarn Cooperative, established in Ambelakia, Thessaly.

1781 *Leonard and Gertrude*, a novel defining the cooperative ideal, began to be published by Henri Pestalozzi in Switzerland.

1794 Watchmakers' commercial associations established in Vienna.

1799 Le Phalanstère, an early cooperative-like community, based on principles of voluntarism, harmony and self-support, founded in France by François Marie Charles Fourier.

New Lanark on the Clyde established in the U.K. by Robert Owen, initiating his experiments with creating cooperative communities.

1806 Worker-run collective dairy farm established in Osoppo, Italy, the world's first dairy cooperative and the first cooperative in Italy.

1808 Gardeners' and farmers' societies established in Luxembourg, the first agricultural cooperatives in the modern cooperative era and the first cooperatives in Luxembourg.

1816 Hrubieszow, an agricultural society, established in partitioned Poland, the first cooperative in that country.

Cheesemakers' cooperative societies established in Bern and Fribourg, Switzerland, the first Swiss cooperatives.

1821 The Cooperative and Economical Society, London, began publication of *The Economist*, the first newspaper dealing with cooperative ideas.

1825 Big Artel, a consumer cooperative, established in Siberia, the first cooperative in Russia.

New Harmony, a cooperative community in the state of Indiana, U.S., founded by Robert Owen. It proved to be unsuccessful as originally planned on utopian principles.

1828 The first U.K. consumer cooperative, the Cooperative Trading Association, organized at Brighton by Dr. William King. It is often cited as the first consumer cooperative of the modern cooperative era. King also established a cooperative newspaper, *The Cooperator*, which was published regularly until 1830.

1829 François Marie Charles Fourier published *Le Nouveau monde industriel et sociétaire* in Paris.

1830 The first cooperative factory in the U.K. established in London.

1831 The first French workers' cooperative established in Paris.

The first British cooperative congress held at Manchester, U.K., the first time representatives of an entire national cooperative movement met in a national congress.

1832 Philippe Buchez, theorist of the workers' cooperative movement in France, founded a review, *L'Européen*, set up a cabinetmakers' cooperative and, for the first time, proposed model cooperative bylaws that included the principle of "a perpetual and untransferable reserve fund."

1835 In the U.K. Robert Owen established the Association of All Classes of All Nations, the first attempt to form an international organization connected with cooperation. The bylaws provided for the creation of a central cooperative society with branches in all parts of the world. The Association and its journal, *The New Moral World,* ceased operations in 1839.

1838 Asociación General de Ganaderos de España (General Association of Spanish Stock Breeders), the first cooperative in Spain, established in Madrid.

1839 Louis Blanc published *L'Organisation du travail* (The Organization of Work) in France, defining the basis of the workers' cooperative movement.

Caja de Ahorros (Savings Bank), the first cooperative in Mexico, established in Orizaba.

1841 Brook Farm organized at West Roxbury (near Boston), Massachusetts, in an attempt to establish a utopian cooperative community in the U.S. It operated until 1847.

1843 Hotokusha, a farmers' and handicraft workers' collective, established as Japan's first cooperative.

1844 The first Icelandic cooperative, a supply association, established.

The Equitable Pioneers of Rochdale Society established near Manchester, U.K. The founding and operation of this cooperative is regarded by many as the event marking the start of the modern cooperative movement.

1845 The first German cooperative established in Chemnitz.

Spolek Gazdovski established in Sobotiste, the first-ever credit cooperative and the first cooperative in Slovakia.

1846 A Bread Committee was established by Friedrich Wilhelm Raiffeisen, the mayor of Weyerbusch, Germany, to combat famine during a period of scarcity. This marked the beginning of Raiffeisen's cooperative activity.

The Friendly Societies Act of the U.K. established the position of Registrar of Cooperatives in the government, the first such governmental position.

1847 J. M. Faibre established Teresa Cristina, a cooperative group, at Paraña; the first cooperative in Brazil.

1848 The first Belgian cooperatives (of bakers) established.

1849 Hermann Schulze-Delitzsch established his first cooperative society (of joiners) in Delitzsch, Germany, followed by a second for shoemakers.

Friedrich Wilhelm Raiffeisen established the Mutual Aid Association of Flammersfeld, Germany, his first credit association, from which the idea of rural credit cooperatives grew.

George Jacob Holyoake published *The Manual of Cooperation* in the U.K.

1850 Germany's first credit society (Vorschuszverein) established by Hermann Schulze-Delitzsch, marking the beginning of an urban credit cooperative movement.

The first Hungarian cooperative, a credit association, established in Beogterce.

Lagunda och Hagunda Haradere Varuanskaffnings Bolaget, Sweden's first cooperative, established in Orsundsbro.

1851 The first landowners' credit cooperative established in Denmark; it was also the first Danish cooperative.

Norway's first consumers' cooperative established by Marcus Thrane, the first cooperative in Norway.

A Schulze-Delitzsch credit cooperative established in Celsvec, the first cooperative in Slovenia, then part of Austria.

1852 The Viennese General Aid Group established, the precursor of the Austrian cooperative movement.

The first savings and food purchasing group established in Prague, becoming Bohemia's (later the Czech Republic's) first cooperative.

The first Romanian cooperative, a credit society, established.

The Industrial and Provident Societies Act enacted in the U.K., the world's first cooperative legislation.

1853 In Germany, Schulze-Delitzsche published his first book, *Assoziationsbuch für Deutsche Handwerker und Arbeiter* (Handbook for German Workers and Artisans).

The Central Cooperative Agency established in the U.K. by Edward Vansittart Neale, the world's first cooperative wholesale society and forerunner of the British cooperative wholesale societies.

1854 The first Raiffeisen rural credit cooperative organized in Heddesdorf, Germany.

Equitable Pioneers of Rochdale Society in the U.K. ceased operations.

1856 *The History of the Equitable Pioneers of Rochdale,* by J. G. Holyoake, published in the U.K. It was used to promote cooperative principles and organization throughout Europe.

1859 The first Australian cooperative society established in Brisbane.

The first Irish consumer cooperative society established in Inchicore (Dublin), the first Irish cooperative.

1860 The first Latvian consumer cooperative established in Riga, the first cooperative in Latvia (then part of Russia).

The first Dutch cooperative, a consumer society, established.

1861 The first Canadian cooperative established in Stellarton, Nova Scotia.

1863 Nemleket Sandigi, a cooperative credit association, established, the first Bulgarian cooperative and the forerunner of the Bulgarian Cooperative Bank.

The first cooperative, an agricultural credit society, established in Turkey.

1864 In Germany, Karl Marx discussed in his *Manifesto* the social value of the cooperative movement.

1865 The first cooperative banks were established in Germany by Schulze-Delitzsch and in Italy by Luigi Luzzatti.

1866 The Geneva Congress of the Workers' International declared that labor unions "should attempt to spread the cooperative movement without directing it or imposing any kind of doctrine on it."

1867 Committee formed in France to organize an International Cooperators' Congress during the Universal Exhibition in Paris. The meeting was canceled due to French government opposition.

1868 In Germany, Otto von Gierke used the term "cooperative law" for the first time.

1869 The London Congress, the first European cooperative congress, held in London, was convened by the British cooperative movement.

The first cooperative established in Lithuania.

1870 The first Finnish cooperatives, consumer societies, established in Viiperi and Tampere.

The first handicraft and consumer cooperatives established in Belgrade, the first Serbian societies in what later became part of Yugoslavia.

1871 Sociedad Cooperativa e Caixa Económica de Porto, the first Portuguese cooperative society, established.

1872 The first Swedish housing cooperative established (the world's first housing cooperative).

1875 The first Argentine cooperative, the Sociedad de Producción y Consumo, established.

1876 Coopvie Les artisans, the first Canadian life insurance cooperative, established in Quebec City.

The first cooperative established in Honduras.

1878 Petach Tikva, the first Jewish cooperative settlement, established in Palestine (now Israel).

1881 The New Zealand Farmers' Cooperative Association of Canterbury, Christchurch, established, the first New Zealand cooperative.

1882 The first pharmaceutical cooperative established in Belgium.

The Advisory Education Committee established in the U.K. This was the forerunner of the Cooperative College at Stanford Hall, Loughborough, the first cooperative college.

1883 Cooperative Women's Guild of England and Wales established in London, marking the beginning of cooperative women's guilds, later established in various countries.

1885 First Canadian consumer cooperative established in Winnipeg.

1886 Société d'économie populaire, an adult education association, founded by Edouard de Boyve and Auguste Fabre in Nîmes, France. Joined later by Charles Gide, it became known as the École de Nîmes (School of Nimes).

At the Cooperative Congress in Plymouth, U.K., Edouard de Boyve proposed the creation of an international cooperative federation.

1887 The first telephone cooperative founded by David Atwell in Buenos Aires, Argentina; it existed until 1925.

First Canadian cooperative legislation enacted in the Province of Manitoba.

1888 Albert Shaw, in conjunction with Johns Hopkins University, published *The History of Cooperation in the United States*.

1890 Coop Suisse, the Swiss consumer cooperative organization, established.

1891 Beatrice Potter Webb of the U.K. published *The Cooperative Movement in Great Britain*.

Herbert Myrick of the U.S. published *How to Cooperate*.

1892 Edward Vansittart Neale and Edward Owen Greening introduced a resolution at the Cooperative Congress in the U.K.; this was approved, endorsing the principle of an "international cooperative alliance."

1893 A general assembly of cooperatives, organized by Edward Owen Greening and Henry W. Wolff, adopted the proposals of George Jacob Holyoake (that the name of the new international organization be the International Cooperative Alliance [ICA]) and Horace Plunkett (that the alliance embrace all the recognized types of cooperatives). An executive committee was put in charge of preparing the bylaws for the organization and preparing for an international congress in 1894 (later changed to 1895).

The first cooperatives (consumer) established in Uzbekistan at Tashkent, Samarkand and Bokhara.

1894   The Congress of the Italian League of Cooperatives proposed the celebration of an annual Cooperation Day; the idea was adopted internationally 30 years later.

1895   The London Cooperative Congress, during which the ICA was formally established, was held.

Preuszische Zentralgenossenschaftskasse (Central Cooperative Bank of Prussia) established in Germany. This was the forerunner of the Deutsche Genossenschaftskasse (DG or German Cooperative Bank).

1896   Second Congress of the ICA held in Paris, France. Principal discussions were held regarding individual and group participation in the Alliance, relationships with agricultural cooperatives, and the role of the organization in international relations.

Appointment of a professor of cooperatives at the National University in El Salvador, one of the earliest such academic positions.

1897   Third Congress of the ICA held at Delft, Netherlands, at which the discussions of the previous year's congress continued. This was the last congress in which individual members not representing cooperative organizations played a prominent role.

1898   The first cooperative established in Estonia (then a province of Russia).

The Moscow Union of Consumer Societies established in Russia; it eventually became the All-Russia Union of Consumers' Societies and joined the ICA in 1903.

1899   First mention of school cooperatives, by L. Mabilleau in the French publication *L'Almanach de la coopération française.*

1900   Fourth Congress of the ICA held in Paris, France. Principal discussions focused on participation and international relations. Wholesale stores were also a matter of concern.

La Caisse populaire de Lévis founded by Alphonse Desjardins in Canada, the first credit cooperative in North America. This marked the beginning of the credit union movement in North America.

Charles Gide published *La Coopération* in Paris, France.

The first cooperatives (credit) established in India.

1901   The first cooperatives, provident societies, established in Algeria.

1902 Fifth Congress of the ICA held at Manchester, U.K. Discussions continued as to what organizations should be encouraged to participate in the Alliance. The most controversy involved those advocating profit-sharing with cooperative employees. Other concerns were for workers' housing, the cooperatives' role and the Alliance's role in achieving and maintaining world peace.

Boers Farmers' Cooperative established in South Africa, the first cooperative in Sub-Saharan Africa.

Territorial Grain Growers' Association established in Regina, Saskatchewan, forerunner of the grain cooperatives in midwest Canada.

1903 The Cooperative Union of India joined the ICA.

Sociedad Cooperativa de Ahorros y Construcciones de Porlamar (Porlamar Thrift and Building Cooperative Society) established in Nueva Esparta, Venezuela. It was the first thrift and building cooperative and the first cooperative in Venezuela.

First Canadian agricultural cooperatives established in Adamsville, Quebec (founded by l'abbé Allaire); in Nova Scotia (L'Assomption); and in Winnipeg (the United Farmers of Manitoba).

1904 Sixth Congress of the ICA held in Budapest, Hungary. Agricultural cooperation was a matter of major concern, as was cooperative credit and the relations between cooperatives and the state.

Two types of cooperatives, consumer and thrift, were organized, the first cooperatives in Chile.

The first cooperative established in what would later become Pakistan. The first use of cooperatives in the health field took place in Denmark with the organization of an association of sanatoria.

1905 El Hogar Obrero, a consumer credit and building cooperative, established in Buenos Aires, Argentina, and entered as the first in the newly established register of cooperatives.

The first cooperative, a credit society, was established in East Bengal, in the area that would later become Bangladesh.

The first cooperative societies established in Myanmar (Burma) and Tunisia.

1906 *International Cooperative Bibliography* published by the International Cooperative Alliance (ICA).

The first cooperatives established in Guatemala and Sri Lanka.

Quebec Syndicates Act passed, the first legislation enacted dealing with Canadian credit unions; general cooperative legislation passed two years later.

1907   Seventh Congress of the ICA held at Cremona, Italy. Particular attention was given to relationships with agricultural cooperatives and to the operation of wholesale stores.

The first cooperatives established in Korea.

Edward A. Filene, a Boston merchant, initiated promotion of the U.S. credit union movement after visiting similar organizations in Germany and India. Activation of a U.S. movement was a key event in the developments leading ultimately to the organization of the World Council of Credit Unions (WOCCU).

1908   *The International Cooperative Bulletin* began publication under the auspices of the ICA; in 1928, it became *The International Review of Cooperation.*

The first cooperatives established in Egypt (agricultural) and in Indonesia (Koperasi Ruruals Tangga).

Bernard Lavergne published *Le Régime coopératif, étude générale de la coopération de consommation en Europe*, one of the earliest transnational studies of a sector of cooperative development.

The Zionist Congress in Palestine adopted a policy of forming cooperative settlements. As a result, the first kibbutz was established in Deganaya.

The first settlers' cooperative, Lumbwa Cooperative Creamery, established in Kenya.

1909   The first edition of the *International Index of the Cooperative Press* published by the ICA. It has since been reissued irregularly, most recently in 1990 when it listed 145 organizations in 42 countries.

The Cooperative Union of Canada (CUC) established in Ottawa, Canada, later renamed the Canadian Cooperative Association (CCA).

The first cooperatives established in Cyprus (agricultural) and Uruguay.

Leo Tolstoy published a *Letter about Cooperation* in Russia, in which he cited cooperatives as ideal instruments for social development.

First credit unions established in the United States, assisted by Canadian Alphonse Desjardin; the first U.S. credit union legislation is passed in the Commonwealth of Massachusetts.

1910   Eighth Congress of the ICA held at Hamburg, Germany. It included a major discussion of "A Platform for Cooperative Socialism."

A mutual aid association established in Niger, regarded as the first cooperative in that country.

The first rural cooperatives established in the Philippines; they were the first cooperatives in the country.

1912 President Sun Yat-Sen of China helped launch the Chinese cooperative movement, and the first cooperatives were established.

A shoemakers' cooperative was established, the first cooperative in El Salvador.

The first congress of collective farms held in Italy.

The first cooperative in Taiwan (then known as Formosa) established during the period of Japanese occupation after the Sino-Japanese war.

The first mutual agricultural credit fund established in My Tho, the first cooperative in what is now the Socialist Republic of Vietnam (then part of French Indochina).

1913 Ninth Congress of the ICA held in Glasgow, Scotland. Intercooperative relations and international relations were the principal matters of attention.

Cooperative Societies Ordinance enacted in Mauritius and credit cooperatives established, the first cooperatives in that country.

The first Ugandan cooperative (agricultural) was established in Buganda.

First cooperative legislation enacted in the three prairie provinces of Canada—Alberta, Saskatchewan and Manitoba—and first cooperative grain elevators established.

1914 The first cooperative established in Nicaragua.

The Clayton Anti-Trust Law enacted in the U.S. To encourage their development, cooperatives were exempted from certain anti-trust provisions affecting other businesses.

The first cooperative established in Zambia by European settlers.

1915 Consorzio Agrario Cooperativo, the first Libyan cooperative, established.

1916 The first Colombian cooperative established.

The first consumer cooperative in French-speaking Africa established in Dakar, Senegal.

The first Agricultural Credit Societies Ordinance enacted in Trinidad and Tobago, leading to the establishment of the first cooperatives that same year.

The Cooperative League of the USA (CLUSA) established in Chicago, Illinois, joining ICA as the U.S. cooperative apex organization. In 1985 it was renamed the National Cooperative Business Association (NCBA).

1917 A Raiffeisen-style credit cooperative established as the first cooperative in Thailand.

The Central Cooperative Parliamentary Committee established in the U.K. to represent cooperative interests in the British Parliament; it became the Cooperative Party in 1919.

1918 Nordisk Andelsförbund (NAF), the Nordic Cooperative Wholesale Society, established in Copenhagen, Denmark. It involved consumer cooperative organizations from Denmark, Norway and Sweden (also from Finland in 1928 and Iceland after 1949).

A decree regarding consumer cooperatives issued by the Russian government. It was the first Soviet law concerning cooperatives, and it authorized placement of communist officials on the boards of directors of Centrosoyus and other cooperatives.

1919 The first use of cooperatives in a public health campaign took place in Calcutta, India, where they organized a network of anti-malaria cooperatives.

Protectora del Obrero (Protector of the Worker), the first Ecuadoran cooperative, established in Guayaquil.

The first school cooperative (student cooperative) in the world established in France.

The first cooperatives established in Mali.

Cooperativa de Consumo de Empleados y Obreros de los Ferrocarriles del Sur (Railway Workers' Consumer Cooperative) established in Arequipa, Peru, becoming the first Peruvian cooperative.

The Horace Plunkett Foundation established in London.

The Cooperative College established in Stanford Hall, Loughborough, U.K.

First invalids' (disabled persons') cooperative established in Poland; members were principally veterans of World War I.

1920 The Cooperative Service created within the International Labour Office, the Secretariat for the International Labour Organisation (ILO). The Service was designed to carry out the ILO's interest and activities in support of the cooperative movement worldwide.

The first edition of the *International Directory of Cooperative Organizations* published by the ILO. This was an attempt by the ILO to list the major cooperative organizations of the world. There have been 13 irregularly produced editions, the latest in 1988.

The first cooperatives established in Costa Rica, Cyprus (Turkish section), Malaysia, Puerto Rico and Suriname.

Caisse nationale du crédit agricole (National Agricultural Credit Bank) established in Paris.

Ukrainian Union of Consumer Cooperatives established.

1921 Tenth Congress of the ICA held at Basel, Switzerland. Relations between trade unions and cooperatives were a major concern of the Congress, along with the issue of international cooperative relations.

Government decree on cooperatives issued in Burundi and the first cooperatives established there.

Manifeste de l'école de Nîmes issued by Charles Gide in France.

Revue des études coopératives began publication in France.

Presses universitaires de France (PUF), a printing cooperative society, established in Paris. It has since been a major publisher of cooperative literature in French.

Moshav Nahalal established in Palestine, the first cooperative in the *moshav* movement.

Central People's Association established in Urga, the first cooperative in Mongolia.

The Cooperative Research Institute established in Krakow, Poland, the first such cooperative institute in the world.

Fédération suisse des pharmacies coopératives (Swiss Federation of Pharmacy Cooperatives) established in La Chaux-de-Fonds, Switzerland, the first federation for the cooperative pharmacy sector.

The Overseas Farmers' Cooperative Federation in London and the Marketing Agency of the New Zealand Produce Association established commercial relations. Similar relationships were developed by British cooperative organizations with cooperatives in Australia and South Africa.

The first International Cooperative Summer School organized by the Cooperative Union in the U.K. It was designed to be an orientation course on the international cooperative movement and the issues confronting it. From 1925 until the late 1970s, when it ceased functioning, it was an ICA-sponsored activity.

The first use of cooperatives to provide general health services took place in Yugoslavia where they were organized by Michael Avramovich.

1922 International Federation of Cooperative Insurers, now the International Cooperative and Mutual Insurance Federation (ICMIF), established as an auxiliary committee of the ICA.

International Cooperative Banking Committee established as an auxiliary committee of the ICA.

La Coopérative fédérée du Québec (Cooperative Federation of Quebec) established in Montreal.

Vsekopinsovet, a council of disabled persons' cooperatives, established in the Soviet Union.

The Fascist party in Italy created its own cooperative organization, Sindicato Italiano delle Cooperative. The Ente Nazionale Fascista della Cooperazione (National Fascist Cooperative Organization) was established by the government in Rome, and persecution of the existing cooperative movement began; a number of cooperative leaders went into exile.

The first cooperatives established in Jordan and Morocco.

Cooperative Societies Ordinance enacted in Malaysia; it established the world's first self-standing government cooperative service.

Division of Cooperative Marketing established in the U.S. Department of Agriculture, a forerunner of the Farmers Cooperative Service, which was set up in 1953.

1923 ICA declared the first Saturday in July as International Cooperative Day.

The Correspondence Committee of Cooperation established by the ILO at its headquarters in Geneva.

The Antigonish Movement was founded in Nova Scotia, Canada, by R. P. Romkins, Dr. Marcus Coady and A. B. MacDonald. Its international cooperative interests were formalized as the Coady International Institute, established in 1959.

The Central Cooperative Union of Japan became a member of the ICA.

Lenin's definition of the role of the cooperative movement in the Soviet system first appeared in the May 26 and 27, 1923, issues of *Pravda*. Cooperatives were acknowledged as a form of "socialist property."

The first cooperatives established in Zaire, then the Belgian Congo (until 1971, when it became the Republic of Zaire; it is now the Democratic Republic of the Congo).

1924 Eleventh Congress of the ICA held at Ghent, Belgium. Major discussions took place regarding the "Thomas Report" on inter-cooperative relations and on the issue of cooperative neutrality in matters of politics and religion.

The ICA established the International Cooperative Wholesale Society as a way of encouraging joint trading by the national wholesale cooperatives. It enjoyed only limited success and was absorbed into the International Trading Agency in 1945.

The ILO published the first issue of *Cooperative Information*; this ceased publication in 1975.

The Byelorussian Union of Consumer Cooperatives established.

A consumer cooperative established in Yaoundé; it was the first cooperative in Cameroon.

Vår Gård, a cooperative college, established in Sweden.

The Bridge, a newspaper of the Credit Union National Extension Bureau, began publication in Boston, Massachusetts, under the editorship of Roy Bergengren. Its name was changed in 1949 to *The Credit Union Bridge* and in 1963 to *The Credit Union Magazine*.

1925   The cooperative/Rainbow Flag, first proposed by F. Bernardot of France in 1896, was adopted by the ICA as an official ensign.

The National League of Italian Cooperative Societies (Lega), which had been established in 1892, was forced to dissolve. The Italian government claimed that it had engaged in "anti-national activity aimed at subverting the institutions and the regime."

The ICA protested to the Italian government regarding dissolution of the Lega.

The first Singapore credit cooperative (for civil servants) established, the first cooperative in Singapore.

The first cooperative in Tanzania, the Kilimanjaro Native Planters' Association, established.

The American Institute of Cooperation (AIC) established in Washington, D.C. It became an important voice, particularly for agricultural cooperatives, through its annual publication *American Cooperation*.

International Wholesale Cooperation published by Kooperativa Förbundet (KF), the consumer cooperative federation in Sweden; it promoted international trading among cooperatives.

1926   L'Amicale, an agricultural supply mutual society, established as the first cooperative in the Republic of Congo (then a French colony).

The first cooperatives established in Iran, Mauritania and Niger.

The first U.S. housing cooperative established in New York.

Midland Cooperative, the first U.S. petroleum cooperative, established in Minneapolis, Minnesota. This was also the first petroleum cooperative in the world.

1927   Twelfth Congress of the ICA held at Stockholm, Sweden. Discussion continued regarding inter-cooperative relations. Cooperation and socialism was also a major matter of attention.

ICA delegates participated in the World Economic Conference held in Geneva. The Congress proposed the establishment of an international commission of agricultural and consumer cooperative movements, but the proposal was never implemented.

Caisse centrale de crédit agricole mutuel (Central Organization of Mutual Agricultural Societies) established in Fort-de-France, the first cooperative in Martinique.

1928 The ICA changed the name of the *International Cooperative Bulletin* to the *Review of International Cooperation.*

The Finnish Cooperative Union joined the NAF (*see* 1918).

Office central de la coopération à l'école (Central Office of School Cooperatives) established in Paris, France. It became the focal point for the international promotion of school cooperatives.

The first cooperatives established in Ghana.

1929 National Congress on Cooperation held in Spain. Spain joined the ICA and requested promulgation of a cooperative law for Spain.

Caisse centrale de crédit agricole mutuel (Central Bank of Mutual Agricultural Credit Societies) established in Saint Denis, Réunion (an Overseas Department of France); it was the first cooperative in Réunion.

A cooperative hospital established in Elk City, Oklahoma; it was the first cooperative hospital in the world.

1930 Thirteenth Congress of the ICA held in Vienna, Austria. The discussions of the Congress focused on economic policy.

The first cooperatives established in Iraq (consumer and agricultural), Jamaica (Jamaica Coconut Producers' Association) and Western Nigeria (consumer cooperatives).

1931 The Correspondence Committee of the ILO became the International Committee on Inter-cooperative Relations. It was disbanded in 1938.

Mutual aid groups were established for the indigenous population in Upper Volta. They were the first cooperatives in what is now Burkina Faso.

The first cooperatives established in Guinea, Madagascar and Togo.

Kolkhozes (collective farms) established in the Soviet Union, and peasant ownership of land abolished.

Cooperative Proclamation issued and Swaziland Cooperative Tobacco Company established; it was the first cooperative in Swaziland.

1932 The first cooperative technical assistance mission undertaken by staff of the ILO, to Morocco. Assistance was provided by Maurice Colombain.

Fédération des caisses populaires Desjardins (Federation of Desjardins People's Banks) established in Quebec.

The first cooperatives established in Côte d'Ivoire (agricultural production) and Guadeloupe.

Van Well established SPAR in the Netherlands. This was part of the beginnings of a European cooperative retail network.

1933 Special ICA conference held at Basel, replacing the scheduled Congress (canceled due to financial problems of member movements); it included discussions of German cooperatives and the Nazi regime.

First English-language Canadian credit union established in Reserve Mines, Nova Scotia.

Central Union of Consumer Cooperative Societies dissolved by the German government; the structure was converted into an "Economic Enterprise of the German Labor Front."

Reichsverband der Deutschen Verbraucher-Genossenschaften (National Union of German Consumer Cooperatives) established; it functioned as an arm of the Nazi government, much like the Ente in Italy (*see* 1922).

The first cooperatives established in Guyana, and the first Arab cooperatives established in Palestine.

A law establishing the Cooperative Farm Credit System enacted by the U.S. Congress. The Farm Credit Administration was established to operate it. Initial financing was regarded as a loan from the U.S. government to be repaid by farm cooperatives. (It was repaid.)

1934 Fourteenth Congress of the ICA held in London. The Rochdale Principles, past and present, were the major concern of the Congress.

Credit Union National Association of Canada established in Hamilton, Canada. It was a predecessor of the present Credit Union Central of Canada.

The Federal Credit Union Law enacted in the U.S.

Credit Union National Association (CUNA) established in Estes Park, Colorado.

Relationships that developed as part of exporting petroleum products from the Consumer Cooperative Association's refinery in Kansas City to Sweden led to a joint proposal with the Swedish cooperative, KF, that an international cooperative petroleum association be launched. Such an organization was established by the ICA in 1947.

1935 The Rural Electrification Administration was established by an Act of the U.S. Congress, and the first U.S. rural electric cooperatives were organized.

1936 The first Canadian housing cooperative established in Reserve Mines, Nova Scotia.

First cooperative established in Sierra Leone.

The first students' cooperative established in the University of Texas.

1937 Fifteenth Congress of the ICA held in Paris. Discussions, continuing those of the 14th Congress, were held on the Rochdale Principles. Another major focus was on the role of cooperatives in various different economic systems.

The first cooperatives established in Haiti and Lebanon.

1938 The International Cooperative Trading Agency established by the ICA; it went out of business in 1952.

The report of the Nowell Commission of the U.K. recommended the establishment of cooperative departments and agricultural marketing cooperatives in the British colonies in West Africa.

1939 First cooperative established in Bolivia.

1940 The first cooperatives were established in Barbados (a livestock cooperative), Korea, and Saint Vincent and the Grenadines.

Central Union of Cooperative Societies of Japan withdrew from the ICA and issued a strong statement of support for the Japanese war in China.

1941 The first cooperatives established in Kuwait.

1942 An Agricultural Cooperatives Law enacted in Paraguay, and the first cooperative societies were established.

National Rural Electric Cooperative Association (NRECA) established in Washington, D.C., to pursue the interests and needs of the U.S. electricity cooperatives.

1943 Toledo Credit Union established, the first cooperative in Belize (then British Honduras).

The first Syrian cooperative established in Deir-Attye.

1944 On the occasion of the centenary of Rochdale and of the 50th anniversary of the ICA, a document was published by the ICA entitled *A Year of Cooperation, Brief History of the Birth and Development of National Movements in 44 Countries.*

Twenty-sixth session of the International Labour Conference, held in Philadelphia, Pennsylvania, adopted Recommendation No. 77, which stressed the national development of cooperatives.

1945 The ICA convened the London Conference in September 1945 to reestablish cooperative contacts and relationships after World War II; it was attended by representatives from Belgium, Denmark, Finland, France, Great Britain, Iceland, Holland, Norway, Palestine (Israel), Poland, Sweden, the U.S. and the USSR.

The ICA established a study committee to examine and make recommendations regarding the proposed establishment of an international cooperative petroleum association.

The Food and Agriculture Organization (FAO) created as part of the United Nations (UN). Agricultural cooperatives and their development were included in its program focus.

Cooperative Union of Bosnia-Herzegovina established in Sarajevo.

The first cooperatives established in Ethiopia (a consumer society) and Fiji.

Sveriges Olijekonsumenternas Riksförbund (OK), the Swedish Federation of Oil Consumers' Cooperatives, established in Stockholm.

1946 Sixteenth Congress of the ICA held at Zurich, Switzerland. The first American, Murray Lincoln, was elected to the executive committee of the Alliance. Discussions focused on the relations between cooperatives and public authorities and on cooperative policy.

The ILO established an advisory committee on cooperation; it operated until 1953.

During 1946, cooperatives were first established in Albania, the Bahamas, Dominica, the Dominican Republic, Lesotho, Malawi, Malta, Papua New Guinea and Saint Lucia.

The United Nations Educational, Scientific and Cultural Organization (UNESCO) was established; among its program concerns was an interest in the development and use of cooperatives as a vehicles for their program interests, particularly in education and literacy. UNESCO, through the ICA, has provided for international in-service training for selected cooperators.

Law 428 is enacted in Italy, dissolving the Ente Nazionale per la Cooperazione, which was established in 1922 by the Fascist government.

Cooperative League of Japan established, one of the moves to reestablish the Japanese cooperatives in the postwar period.

The Colonial Office of the British government published a model Cooperative Societies Ordinance for use in its colonies.

The North American Students' Cooperative League established in Chicago, Illinois.

1947 International Research and Information Center on the Public, Social and Cooperative Economy (CIRIEC), established in Geneva; it was later relocated to the University of Liège in Belgium.

International Cooperative Petroleum Association (ICPA) established.

The ICA proposed the establishment by the UN of a "Cooperative Administration" to manage Middle East petroleum production. The proposed cooperative would include both producer and consumer nations, but was never implemented.

During 1947 the first cooperatives were established in Benin, Hong Kong and Sudan.

Legislation was passed in France to establish general rules for the cooperative movements in the French overseas territories.

Institut für Genossenschaftswesen (Cooperative Institute) established in Marburg, Germany. This was the first of a number of university cooperative institutes established in postwar Germany.

Vaikunth Mehta National Institute of Cooperative Management established in Poona, India.

1948 Seventeenth Congress of the ICA held at Prague, Czechoslovakia. The principal issue discussed was "Cooperation and Nationalization."

The Organization of American States (OAS) established in Washington, D.C. The organization's aims included encouragement of and support for cooperatives in member countries.

Forschungsinstitut für Genossenschaftswesen (Cooperative Research Institute) established at the University of Erlangen, Germany.

Institut für Genossenschaftswesen (Cooperative Institute) established at the University of Munster, Germany.

1949 The first cooperatives (consumer and production) established in Chad.

Iceland cooperatives joined the NAF (*see* 1918).

The Chinese Cooperative League reestablished in Taiwan.

1950 During 1950, the first cooperatives were established in the Gambia, Nepal, the Solomon Islands and Somalia.

1951 Eighteenth Congress of the ICA held at Copenhagen, Denmark. Cooperative policy was the main topic.

Committee for Agricultural Cooperation established within the ICA.

International Federation of Young Cooperators established in Hamburg.

Young Agricultural Producers' Cooperatives established as the first cooperatives in Cuba.

Cooperative movement in Haiti developed with assistance from the U.S. International Cooperation Agency, the predecessor to the U.S. Agency for International Development (USAID). This was the first identified U.S. government assistance for cooperative development.

1952   International Cooperative Housing Committee established in ICA.
The General Cooperative Union of Macedonia established.

1953   East African Cooperative School established in Nairobi, Kenya;
it was designed to train registrars of cooperatives from anglophone
countries.
Canadian Cooperative Credit Society established; the name was later
changed to Credit Union Central of Canada.

1954   Nineteenth Congress of the ICA held in Paris. Discussions were
held regarding international cooperation and the report of ICA director W.
P. Watkins on cooperative development in developing countries.
Nordisk Andels-Eksport (Nordic Export Cooperative) established in
Copenhagen.
The first cooperatives established in Cambodia, Panama and Samoa.
The review *Communités—Archives internationales de sociologie et de
coopération* began publication in France.
Seminar für Genossenschaftswesen (Cooperative Institute) established
in Hamburg, Germany.

1955   The first cooperatives in the Cook Islands established.
The first consumer and supplies cooperatives established in South Vietnam.

1956   The International Cooperative Bank (INGEBA) established in Basel,
Switzerland.
The first meeting of Central America cooperative leaders held in Tegu-
cigalpa, Honduras.
The Caribbean Cooperative Federation established in Kingston, Jamaica.
Editorial Cooperativa (INTERCOOP), the Cooperative Publishing House,
established in Argentina. It began publication of the newspaper *Paz Cooper-
ativa* and the revue *Cuadernos de Cultura Cooperativa*. It has been an im-
portant publisher of cooperative literature in Spanish.
The Pan American Union initiated the Rural Cooperatives Pilot Scheme
in Costa Rica.
National Cooperative Union of India established in New Delhi.
The first cooperatives established in the Gilbert and Ellice Islands, which
became the two independent nations of Kiribati (Gilbert Islands, 1979) and
Tuvalu (Ellice Islands, 1978).
The first cooperative established in Rwanda.
Mondragon, an industrial cooperative complex, established in Spain; it
became an important worldwide model for worker-owned cooperatives.

1957 Twentieth Congress of the ICA held at Stockholm, Sweden. Discussion from the previous congress continued on international cooperation and cooperatives in developing countries.

Agricultural cooperatives established in Libya, the nation's first cooperatives established for indigenous Libyans.

1958 West Indian Confederation of Credit Societies established in Kingston, Jamaica; it was dissolved in 1966.

The first conference of Asian Cooperatives convened by the ICA at Kuala Lumpur.

The first Congress of Student Cooperatives in Asia was held.

Wheising (Sputnik), the first people's commune (an expanded cooperative), established in Honan, China.

The U.S. Credit Union National Association renamed CUNA International, reflecting the growing international character of the credit union movement. A Canadian was elected president of the renamed organization.

Bank für Gemeinwirtschaft (Bank for Collective Economy) established in Frankfurt, Germany. In the 1980s it became a commercial bank.

During 1958, the first cooperatives were established in Antigua, Grenada and Yemen.

1959 Comité général de la coopération agricole (COGECA), the General Committee for Agricultural Cooperation of the European Community, established in Brussels, Belgium.

The International Bank for Reconstruction and Development (World Bank) provided funding to support its first cooperative development project.

Coady International Institute established at the St. Francis Xavier University in Nova Scotia, Canada.

Cyprus cooperative movement divided into separate Greek and Turkish elements.

Institut des hautes études coopératives (Institute for Advanced Cooperative Studies) established in Paris.

College coopératif founded in Paris; it became an important center of training for French-speaking cooperators.

First credit union established in Saint Christopher (St. Kitts)/Nevis and Anguilla, the first cooperative in the country.

Group Health Association of America, a national association of cooperative health groups, established in Washington, D.C. The Association was one of the originators of group health plans in the U.S.

1960   Twenty-first Congress of the ICA held at Lausanne, Switzerland. Deliberations on international cooperation and cooperation in developing countries continued.

International Association of Cooperative Nurseries (for small children) established; initial member societies were in Australia, Canada, England, India and New Zealand.

Parents Cooperative Preschools International (PCPI) established in Canada and the U.S.

Institut für Genossenschaftswesen (Cooperative Institute) established in Hamburg, Germany.

Afro-Asian Institute for Labor Studies and Cooperation established in Tel Aviv, Israel.

A housing cooperative established in Metalanim, Pouape Island, becoming the first cooperative in Micronesia.

The first credit cooperative established in Montserrat; it was the first cooperative in the country.

1961   The first Inter-American Cooperative Conference held in Bogota, Colombia.

The Indian prime minister, Jawaharlal Nehru, suggested that the UN General Assembly establish an International Cooperative Year.

International Cooperative School established in Dresden, Germany. It became an important training center for cooperators from developing countries.

During 1961, the first cooperatives were established in Central African Republic, Gabon, Saudi Arabia and the Seychelles.

First grants from USAID to six U.S. cooperative development organizations for support of cooperative programs in developing countries.

1962   The first Asian Agricultural Cooperatives Conference held in Japan.

OK, Petroleum Import Cooperative Wholesale Society, established in Denmark.

Eurocoop, a coordinating committee of national consumer cooperative federations in the European Community countries, established in Hamburg, Germany.

Foschungsstelle für Agrarstruktur und Agrargenossenschaften der Entwicklungsländer (Research Center for Agricultural Cooperatives in Developing Countries) established in Heidelberg, Germany.

Latin American Center for Cooperative Studies established in Tel Aviv, Israel.

1963   Twenty-second Congress of the ICA held at Bournemouth, U.K. Discussion topics included economic integration and cooperatives in developing countries.

A Women's Consultative Committee established by the ICA, a predecessor of the current ICA Global Women's Committee.

Organización de las Cooperativas de América (OCA), the Organization of the Cooperatives of America, established in San Juan, Puerto Rico.

Instituto Cooperativo Interaméricano (Interamerican Cooperative Institute) established in Panama City, Panama.

Petroleum Products Package Factory of ICPA established in Dordrecht, Netherlands.

OK, Swedish petroleum cooperative, became an inter-Nordic organization.

The first consumer cooperative established in Greenland.

Institut für Genossenschaftswesen in Entwicklungsländern (Institute for Cooperation in Developing Countries) established in Marburg, Germany.

Institute for the Development of Agricultural Cooperatives in Asia (IDACA) established in Tokyo, Japan.

A Cooperative College established in Moshi, Tanzania.

Agricultural Cooperative Development International (ACDI) established in Washington, D.C. It was designed to assist cooperatives in developing countries, particularly those involved in agriculture and farm credit.

1964   The first cooperatives established in Botswana and Tonga.

1965   Sociedad Interamericana de Desarrollo y Financiamiento Cooperativo (SIDEFCOOP), the Interamerican Society for the Development and Financing of Cooperatives, established in Argentina.

A supply cooperative established in Gulzar, the first cooperative in Afghanistan.

International Research Center for Rural Cooperative Communities (CIRCOM) established in Tel Aviv, Israel.

1966   Twenty-third Congress of the ICA held at Vienna, during which the cooperative principles were restated. Continuing attention was given to cooperatives in developing countries.

Caribbean Confederation of Credit Unions (CCCU) established; it replaced the West Indies Confederation.

The 50th session of the General Conference of the ILO adopted Recommendation No. 127 on the role of cooperatives in the economic and social development of developing countries.

1967 The first Pan-African Cooperative Conference voted to create the Pan-African Center for Cooperative Training at Cotonou, Benin.

The Cooperative College of Kenya established in Nairobi, Kenya.

North Efate Transport Cooperative established; it was the first cooperative in Vanuatu.

1968 ICA Regional Office for East, Central and Southern Africa established in Moshi, Tanzania.

First Inter-American Conference on Cooperatives held in Argentina.

African Confederation of Cooperative Savings and Credit Associations (ACCOSCA) established in Nairobi, Kenya. It later became a regional confederation, affiliated with WOCCU.

International Raiffeisen Union (IRU) established in Bonn, Germany.

1969 Twenty-fourth Congress of the ICA held in Hamburg, Germany. The major discussion was on "Contemporary Cooperative Democracy."

General Committee on Cooperation in the Common Market Countries established in Brussels; it was designed to look after cooperative interests in the discussions and actions of the Common Market.

Instituto OCA de Integración Cooperativa para América Latina (Institute for Latin American Cooperative Integration) established by OCA.

A Latin American Congress on Cooperative Law held in Caracas, Venezuela.

The first cooperative in Bermuda, the Bermuda Workers' Cooperative Society, established.

Pan-African Cooperative Training Center opened in Cotonou, Dahomey (now Benin). Management of the Center was later assumed by the African-American Labor Center.

1970 The World Council of Credit Unions established as the international arm of the credit union movement.

Seminar on "Agricultural Cooperation and Rural Development in Latin America" held in Lima, Peru.

The first Asian Conference on Credit and Cooperation held in the Philippines.

The first Latin American Seminar on Cooperatives and Trade Unionism held in Venezuela.

Cooperative Societies Ordinance enacted in Gibraltar.

The first credit union and an agricultural cooperative organized at Foya; they were the first cooperatives in Liberia.

Association of Cooperative Savings and Credit Institutions of the European Economic Community (later known as the European Association of

Cooperative Banks) established. Its goal was to defend cooperatives' interests on a European scale by strengthening collaboration between European cooperative banking groups.

1971   The Joint Committee for the Promotion of Agricultural Cooperatives was established by FAO, ICA, International Federation of Agricultural Producers (IFAP), International Federation of Plantation, Agricultural and Allied Workers (IFPAAW) and ILO. The initiating organizations were soon joined by WOCCU and the UN, and the name changed to the Committee for the Promotion of Aid to Cooperatives (COPAC). The name was again changed in 1988 to its present title—the Committee for the Promotion and Advancement of Cooperatives.

International Organization for Consumer Cooperative Distributive Trade (Inter-COOP) established as an auxiliary committee of the ICA, reflecting a merger of the existing wholesale and retail committees. One aim was to promote economic cooperation between the 12-member consumer cooperative federations and thus to increase their competitive power in both domestic and international markets.

Asian Confederation of Credit Unions established in Hong Kong. It later became a regional confederation of WOCCU and changed its name to the Association of Asian Confederation of Credit Unions (ACCU), with headquarters in Bangkok, Thailand.

Confederación Latinoamericana de Cooperativas de Ahorro y Crédito (COLAC), the Latin American Confederation of Savings and Credit Cooperatives, established in Panama City, Panama; it later became a regional affiliate of WOCCU.

The OAS convened a Technical Conference on Productive and Labor Cooperatives.

In Guatemala, a book on cooperatives published in Braille.

The first cooperatives established in Guinea-Bissau.

1972   Twenty-fifth Congress of the ICA held in Warsaw. A topic of major interest was "Cooperation and Multinational Corporations." Deliberations on cooperatives in developing countries continued.

African seminar, sponsored by the ICA, dealing with "Women's Role in the Cooperative Movement," held at Accra, Ghana.

Cooperative Societies Law enacted in Bahrain and a consumer cooperative established as the first cooperative in that country.

The first cooperative in the Cayman Islands, the Cayman Islands Civil Service Association Credit Union, established.

The Greenland Cooperative League established.

BHF-Bank-DGK International established in Luxembourg as a subsidiary of the DG Bank.

The first European cooperative refinery established in Sweden.

The first cooperative in the United Arab Emirates, a consumer society in Dubai, established.

1973 International Conference of Young Cooperators, sponsored by the ICA, held in Sinaia, Romania.

Caribbean Credit Union Confederation established in Santo Domingo, Dominican Republic; it was later renamed the Caribbean Confederation of Credit Unions (CCCU), the regional affiliate of WOCCU.

The International Cooperative Trading Company established in Singapore by the ICA.

National Cooperative Act proposed in Qatar and the first cooperatives established there.

The Cipriani Labor College established in Port of Spain, Trinidad; it included cooperative training in its curriculum.

1974 The Advisory Group for International Training of Cooperators from Developing Countries (AGITCOOP) established by the ICA. It is now the ICA Global Human Resources Development Committee.

World Council of Churches established the Society for Church Investments, a cooperative development bank to foster investments in projects, including cooperatives, in the Third World.

Eurocophar established, an international pharmacy cooperative association involving cooperatives from Belgium, France, Germany, Italy and Spain.

First Asian Conference of Consumer Cooperatives held in Malaysia.

The Tonga and Fiji Credit Union Leagues formed the Confederated Credit Union Leagues of the South Pacific.

The Gibraltar Society, first cooperative supermarket in Gibraltar, established by the Transport Workers' Union.

1975 The first issue of the *Research Register of Studies on Cooperatives in Developing Countries* published. The Register was a project of the ICA, in collaboration with the Cooperative Research Institutes in Hungary and Poland. It was assisted in its later stages by COPAC.

Cooperative Educational Materials Advisory Service (CEMAS) established by ICA with funding provided by the Swedish Cooperative Center (SCC) and the Swedish International Development Authority (SIDA). It remained active until 1987.

FAO held the first World Food Conference in Rome. The Conference noted the importance of cooperatives in food production, and called on governments to promote their development.

The year 1975 declared International Women's Year by the UN, the central themes being equality, development and peace. This coincided with the first full working year of the ICA Women's Committee, which urged cooperatives worldwide to plan activities in support of the year.

First Open World Conference on Cooperative Fisheries sponsored by the ICA held in Tokyo, Japan.

First cooperative established in Brunei.

1976   Open Asian Conference on Cooperative Credit and Financial Management organized at Madras, India, by the ICA Regional Office.

The UN General Assembly adopted a resolution noting and commending a report of the secretary general on the progress in the development of the world cooperative movement. More than 12 such progress reports have been submitted by the secretary general and adopted by the General Assembly since the first in 1951.

UN held its Conference on Human Settlements (HABITAT I) in Vancouver, Canada. This conference focused on the world's deficit in housing and community facilities. The cooperative movement, through the ICA, emphasized the importance of developing communities, as well as focusing on basic shelter.

Twenty-sixth Congress of the ICA held in Paris, at UNESCO headquarters; principal discussions were held on collaboration between cooperatives, peace, the tasks of the cooperative press, tourism and the cooperative movement, and the role of women within the cooperative movement.

International Disarmament Forum held in York, U.K.; discussions focused on demilitarization, the abolition of armaments and the importance of popular opinion in the campaign against militarism. The ICA and the cooperative movement were expected to play a leadership role, given their continuing emphasis on lasting peace and security and the Alliance's percieved ability to maintain a fast-growing membership, diverse in ideology, race, language and religion.

1977   ICA convened an "Experts Consultation on Cooperatives and the Poor," at the Cooperative College in Loughborough, U.K.

Inter-American seminar on cooperative finance organized by SIDEFCOOP and sponsored by OCA and the OAS.

International Conference on "Cooperatives as an Instrument of Rural Development" sponsored by and held at the University of Ghent.

International Conference on Cooperative Thrift and Credit held at Rio de Janeiro, sponsored by the International Liaison Committee on Cooperative Thrift and Credit (CLICEC).

Conference on "Administration and Management of Cooperatives in Arab Countries" held in Mogul, Iran.

A United Nations Conference on Trade and Development (UNCTAD) study, *Cooperative Insurance—A Suitable Form of Insurance for Developing Countries*, published.

1978 The Executive Committee of the ICA met in Nairobi, the first time an executive body of ICA had met in Africa.

Seminar co-sponsored by the ICA and the OAS, on "The Role of Women in Cooperatives in South America."

ILO publication *Cooperative Information* ceased publication, due to ILO budget constraints caused by temporary withdrawal of U.S. from membership in the organization.

A symposium on cooperative housing organized by the International Cooperative Housing Development Association (ICHDA), held in Copenhagen with participants from Africa, Asia and Latin America.

International Cooperative Trade Conference held in New York, sponsored by CLUSA and the ICA; participants were from 21 countries.

A cooperative training project, Materials and Techniques for Cooperative Management (MATCOM), initiated by the ILO with funding from SIDA.

Pan-African Cooperative Conference held at Cotonou, Benin.

First Open World Conference on Industrial Cooperatives, organized by the ICA International Committee of Industrial, Artisanal and Service Producers' Cooperatives (CICOPA), held in Rome.

Association of European Cooperative Insurers was established, responding to the need for the internationalization of insurance and in anticipation of the single European market.

First cooperative established in Laos.

1979 ICA established a regional office for West Africa at Abidjan, Côte d'Ivoire; it is now in Ouagadougou, Burkina Faso.

UN General Assembly adopted a report of the secretary general on the status of the cooperative movement and passed a resolution supporting the further development of cooperatives in member countries.

ICA's Inter-COOP and the NAF opened a trading office in Hong Kong.

An international symposium on "Schools and Cooperatives as Instruments for Development and International Understanding" was held at UNESCO in Paris, sponsored by the ICA and the French Central Office of School Cooperatives.

Triennial Assembly of WOCCU held at Sydney, Australia.

Project 2000 initiated by the ICA; it was a projective study led by Canadian Alex Laidlaw of the anticipated status of cooperatives in the year 2000.

The UN declared 1979 to be the International Year of the Child. The ICA opted to observe it, in part, through a program to supply clean water to millions of children in developing countries.

An International Conference on "Tourism and the Cooperative Movement" held in Brussels.

European Committee of Workers' Cooperatives established to represent and defend member cooperatives' interests in the European Community.

1980 Twenty-seventh Congress of the ICA held in Moscow; it heard and adopted a report on "Cooperatives in the Year 2000."

Workshop on "Integrated Cooperatives for Satisfying the Basic Need of Shelter in Slum and Squatter Areas" held in Marburg, Germany, sponsored by DESWOS (German Development Assistance Association for Social Housing).

UNDP grants ICA the special status of a "cooperating organization," recognizing its achievements in the development field.

A National Consumer Cooperative Bank founded in the U.S.

1981 The ICA published *Cooperatives in the Year 2000*, a study designed to project current cooperative trends to the end of the century. It included a supplement discussing cooperative developments in communist countries that was prepared by Centrosoyus of the USSR.

Toad Lane, a shop opened in the U.K. by the Rochdale pioneers in 1844, reopened as a cooperative museum.

UN Habitat and ICHDA collaborated in the field to upgrade squatter areas and to develop low-income housing in new areas of Dodoma, Tanzania.

October 16 designated by the FAO as the first World Food Day, to be observed annually. ICA and other cooperatives agreed to participate in and support its observance.

The UN declared 1981 to be the International Year of Disabled Persons. To highlight the relevance of cooperatives, COPAC, in collaboration with the UN, ILO, ICA, and WOCU, prepared a manual on *Cooperatives of the Disabled*.

Fifth International Conference on Cooperative Thrift and Credit, sponsored by CLICEC, held in New Delhi. This marked the first time that the Conference was held in an Asian country.

International Conference on "Cooperative Development and Change" sponsored by the ICA Research Committee and held in Stockholm.

1982 UNIDO, ICA and the government of Tanzania met on the "Economic and Social Potential of Industrial Cooperatives in Developing Countries" in Arusha, Tanzania.

Third International Cooperative Trade Conference, sponsored by ICA, held in Cairo, Egypt.

Triennial meeting of WOCCU held in Toronto, Canada; it approved a long-term planning document.

A Coordination Committee of the Cooperative Associations of the European Community established in Brussels.

European Parliament published the Mihr Report, calling on the European cooperative movement to become a permanent participant in discussions and to set up a federal body to represent itself. The Parliament called on the Commission of the European Communities, inter alia, to promote cooperative development.

CIRIEC held an "International Congress of Public and Cooperative Economy" in Vienna, Austria.

ICA president Roger Kerinec addressed the Special Session on Disarmament of the UN General Assembly. He emphasized ICA's commitment to lasting peace and security as part of the implementation of cooperative principles.

ICA headquarters moved from London to Geneva.

1983 Second International Workers Productive Cooperative Conference held in Warsaw, Poland, sponsored by ICA and CICOPA.

1984 Tortola Cooperative Credit Union established; it was Tortola's first cooperative.

Twenty-eighth ICA Congress held in Hamburg, Germany; Lars Marcus of Sweden was elected president. Robert Beasley of the U.S. was named the new director of ICA.

CLUSA created an affiliate organization, Cooperative Business International (CBI), to help cooperatives around the world with a variety of commercial activities and ventures.

International Alliance of School Cooperatives founded in Paris to foster cooperative principles within the education system and make knowledge about school cooperatives more accessible.

Pope John Paul II, while in Newfoundland, endorsed cooperatives as a way to ensure that "workers have a voice in decision-making affecting their own lives and the lives of their families."

First Meeting of Cooperative Leaders of Balkan Countries held in Sofia, Bulgaria.

1985 Sixth International Conference on Cooperative Thrift and Credit, sponsored by CLICEC, held in Buenos Aires, Argentina.

Seventh Ibero American Seminar on Cooperative Education held in Rio Grande do Sul, Brazil.

ICA Regional Conference on "Cooperatives in the Year 2000" held at Bamako, Mali.

UN Women's Conference held in Nairobi, Kenya. The ICA Women's Committee presented a statement on the position of women in the cooperative movement.

Regional Meeting of Ministers of Cooperatives in the countries of eastern, central and southern Africa organized by the ICA regional office; ministers designated the period from 1985 to 1995 as the "cooperative development decade" for the region.

1986 The UN declared 1986 to be the International Year of Peace. Cooperatives worldwide organized peace-related activities, including preparation and distribution of a peace poster by ICA.

European Committee on Social Housing established. The Committee linked cooperative housing organizations from the countries of the European Union and represented them in European institutions.

1987 UN Seminar on the "Role of Government in Promoting the Cooperative Movement" held in Moscow, USSR.

Report of the UN secretary general on "National Experience in Promoting the Cooperative Movement" adopted by the General Assembly.

WOCCU opened a European office in Geneva. The office was created to bring the developmental needs and requirements of WOCCU members to the attention of European institutions.

UN declared 1987 to be the International Year of Shelter for the Homeless. The ICA Housing Committee reviewed the role cooperatives play and could play in alleviating the problems of homelessness. It published a revised and updated edition of *Cooperative Housing*.

ICA Executive Committee meeting held in Banjul, the Gambia; this was the first ICA executive meeting ever held in West Africa.

The OAS reestablished a cooperative section in its staff, located at its headquarters in Washington, D.C.

A new Rochdale Equitable Pioneer Society created in the U.K. as a means to honor outstanding leaders of the world's cooperatives and to maintain the cooperative site at Rochdale.

Canadian Cooperative Association (CCA) established its first regional field offices, one in Asia (Kuala Lumpur, Malaysia) and one in Latin America (San José, Costa Rica).

Representatives of the European Parliament met in Strasbourg, France; they concluded after discussion that cooperatives should be promoted, especially in less developed areas.

The ICA Consumer Committee designated March 15 as World Consumer Rights Day, commemorating the UN's adoption of a charter giving guidelines for consumer protection.

Second African Ministerial Cooperative Conference met in Lusaka, Zambia. The Conference appraised progress since the first conference in 1984 and set goals for 1987 to 1990.

1988   The 13th edition of the *International Directory of Cooperative Organizations* published by the ILO. It is the most recent version of this publication, which was first published in 1920.

Third World Conference of Industrial Cooperatives held in Paris and sponsored by CICOPA; the conference theme was "The Participative and Democratic Enterprise of the Year 2000."

The Africa Regional Conference of the ILO deliberated on a report by the ILO director on "Cooperatives in Africa." The report examined the experience of the Africa cooperative movement and ILO's experience in working with cooperatives on the continent, and contemplated the prospects for cooperatives in Africa in the future.

An ICA project office was opened in San José, Costa Rica. After one year of existence, the project office was converted into the ICA Regional Office for Central America and the Caribbean. It is now identified as the ICA Regional Office for the Americas.

International symposium on "Food Aid and Cooperatives," organized by COPAC in collaboration with the World Food Program, held in Vienna, Austria.

International Raiffeisen Union organized an international celebration in Frankfurt, Germany, of the centenary of the death of Friedrich Wilhelm Raiffeisen.

Third International Credit Union Forum held by WOCCU in Melbourne, Australia.

A seminar on "Women and Cooperative Credit," organized by the ICA, WOCCU and the International Institute for Development Cooperation and Labor Studies, was held in Tel Aviv, Israel.

Twenty-ninth Congress of the ICA held in Stockholm, where it was addressed by UN secretary general Javier Perez de Cuellar. The main issue discussed was "Basic Values of Cooperation," accompanied by a consideration of cooperatives and development. The Congress proposed that an International Year of Cooperatives be designated by the UN. Bruce Thordarson of Canada was named the director of ICA.

An International Cooperative Youth Seminar was held, concurrently with the ICA Congress in Stockholm, on the themes of international cooperation and peace.

A Center for Cooperatives, the second in the U.S., opened at the University of California at Davis.

1989 The report *The World Bank and the World of Cooperatives*, developed with bank support by ICA senior advisor and director emeritus Robert Beasley, submitted for study and planning for future project activity involving cooperatives.

WOCCU added to the ILO special list of non-governmental organizations.

First consultation on small and medium-scale enterprises, including cooperatives, held by the United Nations Industrial Development Organization (UNIDO).

ICA Central Committee held its meeting in New Delhi. This marked the first time that the Committee had met in Asia.

1990 ICA established a regional office for Central America and the Caribbean at San José, Costa Rica; it was later renamed the regional office for the Americas.

ICA conference on "New Roles for Cooperatives in Central and Eastern European Countries" held in Budapest, Hungary.

ICA-sponsored conferences on industrial/artisan cooperatives held in West Africa (Abidjan, Côte d'Ivoire) and Latin America (Montevideo, Uruguay).

Finnish Cooperative Development Center established by Finnish cooperatives to assist and coordinate cooperative projects in developing countries.

An international symposium on the "Role of the Industrial Cooperative Movement in Economic and Industrial Development" was organized by UNIDO in Moscow, USSR.

The UN declared 1990 to be International Literacy Year. ICA urged cooperatives worldwide to develop literacy programs as part of their regular training and to collaborate with the effort to achieve universal literacy by the year 2000.

International Association of Cooperative Law created with the assistance of the University of Duesto in Bilbao, Spain.

First Asia and Pacific Ministers' Conference held in Sydney, Australia. Discussions included cooperative government collaborative strategies, cooperatives during the 1990s and development of inter-cooperative trade in the region.

Third African Ministerial Cooperative Conference and Exhibition held in Nairobi, Kenya. The Conference adopted resolutions to support the efforts of the Regional Cooperative Development Decade, including the improvement of existing cooperative educational facilities in the region and an examination of the adequacy of cooperative laws.

ICA project office opened in Buenos Aires, Argentina.

Inter-COOP opened an office in Budapest, Hungary, to facilitate trading with its 10 members in Europe, Israel and Japan.

International Seminar on Cooperative Legislation, sponsored by the ICA, held in Prague, Czechoslovakia.

International Conference on the Environment held in Sweden, sponsored by the ICA and the Swedish cooperative KF.

Two meetings of the leaders of cooperatives from eastern and central European countries took place with ICA collaboration; they considered cooperative responses and strategies with regard to the new socio-political situation in those countries.

First American Regional Cooperative Conference held in Guatemala, on "International Cooperation for Cooperative Development."

1991   The International Credit Union Forum was held by WOCCU in Madison, Wisconsin. The theme of the forum was "Economic, Social and Political Dimensions of the International Credit Union Movement."

A special program of support for cooperatives in eastern and central European countries was undertaken by the ICA with support from its member organizations in Belgium, U.K., Israel, Japan and Sweden, and from WOCCU and its members.

A regional conference on "Women and Cooperation" was held in Honduras; it involved some 400 female cooperators from Central American and Caribbean countries.

EURESA, a holding company formed by cooperative insurance firms in Belgium (Prevoyance sociale), France (MACIF), Italy (UNIPOL) and Sweden (Folksam), was created to support cooperative insurance companies from eastern and central European countries.

First Cooperative Seminar of Lusophone (Portugese-speaking) countries was held in Lisbon, Portugal; it discussed the national experiences of cooperatives from the seven Lusophone countries.

1992 A cooperative seminar was held at the UN Conference on Environment and Development in Rio de Janeiro; activities included an ICA booth at the Global Forum of NGOs and a special issue of the *ICA News* dealing with cooperatives and environmental issues.

The second conference of Ministers of Cooperation for the ICA Asia/Pacific region was held in Jakarta, Indonesia; it discussed "Cooperative Government Collaborative Strategies for the Development of Cooperatives."

Thirtieth Congress of the ICA held in Tokyo, Japan, the first congress held outside Europe. The main themes considered were basic values of cooperatives, environment and sustainable development, and ICA structure.

The UN secretary general submitted, and the General Assembly adopted, a report on the "Status and Role of Cooperatives in the Light of New Economic and Social Trends." The report declared an International Day of Cooperatives to celebrate the centenary of the ICA in 1995.

A consultative meeting of ICA member organizations in the Americas was held in Mexico City to prepare for the implementation of the new ICA structure, which called for a regional assembly of the Americas.

WOCCU, ICA and ILO organized a workshop to provide an opportunity to share experiences about the development of credit unions in eastern and central European countries.

International Cooperative Youth Seminar held in Tokyo, Japan, discussed global peace and the environment.

American Cooperative Enterprise Center, with the goal of providing technical assistance, training and opportunities for trade between Polish, Hungarian, Czechoslovak and U.S. cooperatives, opened its headquarters in Prague, Czechoslovakia.

International seminar on "Cooperative Property and Privatization," sponsored by the ICA, held in Geneva.

International conference on "Problems of the Cooperative Movement in the Contemporary World," sponsored by the ICA Research Committee, held in Warsaw, Poland.

Third European Conference on Social Economy held in Lisbon, Portugal.

Second American Regional Cooperative Conference held in Mexico on "Economic Opening: The Cooperative Response."

The International Cooperative Energy Organization (ICEO) established as a specialized committee of the ICA.

1993 The Fourth African Cooperative Ministerial Conference for eastern, central and southern Africa was held in Arusha, Tanzania.

A new organizational structure for the ICA went into effect with the convening of the first biennial General Assembly of the organization (which replaces the former Central Committee). The meeting, held in Geneva in September, elected a board of directors, which replaced its former executive committee and confirmed four regional vice presidents representing Africa, the Americas, Asia and Europe.

With the partition of the country, the board of the Cooperative Union of the Czech and Slovak Federal Republic voted to reorganize itself into a Czech Cooperative Union and a Slovak Cooperative Union.

An ICA-sponsored Regional Conference on "Indigenous Cooperatives and Human Rights" was held in Quetzaltengo, Guatemala.

An International Seminar on "Challenges for Cooperatives in the Contemporary World," sponsored by the ICA Research Committee, was held in the Slovak Republic.

Third American Regional Cooperative Conference held in San Salvador on "Reconversion and Cooperative Competitivity."

Fourth European Conference on Social Economy held in Brussels.

1994 The Third Asia and Pacific Cooperative Ministers Conference was held in Colombo, Sri Lanka. Main discussions revolved around the position of cooperatives in the market-oriented economy.

ICA regional assemblies were held for Africa, America, Asia and Europe.

COPAC organized an open forum at the UN headquarters in New York on the theme "Cooperatives and the World Summit for Social Development."

The International Raiffeisen Union and the ICA organized a joint seminar for their board members during the ICA European Regional Assembly. It was the first occasion for these two groups to collaborate in this way, and both indicated a willingness to find other ways of working together.

WOCCU held the Fourth International Credit Union Forum in Cork, Ireland. Its Women in Development Task Force concurrently held a symposium on "Women and Credit Unions."

ICA president Lars Marcus addressed the ILO at its 75th anniversary conference. He discussed the close collaboration of the two organizations and commended the ILO for its support of cooperatives.

ICA and CIRIEC held an "International Symposium on Cooperative Principles in Contemporary Europe" in Seville, Spain.

1995 The UN World Summit on Social Development was held in Copenhagen, Denmark. The UN Department for Policy Coordination and Sustainable Development, ICA and WOCCU together prepared a series of notes stressing the relevance of cooperatives to the themes of the summit.

Thirty-first and centennial Congress of the ICA met in Manchester, U.K. A statement of cooperative identity, including a restatement of cooperative principles and a cooperative declaration "towards the 21st century," were adopted. The third International Youth Seminar was held in Loughborough, U.K., in conjunction with the ICA Congress.

Fourth World Conference on Women held in Beijing, China. Delegations representing WOCCU and the ICA attended, and a forum was organized on "Women and Cooperatives."

ICA set up its Web site (http://ica.coop.org) to provide easily accessible information on cooperatives to anyone on the Internet.

ICA opened a project office in Sucre, Bolivia.

Fifth American Regional Cooperative Conference held, on the theme "Strategic Alliances."

1996 Continental Forum of Women Cooperators, sponsored by the ICA, held in San José, Costa Rica, the first time the Forum was held in the Americas. A "Platform of Action on Gender Issues" was developed and adopted.

Fifth African Ministerial Cooperative Conference held in Mauritius. Participants reaffirmed their commitment to regional ties and working toward self-reliance.

World Food Summit held at FAO headquarters in Rome. ICA presented the views of the cooperative movement and illustrated the contributions of the cooperative movement to the production and distribution of food, as well as the cooperative role in providing income and employment, which are essential to food security.

Three international meetings were held under the auspices of the ICA Research Committee to discuss themes of timely regional importance to ICA member organizations: Systems of Governance and Management in Cooperatives and Control of Management (in Nitra, Slovak Republic); Innovation and Change (in Tartu, Estonia); and Labor Markets, Unemployment and Cooperatives (in Budapest, Hungary).

ICA Continental Forum on "Strategies for Developing Human Resources in Cooperatives" held in Lima, Peru.

Sixth American Regional Cooperative Conference held on the theme "Globalization: Regional Networks, Local Markets: Cooperative Strategy."

The International Health Cooperative Organization (ICHO) established as a specialized committee of the ICA.

1997 Fifth International Credit Union Forum of WOCCU held in Vancouver, Canada, on the theme of "Diverse Voices in Concert."

ICA held its Europe Seminar on "European Union Enlargement" in Prague, Czech Republic. The purpose of the seminar was to assess the impact of the recent actions of the Union on cooperatives.

Fourth Asia Pacific Cooperative Ministers' and Leaders' Conference held in Chiang Mai, Thailand. The main themes of the conference were gender and development and sustainable development.

International conference on "The Cooperative Advantage in a Civil Economy," sponsored by the ICA Research Committee, held in Bologna, Italy.

Seventh American Regional Cooperative Conference held in Mexico on the theme "Cooperatives Facing Unemployment."

1998 ICA granted consultative status with the Council of Europe as an international NGO.

ICA opened its regional European office in Geneva and appointed its first regional director.

ICA opened its regional office for North Africa and the Arab Countries in Cairo and appointed its first regional director.

Representatives of cooperatives in the Black Sea area met in Varna, Bulgaria, to discuss mutual problems and opportunities.

ICA and FAO signed a "memorandum of understanding" identifying further areas of collaboration between the two organizations on issues of importance to cooperative development.

Two international conferences were sponsored by the ICA Research Committee: "Cooperative Governance and Social Audit Systems" held in Tokyo, Japan, and "Values and Adding Value in a Global Context" held in Cork, Ireland.

Eighth American Regional Cooperative Conference held on "Cooperative Business and Trade, The Human Face of Economy."

Introduction

The story of the cooperative movement in its many and growing manifestations around the world is difficult to capture in a single time and place, in a book such as this. The real story, rather, will only be fully captured in a series of smaller national narratives, some warranting books of their own. It will be found in stories of one, two, three or more individuals fretting about their world and its inequities, inadequacies and injustices, who decide that by working together they can actualize something better for their lives. They begin to develop larger collective visions, create new and better solutions to problems, and establish an organization to give life to their stirring. Cooperation, a basic element in the experience of human life, finds new expression. A cooperative is born, and the story moves on to another place.

Cooperation derives from the Latin *operari* (to work) and the prefix *co* (to work together). It is a social process of working and thinking together to achieve mutually advantageous goals. A cooperative is a voluntarily created organization of people, formed for the purpose of meeting their common needs through mutual action, democratic control and sharing of economic returns on the basis of individual participation.

Some authors point out that cooperation is not new and that there was organized economic cooperation in ancient societies such as Babylon, China, Greece and Rome. Some others contend that cooperation is even more basic than human organization, suggesting, as do some microbiologists, that there is universal evidence that even the simplest forms of life survive and thrive because they work together. Cooperation, they assert, is a part of the driving force of evolution, and human and social advance is dependent upon it.

I will not spend much time on these grander theories, but I do point out some references (see the bibliography) for those who want to explore them. In this book, I will focus on the history of the modern cooperative movement.

This is the history of a series of similar, but generally unrelated, actions beginning in the mid-1700s. They took place in various places in Europe and North America, and soon thereafter in other industrially advancing societies. They represented responses to the problems and needs of farmers and workers confronting the new world created by the Industrial Revolution. It is also the history of a continuing line of theorists who developed or elaborated cooperative ideologies designed to make coherent sense out of changing social and economic conditions, and of their proposed cooperative solutions to these. Theory and action, while not always concurrent, have always been intertwined in modern cooperative history.

In tracing this introductory history, I have generally followed the same outline of topics here and in the bibliography. Hopefully, this will allow for easier cross-referencing.

THE BEGINNING

By 1844, the date of the establishment of the Equitable Pioneers of Rochdale Society in the U.K., from which date many people trace the development of the modern cooperative movement, the first cooperatives had already been organized in a number of countries: Austria (1794), France (1750s), Greece (1780), Iceland (1844), Italy (1806), Japan (1843), Luxembourg (1808), Mexico (1839), Poland (then partitioned) (1816), Russia (1825), Spain (1838), Switzerland (1816), the U.K. (1750s) and the U.S. (1750s). Extensive experimentation with the cooperative form was well under way in France and the U.S., and even more so in the U.K., where by 1830 more than 300 cooperative societies had been officially recognized, 12 cooperative newspapers had been established and in 1831 the first national cooperative congress was held. By 1900, cooperators in 26 additional countries had initiated their first cooperative societies, and the pace accelerated after the turn of the century. By 1925, 74 countries had cooperatives; by 1950, there were 134; and by 1984, when a cooperative emerged in Tortola, there were 165. In an additional 22 countries where cooperatives exist, it has not been possible to identify the exact date when the first cooperative was established. (Appendix 1 contains a list of countries, organized by the date their first cooperative or cooperatives were established.)

NINETEENTH-CENTURY THEORISTS

The cooperative literature of the 19th century, cited in the bibliography, is the product principally of three countries—France, Britain and Germany, with a smattering of works by Italian, Spanish and American authors. Most of them are works written by practitioners who based their views and theories on real cooperative experience or by men who simultaneously set out to establish cooperatives based on their ideas. Five of them, Philippe Buchez, Etienne Cabet, François Marie Charles Fourier, Robert Owen and William Thompson, were born in the last third of the 18th century, and each of them contributed to the intellectual ferment of the emerging cooperative movement. They were concerned in large measure with how cooperatives could serve as an organizational structure for releasing the "ideal good" in human nature, which, they posited, could be brought about most fully in a cooperative environment.

Of the leading 19th-century theorists, only Charles Gide produced important works in the 20th century. Much of his and other cooperative literature of the early 19th century focused on the growing experience with consumer cooperatives in the U.K., as well as on worker production cooperatives in France and credit cooperatives in Germany. The 19th century also saw the beginnings of an attempt to capture the history of different national movements; with publications by George Holyoake in Britain, Ugo Rabbeno in Italy, and the Johns Hopkins University *History of Cooperatives in the United States.* The first "how to" manuals were produced in the latter part of the century, providing experience-based guidance on how to organize and operate cooperative societies. The importance of cooperative literature was emphasized by the ICA as early as 1906, when, shortly after its establishment, it published the *International Cooperative Bibliography* in English, French and German.

TWENTIETH-CENTURY THEORY AND PRACTICE

In 1973 the ILO published a comprehensive bibliography as a special supplement to its journal, *Cooperative Information.* The bibliography was an attempt to list *all* books that had been written about cooperation and cooperatives between 1805 and 1973. It ran to 276 pages. The total list of works written between 1805 and 1899, however, ran to only *eight* pages. With the turn of the century, the pace of production of books on cooperation and cooperatives accelerated (the list of books for the period 1900–1913 ran to nine more pages). The remaining 259 pages represented the output of cooperative books during the next 60 years, through 1973.

More and more literature began to be published in different countries in Europe and in other parts of the world. Books dealing with cooperative theory of a general nature, bearing such titles as *Theory, History and Practice of Cooperation, The Nature of Cooperation, The Cooperative Idea* and

Essays in Modern Cooperation, were published in the 20th century in such diverse countries as Argentina, Austria, Belgium, Canada, China, Colombia, Czechoslovakia, France, Germany, Greece, Haiti, Honduras, India, Ireland, Italy, Kenya, Mexico, New Zealand, Peru, the Philippines, Puerto Rico, the Soviet Union, Spain, Sri Lanka, the U.K., the U.S. and Zambia.

In addition to the geographical diversity of cooperative theorists, viewing the cooperative experience from a variety of national perspectives, there was also ideological diversity among publications viewing cooperation from different ideological perspectives. Among them, the following are of note:

Religious Bases of Cooperation

From the Christian Socialists of Europe and North America to the Hindu philosopher Rabindranath Tagore in his *Cooperative Principle,* from Japan's Toyohiko Kagawa in *Brotherhood Economics* to Roman Catholic papal encyclicals, a variety of voices were raised, proclaiming in different ways that "God" was on the side of cooperation, and identifying the religious principles upon which cooperation was based.

Sociobiology and Cooperation

With the publication of Peter Kropotkin's *Mutual Aid: A Factor of Evolution,* a more secular version of cooperation as being part of the nature of things was introduced into the theoretical discussion. Cooperation, this view holds, is as much an evolutionary favorite as competition is—perhaps even more so. At mid-century, the American author Ashley Montagu joined in this discussion with his *Direction of Human Development.* More recently, Christopher Badcock added his voice with *Evolution and Individual Behavior: An Introduction to Human Sociobiology.*

Human Solidarity as the Basis for Cooperation

The philosophy of humanism, centered on humankind and the maximum achievement of human values, and the utilitarian philosophy emphasizing the "greatest good for the greatest number" have both seen cooperatives and cooperation as an important vehicle for achieving their ends. Erich Loewy's *Freedom and Community: The Ethics of Interdependence* and Donald Regan's *Utilitarianism and Cooperation,* among others, develop these themes.

Cooperation, Mutualism and the Social Economy

Noting that, throughout history, group-based or collective economic activity has been a recurring phenomenon, some theorists have posited that there is a tendency toward mutualism or a social economy in all economies and that cooperatives and other forms of collective ownership are manifestations of this. It is a position that historically has been most actively supported by French cooperators, and the journal *Annals of Public and Cooperative Economy*, established in 1925 by Edgard Milhaud, has been its voice. The International Research and Information Center on the Public, Social and Cooperative Economy (CIRIEC), at the University of Liège, Belgium, with national sections in a number of countries, is the international expression of this view.

Socialism and Cooperation

Modern socialism emerged as a reaction to the mass hardships and inequities of the Industrial Revolution and to the laissez-faire capitalist economic systems that held such conditions to be justified. They were justified as a necessary part of the movement toward a system that would ultimately benefit everyone by allowing aggressive entrepreneurs to pursue unchecked personal gain. The socialist alternative was the social ownership of the means of production and distribution and an equitable sharing of economic benefits and political power. Early skepticism about governments' abilities to organize such a massive transformation, together with fear of unrestrained government power, led to consideration of alternative ways in which social ownership and control might be expressed. The socialist organizational vehicles to achieve these were a workers' political party to take the lead in changing the political order, trade unions to introduce democratic control into industry and the acquisition of social ownership of the means of production and distribution. The emerging cooperative structures of that time were seen as a major alternative form of social ownership, particularly by the Christian Socialists and later by the Fabian Socialists in Britain, as well as by other groups that advocated evolutionary rather than revolutionary change. Of the three vehicles of socialist hopes, cooperatives have been most successful and have continued to grow in number, proliferate in membership and expand in worldwide influence.

Cooperation and Marxism

Communists, with their belief that the proletariat must own and control production and its benefits, and their expectation that socialism would be ushered in by a revolutionary collapse of the capitalist order, were initially reluctant to support cooperatives as part of a solution to social and economic problems. They saw cooperatives as reformist at best and often shied away from them as mere stopgap measures that would only delay the revolution. Consumer societies were seen as simply making life a little better for the working class when it should be steeling itself for the revolution. Converting the new Soviet Union into a communist society and economy in the 1920s proved more difficult than anticipated, and Lenin and others, with some hesitation, agreed that cooperatives, properly controlled to serve the worker state and limited to supplying the consumer sector, could be a legitimate type of "social property." (Whether cooperatives retain legitimacy in their own right, or were only a way station on the road to total state socialism, remained a matter of debate until the collapse of the communist regimes in Europe.) With the expansion of communism into other countries after World War II, the use of cooperatives as a major type of social property became widespread in Eastern Europe and they were to be found in almost all economic sectors except those involving large industrial establishments. The leaders of some developing countries, captivated by a socialist vision, have experimented with moving from a precapitalist economy to a worker-owned state without a capitalist stage, but with limited success.

Rochdale Principles of Cooperation

One of the unique aspects of the Rochdale pioneers was their concern, based on the hard experience of others, that they clearly articulate in advance, the principles and practices they would follow in their cooperative. These are now referred to as the Rochdale Principles of Cooperation. Formulated principally by Charles Howarth, the original principles included the following: that each member was to have one vote and no more; that trading should be no credit, all cash; that sales should be at market prices, with no cut rates; that capital should be restricted to a fixed rate of interest; that there should be equality of the sexes in membership privileges; that accounts should be properly kept and audited and balance sheets presented regularly to the members; that there should be frequent and regular meetings of members to discuss the society's business; and that net savings should be distributed to members in proportion to their purchases.

Cooperative Principles Reformulated

The principles of cooperation have been reformulated by a number of individuals and officially by the ICA at different times since their original expression at Rochdale, most notably in 1937, 1963 and 1995. Discussions of some of the more important of these are cited in the bibliography. The current official statement of these principles, adopted at the Centennial Congress of the ICA in Manchester, U.K., in September 1995, is as follows:

First Principle: Voluntary and Open Membership. Cooperatives are voluntary organizations, open to all persons able to use their services and willing to accept the responsibilities of membership without gender, social, racial, political or religious discrimination.

Second Principle: Democratic Member Control. Cooperatives are democratic organizations controlled by their members, who actively participate in setting their policies and making decisions. Men and women serving as elected representatives are accountable to the membership. In primary cooperatives, members have equal voting rights (one member, one vote) and cooperatives at other levels are organized in a democratic manner.

Third Principle: Member Economic Participation. Members contribute equitably to, and democratically control, the capital of their cooperative. At least part of that capital is usually the common property of the cooperative. Members usually receive limited compensation, if any, on capital subscribed as a condition of membership. Members allocate surpluses for any or all of the following purposes: developing the cooperative, possibly by setting up reserves, part of which at least will be indivisible; benefiting members in proportion to their transactions with the cooperative; and supporting other activities approved by the membership.

Fourth Principle: Autonomy and Independence. Cooperatives are autonomous, self-help organizations controlled by their members. If they enter into agreements with other organizations, including governments, or raise capital from external sources, they do so on terms that ensure democratic control by their members and the maintenance of their cooperative autonomy.

Fifth Principle: Education, Training and Information. Cooperatives provide education and training for their members, elected representatives, managers and employees so that they can contribute effectively to the development of their cooperatives. They inform the general public, particularly young people and opinion leaders, about the nature and benefits of cooperation.

Sixth Principle: Cooperation among Cooperatives. Cooperatives serve their members most effectively and strengthen the cooperative movement by working together through local, national, regional, and international structures.

Seventh Principle: Concern for Community. While focusing on member needs, cooperatives work for the sustainable development of their communities through policies accepted by their members.

Organizing Cooperation

Not many years passed in the evolution of the different facets of the cooperative movement before some people concluded that common mistakes were being made and that the common tasks of organization lent themselves to "how to" manuals or guides. One of the earliest of these, *A Manual for Cooperators*, by Thomas Hughes and Edward Vansittart Neale, was published in 1881. One of the more recent, *Why Cooperatives Succeed and Fail*, was published by the United States Overseas Cooperative Development Committee in 1985 and focused on cooperatives in developing countries. The ILO, in *Cooperative Information,* made an earnest attempt over several years to compile a list of such literature. Their product, covering the period up to the mid-1970s, was helpful but too lengthy to be included here. Somewhere, someone is writing a manual at this very moment.

COOPERATION AND SOCIETY

Cooperatives are and have been primarily economic enterprises whose memberships almost exclusively regard economic achievement as their criterion of success. They hold that cooperatives can only be successful in some larger sense when they are first an economic success. However, different segments of society have come to view cooperatives as having larger roles to play than this.

Cooperation as Economic Democracy

Theorists have long contended that democracy is more than a political process, and that its ultimate achievement will be the institutional structuring of democratic control wherever power plays a role in human society. In the economic sphere, cooperatives quickly became a focus of attention as a way of achieving such economic democracy. Cooperatives by their nature focused on group solutions to problems rather than emphasizing the "rugged individual." The principle of a common sharing of power, regardless of holdings in the cooperative enterprise—one person, one vote, regardless of the number of shares held—structured an opportunity for equal participation in planning and decision making, regardless of wealth. The provision of regular and public meetings, open to all members at all times, made for an openness and transparency in management operations. The concern for continued education provided a means for increasing members' skills on the job and for advancement in group leadership.

Cooperation and Economic Development

While economic advancement was, from the start, an aspect of cooperative development in Europe, North America and other industrializing countries, as groups of farmers and workers wrestled with the conditions caused by the Industrial Revolution, it has been in developing countries that cooperatives have been used most deliberately as instruments of broad-based economic and social development. In these countries, individualistic opportunities and solutions that provide only a trickling-down of benefits were not seen as acceptable strategies. The success of cooperatives in more economically advanced societies suggested that such group-based approaches had relevance to nations and societies undergoing what they hoped would be a more accelerated growth and development. Cooperatives provided structures through which the benefits of innovation and economic growth could be shared more equitably. Cooperatives were "schools of democracy" where the skills necessary for democratic political participation could be acquired by members of cooperatives through the experience of making decisions about their member-owned organizations. But the utilization of cooperatives as strategic elements of economic development strategies was not without its perils. Cooperatives have not been "quick fix" solutions, and few governments, concerned with rapid change and improvement, have been prepared to allow cooperatives to develop naturally at their own pace. Well-meaning government bureaucrats, although they had an advantage over the general population in terms of years of education, were seldom equipped by experience to make business decisions. The authoritarian model of decision making within bureaucracies was hardly one to be emulated in group-controlled organizations. Nevertheless, the growth and expansion of cooperatives in the developing world in the 20th century, and particularly after World War II, are testimony to their relevance in newly independent countries. Further, those elements of the cooperative system in different countries that structured themselves against undue government intrusion have made notable advances. In this respect, credit unions have been particularly successful.

Cooperatives and the Poor

While it may be impossible to define a single rationale for the formation of cooperatives, it is fair to say that they have generally been instruments used by people who were, at their moment in history, not part of the economic and social elite. The roots of most cooperative development are in the population of the dispossessed, and, in fact, that is part of the reason why so many cooperatives have failed. The members have lacked the economic base and the breadth of experience necessary for economic success. In addition, they have not quickly enough acquired the management skills necessary to operate complex economic endeavors successfully. Nonetheless, building on the foundations of their own and others' hard experience, cooperators and their organizations have gradually achieved economic success and provided the opportunity for the dispossessed to become active participants in the benefits of economic growth. Further, cooperatives at their best have retained a sense of solidarity with those still on an upward path and have continued to promote themselves as important vehicles for achieving a better life.

It was because of these roots among the poor that, in an age of international development agencies, some turned to cooperatives with the expectation that they would play a key role in dealing with the problems of poverty and helping the poor of the developing world move out of wretched conditions. While some successes in this regard have been achieved, few cooperative development projects have proven successful on their own in providing comprehensive solutions to societal poverty, an intractable problem even in advanced industrialized countries. Some lessons have been learned, however, and some generalizations can be made. First, cooperatives have been successful among poor people when they have focused their efforts on the problems that drew their membership together and have not tried to become generalized community development organizations. Second, cooperative ideology encourages attention to problems of poverty in ways that transcend that of the average business (and the cooperative movement does agonize about poverty in ways unfathomable to a chamber of commerce), but, like other business undertakings, cooperatives' first concerns are with the success of their own enterprises. Third, cooperatives do not have the means, nor do they perceive themselves to be the vehicle, for the transfer of wealth and resources that are necessary if poverty is to be eliminated. This is a function of government (or revolution) and the larger society. Fourth, individual cooperatives and cooperative systems, beyond impacting the poverty of their own members, do not have the resources to deal with generalized poverty. If they are to be agents of government, acting on generalized problems of poverty because their approach to group organization can be helpful to society, financial and other support for such an activity must be provided by governments or development agencies. Fifth, more visionary cooperators, such as those advocating the establishment of a Cooperative Commonwealth, contend that the answer to poverty lies in a different kind of economic system, one committed to a just and equitable distribution of the fruits of human labor rather than to personal economic aggrandizement. Only when society reflects these values will poverty be eradicated.

THE SOCIAL IMPACT OF COOPERATION

Apart from their worldwide impact as economic institutions, cooperatives are often applauded because of their broad social impact on their members and on the societies in which they function. Cooperatives are cited as having the following influences: encouragement of group harmony in problem solving, enhancement of democratic participation, encouragement of an emphasis on social equality, development of leadership, and growth of human solidarity. The measure of such influences, as well as the specific social impact of cooperatives' operations on their communities, is encouraged and measured by the inclusion, in a growing number of cooperatives, of an annual "social audit" that accompanies the annual audit of business systems.

Cooperation and Peace

While the diverse units of the cooperative movement started as local and then country wide phenomena, it was not long before these groups found each other across national boundaries, and a sense of solidarity with an international movement developed. The need to solve common economic problems led to a sharing of experience and the celebration of individual movements' accomplishments. By the mid-1800s, there were already notions of an international grouping of cooperatives to facilitate interchange and to express a growing sense of human solidarity. Fraternal delegates from other countries were welcomed at national cooperative meetings, and a sense of participation in a common quest for a better, more just cooperative world was quickly established. The founding of the ICA in 1895 brought to fruition these international cooperative longings, and it came as no surprise that the promotion of world peace was an essential part of its ideology. At an early congress of the ICA, a decision was made that each congress should adopt a Peace Resolution, in which the Alliance would state its views on the current state of peace in the world. In less than 20 years, however, the nations whose cooperatives made up the Alliance were confronted with World War I and a nationalism that tugged at every countervailing loyalty. It was a testimony to cooperative solidarity that a semblance of relationships between national movements was maintained during the war and that the international aspects of the movement were reactivated quickly after its end. In 1925 the ICA adopted the Rainbow Flag as an ensign of its commitment to internationalism. World War II was more problematic for the international cooperative movement. In large part this was because the governments of Italy, Germany and Japan had compromised the independence of their cooperative movements, making them mere nationalistic partisans.

The ICA was represented by an observer, Wallace Campbell, at the founding of the United Nations (UN) in 1945 and has had official observer status ever since that time, participating regularly in the deliberations of the UN and its specialized agencies. In 1982 as part of the International Year of Peace, the president of the ICA, Roger Kerinec, addressed a special session of the General Assembly of the UN, expressing the vision of peace and disarmament of the world's cooperators. During the same year, an American and a Russian cooperator jointly designed a poster associating cooperatives and peace, which was published and distributed by the ICA as part of its commemoration of the Year of Peace. Such collaboration was emblematic of a significant aspect of cooperative international relationships. During the Cold War when "eastern" and "western" governments agreed on very little, the cooperative movement was the only major international social movement that did not succumb to the political differences of that dispute and establish corresponding organizations that emphasized differences. Cooperatives, while arguing sometimes rancorously, remained members of one movement under one banner.

Cooperation as the Basis for a Future Society

Every day, in many parts of the world, people are gathering to form cooperatives to help meet their local problems and needs. In other places, cadres of cooperators, frustrated by stagnating economic systems, systemic injustices and world poverty, raise the Rainbow Flag of the cooperative movement as a symbol of their belief that a more cooperative day is coming. They proclaim that human society will evolve to a point at which the values of cooperation will prevail. Some have become authors, proclaiming through the titles of books their belief that cooperation is the answer to the world's ills—Ernest Poisson of France in *La Règublique coopérative*; Surendra Bey of India in *Sahakari Samaj: The Cooperative Commonwealth*; Yugoslavian-Canadian George Davidovic in *Towards a Cooperative World, Economically, Socially and Politically*; and Antonio Fabra Rivas, a refugee from Spain under Franco, in *Hacia un nuevo orden económico* (Toward a New Economic Order).

ECONOMICS OF COOPERATION

By the end of the 19th century, cooperatives had become established; they had functioned long enough and were extensive enough to warrant serious academic efforts to define their place in economic theory and practice. Of particular note were discussions of whether cooperatives were a new economic system in their own right, or whether they simply reflected modifications or adaptations of the approaches of the already-defined capitalist and socialist economic systems. The conclusions of cooperative theorists were mixed, with the predominant view being that cooperation represented reformist adaptations rather than a unique form. But proponents of the other view have continued to make their case.

Comparisons with Other Socio-Economic Systems

With the expansion of democratic socialist governments, the establishment of communism in the Soviet Union, the rise of fascism in Italy and Germany, and the appearance of economic distress within capitalism, a body of literature that tried to place cooperation in or juxtaposed to these systems appeared. Socialists were most comfortable with the growing cooperative movement, seeing it as a principal way in which their economic system would be organized. Communists, particularly those who had lambasted cooperation as mere bourgeois reformism that weakened revolutionary zeal, had trouble acknowledging a role for cooperatives. With a nudge from Lenin, however, and the need to deal with massive problems of social change in the Soviet Union, they came to accept that cooperatives were a type of "social property" alongside state ownership—at least temporarily. Fascism's answer was to coopt cooperatives, rein them in and make them part of a managed state capitalist system. Capitalists held varying views. Some saw cooperatives as simply another type of private ownership (with a more meddlesome group of "stockholders"), while others believed cooperatives to be thinly disguised forms of socialism or communism. Still others saw cooperatives as a useful reform movement that channeled discontent and softened unbridled capitalism. There was another group that saw cooperation as the meeting ground for the best in each of these other systems and believed that the future would be a conscious amalgam of them, with cooperation at its core.

Cooperation and Competition

An early issue of some significance in assessing various economic theories was the role of competition and cooperation. Laissez-faire capitalism, riding the wave of the Industrial Revolution, enthroned the principle of unconstrained enterprise and saw unrestrained competition as the way to achieve great wealth for the enterprising and provide benefits that would trickle down to the masses. Cooperators, reacting to the mass degradations of that same Industrial Revolution, saw collaboration in cooperative organizations as a group-based counterweight to the capitalist system. Introduced into this mix in 1859 was Darwin's *Origin of Species*, describing evolution in the physical world, and its counterpart, Social Darwinism, which projected Darwin's theories onto human society. "Survival of the fittest" became the explanation and rationale for competition among human beings and for the advances of human civilization.

This conception was challenged by many, almost from its inception, but it was Peter Kropotkin's *Mutual Aid, a Factor of Evolution* (1902) that seriously engaged partisans of the two views in what has been a continuing intellectual competition ever since. Social Darwinism has been the dominant view, but there has been a steady stream of treatises by advocates of the cooperative alternative who contend, as did Kropotkin, that physical evolution has involved cooperation as well as competition. They argue that competition is a stage through which human society is evolving and that cooperation will ultimately prove the better survival mechanism.

Believers in this view, and particularly those who contend that competition and cooperation are learned responses rather than reflections of innate qualities, have in recent years developed theories and approaches that they believe will lead to a more "pro-social" human development that will minimize competition and reward cooperation. The "Nurturing Cooperation" section in the bibliography lists some of their material, including various games structured around the principles of cooperation.

Cooperation in Developing Countries

The decolonization process that began to accelerate after World War II produced a group of newly independent countries faced with the dual challenges of nation-building and the social and economic development of their people and institutions. The fact that most of these new countries were preindustrial in economic development, as well as having limited resources and populations living in abject poverty, pushed their leadership to seek ways of accelerating development and of finding the necessary organizational and financial resources necessary to accomplish their development goal.

As soon as their own postwar reconstruction process was well under way, a number of industrialized countries started channeling some resources to assist in Third World development, establishing international agencies to deliver such assistance. The search for indigenous organizational structures through which assistance could be delivered in such a way that it might benefit more than just an entrepreneurial elite led first to support for governmental bureaucracies and then to a search for other alternatives, including cooperatives. These interests in cooperatives led to a flow of literature (see the bibliography) in which the theory and practice of cooperatives in the industrialized countries were adapted to the very different situations of developing countries. That adaptation, now based on growing indigenous experience, continues to the present day.

TYPES OF COOPERATIVES

Cooperative organizations are found in almost every sector of the economy, wherever people have come together to pursue their interests, to ply their trades, or to deal with various problems within their communities. The major sectoral areas of cooperation that have developed are described below. Fuller consideration of them will be found in the literature cited in the bibliography. Appendix 2 identifies the countries in which different types of cooperation are to be found.

Agricultural Cooperatives

Literature on agricultural cooperatives first appeared in the 1850s in France, where it has been a subject of continuing interest. Literature from Germany began to appear in the 1860s and has continued since, with a noticeable reduction during the Nazi period of the 1930s and 1940s. Literature from the U.S. and England appears at the turn of the century, with American publications appearing more regularly and giving particular attention to cooperative marketing. In the period 1910–20, books on agricultural cooperatives appeared in Argentina, Italy and Denmark, followed in the 1920s by works from Luxembourg, Bulgaria and the Netherlands. A surge of books in the 1930s added authors from Europe (Belgium, Czechoslovakia, Ireland, Romania, Spain and Switzerland) as well as from Africa, Algeria, Chile and China. During the 1940s and 1950s, works from Austria, Canada, Hungary, Japan, Sweden and the USSR were published, as well as works from the developing countries of India, Israel, Mexico and Venezuela. Beginning in the 1960s, with growing attention given to social and economic advancement in developing countries, there was a steady addition to the number of countries producing literature on agricultural cooperative theory and practice. The scope of such literature is now almost universal.

Agricultural cooperatives were slower to develop than other types. By 1870 consumer cooperatives had been established in 18 countries, worker production cooperatives in 13, and thrift and credit societies in 12; however, agricultural cooperatives had been initiated in only five—Spain (1837), Australia (1859), Denmark (1860), Switzerland (1860) and the U.S. (1866). As more and more countries moved from subsistence to production agriculture, the relevance of cooperatives, particularly for small farmers, became increasingly obvious. By 1900, agricultural cooperatives were found in almost as many countries as the three other main types of cooperatives. In the years that followed, these became the dominant form, with agricultural cooperatives founded in 79 countries in the next 70 years. Today there are few countries that do not have this form of organization.

Early agricultural cooperatives were usually formed around producers of a particular crop or commodity and generally expressed themselves in form of supply of inputs and/or marketing of produce. The availability of credit to match and support the agricultural production cycle was also important. As farming began to mechanize, cooperatives were formed to make access to such equipment possible without every farmer having to absorb the large costs of individual purchases. Improvements in life on the farm led to expanded needs for credit for improved amenities such as housing.

As industrialization expanded, with a commensurate movement of rural population to urban centers, the number of farmers declined and agricultural operations became increasingly centralized. Large regional cooperative organizations became common. Processing of produce was an important activity, particularly in certain commodities. The export of produce became a significant operation, in which cooperatives took a role. In industrialized countries, the number of farmers has declined dramatically, as has the number of local cooperatives. In most developing countries, however, agricultural cooperatives still exceed all other types in number of societies and size of membership.

The bibliographical material on agricultural cooperatives reflects this diversity and includes specific references on agricultural credit and marketing. It does not attempt, however, to cite the extensive literature on cooperative activity involving individual commodities. The one exception, dairy cooperatives, included because of some particularly interesting developments, illustrates what is available on cooperatives formed around other commodities. Some of this information will be found in the general agricultural cooperative bibliographies cited.

The ILO *International Directory of Cooperative Organizations* (1988) identified agricultural cooperatives in 142 countries. The agricultural cooperatives in 66 of these countries had organized national federations to represent their interests.

Communal Settlements/Farming

Two strains of thought come to mind when considering cooperatives as they are expressed in communal activity. The first is the "intentional communities" whose people move away from the conventional world and adopt a lifestyle that represents their vision of human nature and human society at its best. Their assumption is that general society is corrupt and corrupting and one can only lead the ideal life by getting away from such corruption. This was very much the thought of one group of early cooperative theorists, represented by Charles Fourier and, later in his life, by Robert Owen. The title of Alfred Apsler's book, *Communes Through the Ages: The Search for Utopia*, expresses this theme.

The second strain of communalism is reflected in various structures that have been adopted to help achieve common goals through joint action, including, usually, communal living. The focus in these groups is as much on the efficient accomplishment of tasks as on individual and societal transformation. Collective farming, these advocates assert, is more effective than individual farming and is more socially worthwhile.

Both of these themes are cited for reference in the bibliography, as are the particular cooperative experiences of the communes of China, the kibbutz and *moshav* settlements of Israel, the *ejidos* in Mexico, the state and cooperative farms of the Soviet Union and other countries in Eastern Europe, the *ujaama* villages of Tanzania and the communes (past and present) of the U.S. and other countries. A number of works identify and compare these different national experiences.

Consumer Cooperatives

While consumer cooperatives were generally the first type of cooperative organized in most countries, the literature on this sector of the world movement was slow in developing, and almost all of it has been published in the 20th century. Works by Charles Gide and others in France head the list, followed by early works in Spain, the U.K., Germany, the U.S. and Italy. By the 1930s a geographical spread of new literature had begun, and today locally published materials on consumer cooperatives can be found in most countries.

Consumer cooperatives are generally regarded as having been first initiated by Dr. William King in the U.K. in 1828, followed in 1834 by groups in France and in 1845 in the U.S. By 1871 they were also found in Austria, Canada, Czechoslovakia, Finland, Germany, Iceland, Italy, the Netherlands, Norway, Poland, Portugal, Russia, Spain and Sweden. A second phase of the development of consumer cooperatives covers the period from 1890 to World War II and was characterized by their continuing geographical spread into new countries and the establishment of national federations and national wholesale societies, important steps in integrating the movements. During this time the consumer cooperatives in Germany, Italy and Japan were compromised by the nationalistic zeal of wartime populations and by controls instituted by the governments of these countries. Following World War II they were reconstituted, however, and are important independent cooperative organizations again.

The period after World War II saw consumer cooperatives continue to expand, with the first such societies being started in many developing countries. In the established movements, it was a period of diversification into various fields of consumer services and the emergence of sophisticated networks of supermarkets and department stores. Some of the major movements in Europe had difficulty retaining their economic viability in the face of heightened economic competition from large private marketing operations.

Historically, while opposed in their early days as "only palliative" by militant socialists and Marxists who saw them as only helping to delay the coming of the workers' revolution, consumer cooperatives have been closely aligned with Social Democratic parties in a number of countries, and individuals from their ranks have taken prominent roles in social reform efforts and the peace movement. This more prominent political role has led to tensions with other, more conservative, elements in cooperative movements, nationally and internationally, and has been a hindrance to full cooperative solidarity. On their part, consumer cooperative leaders have held that they are only pursuing a larger cooperative vision.

In recent years, in countries with longstanding consumer cooperative movements, there has been a "new wave" of consumer cooperative development, mostly in food cooperatives emphasizing healthy, naturally grown foods and environmental issues. These have been formed by cooperators seeking new ways to encourage small, worker-owned businesses and to integrate the consumer and producer cooperative movements.

The 1988 edition of the ILO *International Directory of Cooperative Organizations* identified consumer cooperatives in 124 countries, 55 of them having national consumer federations. (See appendix 2.)

Financial Cooperatives

The term "financial cooperatives" was selected for this sector of the cooperative movement, rather than the more traditional "credit cooperatives," to reflect the fact that most of these cooperatives have moved far beyond being mere providers of credit. Whether in industrialized or developing countries, these cooperatives have become or are becoming increasingly sophisticated financial institutions that provide a wide range of financial services to members. Based on the character of their development and operation, they can be placed in three categories: cooperative banks, savings and credit cooperatives (largely, but not exclusively, related to agriculture) and credit unions.

Literature regarding financial cooperatives made its appearance first in 1853 and was mainly related to the thinking and work of Hermann Schultze-Delitzsch in Germany. These works, plus those reflecting the work of Wilhelm Raiffeisen and the developing movement that bears his name in Germany and elsewhere, have made up almost all of the works in German dealing with financial cooperatives. Until 1900 they were almost the exclusive sources of all such literature. After the turn of the century, books began to appear in France and a number of other countries, with a spate of books on the theory and practice of financial cooperatives in Italy and India. In the 1930s in Canada and the U.S., the development of an extensive body of works dealing with credit unions and the Desjardins movement in French-speaking Canada began, and it continues to this day.

Cooperative Banks

Cooperative banks, designed to provide a wide range of financial services to all or to particular sectors of the cooperative movement in a country, appeared for the first time in the final quarter of the 19th century. The ILO *International Directory of Cooperative Organizations* (1988), which listed such banks in 41 countries, identified banks dating from this period in Austria (1872 and 1898), Finland (1902), Germany (1895), the Netherlands (1896), Spain (1901), Switzerland (1902) and the U.K. (1872). Others, notably in Belgium, France and Italy, probably have similar dates of origin but were not so identified in the *Directory*. Banks dating from this period in Bulgaria, Czechoslovakia, Hungary, Poland and Yugoslavia were nationalized or dissolved when communist governments took power in these countries after World War II. In the period leading up to that war, other cooperative banks were established in Europe and elsewhere—Cyprus (1937), Denmark (1925), Israel (1921), Japan (1923 and 1932), Luxembourg (1926), Norway (1936), Sweden (1916) and the U.S. (1933). Cooperative banking began in developing countries, first in Argentina, India, Pakistan and Sri Lanka, during the first quarter of the 20th century, and spread to a number of other countries in the post–World War II period.

Cooperative banks are designed to provide financial services to other cooperative organizations and, in many cases, directly to members of cooperative societies.

Savings and Credit Cooperatives

These cooperatives, like other types, emerged in a number of countries in the mid-1800s in response to the common problems that farmers, artisans, small entrepreneurs and consumers faced as they tried to adjust to and become part of the economies emerging from the Industrial Revolution. With traditional banks showing little interest in serving the needs of these groups, and the increasingly unattractive option of turning to usurious and exploitative money lenders, these groups began to explore cooperative solutions to their savings and credit needs.

In 1854 in Germany, Hermann Schultze-Delitzsch established his first cooperative, aimed primarily at aiding small entrepreneurs in growing urban areas. He was followed within a few years by Wilhelm Raiffeisen, who, dispirited by the lack of benevolence of the established elite in meeting the needs of the poor, started a series of cooperative ventures aimed at serving the rural population in the area where he worked. These efforts took root quickly. Before long they had formed federations that in later years became large banking operations serving cooperative needs. Their cooperative model was emulated in Austria, Bulgaria, the Netherlands, Poland, Romania, Spain, Switzerland and Yugoslavia. By the turn of the century, national unions of savings and credit cooperatives had been established in Austria, Germany, the Netherlands, Romania and Switzerland.

Parallel indigenous developments on a smaller scale were taking place during the same years in Belgium, Bulgaria, Czechoslovakia, Italy, Poland, Turkey and Yugoslavia. In Italy these developments were led by Luigi Luzzatti, a vigorous advocate of "people's banks" or "popular banks" in which ordinary banking services would be made available to ordinary people.

Savings and credit cooperatives quickly began to diversify to serve a variety of needs, as different cooperative sectors became established. The special needs and interests of agricultural cooperatives, of groups of worker producers, small entrepreneurs, consumers and housing cooperatives began to be reflected in specialized organizations designed to meet their credit requirements, usually within the framework of national federations of cooperatives in the various cooperative sectors.

In 1988 the ILO identified 34 countries in which savings and credit cooperatives of this general nature were operating.

Credit Unions

A unique savings and credit cooperative tradition had its origin in North America, first in Canada under the leadership of Alphonse Desjardins and subsequently, with Desjardins's help, in the U.S. under that of Edward Filene and Roy Bergengren. In French-speaking Canada this type of cooperative became known as a *caisse populaire*; in the U.S. and English-speaking Canada, a credit union.

The development of credit unions is described in more detail in the section on WOCCU, later in the introduction.

Fisheries Cooperatives

Literature on fisheries cooperatives was late in developing; the first identified work was published in Algeria in 1932. It was not until the post–World War II years that it began to appear in some volume, very largely the product of the fisheries division of the FAO in Rome. Among these works was *Cooperation for Fishermen* by Margaret Digby, published in 1961 in collaboration with the ICA. From that time on, the literature increased and now includes inter alia works published by the ICA Fisheries Committee, COPAC, the World Bank and the U.S. Department of Agriculture.

For many countries, information about fisheries cooperatives is scanty, and detailed knowledge is sporadic. The first cooperative activity in this sector dates from 1800 in Greece, when the Island Maritime Cooperative was established. Not much is known about it, however, and the next significant event was in 1886 in Japan, when fishermen's groups had become established enough to warrant the issuing of "Regulations on Fishermen's Associations." In the years leading up to World War I, the "Fisheries Organization Society" was established in London and the first fishing cooperatives were organized in France and Indonesia.

The interwar years saw fisheries cooperative activity develop in Canada, Denmark, Italy, Japan, Norway, Sweden and Yugoslavia. An insurance cooperative for fishing vessels was organized in the U.K.

Since World War II there has been an expansion of activities in existing fisheries cooperatives and an expansion of such activities into the developing countries. The ILO *International Directory of Cooperative Organizations* (1988) notes fisheries cooperative activity in 77 countries, including 11 industrialized countries. Most of the citations, however, are for activity in the developing areas of the world, including 23 African countries, 12 in Asia, 13 in the Caribbean, 24 in Latin America and 5 in North Africa and the Near East. (See appendix 2 for details.)

Forestry Cooperatives

Forestry cooperatives are a relatively minor sector in the world cooperative movement. The ILO *International Directory of Cooperative Organizations* (1988) noted their presence in only 12 countries, Chile, Finland, France, Honduras, India, Japan, Morocco, Myanmar, Norway, Panama, Senegal and Sweden. They are also reported to exist on a small scale along the coast of the U.S. While a principal activity of such cooperatives has been the marketing of forest products, in those countries where they remain active economic units, they are now of two principal types. The first type is forest owners' cooperatives, as in Finland, where small holders of forest land join together to obtain necessary supplies used in forest production and for joint marketing of their products. In India, the second type, forest laborer cooperatives, predominates. These are essentially worker production cooperatives, providing manpower to forest owners as an alternative to the owners' hiring individual workers.

The literature on forestry cooperatives, which began to appear in the 1940s, is of only modest proportions. The book by Digby and Edwardson, *Organization of Forestry Cooperatives*, published in 1976 by the Plunkett

Foundation for Cooperative Studies, remains a principal source for placing this type of cooperative in a historical and operational perspective.

Housing Cooperatives

While the tradition of groups associating for housing construction dates far back in human history, formal groups for this purpose are first noted in the U.K. in 1775, and the first formal cooperatives for this purpose were noted around 1850, when housing cooperatives appeared in Denmark, France, Germany, Norway and Sweden. In Germany, housing cooperatives preceded most, if not all, other types of cooperative organizations.

The cooperative response to housing needs grew out of problems associated with the massive movements of populations from rural to urban areas that took place first in the industrializing countries of Europe and North America and subsequently in the developing nations of the world. Most public jurisdictions lacked the experience and resources to deal with this enormous movement of people to the cities and were initially overwhelmed by it. Most employers, intent on maximizing profits, considered employees' housing to be the employees' own problem. The results were squalid slums and squatter communities; people of limited means and power were left to their own devices for lodging.

Faced with such conditions, group-based solutions were, with increasing frequency, chosen by those who wanted something better in housing. Public authorities began to assume responsibility for establishing urban order and providing for public welfare. Groups assisted by socially motivated individuals and organizations began to attack housing problems. The example of cooperatives in other sectors was seen as offering an organizational model for those seeking decent living space.

By the end of World War I, a majority of countries in Europe (plus Argentina and India) had at least the beginnings of cooperative housing movements, and the first national cooperative housing federations had been established in Czechoslovakia, Denmark, France and the Netherlands. By the start of World War II in 1939, cooperatives were found in almost all European countries and in Australia, Canada and the United States Cooperative housing societies had also begun to appear in other developing countries including Chile, Colombia, India, Pakistan and Palestine (Israel).

Partly as a response to the destruction of the war, partly in reaction to the rising tide of urban migration in the developing countries, and partly through the institutionalizing of a successful cooperative model, the post–World War II period saw an increasing spread of cooperative housing.

By 1980 the ICA publication, *Cooperative Housing*, identified 40 countries in which they existed. By 1988, when the ILO *International Directory of Cooperative Organizations* was last published, the number had grown to 73, with national federations of housing cooperatives operating in at least 31 of these countries. (See appendix 2 for a list of countries in which there has been cooperative housing activity.)

International cooperation in encouraging the expansion of housing cooperatives, particularly in developing countries, has been supported not only by established cooperative housing movements in a number of countries (most notably in Denmark, Finland, France, Germany, Sweden and the U.S.), but also by the ICA through its Housing Committee. In the UN system, HABITAT has had a continuing (though sometimes limited) commitment to the advancement of cooperative housing.

For many years, the ICA has had a Housing Committee that encourages interaction among national movements, publishes technical material on the subject and supports assistance to housing cooperatives, particularly in developing countries. In 1964, the International Cooperative Housing Development Association was established by the ICA, and it worked for a number of years in support of cooperative housing, particularly with the UN's HABITAT. The Cooperative Housing Foundation in the U.S., DESWOS (German Development Assistance for Social Housing), and the Scandinavian housing cooperatives have been particularly active in providing technical assistance and training for cooperators from developing countries, in part supported by funds from their governments' development assistance programs.

The literature on cooperative housing appeared initially in Germany, first emerging in the 1860s. Germany continued to be almost the only source of such information in the period leading up to World War I. Published works in Denmark, France, the U.K. and the U.S. appeared during the interwar years. Following World War II the geographical spread of such works was rapid, in its earlier years most prominently in Argentina, Chile and India. It is now quite extensive. Internationally, the ICA Housing Committee has published two editions of its book, *Cooperative Housing*.

Industrial Cooperatives

Cooperators do not agree on how to label these cooperatives. They are variously referred to as "industrial cooperatives," "worker cooperatives," "worker production cooperatives" and "worker productive cooperatives." These terms describe cooperatives in which those who do the work own the business, manage it, and share in the financial returns. The worker-members invest their own money as well as their time and effort.

While industrial production is the predominant type of activity among this form of cooperative, there are also cooperatives that engage in a specialized type of production (e.g., handicrafts), involve a specific population (e.g., disabled persons), or cooperatively provide services (e.g., public utilities and personally oriented services such as health or education).

As industrial cooperatives came into existence and expanded, they offered a variety of things to their owners. For the militant trade unionist or socialist ideologue, they were the first step toward the day when the workers of the world would prevail. As they expanded, they became a tool for moderating the power of capitalism and for lessening the oppression of a debasing industrial order intent on maximizing personal gain at whatever expense. As an expression of the spread of democracy, particularly in France at first, they brought to reality the possibilities of industrial democracy. For the socially restless, they became organizational vehicles for attacking common social and economic needs and problems without waiting for other, grander solutions.

While preceded by some isolated efforts, including collective mills and artisan weavers in England and Scotland in the 1760s, industrial cooperatives as an organized form emerged first in France in the 1830s, building on the thought and actions of Charles Fourier, Philippe Buchez and Louis Blanc. These men undertook experiments that gave industrial cooperatives their form and had published works defining their ideology and organization.

The most common types of industrial cooperative in the early days were those that provided a structure through which skilled artisans could together pursue their trades (carpenters, tailors), often operating in fields, such as baking and food processing, that produced commodities in universal demand. The growth of this form of cooperative was steady in France, was emulated on a smaller scale in Britain (including a workers' building cooperative founded by some of the Rochdale pioneers), and also appeared in a number of other countries. By 1910, such cooperatives could be found in Australia, Belgium, Bulgaria, Czechoslovakia, El Salvador, Germany, Japan, Mexico, the Netherlands, Palestine, Poland, Portugal, Spain, Switzerland and the U.S. During these same years national industrial cooperative federations were established in Britain (1882), France (1884) and Belgium (1897); the first workers' cooperative bank was established in France (1893); and the first legislation directly relating to industrial cooperatives was passed in Japan (1897).

The interwar years saw a progressive growth of industrial cooperatives, including handicraft cooperatives, and the emergence of additional national federations in Hungary (1920), the USSR (1922), Belgium (1924), Italy (1926), Palestine (1928), Poland (1937) and Spain (1942). During the depression years a variety of experiments were tried, particularly in the U.S., to form cooperatives of the poor or unemployed for self-help purposes. The U.S. federal government even funded a project in New York City to document the history of cooperative developments worldwide.

The post–World War II years to the present have been a period of varying tendencies for industrial cooperatives. Many people had great expectations for the newly communist countries, anticipating their emergence as worker states where worker cooperatives would at last come into their own. In Bulgaria, Czechoslovakia, Hungary and Poland, industrial cooperatives came to play significant roles in their national economies. In most of the other communist states, however, cooperatives played minor, specialized roles, with social ownership being expressed mainly through state enterprises.

Furthermore, the long-touted goal of democracy and worker control in the industrial order was obstructed by the roles assumed by communist party functionaries. These tended to be more responsive to state planning directives than to more idealistic theories. Dissenting views were not lacking among cooperators in these countries, however, some even contending that Lenin's real goal, lost in his early death, was a "cooperative socialism" rather than the "bureaucratic" version that actually evolved.

In market-oriented economies, particularly in Europe, industrial cooperatives continued to grow at a modest pace. The persistence of poverty in many of these countries led to government-motivated schemes to form cooperatives for the poor and unemployed, often emulating the experience of the depression years when self-help or labor-pooling cooperatives proved useful.

Another trend in this period was the emergence of industrial cooperatives in a number of developing countries, symbolized by the establishment of a national federation of industrial cooperatives in India in 1951. In the years since then, a total of 69 developing countries have seen the emergence of industrial cooperatives, many of which, however, remain just fledgling efforts. In India, the number of industrial cooperatives now exceeds 60,000, more than the total of all such cooperatives in the rest of the world.

A further trend, found principally in industrialized economies, is the transfer of ownership of failing private enterprises to cooperatives formed by their employees. This allows employment to continue and, for many of these businesses, a reborn ability to function in a competitive environment once traditional stockholder expectations of profits are eliminated.

Another phenomenon of note is the sheer persistence of this type of cooperative organization, given its lesser proliferation in comparison to other types of cooperatives and its inability to achieve the grander aspirations of its founders. Every year in various parts of the world, industrialized and developing, new groups of workers come together to pool their skills and resources and commit themselves to working in a cooperative group. Many of those taking part in these new cooperative enterprises approach their participation with the same zeal as the early cooperative pioneers, and their goals remain similar—utilize one's skills, ameliorate bad conditions, practice solidarity, reshape the world.

The ILO *International Directory of Cooperative Organizations* (1988) cited the presence of industrial cooperatives in 88 countries—18 in industrialized countries, 25 in Africa, 11 in the Asia/Pacific region, 6 in the Caribbean, 16 in Latin America and 12 in North Africa/Near East. (See appendix 2.)

The literature on industrial cooperatives parallels their geographical and historical development. The first works appeared in France in the 1830s, and the French tradition has generated a large portion of the books that have been published. Authors from the U.K. and Germany have also contributed significantly. The period since World War II has been productive, with books from or involving the developing world assuming more prominence after 1960.

Handicraft Cooperatives

Specialized worker production cooperatives of artisans producing handicrafts date from 1842 in Japan and Spain, followed by groups organized in Portugal (1858), El Salvador (1860), Serbia (1870), Mexico (1875), Canada (Quebec) (1876) and Bulgaria (before 1895). The first national federation of such cooperatives was organized in Czechoslovakia in 1910, followed in the interwar years by similar groups in Hungary (1920), Ukraine (1921), Russia (1922), Poland (1937), Tunisia (1937) and Greece (1942).

Since World War II, governments and development organizations have encouraged these cooperatives and provided a modicum of support and technical assistance. The ICA Coop Trade Project, when it was operational during the 1980s, included them in its marketing activities, as have a number of general craft agencies. However, these cooperatives, with a few notable exceptions, tend to be small and struggling and have not yet developed effective international trading structures.

The ILO *International Directory of Cooperative Organizations* (1988) identified a number of countries in which handicraft cooperatives were functioning. A number of other countries may include them under the generic title of "industrial cooperatives." Such cooperatives, however, are known to exist in at least the following countries: Bangladesh, Botswana, Canada, Chile, Côte d'Ivoire, Czech Republic, Guatemala, Hungary, India, Indonesia, Lesotho, Malaysia, Pakistan, Panama, Philippines, Poland, Rwanda, Saint Christopher/Nevis, Slovakia, Somalia, Sri Lanka, Uganda, the U.S. and Uruguay.

A small body of literature exists on these cooperatives. A useful examination of their place among cooperatives in the U.S. is *Finding Coops: A Resource Guide and Directory*, published in 1984 by the Cooperative Information Consortium and available from the National Cooperative Business Association.

Cooperatives of Disabled Persons

Industrial-type cooperatives organized by and for people with physical limitations first appeared in Poland in 1919 to serve the needs of disabled veterans of World War I. By 1922 a similar group of such cooperatives had been established in the Soviet Union. Additional societies were established in Poland, and the "Disabled Persons' Cooperative Union" was established at Warsaw in 1949. Similar cooperatives were launched in Czechoslovakia in 1950 and have grown, as in Poland and Russia, to become major providers of services to the disabled. They provide medical and social services as well as operating enterprises that provide gainful employment.

Cooperatives of disabled people at the local level are of several types: worker production cooperatives involving various trades and branches of industrial production; societies that engage in the sale of articles produced by the first type; labor contracting societies providing direct service to customers such as photography stores and restaurants; home workshops where disabled people work at a trade; and cooperatives that cater to the special requirements of groups, as with credit unions for the blind in the U.S.

As part of the UN International Decade of Disabled Persons (1983–1992) COPAC and the United Nations Center for Social Development and Humanitarian Affairs published *Cooperatives of the Disabled—A Guide for Promotion and Organization*, a work prepared by Johann Gudmundsson, a retired ILO official. This comprehensive guide, including a directory of such cooperatives in 31 countries, builds on the earlier work in this field undertaken by the ILO and the United Nations Development Program.

Insurance Cooperatives

The pre-Rochdale history of the world cooperative movement is considered by many cooperative historians to have begun in Philadelphia, U.S.A., in the 1750s, when Benjamin Franklin and a few neighbors set out to establish the Union Fire Company to protect themselves from fires. In 1752 they organized a mutual insurance society, the Philadelphia Contributionship for the Insurance of Houses from Loss by Fire (which still exists today). Almost simultaneously, similar steps were being taken in London, and life insurance societies were established in both cities in 1767.

A number of small self-help insurance societies were organized in both rural and urban areas in a number of countries in the ensuing 75 years. The first insurance cooperative of lasting influence, the Australian Mutual Provident Society, was established in 1849. It was followed by the Cooperative Insurance Company established in the U.K. in 1867 and the "Coopvie l'es artisans" in Quebec, Canada, in 1876. In the U.S., cooperative insurance groups proliferated to the point that a national association was established in 1895 in Indianapolis, Indiana. That same year livestock insurance made its appearance in Hungary. Mutual insurance cooperatives soon followed with La Solidarité in France (1900), Tryg in Denmark (1903), ASV in the Netherlands (1904), La Prévoyance sociale in Belgium (1907), Folksam in Sweden (1908), Vara in Finland (1910), Volksfürsorge in Germany (1912) and Coop Lebensversicherungs-Genossenschaft in Switzerland (1917).

In the interwar years cooperative insurance federations were established to consolidate and strengthen national insurance efforts, and cooperative insurers developed more lines of coverage appropriate to the needs of cooperatives and their members. This period also saw the establishment of the Credit Union National Association (CUNA) Mutual Insurance Society in 1935 to serve the burgeoning credit union movement in the U.S. and Canada and subsequently in other countries, as the credit union movement expanded into what we know now as the World Council of Credit Unions.

In 1922 the ICA Insurance Committee, now the International Cooperative and Mutual Insurance Federation (ICMIF), was established. Over the years it has provided leadership for what is still an evolving movement, well established in industrialized countries but as yet of lesser standing in the developing world. In 1978 the Association of European Cooperative Insurers was established and within 10 years had affiliated 24 cooperative insurance societies with 50,000,000 policy holders in the countries of the European Community.

The ILO *International Directory of Cooperative Organizations* (1988) cited cooperative insurance organizations in 31 countries: 18 in industrialized countries, 4 in Africa, 2 in Asia, 1 in the Caribbean, 5 in Latin America, and 1 in North Africa/Near East. In 1996 the ICMIF *Membership Directory* listed some 150 cooperative related insurers, 82 of which, in 52 countries, were members of ICMIF. There were also four associations listed as members, five observers, and four regional associations of the federation in Europe, Africa, America and Asia.

CUNA Mutual Insurance Society has had a long history of supplying insurance services to developing credit union movements. Most of these started as joint ventures between CUNA Mutual and national credit union organizations, but a number of them, particularly in Latin America, have spun off as separate credit union insurers. (See appendix 2 for a list of countries with cooperative insurance activity.)

Literature dealing with cooperative insurance appeared in the 1930s and included *Cooperative Insurance*, written by Noah Barou and published in the U.K. in 1936. This work surveyed developments and outlined future development potential for cooperative insurance. Ronald Garnett's *A Century of Cooperative Insurance*, published in 1968, presented a broader picture with 30 more years of experience. Continuing the record of development, the Insurance Federation published *Worldwide Cooperative Insurance in 1983* and periodically publishes a *Members Directory*.

Multipurpose Cooperatives

A review of cooperative experience suggests that most cooperative societies begin by focusing on a narrowly defined problem or need, and success, in most cases, comes from the diligent pursuit of goals established to meet those specific needs. Attempts to meet a diversity of needs or to provide a mixture of services too early in the life of cooperatives is usually a prescription for trouble. Conversely, the members of successful single-purpose cooperatives almost always wish to build on their initial limited success by expanding the focus of their operation to meet additional needs.

So long as the time frame for the growth of a cooperative society is long enough and the pace of its evolution is relaxed enough to allow for gradual development, this problem can be resolved with experimentation. However, when cooperative development is rushed by overzealous participants or external forces, the attempt to do too many things too fast almost always creates serious problems or, at worst, complete failure. This has led some activists to warn that the development of a successful cooperative probably requires a generation of time.

The rapid decolonization of the post–World War II period, combined with a concern for assisting developing countries (which were in only the early stages of industrialization and lacked indigenous institutional structures), led to experiments with cooperative formation. Cooperatives became the externally selected means for achieving a multiplicity of externally defined goals. Quickly established or imposed multipurpose cooperatives were the means selected for many of those efforts. When they achieved only limited success, many people became disillusioned with cooperatives.

The notable lack of success of this approach led to serious reappraisal by cooperators and development specialists, and in the 1970s, with leadership from the ICA Regional Office in New Delhi, a body of literature emerged in which attempts were made to evaluate in more detail the experience with multipurpose cooperatives, to modify the approach, and to factor in the time needed for the internal development of cooperative experience, leadership and sophistication.

It is still uncertain as to whether multipurpose cooperatives can succeed as a starting point for development. Meanwhile, such cooperatives tend to proliferate as a response to the need for different modes of operation in already industrialized economies.

School and Youth Cooperatives

Once organized cooperation had become an established phenomenon, with many of its organizers deeming it "the wave of the future," it was urged that the ideology of cooperation and the structure of cooperatives should be introduced in some systematic way to young people. Three avenues were pursued to achieve this goal. First, it was proposed that cooperatives for primary and secondary school children be organized, so that they could experience cooperation in action in affairs of importance to them. Second, there were moves to introduce cooperation into school curricula. Third, in recognition that many young people were not in formal schools but already in the workforce, special cooperatives were established for particular groups (e.g., young farmers), and training programs were set up to introduce the principles of cooperation and to prepare young people for future leadership in the movement.

The idea of school cooperatives first emerged in Argentina in 1884, when their establishment was authorized in legislation dealing with general education. One of the first general references to such cooperatives was in Mabilleau's *Almanach de la coopération française* in 1899. The record of 20th-century school cooperatives, however, begins with the establishment of La Ruche (The Beehive) cooperative in France by Barthélemy Profit, who later went on to write extensively on the subject. School cooperatives emerged in Latin America in the 1920s, in Argentina (1922), Mexico (1924) and Brazil (1928). They were proposed for Uruguay in 1926 but did not really get started there until 25 years later. National federations of school cooperatives were established in France (1928), Belgium (1954), Saint Christopher and Nevis (1979) and Uruguay (1969).

In the ILO *International Directory of Cooperative Organizations* (1988), school cooperatives are noted as existing in Chile, Costa Rica, France, Kiribati, Montserrat, Peru, Saint Christopher and Nevis, Saint Lucia, and Trinidad and Tobago.

In 1984 the International Alliance of School Cooperatives was established, based at the headquarters of the French school cooperatives in Paris. It reported in 1989 that school cooperatives in Argentina, Côte d'Ivoire, France, Italy, Morocco and Yugoslavia were participating and that expressions of interest had come from such groups in Belgium, Poland, Senegal and Zaire.

The literature on school cooperatives, beginning in the late 1920s, has come principally from France and Latin America and has dealt with theory and practice, operations and management, curriculum (when cooperation is an established subject in schools), and the various national experiences with this type of organization. In 1995 ICA-Europe arranged the publication of an *Anthology on Cooperative Experiences in the European Schools*, a study prepared by the Confederazione Cooperative Italiane and the Centro Studi sulla Cooperazione of Rome.

Youth cooperatives for those no longer in formal schooling have a less structured history than school cooperatives, and their activities are more often organized within already established cooperatives than in separate institutions. Their purpose is to inculcate cooperative philosophy and methods in young people and to identify and train future leaders. In some developing countries such programs have been encouraged as a way of speeding up change and modernization by providing channels of action for young cooperators, allowing them to circumvent older, traditional, more conservative cooperative leadership.

Service Cooperatives

Service structures outside the usual business activity of cooperatives have emerged in a number of countries, as groups of people have turned to cooperative organization as a way of meeting common community and individual needs. These cooperatives have been of two types: those providing public services (e.g., electrification, telephone service, irrigation, petroleum supply and transport) and those addressing common personal needs (e.g., health services, preschool programs and memorial/funeral services).

The term "service cooperative" is also used to refer to specialized cooperatives servicing particular needs within the various cooperative sectors (e.g., artificial insemination cooperatives servicing livestock cooperatives, audit services, specialized wholesalers supplying consumer cooperatives).

Electricity Cooperatives

As electrical energy became increasingly available in the second half of the 19th century, it was quickly accessed as a source of light for towns and cities and as a foundation for the energy needs of their rapidly expanding industries. Meanwhile, candles and kerosene lamps were the dim lights of rural areas, and humans and animals were the primary rural energy sources. The difference between urban and rural lifestyles, based on the different availability of light and power, was obvious, particularly to those in rural areas adjacent to expanding urban communities. This provided the impetus for the first steps taken to light the countryside.

Cooperators in Argentina were the pioneers in this effort, establishing the first electricity cooperative at Punta Alta in 1926. A similar cooperative was established in the Dordogne region of France two years later. In 1935 the Rural Electrification Administration initiated cooperative rural electrification in the U.S. Small local experiments among farmers were also undertaken in Europe. By 1939 a national federation of electricity cooperatives had been formed in Argentina. The National Rural Electric Cooperative Association in the U.S. followed in 1942. In 1945 electric cooperatives appeared in Chile.

Expansion into new countries took place in the 1960s, when NRECA, in collaboration with USAID, undertook projects to establish rural electric cooperatives in Bolivia, Brazil, Colombia, Costa Rica, Ecuador, El Salvador, Nicaragua, Peru and Venezuela, and to provide advice and technical assistance to local interests in other countries, among them India and Indonesia. The next significant effort by the American cooperators, with U.S. government assistance, was in the Philippines, followed by a project, still under way, in Bangladesh, now with additional financial support from the World Bank.

Meanwhile, experiments were being made with electrical generation in small hydroelectric projects and in the use of solar power, both as smaller-scale models for power generation and as ways of offsetting the rising cost of the petroleum products used in the production of electricity. For most of the rural world, adequate night light and electrical energy remain things of the future.

At the present time, in addition to nearly 1,000 in the U.S., approximately 500 electricity cooperatives are known to be operating in the following countries: Argentina, Bangladesh, Bolivia, Brazil, Chile, Costa Rica, El Salvador, India, Indonesia and the Philippines. Of these, some 200 were initiated with the help of the NRECA.

The International Cooperative Energy Organization (ICEO), a specialized body of the ICA, serves the needs of energy consumers and cooperative energy suppliers in regard to energy development, materials and equipment supply, energy efficiency and environmental quality. The ICEO was established in October 1992 in Tokyo, Japan. Its organizational meeting was held in conjunction with the 1993 annual meeting of the NRECA in Dallas, Texas. It is one of the newer specialized bodies of the ICA and has yet to engage itself in a broad scope of work.

Telephone Cooperatives

The first telephone cooperative made its appearance in Argentina in 1887, organized by cooperative pioneer David Atwell in Buenos Aires. It was followed by a similar cooperative founded in the U.S. in 1893. In both countries national telephone cooperative federations were eventually formed, attesting to the growing spread of their services. In these, as in other countries where such cooperatives have been organized, they provide only a very modest amount of the telephone services now available.

Irrigation Cooperatives

The supply of rural water through cooperatives for irrigation purposes has been tried at different times and places and has become more widespread as agricultural production has moved from subsistence to production levels. Irrigation cooperatives are also found in areas where irrigation had been used to supplement rain-fed water supplies. More recently, in rural development projects in developing countries, water cooperatives have become a means for supplying residents of semiurban areas. In spite of the success of some of these user systems, cooperatives have generally played a smaller role in irrigation and water supply than government supplied or regulated systems.

Petroleum Cooperatives

As the need for petroleum products to meet the growing demand of automobile and other transport users expanded, and as farming practices became increasingly mechanized, consumers and farmers in North America and elsewhere looked to their cooperatives to provide them with petroleum products. The first to do so as a supplier was a cooperative in Cottonwood, Minnesota, U.S.A., in 1921. In 1926 Midlands Cooperative Oil Association was organized in Minneapolis, Minnesota, to act as a storage facility to provide petroleum products on a wholesale basis. In 1934 the first cooperative refinery was established at Regina, Saskatchewan. This was followed in 1938 by one at Philippsburg, Kansas, which included prospecting for oil among its activities. Its first cooperative oil well came into production in 1940.

In 1945 in Sweden, OK, the first federation of oil consumer cooperatives was founded, followed in 1946 by Oliufelagid, a cooperative oil enterprise, in Iceland. Similar cooperatives were soon formed in other Scandinavian countries, and in 1963 OK became an Inter-Nordic cooperative structure. In 1972 the first cooperative oil refinery in Europe was established in Sweden.

In 1947 the International Cooperative Petroleum Association (ICPA) was founded, the result of an idea that grew out of a small shipment of lubricating oil from the Consumer Cooperative Association in Kansas City, Missouri, to a cooperative in Estonia in 1934. When such shipments spread to other parts of the world, Howard Cowden, then president of the U.S. cooperative supplier, proposed that an international cooperative trading agency be established to facilitate the growing world trade in petroleum. He was joined in the proposal by Albin Johansson, then president of KF in Sweden. Working together with other cooperative leaders in the ICA, they brought the international association into being.

ICPA has had members in, or made shipments to, all parts of the world, initially mainly as a supplier of lubricating oils and allied products but later trading in crude oil, fuels, waxes, equipment and other products. Its members have included consumer, agricultural, transport and multipurpose cooperatives, as well as national oil companies. The Association has assisted developing countries in meeting some of their petroleum processing needs. In 1963 an oil blending plant was established in Dordrecht, Netherlands, to facilitate more efficient and economic shipments from Europe rather than relying on shipments from the U.S. The Association has played an important role in assisting cooperatives worldwide to deal with the current energy situation caused by the establishment and operation of the Organization of Petroleum Exporting Countries and the steps taken in many countries to deal with exploding oil prices.

Transport Cooperatives

The first identified transport cooperative was founded in Portugal in 1889, but it was not until the 1920s that this form of cooperation began to appear in other countries—a river transport cooperative in Germany (1920), a cooperative shipping service in South Africa (1922), and trucks and buses in Israel (1929). The most significant development has taken place in the period since World War II and most extensively in developing countries. The ILO *International Directory of Cooperative Organizations* (1988) identified 33 countries in which transport cooperatives were active, 5 in industrialized countries, 6 in Africa, 4 in Asia/Pacific, 8 in the Caribbean, 9 in Latin America and 1 in North Africa/Near East.

The predominant transport cooperative activity has been the shipment of farm produce to markets and to processing centers, sometimes by specialized transport cooperatives, often as a service of a cooperative federation or regional union. Consumer transport has been both an urban (buses and taxis) and a rural (interurban and rural bus or minibus systems) phenomenon. A number of transport authorities have been organized on a cooperative basis, most notably the Port of London Authority, the London Passenger Transport Board, and the Compagnie nationale du Rhône in France. Transport cooperatives have proven particularly relevant to the needs of island nations.

New forms have taken shape in more recent years, such as cooperative organization of garages, car repair and servicing, and tourism services. In the U.S., United Airlines, when in economic difficulties, was purchased by its employees and now functions similarly to a worker-owned cooperative.

The literature on transport cooperatives is of modest size and of recent date, reflecting the period of most extensive development.

Health Care Cooperatives

Health care cooperatives are a phenomenon of the 20th century, with beginnings that date to 1904 and the establishment of the first association of cooperative sanatoria in Denmark. During the interwar years, as a number of countries were expanding their public health services, health-oriented cooperatives were introduced in India in 1919 with the establishment of the Central Cooperative Anti-Malaria Society, and in Yugoslavia in 1921 with an extensive movement pioneered by Michael Avramovitch and supported by a network of cooperative sanatoria. In Japan, health societies had expanded to such an extent that a National League of Health Cooperatives was formed in 1933. Developments in Poland followed in 1936, with the introduction of health services by the federation of agricultural cooperatives and the establishment of independent health cooperatives in part of what is now the Ukraine. Expansion into the states of Madras (1938) and Bengal (1939) took place in India, and in 1944 credit unions in the area around Toronto, Canada, formed a Credit Union Benevolent Association to provide medical and hospital care. This activity in Canada was followed the next year by the decision of the Manitoba Pool Elevators to organize group participation in a provincial health services network.

Cooperative hospitals first emerged as a structure for health care services in 1929 in Oklahoma in the U.S. This was followed in 1936 by Sri Lanka, marking the beginning of a network of facilities in that country that were federated in a Union of Cooperative Hospitals in 1970.

In the U.S., growing interest in group health care led in 1946 to the establishment of the Cooperative Health Federation to promote such structures. Groups were established in Washington, D.C., in Washington State, in Minnesota and elsewhere, forming the Group Health Association of America in 1959. These groups were a model for health maintenance organizations (HMOs), now a key ingredient in the mix of health care services in the U.S.

Health cooperatives were established in China in 1958, in France in 1962 as part of the services of the Union fédérale parisienne du bâtiment, and in Spain where by 1989 they had enrolled over 1,000,000 members, almost 3% of the Spanish population. In 1998 ICA, as part of a report on cooperatives presented to the European Commission, identified health cooperatives in Armenia, Belgium, Cyprus, Greece, Poland, the Slovak Republic and Spain.

In 1997 the UN published *Cooperative Enterprise in the Health and Social Care Sectors—A Global Survey*, examining the experience and potential of cooperatives as providers of health care services. The study leading to the publication was actively supported by the ICA that assisted in data collection and with a review of the conclusions. These echoed earlier expressions of UN confidence in the capacity of cooperatives to partner public agencies in expanding social development programs, including health care.

In 1996 a new specialized committee of the world cooperative movement was established to represent and pursue the interests of health care cooperatives—the ICA International Health Cooperative Organization.

Pharmacy Cooperatives

Pharmacy cooperatives have gradually expanded in a few countries. The first were established in Belgium in 1882 and Switzerland in 1906. Noting the popularity of patent medicines and the attraction of indigenous remedies, some people have identified pharmacies as the poor people's health care system.

Pharmacy cooperatives had expanded enough in Switzerland and France to warrant the formation of federations in 1921 and 1925 respectively, and in 1926 the first such pharmacy opened in Argentina, evolving into a national federation 30 years later. In Spain the Pharmacy Federation of Barcelona dates from 1928; upon its experience a national network developed, forming itself into a national association of cooperative pharmacies in 1971. The first Polish cooperative pharmacy was established in 1937.

In the post–World War II period, cooperative pharmacy networks were linked into national federations in Belgium, Britain, Ghana and Spain. The ILO *International Directory of Cooperative Organizations* (1988) noted the existence of the European Union of Social, Mutual and Cooperative Pharmacies, representing 1,384 cooperatives involving 25,590,000 individuals in the European Community.

Cooperative Nurseries/Preschools

These cooperatives, formed by groups of parents who want to provide their children with day care and/or a preschool experience, are predominantly a North American phenomenon. Parents administer and maintain the schools and assist in the classrooms, helping a qualified employed teacher. Classes may vary in length and may take place during single- or multiple-day sessions.

The first identified cooperative nursery school was organized by a group of faculty wives at the University of Chicago in 1916, launching an endeavor that has since grown into an international movement, represented by the Parent Cooperative Preschools International with offices in Canada and the U.S.

In some communities in the U.S., local units of the Parent Cooperative Preschools International have contracted to operate government financed Head Start and similar programs in low-income communities. These programs operate much like cooperatives, with operational and administrative control in the hands of parents.

Cooperative Memorial Societies

At the opposite end of the age span, there is a type of cooperative that arranges, at reasonable cost, for services related to death. Cooperative memorial societies, first organized in a small church in Seattle, Washington, U.S.A., in 1939, arrange with funeral directors to provide the range of services needed for funerals and memorial services.

Some 200 such cooperatives exist in Canada and the U.S., with a membership in excess of 1,000,000. Such services are also an important activity of cooperatives in the U.K.

COOPERATIVE FUNCTIONS AND ACTIVITIES

In the early days of their organization and operation, each cooperative, of whatever type, represented a new group of people experiencing a new type of organization. Cooperatives were usually formed by people with little formal education or training, few resources, limited entrepreneurial experience, and limited experience of working in formal groups. It is hardly surprising, then, that in cooperative history the number of failed ventures has equaled or even exceeded the successes.

Most of the early experience of cooperative formation is lost to us now, for it was local, limited, do-it-yourself, and unobserved by sophisticated researchers and historians. Most cooperatives were exercises in trying to better people's lives, or at least survive, in an indifferent, even hostile world.

Among these cooperators, however, some had a sense that they were doing something more than tinkering with a way of doing business, and had or developed visions of a different kind of society. Cooperative theorists emerged to spell out such a vision and to lay out a conceptual framework. Practical cooperators also started to ask questions about why things did or did not work and, as cooperatives proliferated, began sharing their common experiences and problems. Successful and unsuccessful experiences were noted and reflected upon.

The result was an expanding body of experience dealing with such themes as the operation, management and finance of cooperative groups, participation in and control by members of their own business, and issues related to cooperatives as employers. Cooperators developed a sense of the importance of training in the tasks to be performed within their organization and sought ways of dealing with their other perceived educational needs. The role of women in cooperatives was an early issue, for while most early cooperators were men, the resources they brought to the new enterprises were family resources and soon, as in other enterprises, women became more active participants in the operation, if not always the management, of the businesses.

Cooperatives early on began to tell their story, to themselves and to others, and a cooperative press, and eventually cooperative publishers, emerged. Before long, reflections on successes and failures, as well as on problems and needs, spawned systems for measurement and evaluation, and specialized groups were formed to advocate research and analysis as guides to future action.

Operation and Management of Cooperatives

From their beginning, the operation and management of cooperatives has been a process of trial and error. Most new cooperatives are small, involve persons with limited business experience, and rely almost exclusively (at least in the early stages) on volunteers. Hiring a manager, or even a part-time secretary-treasurer, is a major step. When growth requires the hiring of more employees, the nature of the group changes dramatically, requiring new definitions of relationships between staff and members, new techniques of control, and new delineation of functions and of the meaning of cooperative success. As cooperatives mature, grow in size and become successful businesses (some now giant in scope), their operations and internal relationships continue to evolve and change.

The first known attempt to deal with such complexities in a systematic way was George Jacob Holyoake's *Manual of Cooperation,* published in 1885. This was followed in the years prior to World War I by a number of books by French, German, Spanish and American authors, often combining "how to do it" experience with general theories of cooperatives as a unique element in economies and cooperation as a distinctive way of life. One of the earliest United States Government Printing Office publications on cooperatives was Kerr and Nahstoll's *Cooperative Organization Business Methods,* published in 1915.

As cooperatives grew to be important enterprises and to spread into different sectors and new countries, the scope of the literature followed suit, with new experience from Italy, Belgium, Argentina, Brazil, Canada, Colombia and Mexico being described. In the period since 1960 additional experience from developing countries, most notably India, and the cooperative experience in the communist countries of Eastern Europe has been added to the literature.

Cooperative Finance

Starting as small self-help organizations, cooperatives have had to wrestle from the beginning of their existence with the issue of developing a permanent base of financing. Commercial banks viewed cooperatives with economic and ideological skepticism. Specialized cooperative financial institutions were slow to develop. Cooperative members were undecided as to whether to claim the cooperative's surplus ("profit") for themselves as a benefit or to reinvest it in cooperative growth and expansion.

These problems became the focus of books ranging from Herbert Myrick's *Cooperative Finance* (1912) to the 1986 World Bank publication

Investment and Finance in Agricultural Service Cooperatives by Turto Turtiainen and J. D. Von Pischke.

Financial controls in cooperatives have been another important theme in the development of cooperatives, as novices in finance have had to assume control of the financial affairs of their new enterprises. Accounts have had to be established, bookkeeping methods learned, controls against rash economic moves installed. The presence of some people willing to use either legitimate or illegitimate ways to personally benefit, to the disadvantage of the cooperative group, has been a continuing problem. This has led to the provision of supervisory committees within cooperatives, auditors, government surveillance and a literature dealing with financial controls to better enable cooperatives to protect their interests.

Membership Participation and Control

A unique and central characteristic of a cooperative is the pattern of democratic ownership and control by members. Each member brings resources to the business. Each person participates in the decisions about its operation. Each member shares in the risks and gains.

To foster and perpetuate democratic ownership and control, cooperatives have built certain features into their operations. Regular public meetings are held, and all aspects of the business are open for consideration. Specialized committees, such as those for supervision and member education, ensure that there is openness in all matters dealing with the operation of the enterprise and that the participatory skills of members are enhanced.

Member participation is easier to accomplish when a cooperative is small and relationships between member-owners are close; as a cooperative grows in size and membership and its operations grow more complex, special attention has to be given to maintaining the democratic principles in action. In a cooperative, the degree of participation of its membership must be evaluated equally with its economic accomplishments.

Cooperatives as Employers

A new dynamic is introduced into a cooperative when it arrives at the point where it can no longer rely on its members' voluntary services to carry out all of its operations, when it must employ people to carry these out. Relationships change, new patterns of supervision and accountability are required, and education and training needs are expanded.

Cooperatives have not always made this transition easily. Disputes arise over who (members or nonmembers) should be hired. Wages and working conditions must be established. Power and authority relationships between staff and volunteer leadership must be defined and worked out in practice. Employees must be trained and their work evaluated. As the number of employees expands, labor relations becomes a specialized area of concern for the cooperative, and the question of employee unions arises.

The longitudinal study by G. W. Rhodes, *Cooperative Labor Relations 1900–1952*, considers these and other issues as they manifested themselves during the growth and expansion of British consumer cooperatives.

Cooperative Education and Training

The fifth cooperative principle adopted by the ICA is: "Cooperatives provide education and training for their members, elected representatives, managers, and employees so they can contribute effectively to the development of their cooperatives. They inform the general public, particularly young people and opinion leaders, about the nature and benefits of cooperation."

In pursuit of this goal, cooperatives from their earliest beginnings have given serious attention to the education and training needs of their members, their employees and the general public. One early organized expression of this, on a broader scale than the individual cooperative, was the establishment in Britain in 1882 of an Advisory Education Committee for the British movement; this functioned for many years, and eventually led to the establishment of the Cooperative College at Stanford Hall, Loughborough, in 1919.

The School of Nîmes in France was an early expression of concern for an educated and trained cooperative membership and leadership. Started in 1886 as a circle of workmen under the guidance of August Fabre and Edouard de Boyve, it was joined by Charles Gide, who became its practical leader as an intellectual center for the cooperative movement. This, combined with Gide's tenure of the Chair of Comparative Social Economics at Paris from 1900 to 1921 and the Chair of Cooperation at the College de France from 1924 to 1930, provided him with a rich opportunity to publicize the importance of cooperative education.

Interestingly, one of the other early formal structures for cooperative education was in El Salvador, where in 1896 a professorship in cooperation was established at the National University.

Other early moves included the establishment of a cooperative training school in Austrian Slovenia in 1901, a study group on cooperation at Halle in Germany in 1911, the Museo Social Argentino in Argentina the same year, and a cooperative school at St. Thomas Aquinas College in Quebec in 1916. In quick succession in the postwar years the first cooperative college, in Reykjavik, Iceland, was established in 1918, the U.K. cooperative college and the Horace Plunkett Foundation for Cooperative Studies in 1919, a school for German consumer cooperatives in 1920, and the first Swedish study groups in the same year.

Other formal organizations established between the two world wars included a diverse group of institutions, among them the American Institute of Cooperation (1925), the École technique coopérative in France (1926), the Industrial Cooperative School in Japan, Vär Gärd cooperative college in Sweden (1927), a cooperative college in Denmark (1932), the Institut für Genossenschaftswesen at Frankfurt (1937), the Instituto Cooperativo del Peru (1940), Shahab Cooperative Institute in Iran (1942), the Cooperative College of Western Nigeria (1943), and the Cooperative Institute of Sydney, Australia (1945).

The period since World War II has seen a rapid expansion of such institutions in all parts of the world. The 1988 ILO *International Directory of Cooperative Organizations* identified 86 countries in which there were cooperative education and training organizations or institutes, with the following geographical distribution: industrialized countries—29, Africa—18, Asia/Pacific—15, Caribbean—4, Latin America—14, and North Africa/Near East—6. In addition, 9 international cooperative organizations involved with cooperative training were identified. The 1989 COPAC *Directory of Agencies Assisting Cooperatives in Developing Countries* included a section on opportunities for training abroad for developing country cooperators. It identified 40 such institutions in 33 countries, as well as 6 international organizations providing such training.

Three international programs, described briefly in the dictionary and referenced in the bibliography, are worthy of particular note: AMSAC (Appropriate Management Systems for Agricultural Cooperatives) of the FAO, CEMAS (Cooperative Educational Materials Advisory Service) of the ICA, and MATCOM (Materials and Techniques for Cooperative Management Training) of the ILO. Each made unique contributions to the literature and lore of cooperative education and training.

Activities related to education and training among cooperators have produced a substantial body of literature dealing with theory and history, organization and management, specialized training for leaders, members, employees and the general public, training centers and curricula.

Women in Cooperatives

One of the earliest organized expressions of cooperative women at work was the Cooperative Women's Guild of England and Wales, founded in 1883. Comparable organizations were later established in Scotland (1892) and Ireland (1906). Outside the U.K. similar groups were formed in Sweden (1907), Norway (1910), Switzerland (1921), Belgium (1923), Japan/ consumer (1927), Australia (1930), Poland (1935), New Zealand (1936), France (1937), Japan (1951) and Sri Lanka (1956). The International Cooperative Women's Guild was established in 1924.

These groups were made up of women actively involved in cooperatives in voluntary capacities and/or as staff. Their concerns were a mixture of the normal concerns for cooperative development and of the influence that they as women could exercise, individually and collectively, both inside and outside the cooperative movement. A large measure of their attention was given over the years to the issue of world peace.

The first women's cooperative, Zadruba, was established in Prague in 1900 by the Czech Women's Association. It was followed in Sweden in 1905 by Kvinnornas Andelsförening Svenska Hem. Others were organized in developing countries, in Sri Lanka (1929), Nigeria (1942), Sierra Leone (1954), Saudi Arabia (1966) and Cameroon (1968). In India, the Indira Cooperative Bank, the first women's cooperative bank, was established in 1974.

Within the international movement, the *Review of International Cooperation* in its early issues carried brief articles regarding women's issues and the early work of the cooperative women's guilds. While Henry May was General Secretary of the ICA (1913–1939), attention to the issue of women in cooperatives increased dramatically. Beginning in the 1921 issues of the *Review of International Cooperation* and continuing until 1942, there were regular reports on women's cooperative activities within the ICA and in member countries. It was also during May's tenure that the International Cooperative Women's Guild was most active, organizing, among other things, a series of international cooperative women's conferences and publishing a series of books.

Following May's death in 1939 and the onset of World War II, women's issues received less attention until the 1960s and the establishment within the ICA in 1963 of a Women's Consultative Committee. In 1972 the consultative committee became the ICA Women's Committee, taking on more official status as an ongoing, working part of the ICA. It is now the ICA Global Women's Committee.

By the 1960s the struggle of women to achieve equality with men in social, political and economic spheres had become widespread in industrialized countries and, with assistance from international development agencies, women's issues entered the dialogue with developing countries. Within the UN system the FAO (in the field of agriculture) and the ILO (more generally) began publishing materials elaborating on the subject.

The gender programs of the ICA regional offices for the Americas and Asia-Pacific have been particularly relevant in relating gender issues to the specific situations of the cooperatives in these two regions.

The UN declaration of the Decade for Women (1975–1985), with its international conferences, added broader dimensions to women's issues, and the establishment of the United Nations Development Fund for Women brought to bear new human and financial resources.

In 1985 COPAC, acting for its three UN and four international NGO members, carried out research and, with assistance from the United Nations Development Fund for Women, published *Women in Cooperatives*. This publication identified key constraints confronting women regarding participation in cooperatives. It listed such things as traditional cultural attitudes and organizations, legal restrictions, lack of education, lack of access to credit, and demands on women's time as important limits on women's participation. The publication also undertook to establish a directory of known women's cooperatives worldwide, and outlined organizing steps for those interested in starting such cooperatives. Included was a 57-page bibliography.

The bibliography for this book identifies books dealing with the historical development of women's participation in cooperatives, general works on current gender issues, and selected books documenting national and regional experiences in this field. It also cites material discussing the issue of whether women should be integrated into cooperatives generally or should organize single-sex groups, an issue still widely debated within the cooperative community.

Trade Unions and Cooperatives

The notion that trade unions and cooperatives have a natural affinity and should be part of a larger worker movement grew in part out of the 19th-century socialist theory that the future worker state would be based on three mass movements: a worker (socialist/social democrat) political party, trade unions, and cooperatives. While not accepted by all, the belief that trade unions and cooperatives have so much in common that they should make common cause in building a better future for humankind has remained influential.

Similarities between the two movements that are often mentioned include the following: the two have common roots as organized reactions to the harsh conditions created by industrialization, which gravely disadvantaged industrial workers, farmers and craftsmen; they are both organized on the principles of self-help, mutual aid and unity as the way to achieve improved conditions for their members; they are democratic institutions in which all members have equal rights to make decisions determining organizational directions; both represent organized systems rather than isolated efforts at self-improvement; they collaborate with like-minded organizations at various levels of society; and they have similar visions of what the world will be like when their movements prevail—a worker state for trade unionists, the cooperative commonwealth for cooperators, both built on principles of social and economic equality and democracy.

Despite these similarities, close collaboration between the two movements has not been common. Various factors have tended to distance the two movements rather than draw them together, including: the pursuit of different goals in taking group action, with cooperatives focusing on the general pursuit of the economic interests of their members (some of whom may be employers), while trade unions focus on raising wages and improving working conditions; the fact that cooperators have joined together to establish an economic enterprise, while trade unionists have done so to exercise economic power for workers in collective bargaining with their employers; the fact that cooperatives are established principally to engage in business or trade and define their success in those terms, while trade unions normally define success more in terms of achieving improved benefits for workers through an adversarial relationship with employers (which may on occasion be cooperative organizations); the fact that cooperatives operate in a nonpartisan fashion in the political arena, in part on the assumption that their members represent differing political ideologies, while trade unions are normally closely associated with a particular political party whose platform represents broad worker interests; and the fact that cooperatives and trade unions normally deal with different departments of national governments, cooperatives usually with agricultural or commerce departments, or cooperative departments, trade unions usually with labor departments.

The urge to collaborate, however, has far exceeded separatist tendencies between cooperatives and trade unions, and a number of steps have been taken by the ILO and the ICA to facilitate an expanded relationship. Particularly close affiliation between the two groups can be seen in Singapore, Bermuda, Israel and Trinidad (where cooperatives and trade unions share a common training facility). The ILO International Center for Advanced Technical and Vocational Training at Turin, Italy, includes training for both trade unions and cooperatives. In the U.S., a number of local trade unions have established credit unions for their members. In the U.K., a Cooperative Party has some 25 representatives in the Parliament. It is the largest of the minority parties and aligns itself with the Labour Party on most issues. Consumer cooperative federations in a number of countries have had close relationships with social democratic parties.

Research and Evaluation in Cooperatives

The small self-help and mutual aid efforts of cooperatives in their early, scattered days did not lend themselves to research. Those who sought in desperation to find solutions to economic turmoil and deprivation were action- rather than analysis-oriented. Even when cooperatives had proliferated to the point of forming unions or federations of like-minded organizations, their aspirations were for joint problem solving and for benefits that might flow from united action, rather than conscious self-study of why they succeeded or failed. Trial and error they knew well; systematic study was not their forte.

By the turn of the 20th century, some of the early theorists of the cooperative movement had begun to go beyond simply postulating ideas and theories to studying and analyzing the actual experience of real organizations. As cooperatives became significant in local and national economies, they began to attract the attention of academics and others who wanted to better understand the phenomenon and map its development. Among the earliest such efforts were the École de Nîmes in France and the establishment of the Chair of Cooperativism at the National University in El Salvador in 1896.

Cooperative institutes, some specifically for cooperative research, some with research as only one of their activities, began to appear. In 1917, the Bombay Provincial Cooperative Institute was established in India. The first strictly research institute was established at Krakow, Poland, in 1921. The following year, at the urging of Luigi Luzzatti, the Free University of Mutual Agriculture and Cooperation was established in Italy, becoming the Advanced Institute for Cooperation in 1925. Also established that year were the American Institute of Cooperation in the U.S. and the Center for the Study of Cooperatives in Argentina. Following the establishment of additional provincial institutes in India, an All-India Cooperative Institutes

Association came into being in 1929. The 1930s and early 1940s saw institutes established in Bolivia, Cuba, Germany, Iran, Peru and Romania.

The post–World War II years saw rapid expansion of cooperative institutes, beginning with the establishment of the Cooperative Institute in Sydney, Australia in 1945, and a renewal and expansion of German cooperative interest in 1947–1948 through the establishment of the first university-based institutes. CIRIEC, the International Research and Information Center on Collective Economy, was founded in 1947. In 1957 the ICA established the Research Officers Group to coordinate the growing cooperative research activities. At the end of the 1970s, it reconstituted itself as the Research, Planning and Development Committee and is now the ICA Research Committee. By the mid-1970s there were 29 countries in which cooperatives had developed research activities.

The cooperative research institutes at German universities are of particular note and, combined, probably represent the world's most serious and well-funded cooperative research effort. Located at Erlangen/Nürnberg, Heidelberg, Munster, Cologne, Hamburg, Hohenheim/Stuttgart, Justus Liebig University/Giessen and Philipps/Marburg, they work as individual institutes but coordinate their activities in periodic joint conferences, at which particular bodies of cooperative research are reviewed and discussed by cooperative researchers from around the world.

Also of note was the joint effort of the ICA, the Cooperative Research Institutes in Hungary and Poland, COPAC, and a body of advisors and collaborators from many countries that produced the *Research Register of Studies on Cooperatives in Developing Countries and Selected Bibliography*. During the period 1975–1988, 20 volumes of the *Research Register* and a directory of cooperative research organizations were published. Together they represent the most comprehensive collection of bibliographical material on cooperative activity in developing countries during the period 1968–1988. The project also represents the most serious research collaboration to date by cooperatives worldwide.

The ILO *International Directory of Cooperative Organizations* (1988) identified cooperative research activity in 50 countries, involving cooperative research institutes, university programs, cooperative colleges and training institutions.

For most members of cooperatives, success or failure is not a public policy matter, but one that is defined by the degree to which services carried out on behalf of members are producing a better life for them and enhancing their economic position. The desire for an evaluation of the effectiveness of cooperative organizations and the development of systems to carry out such evaluations has mainly grown out of the efforts of developing-country governments and development agencies to utilize cooperatives as a way of delivering development services or carrying out development tasks. Activities stemming from these interests often forced cooperatives into parastatal roles that were not always in conformity with cooperative principles and did not always reflect the real interests of cooperative members.

COOPERATIVES AND THE STATE

There was little in the early organization of cooperatives to capture the attention of state officials. The organizers were people of little economic or social consequence who had been motivated, in part, by disillusionment about the state ever doing anything for them. The few people of higher status involved in cooperatives were at best regarded as "do-gooders" and at worst as idle dreamers of some far-off better day.

Official recognition and formal registration of cooperatives came first in the U.K., in the provisions of the Friendly Societies Act. In the years leading up to 1830 (14 years before the Rochdale pioneers' society) about 300 cooperatives had registered with government officials. By 1850, cooperatives were being recognized as a different type of organization, and special legislation acknowledging this had been passed in the U.K. Similar legislation was soon passed in a number of other countries.

The number of cooperatives was also expanding significantly in a number of nations. By the end of the century cooperatives could be found in 40 countries, and national unions or federations had been established in the U.K. (1869), Poznan in partitioned Poland (1871), France (1885), Italy (1886), Serbia (1895), Russia (1898), Denmark (1899) and Sweden (1899). Federations in Iceland (1902), Japan (1905), and Czechoslovakia (Bohemia) (1907) and Slovenia (1907) soon followed. Cooperatives were becoming more of an organized force and some of their leaders were assuming political roles in their governments, taking the opportunity to call attention to cooperative matters and interests.

The first half of the 20th century saw a proliferation of cooperatives in countries where they already existed and the spread of cooperatives to new nations and to colonies. They could be found in 72 countries by the end of World War I (1918) and in 119 by the end of World War II (1945). Cooperative legislation expanded at a similar pace. Cooperative laws, which had been adopted in 20 countries prior to 1900, could be found in 52 by 1918 and in 86 by 1945. Today they are almost universal.

Two important historical trends of the 20th century intersected with co-operative expansion and with governments' role vis-à-vis cooperatives. The first of these was the growing acceptance of the idea that national governments should take activist roles in confronting the needs of their entire populations, particularly of those who had received few of the benefits of expanding industrial economies. The plight of small-scale agriculturists and of workers became matters of serious governmental attention, and legislation was enacted reflecting this. Activist government bureaucracies expanded accordingly.

The second trend of note was the changing relationship of colonial governments to their colonies. While this was in no way a uniform process, it could be sensed almost everywhere. The progressive ideas of some colonial administrations were bearing fruit, encouraging the emergence of local leadership. Dissatisfaction with the exploitative economic relationships of colonialism was growing. Frustration with colonial paternalism was becoming endemic, and independence was in the air.

The aftermath of the physical and economic destruction of World War II was the catalyst for the general move to independence for colonies. Hardly a year went by in the next 30 years without an annual roster of new nation-states.

While some consideration may have been given to the idea of independence for colonial possessions by the British and the French, and to a lesser extent by Belgium, the Netherlands and Portugal, in fact very little was done to systematically prepare for such an outcome. However, with regard to cooperatives, the change was beginning. In 1946, the British Colonial Office sent its colonial administrators a model cooperative law and urged local emulation. In 1947 legislation was passed in France regarding cooperatives in overseas territories.

As colonies became independent countries, "nation building" and "social and economic development" became important watchwords. In some countries whose leadership was attracted by socialist ideology, a "socialist path" for development, in which cooperatives were to play important parts, was chosen. Almost everywhere cooperatives, based on their success in industrialized countries, were viewed as an important group-based social tool for achieving needed economic and social advance.

However, there were problems with cooperatives. Most cooperatives during colonial times had been instruments of colonial settlers rather than of indigenous populations, and thus local leaders were inexperienced and lacked the qualities needed for implementation of national development plans. Further, the national leadership, political and bureaucratic, of the new nations was unprepared to let cooperatives naturally develop over time. They were needed now, ready or not! Cooperatives thus came under the tutelage of government officials who had never heard of Rochdale or cooperative principles and who cared less about these than about the national plans they were called upon to implement.

When cooperative performance fell short of expectations, the response was more outside control and more directives. Bureaucracies were given the power and authority to intervene in cooperative affairs whenever they considered it necessary. The results, even in the most benevolent political environments, were cooperative movements that often became instruments of state policies and aspirations rather than instruments for self-betterment.

Nonetheless, cooperatives, as they expanded in number and impact, were able to help meet some member needs and to provide for some improvements in livelihood. Leaders matured and became experienced in dealing with their own governments. International assistance programs more often than not supported cooperative aspirations and advocated more autonomy and independence for cooperative organizations, emphasizing the fact that cooperatives can be the best instruments of development when they are true to their own nature and aspirations rather than implementors of others' aspirations. The ILO called attention to these problems in its Recommendation 127 and urged governments to recognize the need for cooperative autonomy.

In the 1980s, three important attempts were made to wrestle with the dilemma of cooperative-state relations at the international level. First, ICA members, aware of the problems involved, made it a subject of discussion at internal meetings and at congresses. These discussions were summarized in ICA's Studies and Reports #14, *Cooperatives and the State*, published in 1980. The second attempt was the publication by COPAC in 1987 of *Cooperatives and Government*, authored by Swedish cooperator Alf Carlsson. This explored the many facets of the problem and advanced a variety of proposals to meet them.

The third was a UN-sponsored seminar held in May 1987 under the leadership of Murray Silberman in Moscow and attended by representatives of national cooperative organizations, government cooperative officials, and international cooperative and governmental organizations. The *Report of the Seminar on the Role of Government in Promoting the Cooperative Movement in Developing Countries* identified legitimate roles for governments, "if judiciously applied": in establishing a legal framework and favorable political climate, providing financial and other concessional benefits, promoting cooperatives, supporting education and training of cooperators, and as regulators, ensuring that cooperatives and their officials carry out their work in conformity with legal requirements. It also cited three major problem areas that continue to acerbate the relationship: governmental assumption of control over the decision-making processes of cooperatives, provision of assistance in fashions that render cooperatives dependent upon government, and inappropriate use of cooperatives as instruments to promote development in ways that do not also advance cooperative interests.

Between 1993 and 1994, ILO published two reports, generated by its Enterprise and Cooperative Development Department: *Creating a favorable climate and conditions for cooperative development in Africa*, by Hans Münker and A. Shah, and *Creating a favorable climate and conditions for cooperative development in Asia*, by K. K. Taimni. With a backdrop of ILO Recommendation 127, these reports examined the historical and current situation of cooperative movements in these regions and the role governments have played in this regard. They both reflected an ILO interest in steps that could be undertaken to establish a positive environment for autonomous cooperative development based on Recommendation 127.

A 1996 report by the UN secretary general, *The Role of Cooperatives in Light of New Economic and Social Trends*, highlighted the issue of cooperative autonomy; in response, the General Assembly passed Resolution A/RES/51/58 requesting that the secretary general ascertain, in cooperation with COPAC, "the desirability and feasibility of elaborating United Nations guidelines aimed at creating a supportive environment for the development of cooperatives."

In subsequent consultation with its members and with selected cooperative experts and cooperative development practitioners, COPAC prepared *Guidelines Aimed at Creating a Supportive Environment for the Development of Cooperatives*. These were approved by COPAC members and forwarded to the secretary general. It is expected that they will be an annex to his report submitted to the General Assembly in 1999.

If adopted, the guidelines—combined with a parallel effort in ILO to review and amend as necessary Recommendation 127—could go a long way in establishing an international policy environment supportive of cooperative autonomy in relation to governments.

The issues related to the relationship between cooperatives and the state are not limited to developing countries, nor are they limited to current conditions. In one of the early congresses of the ICA, bitter debate was precipitated by a proposal that cooperatives should seek and accept assistance from governments. The debate persists, often defined by the degree of independence achieved by cooperatives in different countries through their growth in numbers and in financial capacity, and through their effectiveness in organizing politically to pursue their interests while remaining independent.

Cooperative Legislation/Law

If the passage of legislation marks the fact that something has become important enough to demand the official attention of the state, then it is interesting that it took the modern cooperative movement over 100 years (from 1750 to 1852) to arrive at that point. Recognition came with the passage of the Cooperative and Provident Societies Act of 1852 in the U.K. But Laszlo Valko's *International Handbook of Cooperative Legislation,* published in 1954, another hundred years later, noted that between 1852 and 1952 more than 5,000 pieces of cooperative legislation had been passed in 125 countries.

Such legislation has been essentially of two types. The first is a general statute, in which an outline of the legal authority of cooperation is provided for, with allowance for further elaboration of this authority in the rules adopted by cooperative societies. Many of the early statutes were of this nature and were favored by the emerging consumer cooperatives as giving them flexibility to adapt their evolving experience in applying cooperative principles to their growing enterprises.

The second type of laws grew out of a need to specifically define provisions for new types of cooperatives, mainly in agriculture, and/or to modify existing laws to provide for their coverage of cooperatives. The Capper-Volstead Act of 1922 in the U.S. exempted cooperatives from some of the restrictions placed on other forms of enterprise, specifically permitting marketing by farmers through their cooperatives in a fashion deemed monopolistic or in constraint of trade when done by groups of other businesses. Various laws were passed, in different countries, conferring a special status on cooperatives in regard to taxation.

Cooperative legislation has at times been hostile to cooperatives. During the 1930s in both Japan and the U.S., organized business interests mounted campaigns, sometimes successful, to limit cooperatives and cooperative practices. More significant were the legislative actions of the fascist governments in Italy and Nazi Germany that led to the elimination of cooperatives or their cooptation to serve the programs of these regimes. In the communist countries of Eastern Europe, cooperative legislation was adopted that, most agree, made cooperatives an integral part of state economic planning and operation. In each of these cases, new legislation more amenable to cooperatives was enacted when these governments failed.

The bibliography includes works that review the history of cooperative legislation. Of particular note are the works by Margaret Digby, *Digest of Cooperative Law at Home and Abroad*, published in 1933, and the books by Laszlo Valko that provide comprehensive historical perspectives. The several books by P. E. Weeraman, director of the ICA Regional Office for Asia at the time of their publication, reveal the implications of cooperative law for developing countries and its ramifications for cooperative autonomy. The ILO has given considerable attention to cooperative legislation, much of it reported in various issues of *Cooperative Information*. Professor Hans Münkner of Marburg University in Germany has been an important figure in this field, relating the issues involved to the emerging cooperative movements in developing countries. Broader discussions of legal principles and of the structure of the "social economy" (including cooperatives) have taken place within CIRIEC.

De-officialization of Cooperatives

Few analysts of cooperatives in developing countries would support a continuation of the central role that many governments have exercised in regard to the cooperative movements in their countries. Some people earlier argued that this role was necessary because these governments have been required to act as instruments of national development and the key component that they perceived cooperatives could and should be in that process. However, most people would now agree that the most viable development role for cooperatives is one similar to that of their counterparts in industrialized countries—as independent socio-economic institutions.

Limiting government involvement in cooperative affairs is not some radical new idea (as the dates of some bibliographical references show). Furthermore, acknowledgment of a need for change by one sector of government has not always resulted in appropriate actions in other sectors needed to bring about the change.

Many politicians are wary of the democratic economic and political practices of cooperatives. This wariness, combined with the reluctance of government cooperative bureaucracies, long comfortable with their role as "guiders" of cooperative movements, to alter that role and the power relationship it represents, is a strong force with which to contend. It will probably take significant international action to bring about the necessary de-officialization. Efforts are under way to convert ILO Recommendation 127 into a convention that would be binding on ILO members. Further, concerted action by ICA and the world cooperative movement should be taken to assume an Amnesty International–like role of advocacy and action, in order to expand and protect cooperative independence whenever it is in jeopardy.

COOPERATIVE EXPERIENCE AND/OR HISTORIES

The literature available on the establishment, development and aspirations of cooperative movements in 186 countries (or other political units) included in this book was too extensive to be included in the bibliography of this volume. Running more than 275 pages, it may one day be published separately or as part of a Cooperative Encyclopedia Project that is under consideration. The literature cited in the bibliography does include coverage of cooperative-like traditions that preceded or paralleled the formal modern movement, chronicles of early cooperative activity, general histories, experience in different regions of the world, and assistance to cooperatives in developing countries.

Precooperative Traditions

One cannot fail to be impressed when reading the histories of cooperative development in individual countries, which frequently note the existence of earlier indigenous traditions of mutual assistance and self-help. The human species has been most inventive in developing ways of collaborating on important common goals. An elaboration of all these did not fall within the purview of this work, but selected citations are included in the bibliography.

Histories of Early Cooperative Activity

By the 1860s cooperative beginnings had been established in a number of countries, and reports of their experience and its relevance to other countries were beginning to be published. These included *Les Associations populaires de consommation, de production et de crédit* by Walras (1865), and *Du mouvement coopératif international, étude théoretique et pratique sur les différentes formes de l'association* by Pelletier (1867), both published in Paris, France. They were followed by Beatrice Potter Webb's *Cooperative Movement in Great Britain* (1898) and George Holyoake's *History of Cooperation* (1908).

General Cooperative Histories

The 20th century has seen the publication of a number of books documenting and discussing the cooperative movement, which started the century in 40 countries and had grown to include more than 186 countries or territories by 1995. The bibliographical entries are divided at midcentury, reflecting the fact that much more has been written in the second half of the century regarding cooperatives in developing countries.

Regional Cooperative Experience

Space limitations have generally precluded consideration of individual national histories of cooperative development, save for the brief entries that are included in the dictionary. The bibliographical entries focus on literature covering groups of countries within regions, rather than individual countries. Where particularly useful national experiences have been identified, however, they are also included.

The beginnings of the cooperative movements in many countries, born out of the efforts of ordinary people who agreed to come together to solve some of the problems of life, are lost in the mists of history. Many of these early efforts ended unsuccessfully, at least in terms of lasting organizations. There is probably one failure (at least) for every successful cooperative. Failures seldom make the history books, particularly those efforts on the scale at which most cooperatives begin.

Thus, establishing firm dates for cooperative beginnings is difficult, and baseline dates are sometimes arbitrary.

Europe and North America

While historians will disagree as to the specific events and dates that mark the beginnings of the cooperative movement, few would dispute the fact that Europe and North America were its cradle and that a series of events in France, the U.K. and the U.S. (then a British colony) during the 1750s permit the designation of that date as its beginning. Most often cited as the salient events are the establishment of mutual insurance companies in Philadelphia and London, and cheesemakers' mutual societies in Franche-Comté in France.

During the next 94 years, before the establishment of the Equitable Pioneers of Rochdale Society in 1844 (which to many marks the advent of the modern cooperative movement), events in at least 11 other countries produced the "first cooperative" in Greece (1780), Austria (1794), Italy (1806),

Luxembourg (1808), Hrubieszow in partitioned Poland (1816), Switzerland (1816), Russia (1825), Spain (1838), Mexico (1839), Japan (1843) and Iceland (1844). With the U.K. in the forefront, cooperatives had been established for agriculture, consumers, dairying, handicrafts, insurance, production and services by 1844. Books had begun to appear touting the virtues of cooperation, and cooperative newspapers begun publication (12 alone in the U.K. by 1830). The first national cooperative congress was held at Manchester in 1831.

By the end of the 19th century, various countries in Europe and North America had added their efforts to the cooperative drive—Germany (1845), Slovakia (part of Hungary) (1845), Belgium (1848), Hungary (1850), Sweden (1850), Denmark (1851), Norway (1851), Czech Republic (Prague) (1852), Romania (1852), Ireland (1859), the Netherlands (1860), Canada (1861), Bulgaria (1863), Turkey (1863), Lithuania (1869), Finland (1870), Serbia/Yugoslavia (1870), Portugal (1871) and Estonia (1898). The ICA had been established in 1895, reflecting the growing international perspective of the movement.

By this time, specialized experience in sectoral activities had begun to emerge among the national movements. Most notably this involved consumer cooperatives in the U.K., worker production cooperatives in France, and savings and credit cooperatives in Germany, each of which were to be important guides for similar efforts elsewhere.

By the outbreak of World War I, most of the European and North American countries had adopted their first cooperative legislation.

In the aftermath of the war, new or newly independent cooperative traditions emerged in Czechoslovakia, Estonia, Finland, Latvia, Lithuania, Poland and Yugoslavia. Russia embarked on its Marxist-Leninist path, rejecting its earlier cooperative experience, which had paralleled that of most of the rest of Europe, for one of collectivized agriculture and cooperatives generally limited to the consumer sector. Cooperatives were incorporated in the planning and operations of the republics making up the new Union of Soviet Socialist Republics.

The interwar years were a period of general growth and elaboration of the cooperative movements in Europe and North America. In the U.S., new and notable cooperative activity emerged in the sectors of savings and credit (credit unions) and rural electrification. These years also saw serious challenges to cooperative independence by the new fascist governments of Italy, Germany and later Spain, which were intent on making cooperatives an integral part of their political and economic programs. As a result, those cooperative movements were seriously compromised, and cooperative leaders were forced into exile as political refugees or silenced in their own lands.

The aftermath of World War II brought a new political reshaping of Europe, with the countries of Eastern Europe, which had been liberated by the Soviet army, soon brought under communist governments. Poland was reshaped with territory ceded to the USSR and ceded from Germany. Estonia, Latvia and Lithuania saw the end of their short period of independence, becoming Soviet republics in the USSR. The Soviet model of cooperation was presented as the way to organize cooperatives and was emulated in Albania, Bulgaria, Romania and the German Democratic Republic. Yugoslavia soon declared "independence" from Soviet models and blended its socialist ideology with some of its earlier cooperative traditions. Its particular focus was on "worker self-management" as a goal for all enterprises, cooperative and otherwise. Czechoslovakia, Hungary and Poland each in their own way opted for a more diverse organization of their cooperatives, maintaining some national sectoral groups affiliated to a national apex organization.

In Western Europe, cooperatives recovered from the effects of World War II and plotted courses in conformity with their earlier traditions. Canada and the U.S. increasingly became involved in international cooperative efforts, assisting in postwar relief efforts and becoming active participants in all aspects of the ICA, providing two consecutive directors of the organization during the last two decades of the 20th century. North Americans were active in the formation of the International Cooperative Petroleum Association and the International Cooperative Housing Development Association, and in the leadership of the international cooperative insurance movement.

One interesting development involving European and North American cooperative organizations during the second half of the century has been the establishment of specialized structures to assist emerging cooperative movements in the developing world on a "movement-to-movement basis." Such cooperative development structures have been operative in Belgium, Canada, Denmark, Finland, France, Germany, Ireland, Italy, the Netherlands, Norway, Sweden, Switzerland, the U.K. and the U.S. In Eastern Europe, training was provided to cooperative leaders from developing countries, in some cases accompanied by technical assistance support within countries. This international development effort is discussed more fully below.

Certain socio-economic trends affecting cooperatives throughout Western Europe and North America during the last half of the 20th century should be noted. The dramatic rural to urban shift of populations has essentially been completed. This has led to a reduction in the number of agricultural cooperatives, mainly through consolidation, and a diminution in membership reflecting the smaller rural population. Integration of functions has taken place, particularly in agricultural processing and marketing, with cooperatives seeking to play important economic roles for their producer members in the stages leading from production to distribution and ultimately to the consumer.

Consumer cooperatives, often credited as the initiators of modern cooperation, have faced growing and strenuous competition from private food combines, with dramatically different results in different countries. In some countries cooperatives have remained competitive and may even have consolidated their position, while others are in serious difficulty. Still others have essentially disappeared from the scene. In the U.S., consumer cooperatives never developed a large or lasting following, though there are a number of small "new wave" societies. The transitions in Eastern European consumer cooperatives are still under way and their final disposition not completely clear. Most seem to be making the changes necessary to recapture a measure of their former membership and enthusiasm, and they expect to maintain an important role in the consumer sector.

Worker production cooperatives have held their own and shown some growth, though they have never become the force for transforming capitalist economies that their early advocates had dreamed of. There are notable localized successes (e.g., Mondragon in Spain), and there has been a growing use of cooperation to handle the transfer of ownership of failing private enterprises to their workers. Another growing phenomenon in the U.S. and elsewhere has been the "employee stock ownership" plan, which provides for a gradual assumption of ownership and ultimately control by workers.

Financial cooperatives, first established in Germany in 1854, continue to show an active and diverse profile with cooperative banks, such as Crédit agricole in France, DG Bank in Germany and Rabobank in the Netherlands rivaling their commercial competitors in international markets. Alongside these are smaller cooperative banks that play a less prominent international commercial role, combining normal banking services with those designed to more directly serve cooperatives and their members. In Canada, Ireland and the U.S., credit unions have become the predominant cooperative sector in terms of overall membership, including respectively 26.0%, 144.9% (including youth members and duplicate adult membership in more than one credit union) and 50.1% of the working-age populations of these countries as members in 1996. Credit union movements are now also found in Poland, Russia, Ukraine and the U.K.

Housing cooperatives, initiated first in Germany in 1845, then in France, Sweden, the U.K., Turkey, Denmark and Czechoslovakia (Bohemia before the end of the 19th century), continue to play an important role in providing shelter for significant segments of the populations of Europe and North America.

Formal collaboration between national sectoral cooperative organizations in Europe began with the establishment of a coordinating organization for consumer federations in 1957, followed in 1959 with one for agriculture. There are now eight such organizations involving, in addition to agriculture and consumers, banks, insurance, pharmacies, tourism, wholesale supply, worker production and tourism. All are based in Brussels and work in a collaborative fashion through the Coordinating Committee of the Cooperative Associations of the European Union.

It is difficult to determine the precise impact of national cooperative movements on national economic and social structures. First, no consistent pattern of data collection exists, and no one currently systematically collects information on cooperatives in all countries. Second, it is not unusual for persons to be members of more than one cooperative, within or across sectors. Third, the numbers identified are for individuals and do not reflect the total number of family beneficiaries that may be represented through an individual cooperator's membership. In this publication, an attempt is made to address these problems by amassing the most recently available statistical information on cooperatives in individual countries and then assessing the percentage of the total population represented in a particular year by cooperative membership—what I have labeled "cooperative penetration." WOCCU, which regularly collects and publishes data on its part of the financial cooperative sector, uses "percentage of working-age population" as its measure of "penetration."

Cooperative penetration in most of the 47 countries of Europe and North America is significant. Disregarding 6 countries for which data was unavailable, the remaining 41 showed the following profile at last report: 6 had penetration of more than 50%; 13 countries between 20% and 49%; 13 countries between 10 and 20%; 5 between 5% and 10%; and only 4 had a penetration of 5% or less. The median penetration for the region was 20.0%. (Appendix 3 lists basic data, by regions and countries, including the penetration rate in each country.)

Africa (Sub-Saharan)

Except for South Africa, where the first cooperative was established in 1902, the early history of cooperative development in virtually the whole of Africa is linked with its history of colonization, particularly by the British and the French. For this reason, countries will be grouped accordingly.

In almost every country, regardless of its colonizer, the first cooperatives and the first cooperative legislation were patterned to serve the needs of colonists, and little attention was originally paid to the potential for cooperatives as a vehicle for the advancement of indigenous people. Any cooperative organization above the primary level usually served the interests of colonial planters engaged in agricultural production for export.

Beyond these similarities, the British and French patterns were quite different in approach and outcome. The French were attentive to establishing "welfare-type" organizations and in a number of their colonies, beginning with Mali and Senegal in 1910, Indigenous Provident Societies were established. These were later, by government decree, restructured as Rural Mutual Provident Societies, then again as Rural Development Mutual Societies. Formal cooperatives did not appear in most French colonies, however, until after independence. By contrast, the British colonialists became intent on establishing cooperatives both for colonist interests and for those of indigenous people. Local societies and higher-level organizations emerged to serve both populations. By the time independence was achieved, national apex federations of cooperatives had already been formed in 9 of the 14 British colonies. The 1988 ILO *International Directory of Cooperative Organizations* identified national apex federations existing in all former British colonies in Africa except Cameroon and Malawi. By contrast, in the 15 former French colonies no national apex federations were in existence at the time of independence, and by 1988 they were to be found only in Mauritania, Niger and Senegal.

The response to calls for colonial independence was also notably different in the British and French cases. Except for Guinea, granted independence in 1958, all other French colonies were awarded their freedom in 1960, a grand year of independence. This was not a process in which consideration was given to the individual colonies' readiness for this important move, nor was time provided for the necessary preparations, for cooperatives or otherwise. By contrast, the British spread out their independence exercise over the period 1957 (Ghana) through 1980 (Zimbabwe).

If cooperative penetration is an accurate indicator, the different approaches adopted by the two colonial administrations had lasting effects on the depth of cooperative development in African countries. In 17 former British and 13 French colonies for which recent information was available, the following was the pattern of penetration:

Penetration	British	French
Less than 1%	1	5
1.0 to 4.9%	6	5
5.0 to 9.9%	6	2
10 to 19.9%	2	0
20% and over	2	1

The median penetration for former British colonies at last report was 5.0%; for the former French colonies it was 1.2%.

A discussion of these two approaches to cooperative development is not just an exercise in comparative colonial administration policy; it also carries messages to those in the developing world who are still at the early stages of trying to establish or enhance cooperative movements. While there are no doubt many lessons to be learned from the British and French approaches, at least four seem obvious. First, if you want to build cooperative movements, then establish cooperatives, not organizations with different names and different agendas. Second, successful cooperative development is built upon independent cooperatives carrying out their own agendas, not the agendas of others. Third, to build extensive independent movements you need effective national apex organizations to promote and represent cooperative interests and needs. Fourth, governments destroy cooperative energy and initiative by making unilateral and arbitrary decisions about cooperative organization and structure.

Little cooperative development took place in the Portuguese colonies of Angola, Cape Verde and Guinea-Bissau until they became independent states in the mid-1970s. Any development that had taken place in Mozambique virtually collapsed with the withdrawal of the Portuguese colonists in 1975. What did not has been further disabled since then by ideological experimentation and civil war. Angola has similarly been caught in a long period of civil war, which has taken its toll on cooperative structures, as on everything else. Promising signs of development since independence (1975) have appeared in Cape Verde, where a combination of agricultural, consumer, fishing and housing cooperatives had resulted in a penetration of 4.5% by 1988.

In the former Belgian colonies of Burundi, Rwanda and Zaire, the pattern has been mixed. Cooperatives, mostly agricultural, have grown slowly and modestly in Burundi since independence in 1962 but at the last report available (1988) had barely penetrated 1% of the population. In Rwanda, after independence in 1962 and before the recent 1994 ethnic conflict, the cooperative movement had been growing more vigorously, incorporating a training center in its activities. In 1986 it reported a penetration of close to 5%. In Zaire, despite earlier unsuccessful colonial administration experiments with cooperative forms, similar to those in French colonies, there was hope that cooperative development after independence in 1960 would be an important part of national development. As with other hopes for Zaire, this one has proven illusory, and no reliable recent reports were available on the current status of cooperatives in the country. Even the diligent statisticians at WOCCU have been unable to provide data in recent years on the credit union operations in Zaire.

The two remaining developing countries in the region, long-independent Ethiopia and Liberia, have shown growth potential for cooperatives, particularly in agriculture and with credit unions, but the continued expansion of both have been hampered in recent years by civil unrest and, in Ethiopia's case, by Marxist ideological experimentation. The most recent reports for Ethiopia (1994) report a cooperative penetration of 8.9% and for Liberia (1990) of 3.4%.

The development of cooperatives in South Africa to date has followed patterns that are more like those of cooperatives in industrialized countries than of those in the other countries of sub-Saharan Africa. In South Africa, the primary activity has been in the fields of agriculture and consumer cooperation. Like most South African institutions, which have primarily served the needs of the white minority, the cooperative movement is now adjusting itself to serve the entire population.

The 42 countries of Africa in which cooperatives have been identified are diverse in their experience and structures and still to some degree reflect their colonial experience. Some have been adversely affected by destabilizing factors such as ideological experiments and military coups. In terms of sectoral activity they have been predominantly agricultural (40 countries), consumer (33 countries), and financial, principally credit unions (29 countries). Worker production cooperatives involving a variety of products, including handicrafts, are found in 35 countries. Small-scale fishing cooperatives are found in 24 countries, housing cooperatives in 13 and insurance cooperatives in 6.

Penetration rates vary from 42% (Lesotho in 1994) to 0.03% (Guinea-Bissau in 1986). Three countries had rates of more than 20%, 2 between

10% and 20%, 11 between 5% and 10%, 15 between 1% and 5% and 8 had less than 1%. The median rate for countries in the region was 3.4%. (See appendix 3 for country details.)

The ICA operates two regional offices in Africa, one for West Africa, located since 1996 in Ouagadougou, Burkina Faso (formerly in Abidjan, Côte d'Ivoire) and one for East, Central and Southern Africa in Nairobi, Kenya, formerly in Moshi, Tanzania. The continent's credit unions, located in 28 countries, are affiliated with the African Confederation of Cooperative Savings and Credit Associations (ACCOSCA), located in Nairobi. WOCCU in its 1997 *Statistical Report* indicated that there were 5,019 credit unions in Africa with a total membership of 2,423,011. Information on credit unions in the Congo, Liberia, Nigeria, Swaziland, Zaire and Zambia was unavailable or considered unreliable. *The Cooperative Network in Developing Countries—A Statistical Profile*, published in February 1987 by COPAC, indicated that there were then 83,634 cooperatives in Africa with a membership of 16,980,605.

Asia/Pacific Region

The emergence of cooperatives in the Asia/Pacific region took place during three broad periods: the late 19th century, the years from 1900 through 1925, and the post–World War II period.

Bracketing 1844, the date of establishment of the Rochdale Society in the U.K., were the first two cooperatives formed in the Asia/Pacific region. Hotokusha, an agricultural and handicraft collective, was organized in Japan in 1843, and the Australian Mutual Provident Society was founded in 1849. Both were portents of substantial national cooperative activities that began soon thereafter and rapidly involved the formation of cooperatives in a variety of economic sectors and in different parts of the two countries. These initial efforts were followed before the end of the century with organized cooperatives in agriculture in New Zealand beginning in 1881 and consumer cooperatives formed in Samarkand, Tashkent, and Bokhara in Uzbekistan in 1893.

In 1900 the first cooperative in India was formed, and it was soon emulated in other parts of the country, including what were to be the first cooperatives in the future Pakistan (1904) and Bangladesh (1905). The first cooperatives soon followed in Myanmar (1905), Sri Lanka (1906), Korea (1907), Indonesia (1908), Philippines (1910), China (1912), Taiwan (1912) (then known as Formosa and under Japanese rule), Vietnam (Indochina) (1912) and Thailand (1917). In the interwar years, groups in Malaysia

(1920) and Singapore (1925) joined the organized cooperative ranks as did those in Mongolia (1921) and in the Soviet republics of Central Asia, Kazakhstan, Kyrgyzstan, Tajikistan and Turkmenistan.

The period following the end of World War II was one of concern for the development of the Pacific islands, a number of which had been devastated by the war. A South Pacific Commission, formed by Australia, France, the Netherlands, the U.K. and the U.S. included cooperative organization among the economic and social development activities that would help lead to independence for new island nations in the 1970s. The first cooperatives were soon organized in Fiji (1945), Papua New Guinea (1946), the Solomon Islands (1950), Samoa (1954), the Cook Islands (1955), Kiribati (1956), Tuvalu (1956), Micronesia (1960), Tonga (1964) and Vanuatu (1967). The first cooperatives also emerged in Hong Kong (1947), Nepal (1950), Cambodia (1954) and Laos (1978).

Cooperatives as they have evolved in the Asia/Pacific region present a diverse picture and are difficult to characterize simply. They are found in the high-income countries (with a per capita GNP of over $11,120) of Australia, Hong Kong, Japan, New Zealand and Singapore. They are also well established in the low-income countries (per capita GNP of less than $650) of Bangladesh, Cambodia, China, India, Indonesia, Laos, Myanmar, Nepal, Pakistan, Sri Lanka and Vietnam.

China, with 160 million cooperators, and India, with over 180 million, though poor, are the world's numerical giants in terms of cooperative membership. By contrast, membership in the Pacific islands as a whole is relatively small. Overall cooperative penetration of the population of the region (median rate of 15.5%) ranks the region after Europe/North America (median of 16.5%) in terms of cooperative membership as a portion of total population. This, however, well exceeds the other developing regions, whose median rates are 3.4% for Africa, 12.7% for the Caribbean, 4.0% for Latin America and 2.5% for North Africa/Near East. (See appendix 3 for national penetration rates.)

In the 33 (out of 39) countries in the region for which information was available (see appendix 3), the predominant cooperative sectors were consumer (in 26 countries), agriculture (23) and finance (22). Other sectors were worker production or services (in 19 countries), multipurpose (16), fishing (14), housing (10) and insurance (8). Cooperatives in 18 of these countries also included other types that did not fall into these eight main sectoral categories.

In 11 countries (Australia, Bangladesh, Fiji, India, Indonesia, Japan, Malaysia, Pakistan, Philippines, Solomon Islands and Sri Lanka), cooperatives were involved in all or almost all major sectors. In 10 countries, cooperatives were involved in only one or two sectors. Most of these were Marxist-oriented countries or former Soviet republics. In eight of the remaining countries, cooperatives were diversified into half or more of the major sectors.

Additional information on cooperative development in the countries of the region is included in the dictionary entries. Several countries represent special situations, as noted below.

The progress of cooperative development in Australia and New Zealand has been strongly influenced by their size and geography. Australia's pattern of cooperative diversity was set early on by a series of unrelated organizing efforts in several sectors, among widely dispersed populations in what were then separate colonies. Cooperatives in New Zealand, in contrast, started principally in the agricultural sector and were national in focus almost from their beginning. Both have continued their development according to these initial patterns. The two countries saw the introduction of credit unions in the mid-1900s, and significant movements have developed in both, the larger in Australia. Australia remains diversified by cooperative sectors and its strength varies between states. It has a national apex organization. In New Zealand, agricultural cooperatives, credit unions and insurance are the significant sectors. There is no national apex organization.

The first cooperatives in China were organized in 1912 under the encouragement of revolutionary leader Sun Yat-Sen and his banner of "democracy, nationalism and socialism." They developed in a fashion similar to other countries, diversifying into various cooperative sectors and spreading to different parts of the country. Within 25 years cooperative legislation had been adopted, the government had established a cooperative department, a national apex union had been organized, and there were reported to be some 47,000 cooperatives with in excess of 2 million members. Expansion continued at a rapid pace during the Sino-Japanese War and during World War II, with a growing number of industrial cooperatives. By 1944, there were reported to be a total of 160,000 primary cooperatives with a membership of more than 15,000,000. Things changed dramatically with the victory of communist forces in the Chinese Civil War in 1949, and cooperative development since that date has followed more of a Soviet model, limiting its function to "supply and marketing cooperatives." The number of primary cooperatives was reduced through consolidation to approximately 32,000, but membership increased dramatically, totaling more than 160,000,000 in 1992.

The pace of development of cooperatives in India, now numerically the largest cooperative movement in the world in terms of primary cooperatives, cooperative superstructure and cooperative membership, seems to have been set at the outset. In just a few years, starting with founding of the first credit cooperatives in 1900, the Cooperative Union of India was established (1903) and joined the ICA, the Cooperative Societies Act was enacted (1904) and the first cooperative bank in Madras was organized (1905). Edward Filene, a Boston merchant, visited India (1907) and was so impressed with what he saw of Indian credit cooperatives that he used them as one model in launching the U.S. credit union movement. In 1910 the first of the provincial (now state) cooperative federations was established. All were encouraged and applauded by the British colonial administration, which was soon using India as a model for cooperative development in its colonies worldwide.

Jawaharlal Nehru, Indian prime minister from 1947 to 1964, called upon cooperation to "pulse the nation," and the cooperative movement has tried to respond. It now counts some 20% of the nation's population as members. Few villages are without their cooperative. Nineteen national federations reflect the role of cooperatives in almost every important sector of the national economy. India has spawned leadership for the worldwide cooperative movement and supplied some of its most thoughtful contemporary theorists. Its publications on cooperatives circulate throughout the world.

While one could almost declare India the cooperative dream come true, it has nevertheless exhibited the frailties of other human institutions and at least one serious and persistent compromise of the cooperative ideal. It has an inappropriately structured authority role for government in cooperative affairs. This has permitted persistent intrusion by government officials and has often given cooperatives the appearance of being mere appendages to governmental plans and programs.

Although nourished by the same 47 years of early cooperative history as cooperatives in India, cooperatives in Pakistan and Bangladesh have not had the same degree of success. Both countries count less than 10% of their population as cooperative members.

In Indonesia, building on initial cooperative development efforts dating from 1908, and augmented by a cooperative law and regulations dealing with indigenous cooperatives in the 1920s, the cooperative movement, established on an extensive network of agricultural and multipurpose societies, grew only slowly until full national independence was gained in 1954. Government has taken an active role in the cooperative movement, often to the detriment of its independence. Growth has been consistent since 1954, however, and the movement currently involves nearly 20% of the total population. Among nations with largely Moslem populations (where cooperative development has generally been modest), Indonesia ranks first in total cooperative membership and is rivaled only by Egypt in terms of population penetration.

The first cooperative in Japan, and probably in all of Asia, Hotokusha, established in 1843, launched a movement that, by the end of the century, though little known outside, was well established as an independent development line of the worldwide cooperative movement. Beside an 1880s study of the German Raiffeisen movement by two Japanese cooperative leaders, there seems to have been little contact with other established movements. The *International Review of Cooperation* first made note of Japanese cooperative experience in 1908. It is interesting to observe, therefore, that Japanese cooperatives, reacting to the industrial transformation of their country, followed much the same path as those in other industrialized countries and became the instrument of urban consumers and small farmers seeking to better conditions for themselves and their families. Alternative systems of worker productive societies emerged as an early concern but have not proved any more expansive than in other parts of the industrialized world. Cooperative education, involvement of women and youth, and cooperative publications were among early concerns of the Japanese movement, as were, in later years, concerns for assistance to cooperatives in the developing world.

Relationships with the world cooperative movement were slow in developing. Japanese cooperatives joined the ICA in 1923 but withdrew in 1940 after international criticism of Japan over the Sino-Japanese War. By 1952, when Japan rejoined the Alliance, the initial post–World War II adjustments were well under way. American occupation forces, utilizing experienced American cooperators, had been active in reorganizing Japanese cooperatives and their federations and were intent on promoting cooperatives as a way of contributing to the further democratization of Japanese life. Growth since that time has been rapid. In 1993, 9,688 Japanese cooperatives could count 57,527,085 members, 45.9% of the total population, among the leading national movements in cooperative penetration.

Growth among cooperatives in other Asian countries with significant penetrations of their populations, e.g., Kazakhstan, Korea (Republic), Malaysia, Sri Lanka and Vietnam, has continued apace, and all show over 20% penetration of their nations' populations.

Cooperative development in the Pacific island nations, almost all of which has taken place since the end of World War II, has been mixed, with most movements still numbering less than 5% of their population. Exceptions are Kiribati (39.5%) and Tuvalu (52.9%) whose penetration percentages would seem to indicate that cooperatives are involved, either directly or indirectly, with almost the entire population.

The former Soviet republics, along with Mongolia, constitute a new cooperative grouping in Central Asia. Their cooperative structures and functions have tended in the past to follow the lead of Centrosoyus, with which they were affiliated when part of the USSR. Their final position in what are now independent states still remains to be seen. All save Mongolia have had significant penetration of their national populations in the past, in consumer cooperatives. In Kazakhstan, Kyrgyzstan and Turkmenistan, penetration has exceeded 20% (though 1996 statistics show a considerable drop in cooperative membership in Kyrgyzstan and a smaller one in Turkmenistan).

Caribbean Region

Cooperatives in the Caribbean are a phenomenon of the 20th century. They were first established in Trinidad and Tobago (1916), Suriname (1920) and Martinique (1927), and in part they reflected the colonial traditions of Britain, the Netherlands and France. The cooperatives of the region, except in the case of Haiti (independent since 1804), were all initiated during the period in which the 22 current nations or territories (eight are still not fully independent) of the region were under colonial administration. Initial cooperative legislation, except in the Bahamas, was also enacted during that period.

The early cooperatives were formed in various cooperative sectors, but agricultural interests generated cooperative activity most frequently. In the 1940s credit unions were initiated, first in Jamaica and Trinidad and Tobago, then later in all of the countries, except for the French territories. Since that date this sector of the cooperative movement has gradually assumed dominance. At the present time, credit union members constitute more than 50% of the cooperative membership in every country except Saint Christopher/Nevis. In a majority of countries, credit union members account for over 80% of national membership.

Despite this, there is considerable sectoral diversity. Jamaica reported cooperatives in 8 sectors, Guyana in 7. In the Bahamas, Barbados, Dominica, Saint Lucia, and Trinidad and Tobago cooperatives are found in 6 sectors. Five countries have societies in 5 sectors, 5 in 4 (see appendix 2). Most of these are small-scale operations, particularly in fishing and worker production cooperatives: in the latter case, they represent small-scale production for local consumption and handicrafts produced mainly for the tourist trade. Statistics in 14 countries list cooperatives other than those in the eight major categories, revealing that the cooperative form is being used for nontraditional activities.

Cooperative penetration of the populations of the countries of the region is significant, the mean for the 19 countries being 12.7%. Dominica, ranking highest among the cooperative movements of the nations of the world, reports a penetration of 74.3%. Four exceed 20%—Belize (20.5%), Jamaica (23.4%), Montserrat (27.9%) and Saint Christopher/Nevis (26.8%). Eleven of the 19 countries exceed 10%. Only Haiti (1.1%), Suriname (3.4%) and Tortola (1.2%) have less than 5%. All penetration figures for countries in the region are strongly influenced by the burgeoning credit unions.

Attempts have been made in the past to establish a Caribbean federation of cooperatives, but these have not been particularly successful. The Confederation of Cooperatives of the Caribbean and Central America has encouraged participation by Caribbean cooperative movements but has elicited little consistent involvement or response.

The Caribbean Confederation of Credit Unions based in Barbados was formed in 1969 and represents the credit union movements in 16 of the 22 Caribbean countries in which cooperatives operate. In 1996, combined membership in the 412 credit unions reported by the Confederation was 1,083,437. WOCCU indicated that this constituted 38.67% of the working-age population in the countries that are associated with the CCCU.

Latin America Region

The Latin America region encompasses 20 principally Spanish-speaking countries that fall into three groupings: South America, Central America, and the three Caribbean islands of Cuba, the Dominican Republic and Puerto Rico. (Some would also include the francophone island jurisdictions of Guadeloupe, Haiti and Martinique, but in my judgment, they are more akin to their English-speaking neighbors in racial background and culture.)

The countries of Latin America generally share certain common heritages—an indigenous Indian population, Spanish language and culture, and early independence from Spain and Portugal (mostly during the period 1809–1825). Oligarchical and authoritarian rulers backed by military force, colonial economies oriented toward mineral extraction, and agricultural production for export to industrialized nations have also been common to most of these countries.

In contrast to Africa and Asia, cooperative development in most Latin American countries was slow to appear following independence. Only four countries saw their first cooperative emerge during the 19th century:

Mexico (1839), Brazil (1847), Argentina (1875) and Honduras (1876). The remainder, except for Cuba (1951) and Panama (1954), took nearly a century or more after independence to evolve the beginnings of cooperative movements.

The movements, once begun, have tended to develop along common lines. First, they have appeared simultaneously in several different sectors. All except Panama report cooperatives in agriculture; save for Cuba and El Salvador, all have consumer societies; financial cooperatives (mostly credit unions) are found in all but Cuba; worker productive cooperatives are found in all but Cuba and El Salvador. Sixteen of the 20 countries have housing cooperatives; 13 have insurance; and 11 have fishing cooperatives. Multipurpose cooperatives are found as organized efforts in Costa Rica, Dominican Republic, Honduras and Panama.

Financial cooperatives, mainly credit unions related to the WOCCU structure, have gradually assumed a dominant position in terms of cooperative membership. Only in Argentina, Brazil and Venezuela are they not the predominant type in terms of membership.

All the national movements, save Argentina, have been slow to grow, and cooperative penetration in the region remains modest. Only in Argentina (27.8%), Puerto Rico (27.0%), Uruguay (18.9%) and Colombia (13.1%) have cooperative memberships exceeded 10% of the population. The median for the countries of the region is 4.0%.

Cooperative penetration (see appendix 3) and growth is modest in all sectors, even in those countries where credit unions predominate. Further, there has been a tendency in Latin American cooperative movements to ignore those societies that do not quickly succeed on their own, and for the more successful to focus on emulating their commercial counterparts rather than helping to build a movement. While there were early "evangelists" in the region, arguing that cooperatives are for everyone, they have not been very obvious and influential among recent cooperative leaders. It appears that the growing ICA presence in the region may moderate these tendencies.

The cooperative movement in Argentina stands out in terms of its size (27.4% of the population), its diversity and its network of cooperative support organizations. It has contributed significantly to the literature on cooperatives and INTERCOOP Editora Cooperativa, a cooperative publishing house in Buenos Aires, is widely respected for its cooperative publications. Significant leaders in various sectors of the international movement have come from the ranks of Argentine cooperatives.

Internationally, the cooperatives of the region have formed several groups to represent their interests and aspirations. They include the following: the Organization of Cooperatives of America (OCA), established in 1963 with headquarters in Bogota, Colombia; the Latin American Confederation of Savings and Credit Cooperatives (COLAC), the regional organization for credit unions, headquartered in Panama (it also has a related education foundation, FECOLAC); an ICA Regional Office for the Americas in San José, Costa Rica, and a project office in Buenos Aires, Argentina; the Inter-American Cooperative Institute, located in Panama; the Latin American Association of Cooperative Education Centers, associated with the OCA but with headquarters in Zaragoza, Spain; and the Interamerican Society for the Development of Cooperative Financing (SIDEFCOOP), headquartered in Buenos Aires, Argentina. The current president of the ICA, Roberto Rodrigues, comes from the Brazilian movement.

North Africa/Near East

The North Africa/Near East region encompasses 19 countries stretching from the Atlantic coast of North Africa through the Near East to Afghanistan. It is, except for Israel and a portion of Lebanon, a predominantly Islamic area in terms of faith, culture and politics. Currently it is undergoing a religious revival with the goal of making Islam ever more fully the core of all activity.

The first cooperative in the region was formed in Israel (then Palestine) in 1878. This was followed in the first quarter of the 20th century by North African cooperatives formed in Algeria (1901), Tunisia (1905), Egypt (1908), Libya (1915) and Morocco (1922). The next 20 years saw cooperatives emerge in the countries north of the Arabian Peninsula, in Jordan (1922), Iran (1926), Iraq (1930), Arab Palestine (1933), Lebanon (1937) and Syria (1943). The first cooperative in Afghanistan was organized in 1965. Save for Kuwait, in which the first cooperative was organized in 1941, cooperative development in the Arabian Peninsula came late in Yemen (1958), Saudi Arabia (1961), the United Arab Emirates (1972), Qatar (1973) and Bahrain.

At present, save for Israel, cooperative movements in the countries of the region, even where they have significant memberships (as in Egypt, Libya, Iran and Syria) are among the less developed movements in the world. Only seven of the countries have a national federations representing sectoral cooperatives. Only six have national apex organizations to articulate with, and represent cooperative interests to, governments and other groups.

Sectoral cooperatives are found principally in the areas of consumers (17 countries), agriculture (15), worker productive (14), and housing (11).

Eleven out of the 18 countries include cooperatives in each of these sectors. In contrast with other regions, financial cooperatives are found in only six countries. This is related in part to the continuing controversy over how interest is to be handled under Islamic law when credit is provided. The Islamic faith is intensely opposed to usury.

Israel has the most developed cooperative movement in the region, with penetration of the national population at 38.3% in 1994. It is longstanding, ideologically rooted and politically connected. It includes cooperative activity in most sectors of the economy of Israel. It has experimented successfully in the kibbutz and *moshav* with collective systems operating in a democratic society. It has shared its experience with less developed countries. If and when real peace with its immediate neighbors comes and movement-to-movement relations are established with cooperatives in those countries, Israel's experience could be highly important to other movements.

Cooperative activity in Egypt dates from 1908 when the first agricultural cooperative was organized. That sector was dominant in cooperative membership until recently, when it was overtaken by an expanding consumer cooperative movement. The Higher Institute of Cooperative and Managerial Studies in Cairo, which offers courses in Arabic for students at the Ain Shams University, has been an important training institution for cooperative leadership, both in Egypt and elsewhere.

Iran, Libya and Syria are the other countries in the region in which cooperative penetration (see appendix 3) has reached more than 10%, a level at which movements are becoming recognizable actors in national economies. The median penetration rate for the entire region, however, was only 2.5% at last report, making it numerically the least cooperatively developed region of the world.

The sole regional cooperative structure, of recent origin, is the Arab Cooperative Union based in Cairo, Egypt. Among the activities of the Union has been the collection of statistical data on cooperatives in the region. Other activities of the Union have not been widely publicized.

ICA opened a Regional Program Office in Cairo in 1998. This, if it follows the pattern of other ICA regional offices, should lead to an increase in regional activities.

Assistance to Cooperatives in Developing Countries

Collaboration between cooperatives in different countries, enshrined as the principle of "cooperation among cooperators," has been evident from the beginning of the international cooperative movement. It has been reflected in the growing understanding of and appreciation for the different paths of development taken by different national movements, through efforts to assist one another and, through development of a common ideology, to shape a common movement. Formal assistance involving serious commitments of people and resources, however, was limited until recent years.

Paralleling the cooperative movement, one of the early organized expressions of an international interest in cooperative development was the establishment of the Cooperative Service within the ILO in 1920 and, beginning in 1923, the publication of *Cooperative Information*, which called attention to the development and needs of cooperatives worldwide. The ILO began formal technical assistance to national cooperative efforts in 1932 with a mission to Morocco.

A resolution passed in 1933 by the Pan American Union called for that organization to "provide guidance to and coordinate the development of the cooperative movement in the western hemisphere." In 1945, a cooperative service was established within the Union to more fully implement the resolution.

The transformation of colonies into newly independent states following World War II introduced a new dynamic into discussions of assistance to the newly dubbed "developing countries" and to fledgling cooperative movements in those countries.

The establishment of the UN and the World Bank (formally, the International Bank for Reconstruction and Development) in 1945 and subsequently of specialized UN agencies, including the United Nations Development Program and FAO, brought attention to the needs of developing countries and the need for a commitment of resources to meet these needs.

By the late 1950s, a number of industrialized countries had established special programs to assist in the developing countries, sometimes creating new agencies for this purpose, sometimes adding a development section to an existing foreign affairs department. In some cases, attention was specifically given to assistance to cooperative development, and some cooperative movements began to plan assistance programs. The first of these, the Swedish Cooperative Center, was formed in 1958.

To further encourage support for development and to call the world's attention to the needs of the "underdeveloped countries," the UN voted to designate the 1960s as the Development Decade. One of the events of this decade was action by the U.S. Congress, later called the Humphrey Amendment, making support for cooperative development a priority interest of the U.S. foreign assistance program. It called on USAID to utilize the expertise of U.S. cooperatives in project implementation. As a result, six U.S. cooperative structures were designated as "cooperative development organizations": Agricultural Cooperative Development International, the Cooperative Housing Foundation, the Credit Union National Association, the National Cooperative Business Association (at that time known as CLUSA), the National Rural Electric Cooperative Association, and Volunteers in Overseas Cooperative Assistance.

In Japan in 1963 the national agricultural cooperative federation established the Institute for the Development of Agricultural Cooperation in Asia (IDACA). In the U.K., cooperatives and the Overseas Development Administration organized international conferences on aid to cooperatives in developing countries. The cooperatives of Scandinavia began "Nordic" projects of support for cooperatives in East Africa. The ICA opened a regional office in New Delhi and, later, one in Moshi, Tanzania, and one in Abidjan, Côte d'Ivoire. In Canada the initial steps were taken that would result in the establishment of three cooperative development organizations: the Cooperative Development Foundation, the Société de développement international Desjardins (SDID) and the Société de coopération pour le développement international (SOCODEVI). In other countries similar actions were initiated.

The designation by the UN of the 1970s as the Second Development Decade was accompanied with actions by the ICA to make this period concurrently the Cooperative Development Decade and to mobilize the world cooperative movement in support of development. One of the outcomes was the establishment of COPAC in 1971 as a joint effort of the UN system and of international NGOs concerned with cooperative development.

One of the early activities of COPAC was a survey of the development community to ascertain the degree of interest in supporting cooperative development. A result of that survey was the publication of the *Directory of Agencies Assisting Cooperatives in Developing Countries,* which has been subsequently reissued at irregular intervals. The 1989 edition of the COPAC Directory listed 306 such groups, including 14 UN agencies, 9 international development banks, 5 intergovernmental agencies, 47 bilateral governmental agencies, 26 international non-governmental groups (including 14 cooperative organizations), 105 bilateral non-governmental development organizations (of which 49 were cooperatives), 47 organizations providing volunteers to assist in cooperative development, and 51 training centers providing international training for cooperative leadership (23 of which are in developing countries).

The COPAC *Directory* included a number of organizations that provide only sporadic help to developing-country cooperatives, as well as to others with major programs. These include the ILO, the FAO and bilateral governmental agencies in Canada, Denmark, Finland, France, Germany, the Netherlands, Norway, Sweden, the U.K. and the U.S.—all of which have been particularly forthcoming with resources. Also included are international cooperative organizations such as the ICA, WOCCU, and national cooperative development organizations (in addition to those already mentioned), such as the Cooperative College CLEAR Unit and the Plunkett Foundation in the U.K., the Cooperative Committee of the Royal Norwegian Society for Rural Development, Cooperative Center Denmark, the Finnish Cooperative Center, the Rabobank Foundation in the Netherlands, Cooptecnital in Italy, the Irish Foundation for Cooperative Development, the Centre Intercoopératif Français, Land O' Lakes and the Overseas Cooperative Development Committee in the U.S., Centrosoyus in Russia, the Central Cooperative Council in what was then Czechoslovakia, and the Cooperative Research Institute in Hungary and Poland.

A Natural History of Cooperative Development

In this brief review of an extensive cooperative history, one is able to discern certain recurring patterns that have been common to cooperative development in many different countries. These may be viewed as the "natural history of cooperative development," which proceeds as follows.

First, a gathering of individuals agrees that it has certain economic needs or problems for which group-based solutions appear to have better prospects than if each person alone tackled the problem. A group is formed, it opts for a cooperative structure, leadership emerges, a program of action is developed and rules are adopted.

As the cooperative carries out its plans, it generates group enthusiasm and gains the attention of others who feel that a cooperative could be of assistance to them in meeting similar problems and needs. Other cooperatives are formed, and cooperative formation becomes a generalized activity.

At a certain point, cooperative groups find that they can accomplish certain things more effectively if they collaborate with each other than if they rely solely on their own group. They come together to form a cooperative union or federation to carry out common tasks.

As cooperative operations become more extensive, legal status is sought for cooperatives. Cooperative legislation specific to a sector or of a general nature is adopted, giving official status to the cooperatives and defining the extent or limits of their legal activity. Official rules are promulgated by the legal authorities.

As cooperatives of a particular type or in a particular sector demonstrate their effectiveness in meeting member needs, groups of people involved in other sectors decide that the cooperative form may also be of assistance to them. Sectoral groups are formed and proliferate. Federations or unions of such groups are formed.

As the number of cooperatives and unions expands, groups within an individual sector find it advantageous to form an organization at the national level to reflect their interests and enthusiasm. A national federation or union is formed. In smaller countries, this national organization may include cooperatives of various types. In larger countries it may be confined to one sector.

If the structure established in the previous step has not already involved a variety of sectors, the next step usually is to form a multisectoral national apex federation.

Finally, national cooperative leaders and organizations form multinational, regional or worldwide associations to address their common cooperative interests and needs.

The maturation of a cooperative movement in a particular country can be assessed by examining the stages it has gone through or reached. A fully mature movement will have primary level cooperatives in a variety of sectors, sectoral organizations at a regional and/or national level, and a national apex organization representing the entire cooperative structure. The national federation will be affiliated with international, regional or worldwide cooperative organizations.

The impact of a national cooperative movement can be assessed, in part, by looking at how much of this network of self-supporting cooperative structure has developed in an individual country. The impact of a cooperative movement may also be assessed by examining the degree to which cooperatives have involved the population of a country in their operation, that is, the penetration of the cooperative into the population. The higher the penetration, the greater the influence of cooperatives in the national economy and the greater the significance of cooperatives in national life.

INTERNATIONAL COOPERATIVE ORGANIZATIONS

The ILO *Directory* (1988) includes a section (pages 3–6) listing 41 "International Organizations" of varying degrees of importance to the international structure and activities of cooperatives. The ILO list (most of the organizations on this list are described in the dictionary) includes several categories of organizations that operate above the national level, some regional in their interests and some with broad international scope; others take particular sectors of the movement as their focus. Based on an analysis of their scope of interest, their operational structure, and the degree of activism of the groups, two stand out and are discussed at some length in this section—the International Cooperative Alliance and the World Council of Credit Unions.

International Cooperative Alliance (ICA)

In 1835 Robert Owen, regarded by many as the "parent" of the cooperative movement, established the Association of All Classes of All Nations, an early attempt to form an international organization connected with cooperation. The bylaws of the Association proposed the establishment of an international cooperative organization with branches in all nations. Owen's idea did not trigger an immediate response and, as in many things dealing with cooperatives, the idea was slow in maturing. It next surfaced in the late 1860s with the following events: Jean-Pierre Beluze proposed formation of an international alliance of cooperatives (1866); an abortive International Cooperative Congress, to be associated with the Paris International Exposition, was attempted by the French cooperatives (1867); and international sponsorship and participation in the 1869 British Cooperative Congress nurtured the growing sense of cooperation as an international concern. By the mid-1880s serious discussions had begun within the French and British movements, and exchanges of visits by their leaders became a regular occurrence. Edouard de Boyve was invited to address the 1886 British Congress at Plymouth where he urged the establishment of organic relationships between cooperators of all nations, a move endorsed by the delegates. Thereafter, discussions became focused informally in a group principally involving Edward Vansittart Neale, Edward Owen Greening, Edouard de Boyve and Charles Gide, who together pushed ahead to make their dreams of an international structure become a reality.

In August 1895 in London, an International Cooperative Congress was held in which internationalization of the cooperative movement was the one clear objective. Some 200 delegates (the largest number representing the U.K.) from cooperative groups in 13 countries—Argentina, Australia, Belgium, Denmark, France, Holland, Hungary, India, Italy, Russia, Serbia, the U.K. and the U.S. (which was represented by three delegates and five visitors)—convened on Monday, August 19, for a week of work and socializing. Clearly the principal objective was to get an organization established, but there were a number of additional agendas. People needed to get to know each other. The four principal branches of cooperation—agriculture, consumer, credit and worker production—needed an opportunity to explicate themselves and to consider their particular problems from an international perspective. Deeply held views about the nature and future of cooperation needed expression.

Congress sessions, chaired by Earl Grey, were plenary, so that all the delegates could participate in all the discussions. Edward Owen Greening gave the keynote address, foreshadowing the main work of the Congress that was crystallized in a series of resolutions. The first of these was:

> That the organizations and individuals who have signified their adhesion be, and they are hereby, constituted the International Cooperative Alliance, to continue the work commenced by the late Edward Vansittart Neale and his friends.

The remainder defined the objectives of the Alliance and the nature of its membership, declared neutrality in matters of religion and politics, established a Central Committee and charged it with reporting back at a subsequent congress on proposals for the organization and operation of the Alliance.

The first Central Committee was elected, with representatives from Belgium (2), France (3), Germany (1), Italy (2), the U.K. (6) and the U.S. (1). The Executive Bureau (later Committee) was elected as follows: Earl Grey, president and chairman, J. W. Wolff, treasurer, E. O. Greening and J. C. Gray, secretaries, and Aneurin Williams, assistant secretary. All the officers were from the U.K., a practical step that continued until the 1920s due to the special support being provided by cooperatives and cooperative leaders in the U.K., and to problems of costs and travel associated with convening a more diverse group involving representatives from other nations.

Subsequent congresses, in Paris (1896), Delft (1897), Paris (1900), Manchester (1902), Budapest (1904), Cremona (1907) and Hamburg (1910) saw the fledgling ICA wrestle with the writing of a constitution and other rules, guided mostly by pragmatic decisions that reflected a concern for unity rather than ideological purity. However, debates over profit-sharing, the relative importance of production versus consumer cooperatives, the role of state support for cooperative development, relationships with other international organizations and similar matters identified sharp differences that led to the withdrawal of major agricultural, credit and worker productive societies. Major decisions were made regarding ICA membership, originally open to individuals as well as organizations, with the gradual elimination of membership for individuals and the decision to become truly a union of national cooperative unions.

The Congress at Glasgow in 1913 confronted two momentous issues, the growing clouds of war in Europe and the role of cooperatives and cooperators in preventing it, and the matter of full-time paid staff leaders for the organization. A Peace Resolution, building on earlier Central Committee and Executive Committee actions, was unanimously and enthusiastically passed. Henry May was named general secretary, beginning an era in which the director of the ICA would play a pivotal role in the thinking and work of the Alliance, augmenting significantly the work done by its elected leadership. There was no further ICA congress until 1921, due to the outbreak of World War I and to postwar reconstruction and reconciliation within the cooperative movement.

At the Congress in Glasgow the participants also agreed that the Executive Committee should include representatives from more than one nation. However, due to the outbreak of World War I, the Executive and Central Committees had difficulty meeting, and therefore the individuals serving on the two committees in 1913 remained in their positions until 1921. Decisions regarding the Alliance were simplified by virtue of the fact that the individuals making the decisions governing it were all from the same country. It may also have been part of the reason why the Alliance survived so well. The leadership did not have to concern themselves with rivalries and resentments of individuals from warring countries. During the war the previously harmonious relations between cooperatives and trade unions became strained because of the different economic pressures on each group.

Notably, during World War I, the Alliance remained active across national lines. The *International Cooperative Bulletin* continued to appear in identical English, French and German editions. Many cooperative movements emerged from the war in strengthened positions, based on their services to consumers in difficult times and the public esteem that they had acquired because of their services to citizens and governments. Further, the Peace Resolution of the Glasgow Congress proved a rallying point for cooperators once nationalistic passions had cooled.

The postwar period saw the Alliance relating to the new international structures that emerged from the war, the League of Nations and the ILO. In the latter case, relationships were facilitated by the appointment of French cooperative leader Albert Thomas as the first director of the ILO and his establishment of a Cooperative Service in the organization to pursue assistance to cooperation. Thomas continued to attend Alliance meetings as a representative of French cooperatives. He also chaired a committee within the ILO, designed to build relationships between agricultural and consumer cooperatives, in which the ICA participated.

Another new dynamic in the international movement emerged from the collapse of the Russian Empire and the emergence of the Union of Soviet Socialist Republics (USSR) with its moves to nationalize industry and to place cooperatives in the context of socialism and central economic planning.

In Geneva in 1920 the Central Committee of the Alliance met for the first time since the outbreak of the war. The members discussed constitutional problems and policy. The constitutional issues included adjustments to the membership rules to account for the new and diverse national populations, new regulations for the election and composition of the Central and Executive Committees, and new rules on payment of dues. The policy questions revolved around how to deal with the exchange of goods and persons on the international level, so as to avoid the ruthlessness that created power conflicts and war. The Committee decided to hold a congress in Basel in August 1921 and deal further with the constitutional and policy issues then. It was no coincidence that both these meetings were held in Switzerland, a country that had remained neutral throughout the war.

Although, since its inception in 1895, the Congress of the Alliance had been the governing body and was declared as such in the constitution, the interwar years found the Central and Executive Committees playing a stronger role. The committees became the initiators of policy, but even so, all procedural changes had to be approved by the Congress.

The Basel Congress (1921) dealt mostly with how to adapt the organization to the newly structured world around it. A new economic policy was discussed, support for the 1913 Glasgow Peace Resolution was reiterated, and an appeal was made to trade unions to recognize that fundamentally the two types of organizations had similar goals. A controversial membership issue at the Congress forced participants to decide between the Central and Executive Committees' views. The USSR government had become involved with the leadership and decision making of Centrosoyus, and a debate had begun as to how far it was still a popular movement or whether it had become completely parastatal. The Congress voted on whether or not Centrosoyus should remain a member of the Alliance, eventually siding with the Executive and continuing its membership. Immediately following the Congress, the Central Committee elected the first international Executive Committee.

Three "Specialized Bodies" have their roots in the Basel Congress. The Alliance's Specialized Bodies are committees that report to the Alliance and bring together the various types of cooperatives from different countries. These bodies are more focused than the Alliance can be and are able to receive input on specific matters relating to individual types of cooperatives as opposed to national cooperative movements in general. The three Specialized Bodies that were founded in Basel were the International Cooperative Banking Committee, the International Cooperative Assurance Committee, and the International Cooperative Women's Committee. The Banking Committee was created in an effort to start an international cooperative bank, the Assurance Committee worked to exchange information and experiences between the assurance cooperatives in different nations, and the Women's Committee sought to organize and draw together women throughout the world who worked with cooperatives. At the 1924 Ghent Congress the Women's Committee was replaced by the International Cooperative Women's Guild.

By the time of the Basel Congress, fascism was on the rise in Italy. Despite aid efforts from the Alliance and attempts to pressure the government, cooperatives in Italy were eventually rendered almost powerless, with the loss of over 80% of their membership and all their funding.

In 1923 the Executive Committee declared the first International Cooperative Day, to be observed on the first Saturday in July. It was designed to be a day when cooperatives around the globe would celebrate and demonstrate to nonmembers the movement's solidarity. This served to unify the members of the Alliance and cooperatives worldwide at a time when national conflicts had strained the Alliance's internal relations. During the same period the Alliance formally adopted the Rainbow Flag as the organization's official ensign.

By the early 1920s the economic worries of the world seemed to be receding. This allowed the Alliance's congresses at Ghent (1924) and Stockholm (1927) to focus on other issues, such as reaffirming the Alliance's neutrality and inter-cooperative relations. The Alliance's growing importance in international affairs was revealed at the Ghent Congress by the presence of parliament members or senior public officials from 10 governments, as well as delegates from several important international organizations, including the ILO. An important outcome of the Stockholm Congress was the adoption of a resolution, still currently in effect, that no country or union of countries could control more than one-fifth of the total voting power at congresses.

Another Specialized Body, the International Cooperative Wholesale Society (ICWS), was created at the Ghent Congress. First suggested at the

1921 Basel Congress, the Society was proposed as a method of gathering information from various national wholesale organizations about their imports and exports. The Society did not become active until 1930.

During the same decade, the issue of the Alliance's neutrality was a pressing subject. Soviet use of the cooperative movement's international contacts to expound communist propaganda began to distress Alliance members in other countries. This resulted in the Central Committee's adopting a memorandum in 1925 stating that political and religious neutrality was an issue that could be regulated in all acts originating with the Alliance. Non-neutral activity and interaction by national cooperative organizations outside their own countries could not be regulated, only considered a breach of good faith. This was the beginning of strained relations between Soviet cooperatives and the Alliance.

By the late 1920s, members of the Alliance were beginning to argue that the cooperative principles were becoming outdated due to drastic changes in the global economic environment. At the 1930 Congress in Vienna a Special Committee to review the Rochdale Principles was called for and approved. This was an important move because, in over 90 years, there had been no definitive restatement of the principles.

The economic depression of 1929 onward began a period of hostility toward cooperatives on the part of private traders and industrialists, a hostility that lasted through World War II. Many governments succumbed to pressures for increased taxation and/or cooperatives' inclusion in trade regulations directed at large capitalist enterprises.

Also during this period, totalitarian regimes in several countries were restricting cooperative freedom. In Germany, under the Nazi party, incidents reminiscent of Fascist Italy began to occur. Cooperatives were subjected to harassment and to acts of violence that were either ignored or condoned by German law enforcement agencies. Cooperatives in Germany were liquidated, with ownership passing into private hands. With the emergence of the Third Reich, cooperatives faced persecution for their democratic character even more than for their economic action. Cooperative offices were seized and leaders in the movement arrested. The German edition of the *Review of International Cooperation*, which was printed in Hamburg, was terminated because it only served to aggravate the Nazi officials.

Similar persecution began to occur in Austria; however, the ICA, represented by director Henry May, came to the aid of the Austrian cooperators. May immediately called for a report on the conditions of cooperatives in Austria. In 1934 he traveled to Austria himself to request clemency for two prominent Alliance leaders who had been arrested. He managed to meet with the chancellor of Austria and clarify the purpose and ideology of co-operatives. The chancellor reassured May that control of the cooperatives would be returned to their rightful member-owners once it was evident that they were no longer involved with opposition political parties. The cooperatives cut their political ties, and soon Austrian representatives again appeared on the Central Committee. Unfortunately, the Austrian cooperative movement's freedom only lasted until 1938 and the German Anschluss.

In the USSR, with the government's decree of 29 September 1935, consumer cooperative societies throughout the Union were disbanded and their operations were transferred to the state trading department. The central import organization, Centrosoyus, also lost its functions to the state trading department.

During the same period many cooperators in Spain were forced into exile to escape persecution by the new reactionary government. The cooperative movement in Spain did not fully distance itself from these influences and as a result only rejoined the Alliance in 1981, following a change of government and a return to democracy.

The Alliance also saw its international influence and even its freedom of existence seriously threatened. Membership of the Alliance decreased due to the political disputes and to the governmental interference in Spain, Germany, Austria and the USSR. The Alliance began to rely heavily on the co-operative movements of the U.K. and France for support, both financial and political.

The acceptance of the redefined cooperative principles and the passing of a resolution that specified the role of cooperatives in differing economic systems marked the Congress at Paris in 1937. The Special Committee formed in Vienna seven years earlier reported back and declared that there were seven fundamental cooperative principles, the first four of which were obligatory for any true cooperative. The seven principles were open membership, democratic control, dividends on purchases, limited interest on capital, political and religious neutrality, cash trading and education. Two other principles were also recommended but not considered to be fundamental. These were trading exclusively with members and voluntary membership.

A resolution on cooperatives' roles in different economies, adopted at the Paris Congress, was significant because it represented the Alliance's position immediately before the war and was one of its last official acts before World War II. It reads as follows:

> That Cooperation, as a form of expression in social activity of its own, is possible and necessary in all the different kinds of economic and political sys-

tems, even though its tasks and importance vary in different systems, principally depending upon the character of the social groups that have obtained possession of the State power.

That the cooperative movement in all economic systems demands for itself complete freedom of activity on the basis of its own principles, and repels all efforts to control politically its activity.

That the cooperative movement, wherever a regulated economy in some form or other has been put into power, rejects measures that hinder the national or international development of its activity, just as it rejects any efforts in a socialist economic system to concentrate the whole economic activity in the hands of public bodies.

During the last years of Henry May's leadership the ICA adopted an active role in opposition to impending war. If war became inevitable, the Alliance would work to provide support and protection to cooperatives during it. In 1939 May published what would be his last article in the ICA *Review of International Cooperation*. The article set forth the following six tasks for the Alliance's wartime agenda and its goals for the future:

1. To maintain communications and, as far as possible, personal contacts with the national affiliate organizations;
2. To maintain the ICA publications, including special features of information of wartime importance to national movements;
3. To consider and prepare for the full range of ICA activities that would need renewal after the war;
4. To seek agreement on the principles and considerations that should govern a postwar world settlement designed to ensure freedom, security and universal peace;
5. To determine the contribution that could be made by organized cooperative movements to the adoption and realization of such a program; and
6. To initiate a more intensive campaign of recruitment to ICA membership of cooperative movements developing outside Europe.

These were of great significance because they served to guide the Alliance during the war, and, with Henry May's death later in 1939, they enshrined his legacy of contending for peace, for economic and social justice and for the expansion of the cooperative movement.

During World War II the Alliance's committee meetings were again disrupted. Members were unable to travel to the U.K. for meetings due to travel and communication problems, and meetings scheduled for other countries were canceled for the same reasons. The president of the ICA at the beginning of the war was Väinö Tanner, a Finn. Due to the Russo-Finnish war he found himself cut off from communication with the Alliance. Tanner's absence, combined with May's death, left the Alliance with no constitutionally delineated leadership. This resulted in the appointing of an acting president who led the Alliance until the Central Committee could meet again after the war. Along with the decrease in international participation and financing, the ICA secretariat saw its staff drop from 20 to eight by 1941. Despite these changes and complications, the Alliance remained strong during and after the war. The *Review* continued to be published, as called for by May, with contributions from numerous countries, including Argentina, Australia, Belgium, Canada, Ceylon, China, Colombia, Estonia, Finland, France, Germany, Great Britain, Holland, India, Norway, Palestine, Romania, Sweden, Switzerland, the U.S., the USSR, Venezuela and Yugoslavia.

Toward the end of World War II the Alliance sent out an appeal to its members in countries that were less damaged by the war to help war-ravaged movements. The Alliance raised over £300,000, as well as large donations of resources from specific cooperatives. This demonstrated just how much the Alliance had expanded its membership and grown in power in the interwar years.

The 1946 Congress, held in Zurich, was marked by a resolution calling for international control of the world's oil resources and the administration of Middle Eastern oil by a UN body. This resolution was strongly supported at the Congress, but the UN did not act on the Alliance's recommendations. A year later the Alliance created a Specialized Body, the International Cooperative Petroleum Association (ICPA), with the goal of assuring supplies of petroleum at reasonable prices to its members. Within its first fiscal year the ICPA had organizations in 20 countries at some point in the membership process.

In 1946 the Alliance was given consultative status with a number of international organizations, among them the ILO, FAO and UNESCO, along with other special councils of the UN. This demonstrated the ICA's growing influence in international politics and affairs and its unique position among cooperative organizations.

In 1947 the number of the Alliance's Specialized Bodies grew from five to eight, with the creation of the previously mentioned ICPA as well as the Auxiliary Committee of Representatives of Workers' Productive and Artisans' Societies (CICOPA) and the International Cooperative Press

Committee. Although first proposed in 1932, partly in response to the world economic depression, CICOPA was not officially active until it held its first meeting in 1957. The goal of the International Cooperative Press Committee was to create an International Press Agency, a goal yet to be fully achieved.

The Cold War began to affect the workings of the Alliance, starting in the late 1940s and continuing until the collapse of the communist regimes in Eastern and Central Europe from 1989 to 1990. The political conflicts between east and west created an atmosphere of suspicion and distrust within the Alliance, evident at the Prague (1948), Copenhagen (1951) and Paris (1954) congresses. Centrosoyus was gaining power and was now the ideological leader of several cooperative movements, rather than merely a lone voice. The western members of the Alliance feared that, through this accumulation of influence, Centrosoyus, as the largest representative from the east, was trying to gain control over the Alliance. These fears were re-inforced by an attempt by Centrosoyus, at the Prague Congress, to amend 14 of the 35 articles of the Alliance's constitution. The articles that the USSR delegates proposed to amend touched on the following issues: including Russian as one of the official languages of the Alliance; excluding fascists from the Alliance; admitting to Alliance membership "associations of persons or organizations . . . provided they observe the Rules of the ICA" (no particular type of organization or association being specified); appointing a Managing Bureau; changing the rule so that decisions at congresses and by the Central Committee would need a two-thirds majority (as opposed to the existing simple majority); expanding the Executive Committee to 22 members (doubling the existing size); and appointing, by the two biggest national cooperative movements, two assistants to the general secretary (the USSR and the U.K. were the two largest movements at the time). None of these proposed amendments was approved, but these internal conflicts caused prolonged discussion at all three congresses and delays in the adoption of the Peace Resolution, an item passed almost unanimously, with no delay, on all previous occasions.

At the 1951 Congress in Copenhagen, based on a recommendation from the Prague Congress (1948), the Specialized Body on Agricultural Cooperation and the International Housing Committee were created. The Agricultural Committee was responsible for agricultural affairs within the Alliance and extensively promoted Alliance membership among agricultural organizations. The Housing Committee helped to raise awareness of housing problems throughout the world and claimed that it was the responsibility of all categories of cooperatives to help solve these problems. The

Copenhagen Congress also created the Committee on the Rationalization of Commodity Distribution. This dealt with keeping costs down and maintaining a healthy competition in commodity distribution in areas where inflation had negatively affected the standard of living.

A historic resolution was approved at the Paris Congress (1954), leading to the establishment of the Alliance's international development fund later in the same year. The resolution was the first to establish cooperative development as an Alliance priority. The resolution attempted to define and identify "underdeveloped" countries that could benefit from assistance from the Alliance, and it called on all members to come to the aid of cooperative pioneers in such countries. This resolution sparked discussions and papers that continued to appear during the Stockholm (1957), Lausanne (1960) and Bournemouth (1963) congresses, and the development program is still currently active and strong. This program was strongly supported in 1966 by the ILO Recommendation 127 that declared cooperatives to be important instruments of economic, social and cultural development and called on governments of developing countries to recognize and utilize them as such. The first region to benefit from the Alliance's development fund was Southeast Asia.

A regional conference was planned for Southeast Asia and was held in Kuala Lumpur, Malaysia, in 1958. At the conference, participants were able to exchange information about the various cooperative movements located in the region, and eventually it was decided that a Regional Office was needed. The Regional Office would be a branch of the ICA secretariat and would involve all the purposes of the Alliance, not only aid to "underdeveloped" countries in the region. By 1960 the Regional Office had been established at New Delhi, India.

In 1958 the Committee on Retail Distribution and the Research Officers' Group, both Alliance Specialized Bodies, were created. The purpose of the Retail Committee was to deal with assortment policy, profit from retailing, education and training of personnel and similar issues. The Research Group was composed of representatives from the planning departments of various national cooperative movements and was to provide leadership in carrying out research on cooperative matters. It is currently referred to as the Research Committee.

At the Bournemouth Congress (1963) the cooperative principles were once again called up for review. They were to be presented, in their restructured form, at the next congress. The year 1963 saw the opening of the first cooperative petroleum manufacturing facility, in the Netherlands, under the ICPA flag. It also was the beginning year of William Gemmell Alexander's five years as ICA director.

The year 1965 marked the 70th anniversary of the Alliance and the 20th of the UN. It was declared International Cooperation Year by the UN, and the Alliance called on all of its members to give special recognition to the UN.

As called for in 1963, the cooperative principles were reformulated and presented to the Congress at Vienna (1966). Instead of the existing seven, the report concluded that there were in fact six essential principles. The reformulation took into account the activities of the Alliance's member cooperatives as well as the means by which the principles, which had been updated in 1937, could be further modernized to reflect current roles and responsibilities of cooperatives. The six updated principles were as follows: open and voluntary membership; democratic organization and administration; limited rewards from share capital; distribution of surpluses among members in three possible ways (further development of the cooperative, common services, or distribution amongst members in proportion to their transactions with the organization); cooperative education of members, staff, employees and the general public; and the duty of the cooperative organizations to actively cooperate at all levels. These principles remained basically similar to those put forward in 1937, but they were slowly becoming more action-oriented and less philosophical.

In 1966 the Alliance realized that the development fund would have to shift focus in order to have a significant impact in developing countries. During the 12 years since its creation, the fund had been used mostly for small projects. Although small projects were still to be supported under the new agenda, the Alliance decided to focus the fund on sizable, meaningful projects that would encourage cooperatives in developing countries within a long-term strategy. The Alliance also began to seek support from other organizations and also to encourage member cooperatives to contribute funds for specific projects. The latter effort was in the hope that contributions would increase because members would know specifically what they were being spent on.

In 1968 the Alliance opened the doors of its second Regional Office, in Moshi, Tanzania. This office served East and Central Africa. This office, like the Regional Office for Southeast Asia, would be an extension of the Alliance's secretariat, but in this case education and technical assistance, trade promotion and public information were declared high priorities. The opening of a second Regional Office reinforced the promise of a future of continued expansion for the Alliance. The East and Central Africa Regional Office moved from Moshi to Nairobi, Kenya, in January 1999.

Only one special subject was prepared for deliberation at the Hamburg Congress (1969): contemporary cooperative democracy. Three papers were presented, by the ICA secretariat, the USSR, and Sweden and France jointly, each representing a different view. The deliberations occupied one entire day of the Congress, without exhausting the list of those who wished to contribute to the discussion. Despite the differing initial viewpoints, the Congress adopted a recommendation affirming that:

> Political democracy is indispensable to the development of cooperation and that reciprocally to economic democracy without which political democracy remains incomplete.

This recommendation, unanimously adopted, represented a reaffirmation of historic cooperative ideology and a belief that, to cooperatives, democracy is a seamless garment.

In 1970, in celebration of its 75th anniversary, the Alliance declared the 1970s the Decade for Cooperative Development. Building on experience gained in the 16 years of the development fund, the Alliance initiated a 10-year program that would increase the promotion of cooperative development in Third World countries. Although the Alliance had, by this point, gained widespread support for its efforts in developing countries, the decade itself proved to be somewhat disappointing. A report to the Moscow Congress (1980) declared the decade to have been "not quite as great or as uniformly successful as had been hoped," but its lack of success was attributed to "unfavorable economic and other circumstances" rather than to any lack of effort by the cooperative movement itself.

The Cooperative Wholesale Committee and the Committee on Retail Distribution merged in 1970 to form the International Organization for Consumer Cooperative Distributive Trades (INTER-COOP). The aim of the committee was to intensify economic collaboration between members and strengthen the power of consumer cooperatives.

In 1971 the ICA, FAO, ILO, International Federation of Agricultural Producers (IFAP) and International Federation of Plantation, Agricultural and Allied Workers (IFPAAW) joined to create the Committee for the Promotion of Agricultural Cooperatives. The initiating organizations were soon joined by WOCCU and the UN, and the name was changed to the Committee for the Promotion of Aid to Cooperatives (COPAC). (It was again changed in 1988 to its present title—the Committee for the Promotion and Advancement of Cooperatives.) The committee would work closely with the ICA, where it is now headquartered.

By the 1972 Warsaw Congress, the Alliance had developed more specific goals and aims for the development fund, and it had identified four specific areas of focus for developed countries: providing training courses and study tours for visiting cooperators from developing countries; providing training courses in the developing countries, either by correspondence or by sending tutors; sending experts, on either a short- or a long-term basis, to provide advice and to fill, on an interim basis, administrative and technical posts in the cooperative movements of developing countries; and raising funds from cooperative members in developed countries and using these for the provision of educational and other equipment needed by cooperators in developing countries. It was felt that these four categories managed to cover most necessary areas.

In 1973 the Alliance's Organization for Cooperative Consumer Policy was founded to work in the field of consumer information, protection, enlightenment and education, while bearing in mind environmental aspects and establishing common lines of action among its members. During the same year the Advisory Group for International Training of Cooperators (AGITCOOP) was created to advise the Alliance on education and training for cooperators in developing countries. AGITCOOP became the ICA Human Resources Development Committee in 1995.

Two important international conferences were held in the late 1970s, beginning a tradition of cooperation among fishery and industrial cooperatives. In 1975 the ICA held its first Open World Conference on Cooperative Fisheries in Tokyo, and in 1978 its first Open World Conference on Industrial Cooperatives in Rome. In Tokyo, fishing cooperatives responded to the international food crisis and the need for development in underdeveloped countries as well as the need to work together to maintain their own survival in an increasingly competitive international market. The participants discussed production, protection of resources, marketing and processing of fish, modernization of the fisheries industry, and the need for assistance to developing countries. In Rome, participants exchanged ideas on the origin and development of industrial cooperatives, the role of such cooperatives in economic and social development, and the role of international organizations in the development of industrial cooperatives. Industrial cooperatives were becoming increasingly popular because they provided an alternative to both capitalist and state enterprises.

In 1978 the Working Party on Cooperative Tourism was created at the Conference on Tourism held in Copenhagen. In 1992 this organization became the ICA Tourism Committee (TICA).

In 1981 the Alliance opened its third Regional Office, in Abidjan, Côte d'Ivoire. This office serves the West African Region, with the purpose of promoting cooperatives in its 16 countries. A special focus on education and training and on promoting cooperatives through the teaching of development, as well as promoting effective management and business methods, was planned. In 1996 the office was moved to Ouagadougou, Burkina Faso.

Starting in mid-1981, with the resignation of Dr. S. K. Saxena (India) after 13 years as director, the Alliance experienced a period of uncertainty within its staff leadership, as five directors came and went. After a long period of deliberation and the last-minute withdrawal of a selected candidate, deputy director R. P. B. Davies (U.K.) was appointed acting director. This lasted until October 1981, when Andre Saenger (Switzerland) was appointed director. In October 1983 Saenger resigned and was replaced by an interim director, Françoise Baulier (France), who had worked closely with the Alliance leadership. She served as interim director until late in 1984 when Robert Beasley (U.S.) was appointed director. Beasley served for four years, stepping down in 1988 to be replaced by Bruce Thordarsen (Canada), the current director-general, who has provided more than a decade of sustained, capable leadership.

In mid-1982, the president of the Alliance, Roger Kerinec, was invited to speak to the UN General Assembly second Special Session on Disarmament. He spoke on behalf of cooperatives and cooperators worldwide, stating that it was "time that nations, all nations, learn that real courage does not consist of facing death bravely but of living with others." Although a Special Session on Disarmament was a step in the right direction, Kerinec observed that not enough was being done and that the UN should use its international influence to work toward gradual and controlled disarmament.

In 1982 the Central Office of the Alliance moved from London to Geneva. This represented a break from what had hitherto been a strong British influence on the organization and was the first time the office had been located outside the U.K.

The main issue discussed at the 1984 Hamburg Congress was a paper, presented by Centrosoyus, on "Global Problems and Cooperatives." Discussions focused on safeguarding peace, helping to deal with the world's food and energy shortages, protecting the environment, and promoting economic growth in developing countries. These are all longstanding issues that the Alliance continues to grapple with.

In 1988, the Alliance's development projects were reevaluated and a program set forth for future aid to developing countries. This plan included work toward the de-officialization of cooperatives, shifting from government to member control; movement-to-movement aid, through the creation of specialized organizations and/or committees; and integrated programming, coordinating the planning of the various development activities and projects going on around the globe. It was hoped that these would lead to improvements over previous efforts.

Also in 1988, the Alliance opened a Project Office in San José, Costa Rica. After a year, it was converted into the Regional Office for Central America and the Caribbean, and it is now the Regional Office for the Americas.

A paper was presented and a resolution adopted at the Stockholm Congress (1988), calling for an attempt to define cooperative identity through the examination of cooperative ideology, principles and values. This was the beginning of a seven-year effort to redefine the philosophical direction of the Alliance. The ideology and principles of the movement had already been thoroughly examined and detailed, so the paper focused on the third category, cooperative values. It presented two separate lists. One was current and included eight advanced concepts (self-help, mutual help, non-profit interest, democracy, "voluntariness," universality, education and purposeful values); the second was drawn from an earlier publication and included seven concepts (association and unity, economy, democracy, equity, liberty, responsibility and education). The basic values were honesty, openness, social responsibility and caring for others. This paper served as the basis for extended discussion and for the resolution calling for a continuing study as a way of establishing basic global values, which, in turn, would establish priorities for the Alliance's long-term program.

The ICA's Executive Committee established a Basic Values Advisory Committee that presented preliminary conclusions in a report to the 1992 Tokyo Congress. This report outlined basic global values, including economic activities for meeting needs; democratic participation; human resource development; social responsibility; and national and international cooperation. The report also suggested approaches for reformulating the ICA's cooperative principles before the 1995 Manchester Congress. The first approach, the more modest, recommended that the principles be revised to include the following: a new principle on capital formation; employees' participation in the management of cooperatives in the principle about democracy; and a new principle to emphasize the autonomy and independence of cooperatives. The second approach recommended two types of principles: the basic cooperative principles that express, at the universal level, the essence of cooperation, and the basic rules and practices essential for cooperative action. Under the second approach, the first category of principles was not subject to change, whereas the second category was expected to be revised and adapted to changes occurring in the world and in the international cooperative movement. Based on these recommendations the Tokyo Congress adopted a resolution calling for the final results of the investigation into cooperative values and principles to be presented at the 1995 Manchester Congress.

Major restructuring of the Alliance had been proposed in Stockholm, and a Structure Committee was set up to assess exactly what changes should be made. The committee presented its evaluation to the Tokyo Congress (1992) and proposed the following changes: the amalgamation of the functions of the Congress and the Central Committee into a new governing body, the ICA General Assembly; the creation of four new Regional Assemblies: Asia/Pacific, Africa, the Americas and Europe, to meet in alternate years during the years in which the General Assembly did not meet; provision for the regional nomination of vice presidents in order to ensure effective regional representation on the ICA board (the current Executive Committee); clarification of the relationship between the ICA and the Specialized (sectoral) Organizations, which should be able to finance their own activities in the future; and a gradual increase in membership fees.

These changes were extensive, affecting most aspects of the Alliance's operations. Even so, the changes were greeted positively by the Congress, in the hope that they would improve and enhance what most regarded as the Alliance's already successful operations. The resolution was approved.

The Manchester Congress (1995) adopted further modifications to the Alliance. As opposed to the structural changes adopted in 1992, these were ideological and included a revision of the values and principles of the Alliance. This revised philosophical direction for the Alliance incorporated a definition of cooperatives, a definition of the values on which they are based, and a set of reformulated principles. A cooperative was defined as "an autonomous association of persons united voluntarily to meet their common economic, social and cultural needs and aspirations through a jointly-owned and democratically controlled enterprise." The revised principles were set forth as guidelines for member cooperatives. The seven revised principles were: voluntary and open membership; democratic member control; economic member participation; autonomy and independence; education, training and information; cooperation among cooperatives; and concern for the community. The principles of autonomy and independence and of concern for the community were relatively new concepts, whereas the remaining five principles were based heavily on the original Rochdale Principles and their reformulations over the years.

The year 1995 marked the centennial anniversary of the Alliance, which was acknowledged by the UN through its declaration of the first Saturday in July as International Cooperative Day, the same day as the cooperative movement's own celebration. This was an important manifestation of the UN's support for the Alliance and the cooperative movement on an international level.

In 1996 the International Health Cooperative Organization (IHCO) was created within the Alliance. The IHCO's objectives include providing a forum for the discussion and exchange of issues relevant to its member organizations; providing information to UN organizations, national governments, the media and the public about the nature and role of health cooperatives; promoting the development of health cooperatives; and collaborating with the other specialized bodies of the ICA.

In 1998 the Alliance opened two Regional Offices: a European Regional Office, with headquarters at the ICA in Geneva, Switzerland, and a North Africa and Arab Countries Regional Office, headquartered in Cairo, Egypt.

World Council of Credit Unions

In 1900 Alphonse Desjardins, after extended correspondence with English cooperator Henry Wolff and a review of available material on the European experience with savings and credit cooperatives, joined with more than 80 people to sign the roll of membership and to subscribe more than 500 shares of the Caisse Populaire de Lévis in Quebec Province of Canada. This was followed by a second society in 1901 and a third in 1905. In 1907 Desjardins accepted an invitation to travel to Manchester, New Hampshire, to advise on the possibility of forming similar groups in the U.S. The result was the establishment of three parish credit unions—St. Mary's in Manchester, New Hampshire, St. Jean-Baptiste in Lynn, Massachusetts, and St. Jeanne d'Arc in Lowell, Massachusetts. At roughly the same time that Desjardins was organizing these credit unions, Edward Filene, wealthy owner of a Boston department store, embarked on a trip around the world during which he was introduced to the savings and credit cooperatives of Germany and India. The latter particularly impressed him, and he returned home convinced that such an organization held great potential for persons of limited means in the U.S. He joined with others in Massachusetts who were exploring similar options and soon emerged in a leadership role, in part because of his willingness to commit significant financial resources to support his efforts. (Filene eventually would contribute a total of more than $1,000,000 to support credit union development in the U.S.) Shortly after World War I Filene recruited a 40-year-old lawyer from Lynn, Massachusetts, Roy Bergengren, to help organize and strengthen the credit union effort in Massachusetts and ultimately to organize the Credit Union National Extension Bureau in 1921. The goals of the Bureau were to obtain credit union legislation in each state, to organize enough credit unions in each state to support a state league and, when there were enough credit unions and leagues, to form a national league. (The formation of a worldwide credit union organization, though often discussed, became a formal goal at a later date.)

Filene's and Bergengren's ideas were viewed as visionary by many, who saw that in 12 years only 90 credit unions had been organized in Massachusetts, some 50 in New York, 33 rural societies in North Carolina, and a scattering of others, totaling 190, throughout the country. But Bergengren's organizing skills became legendary, with much of his time being utilized as a traveling evangelist for credit unions, recruiting and leaving behind local leadership captured by and working for the achievement of the credit union vision. Bergengren also drew into the organizing effort business associations, trade unions, organizations of government employees, and religious and other groups that he had convinced should join in the organizing effort as a way of providing benefits to their employees or members. Thirteen years later, just before a meeting to organize the Credit Union National Association (CUNA) to replace the National Extension Bureau, there were 2,489 credit unions throughout the U.S., with 427,097 members. A federal credit union law had been passed earlier that year, supplementing laws in 32 states. State leagues had been formed or were forming in 34 states.

Growth under CUNA continued at a rapid pace. Twelve years later, at the start of 1946, there were 8,683 credit unions with 2,842,989 members. In 12 more years (1958) the totals were 18,838 credit unions and 10,431,606 members. Another 12 years later (1970), 23,761 credit unions existed with a membership of 21,630,958. Twenty-six years later, in 1996, after a period of consolidation of smaller credit unions, there were 10,569 credit unions with 63,788,693 members, 47.4% of the working age population of the U.S. Clearly the three early goals of the Credit Union Extension Bureau had been accomplished.

The fourth goal, a worldwide movement of credit unions, was never out of mind. As early as the 1920s, Bergengren was in touch by correspondence with people around the world, and the mailing list of *The Bridge*, the publication of the Extension Bureau, included a variety of foreign addresses. When CUNA came into existence in 1934, with Bergengren as its head, international interest persisted, focusing initially on credit unions in English-speaking Canada. By 1938 credit union legislation had been adopted in all the Canadian provinces, and CUNA credit union insurance and supply services were available in Canada. By 1940 there were 1,167 credit unions in Canada with a membership exceeding 200,000. By 1945 this had grown to 2,219 credit unions with approximately 590,000 members. Provision for membership in CUNA by Canadian provincial leagues had been approved in 1939, and by 1944 eight leagues were members. Growth has persisted, and in 1996 there were 905 credit unions in English-speaking Canada with a membership of 4,105,730.

Parallel developments were taking place elsewhere, some with CUNA assistance, some independently. By the late 1930s, 30 credit unions had been developed in the Philippines with the aid of a Protestant missionary. In 1940 the first credit unions were organized in Australia and El Salvador. In 1943, with assistance from Catholic missionaries, credit unions were founded in Belize and Jamaica. In Trinidad and Tobago and the Dominican Republic active organization of credit unions was undertaken, with national leagues soon established. In the post–World War II years, provision was made for membership in CUNA for national leagues in the Western Hemisphere, and by 1953 leagues from Canada, Puerto Rico, Jamaica and the Dominican Republic had representatives on the CUNA board of directors.

The year 1953 was significant for international credit union development. In resolutions adopted that year, CUNA resolved to formally become involved in international development activities; formulated plans to expand the use of credit unions as one of the tools to win permanent international peace; prepared and distributed materials regarding credit unions to the U.S. foreign assistance program, the UN, the FAO and the ILO; established a Foreign Credit Union Study Committee; and voted to establish the World Extension Division, with staff and budget, to formalize its international credit union development activities.

The World Extension Division began work in October 1954, and its staff immediately moved to reactivate contacts that had been unofficially established in earlier years. The division's report for 1955 gives some sense of the scope of its activity: contacts with 82 countries and territories; training given to 65 people from 40 countries; credit unions organized in India, Guatemala, New Zealand, Nigeria and the Philippines; passage of credit union legislation and organization of the first credit unions in Peru; and assistance to leagues in Jamaica and Trinidad and Tobago.

In 1958, with World Extension Division staff assistance, the West Indian Confederation of Credit Societies was established, the forerunner of the present Caribbean Confederation of Credit Unions and the precursor of similar confederations in Africa (1968), Latin America (1970) and Asia (1971).

In 1961 CUNA signed its first contract with the U.S. Agency for International Development, making available U.S. foreign assistance funds to support credit union development. These funds eventually permitted the establishment of the CUNA Global Projects Office, with staff in Washington, D.C., and of the Latin America Regional Office in Panama, which reflected a priority interest at that time in the development of credit unions in the Western Hemisphere.

By 1964 CUNA was committing 9.5% of its budget to international credit union development. However, there were growing concerns among some leaders of the American movement that international activities were diluting attention from credit union problems and needs in the U.S. To accommodate these views, CUNA International was established in 1964 with three separate forums, in which the U.S., Canada and the developing movements might each pursue their individual interests while remaining part of the whole.

This new arrangement did not prove completely satisfactory to everyone, and, while international activities continued and grew, attention shifted to an alternative model for a world credit union organization, an international organization in which national movements, including the U.S., would be represented. After much discussion, the World Council of Credit Unions (WOCCU) was established in 1970, with provisions for membership for certain established national associations and for regional confederations in Africa, Asia, the Caribbean and Latin America. Initial policies provided for membership on the World Council Board of Directors to be partly based on movement size. Other provisions ensured that no movement (meaning the U.S.) could dominate the body. In fact, the U.S. movement has, over the years, voluntarily accepted a smaller proportion of board membership than would be justified by its membership, which accounts for about 70% of credit union members worldwide.

As WOCCU came into existence in 1970, the extent of credit union development was as follows: Africa—1,795 credit unions; Asia—16,827; Australia—848; Canada—4,214 (1972); Caribbean—610; Europe—341; Latin America—4,168; South Pacific—413; and the U.S.—23,761.

In the 1970s WOCCU established its offices at the CUNA Credit Union Center in Madison, Wisconsin, and moved ahead to develop operating procedures to represent credit unions worldwide. Technical assistance efforts on behalf of developing credit union movements, funded principally by the Agency for International Development, continued to be carried out by the CUNA Global Projects Office in Washington. This separation was deemed appropriate due to a need to conform to provisions of the U.S. Foreign Assistance Act, which called upon USAID to utilize "American cooperatives" in providing assistance to cooperatives in developing countries. During 1980–1981, an agreement acceptable to USAID was arrived at between CUNA and WOCCU, whereby CUNA remained the actual signatory of grants or contracts but delegated responsibility for their implementation to WOCCU. This remains the way in which U.S. foreign assistance funds are channeled for support of international credit union development.

A chief executive officer was named for the World Council, and the staffs of WOCCU and the CUNA Global Projects were merged, most of them being located in Madison, Wisconsin. A small Washington, D.C. office was maintained, to handle day-to-day relationships with USAID and other funding sources and to act as North America Regional Office for the world credit union movement. Technical assistance to new and established national movements became increasingly a joint effort by WOCCU and the regional confederations that were establishing themselves as functional bodies in Africa, Asia, the Caribbean and Latin America.

WOCCU actively pursued its role as an international organization. It became a member of the ICA, achieved official observer status with the UN, and was one of the group of international organizations that established COPAC. It cultivated relationships with the World Bank and the Inter-American Development Bank.

The worldwide credit union movement has continued to grow and develop, with new national movements being organized while some established movements have waxed and waned due to changing conditions and leadership. Political turmoil has almost always adversely affected credit union membership. Economic distress in countries and regions has taken a toll. However, at times these have provided new opportunities, as in Europe where, after the collapse of the communist governments, fledgling credit union movements in the Czech Republic, Hungary, Poland, Russia and the Ukraine have emerged, the last-mentioned three now full-fledged members of WOCCU.

The dynamic of the movement is partially reflected in its statistics. At the end of 1997, WOCCU reported credit union statistics by region:

Region	Credit Unions	Members	Penetration
Africa	5,019	2,423,011	1.66%
Asia	13,988	8,566,474	2.31%
Caribbean	351	1,026,435	33.68%
Europe	1,251	2,502,062	1.64%
Latin America	1,871	5,246,039	2.84%
North America	11,290	72,578,655	47.54%
South Pacific	342	3,147,181	27.19%
WOCCU Total	34,112	95,489,857	9.36%

*Population penetration is calculated as a percentage credit union members are of total labor force of WOCCU member countries.

If success is measured by the degree to which credit unions have enrolled as members a significant portion of the working-age population, then it has been considerable in a number of places. In 28 countries in 1997, credit unions had enrolled at least 10% of their working-age populations as members. Assuming that each member represented a family of at least five, these figures suggest that credit unions provided services to an estimated 50% or more of the population in the following countries: Antigua and Barbuda (39.4%), Australia (31.9%), Bahamas (18.9%), Barbados (15.9%), Belize (26.2%), Bermuda (10.3%), the Cayman Islands (17.6%), Canada (26.0%), Colombia (13.9%), Costa Rica (15.1%), Dominica (168.5%), Ecuador (19.4%), Grenada (35.0%), Honduras (10.8%), Ireland (144.9%), Jamaica (40.7%), Korea (24.4%), Netherlands Antilles (16.2%), Panama (12.2%), Rwanda (13.7%), Saint Christopher and Nevis (43.5%), Saint Lucia (29.1%), Saint Vincent and the Grenadines (36.2%), Seychelles (17.9%), Sri Lanka (10.2%), Suriname (10.1%), Trinidad and Tobago (44.1%) and the United States (50.1%). (The penetration figures for Dominica and Ireland, and perhaps others, reflect the inclusion of youth accounts and duplicate membership by adults who belong to more than one credit union—e.g., my wife is a member of three.)

It would be a mistake, however, to declare the movement a universal success. Impressive as progress has been in the years since Desjardins established the first credit union in Lévis, Quebec, in 1900, there is still a long way to go. The movement, though well established in many countries, still counts among its membership some countries with only modest, sometimes minuscule, portions of working-age populations as credit union members. In 1997 there were 26 countries in which credit unions have had a presence for long periods of time, but in which membership penetration was less than 1% of the working-age population. In these countries, an organizing zeal for credit union development comparable to that found in a Bergengren or a Desjardins appears to be currently lacking.

There is also a tendency for credit union movements to turn their attention too early, after an initial period of organizing zeal, to becoming sophisticated financial institutions. In the process of trying to do so, they end up serving only a small and comparatively better-off part of the population. This is probably most evident in Latin America, where after 30 years of assistance and activity, total regional penetration was only 2.84% in 1997. Further, in only five countries did penetration of the working-age population exceed 10%—Colombia (13.9), Costa Rica (15.1%), Ecuador (19.4%), Honduras (10.8%) and Panama (12.2%).

Certain areas of the world have been little touched to date by the international credit union movement. A world map coded for the presence of credit union organizations would show large blanks in North Africa and the Near East, in Europe and in the island nations of the Pacific. Each of these areas poses particular challenges and opportunities to WOCCU and its members if the goal of a worldwide movement is to be fully achieved.

Note: The format for this book calls for the dictionary chapter that follows to include a brief presentation of facts about cooperatives and the cooperative movement. Included are prominent persons important in making events such as those in the chronology happen.

Choosing individuals from any group of peers for special attention is always a daunting task. Choosing from among the thousands of eminent cooperators, each of whom is memorable in his or her own national movement, and from a movement that emphasizes the group, was even more so.

Recognizing that it was necessary to go beyond any author's personal contacts and judgments, the following criteria were generally followed:

1. Deceased persons important to each national movements should be considered.
2. All regions of the world should be represented.
3. The time frame to be considered was 1750 to present.
4. Persons included should have been noteworthy in their own national cooperative movement as well as effective participants in the activities of the growing international structures of the cooperative movement.

The author has tried to be true to the criteria, but the sheer number of national movements has sometimes necessitated regional rather than national lists. Further, because the final criterion of participation in the world movement has involved, with a few notable exceptions and until the mid-20th century, mainly cooperators from the industrialized countries, the list includes a disproportionate number of persons from Europe and North America.

If at some later date a *Cooperative Encyclopedia* is developed, extended entries can be elicited for each country. Providing these will more adequately recognize and acknowledge the leadership provided the cooperative movement everywhere.

In geographical citations an attempt was made to be totally inclusive. There is a listing for each country and certain territories in which it was possible to identify and confirm cooperative organizational activity. The most current information about the status of national movements varies greatly, so the latest year for which statistics were generally available for all of a national movement were utilized. Given the lack of an established worldwide system of gathering and publishing data regarding cooperatives, some information included here may be so dated that it does not represent the current cooperative situation in individual countries, and allowances have been made for this fact. (Clarifying statements from national movements correcting inaccuracies are welcomed by the author.) Overall, however, the listings reflect much of the flavor of a worldwide popular movement and its past leadership.

In statistical citations, if data is lacking for a particular item that fact is noted with "na."

The Dictionary

A

ACLAND, ALICE. One of the founders of the Women's League for the Spread of Cooperation which later became the Cooperative Women's Guild of England and Wales, a precursor to the **International Cooperative Women's Guild** and later the **ICA** Global Women's Committee. She was the wife of **Arthur Acland**.

ACLAND, ARTHUR (1847–1926). British cooperator and leader of the Liberal Party, he participated in some of the early French cooperative **congresses**, establishing relationships and sharing approaches to the issues and problems facing the nascent cooperative movements, which contributed to its internationalization. He established the Acland Scholarships, administered by the **Cooperative Union (U.K.)**, "in order to enable young men and women under 30 to reside abroad for the purpose of studying economics and social problems." He was the husband of **Alice Acland**.

ACT. A law or decree passed by a parliament or issued by a government. Most countries have a specific cooperative act dealing with the legal recognition of cooperatives and their regulation. *See also* COOPERATIVE LAW.

AFGHANISTAN. Cooperatives are a recent phenomenon in Afghanistan; the first (a **supply cooperative** at Gulzar) was organized in 1965. The first **consumer cooperative** was organized in 1967; the first in agriculture in 1968. An expansion of these initial efforts was facilitated by external assistance during the 1970s, much of which was provided by the **FAO**. In 1980 a cooperative conference was held in Kabul, attended by 650 representatives from all parts of the country. The **ILO** *Directory* **(1988)** reported that in 1986 there were 671 cooperatives with a total membership of 147,600 in the following sectors: agricultural—459 with 73,000 members; consumer—179/73,300; and industrial—33/1,300.

The combined membership constituted approximately 0.9% of the population. Further development of this base has been difficult in recent years because of the continued civil war in the country.

AFRICAN CONFEDERATION OF COOPERATIVE SAVINGS AND CREDIT ASSOCIATIONS (ACCOSCA). The continental organization of **credit unions** in Africa with headquarters in Nairobi, Kenya, in 1997 it had 28 national **credit union confederations** as members. Twenty-five of them reported 2,423,001 individual members in some 5,019 credit unions. ACCOSCA assists in the organization and promotion of cooperative savings and **credit** societies through technical assistance and resource mobilization. It is a member of **WOCCU.**

AGRICULTURAL COOPERATIVE. An **association** of farmers for the mutual benefit of its members as **producers**; it may include among its activities farm supply, processing and marketing. Some agricultural cooperatives are organized collectively—all the assets of the cooperative are held and the work is done in common.

AGRICULTURAL COOPERATIVE DEVELOPMENT INTERNATIONAL (ACDI). One of the U.S. **cooperative development organizations** created by American cooperative and farm organizations to provide assistance to **agricultural cooperatives** and cooperative **credit** systems in **developing countries**. It is affiliated with the **National Council of Farmer Cooperatives** and receives financial assistance for its work from **USAID.**

AGRICULTURAL CREDIT. A loan given by a bank, a cooperative, or other organization or individual for a specific purpose related to agricultural operations.

ALAJOKI, E. A Finnish cooperative leader who achieved prominence in the first half of the 20th century, he was born and raised on a farm in the Parish of Lapua in northern **Finland**. He was, at an early age, one of the founders of the Cooperative Society of Lapua. He was the first chairman of the nationwide Central Organization of Agricultural Producers and remained active in various **agricultural cooperative** organizations. Alajoki was elected to the Board of Administration of S.O.K., the Finnish Cooperative Wholesale Society, in 1917 and became chairman in 1934, a position he held until his death.

ALANEN, JULIUS (1882–1952). Finnish cooperator, he was active in the leadership of the Progressive Consumer Cooperative Movement (OTK) in **Finland**, where he served from 1917 on its board of directors and was its general manager. He was active in the **Nordisk Andelsförbund** and the International Cooperative Trading Agency. He was a member of the **ICA** Central Committee at the time of his death.

ALANNE, VIENNO SERVERI (1878–1960). Finnish born, he was a professor at Helsinki University before moving to the **United States**, where he was active in the Northern States Cooperative League. He wrote extensively on cooperative matters and is most widely known for his books dealing with **consumer cooperatives**. He was a member of the board of directors of **CLUSA**.

ALATRISTE, SEALTIEL L. An early leader among cooperators in **Mexico**, he attempted to organize a cooperative movement in 1906 but was opposed by the government to such a degree that he fled as a political refugee to the **United States**. He returned later and was a major force in the success of the Sociedad Nacional Cooperativa, organized in Mexico City in 1915.

ALBANIA. Cooperatives in Albania are a phenomenon of post–World War II economic and political conditions. The first cooperative (consumer) was established in 1945, as was a Cooperative Committee in the Office of the Prime Minister. The first agricultural **marketing** and **worker productive cooperatives** were established in 1946. By 1947, 160 cooperatives had been formed. A Central Union of Cooperatives was subsequently organized to coordinate the varied cooperative activities. The famed secretiveness of Albanian society applies equally to cooperatives. The **ILO** *Directory* **(1988***)* contains no statistical data regarding Albanian cooperatives. No current data could be identified. With the recent changes of government, it is expected that it will be possible to develop a fuller profile and history of Albanian cooperation.

ALEXANDER, WILLIAM GEMMELL (1918–). A British cooperator, he served as director of the **ICA** for the period 1963–68. Previously he had been involved with cooperative development in the Gilbert and Ellice Islands (*see* KIRIBATI and TUVALU) and served for a time as Registrar of Cooperatives in **Mauritius** and **Cyprus**. Immediately before his selection as director of ICA, he was managing the Agricultural Department of the **English Cooperative Wholesale Society**.

ALGERIA. Cooperative activity in Algeria dates from a legislative initiative in 1893 authorizing the establishment of local provident societies. The first formal organization of one of these, however, took place only in 1901. A diversified network of agriculture-related cooperatives emerged shortly thereafter, and growth continued through the World War II years. Cooperatives were involved in the production of cereals, citrus fruits, cotton, olive oil, tobacco and wine; in the operations of distilleries and dairies; and in supplying agricultural machinery and providing **agricultural credit**. By 1945 there were 365 **agricultural cooperatives** and 204 rural **credit cooperatives**. Agitation for independence and a redistribution of power and resources, followed by an armed uprising, led to independence in 1962 and with it the exodus of over half a million French settlers. Experiments in group farming on expropriated land, agricultural **credit** for the indigenous population, cooperatives among the military, **production cooperatives** paralleling state industries, and **housing** and **consumer cooperatives** have marked the years up to the present. The **ILO** *Directory* **(1988)** reported 6,060 agricultural (including credit) cooperatives, 890 consumer, 10 industrial, and an undetermined number of **housing cooperatives**. Complete information on numbers of members was unavailable.

ALLAIRE, ABBÉ. A priest and **cooperative pioneer** in **Canada** in the early 20th century, he helped establish **agricultural cooperatives** in Quebec, beginning with one at Adamsville in 1903. In 1912 he was director of a cooperative training center in Quebec.

ALLEN, SIR THOMAS W. (1864–1943). A cooperative leader in the **United Kingdom**, he was president of the **English Cooperative Wholesale Society** from 1929 to 1933. He had earlier established his cooperative credentials as General Manager and Secretary of the Blaina Cooperative Society, which he served for many years. In 1906 he was appointed a director of the Cooperative Insurance Society. In 1910 he became a director of the **English Cooperative Wholesale Society** and was a leading figure in the government's food distribution program during World War I. Allen became active in the **ICA** from 1929 to 1933, serving on its Executive Committee and as a vice president. He was highly regarded for his religious dedication, his business acumen and his commitment to supplanting the capitalist system of commerce and industry by "a more excellent system based on cooperatives."

ALLEY, REWI (1897–1987). A New Zealander who moved to **China** in the 1930s and who remained there and was involved in the evolution of the cooperative movement before and after the communist revolution. From 1938 onward he was an active participant in the formation of the Chinese industrial cooperatives movement which adopted the motto *gung ho*, meaning to work together. Alley was a teacher and headmaster of a school in China and the author of more than 60 books.

ALLIANCE, THE. *See* INTERNATIONAL COOPERATIVE ALLIANCE.

AMERICAN INSTITUTE OF COOPERATION (AIC). An **association** of state and national cooperative organizations in the **United States** with headquarters in Washington, D.C., currently affiliated with the **National Council of Farmer Cooperatives**. Its purpose is to promote better understanding of the cooperative way of doing business. AIC holds an annual National Institute of Cooperative Education conference in which there are discussions of topics of current cooperative interest, including developments in the international cooperative movement. The proceedings of the conferences have been published annually since 1925 under the title *American Cooperation.*

ANDERSON, CARL ALBERT (1892–1979). A cooperative leader in **Sweden**, he began his cooperative work as a shop assistant with the Cooperative Society of Stockholm. He assumed increasingly important positions with that organization and in 1937 became a director and member of its board. In 1945 he became the society's chairman, a position he held until retirement in 1965. Anderson was a member of the **Kooperativa Förbundet (KF)** Administrative Council from 1946 to 1957, when he became chairman of the KF board of directors. Within the international cooperative movement, he was a member of the Central Committee of the **ICA** from 1948 and chairman of the ICA's Retail (**consumer**) Committee. For many years he was chairman of the board of **Nordisk Andelsförbund,** the Scandinavian Cooperative Wholesale Society. Outside the cooperative movement Anderson was a dedicated public servant, serving for 26 years prior to his death as chairman of the Stockholm City Council, as a member of the First Chamber of the Swedish Parliament, and as an official of both the Swedish Gymnastics and Sports Associations.

ANDERSON, GLENN (1927–1980). A cooperative leader in the **United States** who worked actively in the cooperative movement in Minnesota and Wisconsin. He was executive secretary of the Wisconsin Federation of Cooperatives before becoming the president of **CLUSA**, a position he held from 1978 to 1980. He served on the Executive Committee of the **ICA**.

ANGOLA. Angola in recent years has been caught up in internal conflict, compounded by East/West ideological confrontation and disputes with South Africa related to the move to establish the nation of Namibia. The confusion resulting from these has left only vestiges of a cooperative movement, whose current status is unclear. The latest available statistics are from 1979, when it was reported that there were 380 agricultural and 560 consumer cooperatives with a membership of 440,000 (5.8% of the population at that time).

ANGST, E. (1862–?). A cooperative leader in **Switzerland**, he was active in the management of the General Consumer Society of Basel from 1901 to 1935, serving as its chairman from 1910 to 1935. Concurrent with his activity in Basel, he was active in the Swiss Union of Cooperatives, serving on its executive board from 1902, as vice president from 1909 to 1923, and as president from 1923 to 1935. He was an active promoter of **insurance** and **housing cooperatives.** Angst was named a member of the **Committee of Honor of the International Cooperative Alliance** in 1936, in recognition of his work in the Swiss and international movements.

ANGUILLA. Originally a part of **Saint Christopher (St. Kitts)/Nevis** and Anguilla and administered from St. Kitts, Anguilla separated itself in 1971 and became a British dependent territory. In the previously combined territory, **cooperative legislation** was passed in 1956 and the first cooperative (a **credit union**) established in 1959. Formal registration of cooperatives began in 1969. The **ILO** *Directory* (**1988**) reports that in 1985 there were 1 credit union, 1 consumer, 1 transport and 3 other societies. No data was available on membership. *See also* SAINT CHRISTOPHER (ST. KITTS)/NEVIS.

ANIMALS, COOPERATION AMONG. Animals cooperate as well as fight in order to survive. Cooperation among them as described by **Peter Kropotkin** in his book *Mutual Aid* is highly significant. W. C. Allee, a zoologist, in his *Social Life of Animals*, shows how even protozoa, one-celled organisms, "work together." He concludes that humans in their move toward increased cooperation are following the primitive drives of protoplasm itself, and that it is as natural for humans to cooperate as it is for them to be intelligent.

ANNUAL GENERAL MEETING. The main meeting of a cooperative society, held once a year. It is generally at this meeting that an annual report regarding the cooperative's operation, including its finances, is presented by the **chairman, manager,** or management committee and the main policy decisions are made, **bylaws** changed, and other important matters decided. It is often referred to as "the AGM."

ANSEELE, EDOUARD (1857–1938). A cooperative leader in **Belgium,** he was an agitator for labor rights, social justice and economic democracy and was one of four socialist ministers in the post–World War I Belgian government. He was among the founders of the Vooruit Distributive Society at Ghent in 1874 and was a proponent of the **worker productive cooperative** movement, which he believed had the greatest potential for undermining **capitalism.** Anseele was a regular participant in the **ICA** congresses from 1900 to 1924, strongly upholding cooperation as the basis for all social organization.

ANTIGONISH MOVEMENT. A movement designed to utilize a variety of types of cooperatives—**credit unions** and **consumer, production** and **housing cooperatives**—among the residents of Nova Scotia in **Canada** as a means of enhancing their social and economic development. It was inaugurated in 1923 by Father **M. M. Coady, A. B. MacDonald, R. P. Romkins, Father James J. Tompkins** and others connected with the Extension Department of St. Francis Xavier University at Antigonish. The key to the success of the movement has been its program of adult education and its varied activities in community development.

ANTIGUA AND BARBUDA. In this island nation in the Caribbean, cooperatives are a relatively new phenomenon. Initial **cooperative legislation** passed in 1948 was replaced by the Cooperative Societies Ordinance adopted in 1958, and the first cooperative was organized that same year. Modest growth followed, most notably with the formation of **credit unions,** allowing the **ILO** *Directory* (**1988**) to report 14 cooperatives (agriculture—4; credit unions—7; transport—1; and others—2) with 2,300 members. By 1996, credit union membership had grown to 12,704 and had been consolidated into three societies. Assuming a modest rate of growth in other types of societies, **cooperative penetration** of the national population was estimated to be 19.6% that year.

ANTON, JUAN SALAS (1854–1931). A cooperative leader in **Spain,** he studied law at Barcelona and Paris, but gave up law when he turned to the cooperative movement in 1890 as a vehicle to help the working classes and to transform Spanish society economically and socially. He assisted in the formation of the Regional Chamber of Cooperative Societies of Catalonia and the Balearic Islands and in 1899 founded the journal, *Revista Cooperativa Catalana.* In 1902 Anton was elected to the Executive Committee of the **ICA,** representing Spanish cooperatives.

APARTMENT, COOPERATIVE. A type of housing acquired or built which is owned and operated by a group of people formally organized into a cooperative **association.** The cooperative sells units within the building to members and manages the apartment complex cooperatively. Individuals usually sell their apartments only to the association at an appraised value, or to others with the association's approval.

APEX COOPERATIVE ORGANIZATIONS. The term "apex" is used to describe the top organization in a national cooperative structure whose membership is usually made up of the individual cooperative societies of a particular type, e.g., agricultural or housing, or of their **federations,** or of federations of cooperatives from geographical areas. There are international apex organizations whose membership is made up of national cooperative organizations, e.g., the **ICA,** the **International Raiffeisen Union,** or of national and **regional cooperative** organizations, e.g., **WOCCU.** There are also apex organizations for regions of the world, e.g., the Coordinating Committee of the European Community Cooperative Associations, the **Organization of Cooperatives of the Americas,** the **Arab Cooperative Union** and regional **credit union confederations.**

APPROPRIATE MANAGEMENT SYSTEMS FOR AGRICULTURAL COOPERATIVES (AMSAC). A plan initiated in 1977 by the **FAO,** to develop and implement a system of management for farmer cooperatives in **developing countries** based on the cumulative experience of FAO and associated organizations. Its goal is to enhance their capacity for effective organization of their activities and lead to an expanded scope of benefits for cooperative members. AMSAC activities are structured on regional and national bases, recognizing the cultural and historical differences between various parts of the developing world. The activities include the formation of national plans and the development of materials to assist in their implementation. On the request of governments, the FAO organizes national workshops and training courses, prepares national management guides, carries out feasibility studies, and develops proposals for pilot projects to implement the AMSAC approach.

ARAB COOPERATIVE UNION. An **association** of **apex cooperative organizations** from countries that are members of the Arab League, its headquarters are in Cairo, Egypt. One of its accomplishments is the collection of statistical information on cooperatives in its member countries, published in 1994. Current information on the present status of the organization was not available.

ARGENTINA. The cooperative movement in Argentina was the first to begin in a country outside the industrialized countries of Europe, **Australia**, **Canada**, **Japan** and the **United States**. The first society was established in 1875, followed by two other successful societies in 1884 and 1885. The first **cooperative legislation** was enacted in 1905 and the first national **union** formed in 1922. The movement has gradually developed into a network of diverse types of cooperatives and has continued to grow in spite of the periods of political turmoil that have been a part of the nation's history. A total of 721 cooperatives with 417,124 members at the end of World War II grew to a total of 3,839 with 4,184,342 members in 1970, and to 4,383 societies with 10,180,859 members in 1986 (more than 33% of the total population). In recent years the number of cooperatives has increased, but total membership has declined by nearly 10%. In 1991 cooperatives were found in the following sectors: agriculture—1,492 societies/with 442,991 members; consumer—476/1,000,000; housing—1,428/243,973; insurance—49/3,727,097; savings and credit—301/1,530,000; public services—1,476/1,997,905; worker productive—2,111/33,329; and others—809/127,974. In all there were 8,142 cooperatives with a combined membership of 9,103,269, equaling 27.8% of the national population. The cooperative movement in Argentina is as established, independent and diverse as any in the world. Its diversity is reflected in a network of national **federations**, financial institutions, education and training structures, and a cooperative publishing house, INTERCOOP Editora Cooperativa Limitada, of international repute.

ARIZMENDI, FATHER JOSÉ MARIA (1915–1976). A Basque priest who developed a concern for education and employment in his parish at Zaragoza. After release from prison for opposition to the Franco regime in **Spain**, he established a school of engineering in 1943 and, with five students who graduated from there in 1952, launched a **production cooperative**, ULGOR, in 1956. This initial effort, now known as the **Mondragon Cooperatives**, has grown to include a number of other producer cooperatives and employs thousands of people.

ARMENIA. While Armenia was part of the **Union of Soviet Socialist Republics**, cooperatives were organized as part of **Centrosoyus**. Since Armenia's establishment as an independent state, the cooperative movement has diversified, though membership remains principally in **consumer cooperatives**. In 1996, the **ICA** reported that there were 5,725 cooperatives with a membership of 571,065 in the following sectors: agriculture—356 societies/with 1,620 members; consumer—2,874/558,230; fisheries—35/145; worker productive—1,861/8,630; transport—116/490; health—18/65; utilities—148/635; and others—317/1,250. Cooperative membership was 16.5% of the national population.

ARNESEN, RANDOLF (1881–1958). A pioneer in the cooperative movement of **Norway**, he was also an active member of the Labor Party, a trade unionist and, for 24 years, a member of the Oslo Town Council. He became general secretary of the Norwegian Cooperative Union and Wholesale Society and held that position until his retirement in 1948. Arnesen was also, for the same period, the editor of the cooperative journal *Kooperatören,* from which position he exerted great ideological and organizational influence on the growing cooperative movement in Norway. A collection of articles from his pen has been published by the Norwegian cooperatives.

ASHWORTH, MILES (1782–1868). First president of the **Rochdale Society of Equitable Pioneers**, he was an Owenite socialist and active in textile manufacture. He was the father of **Samuel Ashworth.**

ASHWORTH, SAMUEL (1825–1871). One of the **Rochdale pioneers**, he was one of the volunteers working at the cooperative's **Toad Lane** store when it opened in December 1844. At age 19 he was probably the youngest of the founding group. He served the **Rochdale Society of Equitable Pioneers** for 20 years as buyer and manager and, in 1866, became manager of the Manchester Wholesale Society. He was the son of **Miles Ashworth**.

ASIAN CONFEDERATION OF CREDIT UNIONS. *See* ASSOCIATION OF ASIAN CONFEDERATION OF CREDIT UNIONS.

ASOCIACIÓN LATINOAMERICANA DE CENTROS DE EDUCACIÓN COOPERATIVA. An **association** of Latin American cooperative training centers, associated with the National Cooperative Education Center in Zaragoza, **Spain**, it meets periodically to assess and plan for effective **cooperative education** and training programs in Latin America.

ASSOCIATION. An organization of persons or groups with a common interest or common aims. Cooperative societies are sometimes referred to as "cooperative associations."

ASSOCIATION OF ASIAN CONFEDERATION OF CREDIT UNIONS (ACCU). A **federation** of the **credit union** movements in 13 Asian countries with headquarters in Bangkok, Thailand, it was organized in 1971. In 1997 its national federations reported a combined membership of 8,566,474 people organized in some 13,988 credit unions. ACCU serves as a vehicle for pooling the human and financial resources of the region for credit union development. It is a member of **WOCCU**.

ATATURK, KEMAL (1880–1938). Originally named Mustafa Kemal, he took the name Ataturk, "Father of the Turks," after being a leader in the Turkish war of independence and becoming the first president (1923–38) of modern **Turkey**. As president he took important steps to create a modernized Turkish society, lessening the political power of Islam by abolishing the caliphate and outlawing certain sects. He introduced the Roman alphabet to replace Arabic lettering, and he modernized the Turkish economy. Ataturk saw cooperatives as a tool for modernization and promoted their formation. In 1923 he had a brochure printed and circulated regarding the cooperative movement and in 1931 issued guiding rules for cooperatives, patterning these on the established experience of the growing European movements.

ATWELL, DAVID. An Argentine cooperative pioneer who in 1884 established the first **consumer cooperative**, which some regard as the first successful cooperative in **Argentina**. He was also instrumental in the establishment of the first **telephone cooperative** in the country.

AUDIT. An examination of the accounts of a cooperative society made periodically by a person not directly connected with the operation of the society. In some countries, audits are carried out by the government department responsible for the registration or certification of cooperatives, in others by a certified accounting body (cooperative or private) whose independent status and reliability are accepted by cooperative members and the government. Societies may also appoint their own internal auditors to periodically check their accounts. It is the purpose of an audit to publicly review the financial condition of a cooperative and to provide open access for members to their organization's financial and management operations.

AURELIAN, P. S. A politician and economist in **Romania** who was a **cooperative pioneer** in his country. He considered that the political independence of the working class ought to be preceded by economic independence. In active pursuit of these views, he founded the first distributive (**consumer**) and **credit** societies in Bucharest.

AUSTRALIA. The cooperative movement was initiated in Australia with the establishment of a mutual provident society (**insurance**) in 1849 followed by a cooperative society in Brisbane in 1859. The first **cooperative legislation**, a building societies **act**, was enacted in 1881, followed by a more extensive law in 1903. By 1918 the development of cooperatives had become extensive enough in various parts of the country to lead to the convening of the first All-Australian Conference of Cooperatives, held in Melbourne. This was soon followed by the first Australian Congress of Consumer Cooperatives, held in Sydney in 1920. Statewide cooperative **federations** and state cooperative laws came next, parallel with the development of agricultural commodity societies, particularly in Western and South Australia. A fledgling **credit union movement**, which began in the 1940s, spread quickly throughout the country, resulting in the formation of state credit union federations and a national federation by the mid-1960s. The national Cooperative Insurance Company of Australia was founded in 1947. **Housing cooperatives** have flourished, particularly in New South Wales. By 1992 the **ICA Regional Office for Asia and the Pacific** reported that there were 9,232 cooperatives in the country involving 2,880,810 members (14.8% of the national population) in the following sectors: agriculture—234 societies/with

371,235 members; consumer—480/514,580; fisheries—38/4,306; housing—5,429/1,029,008; multipurpose—2,346/434,857; savings and credit—415/445,237; and others—290/81,587.

AUSTRIA. The first Austrian cooperative, a Schulze-Delitzsch **credit** society, was established at Klagenfurt (then Celsvec) in 1851. It began a movement within the then Austro-Hungarian Empire which spread rapidly and was extensive enough to federate nationally in 1872. The first **cooperative legislation** followed a year later. A parallel development of **credit cooperatives** among farmers led to the formation of the Austrian Raiffeisen Union in 1898. A federation of **agricultural cooperatives** was formed the same year and a consumer federation in 1901. This network of cooperatives grew vigorously in many corners of the empire in the years leading up to World War I.

Dissolution of the Austro-Hungarian Empire as a result of the war, however, brought into being a smaller Austria, both in size and in influence. The empire's widely dispersed cooperative experience took new roots in partitioned Hungary and in cooperative movements in newly established **Czechoslovakia** and **Yugoslavia**. The cooperative movement restructured itself, and the main lines of activity, credit, agriculture and consumer societies began a new phase of development. These were augmented in the interwar years by a central **cooperative bank**, a national **housing cooperative federation** and a national **insurance** society. Vienna was the venue for the 13th Congress of the **ICA** in 1930, attesting to the recovery of the movement's international status. The German takeover of **Austria** in 1938 and its incorporation into the German Reich led to the forced dissolution or manipulation of much of the cooperative structure. Particularly targeted was the **consumer** movement, which was deeply rooted in the trade unions and the socialist political structure.

The cooperative movement restructured itself after World War II in a new Austrian Republic, while **Karl Renner**, a key leader in the consumer cooperative movement and an important participant in the ICA, was the first president of the Republic. The subsequent period has seen the Austrian movement return to its traditional sectors, agriculture, consumer, credit and banking, and housing. In 1966 the 24th Congress of the ICA was held in Vienna and included an intensive debate on and restatement of **cooperative principles**. A profile of the movement in 1996 was prepared by ICA, showing 1,485 societies with 3,839,376 members in the following sectors: agriculture—1,067 societies/with 444,139 members; banking—763/2,388,450; consumers—76/648,575; housing—

108/332,842; worker productive—12/1,160; and others—102/24,201. **Cooperative penetration** that year was 47.9% of the population.

AVRAMOVITCH, MICHAEL (1864–1945). A pioneer of the Serbian cooperative movement, he took the leadership in the foundation of the first rural credit society in Serbia based on the model of the Raiffeisen credit cooperatives in **Germany**. He was the founder of the Union of Serbian Agricultural Societies and served as its director for 30 years. He had a particular interest in the establishment of medical cooperatives, the first of which he helped establish in 1921. Avramovitch was in attendance at the 1st Congress of the **ICA** in 1895, representing Serbia; he was elected to the ICA Central Committee, on which he served until 1930. The government of **Yugoslavia** presented him with an award in recognition of his work in the cooperative movement and in other important aspects of Yugoslav national life.

AZERBAIJAN. The Union of Cooperative Societies was established in 1915. In 1924 the *Review of International Cooperation* reported the presence of 177 **consumer cooperatives** with 118,809 members and 27 **worker productive cooperatives** with 2,815 members. During the time that Azerbaijan was a republic in the **Union of Soviet Socialist Republics**, its cooperatives were a constituent part of **Centrosoyus**. As part of a now independent state, consumer cooperatives have restructured themselves and constitute most of the cooperative movement. Data for 1995 indicated that there were 79 consumer societies with a membership of 920,000. In 1996 an **ICA** report indicated that there were 79 societies with a membership of 660,000 (9.0% of the population of the Republic).

B

BAHAMAS. The earliest cooperative, a **credit union**, was organized in 1946 through the efforts of a local Catholic church. More systematic cooperative development efforts were undertaken after the passage of the Cooperative Societies Act and Regulations in 1974, the subsequent establishment of a government cooperative office, and assistance provided by international development agencies. By 1986, the **ICA** reported, there were 30 cooperatives with an estimated 8,000 members. Credit union membership was predominant and the credit unions had formed a national league (**federation**) in 1980, the only higher-level cooperative federation in the country. Other cooperatives were in agriculture, fisheries, housing and handicrafts. In 1996, **WOCCU** reported that credit union membership had grown to 28,431. Total **cooperative penetration** of the national population that year was estimated to be 11.4%.

BAHRAIN. Cooperatives are a recent phenomenon in Bahrain, but growing. The **ILO** *Directory* (**1988**) reported 1 agricultural, 1 credit and 5 consumer cooperatives. In 1994 the **Arab Cooperative Union** reported 17 cooperatives (agricultural—1; consumer—11; fisheries—1; and multipurpose—4) with a total membership of 8,218 (1.5% of the population).

BAKER, CHRISTOPHER (1941–). An American cooperator and now chief executive of the **World Council of Credit Unions** (WOCCU), Baker has worked with the credit union movement since 1974. With WOCCU, he has served as director of technical assistance and project development, director of planning and evaluation, director of corporate development and director of the Washington regional office before being named chief executive in 1993.

In his international credit union career, he has worked at all credit union levels and in many cultural settings. From 1969 to 1974, he was a visiting professor at the University of Costa Rica. From 1944 to 1959, he lived in Cuba. He is a graduate of Middlebury College and holds an M.A. and Ph.D. from the University of Florida.

BALANCE SHEET. A statement of the accounts of a cooperative society, showing its debits and credits as well as its assets and liabilities at a particular point in time. The balance sheet provides a snapshot of the financial condition of a society.

BALDINI, NULLO (1862–1945). In 1885 the Ravenna Workers' Association, a workers' cooperative under the leadership of Nullo Baldini, began an operation to drain marshlands in the Rome suburbs of Ostia and Fiumicino.

BANGLADESH. The history of Bangladesh cooperatives is intertwined with those of **India** and **Pakistan**. The passage of the Indian Cooperative Law in 1904 and the subsequent cooperative organizational effort were reflected in events in the province of Bengal, where the first cooperative was organized in 1905. In 1947, the new independent states of India and Pakistan were formed, with predominately Hindu and Moslem populations respectively. Bengal was similarly partitioned, West Bengal remaining in India and East Bengal becoming East Pakistan. An East Pakistan Cooperative Bank was established in 1948 and a cooperative law passed in 1964. A pilot project to organize cooperative villages, the Comilla Project, was initiated in 1960 and was the source of considerable cooperative innovation. It was expanded as the Integrated Rural Development Program in 1970 and was continued after Bangladesh became independent of Pakistan in 1971. These programs and the interest of the government of Bangladesh contributed greatly to the dramatic growth of cooperatives in Bangladesh after independence. In 1970 the **ILO**'s *Cooperative Information* reported 2,023 cooperatives with 475,000 members. A 1994 **ICA Regional Office for Asia and the Pacific** statistical report indicated that in 1993 Bangladesh had 130,022 cooperatives with a membership of 7,131,933 (6.2% of the population) in the following sectors: agriculture—108,895 societies/with 4.5 million members; fisheries—3,302/379,745; housing 131/28,005; multipurpose—3,798/697,735; savings and credit—216/783,000; worker productive—2,256/381,769; and others—11,424/361,679. The cooperative structure includes a national confederation, 18 national federations and 868 regional federations. The **ICA** in 1996 reported a cooperative membership of 7,467,967, 6.1% of the population.

BANK, COOPERATIVE. A cooperative bank is a financial institution owned and operated by cooperative depositors, or a banking business owned and operated by a cooperative organization for the benefit of cooperatives and their members. On occasion, governments have created cooperative banks for the purpose of providing credit to cooperatives. Some national cooperative banks have become major international financial institutions, among them **Crédit Agricole** and **Crédit Mutuel** in France, **DG Bank** in Germany and **Rabobank** in the Netherlands. Cooperative banks are organized to represent their interests through groups such as the ICA Banking Committee and, in Europe, the Association of Cooperative Banks of the European Community. *See also* CREDIT COOPERATIVES.

BARBADOS. The first cooperative, a livestock society, was established in 1940, initiating an official governmental interest in cooperatives, which was added to that of local people. The Cooperative Societies Act was enacted in 1949, and the first **credit union**, the Shamrock Society, organized by a Catholic church congregation, was established in 1950. Independence in 1966 brought a new surge of interest in cooperatives, and by

1969 there were 80 cooperatives in existence with a membership of 6,292. In 1972 the first national cooperative **federation** was formed, the predecessor of the current Barbados National Association of Cooperative Societies. A 1986 **ILO** report on cooperatives in Barbados reported 61 cooperatives with a membership of 23,590 in the following sectors: agriculture—4 societies/with 62 members; consumer—5/1,669; credit unions—45/20,871; fisheries—1/415; and transport—6/234. In 1997 **WOCCU** reported that the Barbados Cooperative Credit Union League represented 43 credit unions whose 21,497 members made up nearly 90% of Barbados's cooperators. At that time, overall cooperative membership was estimated to be 24,290 (9.5% of the population).

BARBIER, CHARLES HENRI (1902–1984). A cooperative official in Switzerland who served for 22 years on the board of the Swiss Union of Consumer Societies and as director of its Department for Press, Propaganda and Education. His cooperative **association**s, which began with the **consumer cooperative** at La Chaux de Fonds, took him into the Central and Executive Committees of the **ICA** as well as to **UNESCO**, whose adult education programs captured his interest and ability. When the Swiss consumer cooperatives initiated a program of assistance to the cooperatives in Benin, Barbier was called on to direct their efforts. This was one of the earliest examples of **movement-to-movement assistance**.

BAROU, NOAH (1889–?). He served for many years in London as the director of the Moscow Narodny (People's) Bank, which financed the export and import activities of the central cooperative organizations of the **Union of Soviet Socialist Republics**. He wrote extensively on **cooperative banks** and other subjects in the publications of the **ICA** and other organizations.

BASEVI, ALBERTO (1882–1956). Born in Modena, of a wealthy middle-class family, he dedicated himself to making cooperatives an instrument for furthering the welfare of workers and peasants and to building a viable cooperative movement in **Italy**. Basevi took a degree in law at Modena and shortly thereafter became **secretary** to cooperative pioneer **Luigi Luzzatti**. In 1909 he established the Rome office of the Lega Nazionale delle Cooperative and became its director. In 1914 he became secretary general of the National Credit Institute and, when it was merged by the Fascist government in 1927 with Banco del Lavoro, became director general of the Bank. In 1946 Bavesi became director general of cooperation in the Ministry of Labor and Social Security, where he founded the journal *Rivista della Cooperazione*. Disagreements over cooperative policy in the government led to his resignation and to the dedication of his final years to work within the Lega Nazionale delle Cooperative, which named him honorary president.

BATH, THOMAS H. (1875–1956). A **cooperative pioneer** in **Australia,** he became a farmer in Western Australia after a period as Minister of Lands and Agriculture in the Labor government of that state. His farming activities brought him to cooperation and he became a powerful influence in the cooperative movement in Western Australia, serving for many years as a trustee of the West Australian Wheat Pool. It was in this capacity that Bath represented Australia at the 1927 International Wheat Pool Conference in **Canada** and became a recognized leader in world agricultural cooperation. He was also important in establishing commercial relations between Australia and the **English Cooperative Wholesale Society**. Bath served for several years as the volunteer secretary of the Cooperative Federation of Australia.

BEASLEY, ROBERT (1929–). An American cooperator who spent most of his U.S. career with Farmland, a large **regional cooperative** in the midwestern **United States**. He served as chairman of **CLUSA** and was active in the **Overseas Cooperative Development Committee** before becoming director of the **ICA** for the period 1984–88 and director emeritus for 1989. During this later period Beasley authored an important report on the **World Bank** and cooperatives.

BEATON, NEAL S. (1880–1960). A Scottish cooperator, he started his career as an employee of St. Cuthbert's Cooperative Association in Edinburgh. He was an organizer of the Shop Assistants Union from 1911 to 1919 and became the union's national president in 1921. He was president of the Scottish Trade Union Congress. Beaton was elected to the board of the Scottish Cooperative Wholesale Society in 1924 and became its president in 1932, serving until 1946. He was among the leaders of the **ICA**, serving on its Executive Committee in 1946.

BELARUS. The Byelorussian Union of Consumer Cooperatives was founded in 1924 and had developed by 1987 into a structure with 6 regional unions, 70 district unions and 47 district societies with a membership of 21,851,200 (28% of the population). It is around this structure that the newly independent Belarus is reconstituting its cooperative movement. In 1995 the **ICA** reported that there were 150 **consumer cooperatives** with a total membership of 1,921,028 (18.5% of the population). A similar report for 1996 showed 147 cooperatives with a total membership of 1,927,100, still 18.5% of the population.

BELGIUM. The first Belgian cooperative (of bakers) was established in 1848, initiating a type of **worker productive** activity that would be emulated and become an important part of the **consumer** movement as it developed. The first Belgian cooperative **credit** institution was established in 1860. These and other cooperatives had multiplied to the point that a **cooperative law** was proposed and enacted in 1873. The foundation of new cooperatives moved slowly up to 1886, averaging seven new societies per year, but from 1887 to 1896 the pace quickened with an average of 37 per year, increasing to 97 per year in the years leading up to 1908. Indicative of the variety of cooperatives formed during this period were a pharmaceutical society, the first socialist society, an **agricultural credit** group, a farmers' guild, a cooperative corporation for public services, an **insurance** society and worker productive cooperatives, which would become part of the future Christian Cooperative Federation. Each of these were followed by similar organizations and the formation of **federations** became an important aspect of the period. Included among these were the Belgian Federal Cooperative Society, the Belgian Boerenbond and the Belgian Cooperative Federation. The **ICA** *Review of International Cooperation* reported that in 1908 the profile of 945 Belgian cooperatives included 24 building, 391 consumer, 45 credit, 29 dock worker, 66 insurance, 17 pharmacy, 82 supply and marketing, 96 worker productive and 195 other societies; membership was estimated to be 324,700. A history of this early period of Belgian cooperative development, written by Louis Bertrand, was published in 1902. Development of the movement continued at an increasing pace, interrupted by World War I. A further ICA report, in 1922, showed that the movement had grown to 1,483 societies with 517,122 members.

The growing significance of the Belgian movement was reflected in the ICA decision of hold its Tenth Congress in 1924 in Ghent. Cooperative development remained important in Belgium through the interwar years and beyond and has reflected many of the trends in other European countries, including an agricultural sector that has consolidated into fewer farms and developed sophisticated support systems, and a consumer sector that has wrestled with retail store modernization and competition from private enterprise. The Belgian movement has maintained its "sectarian" character and structure with three major wings, socialist, Christian and neutral. A 1998 ICA report to the European Commission indicated, in 1996, a total of 1,553 cooperatives with a membership of 3,597,262 in the following sectors: agriculture—1,264 societies/with 398,000 members; banking—249/1,199,262; health—10/2,000,000; insurance—4/na (membership not indicated); worker productive—26/membership not available; and others—70/60,000. **Cooperative penetration** in 1996 was 35.4% of the national population.

BELIZE. St. Peter Claver Credit Union in the Toledo District, the first cooperative in Belize, was established in 1943 with the assistance of Rev. **Marion Moses Ganey**, S.J. **Cooperative legislation** was enacted in 1948. In 1950 a **consumer cooperative** was organized in Belize City, and in 1954 a government Department of Cooperatives was established. The Belize Credit Union League was formed in 1956. From these beginnings, the development of cooperatives spread to other areas of the country and involved different types of cooperatives. The **COPAC** Country Note on Belize (1986) reported 130 cooperatives with a combined membership of 38,681. By 1991, the number of cooperatives had increased to 183 with an estimated membership of 39,171 (21.8% of the population). Cooperatives were found in the following sectors: agricultural (91), consumer (1), credit union (40), fisheries (13), worker production and transport (13) and others (25). Eighty-four percent of cooperative membership was in the 40 **credit unions**. In 1996, **WOCCU** reported that Belize had 12 credit unions, with a total membership of 19,911. Data regarding cooperatives in other sectors was not available. Assuming a modest growth in the membership of such groups since 1991, it was estimated that total membership of all cooperatives that year was 23,518 (10.7% of the population.) National **federations** have been organized in the fields of agriculture, beekeeping, credit unions and fisheries.

BELUZE, JEAN-PIERRE (1821–1908). A French cooperator, a joiner by trade, and a follower of **Etienne Cabet**, in 1863 he founded the Banque du crédit au travail to finance **worker productive associations** and cooperatives of other types. He also published the periodical, edited by Elie Reclus, *L'Association*, later known as *La Coopération*. It was in an article in *L'Association* on July 29, 1866, that he argued that cooperation should be international in character, and he used the title "International Cooperative Alliance." Beluze had hoped to encourage the foundation of such an organization at the Cooperative Congress scheduled for Paris in 1867, but his move was frustrated when the Congress was canceled by the French government.

BEN-GURION, DAVID (1886–1973). A Polish-born immigrant to Palestine, he became the first prime minister of **Israel**. Earlier, after World War I, he cofounded Haganah, the underground Jewish army, and Histadrut, the General Federation of Jewish Labor. In 1923, in collaboration with **Levi Eshkol**, another future prime minister, **Itzhak Ben-Zvi**, a future president of Israel, and others, he established Hevrat Ovdim, the General Cooperative Association. Ben-Gurion remained an active cooperator and returned to live on his **kibbutz** when he left active political life.

BEN-ZVI, ITZHAK (1884–1963). The Russian-born second president of **Israel** (1952–63), he was active in early Jewish pioneer and defense groups in Palestine from 1907 onward. In 1923 he cofounded, with **David Ben-Gurion, Levi Eshkol** and others, Hevrat Ovdim, the General Cooperative Association.

BENIN (formerly Dahomey). The first cooperative (agricultural marketing) was established in 1947, and a national **federation** of such cooperatives was established in 1949 (now inactive). At independence in 1960 there were 60 cooperatives, mainly agricultural, but a new law in 1961 required the recertification of all societies. By 1971 there were 45 active societies and 300+ **precooperatives**. Several **regional cooperative unions** were established at different times, with 5 listed in the **ILO** *Directory* **(1988)**, associating cooperatives in the sectors of **credit** and savings, fisheries, worker production and rural development. The profile of cooperative development for 1985 reported in the *Directory* showed that there were 2,085 cooperatives (agricultural, consumer, credit, fisheries, industrial and others) with a total of 30,337 members. A 1987 **ILO** report differentiated between cooperative and precooperative organizations as follows: precooperative—1,849 societies with 38,295 members; cooperatives—242 societies with 48,451 members. **Cooperative penetration** at that time was 1.1% of the population if cooperatives alone are considered; it was 2.0% if precooperatives are also included. A 1998 report by the **ICA** indicated that cooperative membership had grown to 191,000 (3.3% of the population). The increase was attributed principally to savings and **credit cooperatives**.

BERGENGREN, ROY F. (1879–1955). An American lawyer who was attracted into the **credit union movement** by **Edward Filene**. With Filene, he established the National Extension Bureau in 1921 to develop credit unions across the **United States**. The Bureau existed until 1935, when the **Credit Union National Association (CUNA)** was founded. Bergengren gave early attention to the enactment of credit union legislation and was instrumental in gaining the passage of numerous state laws. Beginning in 1924 he edited a monthly magazine, *The Bridge* (the name was changed in 1949 to *The Credit Union Bridge* and in 1963 to *The Credit Union Magazine*), and a series of books dealing with the organization and operation of credit unions. In 1935 he became the managing director of the Credit Union National Association, a position which he held until his retirement in 1945. Bergengren was also active in the foundation of cooperatives in **Canada**, working among farmers and fishermen in Nova Scotia in 1932 and organizing the first credit union in Welland, Ontario. His autobiography is entitled *Crusade*. He was inducted into the U.S. **Cooperative Hall of Fame** in 1979.

BERMUDA. The **ILO** *Directory* **(1988)** reported three cooperatives in Bermuda, a **credit union** established in 1972, a **consumer cooperative** formed in 1969 and a taxi cooperative set up in 1985. The membership totaled 3,816. By 1996, based primarily on an increase in credit union membership, the total was estimated to be 4,847 (7.8% of the population).

BERTRAND, LOUIS (1856–1943). A **cooperative pioneer** in Belgium, he helped establish the Belgian Cooperative Federation, and in 1902 he published his *Histoire de la coopération en Belgique*. In 1907 La Prévoyance sociale, a cooperative **insurance** company based on his ideas, was established.

BLAIS, RAYMOND (1935–1987). A leading cooperator in **Canada**, after an initial period of work as a government official and part-time lecturer at Laval University, in 1968 he began a career with the **Desjardins Group**, becoming its president from 1981 to 1986. He was a member of the board of directors of the **International Raiffeisen Union** from 1981 to 1987.

BLANC, LOUIS (1811–1882). A French author and cooperative activist who was part of the **utopian** tradition of French cooperatives. He advocated the formation of worker-owned productive associations as the way for average people to help themselves to raise their own living standards, and he organized such a cooperative in Paris in 1848. Blanc authored the book *The Organization of Labor* in 1839, spelling out his ideas and approach. It became a text used throughout Europe for those wanting to initiate **worker productive cooperatives**. Recognizing the difficulty of generating the capital needed for industrial cooperatives, he advocated governmental intervention and assistance to initiate such cooperatives, with the government withdrawing as the cooperatives became capable of self-management. This approach proved successful in the **United States** in the cooperative **farm credit system** and **rural electric cooperatives**, but has proven troublesome in most **developing countries,** where governments once involved are reluctant to withdraw from the direction of cooperative systems.

BOARD OF DIRECTORS. A body elected by the members of a cooperative society to manage its affairs. The times and places of the meetings of the board are usually specified in the **bylaws,** as well as the nature and timing of the reports of the board of directors to be made to the members.

BOGARDUS, EMORY S. (1873–1964). Professor of sociology and dean of the Graduate School at the University of Southern California in Los Angeles, he was introduced to cooperatives as a college student and was strongly influenced by **Toyohiko Kagawa** and by his visits to cooperatives in Europe, including Great Britain and Scandinavia. Bogardus was author of over 30 books, including several on cooperative subjects. He was the author of the *Dictionary of Cooperation,* published in 1943.

BOLIVIA. Bolivia was the last of the South American countries in which cooperatives were introduced and took root. The beginnings are found in a legislative decree issued in 1939 regarding **health cooperatives** and, in the same year, the organization of the first miners' cooperative at Potosi. These were followed in short order by **cooperative legislation** related to **consumer cooperatives,** the establishment of the first **agricultural cooperative,** a cooperative institute and, in 1953, the beginning of the journal *Cooperativas,* published by the government. By 1960 national **federations** for agricultural cooperatives and **credit unions** had been formed, a regional miners' federation established, a **cooperative law** enacted, a Cooperative Development Department in the government organized, and a cooperative training center established at La Paz. The **ILO** *Directory* **(1988)** reflected the continued trends of development—4 national federations and a total of 2,337 cooperatives with 1,317,030 members (18.8% of the population). Data prepared on Bolivia by the **Organization of Cooperatives of the Americas** in 1991 indicated 4,121 cooperatives with a membership of only 447,490 in the following sectors: agriculture—1,443 societies/with 64,200 members; consumer—230/19,663; housing—173/10,234; multipurpose—38/65,926; savings and credit—343/19,091; worker productive (industrial and services)—1,828/264,879; others—66/3,497. This represented a **cooperative penetration** of 6.4% of the population. A notable development has taken place in the district of Santa Cruz, where cooperatives, together with other more traditional activities, have been organized to provide basic community services such as water, electricity, telephone and sewage disposal.

BONNER, ARNOLD (1904–1966). Senior tutor at the **Cooperative College, Loughborough**, he began his work there in 1930, dedicating himself to **cooperative education** and to the study of European cooperatives, particularly in prewar **Czechoslovakia, Sweden, Denmark** and **Germany**. Three times during the 1950s, he visited the West Indies at the request of the British Council to lecture on and stimulate cooperative activities. Bonner was a member of the five-person **ICA** Commission on Cooperative Principles and was a prolific writer. His former students established a memorial fund to honor his work, and the College produced a commemorative volume in his honor.

BONOW, KARL DANIEL MAURITZ (1905–1982). A cooperator in **Sweden** who served as president of the **ICA** for the period 1960–75, he was born in Lulea in northern Sweden and attended Uppsala University. In 1933 he joined **Kooperativa Förbundet (KF),** the Swedish consumer cooperative federation, as assistant to the chief of the organization department. In 1941 Bonow became general secretary of KF. Elected a member of the ICA Executive Committee in 1946, he became vice president in 1957 and president in 1960. During his period as president of ICA, he was a tireless promoter of cooperatives in **developing countries**, of the status of women throughout the cooperative movement, and of ICA's traditional position on cooperative membership, i.e., voluntary, democratic, politically neutral and independent of government dictates. The headquarters of the **ICA Regional Office for Asia and the Pacific** in New Delhi is named Bonow House in recognition of his work and of his assistance to Asian cooperative movements. Bonow was an author of note, writing on numerous aspects of the Swedish economy. He was a frequent member of governmental commissions and represented Sweden at international meetings.

BOSNIA-HERZEGOVINA. The history of cooperatives in Bosnia-Herzegovina is entwined with that of **Yugoslavia,** of which it was a part from 1919 onward, until 1991 when it became an independent state. The Cooperative Union of Bosnia-Herzegovina was established at Sarajevo in 1945. No separate statistics were available for the region when it was part of Yugoslavia, and the conflict in the country since its independence has hampered any rational development of the cooperative movement. The **ICA** reported that in 1996 there were 70 **agricultural cooperatives.** Information regarding membership was unavailable.

BOTSWANA. The Botswana cooperative movement is one of the younger movements in Africa. The first society was registered in 1964. Since then, growth has been steady and substantial. The cooperators, government and assistance agencies have all pursued a policy of controlled expansion, carefully guiding the development of an infrastructure of viable and independent societies. There was concern that effective management, administrative and control systems be developed and that trained manpower be provided to ensure continued stable development. All these efforts have paid off for the movement and its members. A 1995 report of the **ICA Regional Office for East, Central and Southern Africa** indicated that there were 180 cooperatives in the following sectors: agriculture—15 societies/with 5,072 members; consumer—13/32,151; credit unions—86/9,270; industrial—6/175; multipurpose—60/13,068, plus a **cooperative bank** and cooperative development center. Total membership at that time was 59,736. An ICA report for 1996 indicated a membership of 77,736 (5.3% of the population of the country).

BOWEN, EUGENE R. (E. R.) (1882–1974). A cooperator in the **United States,** he worked for 25 years in farm machinery businesses before becoming executive secretary of **CLUSA,** serving in that position from 1934 to 1946. He was instrumental in bringing more **agricultural cooperatives** into CLUSA membership and strongly advocated that **cooperative education** and promotion, as well as business activities, should be embodied in the same cooperative organization, rather than separated. Bowen promoted interest in cooperatives among labor, religious, educational and professional organizations and urged them to organize such groups among their membership. He was the author of a number of books on cooperatives and was inducted into the U.S. **Cooperative Hall of Fame** in 1978.

BRADSHAW, SIR WILLIAM (1887–1955). A cooperator in the **United Kingdom**, he was the son of a Derbyshire miner. He went to work for a cooperative at age 13 and was manager of the society at age 23. At 27 he was named manager/secretary of the Midlands Cooperative Society and in 1921 was elected to the board of the **English Cooperative Wholesale Society**, becoming its president in 1936. Bradshaw represented British cooperatives on the **ICA** Central Committee from 1930 onward and was elected to the Executive Committee in 1934.

BRAUN, THEO (died 1994). A 20th-century French cooperative leader, he served for many years as president of the Confédération nationale de crédit mutuel. He was also president of the **International Raiffeisen Union** from 1981 to 1988. In this capacity he was influential in shaping the direction and management of the organization. Braun was also the initiator of the International Raiffeisen Cooperative Seminars, which were designed to share the experience of established cooperative movements with emerging movements. He served for a period as Minister for the Affairs of the Aged in the government of François Mitterand.

BRAZIL. The start of the Brazilian cooperative movement dates from 1847, with the establishment of a rural society in the state of Paraña by a French medical doctor, Jean Maurice Faibre. By 1888 cooperative stirrings had developed to such a point that a national publicity campaign was organized. Government decrees in 1903 and 1907 enhanced the cooperative effort, and individual cooperatives were soon to be found in all parts of the country. These had developed in sufficient number by 1925 that they began to form regional **federations**. Organized throughout the nation, they were seen as a way to maximize the advantages to be achieved by cooperative collaboration. In 1994 there were 92 such federations representing the interests of different types of cooperatives. A national confederation emerged in 1956 with the formation of the National Union of Cooperative Societies, followed in 1964 by the Brazilian Cooperative Alliance. In 1971 the Organization of Brazilian Cooperatives (OCB) was formed to represent all cooperative interests in the country, a responsibility it still carries. In 1991 OCB published *The Brazilian Cooperative System,* outlining the status of the cooperative movement, indicating 3,589 societies with 2,978,000 members (approximately 2% of the population). A report of the **ICA** in 1998 indicated that there were 5,399 Brazilian cooperatives with a membership of 3,741,667 (2.3% of the population) in the following sectors: agriculture—1,496 societies/with 918,883 members; consumer—238/1,221,985; credit (banks)—842/655,896; electricity and telephone—205/270,000 (1991); fisheries—25/16,209; health—862/595,105; housing—170/36,468; worker productive—1,103/297,121; and others (including transport)—458/na. The current (1999) president of the ICA, Roberto Rodrigues, comes from the Brazilian movement.

BROBERG, LAURITS P. (1859–1937). Originally a peasant farmer in Denmark, he served as president of the Federation of Danish Cooperative Societies, as chairman and managing director of the Wholesale Society of Danish Consumer Cooperative Societies, and as chairman of the board of **Nordisk Andelsförbund** from its founding in 1918 until 1933. Broberg was a member of the Danish Parliament from 1906 to 1914 and a longtime member of the **ICA** Central Committee.

BRODERICK, SIR THOMAS (1856–1925). An activist in the **United Kingdom** cooperative movement for 50 years, he was secretary of the **English Cooperative Wholesale Society** from 1899 to 1923. From this position, he saw the value of an international cooperative wholesale structure as a potential benefit to many movements and proposed its establishment to the **ICA** in 1920. Broderick chaired the ICA International Wholesale Society Committee when it was established.

BROOK FARM. A **utopian** cooperative community established in West Roxbury (near Boston), Massachusetts, in 1841. Like similar organizations, it was established to provide an alternative social and economic environment for its members, in which they could practice their group ideals and provide a model society for the achievement of humanistic ideals. In the case of Brook Farm, the aspirations of its organizers exceeded their capacity to achieve them, and it terminated its operations in 1847.

BROOKS, D. W. (1901–). A cooperative leader in the **United States**, he was the organizer of the Cotton Producers' Association (later Gold Kist) and general manager of Gold Kist Inc. of Atlanta, Georgia, building it into a large and successful cooperative engaged in worldwide business (former U.S. president Jimmy Carter was a member). He served on numerous governmental advisory bodies and was an active proponent of utilizing food as an instrument for the maintenance of world **peace**. Brooks was a delegate to the American Assembly, a group designed to propose changes which would make the **United Nations** a more effective organization. He was twice president of the **National Council of Farmer Cooperatives**, the principal national **agricultural cooperative** organization in the **United States**.

BROT, MARCEL (1887–1966). A physician by training, he was a cooperative leader in **France** who served as president of the **ICA** from 1955 to 1960. During this period he was also president of the National Federation of Consumers' Cooperatives of France (FNCC) and of the Union of Cooperators of Lorraine. It was during Brot's presidency of ICA that the first phase of ICA's technical assistance program to assist cooperatives in **developing countries** took shape, and he was instrumental in the preparatory work leading up to the establishment of the ICA Regional Office in New Delhi. While not a prolific author regarding things cooperative, over the years he contributed brief articles to *Le Coopérateur de France* and other journals. A collection of these was published in his honor by his colleagues in the FNCC.

BRUNEI. The cooperative movement began in August 1974 when the Cooperative Development Department was established by the government. This was followed in 1975 with the promulgation of the Cooperative Societies Act designed to register, regulate and give legal structure to the movement. Since that date over 100 cooperatives have been registered, and a number of **school cooperatives** have been organized. More detailed data was unavailable.

BRYN, WILLIAM. An early 19th-century cooperator, in 1830 he founded a cooperative shop in New York that is regarded as among the important forerunners of the **consumer cooperative** movement in the **United States**.

BUCHEZ, PHILIPPE (1796–1865). An author of early works on cooperatives, he was part of the **utopian** tradition in French cooperative thought and a theorist of the workers' cooperative movement. In 1832 he founded *L'Européen*, set up a cabinetmakers' cooperative and proposed a set of model cooperative **bylaws** including the principle of "a perpetual and untransferable reserve fund." This was an important step in encouraging cooperatives to expand the capital bases of their enterprises.

BUFFOLI, LUIGI (1850–1914). A pioneer in the cooperative movement in **Italy**, in 1886 he established the Unione Cooperativa di Milano, the first Italian **consumer cooperative** based on the **Rochdale Principles**. Over the years this effort in the interest of consumers grew into a large-scale integrated operation in Milan, with international business connections, and into a network of consumer cooperatives throughout the country. Buffoli was one of the founders of the National Federation of Cooperative Societies, the present Lega Nazionale. His literary skills found expression in numerous articles and pamphlets and in the establishment of the journal *L'Idea Cooperativa*. He was for many years a member of the **ICA** Central Committee.

BUGNON, EMILE (1880–1963). A French professor and cooperator, he was among the founders in 1918 of the Union des coopérateurs de Lorraine, which became one of the most successful French consumer societies. In 1928 he helped create the Central Office of School Cooperatives, which groups together and stimulates **school cooperatives** in France and, through its international arm, similar groups around the world.

BULGARIA. With the disintegration of the Ottoman and the Austro-Hungarian Empires, there was a gradual infiltration of Western European influence into Bulgaria and other parts of the Balkan region. A growing knowledge of the experience of the German **Raiffeisen credit cooperatives**, the French **production cooperatives** and the British **consumer cooperatives** led to efforts to emulate these as ways of improving the lot of Bulgarians. The first credit society was established in 1863. The period from 1890 to the end of the century saw the establishment of the first agricultural credit society (Oralo, at Mirkovo, now part of Sofia), the first consumer cooperative, and the first production society (Rabotnik). A wine producers' cooperative, a cooperative bakery, and a sericulture cooperative were soon started and were quickly emulated. By 1918 there were 994 cooperatives, and 6 national and regional unions had been organized. These efforts continued with growing success, and by 1946 there were 4,603 cooperatives with 83 regional and national unions.

During the first five years of the communist government (1944–48), the banking and industrial sector were nationalized, and the collectivization of land was begun. Collective farms and **production cooperatives**, based on the pooled land of farmers, were promoted, with some notable successes. **Worker productive cooperatives** were more tolerated than encouraged and had only a minor economic impact, but they did provide needed artisanal and repair services. They also became utilized for certain social services, and included a network of cooperatives of the disabled. Consumer cooperatives were strengthened both in number and in the scope of their activities, and they became involved in almost all aspects of the production and supply of goods and services to the entire populace. They also established and operated an education and training structure to serve their leadership and manpower needs, and through their membership in the **ICA** became the contact point of Bulgarian cooperatives with the international cooperative community.

Since the 1989–90 collapse of the centrally planned communist system, cooperatives have made a transition to a more market-oriented future and have, with ICA and other international intervention, established their legitimacy as private economic institutions. New **federations** and a **cooperative bank** have been formed, and a restructuring of the movement is still under way, as is a redefinition of the property rights of the formerly state-controlled cooperative institutions. An ICA report (1998) provided the most recent statistical data showing, for 1996, 4,814 cooperatives with 1,213,000 members (14.0% of the population) in the following sectors: agriculture—3,267 cooperatives/with 743,000 members; consumer—1,121/430,000; and worker productive—42/40,000. There was also a cooperative bank used widely by the cooperative movement.

BURIAL COOPERATIVES. *See* FUNERAL COOPERATIVES.

BURKINA FASO (formerly Upper Volta). Cooperatives are not yet widely developed in the former Upper Volta. Initial efforts aimed at their establishment can be dated from the French colonial period in the 1930s when **mutual aid** groups were promoted among the indigenous population. The first of these was formed in 1931. Since independence in 1960, as well as in the precursor colonial period, the development of cooperatives has been very much a part of and subordinated to official government schemes to achieve rural development. This has been moderated to a degree by assistance to fledgling cooperatives provided by nongovernmental organizations and a growing skepticism about government-directed and -implemented development. However, a truly viable and independent cooperative movement is still a thing of the future. Cooperative activity has been mainly in the areas of agriculture, **credit,**

production and **precooperative** associations. The **ILO** *Directory* **(1988)** described these sectors as involving 160 cooperatives with 61,345 members (0.78% of the population). An ICA report for 1998 indicated that cooperative membership had declined to approximately 20,000.

BURMA. *See* MYANMAR.

BURR, CARLOS. Director of the government support services for cooperatives in **Chile,** which were consolidated under his leadership in 1942, he is widely regarded as the father of the modern Chilean cooperative movement.

BURUNDI. The first stirrings of cooperation began in 1921 with the issuance of a government decree and the establishment of the first cooperative society. The principal increase in cooperative activity has taken place since 1955, following a decree regarding the formation of **indigenous cooperatives**. A national association was established in 1963 but dissolved two years later. Six **regional cooperative unions,** representing 207 cooperatives with 48,751 members, were listed in the **ILO** *Directory* **(1988)**. At that time **cooperative penetration** was 1.04% of the population, almost exclusively among agriculturalists.

BUTCULESCU, D. C. A pioneer in the Romanian cooperative movement, he was an effective propagandist for cooperative ideas and organization. He contributed his own money to the cooperative effort and was instrumental in the organization of cooperative training, as well as helping to found and publish the first cooperative journal in **Romania**. He was also the instigator of a number of cooperative workers' organizations.

BUYING CLUB, COOPERATIVE. An organization of persons to purchase goods from a wholesaler for their own needs according to **Rochdale Principles**. Such groups are most frequently formed as a preliminary step in the process of establishing a consumer cooperative.

BYLAWS. The regulations made or adopted by each cooperative society, they govern the actions of the society and put into practice its aims and constitution. Bylaws usually have to be registered with the government official or body that certifies the official status of cooperatives. In many countries this is a **commissioner** or **registrar of cooperatives**.

C

CABANETTES, CLEMENT. A cooperator in **Argentina**, in 1898 he founded El Progreso Agrícola de Pigüe, the first mutual assistance cooperative in Latin America.

CABET, ETIENNE (1788–1856). Author of early works on cooperatives, including *Voyage en Icarie*, published in Paris in 1840, in which he advocated the establishment of **utopian** communities. He joined an "Icarian Colony" in Texas but later left it to help organize colonies in Illinois and Missouri, where he died in 1856.

CAISSE POPULAIRE. People's bank in the French-speaking parts of **Canada,** similar to a **credit union** in English-speaking Canada and the **United States**.

CAISSE POPULAIRE DE LÉVIS, LA. The first *caisse populaire* established in North America in 1900 by **Alphonse Desjardins**. It is still in operation and in 1988 had 26,000 members, 77% of the population of Lévis, Quebec, **Canada**.

CAMBODIA (also known as Kampuchea and the Khmer Republic). There were cooperative development efforts dating back to 1940 (forestry and fisheries) and some post–World War II organizing at the national level and in local communities, but these had only limited success. The same was the case for the attempts to form cooperative/communal farms during the communist period. The level of political turmoil and armed violence in Cambodia during the past 30 years and more has precluded anything resembling a systematically developed cooperative movement in the country. No recent statistics were available. The **ILO** *Directory* **(1988)** reported data for 1974—700 cooperatives with 430,000 members (7.7% of the population). These statistics, however, are of only historical interest and have little relevance to the current situation.

CAMEROON. Though the first cooperative in Cameroon was a consumer society started in 1924, the cooperative development efforts in the 1930s and for some time thereafter focused largely on agriculture—principally cacao, coffee and cotton production, processing and marketing. The **credit** sector, a later development involving the Union des caisses populaires in French-speaking areas, and the Cameroon Cooperative Credit Union League, based in Bamenda, in English-speaking Cameroon, now exceeds in number the cooperatives in other sectors. The latest statistics (1985) reported a total of 404 cooperative societies (but did not indicate the number of individual members) in the following sectors: agriculture (77), consumer (1), credit and savings (290), fisheries (2), worker productive (11) and others (23). No more recent statistics were available, except for credit unions. WOCCU reported that in 1996 that there were 314, with a membership of 112,420.

CAMPBELL, WALLACE (1911–1998). An American cooperator, he was employed for many years by the **Cooperative League of the U.S.A. (CLUSA)** and was active in both national and international cooperative affairs. He was an official observer at the founding conference of the **United Nations,** representing the **ICA,** and later became the ICA's official representative in New York. Campbell was among the organizers of the **Cooperative Housing Foundation** and served as its president. He played similar roles in the International Cooperative Housing Development Association, which was affiliated with the ICA. He was among the organizers of **CARE,** served in its leadership for many years, and was the author of a definitive history of the organization. Campbell was named to the U.S. **Cooperative Hall of Fame** in 1981.

CAMPBELL, WILLIAM. A British cooperator, he was active in studying and structuring cooperative movements during the period of British colonialism. In the 1920s he was in charge of cooperative development in Ceylon (now **Sri Lanka**) and later was an advisor on cooperatives to the government of **China** under the auspices of the League of Nations. Campbell was also involved with cooperatives in **India** and in 1944 in **Uganda** and **Kenya.** He was the author of *Studies in Cooperation.*

CAMPUS COOPERATIVE. An organization of college students, conducted on a **mutual aid** basis, to provide services such as housing, book purchase and canteens. In 1968 a group of campus housing societies established the **North American Students of Cooperation (NASCO)** to provide a forum for the exchange of information and ideas, financial planning and assistance, and organizational and educational support to campus cooperatives in the **United States** and **Canada.**

CANADA. With the start of a cooperative at Stellarton, Nova Scotia, in 1861, preceded by a mutual fire **insurance** society in 1852, Canada became the third country outside Europe (after **Japan** and the **United**

States) to see a cooperative movement initiated. By the turn of the century, cooperative activity had begun among producers (1876) and consumers (1885), **cooperative legislation** had been initiated in the province of Manitoba (1887), the cooperative movement in the province of Quebec had been started, farmers on the western plains had initiated cooperatives and, in 1900, the first **credit union** in North America, **La Caisse populaire de Lévis,** had been founded by **Alphonse Desjardins**.

Provincial and regional sectoral cooperative structures soon emerged, and further cooperative legislation was enacted in other provinces (the first national legislation came only in 1949). In 1909 the **Cooperative Union of Canada** was formed to represent the now nationwide phenomenon of cooperatives. In Quebec the Desjardins movement expanded from its credit union base into a multisectoral organization now known as the **Desjardins Group. Agricultural cooperatives** expanded rapidly in most provinces, and grain pools were formed to represent major agricultural interests in the west. In the Maritime Provinces, cooperative activity was given a boost through the activities of Dr. **Wilfred Thomason Grenfell** and in Nova Scotia through the establishment of the **Antigonish Movement** by **James J. Tompkins, M. M. Coady** and others. In 1924 the first **fishery cooperative** was established, and in 1930 the first cooperative building society. National **federations** for these two sectors soon followed, and in 1932 the forerunner of the **Canadian Cooperative Credit Society**, for English-speaking credit unions, was established.

The post–World War II period saw the establishment of national cooperative **insurance** structures in both English- and French-speaking communities and the formation of a medical services federation. In 1953 the Cooperative Union of Canada adopted a resolution acknowledging the importance of assisting cooperatives in **developing countries** and called on the government to enter into a partnership with the cooperative movement to facilitate this. A similar concern was soon expressed for the native Canadian Indian and Eskimo communities. A cooperative college was established in 1955 in Saskatoon, Saskatchewan, and in 1960 **preschool cooperators** joined with those in the **United States** to form the Parent Cooperative Preschools International.

In the intervening years Canadian cooperatives have continued to grow. Consolidation into fewer, larger societies has characterized much of the movement, particularly in agriculture. Credit unions have become the predominant sector by membership, in 1993 constituting over 50% of the total cooperative membership, which that year was reported to be

7,868,046. By 1996 the cooperatives in Canada totaled 7,870, with a combined membership of 14,518,682, 50.4% of the country's population. The sectoral profile of cooperatives was as follows: agriculture 904 cooperatives/with 623,339 members; consumer—582/2,976,513; credit unions—2,448/10,014,000; fisheries—61/9,813; forestry—88/8,664; health—28/316,304; housing—2,001/116,276 (units); social care—446/32,812; transport—64/7,972; utilities—397/142,537; worker productive—62/4,171; and others—779/266,281. **Insurance cooperative** activity was also significant nationally as well as in the provinces. In 1996 there were 10 such national cooperatives. Collectively they had issued over 10,000,000 policies.

Nationally the cooperative movement is divided into English- and French-speaking organizational structures, represented respectively by the **Canadian Cooperative Association** and the **Desjardins Group**.

CANADIAN COOPERATIVE ASSOCIATION (CCA). This is the national association of English-speaking cooperative organizations, formed in 1987 by a merger of the **Cooperative Union of Canada** and the Cooperative College of Canada. In addition to its domestic program of promoting and representing Canadian cooperatives, it operates an international development program that assists cooperatives in Africa, Asia, the Caribbean and Latin America. *See also* CANADA.

CANADIAN COOPERATIVE CREDIT SOCIETY (CCCS). *See* CREDIT UNION CENTRAL OF CANADA.

CANADIAN INTERNATIONAL DEVELOPMENT AGENCY (CIDA). A government department, it is responsible for most of **Canada**'s official assistance to **developing countries**. It supports developing country government projects, international development institutions and the work of non-governmental organizations. It has an Institutional Cooperation and Development Services Division makes funds available to Canadian **cooperative development organizations**.

CANCE, ALEXANDER E. (1874–?). An American educator and cooperator, in 1910, at the Massachusetts Agricultural College, he offered the first course on cooperatives in an American university. He traveled to Europe in 1912 to study cooperatives, returning there the next year as part of an official delegation of seven to study European cooperative work and credit. Their report, submitted to President Theodore Roosevelt and the United States Congress, became a blueprint for many cooperative developments in the **United States**.

CAPE VERDE. Cooperative development is a recent phenomenon in Cape Verde, with most activity having taken place after independence in 1975. By 1980 there were 25 cooperatives with 2,239 members. Latest available statistics (1988) from the Instituto Nacional das Cooperativas indicate a rapid growth to 216 cooperatives with 20,165 members (4.5% of the population) in the following sectors: agriculture—49 societies/with 857 members; consumer—95/17,532; housing—18/319; savings and credit—24/1,088; and worker productive—30/369. In addition, the Institute reported 39 **precooperatives** and 75 **mutual aid** groups. In the past, the vast majority of cooperative members were affiliated with the **consumer cooperatives**. Since 1991, a growing number of **production cooperatives** has been noted.

CAPITALISM. An economic system based on private capital, in which ownership and control of productive and distributive businesses operate on the principle of maximizing **profit**. Control of such institutions is based on the amount of capital owned and, where voting is involved, on the number of shares owned.

CAPPER, ARTHUR (1865–1951). An American publisher, philanthropist and politician, he served 30 years in the **United States** Senate, where he co-sponsored the **Capper-Volstead Cooperative Marketing Act** of 1922. This law permitted farmers to lawfully unite to collectively market their production. Prior to this time, various measures had been taken to limit such **cooperation** as being monopolistic and in constraint of free trade. In 1984 the Arthur Capper Cooperative Center was established at Kansas State University; it provides classes and information on cooperatives to all segments of the population.

THE CAPPER-VOLSTEAD COOPERATIVE MARKETING ACT. A law passed in the **United States** in 1922 making it lawful for farmers to unite to collectively market their products. Prior to its passage, various regulations and laws that barred combines and cartels from restricting trade were being applied to cooperatives, to keep farmers from acting together to sell their products. The new law provided that, under certain conditions, farmers could now handle, process and market these together unless cooperatives acted in a monopolistic or trade-restricting fashion.

In such cases the Secretary of Agriculture could initiate governmental action against them.

CARE (COOPERATIVE FOR AMERICAN RELIEF EVERY-WHERE). Established in 1945 as part of the response to the International Reconstruction Conference, which was organized by **CLUSA** to see how cooperatives might assist people in Europe in the aftermath of World War II. Originally organized as the Cooperative for American Remittances to Europe with **Murray Lincoln** as its president, its name was later changed to reflect its program outreach to all parts of the world involving different types of programs. CARE implements a variety of programs, including provision of assistance to cooperatives. It is a major provider of assistance under the United States Food for Peace Program. CARE International, an international coordinating agency, was organized to reflect the fact that CARE organizations, in addition to the original one in the **United States**, have been established in **Austria**, the **United Kingdom**, **Canada**, **France**, **Germany**, **Italy**, **Japan** and **Norway**.

CARIBBEAN CONFEDERATION OF CREDIT UNIONS (CCCU). The first attempts to establish and maintain a **federation** of West Indian **credit unions** date from the 1950s, but the present Caribbean-wide organization of English-speaking credit unions dates from 1972. It has its headquarters in **Barbados**. In 1997 the Confederation reported members in 18 countries, encompassing 351 credit unions with 1,026,435 members, nearly 25% of the working-age population of the region. CCCU promotes the organization and development of credit unions throughout the Caribbean through training and technical assistance for its member institutions. It is a member of **WOCCU**.

CARLSSON, ALF (died 1994). A Swedish cooperative leader, he was director of the **Swedish Cooperative Center** and closed out his cooperative career at the Swedish Cooperative Institute. He served for a short period as development director for the **ICA** during 1985. He was a frequent contributor to the literature discussing current cooperative and development issues, including those dealing with the role of government in cooperatives (he prepared the **COPAC** discussion material on that subject) and **movement-to-movement** support.

CARPENTER, J. HENRY (1893–1954). An American religious leader and cooperator, he was head of the National Council of Churches Industrial

Division and of its Committee on the Church and Cooperation. He was chairman of the American Committee in Aid of Chinese Industrial Cooperatives and took a leadership role in organizing the 1930s tours of **Toyohiko Kagawa** in the **United States** promoting **cooperation**. He was author of *Peace Through Cooperation.*

CARTER, SAMUEL (1859–?). Born in England, he migrated to North America in the 1870s, working first in the American cotton industry before locating in Guelph, **Canada**, where he established a knitting mill. He was active in a number of social causes, including the Workingman's Cooperative Association, and was mayor of Guelph for a period. Carter was a participant in the first congress of the **Cooperative Union of Canada** in 1909, where he was elected its first president, a position he held until 1921. He was widely regarded as a Canadian counterpart to **Robert Owen**, a practical businessman with genuine concern for working people and committed to social reform.

CASTRO POZZO, HILDEBRANDO (1890–1945). A Peruvian author who published, in 1936, *Del ayllu al cooperativismo socialista*, regarded as an original contribution to Latin American cooperative thought, urging that cooperatives be built on indigenous foundations. *Ayllu* was an organizational form used by the Incas.

CAYMAN ISLANDS. The only known cooperative activity in the Cayman Islands is the Cayman Islands Civil Service Association Cooperative Credit Union, founded in 1973. In 1996 it had 3,823 members (10.5% of the population of 36,400).

CENTRAL AFRICAN REPUBLIC. After earlier unsuccessful attempts dating from 1946, the first cooperatives, as well as a related **cooperative law,** were initiated in 1961, a year after independence from France. Growth and development was slow. When an **ILO** consultant prepared an overview report in 1987 he found that there were 29 cooperatives in the following sectors: agriculture (15), consumer (4), fisheries (6), savings and credit (1), and worker productive (3). They had a combined membership of 30,488 (1.2% of the population). A national cooperative **federation** was established in 1973, with membership required of all cooperatives. It had become inoperative by the time information was collected for inclusion in the **ILO** *Directory* **(1988)**. No more recent data was available.

CENTRAL FINANCE FACILITY. Established in **credit union movements**, this is a facility in which surplus liquidity in a local credit union can be deposited, receiving interest, and where funds can be borrowed by other credit unions to meet liquidity shortages. The Central Finance Facility may invest or deposit surplus funds to generate additional revenue for the movement. **Surpluses** generated by the operations of a Central Finance Facility are distributed to member credit unions based on their patronage.

CENTRE INTERCOOPÉRATIF FRANÇAIS D'AIDE AU DÉVELOPPEMENT. The Center is a coordinating and consultative body established by the French national **apex cooperative organization**, Groupement national de la coopération, as a clearinghouse for requests for assistance from French cooperatives to cooperatives in **developing countries**.

CENTROSOYUS. The Central Union of Soviet Cooperative Societies, organized in 1898 in **Russia**, later the **Union of Soviet Socialist Republics**. It provided almost all consumer services to rural areas, to which it was restricted in 1935. It has been an important participant in the **ICA,** with several Centrosoyus representatives serving as vice presidents. In the post–World War II period it has played a leadership role among the cooperatives of the communist states of East and Central Europe and of those **developing countries** that opted for a socialist path to development. The **Moscow Cooperative Institute**, the principal training center of Centrosoyus, has provided short- and long-term training to cooperators from the developing world, including an extensive five-year course. *See also* SOCIALISM.

CERUTTI, LUIGI (1865–1932). A **cooperative pioneer** from **Italy**, in 1892 he established a Catholic movement to form rural banks. He was partially motivated by his opposition to a similar secular movement established by Dr. **Leone Wollemborg**.

CHAD. The first cooperative activities noted in Chad were a **cooperative law** enacted under the French in 1946 and the establishment of urban **consumer** and **production cooperatives** in 1949. Progress was limited, and problems associated with cooperatives in generaled to their total abolition in 1952. A government Office of Inspection of Cooperatives was established in 1959 and a Cooperative Decree issued in 1961. There have been a few sporadic attempts to organize cooperatives since independence, mostly focusing on **precooperative** groups, but the results have been meager. By 1974 there were 16 cooperatives with 1,796 members. By 1986 these had increased to 32 with an estimated 3,600 members (0.07% of the population).

CHAIRMAN. Every cooperative society has an elected chairman who presides over the **board of directors'** and other meetings, carries out designated responsibilities, and acts as a spokesperson for the cooperative. Sensitivities to gender considerations have led to suggestions that this position be designated as chair, chairperson or president.

CHARBO, J. J. A. A cooperator in the **Netherlands**, from 1946 to 1966 he was a member of the **ICA** Central and Executive Committees representing the Dutch movement in which he was an active participant for 31 years. He was manager of the National Cooperative Council (in which all Dutch **agricultural cooperatives** are represented) from 1943 to 1946, leaving that position to join the managing board of the Dutch Cooperative Wholesale Society in 1947. During the postwar years Charbo was an important influence in bringing about the amalgamation of the three national consumer cooperative unions into one national **apex organization**, COOP Nederland.

CHARIAL, ANTOINE (1885–1965). A cooperator in **France**, he was a leader in the **worker productive cooperative** movement. Apprenticed as a mason in Lyon, he became a militant socialist and trade unionist and at age 25 became secretary of the Masons' Union in Lyon. Charial worked with **Albert Thomas** during World War I and was introduced to the cooperative idea, which he used in establishing the first worker productive cooperative, L'Avenir. In addition to his cooperative work, he was deputy mayor of Lyon, director of the welfare department and hospitals of that city, and founder of homes for the aged. He started the Union of Worker Productive Societies of the South-East Region, initiated a pension fund for retired members of L'Avenir, and organized a center for young people and a technical school for young workers in the building trades. After World War II Charial took an active interest in international cooperative activities, serving from 1949 to 1963 as a member of the **ICA** Central Committee.

CHAVEZ NUÑEZ, FERNANDO. During the mid-20th century he served as chief, Cooperative Section, Division of Labor and Social Affairs, Pan

American Union, and was the author of numerous publications on co-operative themes.

CHILE. The first stirring of a cooperative approach in Chile was an attempt in the mid-1800s by Ramon Picarte to create a cooperative community at Chillán, based on the **utopian** ideas of **François Marie Charles Fourier**. It proved transitory, but the next, more successful efforts led to the establishment of thrift and **consumer cooperatives** in 1904. Related organizational efforts were carried out in different parts of the country, and cooperatives assumed official status with the passage of the first **cooperative law** in 1924, followed by legislation related to **agricultural cooperatives** in 1929. The 1930s and 1940s saw continued, gradual growth with new cooperatives formed for rural electrification and housing. The 1950s were a period of consolidation and the beginning of national **federations** for specific cooperative sectors, the first of which (1953) was for savings and **credit cooperatives**.

The 1960s saw the emergence of a series of cooperative support organizations related to education and technical training, agrarian reform and general cooperative promotion, reflecting the continuing growth of the cooperative sector. A national confederation of cooperatives was established in 1968.

The 1970s and 1980s found the cooperatives caught in the middle of the political and military struggles of Chile, with their overtone of Cold War ideologies. However, controlled growth and experimentation continued as cooperative leaders, with associations in different political camps, still tried to pursue a cooperative agenda.

The **Organization of Cooperatives of the Americas** reported that in 1991 there were 1,960 cooperatives with 581,593 members (4.3% of the population) in the following sectors: agriculture—425 cooperatives/with 33,924 members; consumer—70/88,747; fisheries—46/1,494; housing—946/102,249; multipurpose—9/6,022; savings and credit—105/159,754; worker productive and services—236/97,219; and others—556/92,184.

CHINA. Encouraged by directives issued by President **Sun Yat-Sen**, the first Chinese cooperatives emerged in 1912, starting a process that by the end of the 1920s would see the establishment of a Committee on Rural Cooperation by the International Famine Relief Commission, the enactment of **cooperative legislation**, and the formation of the China Cooperators' Union. By 1937 there were nearly 47,000 cooperatives (predominantly for **credit**) with more than 2,000,000 members, and a government cooperative department had been established. The outbreak of the Sino-Japanese War and the subsequent disruption of the Chinese economy led to the formation, with international assistance, of the Industrial Cooperative Movement. Other types of cooperatives continued to expand as well, and by the end of 1944 there were 160,229 **primary cooperative** organizations in China with a combined membership of 15,341,730.

With the victory of the communist forces in the civil war that followed the defeat of the Japanese, a new cooperative era was initiated, focusing mainly on the formation of **supply** and **marketing cooperatives,** organized in rural areas and designed to service farmer needs and to provide a consumer supply structure that could service the entire country. At the meeting of the newly established All-China Federation of Cooperatives, held in Beijing in July 1950, it was announced that there were then 38,000 cooperatives with 20,000,000 members. A year later it was reported that there were 51 million members in 42,425 cooperatives, 80.7% of which were supply and marketing cooperatives, 15.4% consumer, 2.1% producer and 1.8% other types. Although influenced sharply by the changes in Maoist policy and by accompanying political changes, and by controversies over **communes** and over the place and rewards for private initiative, the All-China Supply and Marketing Cooperative Federation has continued to grow and diversify and has become a major production and distribution organization for much of Chinese society. The **ICA Regional Office for Asia and the Pacific** statistics for 1992 reported 32,000 cooperatives with a membership of 160,000,000 (13.8% of the population for that year). A subsequent report of the All-China Federation of Supply and Marketing Cooperatives indicated that in 1998 membership had grown to 180,000,000 farm households, 80% of the national total. Using membership as a criterion, China is now numerically the second largest national cooperative structure in the world, exceeded only by **India**.

The All-China Federation of Supply and Marketing Cooperatives is a pervasive structure in Chinese society. It has 5.8 million employees and nearly a million business and service facilities. The Federation is the nationwide **apex organization** of Supply and Marketing cooperatives, operating through a network of regional and county organizations to service the widespread primary groups. Its main business activities include farmer and production guidance, supply of needed agricultural inputs, marketing, retail sales, processing and manufacturing, storing and transportation and waste material recycling. It also provides tourist and catering services, science and technology education and international economic and trade activity.

CICOPA. *See* INTERNATIONAL ORGANIZATION OF INDUSTRIAL, ARTISANAL AND SERVICE PRODUCERS' COOPERATIVES.

CIRIEC. *See* INTERNATIONAL CENTER OF RESEARCH AND INFORMATION ON THE PUBLIC, SOCIAL AND COOPERATIVE ECONOMY.

CLEAR UNIT. *See* COOPERATIVE LIAISON, EDUCATION AND RESEARCH UNIT.

CLEUET, AUGUSTE J. (1876–1956). A leader of the **consumer cooperative** movement in **France,** he began his cooperative work in the celebrated consumer society, L'Union, in Amiens. From there Cleuet was appointed to the management of the Magasin de gros, the consumer wholesale organization. When it united with the **distributive societies** in 1912 he became its managing director. He was elected to the Central Committee of the **ICA** in 1921 and reelected successively until 1954. He represented French cooperatives on the ICA International Committee of Cooperative Wholesale Societies, later the International Cooperative Wholesale Society. Cleuet was elected its chairman in 1934 and led the effort to establish the International Cooperative Trading Agency. World War II and the German occupation of France disrupted his cooperative career, but when the consumer cooperative movement was reorganized at the end of the war he reassumed active leadership.

CLUSA. *See* COOPERATIVE LEAGUE OF THE U.S.A.

COADY INTERNATIONAL INSTITUTE. Established in 1959 by the board of governors of St. Francis Xavier University in Nova Scotia, **Canada,** and named for Dr. **M. M. Coady**, a leader of the **Antigonish Movement** upon which the Institute was patterned, the institute emphasizes the building of human capacity through self-help organizations for the economic welfare of common people and the training of leaders for such efforts. The Institute, while not sectarian in its clientele or approach, has been continually enriched by the insights of Catholic social teaching and ethics, adapting these to the needs of a changing and developing world. The Institute's program combines training at the center in Nova Scotia with overseas training activities. In a recent year 70 leaders from 23 Third World countries participated in the Canada-based training, while 850 development workers from 19 counties were involved in 32 overseas training activities.

COADY, M. M. (1882–1959). A priest and educator in **Canada**, a native of Nova Scotia, Moses Michael Coady became a cooperative leader through his work as the founder and first director of the Extension Department of St. Francis Xavier University in Antigonish, Nova Scotia. With his cousin and fellow priest, **Father James J. Tompkins**, and cooperative activist **A. B. MacDonald**, Coady was co-founder in 1923 of the **Antigonish Movement**. This movement used community development techniques, usually organized around cooperatives, to empower common people to establish social and economic structures to meet their self-identified needs. In 1959 the board of governors of St. Francis Xavier University established the **Coady International Institute**, a training center where representatives from **developing countries** could assemble to study ways of affecting social change in their own countries through the organization and enhancement of cooperative organizations.

COHN, HYMAN I. (1870–1941). Born in **Russia**, he migrated to the **United States** in 1895, becoming an indefatigable promoter of cooperatives and of the efforts to unite such groups on a nationwide basis. He was one of the organizers in 1909 of the Cooperative League of America, a forerunner of **CLUSA**. The move proved unsuccessful, and the League was disbanded in 1914. However, Cohn and **Albert Sonnichsen** prevailed on Dr. **James Peter Warbasse** to convene a meeting of his associates to hear the case for a new national cooperative organization. The result was the establishment of the **Cooperative League of the U.S.A. (CLUSA)** in 1916. Cohn was on the board of directors from 1916 to 1920 and continued his enthusiastic interest in cooperatives until his death.

COLE, GEORGE DOUGLAS HOWARD (G. D. H.) (1889–1959). British academic, journalist, socialist and labor activist who was professor of social and political thought at Oxford University. He believed that socialist philosophy must be international and universal, and that the achievement of economic democracy was essential before there could be a fulfillment of the democratic political ideal. Cole felt that cooperatives were the best way of achieving this. He published, along with numerous articles and pamphlets, two notable books on cooperatives in the **United Kingdom**—*A Century of Cooperation* (1945), and *The Cooperative Movement in a Socialist Economy* (1951).

COLLÈGE COOPÉRATIF. A French cooperative training institution, located in Montrouge, under the direction of professor **Henri Desroche**. It was associated with the Écôle des hautes études en sciences sociales and provided training for undergraduate and postgraduate students. The Collège coopératif was the principal organizer of the programs of the **International Cooperative University**. Some question whether the college will continue without the leadership of Professor Desroche, who died in 1994.

COLLIN-BERNOULLI, BERNHARD. A cooperative leader in **Switzerland**, he is generally regarded as the founder of the Swiss **consumer cooperative** movement.

COLOMBAIN, MAURICE (1887–1966). A colleague of cooperative theorist Dr. **Georges Fauquet** in Strasbourg, he went to work for the **ILO** when its cooperative section was established in 1921 and Fauquet was named as its head. Colombain succeeded him in that position in 1932 and remained head until 1947. In 1932 he traveled to **Morocco** to implement the first cooperative technical assistance mission on behalf of the ILO. Following his retirement from the ILO, he joined the board of the French Central Office for School Cooperatives and was a cooperative advisor to the Ministry of Overseas Affairs. Colombain served as president of the National Committee of the Federation of French Consumer Cooperatives and director of the Institute of Cooperative Studies in Paris. He was a prolific writer on cooperatives.

COLOMBIA. The first recognized cooperative in Colombia, an **agricultural cooperative**, was founded in 1916, followed by a **credit cooperative** two years later. In 1918 the first cooperative **act** was passed. Growth of the movement was slow, however, with only 25 recognized cooperatives by 1935. After that date growth was more rapid: 248 in 1945, 385 in 1955, 1,553 in 1965, 1,874 in 1975, and 2,911 in 1987. These developments have taken place against a backdrop of frequently changed **cooperative legislation** and the establishment of cooperative bureaucracies in various government departments as new cooperative sectors have emerged. There has been a proliferation of national **federations** (19 in 1987), representing sectoral interests, and two national confederations have been formed. Predominant in the number of cooperatives and membership in 1987 were the savings and credit societies, mainly credit unions (1,173 with 597,500 members), followed by consumer, agriculture, worker productive, housing, and others, mainly cooperative schools. Total cooperative membership that year was 1,383,300 (4.6% of the population). The **ICA** statistics for 1996 show Colombia with 1,936 cooperatives and a total membership of 4,818,250 (13.1% of the population) in the following sectors: agriculture—332 societies/with 1,060,310 members; consumer—13/38,897; banking—4/na; credit unions—84/ 2,111,172; insurance—1,492/1,601,443; and others—11/6,428.

COMMISSIONER. In some countries, a person appointed by a minister or cabinet member to be head of a government department, e.g., Commissioner for Cooperatives. *See also* REGISTRAR OF COOPERATIVES.

COMMITTEE. A group of people elected by and from the members of a cooperative society (usually at the **annual general meeting**) to carry out certain responsibilities defined in the **bylaws**. The bylaws also define the number of people who will be elected to serve on each committee.

COMMITTEE FOR THE PROMOTION AND ADVANCEMENT OF COOPERATIVES (COPAC). Established in 1971 as the Joint Committee for the Promotion of Aid to Agricultural Cooperatives, its initial sponsors were the **FAO, ILO, ICA, International Federation of Agricultural Producers** and **International Federation of Plantation, Agricultural and Allied Workers**. Its formation was among the activities undertaken as part of the **Cooperative Development Decade**. The membership was expanded shortly thereafter with the addition of the **United Nations** and **WOCCU**, and "Agricultural" was dropped from its title in recognition of a change in scope to include a concern for all types of cooperatives in **developing countries**. Its current title was adopted in the late 1980s. COPAC has published a *Directory of Agencies Assisting Cooperatives in Developing Countries*, a series of country information notes describing the status of cooperatives in individual countries, and a newsletter providing general information about cooperative development. It has organized periodic international conferences discussing themes of relevance to cooperatives in developing countries. For many years the COPAC secretariat was located in Rome at the FAO but recently relocated to Geneva, where it is housed at the ICA in an office building adjacent to the ILO.

COMMITTEE OF HONOR OF THE INTERNATIONAL COOPER-ATIVE ALLIANCE. A committee formed at the Basel Congress of ICA in 1921 to honor those who had made unique and important contributions to the development of their national movements and to the international cooperative movement. It provided for their ongoing participation in the deliberations of the **ICA** in a consultative capacity as individuals. With the decision in 1930 to eliminate individual membership in the ICA, the Committee was disbanded.

COMMON BOND. In **credit unions** it is important for members to have a common bond (affiliation), as this adds to a feeling of mutuality, trust and loyalty. The common bond usually means people living in the same community, working in the same place, or already belonging to a common organization such as a cooperative or trade union. In the **United States,** the existence of a common bond has been a legal requirement for membership in credit unions.

COMMUNES. A commune is a cooperative community, formed for ideological, political or religious reasons, in which all resources of the group are held in common and in which the activities of the group are carried out collectively. Communes are found in many countries and are seen by their members as important in permitting a group to live according to more ideal standards. Communes are usually organized without affiliations with one another. However, in the 20th century there have been experiments with groups of communes, such as the **kibbutz** and *moshav* in **Israel** and communal farms in **China** and elsewhere.

CONFEDERACIÓN LATINOAMERICANA DE COOPERATIVAS DE AHORRO Y CRÉDITO (COLAC). The Latin American Confederation of Savings and Credit Cooperatives was established in 1971 to represent the **credit unions** in Spanish-speaking countries of Latin America. It currently has 17 national credit union **federations** among its members, and its headquarters is in **Panama**. In 1997 its members reported a total of 1,871 credit unions with a combined membership of 5,248,039. It is a member of **WOCCU**. COLAC has an affiliated foundation (FECOLAC) that acts in the areas of education, training and other member services.

CONFÉDÉRATION DES CAISSES POPULAIRES D'ÉCONOMIE DESJARDINS. The confederation of French-speaking *caisses populaires* and their related activities in Quebec and three other provinces in

Canada. It is responsible for the planning and coordination of all **Desjardins Group** activities, including the **audit** of *caisses* and their **federations**. It is the French-speaking equivalent of national **credit union** federations in other parts of the world. In English-speaking Canada its counterpart is the **Credit Union Central of Canada**.

CONFEDERATION OF COOPERATIVES OF THE CARIBBEAN AND CENTRAL AMERICA (CCC-CA). A confederation of cooperatives, originally established in 1957 and revived in 1979, that seeks to draw together and represent cooperatives in both English-speaking and Spanish-speaking countries bordering the Caribbean Sea. It has its headquarters in San José, **Costa Rica**.

CONGO (BRAZZAVILLE). Little information was available concerning the establishment, history, progress and problems of cooperative development in the then French Congo. The first cooperative was established in 1926, the first **indigenous societies** were initiated in 1937, and the first **cooperative law** enacted in 1946. The French colonial government gave only modest encouragement to cooperative efforts before independence. The newly independent government issued a decree in 1963, essentially abolishing all cooperatives that then existed and establishing a special board to approve any new ones founded in the future. Some were approved, but little support or assistance was provided by the government department charged with such tasks. The **ILO** *Directory* **(1988)** contained statistics for 1981 showing 841 cooperatives (799 agricultural, 19 consumer, 3 fisheries and 20 industrial) with a total membership of 20,908 (1.8% of the population).

CONGRESS. A formal business meeting, usually of a national or international cooperative organization, e.g., the **annual general meeting** of a national cooperative **federation** or the Congress of the **ICA**.

LE CONSEIL CANADIEN DE LA COOPÉRATION. This is the equivalent of a national **federation** of cooperatives for French-speaking areas of **Canada**, representing their interests and promoting cooperative philosophy in the areas covered by its nine provincial councils. It has provided some assistance to cooperatives in **developing countries**.

CONSUMER. A person who consumes goods or services; the opposite of a **producer**. Consumer goods are articles that are used to satisfy daily needs and desires, such as food, clothing and household goods.

CONSUMER COOPERATIVES. Cooperatives organized to provide access to consumer goods; also referred to as **distributive societies**. Such cooperatives may take a variety of forms ranging from simple **buying clubs** for joint purchasing of goods to other forms of shops, including supermarkets and department stores.

COOK ISLANDS. An independent Pacific island nation, aligned as an Associated Territory to **New Zealand**, it has had a cooperative tradition since 1953 when the Cook Island Cooperative Regulations were issued. In 1955 the first thrift and **credit cooperative** societies were formed. The Cook Islands Cooperative Union was established in 1958 and transformed in 1960 into the Cook Islands Cooperative Bank. A **cooperative wholesale society** to service the **consumer cooperatives** was established in 1966. In a 1972 article in the **ILO** publication, *Cooperative Information,* it was noted that there were 54 cooperatives with 4,750 members (22.3% of the population). There were also 20 school savings societies. Much of the economy at that time was organized around cooperative structures. No recent data was identified.

COOPER, WILLIAM (1822–1868). First cashier of the **Rochdale Society of Equitable Pioneers,** he was an avid correspondent, writing letters, disbursing information about cooperatives and speaking on their behalf at every opportunity.

COOPERATION. From *operari*, "to work," and *co*, "together," it is the act of thinking, planning and working together for or toward a common economic and/or social goal.

COOPERATIVE. A voluntary organization of people formed for the purpose of meeting their common needs by mutual action, democratic control, and sharing of economic returns on the basis of participation. In 1995, at its Centennial Congress, the **ICA** adopted the following definition: "A cooperative is an autonomous association of persons united voluntarily to meet their common economic, social and cultural needs and aspirations through a jointly-owned and democratically-controlled enterprise."

COOPERATIVE BANK. A bank owned by cooperatives or one formed to provide credit to cooperatives.

COOPERATIVE BIBLIOGRAPHIES. The international cooperative movement early in its history realized the importance of chronicling the growing body of literature about cooperation and cooperatives. Within 10 years of its founding the **ICA** had assembled and published in English, French and German the *International Cooperative Bibliography*. During the period 1973–75, the **ILO** published its *Bibliography: Survey of Cooperative Literature From 1813 to 1973*, a list of every book that the ILO could identify as having been written about cooperatives up to that date. The **Plunkett Foundation for Cooperative Studies** for many years included an extended bibliographical listing in its annual *Year Book of Agricultural Cooperation*. An important new source appeared in 1975 (continuing until 1988 in volumes 1–20), the *Research Register of Studies on Cooperatives in Developing Countries and Selected Bibliography*. This was compiled by an international panel (later by **COPAC**) and prepared and published jointly by the ICA and the Cooperative Research Institutes in **Hungary** and **Poland**. The number of cooperative bibliographies has grown over the years and now includes many that document the literature on national and international cooperative movements and on various cooperative sectors.

COOPERATIVE CENTER DENMARK. Established in 1985 by the three Danish **apex cooperative organizations** as a **cooperative development organization**, it provides advice and acts to strengthen the capacity of cooperatives in **developing countries**. One of its aims is to provide such assistance on a **movement-to-movement** basis, bypassing governmental involvement in the cooperative development process, a move deemed important in achieving cooperative independence and viability.

***COOPERATIVE CHRONOLOGY*, ILO.** Issued as Supplement No. 2 of the 1973 issues of *Cooperative Information,* published by the **ILO**, the first half of the publication contains a discussion of various cooperative subjects, tracing their chronological development. The second half is a series of brief references to important events in the cooperative movement throughout the world, by year and country, covering the period 1750 to 1973. The 1973 *Cooperative Chronology* was supplemented with additional information in subsequent issues of *Cooperative Information*. It was a major source of information for the chronology included in this book.

COOPERATIVE COLLEGE, LOUGHBOROUGH. *See* INTERNATIONAL COOPERATIVE TRAINING CENTRE, LOUGHBOROUGH.

COOPERATIVE COLLEGES. Central educational institutions (also referred to as training centers or institutes) established to train cooperative officials, staff and **committee** members. Some colleges have correspondence courses in addition to residential courses. Courses may vary in length from a few days to several years and are usually designed to provide specialized information or skills training. The **ILO** *Directory* (1988) listed 181 such institutions in 75 countries in all parts of the world.

COOPERATIVE COMMONWEALTH. The proposal by some cooperative theorists that society be organized according to a cooperative political system managed by a cooperative congress, paralleling an economy that would be almost entirely structured along cooperative lines. The plan is regarded as visionary by most cooperators, but many writers on cooperation favor change in the direction of a cooperatively motivated public opinion, informed by the teaching of cooperation in schools and an increasing emphasis on the achievement of cooperation through legislation.

COOPERATIVE DEMOCRACY. A socio-economic and political system in which all the major relationships of life, including economic organizations, are structured on the basis of control by the people, each having one vote, thus limiting the power of wealth. **Mutual aid** is the chief motivating force in such a system.

COOPERATIVE DEVELOPMENT DECADE. A campaign organized by the **ICA** during the 1970s to draw attention to and encourage support for cooperatives in the developing nations. It was designed to be part of the cooperative movement's support of the Second United Nations Development Decade. Activities were carried out to encourage cooperatives in developed countries, government bodies, non-governmental organizations, and **United Nations** agencies to support the expansion and strengthening of cooperatives in the developing parts of the world. Among the major ICA activities were an expansion of the scope and work of **COPAC**, the publication of the *Research Register*, expansion of the development work of the ICA regional offices, including the opening of an office in West Africa, and the formalization of an ICA development strategy and generation of the resources needed to support it.

COOPERATIVE DEVELOPMENT ORGANIZATIONS. Specialized organizations or sections of organizations established by cooperative groups in industrialized countries to provide assistance to cooperatives in **developing countries**. The 1989 edition of the *Directory of Agencies Assisting Cooperatives in Developing Countries*, published by **COPAC**, identified 16 international cooperative structures functioning in this capacity and 45 national cooperative groups from 20 industrialized countries, some of which provide only limited assistance.

COOPERATIVE DICTIONARIES. Glossaries of terms commonly used in discussions of cooperative organizations and their operation. The first noteworthy dictionary, edited by **Vakhan Totomiants** and Robert Schloesser, was published in 1928 (see bibliography). Others have followed periodically. These dictionaries have become increasingly multilingual as the cooperative movement has become increasingly international and the need to translate common cooperative terms from one language to another has arisen.

COOPERATIVE EDUCATION. Educational programs to inform cooperative members and others of the principles and practices of cooperatives as well as to teach skills needed to effectively operate a cooperative organization. It may also include special curricula for use in schools to introduce the principles and practices of cooperation to students. The Principles of Cooperation adopted by the **ICA** state: "All cooperatives should make provision for education of their members, officers, and employees, and of the general public in the principles and techniques of cooperatives, both economic and democratic."

COOPERATIVE EDUCATION MATERIALS ADVISORY SERVICE (CEMAS). A project of the **ICA,** initiated in 1974 as a way of improving the materials and methods of cooperative training in **developing countries** and as a clearinghouse for information and advice on education and training for ICA member movements. Its focus was on making materials and methodology available for training at the **primary cooperative** level in these countries. A list of its publications is available from the ICA. The project was terminated in 1987 when external funding was exhausted.

COOPERATIVE FARMS. A form of collective agricultural organization in which land and the means of production are jointly utilized by the members of a cooperative organized to engage in agriculture-related activities. Title to land, livestock and equipment may be owned individually, or these items may be combined in a collective pool.

COOPERATIVE FLAG. The **ICA** in 1925 adopted as its ensign the "Rainbow Flag." Such a flag was first proposed in 1896 by F. Bernardot, a delegate from the Familistère de Guise at the Second Congress of the ICA, and then promoted for many years by **Charles Gide** and others. The flag, seven parallel bands representing the seven colors of the spectrum, was first introduced into cooperative lore by **François Marie Charles Fourier,** who adopted it as the banner of his ideal community, representing diversity in unity.

COOPERATIVE GAMES. Games and sports designed to inculcate a cooperative practice or viewpoint as opposed to a competitive form. They may include dramatic works designed to entertain or educate about cooperatives.

COOPERATIVE HALL OF FAME, UNITED STATES. The Cooperative Hall of Fame and Historical Society was established in 1974 by **CLUSA** (now the **National Cooperative Business Association**) to honor those distinguished individuals in the **cooperative movement,** living and dead, who have made unique and lasting contributions to the movement in the **United States.** A commemorative plaque at the National Cooperative Business Association in Washington, D.C., tells of the accomplishments of each person inducted into the Hall of Fame. Between 1974 and 1990 64 individuals were so honored.

COOPERATIVE HOUSING FOUNDATION (CHF). Established in 1952 to promote and provide assistance to cooperative housing in the **United States,** it established CHF International in 1965 to carry out a similar program in **developing countries.** It is one of the U.S. **cooperative development organizations** supported by **USAID.**

COOPERATIVE INFORMATION. A publication of the Cooperative Section of the **ILO,** inaugurated in 1924 and published in English, French and Spanish. It ceased publication in 1975, due to a budgetary crisis created by the withdrawal of the **United States** from membership in the ILO. It was an important source of information about cooperative developments in different countries and internationally. It produced major works dealing with **cooperative bibliography** and the history of the cooperative movement.

COOPERATIVE LAW. Act(s) or decree(s) passed by a legislative body or issued by a government referring to cooperatives. They usually deal with the constitution, registration and regulation of cooperative societies. The first known cooperative law, the **Industrial and Provident Societies Act** in the **United Kingdom**, was passed in 1852. Attempts have been made from time to time to draft a model cooperative law. Notable in this regard are P. E. Weeraman's *Model Cooperative Law* (New Delhi: ICA, ROECSEA, 1971), and *Model Credit Union Act and Commentary* (Madison: CUNA, Governmental Affairs Division, 1987). *See also* ACT.

COOPERATIVE LEAGUE OF THE U.S.A. (CLUSA). Established in 1916 by **James Peter Warbasse** and **Agnes Dyer Warbasse** and associates as an organization of cooperatively minded people, it later became a national **federation** of regional and national cooperative societies. It has been the **United States apex cooperative organization** represented in the **ICA** since 1916. At first it maintained offices in New York and Chicago but it was later located in Washington, D.C. In 1985 the name was changed to the **National Cooperative Business Association**, in part to acknowledge that by then it included members from all types of cooperatives in addition to its earlier primary constituency, **consumer cooperatives**. It is one of the U.S. **cooperative development organizations**, assisted by **USAID**, providing assistance to cooperatives in **developing countries**.

COOPERATIVE LEGISLATION. *See* COOPERATIVE LAW.

COOPERATIVE LIAISON, EDUCATION AND RESEARCH UNIT (CLEAR UNIT). The development arm of the **Cooperative College, Loughborough**, the CLEAR Unit provides a wide range of consultancy, research and training development services to all forms of cooperative organizations, governments and international agencies in the **United Kingdom** and **developing countries**.

COOPERATIVE MAGAZINE, THE. A periodical sponsored by **Robert Owen** and published during 1826–27.

COOPERATIVE MOVEMENT. The collection of organizations that are committed to following **cooperative principles** and act collectively to implement and expand their use in economic and social activities. The term is used on occasion to describe a particular sector of the overall cooperative movement, e.g., the **credit union** movement, a national movement, e.g., the Swedish cooperative movement, or the international movement, reflected most fully in its diversity by the **ICA**.

COOPERATIVE NEWS, THE. A publication of the Cooperative Union in the **United Kingdom**. It is the oldest cooperative publication still in existence.

COOPERATIVE NEWS SERVICE, ICA. A publication of the **ICA,** established in 1928 to provide information about the worldwide cooperative movement and activities of cooperatives in individual countries. It was discontinued in 1982 and replaced by the *ICA News*, which is currently issued six times a year and distributed from the ICA headquarters in Geneva, Switzerland. These publications were major sources of information for the chronology included in this book.

COOPERATIVE PARTY. A political organization comprised of members of cooperative societies in the **United Kingdom,** established in 1919 for the purpose of gaining seats in the House of Commons as a means of supporting the cooperative movement and of opposing adverse legislation. It never has been able to elect more than a few members. It is regarded by some as transgressing the **cooperative principle** of political neutrality and has remained a matter of controversy among some cooperators.

COOPERATIVE PENETRATION. A measure of the percentage of a national population that is involved in cooperative organizations. In this book, cooperative penetration is defined as the percentage of a country's total population represented by cooperative membership. In the statistical reports of the **World Council of Credit Unions**, penetration represents **credit union** membership as a percentage of working-age population. The larger the percentage of penetration, the greater the possibility that cooperatives in a country will be an important economic and social force.

COOPERATIVE PIONEERS. The principal leaders in the establishment or early years of the cooperative movements nationally or internationally.

COOPERATIVE PRESS. A generic title for newspapers and periodicals published by cooperative organizations in different countries. Since 1909, the **ICA** has published on an irregular basis a *Directory of Cooperative Press*, last published in 1990. It listed 145 cooperative press sources in 42 countries.

COOPERATIVE PRINCIPLES. Basic guidelines for cooperation and characteristics that distinguish cooperative organizations from other groups. They are applied to societies all over the world and are usually identified with the organizational characteristics adopted and utilized by the **Rochdale pioneers**. They were restated in 1995 by the **ICA** as follows: (1) voluntary and **open membership**; (2) democratic member control; (3) member economic participation; (4) autonomy and independence; (5) education, training and information; (6) cooperation among cooperators; and (7) concern for community. They and the process utilized in their restatement are discussed in the ICA publication *Cooperative Principles for the 21st Century*.

COOPERATIVE PROJECT, THE. An organization of **cooperative research** workers established in New York in 1938 as a project of the Works Progress Administration (WPA), a temporary **United States** government employment program established during the depression of the 1930s. Under the leadership of V. J. Tereshtenko, it analyzed literature in various languages on various phases of the cooperative movement and issued reports on the results of its research. The project had the ambitious idea of producing an *Encyclopedia of Cooperatives* but was unable to accomplish it, as funding for the project was eliminated before its goals could be accomplished. Among the reports produced by the project were *Cooperative Education*, *Legal Phases of Cooperation*, *Cooperative Housing*, and *Cooperation in Latin America*.

COOPERATIVE RESEARCH. Research into the theory and practice of cooperation and cooperative organizations, it has been carried out by disparate parts of the world cooperative movement. The **ICA**, through its Research Committee, acts to rationalize the effort. During the period in which the *Research Register* was published by the ICA and the Cooperative Research Institutes in **Poland** and **Hungary,** there was some common effort dealing with research on cooperatives in **developing countries**. After World War II a number of universities in **Germany** individually initiated cooperative institutes that include research among their activities. They have jointly sponsored a number of international seminars in which there is joint consideration of a particular cooperative theme.

COOPERATIVE SCHOOLS. These are formal education programs established by one or more cooperatives to provide a cooperative education program. Such programs may focus on member needs to improve their skills as cooperators or on the staff of cooperatives, where attention is given to necessary job-related skills. As cooperative movements have become more established, a number have built or otherwise acquired facilities for a school or training center in order to carry out such programs. There are also examples of cooperatives being organized to establish and operate schools that parallel other education systems, public or private. Cooperative schools are not to be confused with school cooperatives, which are extra curricular programs in schools established by or for students, the main purpose of which is to provide experience in the principles and practice or a cooperative.

COOPERATIVE SERVICE. The organizational unit within the **ILO** that plans and implements ILO program interests in support of **cooperative development**. Established in 1921, it published *Cooperative Information* from 1923 to 1975. In 1932 in **Morocco,** it initiated a program of technical assistance to member governments that request assistance with cooperative development in their country. A modest effort in the beginning, it has become a major part of Cooperative Service activities during the period in which funding has been available for international development programs. It is a major implementing agency for cooperative development programs funded by the **United Nations Development Program (UNDP).**

COOPERATIVE SOCIETY. A formally established and registered organization consisting of a group of persons who have agreed to work together for common economic and social goals utilizing **cooperative principles**. Often the organization is referred to simply as "a cooperative" or "a society." The terms are interchangeable.

COOPERATIVE UNION, LTD., THE, ENGLISH. Established in 1868 in Manchester to represent the growing **consumer cooperative** movement, it is the organization of central importance in influencing the cooperative movement in the **United Kingdom**. It has grown until its member societies represent several million households and its structure and staff support all aspects of the movement in its educational, promotional and representational activities. It is not a trading organization. The Cooperative Union hosted the Centennial Congress of the **ICA** in 1995, reflecting the important role that it has played in the history of the international cooperative movement.

COOPERATIVE UNION OF CANADA, THE (CUC). Established in 1909 as a national institution to represent and promote cooperative interests in **Canada**. In 1987 it merged with the Cooperative College of Canada to form the **Canadian Cooperative Association**.

COOPERATIVE WHOLESALE SOCIETY, LTD., UNITED KINGDOM. Established in 1863 as the North of England Cooperative Wholesale and Depot Society, it is among the world's largest associations of retail cooperatives organized as a wholesale business. It does hundreds of millions of dollars' worth of business annually. It owns and operates many factories and farms in the U.K. and has had estates in West Africa and tea plantations in **Sri Lanka**. It employs many thousands of workers. A member of the **ICA** since its inception, it has provided significant leadership to the international movement over the years. Its organization and functioning have been a model for many **consumer cooperative** movements in other parts of the world.

COOPERATIVE WOMEN'S GUILDS. Organizations that were formed by women cooperators in a number of countries in the early days of the cooperative movement. They envisioned their work as educating cooperative members, young people and the general public about cooperation. The first such group was formed in the **United Kingdom** in 1883 at a meeting of the Congress of the **Cooperative Union**. The guilds provided a way for women to participate in cooperatives, which were at that time, and still are largely today, dominated by men. An **International Cooperative Women's Guild** was formed in 1924, affiliating the guilds from a number of countries. Women's guilds were active in the **United States** from the 1920s through the 1960s.

COOPERATOR. A person who subscribes to **cooperative principles** and who belongs to and participates in a cooperative society.

COOPERATOR, THE. The first known cooperative newspaper, established in 1828 by William King in Brighton, **United Kingdom**. It ceased publication in 1830.

COPAC. *See* COMMITTEE FOR THE PROMOTION AND ADVANCEMENT OF COOPERATIVES.

CORONA MARTINEZ, ENRIQUE U. (1897–1964). An Argentinean lawyer and cooperative leader, he was for many years a member of the board of directors of the cooperative El Hogar Obrero in Buenos Aires. He was also a member of the board of the Argentine Federation of Consumer Cooperatives, president of the Argentine Federation of Electrical Cooperatives, and vice president of the National Council of Cooperatives of the Republic of **Argentina**. He was a member of the **ICA** Central Committee and a vice president of the **Organization of Cooperatives of the Americas**.

CORT, EDWIN GALLATIN (E. G.) (1885–1944). An American farmer and government agricultural extension agent, in 1923 he helped establish the Freeborn County Cooperative Oil Company, the first of its kind in the **United States**. A group of such cooperatives, under Cort's leadership, formed the Minnesota Cooperative Oil Company in 1926, expanding its territorial base and activities in 1930 and becoming Midland Cooperative, an organization of which Cort was manager until his retirement in 1940. He was a longtime member of the board of directors of **CLUSA**. He served on the Board of National Cooperatives, an important **consumer cooperative** network. He was inducted into the U.S. **Cooperative Hall of Fame** in 1986.

COSTA RICA. The hardships growing out of the depression following World War I, plus the earlier experience with cooperatives of European immigrants who moved to Costa Rica, were the ingredients that encouraged the formation of cooperatives in the 1920s and 1930s and the enactment of the first **cooperative legislation** in 1925. These early efforts, memorable as they were, had all but vanished by the late 1940s (save for the Victoria Cooperative Society, the oldest cooperative still in existence in Costa Rica). With the support of a cooperative department in the National Bank, established in 1947, a new era began, which saw cooperatives take deeper root. A slow but steady growth began, and by 1959 there were 43 cooperatives registered (one-third of which were **credit unions**); by 1969 there were 221, and by 1979 there were 337. A national **apex organization** was established in 1969, and there are 12 national **federations**, 7 **regional unions** and a **cooperative bank**. Since the early days, the **credit union movement** has been the leader in the number of cooperatives and members. In 1992 there were 359 cooperatives, with a total of 293,608 members (9.5% of the population), in the following sectors: agriculture—39 societies/with 17,660 members; consumer—15/3,149; housing—9/976; multipurpose—81/94,413; savings and credit—87/103,607; worker productive—43/64,159; and others—85/9,644. No statistics covering all sectors were identified for more recent years, though there were clear indications of continued membership growth and consolidation of smaller cooperative units into larger ones.

CÔTE D'IVOIRE. The first cooperatives in Côte d'Ivoire were established by French colonists in 1932, and native provident societies were mandated by the French colonial administration. Even with **cooperative legislation** passed in 1946, neither developed to any significant size until the 1950s. The establishment of a banana producers' cooperative (1953), the enactment of a cooperative decree by the government (1955), and the establishment of a cooperative training center at Tiébissou (1957) marked a new period of development with a focus on **agricultural cooperatives.** By 1963 there were 23 active cooperatives and 772 "cooperative-oriented groups," essentially **precooperatives,** 431 of which were fairly well along in their development. Out of the "cooperative-oriented groups," 628 were coffee and cacao marketing groups; 27 were non-agricultural groups. The establishment by the **ILO** of the National Center for the Promotion of Cooperative Enterprises (CENAPEC) in 1969, as part of a **United Nations Development Program** support effort, was an important step forward in providing the necessary expertise for a modern cooperative movement, both to cooperators and to the government officials involved with them. In 1996 the **ICA Regional Office for West Africa** indicated that there were 3,342 cooperatives with a membership of 213,405, 95% of which was in the agricultural societies. Cooperative members comprised 1.4% of the population and were in the following sectors: agriculture—3,217 societies/with 203,448 members; credit unions—70/8,811; fisheries—44/541; and worker productive—11/605.

COWDEN, HOWARD (1893–1972). A cooperative leader in the **United States,** born into a farm family of nine children in the midwest, he was a high school teacher before entering a cooperative career, starting with the Missouri Farmer's Association. In 1929 with a few friends Cowden established the Union Oil Company in Kansas City, a wholesale **petroleum cooperative** for cooperatives in the midwest. In 1934 its name was changed to the Consumers Cooperative Association and in later years to Farmland Industries. It is now among the largest U.S. cooperative organizations. Cowden was one of the founders and leaders of National Cooperatives, a central **supply cooperative** for other cooperatives. Cowden became one of the United States representatives to the **ICA** and served on its Central Committee for many years. In 1946 he proposed, and the ICA Congress adopted, a proposal to form the **International Cooperative Petroleum Association** to serve the growing petroleum needs of cooperatives in various parts of the world. In 1950 he was awarded an honorary degree from St. Francis Xavier University, Nova Scotia, and he was inducted into the U.S. **Cooperative Hall of Fame** in 1976.

CREDIT. A sum of money placed on loan at the disposal of a member of a cooperative or of a society for use for agreed-upon purposes. Such credit is predicated on trust in the person's/organization's ability and intention to repay the loan.

CRÉDIT AGRICOLE. A French agricultural **cooperative bank,** established in 1920 with its headquarters in Paris. It has become one of the largest international banks.

CREDIT COOPERATIVES. Cooperatives organized to provide credit. These cooperatives are usually structured to serve particular sectors of the cooperative movement in a country, e.g., agriculture, housing, worker productive.

CREDIT UNION. A form of cooperative savings and **credit cooperative** that had its origins in **Canada** and the **United States**, but has since spread around the world as an alternative to banks that are reluctant to serve persons of modest means. They concentrate on mobilizing the savings of their members as the source of their funds for lending for productive and provident purposes. A unique feature of their organization, and until recently a legal requirement in the United States, is their insistence that the membership of each credit union have a **common bond**, e.g., have a common employer, be civil servants, or consist of people living in the same community; this makes more feasible the granting of credit on a personal basis without the security required by other financial institutions.

CREDIT UNION CENTRAL OF CANADA. This is the national trade association of the English-speaking **credit unions** in **Canada**, providing financial services to its members, mainly provincial central credit unions. Originally established in 1953 to provide financial services, it merged in 1977 with the National Association of Canadian Credit Unions, becoming the **Canadian Cooperative Credit Society** and assuming its current dual roles. A subsequent reorganization produced its current title. It actively supports international credit union development through the **Canadian Cooperative Association** and **WOCCU**.

CREDIT UNION CONFEDERATION. A regional association of national **credit union leagues**, e.g., the **Caribbean Confederation of Credit Unions**, which is associated with **WOCCU**. Confederations exist in Africa, Asia, the Caribbean and Latin America. Discussions regarding the formation of one in the Pacific have been going on for some years.

CREDIT UNION LEAGUE. A form of higher-level organization for **credit unions** in a particular geographical area, equivalent to a regional union or **federation** of other types of cooperatives. In the **United States**, leagues are an intermediary structure at the state level, between the primary-level credit union and the national credit union association. In **Canada,** "provincial centrals" are the equivalent of leagues. In some countries the national credit union federation is called a league, e.g., the Russia Credit Union League.

CREDIT UNION MOVEMENT. At the international level, a network of **credit unions** in more than 80 different countries that are joined together in common affiliation through **WOCCU**. In individual countries, the term refers to one sector of a national cooperative movement.

CREDIT UNION NATIONAL ASSOCIATION (CUNA). The national association of **credit unions** in the **United States,** established in 1934 with **Roy F. Bergengren** as its first managing director. Its membership includes **credit union leagues** from each of the states, representing in 1997 10,417 credit unions with 72,578,656 members. Its headquarters are in Madison, Wisconsin. **WOCCU**, of which CUNA is a member, has its offices in the same building complex as CUNA, reflecting the importance the United States **credit union movement** has had in supporting the worldwide expansion of credit unions, now found in over 80 countries. In 1962 CUNA formed the CUNA Global Projects Office to implement an assistance program to credit unions in **developing countries** as one aspect of the cooperative support provided by **USAID** to U.S. **cooperative development organizations**. CUNA is still the recipient of USAID funds but has delegated program implementation of these to **WOCCU**. In 1980 the CUNA Foundation was established to raise funds from U.S. credit unions and credit union members for development purposes in low-income communities in the U.S. and in developing countries.

CROATIA. The history of cooperatives in Croatia is entwined with that of **Yugoslavia,** of which it was a part from 1919 to 1991, in which year it became an independent state. While it was part of Yugoslavia, the Cooperative Union of Croatia was established, as well as a cooperative correspondence school in 1954. No separate statistics were available for the region while it was part of Yugoslavia. An **ICA** statistical report for 1996 indicated that there were 470 agricultural cooperatives, 164 credit unions, and 568 housing societies, a total of 1,211. No information was available on individual membership.

CRÜGER, HANS (1859–1927). An early theorist and historian of the cooperative movement in **Germany**. He was the first German participant in the **ICA** congresses and wrote a book on the 1900 ICA Congress that was important in informing German cooperators of the emerging international cooperative movement reflected in ICA activities.

CUBA. In 1943 a National Cooperative Institute was established to provide leadership in the development of cooperatives in Cuba. **Agricultural cooperatives** were supported by the Agricultural Development Bank, which was established in 1950. **Cooperative legislation** was passed in 1951, and a National Federation of Cooperatives came into being in 1954. A new **cooperative law** followed in 1960, but its intent was aborted by the revolution of that year, and it was replaced in 1963. Cuba under the Castro government has mainly developed a collectivized agriculture that does not claim to be cooperative. It has, however, permitted the establishment of private farmer cooperatives on a small scale, as well as "voluntary collectives" of private farmers. There is a small **credit cooperative** sector. Current information on cooperative structures in Cuba is sketchy, and there is as yet no indication that cooperatives will have a greater place in the national adjustments that are being made, adjustments both to the demise of the Eastern European communist partners of Cuba and to the need to develop alternative economic vehicles for maintaining Cuban **socialism**. Statistical data on Cuban cooperatives was incomplete.

CUNA. *See* CREDIT UNION NATIONAL ASSOCIATION.

CUNA MUTUAL INSURANCE SOCIETY. Incorporated in 1935, a year after the establishment of the **Credit Union National Association**, it currently operates in all of the states of the **United States** and in 56 international areas, providing **insurance** services to **credit union** systems.

It is the parent company of the CUNA Mutual Insurance Group, which is a network of insurance and financial companies providing services of benefit to the **credit union movement**.

CUSO VOLUNTEERS. Members of a Canadian program, financed by the Canadian government, that provides volunteers to work in **developing countries**. Many CUSO volunteers have assisted in **cooperative development** projects.

CWS. The initials of a **cooperative wholesale society**. They designate similar cooperative organizations in a number of countries. *See also* WHOLESALE COOPERATIVES.

CYPRUS. The start of the cooperative movement in Cyprus dates from the period 1909–14, the earlier date marking the establishment of the first cooperatives (agriculture and savings) and the latter the passage of the first **cooperative law**. Cooperatives have shown steady growth since then, hindered principally by the ethnic conflict between Greek and Turkish residents, backed by **Greece** and **Turkey**, which has led to the current division of the country. An **ICA** statistical report for 1996 indicated that in the Greek portion of Cyprus there were 690 cooperatives with 515,352 members (69.2% of the population). They were found in the following sectors: agriculture—36 societies/with 15,727 members; consumer—127/69,880; housing—1/5,581; insurance—1/na; savings and credit (banks)—477/420,057; worker productive—11/2,026; and others—37/2,081. In 1994 the Turkish-controlled section of the country reported having 272 multipurpose cooperatives with 28,227 members (21.1% of the population). The savings and **credit cooperatives**, with supporting **cooperative banks** in each community, have remained the predominant type of society.

CZECHOSLOVAKIA. *See* CZECH REPUBLIC.

CZECH REPUBLIC. The beginnings of organized cooperation in the Czech Republic (then Bohemia and part of the Austro-Hungarian Empire) date from 1852 when the first savings and first food purchasing groups were established in Prague. In 1870 the first consumer society came into existence, and in 1873 the first **cooperative legislation** was enacted. **Agricultural cooperatives** were initiated in 1880 and by 1896 had developed sufficiently to warrant establishment of a central **union**.

Worker productive cooperatives emerged in the 1890s and by 1897 were being serviced by a central supply union. The first housing society was established in Brno in 1900, inaugurating a period of rapid expansion of such groups, which by 1908 were being serviced by a central union of **housing cooperatives**.

Czechoslovakia was created as an independent state following World War I by merging Bohemia, Moravia and **Slovakia**. Its newly constituted movement was structured on the rich and diverse background of earlier sectoral cooperatives, augmented by societies for such specialized interests as disabled persons, travel and foreign trade. The movement grew in the interwar years, from 5,839 societies in 1922 to 11,568 in 1937. The movement was seriously disrupted during World War II by German occupation, a war of liberation, and subsequent political turmoil, which led to the establishment of a communist government in 1948. This gave birth to a period of nationalization of enterprise and a restructuring of the cooperative movement to serve the social and economic interests of a nationally planned economy. During this period cooperatives were focused in the sectors of agriculture, consumers, housing and worker production. **Federations** for these sectors were established in the Czech and Slovak Republics and at the national level. A national Central Cooperative Council was established to guide the entire structure. Growth of cooperatives was significant, reflecting the government's acceptance and use of cooperatives as expressions of socialist property. By 1987 there was a total of 2,518 cooperatives with 4,875,883 members (31.3% of the population).

The demise of the communist government in 1989–90 and the subsequent separation of Slovakia as a separate state brought major changes to the cooperative structure. However, most major segments of the movement appear to be adjusting to the new political and economic realities of the country. A 1998 statistical report of the **ICA,** covering the year 1996, reported that there were 2,185 cooperatives in the Czech Republic with a total membership of 1,381,583 (13.4% of the population).

D

DAHL, G. W. (died 1920). An early Swedish cooperative leader, he was instrumental in the organization of the Swedish Cooperative Society, **Kooperativa Förbundet,** of which he later became head. He was elected a member of the **ICA** Central Committee in 1913 and served until just before his death.

DAHRENDORF, GUSTAV (1901–1954). A German editor, politician and cooperator, he was an active socialist before World War II and editor of the *Hamburger Echo*. In 1927 he was elected to the Hamburg Senate and in 1932 to the Reichstag, in which he was the youngest member. Dahrendorf suffered under the Nazi regime and was twice imprisoned. After World War II he offered his services to help rebuild the German **consumer cooperative** movement. In 1946 he was elected manager of the Hamburg consumer cooperative society, Produktion. In 1954 he became president of the German Cooperative Wholesale Society. Dahrendorf was elected to the **ICA** Central and Executive Committees in 1951 and served until his death.

DAIRY COOPERATIVE. An association of people engaged in the production, processing and marketing of dairy products. The first **agricultural cooperative** in the world was a dairy society established in 1806 in Osoppo, Italy. In the **United States**, the **dairy cooperatives** are by far the largest, in business volume, of the cooperative marketing systems.

DANEAU, YVON (1932–?). A 20th-century French-Canadian, he was introduced to cooperatives while a student at the École des Pêcheries, noting that forming a cooperative was a key action of successful fishermen. He combined his academic and cooperative interests in 1965 to 1970 when he served on the faculty of Laval University and also as director general of the Cooperative Council of Quebec. From 1974 until his death, Daneau was associated with the **Confédération des caisses populaires d'économie Desjardins du Québec**, serving in its research and development department before becoming president/director of the **Société de développement international Desjardins** (SDID). In 1981 he was made head of the international sector of the Desjardins Confederation and their representative to the **ICA** Central Committee. From there he was elected ICA vice president, the first Canadian to occupy such a leadership post in the international cooperative movement.

DANISH INTERNATIONAL DEVELOPMENT AGENCY (DANIDA). The government agency in **Denmark** providing assistance to **developing countries**. Assistance to projects supporting cooperatives has been a priority, with most assistance concentrated on cooperative development in **Kenya** and **Tanzania**. DANIDA support is provided to **Cooperative Center Denmark** to help Danish cooperatives assist their counterparts in **developing countries**.

DAVIDOVIC, GEORGE (1901–1988). Born in **Serbia**, educated in **Switzerland**, he served as secretary-general of the Cooperative Union of **Yugoslavia**. He taught about cooperatives at the Belgrade School of Economics and for 10 years edited the journal *Economic and Financial Life*. Opposing both Nazi and communist threats to the independence and democracy of the cooperative movement, Davidovic's life and freedom were threatened to such an extent that he fled his homeland, escaping to Switzerland. He later moved to London where he served from 1958–62 as secretary for agricultural cooperatives at the **ICA**. In 1962 he became director of research for the **Cooperative Union of Canada** and was a frequent lecturer at the **Coady International Institute**. He was author of *Towards the Cooperative World—Economically, Socially, Politically.*

DAVIDSON, JOHN M. (1890–?). A Scottish cooperator, he was trained as a boiler molder and by 1913 was an officer in the Scottish Brass Makers Association. His cooperative involvement began in the Kinnick Park Cooperative Society where he served on the board of management and later as president of the society. Davidson was also president of the United Cooperative Bakery Society. In 1931 he was elected a director of the **Scottish Cooperative Wholesale Society** and became its chairman in 1946. In the Scottish Cooperative Wholesale Society he served in a wide range of cooperative business undertakings, including the Cooperative Insurance Society and the LUMA Cooperative Electric Lamp Society. He was for many years a member of the **ICA** Executive Committee.

DAVIES, MARGARET LLEWELYN (1862–1944). She served for 32 years (1889–21) as the general secretary of the English Women's Cooperative Guild and was instrumental in the organization of the International Conference of Women Cooperators, a predecessor of the **International Cooperative Women's Guild**. In 1922, in Brighton, Davies was the first woman to preside over an **ICA** congress.

DEANS, JAMES (1845–1935). A Scottish cooperative leader, his interest in cooperative work extended over 56 years. From humble beginnings, which required him to begin to earn his own living at age nine, he pursued his own education in his spare moments and became a librarian. Active in local and district cooperatives in Ayrshire District of Scotland, Deans was elected to the Scottish Sectional Board of the Cooperative Union, and in 1884 became its president and chairman, positions that he held for 40 years. In the international movement he was from 1910 to 1921 on the Executive and Central Committees of the **ICA** and was one of the stalwarts who maintained the communications of the **Alliance** with its membership throughout World War I. Deans envisioned the establishment of a **Cooperative Commonwealth**.

DE BACKER, ADOLPH (1863–1937). A militant cooperator and trade unionist in **Belgium,** he was one of the founders of Vooruit, an important cooperative in Ghent. He was director of the Imprimerie Populaire, a cooperative printing society, also in Ghent.

DE BALOGH, ELEMÉR (1871–1938). An early leader in the cooperative movement in **Hungary** who went to work with Hangya when it was founded in 1898, serving as director general and helping it to grow to some 3,000 societies by the end of World War I. In 1916 he founded the Hangya Industrial Company to produce goods for **consumer cooperatives**. De Balogh represented Hungarian cooperatives in the **ICA** Central Committee for 25 years. After his retirement in 1934 he was awarded the Hungarian Cross of Merit in recognition of his work with the cooperative movement.

DE BOER, KLAAS (died 1945). A Dutch cooperator, he was secretary of the Central Union of the Netherlands Cooperative Societies. From 1908 he was an active participant in the **consumer** and **production cooperative** movements, serving as president of local societies and on the directorates of HAKA, the Dutch cooperative **wholesale society**, and the National Cooperative Council. De Boer was elected to the **ICA** Central and Executive Committees in 1937, serving until his death.

DE BOYVE, EDOUARD (ÉMILE) (1840–1923). Son of a Huguenot father and a British mother, he was at the center of the moves in **France** and England to ensure that the burgeoning cooperative movement was international in character. In France he advocated and urged that the **Rochdale Principles** be adopted as the basis for the French movement. After living in Paris for a number of years, de Boyve came under the influence of a Protestant minister there and, when he married at the age of 32, he settled in the Huguenot town of Nîmes in southern France. There he interested himself in religion, the savings bank and the society for **mutual aid**. English journals, including those on cooperatives, were part of his regular reading, and he was soon captured by the Rochdale ideals (*see* COOPERATIVE PRINCIPLES). In 1883, with a group of others, he founded a consumer society, the Abeille Nîmoise, alongside the cooperative bakery, La Renaissance, which had been established in 1879. These were precursor steps to his work, with **Auguste Fabre** and **Charles Gide**, in the Ecôle de Nîmes.

In 1885 de Boyve convened and presided over the first French Cooperative Congress in Paris, which resulted in the establishment of the first national **federation**, known later as the Union coopérative. Participation in subsequent British congresses provided de Boyve with an opportunity to expound his ideas regarding the international aspect of cooperation and to propose the establishment of a Managing Committee of International Cooperation. He was to see the realization of his ideological and organizational dreams in the establishment of the **ICA** in 1895, and later to have his spirit of internationalism enshrined in the ICA practice of adopting a Peace Resolution at each of its congresses. On his retirement in 1913 de Boyve was named honorary general secretary of the ICA. At Nîmes, in addition to his active cooperative organizational activities, for 30 years, until his death in 1923, he edited the journal *L'Émancipation*, an important forum for defining and refining cooperative ideologies and strategies.

DE BROUCKERE, LOUIS (1870–1951). Professor of Cooperation at the Free University of Brussels from 1926 to 1938, he was an advocate of worker education and a prolific writer, publishing at least one book a year while teaching in Brussels. De Brouckere was a frequent contributor of articles published in the *International Review of Cooperation* and a participant in the **International Cooperative Schools** held annually by the **ICA**. He was a member of the ICA Central Committee from 1946 until his death.

DEHLI, OHLI (1851–1924). A lawyer in **Norway**, he was a leader of the Norwegian League of Students and similar Scandinavia-wide student activist organizations before becoming president in 1893 of the Kristiania Workingmen's Union. From this position he used his energies to find solutions to working-class problems and to achieve major reforms of Norwegian society. In 1892, while on a government-sponsored study of working-class problems in England and the **United States**, Dehli became acquainted with the cooperative movement and on his return founded the Kristiania Kooperative Selskap. He was one of the founders of the Norwegian Cooperative Union and Wholesale Society in 1906, serving as its president until his retirement in 1919. He served on the **ICA** Central Committee from 1910 to 1921 and on his retirement was elected a member of the ICA's **Committee of Honor.**

DEMOCRATIC CONTROL. In cooperatives, this means that the affairs of a society are administered by people selected or appointed in a manner agreed by the members and accountable to them. All final decisions made in a cooperative are made by members of the society on a one-member-one-vote basis, regardless of the size of individual shareholdings.

DENMARK. The stirrings of cooperation that have resulted in the Danish movement date from the 1850s and 1860s, during which time the first **agricultural, consumer, credit** and **production cooperatives** emerged, the first society dating from 1851. All these types have flourished over the years, producing a strong rural agricultural producer network as well as worker productive and consumer systems. A unique feature of Danish cooperation is that there has never been legislation adopted to give cooperatives a special legal status. Cooperatives are covered by the same laws that affect other forms of business enterprise, and many Danish cooperators pride themselves in this uniqueness. Danish agriculture has thrived under the cooperative form, but, as in other industrialized countries, its organization has become concentrated in a few large commercial operations, and the number of local agricultural cooperatives and farmer members has declined with the transition to a more urbanized population. (For example, 1,400 Danish dairy factories in 1935 had, by 1992, concentrated into 42.) Agricultural cooperatives' interests and their dominant place in the agricultural sector are represented by 21 national commodity or functional **federations.** Consumer cooperatives are the most extensive sector in Denmark—683 local societies with 1.2 million members in 1993 (approximately a quarter of the Danish population). **Housing cooperatives** (721 in 1993) provided housing for more than 400,000 families, supplying over 18% of Danish housing units. There are also well-established cooperative networks in the **insurance** and **credit**/banking sectors.

The national Central Union of Urban Cooperative Societies has close ties to the trade union movement and to the Social Democratic Party. It includes in its membership **worker productive** and **service cooperatives.** It has been aggressive in trying to establish a more influential role for cooperation in all aspects of the Danish economy. The other, and oldest (1899), nationwide cooperative organization is the Central Cooperative Committee of Denmark, which draws together all cooperative sectors. A 1998 **ICA** report of member statistics reported that there were 1,445 cooperatives in Denmark with an estimated 1,797,067 members (34.2% of the population) in the following sectors: agriculture—65 societies/with 113,000 members; consumer—526/1,226,867; housing—695/400,000 (units in 1993); savings and credit/banking—41/52,000; and worker productive—115/5,200. There were also 3 insurance cooperatives. In 1986, **Cooperative Center Denmark** was established to represent Danish cooperative interests in providing assistance to cooperatives in the Third World.

DE-OFFICIALIZATION OF COOPERATIVES. A process of eliminating inappropriate governmental involvement in cooperative affairs, limiting it to such roles as official recognition and ensuring that cooperatives, like other organizations, are legally carrying out their appropriate functions.

DE QUENTAL, ANTERO. A late 19th-century Portuguese **cooperative pioneer**, in 1870, with **Jose Fontance**, he attempted to organize cooperative societies in Portugal.

DESJARDINS, ALPHONSE (1854–1920). Born in Quebec, **Canada**, he is regarded as the founder of the **credit union movement**, building upon the experience of **Friederich Wilhelm Raiffeisen** in **Germany**, whose work Desjardins studied while he was working as a verbatim transcriber in the Canadian Parliament. Convinced of the merit of this form of cooperative as a practical tool to alleviate the problems of the poor in his native Quebec, he drew together a group to form **La Caisse populaire de Lévis** in 1900. Operating out of his home and with the active participation and leadership of his wife, **Dorimene Desjardins**, he perfected the operations of the *caisse* and gradually moved to expand them across Canada, particularly in the Province of Quebec. With his experience in Parliament he was able to formulate and see enacted **cooperative legislation** that would benefit all cooperative sectors. In 1909 he assisted in the formation of the first **credit union** in the **United States**, St. Mary's Cooperative Credit Association in Manchester, New Hampshire. In 1913 he was knighted by the Pope as a Commander of the Order of St. Gregory. The Pope particularly cited Desjardins's work with Catholic clergy, many of whom became "missionaries" of the credit union movement.

DESJARDINS, DORIMENE (1858–1932). Wife of **Alphonse Desjardins**, she was an active participant in the work to establish *caisses populaires*. She carried full responsibility for the daily operation of **La Caisse populaire de Lévis** during Alphonse's absence and illness. Without her work, the first **credit union** in North America would probably not have succeeded. After his death she participated in the organization of the "Union régionale des caisses populaires de Québec.

DESJARDINS GROUP. The term used to encompass the complex of activities to meet the financial needs of people in French-speaking **Canada**. It involves some 1,400 affiliated *caisses populaires*, 11 regional **federations**, a confederation, a central bank and 13 related corporations, among which is the **Société de développement international Desjardins**, which is involved in assistance to national and international **credit union** development.

DESROCHE, HENRI (died 1994). A distinguished cooperator in **France**, he was a world-renowned cooperative thinker who deliberately extended his influence through the thousands of cooperative leaders who were his students. He was formerly the director of the Centre national de la recherche scientifique. Desroche is cited 16 times in the bibliography of this book, for works dealing with the early history of the cooperative movement to its current manifestations in the developing world. Desroche was learned and eloquent on most cooperative subjects and activities.

DEUTSCHE GENOSSENSCHAFTSKASSE. The German Cooperative Bank, more popularly known as DG Bank, is now one of the major international banks. It was founded originally in 1895, with government financial assistance, as the Preussische Zentralgenossenschaftskasse in Prussia, to provide supplemental credit to the **Raiffeisen** and **Schulze-Delitzsch** cooperative financial systems. Its operations soon expanded, and it evolved into an all-German financial institution, recognized officially as the Zentralgenossenschaftskasse in 1932. It now represents German cooperative interests domestically and internationally. Following World War II and the consolidation of the three western zones of occupation into the German Federal Republic, the bank was reconstituted under its present name, with financial and management control dominated by the four branches of the German cooperative movement—agriculture, producer/artisan, consumer and housing. In 1957 it was given authority to issue bonds and thus gain access to wider capital markets.

DG Bank has assisted the cooperative movement in a variety of ways including publishing important literature, collecting detailed statistical data, and giving generous financial support to the work of several cooperative institutes at major universities in **Germany**.

DEVELOPING COUNTRIES. Countries with low levels of per capita income, low levels of industrial production, low levels of public services (education, health, etc.), and in which most of the population resides in rural areas and is engaged in agriculture, much of it of a subsistence nature. These countries are usually contrasted with industrialized countries. They are poor in economic terms, in contrast to rich countries. Most of the countries of the world fall into this category. Most of the world's population resides in them.

DEVERICK, BARBARA (1925–1989). A cooperator in the **United States**, she was active in the **rural electric cooperative** movement in her native state of North Carolina as well as in the national and international cooperative movements. She served as chair of the **National Cooperative Business Association** and the **Overseas Cooperative Development Committee**. She was a member of the **ICA** Central Committee and an active participant in the ICA Women's Committee. She was inducted into the U.S. **Cooperative Hall of Fame** in 1989.

DIETL, ANTON (1868–?). Leader of the German section of the Czechoslovakian cooperative movement in the interwar years, he began his work in a metal factory where he became an early activist in the trade union movement, editing a trade union newspaper. Dietl became active in cooperatives in 1907, first in a new consumer society and then as director of the Prague Secretariat of the Central Union of Austrian Consumer Societies. After Czechoslovakia gained its independence at the end of World War I, he was appointed secretary of the Union of German Economic Societies and served as a member of the Czechoslovakian Parliament. Dietl served on the **ICA** Central Committee from 1921 until his retirement in 1936.

DIGBY, MARGARET (1900–1985). Associated for over 50 years with the **Plunkett Foundation for Cooperative Studies**, first as research assistant (1927–34), then as secretary (until her retirement in 1968), and consultant thereafter. Digby established an international reputation as the author of books and articles on almost all aspects of cooperation. She edited the Plunkett Foundation *Year Book of Agricultural Cooperation* for many years and was the author of various studies and reports on cooperatives for **United Nations** specialized agencies. Digby was secretary of both the Agricultural Managers' Association and the Federation of Agricultural Cooperatives of Great Britain and Ireland. Her internationally acknowledged authority in the field of cooperation was recognized when she became an officer of the Order of the British Empire (OBE) in 1950 and was awarded an honorary degree by Exeter University in 1966.

DIRECTORY OF AGENCIES ASSISTING COOPERATIVES IN DEVELOPING COUNTRIES. A publication of **COPAC**, issued from time to time, which lists, describes, and provides contact information for all known agencies providing assistance to cooperatives in **developing countries**. It includes international governmental organizations such as those that are part of the **United Nations**, bilateral governmental agencies such as **USAID** and the **Canadian International Development Agency**, and international and national non-governmental organizations. It also includes sections listing international training opportunities for cooperators and information on a variety of organizations, such as the United Nations Volunteers and the **Peace Corps**, which provide longterm volunteers to work with cooperative organizations.

DISTRIBUTIVE SOCIETIES. *See* CONSUMER COOPERATIVES.

DJIANG, Y. S. Early cooperative leader in **China**, he was one of the principal promoters of the Chinese cooperative movement. He served as secretary of the Committee on Rural Cooperation of the China International Famine Relief Commission. In 1934 he was named head of the Department of Cooperatives in the Ministry of Industries.

DOIGS, THOMAS WILLIAM (1896–1955). American **credit union** leader, in 32 years of work in the movement he personally organized over 1,000 credit unions, beginning as a volunteer in Minnesota, where he was a postal employee. He was assistant managing director of the **Credit Union National Association** and was named managing director to succeed **Roy Bergengren** in 1945.

DOMINICA. Preceded by some agricultural associations, mainly involving banana production, formal cooperatives were first established in

1946. A legal framework was established in 1950 and the first **credit union** (assisted in its formation by Belgian nuns) was started in 1951. **Agricultural cooperatives** and credit unions have been the predominant types of societies, with the credit unions overwhelmingly dominant in membership (90% of the total). Both have national associations. The **ILO** *Directory* **(1988)** reported a total of 57 cooperatives with a membership of 37,168 (46.5% of the total population). The **WOCCU** *1997 Statistical Report* indicated that in 1996 there were 19 credit unions with 60,658 members (65.7% of the nation's 83,000 citizens). Total **cooperative penetration** in that year was estimated to be 78.6%.

DOMINICAN REPUBLIC. While there were stirrings of cooperation in the 1920s, and indigenous traditions prior to that, formal cooperatives with some staying power first emerged only after World War II, with the establishment in 1946 of two **credit unions**. The Catholic Church, particularly the Scarboro Order, were active in this and subsequent efforts, seeing cooperatives of all types as deserving of church support. A particularly prominent figure was Rev. Pablo Steele. The history of cooperative development, however, has been one of ebb and flow, with political and economic events radically affecting its development. Even with a governmental and legal structure set up in 1952 and the emergence of national **federations**, progress has been sporadic. The **COPAC** Cooperative Information Note on the Dominican Republic (1985) provides the latest stark picture—only 51% of registered cooperatives were still active, and membership in all sectors was in decline. Political and economic turmoil have not eased since then, and any cooperative prospects, whatever they may be, lie in the future. The **ILO** *Directory* **(1988)** reported 238 cooperatives with a membership of 157,993 (2.0% of the total population).

DOWNIE, JOHN (1871–1949). A Scottish cooperator, he was a writer and linguist who translated Swedish and other books on cooperatives into English. He started work as a railway porter, was self-educated, and became a civil servant. For over 20 years he was president of the Wishaw Cooperative Society and chairman of the Scottish section of the British Cooperative Union. He also served on the **ICA** Executive Committee.

DREJER, AAGE AXELSEN. A Danish cooperative leader active in the first half of the 20th century, he was an administrator, author, journalist and educator who served as secretary of the Danish Federation of Dairy Societies (1917–28) and of the Central Cooperative Council of **Denmark**.

In 1929 he published a general study of the cooperative movement in Denmark. Drejer served on the **ICA** Central Committee beginning in 1924, and from 1946 on the Executive Committee. He was the first chairman of the ICA Agricultural Committee, and was director of the **ILO** training courses held in Denmark. He was an active member of the Cooperative Committee of the **International Federation of Agricultural Producers**.

DUTTWEILER, GOTTLIEB (1888–1962). A Swiss food executive who started his career as an apprentice in a wholesale grocery. After a period as a coffee grower in Brazil, he returned to **Switzerland** and in 1925 launched an itinerant consumer goods retailing association with five trucks. In 1941 Duttweiler converted his now successful nationwide business venture into the cooperative **Migros**. Migros became notable for emphasizing social responsibility in business, providing a percentage of profits for social and cultural purposes, and refusing to sell personally or environmentally harmful items. Duttweiler provided a personal example of his cooperative ideals by setting his own salary as general manager at the same level as that of his managers. Migros, along with Coop Switzerland, now services a large majority of the Swiss retail food and related consumer goods market.

E

ECUADOR. The beginnings of the cooperative movement in Ecuador date from the first cooperative, Protector of the Worker, established in 1919 in Guayaquil. Growth was slow even after the passage of **cooperative legislation** in 1937, and it was not until the 1960s that a "movement" could be identified. The establishment of a cooperative department in the government in 1961 was followed later in the decade by national **federations** for the housing and **credit union** sectors and agricultural producers' federations for bananas, coffee and rice. A **cooperative bank** was established in 1964 and a federation of **worker productive cooperatives** in 1972. Each of these types, except housing, has grown, and in an **ICA** regional publication covering 1987, a total of 6,048 cooperatives was reported with 898,295 members (9.02% of the population of Ecuador). They were in the following sectors: agriculture—2,583 cooperatives/with 91,545 members; consumer—1,233/132,000; credit unions—822/632,000; and worker productive—1,410/42,750).

EGYPT. The prospects for cooperative organizations in the fields of agriculture and among consumers were promoted at an early period (1908) in Egypt by **Omar Lutfi**, considered a leading pioneer in the Egyptian cooperative movement. The initial response to his efforts was limited, but there was a gradual buildup of societies in the ensuing years, enough to warrant passage of the first **cooperative law** in 1923. A surge of new activity followed the end of World War II, and a National Cooperative Union (now defunct) was established in 1947. Following the revolution of 1952, serious cooperative development efforts, with strong governmental involvement and assistance, were begun in connection with agrarian reform measures. New activity was stimulated as well in **consumer, housing** and **worker productive cooperatives**. By the early 1960s national **federations** existed in each of these three sectors, and in the agricultural sector specialized federations for particular crops had begun to emerge (by 1978 there were 11). In the government, some confusion about responsibility for cooperatives has arisen due to the lack of a single cooperative department; different ministries have set up cooperative support and supervision units for their own sectors. A Higher Institute of Cooperative and Management Studies was established at Ain Shams University in Cairo. Growth in the cooperative movement has been steady since the 1950s, generally unimpeded by political events. In 1994 the General Cooperative Union of Egypt reported that there were 18,165 cooperatives with 11,466,200 members (20.3% of the national population). By sector they divided as follows: agriculture—6,360 cooperatives/with 4,200,000 members; consumer—9,762/5,450,000; fisheries—91/86,200; housing—1,459/1,500,000; and worker productive—493/230,000.

EIKEL, CHARLES F. (1908–1988). A **credit union** leader in the **United States**, he started his work with cooperatives by organizing a local credit union in Louisiana in 1935. He expanded his efforts, first becoming the managing director of the Louisiana State Credit Union League, then an area representative for the **Credit Union National Association (CUNA),** and in 1956 chief executive officer of CUNA. He is credited with starting the observance of Credit Union Day, now observed around the world. Under Eikel's leadership, the **CUNA Mutual Insurance Society** building was opened in Madison, Wisconsin, providing space for many credit union operations, including **WOCCU.**

EJIDO. A traditional Indian form of communal ownership in **Mexico**, in which individual families use designated plots of land within the

commune. The system was badly abused during the 19th century with large haciendas (estates) acquiring Indian lands, which were often expropriated to meet debts and other obligations. After the Mexican Revolution of 1910, a land reform program was initiated, one of the goals of which was to abolish institutionally and ecclesiastically owned estates, returning illegally acquired land to the Indian population and reestablishing their *ejidos*. Some cooperatively owned *ejidos* were also established, as a way of providing land to the landless and increasing agricultural production. Expansion was slow and uneven in the early years, but during the presidency of Lazaro Cardenas (1934–40), communal collectives were organized and given *ejido* status. By the close of his term, nearly 15,000 *ejidos* had been established and some 5,000,000 people (one quarter of the population) inhabited them. Currently it is estimated that 55% of Mexico's cultivated land is farmed by *ejidos*. Their operations vary greatly as to sophistication and success. At one extreme are those, largely in cotton-growing areas, which have shown significant development. In less developed areas they are economically and socially marginal. In 1980 a study by the **FAO** estimated that there were 24,000 *ejidos* with 2,600,000 members.

ELECTRIFICATION COOPERATIVE. An organization of people who own and operate electric power systems including, in some cases, power-generating facilities. There has been only limited development of urban electrification cooperatives, but **rural electrification cooperatives** have been established in many countries, ranging from **Bangladesh** to the **United States**, where almost all of the rural areas of the country are provided with power by a network of almost 1,000 rural electric cooperatives, most of them established in the 1930s. A number of European countries developed electrification cooperatives in the interwar years, but they have been largely replaced by publicly owned electric companies. Electrification cooperatives have been developed in a number of countries in Latin America.

ELIAS, A. E. (died 1919). One of the foremost leaders of the early cooperative movement in the **Netherlands**, he was among the founders of the Eigen Hulp cooperative society in the Hague and was largely instrumental in establishing the Dutch Cooperative Union, which he served as chairman. For a number of years he was a member of the **ICA** Central Committee. In addition to his work with cooperatives, he held a number of high governmental positions including Under-Secretary of State for the Colonies and was a member of the Dutch State Council.

ELLDIN, HARALD (died 1968). The first principal of **Vår Gård,** the co-operative school of the Swedish **consumer cooperatives.** He was responsible for the training of almost two generations of the staff and leadership of **Kooperativa Förbundet** during critical years in the development of Swedish consumer cooperatives.

ELLERBE, THOMAS F. (1892–1987). An architect and cooperator in the **United States.** His firm designed the first cooperative hospital in Elk City, Oklahoma, and was later deeply involved in the design of **rural electric cooperative** systems and facilities. Ellerbe established the NRECA Fund (in 1977) to support the work of rural electric cooperatives and the Cooperative Foundation, which awarded grants for **cooperative education.** He was a member of the board of directors of **CLUSA** and was inducted into the U.S. **Cooperative Hall of Fame** in 1978.

ELLIS, CLYDE T. (1908–1980). An American politician and cooperator, he was elected to the **United States** Congress after service in the legislature of the state of Arkansas. After two terms in Congress, during which he had been a leading advocate of **rural electrification,** Ellis was chosen to be the first executive manager of the newly established **National Rural Electric Cooperative Association (NRECA),** a position he held until 1967. Working through an International Programs Office established in NRECA in the early 1960s (which acts as a **cooperative development organization**), he helped to introduce electric power programs to people in more than 30 countries.

EL SALVADOR. The establishment in 1898 of a professorship in cooperation at the National University marks, for most people, the first stirrings of cooperation in El Salvador. However, a shoemaker cooperative established in 1912 was the first formal cooperative. It soon failed but was followed by similar attempts, also short-lived. The problems of the economic depression of the 1930s produced the first cooperatives with staying power, **credit unions** and small **worker production cooperatives.** These grew slowly, and it was not until 1955 that a national credit union **federation** was established. Programs established in the 1960s as part of the **United States** government's "Alliance for Progress" stimulated new **cooperative development.** New legislation was passed, and steps were taken to promote agrarian reform, which followed in the 1970s. For much of the time there was serious political unrest including armed conflicts in the country, a situation that has persisted to the present.

There is now a two-pronged cooperative effort in El Salvador, the so-called traditional sector cooperatives and the reformed sector. The latter are primarily **agricultural cooperatives** and a network of **credit cooperatives** that were formed in response to agrarian reform. The traditional sector includes agricultural and livestock **production cooperatives**, credit unions (affiliated with the **WOCCU** network), fisheries, school, transport, and worker production cooperatives. The **ICA Regional Office for Central America** reported in 1993 that there were 1,039 cooperatives with 133,512 members in the following sectors: agriculture—660 societies/with 50,562 members; credit and savings—206/60,626; and others—173/13,324). Cooperative membership was 2.3% of the population.

EMRE, CEVAT (1887–1961). A Turkish cooperative pioneer, he published a study of **consumer cooperatives** in 1913.

ENFIELD, A. HONORA (1882–1935). A British cooperator, she began work with the English Cooperative Women's Guild in 1917, first as the private secretary to its president, **Margaret Llewelyn Davies,** and, from 1922, as its general manager. In 1921 she took on work with the **International Cooperative Women's Guild**, serving as its full-time secretary from 1927 until her death. She prepared publications on general cooperative matters and on disarmament, a major interest of the Guild. Enfield traveled extensively in Europe, promoting the interests of the Guild and the cooperative movement generally.

ENGLISH COOPERATIVE WHOLESALE SOCIETY. *See* COOPERATIVE WHOLESALE SOCIETY, LTD., ENGLISH.

ENTRANCE FEE. A sum of money, usually a nominal amount, payable by all who become members of a cooperative society. It is in contrast with share capital, which members invest in their cooperative, and is usually a variable amount based on the economic means of individual members and on their commitment of support to the cooperative as an economic institution.

EQUITABLE PIONEERS OF ROCHDALE, THE. *See* ROCHDALE SOCIETY OF EQUITABLE PIONEERS.

ERDÉLYI, MORITZ (1877–1929). A printer by profession, he was an important activist in the consumer and worker cooperative movements in

Hungary. He helped establish the General Consumers' Society of Budapest in 1904 and later became its managing director. He was active in Hungarian governmental affairs after World War I.

ESHKOL, LEVI (1895–1969). Prime Minister of **Israel** after independence, he was among the leading founders of Hevrat Ovdim, the General Cooperative Association, in 1923.

ESTONIA. Dominated at different times by Danes, Swedes, Germans, Russians and Poles, Estonia has had only brief periods of modern independence (1918–1940 and 1991 to the present). During the earlier period, Estonian cooperatives had a vigorous and rapid growth starting with **agricultural** and **credit cooperatives** established during the period 1898–1918 (under a suspicious Czarist administration). **Cooperative legislation** was passed in 1917, and the movement burgeoned by 1938 into a flourishing structure with banking, industry, **insurance**, service, and trade sectors with 15 cooperative **federations/unions**, 2,993 local societies, 264,390 members and a national cooperative **apex organization.** During the period from 1940 to 1991, when Estonia was part of the **Union of Soviet Socialist Republics,** all of this organization was eliminated except for the consumer cooperative structure. With a newly independent Estonia in 1991, and with assistance from the **ICA** and national cooperative bodies, particularly from the Scandinavian countries, the cooperative movement has begun to reemerge, building on its previous history and experience, but finding 50 years of state and party domination and direction to be a formidable countertradition. **Consumer cooperatives** have been reconstituted as an independent force and have returned to membership in ICA. There is growing interest in agricultural cooperatives, organized among farmers in privatized state and collective farms, and small cooperative production units have been formed. Cooperative credit and insurance is under consideration. A 1998 ICA statistical report noted that in 1996 there was a much reduced movement of 30 consumer cooperatives with a membership of 53,528 members (3.7% of the population). Expectations are that cooperatives in Estonia will soon return to their earlier lively tradition.

ETHIOPIA. Cooperatives were a post–World War II phenomenon in Ethiopia, starting with a **consumer cooperative** established in 1945, during a period of British involvement in the country. The Haile Selassie government issued cooperative-related proclamations in 1960 and established a government Cooperative Development Department. During that decade **agricultural, credit**, and industrial **cooperatives** became well established. A military coup in 1974 deposed the emperor, abolished the regime and instituted military control. After three years of internal struggle within the military itself (including the execution of a series of military heads of state), a faction made up of officers trained in communist Eastern Europe prevailed, and the country committed itself to a Marxist development path. Plagued by internal revolt in Eritrea and other parts of the country and continued disputes over policy, the government saw few of its plans through to fruition. Through all of this the cooperative movement maintained itself, sometimes helped and sometimes hindered by external events. By 1982, the **ILO** *Directory* **(1988)** indicated, there were 4,052 agricultural cooperatives with 4,643,533 members, 171 **credit unions** with 30,815 members, and 817 **worker productive cooperatives** with 51,085 members. An **ILO** report in 1994 indicated that there were then 4,274 cooperatives with 5,122,856 members—8.9% of the population.

EUROPEAN UNION COOPERATIVES. The European Economic Community, established in 1958, and since then evolving into the European Community and the European Union, gradually expanded its influence in its member countries, originally six, currently 12. In order to cope with these and related developments, the national cooperative organizations in these countries have established a series of bodies reflecting different sectors of the economy to more fully coordinate their interests and represent them before European Union institutions. The nine such groups, all located in Brussels, **Belgium**, are as follows: the Coordinating Committee of the European Union Cooperative Associations; the Association of Cooperative Banks of the European Union; the Association of European Cooperative Insurers; the European Committee for the Coordination of Cooperative Tourism; the European Committee of Workers' Cooperatives; the European Community of Consumer Cooperatives; the European Union of Social, Mutual and Cooperative Pharmacies; the General Committee for Agricultural Cooperation in the European Union; and the Union of Retailer-Owned Wholesalers in Foodstuffs.

EVERLING, HENRY (1873–?). A German consumer cooperative leader who spent two-thirds of his life in active service to social movements toiling for the welfare of working people. In 1898 he was involved with others in the formation of Produktion, a consumer, housing and thrift society in Hamburg. He became its full-time secretary in 1908. After several years in the council and senate of the city of Hamburg, he joined the German **cooperative wholesale society** and came to be regarded as the organizing genius of the **consumer cooperative** movement in **Germany**. He not only worked out its democratic pattern in the early 20th century but emerged from retirement in 1945, after 12 years of Nazi oppression, to act as chief of the cooperative wholesale society and to lead the movement's revival. He retired in 1949 but remained on the Central Committee of the **ICA** as a representative of the German consumer cooperatives.

F

FABRA RIBAS, ANTONIO (1881–1958). A militant socialist cooperator, a native of **Spain**, he was active in cooperative affairs there until the end of the Spanish Civil War. During that period he was professor of cooperation at the School of Social Studies in Madrid and a Spanish delegate to several sessions of the International Labour Conference, where he worked with his longterm friend **Albert Thomas** on cooperative and other matters. Fabra Ribas was among the drafters of the Cooperative Law that was introduced in 1931 when the Spanish Republic was founded. Exiled after the civil war, he moved to **Colombia** and worked at the Institute of Cooperative Study at the University of Cauca at Popayan from 1943 to 1945. In 1946 he was in **Costa Rica,** and then in **Venezuela** from 1947 to 1949. Fabra Ribas eventually went to the **United States** where he published a number of books and articles on cooperation. He returned to Spain in 1950 and remained an active author and cooperative advocate until his death.

FABRE, AUGUSTE (1839–1922). An early and enthusiastic cooperator in **France** who was an advocate of the socialist ideas of the *phalanstères* of **Charles Fourier**. At Nîmes, in 1878, he founded a small circle for education, from which emerged the consumer society, La Solidarité. Shortly thereafter he met **Edouard de Boyve** and established with him, in 1884, the Society of Popular Economy, which was to give birth to the celebrated **School of Nîmes**. Fabre was a contributor to its journal, *Emancipation*, and was the author of various pamphlets on the subject of the social economy. He was among the conveners of the first French Cooperative Congress in 1885, and was active in the leadership of the **federation** that grew out of the meeting.

FAO. *See* FOOD AND AGRICULTURE ORGANIZATION.

FARM BUREAU FEDERATION, AMERICAN. A national association of farmers formed in 1919. Functioning through county and state bureaus, it endeavors to help farmers solve their agricultural problems. In some states the farm bureau has taken the lead in sponsoring cooperative societies for the purpose of farm supply, bargaining, marketing and **mutual insurance**. The bureau has a long history of lobbying for the agricultural interests it supports.

FARM CREDIT SYSTEM, UNITED STATES. Initially established by the United States Congress in 1916 to provide longterm mortgage loans to farmers, it has grown over the years on its own initiative and through further action of Congress to become a comprehensive multi-billion-dollar financial system serving the varied credit needs of cooperators and farm cooperatives in all parts of the **United States**. It is organized on a regional basis and administered centrally by the Farm Credit Administration. Originally capitalized with government funds, the cooperative credit system by 1968 had completely repaid this government seed capital. The farm credit system supports international **cooperative development** through membership and participation in **Agricultural Cooperative Development International**.

FARMERS UNION, NATIONAL. Officially known as Farmers' Educational and Cooperative Union of America, it was founded in 1902 as a national association of farmers and serves a wide range of farmer needs. Its symbol is a triangle, reflecting the organization's three principal interests—education, cooperation and legislation. It has been influential in the organization of a number of major farmer cooperatives and **mutual insurance** societies.

FARM SUPPLY COOPERATIVE. *See* SUPPLY COOPERATIVE.

FAUQUET, GEORGES (1883–1953). A French cooperator, he was an eminent cooperative theorist, best known for his principal work, *The Cooperative Sector*, in which he defined the specific role of cooperatives as part of national and international economies, rather than as separate and distinct economic systems as proposed by the advocates of the **Cooperative Commonwealth**. He was named chief of the Cooperative Section of the **ILO**, serving from its inception in 1921 until 1932. Fauquet was active in the **ICA**, representing French cooperatives on the Central Committee from 1934 to 1953.

FEDERAL CREDIT UNION ACT OF 1934. A national law permitting the establishment of **credit unions** in any state of the **United States** and defining the methods for chartering, supervising and examining the operations of such groups. Prior to this act, legislation regarding credit unions had all been at the state level.

FEDERATION. A regional or national organization of cooperatives of a similar kind from within one area or country. The term is used interchangeably with **union**, e.g., national federation = national union.

FERNANDEZ PRADEL, JORGE. A Jesuit priest who, in the 1920s and 1930s, actively organized **consumer**, **credit** and **housing cooperatives** in **Chile**. He regarded his cooperative activity as part of the social action mission of the Christian church.

FIJI. The first Fijian cooperative was established in 1945 while the country was still a colony of the **United Kingdom**. The first **cooperative legislation** followed two years later and presaged the early growth of a number of types of cooperatives. Just prior to independence in 1969, the **ILO** reported that there were 716 cooperatives with 14,442 members. Fiji, whose indigenous population is now a minority (the majority is composed of descendants of Indian immigrants), has been since independence a racially polarized society, a fact that led to a military coup in 1987 after an Indian-majority government was elected. This polarization has affected the cooperative movement and been a deterrent to growth. A 1998 **ICA** statistical report noted that in 1996 there were 532 cooperatives with 28,961 members, 3.7% of the population. Cooperatives were noted in the following sectors: agriculture—202 cooperatives/with 9,957 members; consumer—130/7,301; housing—8/264; savings and credit—122/6,194; worker productive 13/399; and others—57/4,846.

FILENE, EDWARD (1860–1937). An American entrepreneur and philanthropist who, along with his business endeavors (the Filene's stores in Boston) and his assistance in establishing local, national and international chambers of commerce, became enamored with the idea of **credit cooperatives** as a vehicle for serving the savings and credit needs of people of modest means. In 1907–08 Filene traveled to **Germany** and then to **India,** where he was introduced to the work of cooperatives by the Englishman W. R. Gourlay, who was assisting in their establishment. In 1909 he helped found the first **Desjardins** credit society in the **United States,** thus launching the U.S. **credit union movement.** Filene financed the early credit union organizing work and formalized this effort through the establishment of the Credit Union National Extension Bureau in 1921. In 1934 he became the first president of the newly established **Credit Union National Association.** He was also founder and president in 1935 of Consumer Distribution Corporation, a central organization for a national league of cooperative department stores. Filene held that cooperation was a key ingredient in the establishment and maintenance of world **peace**, and he organized and financed peace awards in Europe, an effort that brought him formal recognition and awards from several countries.

FINLAND. Organized cooperative activity began in Finland (at the time a part of **Russia**) in 1870 with the establishment of **consumer cooperatives** in the communities of Viiperi and Tampere. The first **agricultural cooperative** followed in 1880, and by 1895 **Hannés Gebhard**, regarded as the father of the Finnish cooperative movement, was expounding the cooperative idea and encouraging the organization of Finland Pellervo Seura, the Central Organization of Farmers' Cooperatives. Tensions soon developed between urban and rural cooperatives, eventually leading to a division of the movement into "progressive" and "neutral" factions and later to separate national organizations—a division that still persists. In 1902 a cooperative central bank, now OKOBANK, was established marking the beginning of efforts to organize **credit cooperatives** and to provide an independent financial base for the cooperative movement. Both the agricultural and consumer movements grew and diversified, little hindered by the disruptions of World War I and the achievement of Finnish independence. By 1923 there were 10 national organizations representing 3,626 societies with more than 540,000 members.

The interwar years saw further elaboration of both movements, including the beginning of participation by the Finnish consumer movement in the international Nordic Wholesale Cooperative Society **Nordisk Andelsförbund.** The World War II period was a difficult time for Finland and Finnish cooperatives that were caught between an expansionist **Union of Soviet Socialist Republics** and the moves of Nazi **Germany**, which played to the Finnish fear of its giant communist neighbor. The national and international cooperative movements were caught in these moves, in part because **Väinö Tanner,** who played a key role in the wartime Finnish government (and was jailed for this after the war), was also president of the **ICA**.

In the postwar period the establishment of cooperative educational institutions was an important development, with separate organizations for the different wings of the movement established, along with a Department of Cooperative Studies at the University of Helsinki. Cooperatives continue to play an important part in the life and economy of Finland, which has become increasingly urbanized and industrialized. Agricultural production and forest products, both of which are highly organized as cooperatives, are key elements in the Finnish economy. Consumer cooperatives continue to be significant in meeting the needs of the general public. In 1998, an ICA report indicated that there were 1,664 cooperatives with a membership of 2,337,374+ (membership figures were unavailable for 1,140 cooperatives: 285 worker productive, 23 social care, 390 utilities and 442 other cooperatives). In the following sectors the cooperative situation was as follows: agriculture—64 cooperatives/with 134,800 members; consumer—46/1,066,774; forestry—1/117,800; insurance—115/350,000; and savings and credit (banking)—298/668,000. At least 45.8% of the population were cooperative members.

FISHERY COOPERATIVES (FISHERIES). These are cooperatives that have been formed by people associated with the fishing industry, and may be involved in the harvesting, processing and marketing of fish and related products. They will usually be found supplying needed equipment and fishing gear for purchase by their members. These cooperatives, which the **ILO Directory (1988)** identified as operating in 77 countries, may range from those involving fishermen in oar-powered canoes selling their catch on a beach to those in a country such as Iceland, which are complex, integrated industries with international markets.

FLEMING, ROBERT (died 1939). A cooperative activist in Northern Ireland, he became secretary of the Belfast Cooperative Society in 1898 and later chairman of the first Irish Executive of the U.K. Cooperative Union, serving as its full-time secretary beginning in 1909. Fleming was elected to the board of directors of the **English Cooperative Wholesale Society** in 1917 and during the same period was a member of the **ICA** Central Committee.

FOLK HIGH SCHOOLS IN DENMARK. The first successful *folkschule*, or folk high school, was started in 1850 in Ryslinge by Christen

Kold. The movement to establish such schools was strongly supported by **Bishop Nicolai Grundtvig,** who saw it as a way of recruiting and training young leaders for Danish rural society. Many cooperative leaders in **Denmark** are products of the folk high schools.

FONTANCE, JOSÉ. A 19th-century Portuguese cooperative pioneer who first attempted, along with **Antero de Quental**, to organize cooperative societies in **Portugal**.

FOOD AND AGRICULTURE ORGANIZATION (FAO). The FAO was created in 1945 to raise levels of nutrition and standards of living, improve the conditions of rural life, and encourage an expanded world economy. To support these aims, a resolution was adopted at the founding conference, endorsing cooperatives as an important economic vehicle and commending them for providing experiences in **democratic control** and management. All member countries were urged to study ways of establishing and strengthening cooperative societies. In the FAO staff structure there has been for many years a section dealing specifically with cooperatives; it has emphasized popular participation and the training of cooperative leadership. The FAO has been the source of much useful literature on cooperatives and has organized important international conferences to discuss issues relevant to various sectors of the cooperative movement. When **COPAC** was organized as an interagency committee, the FAO, as part of its contribution, agreed to house and support, at no cost, the secretariat of the Committee.

FOURIER, FRANÇOIS MARIE CHARLES (1772–1837). A French social philosopher, he was the author of early works on cooperation that were a part of the **utopian** tradition in French cooperative thought. He emphasized the necessity of establishing voluntary, harmonious self-supporting communities, *phalanstères*, the first of which he formed in 1799. He contended that such groups would lead to the eventual elimination of governing authority. Fourier's ideas are often cited by those advocating communal living and are considered important as background to the **kibbutz** movement in **Israel**. **Brook Farm**, near Boston, Massachusetts, was an experiment in Fourier's philosophy. It was short-lived and provided evidence that what Fourier advocated in theory was difficult to achieve in practice. He was also a strong opponent of militarism.

FOWLER, HENRY L. (HARRY) (1876–1980). A Canadian cooperator, he was manager of an oil distribution cooperative in Saskatchewan in the

1930s and played an important role in the organization in 1935 of the world's first cooperative refinery. He was active in the promotion of a number of related cooperatives, including Interprovincial Cooperatives, which had operations in several provinces in **Canada**. Fowler served at the close of his career as head of Federated Cooperatives, a cooperative retailing system in Western Canada.

FRANCE. The establishment of cooperatives in France dates from the 1750s when several cheesemakers' **mutual** societies were established in the Franche-Comté region. However, apart from some early important theorizers about cooperation, e.g., **Charles Fourier, Philippe Buchez** and **Louis Blanc**, active organization of cooperatives throughout the country dates from the 1830s when the first **agricultural, consumer** and **worker productive cooperatives** were organized and the different facets of the cooperative movement began to proliferate. Worker productive cooperatives were most prominent in formation in the following years, under the leadership of Buchez and Blanc. The first **credit cooperative** in France, established in 1863, focused its assistance on workers' groups, and in 1884 the General Confederation of Workers Production Cooperatives came into being. In 1865 the first proposal of **cooperative legislation** was made, and a law was enacted two years later.

Contacts with cooperatives in the **United Kingdom** and elsewhere in Europe developed during this period, and French cooperators proposed the holding of an international cooperative **congress** concurrent with the Universal Exhibition held in Paris in 1867. Plans were aborted, however, after opposition from the French government. The movement continued to grow and produced more organizations and a new generation of cooperative theorists, among them **Edouard de Boyve, Auguste Fabre**, and **Charles Gide** (organizers of the **School of Nîmes**). They also authored a series of cooperative publications, a number of them published by worker-owned printing cooperatives.

The 1890s were an active period related to cooperative credit. A **cooperative bank** of worker productive societies was organized, an agricultural cooperative credit law enacted, and new agricultural credit cooperatives established that were organized into regional unions that eventually became **Crédit agricole**.

The new century saw the cooperative movement in France growing vigorously and actively participating in the newly established **ICA,** which had held its second and fourth congresses in Paris in 1896 and 1900. **School cooperatives** became a matter of discussion, and the first **mutual insurance** society was established. Cooperatives were increasingly joining in regional and then national **federations**, particularly for consumers, credit, agriculture and housing. A national **cooperative wholesale society** was organized, and in 1917 a central cooperative bank was established in Paris.

Speedily recovering from the effects of World War I, French cooperatives moved into a new period of growth and proliferation. New legislation was passed, the first **fishery cooperatives** organized, the *Revue des études coopératives* began publication, Crédit Agricole was established, the Central Organization of Peoples' Banks organized, and a national **apex organization** formed. The interwar years were a period of continued growth in size, complexity, and sophistication for cooperatives. Membership growth matched these trends, and French cooperative leaders assumed increasingly large roles on the international scene. Included among them were **Albert Thomas,** who became the first director of the **ILO.** He quickly took steps to structure cooperative issues and concerns into the work of ILO, including the creation of a **Cooperative Service,** led in its early development by a series of French cooperators.

World War II and the German occupation of the country were disruptive, often destructive, to cooperative infrastructure and organization. With the end of the war, such disruption was soon overcome and the cooperative movement reactivated. During the period 1945–48 agricultural cooperatives were reconfigured in 15 new or revitalized national **federations,** precursors of the dramatic restructuring of French and European agriculture and agricultural cooperatives which have characterized the post–World War II period. Consumer cooperatives elaborated their activities to provide a growing range of consumer services in larger and increasingly complex organizational structures. In the 1980s, however, such sophistication almost overwhelmed the consumer cooperatives, forcing major bankruptcies and a radical restructuring of the movement into a leaner and more decentralized structure. **Worker productive cooperatives** continued to grow, and French leadership was prominent in this sector of the international movement. A move to nationalize all French banking impacted the cooperative banking and credit structures in the 1980s, but subsequent reconsideration by government has left these structures an important cooperative force in France, in Europe and on the international scene.

The Groupement national de la Coopération, established in 1968 as the new apex organization for French cooperatives, reported in 1988 that there were 25,008 cooperatives in France with a membership of 13,175,238 in the following sectors: agriculture, consumer, commerce, fisheries, housing, savings and credit, school, transport and worker productive. A more composite view in 1990, utilizing information from the

Groupement, the ILO and the European Community, identified 24,415 cooperatives with 16,228,755 members, 28.5% of the French population. An ICA statistical report in 1998 noted that in 1996 there were 23,573 cooperatives in France with a total membership of 17,485,573, 30.1% of the population, in the following sectors: agriculture—16,800 cooperatives/with 1,300,000 members; consumer—97/3,400,000; fisheries—161/17,000; housing—157/70,000; independent retailer—35/9,600; savings and credit (banks)—4,699/12,631,800; transport—31/733; and worker productive 1,593/56,440.

FRANKLIN, BENJAMIN (1706–1790). Writer, publisher, philosopher, scientist, and statesman of the American Revolution, he inspired the formation in the 1750s of the first **mutual insurance** association in the **United States**, the Union Fire Company. This developed in 1752 into the **Philadelphia Contributionship for the Insurance of Houses from Loss by Fire**, regarded by many as the oldest cooperative society in the country. As a prominent political figure, his promotion of mutual insurance helped to positively influence American attitudes toward cooperation. In 1987 Franklin was inducted into the U.S. **Cooperative Hall of Fame**.

FREUNDLICH, EMMY (1878–1948). An Austrian consumer cooperative leader, she was for many years on the board of directors of the Austrian Central Cooperative Union and on the Supervisory Committee of the Austrian Cooperative Wholesale Society. She headed the women's section of the Cooperative Union and was editor of its official publications. In 1921 she became president of the **International Cooperative Women's Guild**, a position she held for 25 years. Freundlich was elected to the **ICA** Central and Executive Committees in 1921, serving until 1937. She was a socialist member of the Austrian Parliament until 1934 when she was arrested during an attempted military coup; her release was made dependent upon her withdrawal from political activity. After World War II, she and her family moved to the **United States,** where she served for a time as **United Nations** representative of the International Cooperative Women's Guild.

FRUITÈRIES IN THE FRANCHE-COMTÉ (NOW HAUTE SAÔNE) IN FRANCE. Cheesemaking cooperatives established around 1750 in France, they are regarded as among the early activities in the history of the modern cooperative movement.

FUNERAL COOPERATIVES. Also known as burial associations or memorial societies, these are designed to provide simple and inexpensive burial services to members and their families. They are sometimes organized as separate cooperative societies, or, in other cases, they constitute a special program made available by a cooperative society as "the ultimate consumer service" to its members. They are found most extensively in **Canada**, the **United States** and the **United Kingdom**.

G

GABON. Organized cooperation came to Gabon only after independence from **France** in 1960. A General Cooperative Decree was issued the next year by the new government, replacing the legislation enacted in 1946 in response to a French colonial directive. The first cooperative was established in 1961, but further implementation of cooperative interests in terms of organization has been slow to come and is still only small. By 1975 there were 13 cooperatives; by 1984 there were 40 (all in agriculture) with 1,142 members, 0.11% of the population.

GADGIL, D. R. (1901–1971). An Indian cooperator, he wrote and spoke extensively about cooperatives and **cooperative development**.

GALLAGHER, PATRICK (1871–?). A cooperative leader in **Ireland**, he helped to organize Templecrone Coooperative in Donegal, of which he was the longtime manager. He was widely known for his cooperative activities and became known as Paddy the Cope. This became the title of his autobiography, which, along with his own life story, included an account of the growth of the Irish cooperative movement.

GAMBIA, THE. While a cooperative-like marketing association was established in 1920, the first formally recognized cooperatives were established in the Gambia only in 1950, followed by the adoption of a Cooperative Societies Law in 1951. A **marketing cooperative**, dealing mainly in groundnuts, the Gambia's principal export, was established in Kombo in 1955. Growth in numbers of cooperatives warranted the formation in 1959 of a national **union**, the Gambia Cooperative Central Banking and Marketing Union (later renamed the Gambia Cooperative Union). While there have been some efforts to create consumer and **fishery cooperatives**, they have not been very successful. In 1986 the **ICA West Africa Regional Office** reported the presence of 62 **agricultural**

cooperatives with 100,000 members and 65 **credit unions** with 3,500 members. The **ICA** Regional Office reported in 1996 that there was a total cooperative membership of 100,000, 8.3% of the population.

GANEY, MARION MOSES (1904–1984). An American Catholic priest who organized the first **credit union** in **Belize** in 1943 and who subsequently worked full-time for credit union development in that country, organizing 22 credit unions and a league by 1953. Reassigned by the Church to **Fiji**, he undertook credit union development there, including the establishment of a training school named in honor of the American credit union leader **Roy Bergengren**. Ganey was also active in initiating credit union activity in Western **Samoa**.

GARBADO, GEORGE (1863–1928). A French **consumer cooperative** activist, his early efforts included co-founding the Union d'Amiens in 1892; he became its manager in 1898. He was also instrumental in forming Le Cordonnière Ouvrière, a **production cooperative**, in 1902. He joined the French cooperative **wholesale society** in 1908 and was active in its leadership. From 1918 to 1922 he served on the Superior Cooperative Council of **France**.

GARIBOTTI, GIUSEPPE (died 1930). An Italian cooperative leader, he held important positions in government, cooperatives and provident institutions. He was active in cooperatives in Cremona and Brescia, and was for a number of years a member of the Advisory Committee of the National League of Cooperatives of **Italy;** he was appointed its general secretary in 1922. He served as a member of the Italian Parliament.

GARRIDO TORTOSA, FERNANDO (1821–1883). A pioneer of the Spanish cooperative movement, in 1864 he established the Obrera Mataronense at Mataro, a workers' cooperative for spinners and weavers. He wrote two books that are important to the emerging cooperative movement in **Spain** and also part of the early defining of cooperative theory: *El trabajador asociado* in 1873 and *La cooperación, teorético-practico* in 1879.

GEBHARD, HANNÉS (1864–1933). An academic and cooperator in **Finland**, he is considered the father of the Finnish cooperative movement, which he helped found in 1895. He devoted most of his life to the development of **agricultural cooperatives**. In 1899, before there was any formal Finnish legal authority for such action, he was one of the organizers of the Pellervo Society, which became a national cooperative association. By 1902 it had 50 affiliated cooperative societies, 596 by 1905, 1,930 by 1910, and 6,835 (with over 800,000 members) by 1932. Internationally, Gebhard was associated with the activities of the **ICA** but was never active in the day-to-day leadership. He was involved in a League of Nations study of cooperatives in **Bulgaria**. For the last 10 years of his life he was the manager of the **credit cooperative** movement.

GEIGER, ERIK GUSTAV. A Swedish poet and historian who in 1825 introduced the cooperative idea to **Sweden**. He was the author of early works in Swedish on cooperatives.

GENERAL MANAGER. A person employed as the principal officer to run the business affairs of a large cooperative. The general manager is answerable to the **board of directors** and through it to the **annual general meeting** of the members. This position may alternatively be designated as managing director or chief executive officer.

GENERAL MEETING. An assembly where all members in good standing of a cooperative may attend and vote, and where all important matters are discussed and decided upon. Provisions for the scheduling and agendas of such meetings are usually included in the **bylaws** of the society. *See also* ANNUAL GENERAL MEETING.

GEORGIA. The General Union of Consumer Societies was established in 1919 and was an **ICA** member from 1921 to 1924 during a period of Georgian independence. While Georgia was a republic in the **Union of Soviet Socialist Republics**, cooperatives were incorporated in the national **Centrosoyus**. Since Georgia's latest independence, the cooperative movement has been in some turmoil and is still in the process of refining and reconstituting itself. In 1993, ICA reported a membership of 1,700,000 in 128 primary societies. In 1996, they reported there were 105 **consumer cooperatives** with a membership of 200,000, 3.8% of the population.

GERMAN DEVELOPMENT ASSISTANCE. Assistance to cooperatives is viewed as important in the German development assistance program, as part of its support to self-help organizations. Most German assistance to cooperatives, however, is channeled through non-governmental organ-

izations with the largest portion going through three political foundations, the Konrad Adenauer Foundation, the Friedrich Ebert Foundation,
and the Friedrich Naumann Foundation. The Adenauer Foundation has
been particularly supportive of **credit union** development.

**GERMAN DEVELOPMENT ASSISTANCE ASSOCIATION FOR
SOCIAL HOUSING (DESWOS).** An arm of the German cooperative
housing movement, it supports development projects, conducts training
programs and seminars, and is involved in other housing-related activities in **developing countries**. In 1987 it was supporting 27 projects in 13
countries.

GERMANY. The year 1845 is noted as the beginning of cooperatives in
Germany. It was the year in which the first German society was organized in Chemnitz, and **Victor Aimé Huber** was advocating cooperation
as an economic solution, particularly for the problem of housing. In 1846
Friedrich Wilhelm Raiffeisen began his work in support of cooperation,
followed in 1849 by **Herman Schulze-Delitzsch**'s establishment of cooperatives for shoemakers and joiners. The next 30 years of German cooperative history belonged essentially to these two men and their collaborators. Raiffeisen oversaw the emergence of a rural credit and
agricultural network based on strong local units, federated regionally and
united nationally into a central **cooperative bank** and a **federation** of
agricultural cooperatives. Schulze-Delitzsch operated in more urban
areas, developing credit structures for artisans and small entrepreneurs.
By 1864 there were 400 such local groups. The next year a central cooperative bank to service their needs was established at Weimar. Two years
later Schulze-Delitzsch, during his membership in the Prussian Parliament, engineered the passage of the first German **cooperative legislation**.

Subsequent years, up to World War I, saw the establishment of the
consumer movement with a national wholesale organization in 1897 and
a national **consumer cooperative union** in 1903 under the leadership of
Heinrich Kaufmann. Housing cooperatives began their period of organization in 1889. An alternative national agricultural cooperative
union, later to unite with the Raiffeisen groups, was organized in Hesse
by **Wilhelm Haas**. The Central Cooperative Bank of Prussia, later to become the **Deutsche Genossenschaftskasse (DG Bank),** was organized
in 1895. A national association representing the growing number of non-
agricultural **production cooperatives** was formed in 1901 under the

leadership of Karl Korthaus. Auditing unions formed in increasing numbers in response to changes in the **cooperative law** that made audits mandatory in the various sectoral cooperatives.

At the outbreak of World War I there were 34,568 cooperatives in Germany with a total membership of 6,250,000. During the war the German national associations formed the Freier Ausschuss der Deutschen Genossenschaftsverbände (Free Committee of German Cooperative Associations), which still exists as a loose national confederation. The post–World War I years were a period of further growth and elaboration, mergers of rival sectoral associations and establishment of central business organizations to carry out specialized functions for various sectors or for the entire movement. By the end of 1934 the number of cooperatives and members reached a peak of 53,348 societies with a membership of nearly 9,000,000. All was to change quickly, however, with the onset of a National Socialist (Nazi) government that was hostile to **cooperative democracy** and independence and that found the socialist orientation of the consumer movement particularly offensive. The organizational structure of the consumer cooperatives was quickly abolished and its functions assumed by the Nazi Deutsche Arbeitsfront. Other sectoral unions were placed under strong, centralized governmental supervision and control. The downward spiral of German cooperatives was completed with the liquidation of all central organizations at the end of World War II in 1945.

Reconstruction of the cooperative movement was quick in coming, however, and in all the four zones of postwar occupation there were new or revived cooperative structures. In the Russian zone, soon to become the German Democratic Republic (GDR), a consumer movement emulating that in the **Union of Soviet Socialist Republics** was established. **Audit** unions in all three western zones were reactivated, the first as early as in 1945, and by 1949, with the establishment of the Federal Republic of Germany (FRG), they were a national reality. In 1948 the consumer federation and the Raiffeisen union were reestablished. The housing cooperatives federation followed in 1949. A loose union of central associations was revived in the FRG. Growth and elaboration of the sectoral movements in both parts of Germany continued, and soon they had reestablished themselves as key elements in the national economies. A publication of the DG Bank reported that in the FRG at the beginning of 1985 there were 10,185 cooperatives with 14,018,037 members (22.8% of the population).

The GDR was created in 1949, encompassing the area of the Russian zone of occupation of Germany after World War II. It adopted an orthodox Marxist-Leninist model for its economy with most industry nation-alized and a collectivized agriculture imposed. Provision was made for cooperatives to be the principal economic structure in the consumer sector and the Verband der Konsumgenossenschaften der DDR, established in 1945, was acknowledged as the vehicle for its implementation throughout the country, including a comprehensive production and distribution system. A **cooperative college** was established in Dresden, and the movement assumed a role in international cooperative affairs, including membership in the **ICA**. It sponsored activities designed to support cooperatives in **developing countries**, particularly those that had opted for "socialist paths for development," and to support cooperative leaders in other countries who shared this perspective. Just prior to the collapse of the East German system in 1989–90 the ICA reported a GDR cooperative membership of 4,600,000 (28.3% of the population) in 198 consumer cooperatives. Since that date and the reintegration of the former GDR into Germany, steps have been taken to integrate the consumer cooperatives with those in the rest of the country and to reintroduce cooperatives in other economic sectors.

The collapse and dissolution of the GDR and its reintegration into a united Germany has posed adjustment problems for cooperatives, problems that are still playing themselves out in a united Germany where the national economic policy is one of a "socially responsive market economy" and where cooperatives are striving to be a system beyond both individualism and collectivism.

Recent ICA statistics on the status of the combined movement in the unified Germany showed that in 1996 there were 10,320 cooperatives with a membership of 22,322,050 (27.9% of the population) in the following sectors: agriculture—4,434 cooperatives/with 3,100,000 members; consumer—47/1,580,000; housing—1,940/3,151,050; insurance—1/na; savings and credit (banks)—2,421/14,200,000; and worker productive—1,477/291,000.

Support of the international development of cooperatives has been a continuous part of the activities of German cooperatives. During the period since World War II this has manifested itself in a number of ways. The **International Raiffeisen Union** was established in 1968, bringing together sectors of movements in other countries that shared its orientation. The German political foundations, Konrad Adenauer, Friedrich Ebert and Friedrich Naumann, have all included assistance to cooperatives in developing countries as part of their programs. The German universities have formed a network of cooperative institutes, which in international conferences have elaborated the present condition and future possibilities of cooperatives throughout the world.

GHANA. Cooperatives emerged in Ghana (then the Gold Coast) in 1928 as a mechanism for dealing with the country's major crop and export commodity, cacao. That remains the main focus of the **agricultural cooperatives.** A Cooperative Societies Ordinance was passed in 1931, modeled after the **cooperative law** in **India.** In the 1940s a national **federation** was organized, a government department concerned with cooperative promotion and supervision established, a **cooperative bank** initiated, and a Cooperative Wholesale Establishment organized as a source of supply to the consumer sector of the movement. **Credit unions,** initially assisted by missionaries and encouraged by the government, were first formed in the 1950s. From that period to the present, the status of the cooperative movement has waxed and waned with changing governments and a number of military coups, some of which have viewed cooperatives very positively, others with indifference or even disdain. The cooperatives, in response, have tended to wait until a new government indicated to them what it wanted them to do. Despite all this, the movement grew over the years (though it is difficult to find consistent, comparable statistics). An **ICA** study done in conjunction with assistance organizations from **Germany** and **Norway** in 1986 reported that there were 8,085 cooperatives (3,935 agriculture; 385 credit unions; 1,818 service; and 1,947 worker productive) with a total membership of 3,500,000 (memberships by types of cooperatives were not reported). This constituted 27.6% of the national population at that time. Difficult economic conditions in recent years have taken their toll on the cooperative movement, as on the whole country.

GIDE, CHARLES (1847–1932). Born of a Huguenot family in Uzès, **France,** he was a lawyer, academic, economist and cooperator. He served on the law faculty at Bordeaux and in 1883 published *Principles of Political Economy,* which has been translated into over 50 languages and by 1932 had gone through 27 editions. He was a co-worker with **Edouard de Boyve** and **Auguste Fabre** in the **School of Nîmes** where for 46 years he contributed to *L'Émancipation—Journal d'éducation coopérative.* In 1900 he published *La Coopération,* in which he tied his cooperative philosophy to the **Rochdale Principles.** He was among the French delegates to the **ICA** Congress at Manchester in 1902, which gave him an opportunity to make a pilgrimage to Rochdale. From 1900 to 1921 he held the chair of comparative social economics in Paris and from 1920 to 1930 the chair of cooperation at the College of France. Twenty volumes of his works, published by the National Federation of Consumers' Cooperatives of France, reveal the significant economic theory that he developed for cooperatives during his 40 years of participation in the movement. Gide was an important influence in developing and maintaining the political (party) **neutrality** of French cooperatives. He served on the ICA Central and Executive Committees for 30 years. Among the results of his influence on the international movement were the continuing emphasis on the role of cooperatives in achieving and maintaining international **peace** and his advocacy of an international **cooperative flag**.

GIERKE, OTTO FRIEDRICH VON (1841–1921). A cooperative pioneer in **Germany**, he developed the rationale for **cooperative legislation**. In 1868 he introduced the term **cooperative law** into the vocabulary of the movement.

GILL, T. H. (SIR HARRY) (1885–1955). A British cooperator, trade unionist and politician, he started his career as a railway clerk, becoming president of the Railway Clerks Association from 1919 to 1932, during which time he also served as a Labour Member of Parliament and as president of the York Cooperative. In 1932 Gill was elected a director of the **English Cooperative Wholesale Society**, then its president in 1948. He served as the president of the **ICA** for the period 1948–55. He was knighted by the British government in 1950.

GJÖRES, AXEL. A mid-20th-century cooperative leader in **Sweden**, he set up the first Swedish cooperative study group in 1920. He served for a number of years as editor of *Konsumentbladet*, the publication of **Kooperativa Förbundct (KF)**, and later he became general secretary of KF. In 1938 he was Minister of Supply in the Swedish government. Gjöres was a member of the **ICA** Executive Committee for a number of years. He was author of *Cooperatives in Sweden*.

GLEN, A. ROD (1919–1980). Journalist, trade union officer, municipal official and **credit union** pioneer in **Canada**, his initial cooperative activity was in British Columbia. In 1960 he was elected the first non-U.S. citizen to be president of the Credit Union National Association International, later to become the **World Council of Credit Unions**. Glen was among the founders of the **Canadian Cooperative Credit Society**, the national **apex organization** for Canadian credit unions at the time.

GODIN, J. B. (1817–1888). Leader of the fledgling cooperative productive societies in **France**, Godin was attracted to the **utopian** ideas of **Charles Fourier**, who advocated combining capital, labor and talent into cooperative production societies. In 1840, Godin set up a small workshop employing 30 workers. He later moved to Guise where by the time of his death his **production cooperatives** were employing over 1,500. To service the needs of his members he reduced working hours, established funds for mutual aid and medicine, and constructed housing in which a wide range of social and economic services was provided to residents.

GOEDHART, G. J. D. C. (1857–1945). By profession Goedhart was head of the Bureau of Official Reporters of the Dutch Parliament. However, he found his real life's work in propagating the cooperative idea and building the cooperative movement in the **Netherlands,** a task on which he worked for 63 years. At the Hague he was soon elected to the board and later became chairman of the cooperative, Eigen Hulp (Self Help). Subsequently he became a member of the Executive Committee of the Dutch Cooperative Union and was for many years its president. Goedhart was also, from 1914 to 1926, the chairman of the directors of the then Handelskamer, the Dutch Cooperative Wholesale Society. He was prominent as a representative of Dutch cooperatives in the **ICA**, serving on the Central Committee beginning in 1900 and as president for the period 1921–27, a critical time in which relationships were being reestablished among cooperators who had been opposing national partisans during World War I. Goedhart completed a history of the Dutch cooperative movement just prior to his death. A foundation, the Goedhart-Stichting, was established in 1938 by Dutch cooperatives in his honor. The foundation has produced materials in Dutch of relevance to cooperative development and operation.

GOOD, WILLIAM C. (1876–1967). A Canadian cooperative leader, he was among the founders of the **Cooperative Union of Canada** in 1909, later serving as vice president (1915) and president (1921). An important agricultural leader in **Canada**, he helped organize the United Farmers Cooperative in 1914. Elected to the Canadian Parliament, he was a strong advocate for cooperative development.

GRANGE. *See* NATIONAL GRANGE OF THE PATRONS OF HUSBANDRY.

GRAY, J. C. (1854–1912). Son of a Baptist minister, he was raised in Yorkshire. He left school at 13, taking employment with the Lancashire and Yorkshire Railway Company. At 20 he became assistant secretary to the Hebden Bridge Cooperative Fustian Productive Society, and soon he became its secretary. Gray's activities as a cooperative leader, his writings, and his lecturing at cooperative meetings brought him to the attention of **Edward Vansittart Neale,** who recruited him as assistant secretary to the Central Committee of the British Cooperative Union in 1883. Eight years later he succeeded Neale as general secretary of the Union. As the international movement was emerging he took it as a particular interest and was a key figure in the formation of the **ICA,** smoothing over the ideological and organizational disputes that beset its early days. Gray served as the secretary of the ICA for the period 1902–07.

GREECE. Even though one of the earliest cooperatives in Europe, the Red Yarn Society, was established at Ambelakia in 1780 and there were island shipping and mining cooperatives in the 19th century, the modern cooperative movement in Greece is essentially a 20th-century phenomenon with the first **agricultural cooperatives** dating from 1900, the first **cooperative law** from 1914 and the first **federation/union** from 1924. The Greek movement has been and remains mainly an agricultural cooperative structure—7,255 societies with 934,863 members in 1990. While a majority of agricultural cooperatives have provided **agricultural credit,** they have also organized around specific products—honey, cattle, figs and other fruits, olive and olive oil products, sultanas, tobacco and wine. A network of urban cooperatives makes up the remainder of Greek cooperatives, 191 with 48,034 members in 1990. These cooperatives engage in diverse activities: consumer societies that provide products and services to members and non-members; professional and manufacturing societies that either provide members with raw materials and products or establish cooperatives for the collective work of their members; construction cooperatives; and workers' cooperatives where groups of people own and produce collectively. There are also forestry, **school** and **transport cooperatives.** Special cooperatives for women are a recent development. The government has taken a keen interest in and had an active involvement in cooperatives, with the Agricultural Bank of Greece being a major source of credit, particularly for agricultural cooperatives. The **cooperative legislation** of the country has structured and legitimated this role for government, some would say to the detriment of cooperative independence. The **ICA** reported that there were

6,970 cooperatives in 1996 with memberships totaling 1,043,381 in the following sectors: agricultural—6,800 societies/with 782,000 members; consumer—84/200,000; credit unions/banks—32/55,431; insurance—1/na; worker productive—23/2,000; and other—30/3,950. Cooperative membership was 9.9% of the population.

GREENING, EDWARD OWEN (1836–1923). One of the leading pioneers of British cooperation and of the international cooperative movement, he became involved with cooperatives in Manchester and was among those who founded the **Cooperative Union of the U.K.** in 1869. The first congress of the Union that year was organized largely under his stimulus. Greening was among the founders of the Cooperative Productive Federation in 1882 and the Labor Co-partnership Association in 1884. He also acted as manager of the Agricultural and Horticultural Association. He was attracted from an early date to those involved in the Christian Socialist movement and became a leading figure in their activities. In 1892 he, with **Edward Vansittart Neale**, introduced a resolution at the British Cooperative Congress, endorsing the principle of an international cooperative alliance (the resolution was approved). From that point on, Greening was a leader in the formation of the **ICA**, the original statutes of which were drafted in his home. Greening served as the secretary of the **Alliance** for the period 1895–1902. He prevailed upon the British Foreign Office to solicit, through British embassies, information on the status of cooperative development in European countries, and a collection of this information was issued as a Blue Book in 1886, the first international survey of cooperation. He was a prolific writer on social, political and horticultural subjects in addition to cooperation. His literary works include *A Cooperative Traveler Abroad* and *A Democratic Co-partnership*. He was also the editor of several journals.

GREENWOOD, ABRAHAM (1824–1911). A British cooperator from **Rochdale**, he was a wool sorter for 26 years. He authored the plan for the **English Cooperative Wholesale Society** and served as its first president in 1863. He was from 1874 to 1898 the manager of the Society and its **cooperative bank**.

GRENADA. The political unrest and economic difficulties that Grenada has experienced in its 20-plus years of independence, including an armed intervention by the **United States**, have not provided a congenial environment for cooperative development in this small island country. A Cooperative Societies Ordinance was passed in 1955 in pre-independence Grenada, and the first product of it and other cooperative interests was **credit unions**, the first six of which were established in 1958. A total of 28 had been established by independence in 1974, and credit unions still essentially constitute the cooperative movement in Grenada. **WOCCU** cited 19 active societies with 17,635 members in 1996. The **COPAC** Country Information Note on Grenada, published in 1985, identified 15 other cooperatives with a total of 599 members. None of them was of great economic importance at the time, but they indicate interest and experience upon which future structures might be built. Membership in cooperatives in Grenada in 1996 of 18,344 involved an estimated 19.3% of the population.

GRENFELL, WILFRED THOMASON (1865–1940). A British-trained physician and surgeon who moved to **Canada** in 1892 and took up work and residence in Labrador and Newfoundland. He was instrumental there in the formation of basic health and social service infrastructures— five hospitals, seven nursing stations, two large schools and cooperative stores. He acted as an itinerant doctor on ships he owned that annually plied the coastal waters off Newfoundland and Labrador, servicing the health needs of coastal towns. In 1895 he founded the first cooperative in the Province of Newfoundland at Red Bay. Dr. Grenfell organized two trappers' cooperatives, Flower's Cove and the Caribou Trading Company, at Brig Bay, but both were forced out of existence by the opposition of local merchants. The Spot Cash Cooperative Company was established at Saint Anthony, Newfoundland, in 1913. It prospered and was reorganized in 1940 according to **Rochdale Principles** and renamed in his honor as the Grenfell Memorial Cooperative.

GREY, EARL ALBERT HENRY GEORGE (1851–1917). Son of a general, grandson of a prime minister, inheritor of a landed estate, Earl Grey could have been, like many of his counterparts, a person of ease and comfort. Instead, partly motivated by an early introduction to **cooperative principles** and ideals, he was a man of action, committed to reform and to support for the needs of working people. In 1895 he was asked to preside at the founding **congress** of the **ICA**. The next year found him administrator of Rhodesia, and in 1904 he became governor general of Canada. Keeping in touch with cooperative leaders wherever he was in the world, Earl Grey took an interest in local cooperative affairs. In Canada he was particularly taken with the work of **Alphonse Desjardins**

and the emerging *caisse populaire* movement. He acted as honorary president of the ICA for the period 1895–1917, lending his prestige to the growing international cooperative movement.

GRUNDTVIG, BISHOP NICOLAI F. S. (1783–1872). A Danish bishop of the Lutheran Church who gave particular attention to the harsh economic life of Danish peasants. He urged farmers to join together cooperatively and to ameliorate their own problems. Further, he felt that the cooperative approach, through its emphasis on democratic participation and control, offered better prospects for significant accomplishments through evolutionary change than the revolutionary approach being urged by others. An outgrowth of Bishop Grundtvig's thinking and work were the **folk high schools in Denmark**.

GUADELOUPE. Formerly a colony, now an overseas territory of France in the Caribbean. No current information about the status of cooperative development was obtained. In the early 1950s the **ILO** reported the presence of 9 cooperatives of banana producers with an associated cooperative union. Six distillery cooperatives were also carrying on operations, as were 2 **credit cooperatives**, a cooperative book shop, and several **school cooperatives**. No recent data or statistics on cooperative development were available.

GUATEMALA. While **cooperative laws** were enacted in 1903 and 1906 to structure and encourage cooperative development, little remains today of this initial effort—a **mutual aid** society in Guatemala City and a shoemaker society in Coatepeque. A popular revolt in the country in 1944–45 inaugurated a new period of cooperative interest, and provisions were included in the new constitution endorsing cooperatives. A government cooperative department was created in 1945 and further **cooperative legislation** passed in 1949. Active organization of credit and other types of cooperatives began in the late 1940s and early 1950s, and by 1970 there were 411 **registered societies**, 286 in agriculture, 113 savings and credit societies and small numbers of consumer, fisheries, housing, and industrial cooperatives. Most of these had developed in response to private initiatives rather than active government promotion and organization. National **federations** representing the major cooperative sectors emerged in the 1950s, accompanied by regional federations in certain areas of the country. A national confederation was established in 1968. Cooperative growth continued, impacted, as was all in Guatemala, by military coups and armed insurrection. However, in recent years there has been a falling-off in organizations after they had reached a peak in 1985 of 939 cooperatives with a membership of 212,000—2.4% of the population. An **ICA Regional Office for Central America** report in 1997 reported 1,174 cooperatives with a membership of 277,134 in the following sectors: agriculture—554 cooperatives/with 61,628 members; consumer—171/19,775; fisheries—4/127; housing—83/10,264; savings and credit—220/177,913; worker productive and services—136/7,287; and others—6/140. Cooperative membership was 2.9% of the population. A **USAID** assistance program involving U.S. cooperative organizations has been working in the 1990s to help strengthen the country's cooperative structures.

GUINEA, REPUBLIC OF. Guinea, like most francophone African countries, experimented in fairly rapid order with a variety of structural arrangements, urged by France, that it was hoped would coordinate cooperative development with national development planning and contribute to efforts aimed at development of the rural areas in which most of the population resided. All of this emphasis on planning, however, produced very little cooperative structure in Guinea. The first cooperative was formed in 1931, serving mainly the colonist population. A system of **mutual** societies for the indigenous population was established in 1936. **Cooperative legislation** was passed in 1946. **ILO** publications in 1975 and 1988 did not include any statistical data attesting to the number and types of cooperatives in the country. The **ILO** *Directory* **(1988)** reported only the existence of a Department of Cooperative and Mutual Benefit Societies in the Ministry of Agriculture and a National Agricultural Development Bank, with no details on cooperative organizations. An ILO Mission Report in 1989 identified 104 cooperatives with 4,323 members in the following sectors: agriculture—59 cooperatives/with 2,077 members; building/housing—12/546; and industrial—33/1,700. In total they constituted 0.06% of the population.

GUINEA-BISSAU. The Portuguese left little development heritage in their African colonies that became independent in the 1970s. Guinea-Bissau was among the least affected by development efforts and in current **World Bank** statistics, in almost any category, it is still among the least developed countries. The first **cooperative law** and the first cooperatives were established only in 1971. The first union of cooperatives, made up of veterans of the war for independence, came into being in

1973. The **ICA Regional Office for West Africa** reported in 1986 that there were 11 cooperatives (2 agriculture and 9 worker productive) with 326 members in a country with a population of about one million. Cooperative membership constituted 0.03% of the population.

GUYANA. The beginnings of a cooperative tradition in Guyana date from the period after 1839, when newly freed slaves worked and saved money, which they used to make joint purchases of large tracts of land that formerly were cotton and/or sugar plantations. Thirty-eight such cooperative villages were established between 1839 and 1849, covering over 15,000 acres of land. Over the years they disappeared as organized units, and it was not until a hundred years later, in 1933, that Guyana saw its first modern cooperatives, consumer and credit, but these too were short-lived. In 1945 a government cooperative officer was appointed, and he launched a serious effort to encourage organized cooperation, with a focus on credit societies. Responding to a directive from the British Colonial Office, a **cooperative law** was passed in 1948 and a cooperative department established. The first cooperative **union** followed in 1949. From that point there was a rapid growth of cooperatives of many types, so that by 1964, just prior to independence, there were 567 societies with 42,551 members and a national cooperative **federation** had been established. In the first post-independence election, Forbes Burnham was elected prime minister, and in 1970 he proclaimed Guyana a "Cooperative Republic," a title that the country still officially bears. He and his government articulated elaborate schemes for achieving such a republic, but political and economic events have largely frustrated their grand design. Cooperatives have continued to grow nonetheless, so that the **ILO** *Directory* **(1988)** could report that in 1985 there were 1,505 societies with 165,797 members. More than half of these were members of **credit cooperatives** (765 societies with 114,431 members). Other types of cooperatives reported included **agricultural, consumer,** fisheries, **housing, worker productive,** and others. Cooperative membership was 17.5% of the national population.

GYÖRGY, ANDREAS (1848–1927). A lawyer, Minister of Agriculture, and one of the earliest pioneers of the Hungarian cooperative movement, he was a representative of his country's cooperatives in the **ICA** for many years. He was active in Protestant movements and was among the founders of the Presbyterian World Alliance. When cooperation was introduced in **Hungary,** he worked with **Count Alexander Karolyi** and actively promoted the establishment of several hundred societies in Eastern Hungary (Transylvania). While employed in the Ministry of Agriculture, he was responsible for the organization of Hungarian agricultural representation in foreign countries. During this period György attended cooperative congresses in many countries and established a network of international cooperative collaboration. He was named to the **Committee of Honor of the International Cooperative Alliance** in recognition of his work.

H

HAAS, WILHELM (1839–1913). A German **agricultural cooperative** leader, he was born in Darmstadt, studied law at the University of Giessen, and entered the service of the state of Hesse. He established an agricultural distributive society at Friedberg in 1872 and was elected director of this society. The following year he organized an agricultural cooperative **union**. These proved to be significant beginnings from which Haas, while in public service and in local and national parliaments, gave leadership to the organization of German farmers into a national organization to represent their interests. This eventually became the Imperial Union of German Agricultural Societies, which, at the time of his death, is said to have included 24,800 agricultural cooperatives societies having about 2,200,000 members. Building upon his experience in Germany, he was instrumental in the formation of the International Federation of Agricultural Societies, of which he became president.

HAITI. The first Haitian cooperative was established in 1937, three years after the close of a period of **United States** military occupation from 1915 to 1934. The first **union/federation**, at Point-à-Piment, was established the next year and **cooperative legislation** was enacted in 1939. **Cooperatives** for **consumers**, **credit** and **transport** were formed in the 1940s, followed by a **cooperative development** project financed by the United States Government in 1951 and the formation of a National Cooperative Council in 1953. The cooperative movement grew slowly during the period of the Duvalier government, and by 1973 there were 61 cooperatives (19 in agriculture, 37 savings and credit, and 5 miscellaneous others) with a membership of 16,994 (0.3% of the population). Since that time political and economic turmoil, accompanied by coups and countercoups, has seriously eroded even these modest beginnings. A **UNDP** survey in 1990, the latest date for which statistical data was available, reported that there were 300 cooperatives with 100,000 members, 1.45% of the population.

HALL, FRED (1866–1938). Born in Rochdale and educated at the University of Manchester, he was an early advocate and then founder and principal of the **Cooperative College, Loughborough,** where full-time classes began in 1919. He also served as advisor of studies in the Education Department of the **Cooperative Union.**

HANDICRAFT COOPERATIVE. A cooperative association organized to benefit a group of craftspeople through one or more of the following: joint production, purchase of supplies, provision of technical aid and marketing of products.

HARPER, R. K. A British cooperator, in the 1950s he was head of an **ILO** cooperative project in the **Philippines,** during which he developed a wide range of materials to be used in the development of cooperatives in that country. He had formerly served in the Indian Civil Service.

HASUMI, YASUYSHI (1891–1964). On concluding his law studies at Tokyo University, he joined the Ministry of Home Affairs and subsequently became head of the Cooperative Section in the Ministry of Agriculture. In 1940 he was named president of the Central Cooperative Bank. In 1951 he became president of the Central Union of Agricultural Cooperatives, where he remained until his death. He was also a director of the Cooperative College. He was elected to the Central Committee of the **ICA** in 1957 and served there until his death.

HAYWARD, SIR FRED (1876–1944). A British cooperative leader, he was one of the founders of the Burslem Cooperative Society in 1901 and served as its managing secretary from 1920 to 1936. He was chairman of the British National Cooperative Authority. In the **ICA** he was a member of the Central Committee, 1921–44, and of the Executive Committee, 1934–44.

HEALTH COOPERATIVE. An organization of people who join together to make cooperative group arrangements to meet their health care needs.

HEDBERG, ANDERS (1881–1985). A cooperator in **Sweden,** he was a leading theorist of the Swedish **consumer cooperatives**, focusing much of his concern on matters of production, particularly for international trade among cooperatives. This interest led to the formation in 1931 of **Nordisk Andelsförbund,** a five-country Scandinavian **wholesale society.** Hedberg was a frequent contributor of articles to the *Review of International Cooperation.*

HERLIHY, NORA (1919–1988). A pioneer leader in the Irish **credit union movement.**

HERMES, ANDREAS (1878–1964). Described in the *Review of International Cooperation* as the greatest leader of German agricultural cooperation since **Friedrich Wilhelm Raiffeisen,** he first came to international attention as director of the scientific and technical division of the International Institute of Agriculture at Rome, the forerunner of the **FAO,** where he served from 1911 until the outbreak of war in 1914. Hermes spent the decade following the war in service to German agriculture and the national economy, in the public sector as Minister of Food and Agriculture and Minister of Finance and among cooperators as president of the Christian Peasants Union and the National Union of Agricultural Societies. He was a member of the **ILO**'s joint committee of cooperative producers' and consumers' organizations. An open and uncompromising foe of the Nazi regime, he experienced 12 years of imprisonment, exile, war and conspiracy against the Nazi regime, narrowly escaping death at their hands. With the joining of the three western zones of occupation in Germany following the war, an opportunity presented itself to him to reorganize the Raiffeisen **agricultural cooperative** movement, reuniting the regional unions and reestablishing the authority of the **apex federation.** Hermes was instrumental in the formation of the **International Federation of Agricultural Producers** and in the revival of the European Confederation of Agriculture.

HIGHER INSTITUTE OF COOPERATIVE AND MANAGERIAL STUDIES. In association with the Egyptian Society for Cooperative Studies and the University of Ain Shams, the Institute, located in Cairo, Egypt, provides courses in Arabic dealing with cooperatives for students from Middle Eastern countries. It also engages in **cooperative research,** organizes meetings and international conferences and publishes the *Egyptian Magazine of Cooperative Studies.*

HIRATA, COUNT (1849–1925). Co-founder with Viscount Shinagawa (who died in 1900) of the Japanese cooperative movement, he was active from 1890 in diffusion of the cooperative ideal in **Japan**. He was introduced to cooperation while a student of law at Heidelberg University and had an opportunity to see its development on a trip to Germany 10 years later. He initiated the Central Union of Cooperative Societies in 1905 and was its first president, holding that office until 1922. He held high office in the Japanese government and was Keeper of the Privy Seal at the time of his death.

HÖGSBRO, SVEND (1855–1915). Son of the local superintendent of the Danish National High School, he studied law and became a parliamentary reporter, which afforded him an intimate knowledge of political, social and economic conditions. It was as a lawyer that he became involved with cooperatives, representing their interests in many important lawsuits. In 1892 Högsbro was elected to the central board of the Danish Wholesale Society. In 1898 he founded the Andelsudvalg, the Central Union of Danish Societies. He served in the Danish government as Minister of Public Works and later as Minister of Justice. He was elected a member of the **ICA** Central Committee in 1902 and served until 1909.

HOLMAN, CHARLES W. (1886–1971). An American **agricultural cooperative** leader who provided leadership in some of the most important legislative battles affecting cooperatives, including the **Capper-Volstead Act** (1922) and the Cooperative Marketing Act of 1926. Holman was among the founders of the National Milk Producers' Federation and headed the organization until his retirement in 1955. He was one of the organizers of the **American Institute of Cooperation** and was instrumental in obtaining a grant from the Rockefeller Foundation for the provision of its initial funding and for the establishment of its first national institute in 1925. He headed the American Institute of Cooperation until after World War II. Holman was a key organizer in the establishment of the **National Council of Farmer Cooperatives** in 1929. He was elected to the U.S. **Cooperative Hall of Fame** in 1985.

HOLYOAKE, GEORGE JACOB (1817–1906). A self-educated writer, publisher, politician and man of public affairs, he was a fighter for religious freedom, a free press, and the principles of **Rochdale**-style cooperation. He was an early disciple of **Robert Owen,** whose ideas of religious heterodoxy and **utopian** cooperation he shared. In 1843 Holyoake visited Rochdale and encouraged the early cooperators in their move to establish the now famous store in **Toad Lane**. He became their biographer as well, publishing his *History of the Equitable Pioneers of Rochdale* in 1856. He was among the founders of the **Cooperative Union** and served for many years on its board of directors. During this time Holyoake authored a history of the cooperative movement in England. His importance in the British movement is attested to by the fact that the headquarters of the Cooperative Union is named Holyoake House. Early on he was an advocate for internationalizing the cooperative movement and threw himself into the effort to form the **ICA**. He is recorded as the mover of the motion that named the new organization, "The International Cooperative Alliance." He remained active in its deliberations and operations until just prior to his death.

HONDURAS. The first society formed according to modern cooperative ideology was the Sociedad de Ladinos, established in 1876 in Marcala (still in existence and registered since 1954 as a savings and credit society). Sporadic organizing efforts of a similar nature, however, had limited success, and it was not until the 1930s that cooperatives of a lasting character were established. In 1936 the first cooperative **act** was decreed by the government. The 1950s were a time of serious organization on the part of cooperatives and of the establishment of a government agency to work with and supervise the emerging movement. The 1960s saw the formation of national **federations** for **agricultural**, **housing**, savings and **credit** and **transport cooperatives**. A national confederation emerged in 1974, the same year that a privately financed Cooperative Development Institute came into being. In 1991 the Honduran Confederation of Cooperatives reported that there were 767 cooperatives with 124,819 members (2.4% of the population). Cooperatives and their members were in the following sectors: agriculture (including forestry)—417 societies/with 21,460 members; consumer—16/506; fisheries—4/101; housing—35/4,491; multipurpose—29/5,236; savings and credit—188/90,050; student—4/270; and worker productive (including transport)—74/2,705. A 1998 report of the **ICA** indicated that cooperative membership that year had grown to 225,000 (4.0% of the population).

HONG KONG. Cooperatives were first organized in Hong Kong after World War II and consisted of horticultural, pig production and fishery societies. These had expanded in number sufficiently to warrant the organization of **federations** in the early 1950s. **Credit unions** were a later development, with credit union legislation passed in 1970 and a **credit union league** (federation) organized in 1972. The **ILO *Directory* (1988)**

reported that there were 151 **agricultural cooperatives** with 13,478 members in 1980 and 53 credit unions with 20,958 members in 1984. More recent statistical data on agricultural cooperatives was unavailable, but one source indicated that they were known to produce over half of the food provided in the local markets. The *1996 Statistical Report* of **WOCCU** shows Hong Kong as having 37 credit unions with a membership of 51,317. This would suggest a **cooperative penetration** of approximately 0.81% of the population. The effect on the cooperative movement of the return in 1997 of Hong Kong to Chinese rule remains to be seen.

HOUSING COOPERATIVE. An organization of people who join together to cooperatively provide housing to meet their needs. The organization may take a variety of forms, ranging from the joint construction of individually owned homes within a cooperatively owned housing estate to cooperatively owned apartments.

HOWARTH, CHARLES (1818–1868). A British cooperator, he was among the 28 founders of the **Rochdale Society of Equitable Pioneers** and is given the credit for formulating (at age 26) the **Rochdale Principles**. By trade he was a warper in a cotton mill.

HTTP://WWW.COOP.ORG. *See* INTERNET.

HUBER, JOHANNES (1879–1948). A **consumer cooperative** leader in **Switzerland**, his local cooperative activity was in Rorschach where he served on the board of directors and, from 1938 to 1948, as president. He was active in the work of the cooperative seminary at Freidorf and was president of the Swiss Committee on Inter-Cooperative Relations. He was active in the **ICA**, serving as part of an ICA delegation to **Russia** in 1922, and as a member of the Central and Executive Committees in the post–World War II period. He was a member of the ICA delegation to **Germany** in 1947 that assessed the postwar state of the German movement.

HUBER, VICTOR AIMÉ (1800–1869). A professor and pioneer cooperative organizer in **Germany**, he was an early leader in the activities that led to the establishment of the German **consumer cooperative** movement. He was also a major theorist of cooperative **housing**. Huber urged that such housing development be under collective ownership and that it be constructed using self-help and mutual assistance activities of the working class.

HULL, ISAAC HARVEY (1884–1972). A cooperator in the **United States**, he was author of important **cooperative legislation** while briefly (1923–25) a member of the Indiana state legislature. He was a member of the board of directors of the Indiana Farm Bureau Cooperative Association from 1921 to 1926 and its general manager from 1927 to 1946. He was among the founders of United Cooperatives (1930) and National Cooperatives (1933), two **unions** of **regional cooperatives**, and served as president of both for 12 years. (These two merged in 1972 to form Universal Cooperatives.) Hull was among the group organized by **CLUSA** in 1934 to visit European cooperatives, and he returned with an expanded enthusiasm for such organizations. He was instrumental in organizing **credit unions** among farmer cooperatives and was an early advocate and promoter of **rural electric cooperatives**.

HUMPHREY AMENDMENT. *See* HUMPHREY, HUBERT.

HUMPHREY, HUBERT (1911–1978). Mayor of Minneapolis, U.S. senator, and vice president of the U.S.A., he was a staunch legislative supporter of cooperatives and cooperative interests. He is widely recognized for the passage in 1961 of the Humphrey Amendment to the Foreign Assistance Act, an amendment that mandated U.S. governmental assistance for the promotion of cooperatives, in **developing countries**. This step led to the designation of **cooperative development organizations** in the **United States;** these have been given grants for work in the developing regions of the world. In 1973 Humphrey received the National Cooperative Statesmanship Award and in 1979 was inducted into the U.S. **Cooperative Hall of Fame**.

HUNGARY. The first Hungarian cooperative, a credit association at Beogterce, was established in 1850. The first **cooperative legislation**, which remained in effect until 1947, was passed in 1875. The first **federation**, Hangya, was established in 1898 by **Count Alexander Karolyi**, and the first national union was established in 1909. The development of the cooperative movement in Hungary in the early part of the 20th century followed much the same pattern as the rest of Europe, and cooperatives emerged and grew in the sectors of agriculture, consumers, credit, fisheries, housing, insurance and small industry (artisans). Readjustments in cooperative relationships took place with the dissolution of the Austro-Hungarian Empire at the end of World War I, and specific Hungarian national federations for each sector were established during the 1920s. These guided the movement through the World War II period. With the advent of a communist government after the war, cooperatives became integrated into and responsive to the centralized planning of that system. Cooperative growth, not always completely voluntary, continued until the collapse of that system in 1989–90.

New cooperative legislation, the Unified Cooperative Act and the Cooperative Transition Act, were passed in early 1992 and provided for conversion of the cooperative network into a private system, a transition that was mandated to be accomplished that year. The cooperative federations were reconstituted and the necessary transition completed, at least in a rudimentary sense, a process made simpler than in some other Eastern European countries by the fact that Hungarian cooperatives had increasingly established a growing independence under the former system.

A 1992 **ICA** study reported that a national cooperative union had been restructured, that 6 national sectoral organizations had been reconstituted or initiated, and that the movement was reporting a total of 8,651 cooperatives with 4,408,600 members (42.8% of the population). A subsequent report in 1998, reflecting 1996 statistics, noted a cooperative structure including 3,497 cooperatives with 3,013,000 members in the following sectors: agriculture—1,345 societies/with 300,000 members; consumer—260/559,000; housing—1,060/304,000; savings and credit—226/1,800,000; and worker productive 606/50,000 (est.). Cooperative membership in 1996 was 30.1% of the population.

I

ICA. *See* INTERNATIONAL COOPERATIVE ALLIANCE.

ICELAND. While the earliest stirrings of organized cooperation date back to as early as 1830, the first permanently established cooperatives date from 1882—two **supply** and **marketing cooperatives**. The first **consumer cooperative** dates from 1886 and the first national cooperative **federation**, a forerunner of the Iceland Cooperative Federation, was established in 1902. A **cooperative law** was enacted in 1937. Organized societies grew in number and importance and were involved in different sectors—animal husbandry (including slaughterhouses and meat exports), consumer supply, dairying, fisheries and various industries. Most of Iceland's cooperatives are members of Samband Islenskra Samvin-nufélaga, the Samband Federation of Iceland Cooperatives, and consti-tute a multipurpose enterprise that has a presence throughout the island, operating through some 250 outlets. The Federation has a shipping serv-ice, handling much of Iceland's imports and exports, a fish-processing enterprise in the **United States** and representational offices in **Denmark** and the **United Kingdom**. It is a member of the Nordic Cooperative Wholesale Society (NAF). It owns an oil distribution company, indus-trial enterprises and insurance companies, and operates a **cooperative college**. Collectively it is the largest business enterprise in Iceland. In addition to Samband, there is a national Icelandic Dairy Marketing As-sociation with 17 affiliated cooperatives and the Producers' Cooperative Society of Slaughterhouses of Southern Iceland with 4,561 individual members. In the **ILO** *Directory* **(1988)** Samband was reported to have 43 affiliated cooperatives with a membership of 46,804 (18.7% of the population). Taking Samband and the other national groups together, total cooperative membership in Iceland exceeds 20% of the population.

ILO. *See* INTERNATIONAL LABOUR ORGANIZATION.

ILO *DIRECTORY* (1988). The most recent (13th) edition of the *Interna-tional Directory of Cooperative Organizations* was published by the **ILO** in 1988. It identifies most of the important cooperaative organiza-tions in the world, and in a number of cases provides the most recent sta-tistical data available on the status of cooperatives in individual countries.

INDIA. Building on earlier indigenous traditions, the beginnings of a mod-ern cooperative movement in India date from the end of the 19th century. An organized system of cooperation, based on a Western model, was in-troduced in 1904 with the passage of the Cooperative Societies Act, fo-cusing on the encouragement and establishment of **credit cooperatives**. By 1906–07, 843 such cooperatives had been formed. The law was amended in 1912 with passage of the All-India Cooperative Societies Law, broadening the focus to include all types of cooperatives in all parts of the country. The response, voluntary as well as officially encouraged, was dramatic, with the number of cooperatives increasing by 50% in 1912 alone—from 8,177 to 12,324. A pattern of rapid growth of coop-eratives in most sectors of the economy continued, accompanied in 1919 with an **act** transferring primary responsibility for cooperative develop-ment and supervision to the then provincial (now state) governments.

Provincial legislation proliferated, as did accompanying bureaucracies. By 1922–23 there were 56,136 cooperatives with 2,102,446 members.

Growth and expansion of activities continued during the next 25 years, including the establishment of the National Cooperative Union of India in 1929. By independence and the partition of India and **Pakistan** in 1947, the local cooperative society had become a component part of village life in rural India, with cooperation expanding in urban areas as well. A national movement had emerged, reflected in the establishment of the National Cooperative Union of India in 1956. The newly independent government of India committed itself to being a planned welfare state with cooperatives as an integral institution, and by the time of the second five-year plan (1956–61) it had adopted a goal for the country of becoming a Socialist Cooperative Commonwealth. Implementation of these goals involved the government and government officials closely and deeply in the day-to-day affairs of cooperatives at a time, most now agree, when the emphasis should have been on expanding the independent character of the cooperatives as private, non-governmental economic and social endeavors. Between the dual forces of an increasingly sophisticated cadre of cooperative leaders, who wanted their movement to be theirs and to grow in scope and influence, and the (state and national) governments' determination to have cooperatives play vital and controlled roles in national development, conflict was assured. The cooperatives continued to grow and develop and to assert independent tendencies, while still bound by financial support and legislation that literally required the government to stay intimately involved in their operations. Clear plans and action to resolve this predicament await decisive moves on the part of both parties, but particularly on the part of the cooperative movement, which needs to risk giving up a preferential position as it asserts independence.

The decision of the **ICA** to hold its Central Committee meeting in India in 1989, the first such in a **developing country**, attested to the importance and influence of Indian cooperatives in the international cooperative community. India's movement is now the largest national movement in the world, both in numbers of cooperatives and in numbers of members. In 1991 the movement reported 401,139 cooperatives with 166,336,000 members (19.2% of the population). Its economic importance is reflected in the following facts: there are 19 national **federations** active in different sectors of the economy, with 124 counterparts in the different states of India; over 50% of the sugar produced in the country comes from cooperative sugar factories; two cooperative fertilizer companies supply some 70% of the fertilizer market; and there have been major cooperative achievements in dairy development. The above, as well as other measures to make cooperatives particularly relevant to the poor (still the vast majority of the Indian populace), all attest to the importance of cooperatives in Indian society. By 1995, membership had grown to 182,921,000 in 446,784 societies in the following sectors: agricultural—102,935 societies/with 20,244,000 members; consumer—23,903/11,234,000; fisheries—10,763/1,122,000; housing—71,040/5,933,000; savings and credit (banking)—41,500/43,716,000; worker productive—56,852/4,064,000; and others—139,191/96,608,000. Cooperatives at that time included 19.7% of the population.

INDIGENOUS COOPERATIVES. A term used (particularly in Africa) to differentiate cooperatives formed by or for local, domestic populations from those established to serve the interests and needs of colonists. Sometimes referred to as "native cooperatives."

INDONESIA. It was not until the first decade of the 20th century that there was an effort on the part of the Dutch to encourage and initiate cooperative societies for the indigenous population in Indonesia, and their efforts had only limited success. More serious efforts began in the 1920s, including the issuance of Indigenous Cooperative Societies Regulations in 1927, and the holding of a National Cooperative Congress in 1929. By 1934 there were 249 cooperatives (210 of them credit societies) with 18,606 members (14,889 in the credit societies). By the end of 1939 there were 560 societies with 52,555 members. Growth continued, even under Japanese occupation during World War II, and by the end of 1946 there were 2,500 cooperatives of different sorts throughout the country. The struggle for independence further encouraged growth, and by 1953 there were 8,624 **agricultural production, consumer, credit,** paddy storage, village **multipurpose** and **worker productive cooperatives.** A 1977 article in the **ILO's** *Cooperative Information* indicated that 23,679 cooperatives with 7,446,096 members were active in the production, processing and marketing of agricultural products (cloves, coconuts, coffee, rubber, sugar cane and tobacco), as well as in animal husbandry, dairying, distribution of consumer goods, fisheries, handicrafts, quarrying and mining, ship building, and textile and salt production. The government, through a Ministry of Cooperatives and the Directorate General of Cooperatives, has taken a direct and active interest in cooperative matters. The Directorate has had a staff of cooperative officers far outweighing in numbers and authority the leadership of the cooperative movement. Growth of the Indonesian movement has continued, and the **ICA Regional Office for Asia and the Pacific** reported that there were 32,249 cooperatives with 35,715,623 members in 1992 in the following sectors: agriculture—8,040 cooperatives/with 18,333,328 members; consumer—3,592/63,539; fisheries—736/67,793; multipurpose—8,596/13,800,000; savings and credit—4,205/685,983; worker productive—6,634/2,719,980; and others—446/45,000. Cooperative members made up 19.2% of the total population.

INDUSTRIAL AND PROVIDENT SOCIETIES ACT OF 1852. The world's first **cooperative legislation**, enacted in the **United Kingdom**.

INDUSTRIAL COOPERATIVES. *See* CICOPA; PRODUCTION COOPERATIVES.

INSTITUTE FOR THE DEVELOPMENT OF AGRICULTURAL COOPERATIVES IN ASIA (IDACA). The Institute, located in Tokyo, was established in 1963 by the Central Union of Agricultural Cooperatives for the purpose of providing opportunities for cooperative leaders from **developing countries** (particularly in Asia) to study Japanese **agricultural cooperatives** and to learn from their experiences. Cooperators from Africa, Asia and Latin America have attended IDACA training programs, held eight to 10 times per year, and lasting from two weeks to two months.

INSTITUTO COOPERATIVO INTERAMERICANO. The Interamerican Cooperative Institute, established in 1963 and located in **Panama**, provides cooperative training to Latin American cooperators. It is structured in two classes each year covering cooperatives, sociology, political economy and communications. Its staff also engages in micro-project consultation.

INSURANCE. A contract binding a company or government to indemnify an insured party against specific loss in return for specified premiums paid to protect against the risk of loss.

INSURANCE COOPERATIVES. Cooperatives established to provide insurance services to cooperatives and/or cooperative members to protect against unexpected losses. Among the first cooperatives of the modern cooperative era were mutual fire insurance societies established in the 1750s in the **United Kingdom** and in the pre-independence **United States**.

INSURANCE DEVELOPMENT BUREAU. A specialized arm of the **ICA** International Cooperative and Mutual Insurance Federation, it was established to encourage and assist cooperative insurers in **developing countries**. Important leadership in its work has been provided by cooperative insurers in **Canada, Sweden,** the **United States** and the **United Kingdom**.

INTERNATIONAL ALLIANCE OF SCHOOL COOPERATIVES. Established in 1984 with headquarters in Paris at the Office central de la coopération à l'écôle, the Alliance promotes the principles of **school cooperatives**, assists cooperative movements wishing to initiate such cooperatives, and actively encourages their formation in **developing countries**.

INTERNATIONAL CENTER OF RESEARCH AND INFORMATION ON THE PUBLIC, SOCIAL AND COOPERATIVE ECONOMY (CIRIEC). Established in Geneva in 1946 by Professor **Edgard Milhaud** and others as the International Center of Research and Information on Collective Economy, it is now located at the University of Liège in Belgium. It has national sections in a number of countries and publishes the periodical, *Annals of Public and Cooperative Economy.*

INTERNATIONAL COOPERATIVE ALLIANCE (ICA). The worldwide organization of cooperatives, founded in 1895 and including in its membership national cooperative organizations from all sectors. In July 1998 ICA's membership of 236 national **federations** from 93 countries encompassed 724,904,821 individual members in 749,100 cooperatives. Its headquarters office is in Geneva, **Switzerland**, and it has regional offices located in Ouagadougou, **Burkina Faso**; Nairobi, **Kenya**; New Delhi, **India**; San José, **Costa Rica**; and Geneva, Switzerland. Program offices are located in Buenos Aires, **Argentina,** and Brasilia, **Brazil**. A new office, in Cairo, **Egypt**, opened in 1999. These offices provide promotion and assistance to cooperatives in the regions. The ICA carries out much of its work through specialized organizations and working parties including the following: the International Cooperative Agricultural Organization (ICAO), International Cooperative Banking Association

(ICBA), International Organization of Industrial, Artisanal and Service Producers' Cooperatives (CICOPA), International Consumer Cooperative Organization (ICCO), International Cooperative Fisheries Organization (ICFO), ICA Housing Organization (ICHO), International Cooperative Energy Organization (ICEO), International Cooperative and Mutual Insurance Federation (ICMIF), International Organization for Consumer Cooperative Distributive Trade (INTERCOOP), International Cooperative and Associated Tourism Organization (TICA), International Cooperative Health Organization (ICHO), ICA Global Human Resources Development Committee, ICA Communications Committee (ICACC), ICA Global Women's Committee, and ICA Committee on Cooperative Research.

INTERNATIONAL COOPERATIVE ALLIANCE REGIONAL OFFICE FOR ASIA AND THE PACIFIC. Established in New Delhi, **India,** in 1960 as the Education Centre for South-East Asia, it became the ICA Regional Office and Education Center for South-East Asia in 1965. Its name was recently changed to reflect a broadened geographical area of concern that now includes, in addition to Asian movements, those in the countries of the Pacific as well as the Middle East. Most of its program activities in the past have focused on Asian cooperative movements.

INTERNATIONAL COOPERATIVE ALLIANCE REGIONAL OFFICE FOR CENTRAL AMERICA AND THE CARIBBEAN. Established in 1990, its offices are in San José, **Costa Rica**. Its principal activities initially involved the cooperative movements in Central America and the Caribbean, but increasingly its focus is on all the Americas. It is now named the Regional Office for the Americas.

INTERNATIONAL COOPERATIVE ALLIANCE REGIONAL OFFICE FOR EAST, CENTRAL AND SOUTHERN AFRICA. Established in 1968, its offices were in Moshi, **Tanzania,** until the end of 1998 when they were relocated in Nairobi, **Kenya**. Its activities have principally involved the cooperative movements in the English-speaking countries of eastern and southern Africa.

INTERNATIONAL COOPERATIVE ALLIANCE REGIONAL OFFICE FOR WEST AFRICA. Established in 1979, its offices are in Ouagadougou, **Burkina Faso** (formerly in Abidjan, **Côte d'Ivoire**). It is involved with 17 (mainly francophone) West African countries in which the cooperative movements use the English, French and Portuguese languages.

INTERNATIONAL COOPERATIVE BULLETIN. *See* REVIEW OF INTERNATIONAL COOPERATION.

INTERNATIONAL COOPERATIVE DAY. Established by the **ICA** in 1923, it is observed annually on the first Saturday of July to commemorate and celebrate **cooperative principles** and the cooperative movement worldwide. It is accompanied by an official message, usually relating cooperative concerns to contemporary problems or issues, one continuing theme of which has been a goal to institutionalize world **peace**.

INTERNATIONAL COOPERATIVE PETROLEUM ASSOCIATION (ICPA). An international association of most major **petroleum cooperatives,** it was formed in 1947 at the **ICA** Congress in Zurich, **Switzerland,** to operate as an international trading body. Under the initial leadership of **Howard Cowden (United States)** and **Albin Johansson (Sweden),** it focused its attention on both production and conservation. ICPA has emphasized making the trade in petroleum benefit common people, not only a few international corporations and privileged countries.

INTERNATIONAL COOPERATIVE SCHOOL. Organized and held annually from 1925 by the **ICA,** it was designed to provide training to the leadership of the international cooperative movement. The schools were held in different locations in Europe and were staffed by education specialists from the movement and prominent cooperative personalities. The first school was organized in 1921 by the Education Department of the British **Cooperative Union,** which continued to operate the schools under the name International Cooperative Summer Schools. Sponsorship was taken over by the ICA in 1925, and "Summer" was removed from the title. The schools continued to be held annually until 1938, after which they were held irregularly. After 1967 they became known as International Seminars. The schools ceased functioning in the late 1970s.

INTERNATIONAL COOPERATIVE TRAINING CENTER, UNIVERSITY OF WISCONSIN. Established in 1963 and funded originally by **USAID** until 1970 as part of its response to the **Humphrey Amendment** to the Foreign Assistance Act, the Center offered training to cooperators from overseas and published a journal supporting these efforts. After the USAID funding was terminated, the Center was merged with training programs for U.S. cooperators and became the **University Center for Cooperatives** on the Madison campus of the University of Wisconsin. The University Center for Cooperatives, among its activities, maintains a significant library of cooperative books and materials and has been is under contract to the **ICA** to maintain its Web site, **http://www.coop.org**.

INTERNATIONAL COOPERATIVE TRAINING CENTRE, LOUGH-BOROUGH. The Centre, located at the Cooperative College in Loughborough, **United Kingdom**, provides cooperative training for cooperative leaders from the United Kingdom and abroad. It offers courses, one academic year's duration, in cooperative development and organization, cooperative accounting and financial management, and **cooperative education** and training. It also offers a certificate course in cooperative management and supervision. It has about 40 places annually for students from **developing countries**. The Centre operates the **CLEAR Unit**, a consultancy, research, training and development service for cooperatives in the United Kingdom and in developing countries.

INTERNATIONAL COOPERATIVE UNIVERSITY. Organized by Professor **Henri Desroche** and others of the **Collège coopératif** in France with the participation of the **Desjardins Group** in **Canada**, the University arranged, during the 1980s and 1990s, four training sessions a year, of two weeks' duration each, for cooperative leaders and officials in Africa, Canada/North America, **France** and Latin America. The language of communication was French.

INTERNATIONAL COOPERATIVE WOMEN'S GUILD. An association organized in 1921 to further the principles and practices of **cooperation** and to promote the interests of world **peace**. Its affiliated members have included a number of national women's guilds, which met periodically in international conferences. It was replaced by the Women's Committee of the **ICA** (now the ICA Global Women's Committee) in 1963. *See also* COOPERATIVE WOMEN'S GUILDS.

INTERNATIONAL DIRECTORY OF COOPERATIVE ORGANIZATIONS. A publication of the **ILO**, published irregularly. The first edition appeared in 1921 and the latest edition, the 13th, was published in

1988. The International Directories have contained information about cooperatives in all the countries in which cooperative organizations were identifiable at the time. Entries include information about the governmental structures that supported the cooperative system and names, addresses and basic information on national cooperative organizations.

INTERNATIONAL FEDERATION OF AGRICULTURAL PRODUCERS (IFAP). With the end of the devastation of World War II, the emergence of a new internationalism represented by the organization of the **FAO** and the **United Nations**, the emergence of newly independent nations in the developing parts of the world, and a widening recognition that agriculture was in the midst of a technological advance that was changing its whole character, there was a growing sense that the farmers of the world needed to reunite. The result, in 1946, was the formation of the International Federation of Agricultural Producers to act as the nongovernmental spokesman at the international level for farmers around the world, and to act as a forum for the exchange of information and views on farming and general agricultural issues. From its beginning IFAP has recognized the critical role that **agricultural cooperatives** play in these discussions and deliberations and has organized a special committee within its organization to focus on these. IFAP was one of the groups that joined together to form **COPAC** in 1971.

INTERNATIONAL FEDERATION OF PLANTATION, AGRICULTURAL AND ALLIED WORKERS (IFPAAW). An international trade union drawing together the national unions representing workers in the field of agriculture, particularly plantation workers and workers in an increasingly mechanized and technologically advanced agriculture. IFPAAW soon recognized that cooperatives could be an important tool in helping to ameliorate the economically disadvantaged position of their members. Special materials were developed and meetings and workshops held to spread cooperative expertise. When **COPAC** was being organized, with an original focus on **agricultural cooperatives**, IFPAAW was a participant in its formation and has remained one of its sponsoring organizations. Recently, IFPAAW's name was changed to the International Union of Food, Agricultural, Hotel, Restaurant, Catering, Tobacco and Allied Workers' Associations (IUF).

INTERNATIONAL LABOUR OFFICE (ILO). The secretariat of the **International Labour Organization** with headquarters in Geneva,

Switzerland, and regional field offices in different parts of the world to implement its policies and programs. In 1920 a Cooperative Service was added to the secretariat by the ILO's first director, **Albert Thomas,** a French cooperator and active participant in the **ICA.** Through many reorganizations and name changes the Cooperative Service has acted to inform and act on issues of relevance to cooperatives. From 1924 to 1975, the ILO published *Cooperative Information*, an important source of information on the cooperative movements in many countries. Special issues of that publication have collected bibliographical material on cooperatives and chronicled the history of the cooperative movement worldwide. These were invaluable in preparing this book. The ILO has also published the *International Directory of Cooperative Organizations*, the first edition of which was issued in 1921, and the latest, the 13th, in 1988. In 1932 the Cooperative Service undertook the ILO's first technical assistance mission, to aid cooperatives in **Morocco,** the start of what became an extensive program of advice and support to the governments of **developing countries** on matters dealing with cooperatives. It is an important implementer of cooperative development projects funded by the **United Nations Development Program** and by certain bilateral assistance agencies.

INTERNATIONAL LABOUR ORGANIZATION (ILO). Founded in 1919, it provides a meeting ground for business, trade unions and governments to discuss and take action on issues related to labor. The International Labour Organization became a part of the **United Nations** system in 1946. Its governing body is an annual conference, with secretariat (the **International Labour Office**) to implement the policies and programs of the Organization. The annual conference has on occasion addressed cooperative issues and has adopted two formal recommendations, **Recommendation No. 77**, which emphasized the importance of cooperatives in social and economic development, and **Recommendation No. 126,** which defined the nature of cooperatives and addressed the issue of government support to them. The ILO is one of the sponsoring organizations of **COPAC.**

INTERNATIONAL LIAISON COMMITTEE ON COOPERATIVE THRIFT AND CREDIT (CLICEC). Established in 1970, it was a coordinating group for those bodies concerned with the organization and operation of savings and **credit cooperatives.** Among its members were the **ICA, WOCCU** and the **International Raiffeisen Union**. The French cooperative, Crédit mutuel, was an important participant. CLICEC held a series of international conferences to explore the current and potential position of savings and credit cooperatives in the international cooperative movement. It has not been functional in recent years.

INTERNATIONAL ORGANIZATION OF INDUSTRIAL, ARTISANAL AND SERVICE PRODUCERS' COOPERATIVES (CICOPA). CICOPA, known by its French acronym, is a specialized organization of the **ICA**. Its members are producers' cooperatives from different fields, among them construction, industrial production, general services, transport, intellectual skills, artisanal activities, health and social care. The over 70 organization from 57 countries that make up CICOPA see their primary tasks as contributing to the development of already existing organizations, fostering the creation of national organizations of producers' cooperatives all over the world, and promoting the development of such cooperatives, particularly in developing countries. CICOPA sponsored and organized world conferences on industrial cooperatives in 1978, 1983 and 1985.

INTERNATIONAL RAIFFEISEN UNION (IRU). Established in 1968 on the 150th anniversary of the birth of **Friedrich Wilhelm Raiffeisen**, its purpose is to draw together the cooperatives of the world that share Raiffeisen's ideals of self-help, self-administration and self-responsibility and have shown a willingness to share such experience with other cooperatives at earlier stages of development. The IRU is a focal point for collection and evaluation of relevant cooperative information and organizes periodic international conferences, which focus on the needs of cooperatives in **developing countries**. Originally organized by 19 cooperative organizations from 9 European countries, in 1990 its membership included 82 organizations from 47 countries in all parts of the world. Its headquarters are located in Bonn, **Germany**, where it operates one of three Raiffeisen information centers. The other two are in Lévis, Quebec, **Canada**, and in Bombay, **India**.

INTERNATIONAL RESEARCH CENTER ON RURAL COOPERATIVE COMMUNITIES (CIRCOM). Established in **Israel** in 1965 to explore the growing interest in cooperative communities, the Center carries out research and publishes the *Journal of Rural Cooperation.*

INTERNATIONAL UNION OF FOOD, AGRICULTURAL, HOTEL, RESTAURANT, CATERING, TOBACCO AND ALLIED WORK-

ERS' ASSOCIATIONS (IUF). *See* INTERNATIONAL FEDERATION OF PLANTATION, AGRICULTURAL AND ALLIED WORKERS.

INTERNET. The Internet is a worldwide network (World Wide Web) of computerized information systems. In 1995 the **ICA**, in collaboration with the **University Center for Cooperatives, University of Wisconsin**, established an Internet Web site, the Cooperative Gopher, where information is available regarding cooperatives. The information is accessible through Cooperative Gopher at gopher://wiscinfo.edu:70/11/.info-source/.coop.

The ICA home page is located at http://www.coop.org on the Internet. The **ICA Regional Office for the Americas** in collaboration with the ILO COOPNET regional program in Latin America has published *Directorio Paginas Web de Cooperativas en Internet—El Mundo Cooperativo al Alcance de su Mano*, a useful guide to cooperative information in various Web sites worldwide. Its Web site address is http://www.alianzaaci.or.cr.

IRAN. A consumer cooperative, Maine, was established in Teheran in 1926 and, with two others started about the same time, constituted the beginnings of organized cooperation in Iran. Growth was slow, impeded in part by political instability and then by events related to World War II. The first **cooperative law** was enacted in 1952, and in 1963 a national cooperative **federation**, the Central Organization for Rural Cooperatives, was established. An attempted modernization of the country, including a strong push for cooperatives, assisted by both the **FAO** and the **ILO**, was undertaken during the government of Shah Reza Pahlevi in the 1950s; this continued until a fundamentalist Islamic revolution under Ayatollah Khomeini altered the national course in 1979. By that date a combination of **agricultural, consumer**, fisheries, **housing**, and industrial **cooperatives** had been organized, and an **ICA** survey of cooperatives reported the presence in 1978 of 3,063 societies with 2,985,726 members in Iran (8.9% of the population).

The national mood since the 1979 revolution has been set by militant clerical leaders intent on having Iran return to Islamic roots. Cooperatives have evidently remained in favor, and the Minister of Cooperatives reported to the ICA that in 1994 the same combination of types of cooperatives, with the addition of 523 savings and **credit cooperatives**, had grown to 26,107 cooperative societies with 8,174,140 members (12.9% of the population). A similar report in 1997 noted 34,867 cooperatives with a membership of 9,227,418 in the following sectors: agriculture—5,102 cooperatives/with 70,319 members; consumer—9,651/6,507,117; housing—7,530/1,468,989; multipurpose—330/136,850; savings and credit—705/225,594; worker productive and services—9,908/794,251; and others—1,641/24,298. Cooperative membership at that time constituted 14.0% of the national population.

IRAQ. The first cooperatives in Iraq (consumer and agricultural) were organized in 1930 and the first **cooperative law** enacted in 1944. Cooperatives had been planned and developed to the point that a **cooperative bank** was established in 1956 to act as their base of finance. With technical assistance from the **FAO** there was a significant buildup of cooperatives through the 1970s, among them **agricultural, consumer, housing**, and industrial **cooperatives**. By 1978 the General Cooperative Union, the Iraqi cooperative **apex organization**, could report the existence of 2,593 societies with a membership of 800,156. The **ICA Regional Office for Asia and the Pacific** reported that in 1992 there were 2,600 cooperatives with 1,200,000 members in the following sectors: agriculture—2,315 societies/with 480,000 members; consumer—105/300,000; housing—150/350,000; industrial—25/50,000; and others—5/20,000. Cooperative membership was 6.5% of the population.

IRELAND. Fourteen years after the organization of the **Rochdale Society** in England, the first **consumer cooperative** was established in Dublin in 1859, and it was soon emulated in other parts of the country. The first agricultural society dates from 1883 and cooperatives had become frequent enough by 1888 that they joined together in the Irish Cooperative Union. Legislation, the Industrial and Provident Societies Law (1893) and the Friendly Societies Law (1896), followed. Cooperative development in the early period paralleled developments in the **United Kingdom** until partial independence (Dominion status) was achieved in 1922. **Agricultural cooperatives** predominated, encouraged by the formation of the Irish Agricultural Organization by **Horace Curzon Plunkett** in 1892 and the establishment of the Irish Agricultural Wholesale Society in 1897. A number of **housing** and industrial **cooperatives** developed over the years, but it was with the introduction of **credit unions** in 1958 and the passage of an accompanying Credit Union Law in 1966 that a new, dynamic, and now dominant, cooperative sector emerged. Travelers in Ireland will find small credit unions in even the most out-of-the-way communities. A publication of the European Community in 1993 identified 513 credit unions with 1,100,000 members, 107 agricultural cooperatives with 166,539 members, 75 housing cooperatives with 6,005 members, and 18 other cooperatives with a membership of 3,500. In total they represented 36.4% of the Irish population. In 1994 **WOCCU** reported that there were 526 credit unions with 1,637,538 members (nearly 46% of the population of the country at that time). An **ICA** report of national cooperative statistics for 1996 noted 723 cooperatives with 2,123,576 members in the following sectors: agriculture—133 societies/with 186,097 members; banking—1/1,374; credit unions—532/1,935,889; insurance—1/na; and workers productive—56/216. Cooperative membership was 59.5% of the national population at that time.

IRRIGATION COOPERATIVE. An organization of farmers in a particular locality who unite to cooperatively obtain water rights and to jointly distribute the flow of water for their crops at reasonable prices.

ISRAEL. Some 20 years before Theodor Hertzl wrote his book *The Jewish State* and launched the world Zionist movement, the first Jewish cooperative settlement, Petach Tikva, had been established in **Palestine** at a time (1887) when Jews were but a small minority of the population of the then Turkish colony. Growth of similar efforts was slow until the turn of the century, which then saw in quick succession the establishment of Pardessa, a citrus growers' cooperative (1900), the Zionist Congress's adoption of a policy of forming cooperative settlements, the establishment of Deganaya, the first **kibbutz** (1908), the first urban producers' cooperative, Achdout (1909), the first village cooperative at Mervahia (1910), a cooperative **wholesale society**, Hamashbir Hamerkazi, and the first **consumer cooperatives** (1916).

The end of World War I brought a change in status to Palestine from that of Turkish colony to a League of Nations–approved British Mandate based on the Balfour Declaration of Britain's intention to help establish a Jewish homeland in Palestine. Jewish immigration soared and with it the structure for cooperation. The Palestine Cooperative Ordinance was enacted in 1920 and the same year Histadrut, the General Federation of Jewish Labor in Palestine, was established. Histadrut's cooperative arm, Hevrat Ovdim, was established in 1923 with two future prime ministers of Israel (**David Ben-Gurion** and **Levi Eshkol**) and a future president (**Itzhak Ben-Zvi**) among its leadership. A workers' bank and a **cooperative bank** became principal financial arms for the growing movement. During the 1920s the *moshav* movement was established, as well as a structure for **housing cooperatives**. By 1935 there were 623 cooperatives (including 45 Arab societies) with over 75,000 members. By 1939 these had grown to 1,081 societies (124 of them Arab societies), including 125 registered cooperative settlements and collective farms.

Cooperatives became important structures in absorbing the growing number of immigrants from Europe and elsewhere following the end of World War II and in providing vehicles for many of the nation-building activities of the post-independence period. By the end of 1950 there were some 2,179 cooperative societies, 672 agricultural (including 239 kibbutzim and 176 moshavim), 304 consumer, 403 credit and provident fund, 366 housing and 434 industrial and service societies. (Arab cooperative societies were a significant casualty of the first Arab-Israeli war in 1948; only 55 were cited as still active at the end of 1950.) Growth continued in ensuing years in the agricultural sector, accompanied by consolidation of smaller societies in the other sectors. By 1972 there were 2,087 cooperatives (including 197 Arab societies).

During the 1960s there was a growth of cooperative infrastructure, one notable part of which was the establishment of institutes designed to share the Israeli cooperative experience with **developing countries**. An Afro-Asian Institute was established in 1960, a Latin American Center in 1962, and the **International Research Center on Rural Cooperative Communities (CIRCOM)** in 1965. Statistics on cooperatives in Israel, prepared by the **ICA Regional Office for Asia and the Pacific** in 1994, showed a total of 2,677 cooperatives with a membership of 1,877,276. (These figures did not include a separate break-out of Arab cooperatives.) By sector, the non-Arab coops were the following: agriculture—1,482 cooperatives/with 520,000 members; consumer—22/550,000; housing—174/150,000; industrial—123/30,000; insurance—2/50,000; multipurpose—745/126,276; savings and credit—58/450,000; and others—71/1,000. Cooperative membership was 38.3% of the non-Arab area population. *See also* PALESTINE (ARAB).

ITALY. In the history of the modern cooperative movement, Italy was the fifth country (after the **United States, United Kingdom, France** and **Greece**) to record the start of a cooperative organization. In the case of Italy this was a workers' collective dairy established at Osoppo in 1806. Serious emulation of this initial effort was slow in developing, and it was not until the mid-1800s that the ferment of cooperation began to regularly produce lasting results in Italy, in the form of **mutual aid** societies, joint purchasing of agricultural supplies, a printing works, the first consumer society, and a workers' bank established in Milan in 1860 by **Luigi Luzzatti** (whose name, for 60 years, was intertwined with the history of cooperative action in Italy and internationally). The year 1886 saw the passage of the first **cooperative legislation**, the organization of the first national cooperative **federation**, Federazione fra le Cooperative Italiane, and the publishing by **Ugo Rabbeno** of *La Cooperazione in Italia*, a study of the emerging Italian cooperative movement.

Before another 10 years had passed, sectarian divisions in the Italian cooperative movement, along religious and political lines, had begun. They persist to this day, characterized by some as the Red, White and Green Cooperatives (socialist/communist, Catholic and Liberal). Growth and elaboration of societies continued unabated, and the **ICA**, recognizing the importance of Italian cooperatives, held its Sixth Congress in Cremona in 1907. By 1910, when the government compiled for the first time detailed statistical data on the movement, the number of societies had reached 5,065 and membership had reached 1,165,702 (plus an uncompiled number of people's banks and credit societies). The first serious setback to Italian cooperatives came with the seizure of power in 1922 by the Fascists, who coopted what they could of the cooperative movement, abolished or exiled whatever they could not, and restructured all to serve their political ends.

Still the cooperative movement grew and, with the end of World War II and the declaration of an Italian Republic, immediately restructured itself, reaffirmed its sectarian differences (reinforced by Cold War feuding) and took off on a new spurt of growth. By 1974 the **ILO** reported that there were 51,797 registered cooperatives in Italy (with an undisclosed membership). Growth with consolidation into larger and integrated units has characterized recent years, as in other industrialized countries, and a 1998 ICA review of European Union cooperatives identified a complex Italian cooperative movement dealing with agriculture, banks, computers, construction, consumer trade, cultural activities, dairies, fisheries, fruits and vegetables, housing, industrial production and labor societies, insurance, multipurpose activities, retail trade, services, transport, travel and tourism, training, and wine cellars—in all 38,194 societies with a combined membership of 7,624,430 (13.3% of the Italian population).

J

JACOBSON, DOROTHY HUSTON (1907–1985). An American academician and cooperator, she assisted in the preparation of legislation in the state of Wisconsin that mandated teaching of cooperatives in all state schools and prepared a textbook on the subject. With her husband she helped organize the Group Health Mutual Insurance Company in 1938 in St. Paul, Minnesota. Appointed an Assistant Secretary of Agriculture in the Kennedy administration, Jacobson assisted in the development of the Food for Peace Program and was a delegate to the **FAO** conferences. She was inducted into the U.S. **Cooperative Hall of Fame** in 1982. She was the wife of **George Jacobson**.

JACOBSON, GEORGE (1900–1988). An American teacher and cooperative official, his first work with cooperatives was as an organizer for northern states in Minnesota and Wisconsin, followed in 1930 by a period with Midland Cooperative, where he became assistant general manager in 1935. With his wife he organized the Group Health Mutual Insurance Company in St. Paul, Minnesota, in 1938 and he helped organize the Group Health Association of America in 1946. Following passage of the **Humphrey Amendment**, Jacobson was employed by **USAID** to help implement the mandate that the United States foreign assistance program should assist in the promotion of cooperatives in **developing countries**. His work in this regard concentrated on cooperatives and **credit unions** in Latin America. He was inducted into the U.S. **Cooperative Hall of Fame** at the same time as his wife, **Dorothy Huston Jacobson**, in 1982.

JÄGGI, BERNHARD (1869–1944). A cooperator in **Switzerland**, he served from 1909–34 as president of the Administrative Council of the Union of Swiss Consumer Societies in Basel and helped develop the particular operating style of Coop Switzerland. Under his leadership the cooperative village of Freidorf was organized and the cooperative school at Freidorf established. He was also instrumental in the establishment of the Swiss Cooperative Central Bank in 1928. In 1923 Foundation Jäggi, a cooperative studies center, was established at Muttenz. It was later converted into a training center for women. Jäggi was a member of the **ICA** Central Committee from 1913 to 1944 and of the Executive Committee from 1934 until his death.

JAMAICA. An attempt to start a banana **production cooperative** in 1904 and the organization of the first indigenous credit structure in 1905 were the beginnings of what has grown into the Jamaican cooperative movement. Though unsuccessful at that time, these organizations were forerunners of the two major components of the movement as it developed—**agriculture cooperatives** and **credit unions**. In the early 1930s, under the leadership of Jamaica Welfare Limited, led by Norman Manley, a future prime minister, a cooperative development program was initiated and groups interested in cooperatives (including the government) were invited to collaborate. This program encouraged what became the credit union movement (the first unit of which was established in 1941), and organized an independent structure, the Jamaica Cooperative Development Council, in 1944, to encourage and coordinate **cooperative development**. The credit unions were the movement's initial success story, and by 1947 they had evolved to the point where a national **federation**, the Jamaica Cooperative Credit Union League, was established. In 1949 **cooperative legislation** was passed and a government cooperative department established the following year. **Housing cooperatives** became a reality with the establishment of the first in 1951. Since then the movement has grown, and there are now three national federations representing the interests of agriculture, fisheries and credit unions. A national **apex organization**, the National Union of Cooperative Societies, established in 1959, represents the overall movement. The **ILO** *Directory* **(1988)** indicated that in 1986 there were 240 cooperatives with 430,729 members (19.5% of the population); 69% of the membership were in credit unions. The **WOCCU** *Statistical Report* for 1997 indicated that credit union membership had increased to 522,514, raising overall **cooperative penetration** to an estimated 25.3% of the population.

JAPAN. The year 1843 is the generally accepted date for the start of the Japanese cooperative movement, with the inauguration of Hotokusha, a farmers' and handicraft workers' collective. However, it was not until the 1870s that there began a proliferation of cooperative societies, both in number and in type—for example, a salt marketing society in Hiroshima, consumer societies in various cities, a farmers' association of former samurai, farmers' marketing societies and the beginnings of credit societies. Silk production and processing societies as well as those for fisheries, industries and students were next to emerge. By 1900, after several abortive efforts, general **cooperative legislation** had been adopted and growth was in full swing, augmented by a growing network of cooperative **unions**. By 1912 there were 9,683 cooperative societies functioning mainly in the areas of credit, production and marketing (farm and industrial), with 34 unions and a membership exceeding

1,000,000. Ten years later, in 1922, these numbers had increased to 14,047 cooperatives, 191 unions and 2,734,695 members. Japanese cooperatives emerged in 1923 on the international scene as members of the **ICA**. By the 1930s, Japanese cooperative structures had grown to where they were perceived as a threat by other economic interests in the country. An anti-cooperative campaign was organized by chambers of commerce and resulted in repressive legislation adopted by the Japanese Parliament. By the end of the decade this effort had been blunted by the cooperatives, and Japanese attention was diverted by a second Sino-Japanese War, strongly supported by the Japanese cooperative movement. Such support attracted criticism from the international movement and ultimately, in reaction, led to the Japanese withdrawal from ICA.

World War II soon followed, and after the Japanese defeat the cooperative movement attracted the attention of the American occupation forces, which brought in American cooperators to help in the restructuring of the Japanese movement. The result was new legislation and a network of new national **federations** and related structures, which recast the various sectors of the cooperative movement. Growth and progress have been continuous since then, with consolidation of smaller groups into larger societies. The Japanese cooperatives rejoined the ICA in 1952. By 1972 the **ILO** reported that Japanese cooperative membership had risen to 21,600,000 (19.9% of the population). Japanese status in the worldwide movement was reflected in the fact that the ICA's 30th Congress met in Tokyo in 1992. The following year the ICA regional office reported that Japanese cooperative societies then totaled 9,688 with a combined membership of 57,527,085 in the following sectors: agriculture—3,204 societies/with 8,843,705 members; consumer—663/16,252,375; fisheries—3,894/836,403; housing—48/1,076,832 insurance—55/12,000,000; services—117/1,618,823; worker productive—113/5,947; and others—1,594/16,893,000. Cooperative membership was 45.9% of the national population.

JIRASEK, FERDINAND (1871–1931). A Czechoslovakian cooperative leader, he was an active trade unionist in the bakery industry before joining the cooperative movement. In 1905 he joined in the formation of the Workers' Distributive Society. A Central Cooperative Union was established in 1907 and he served as its secretary. In 1909 he was among the founders of the V.D.P. Cooperative Wholesale Society. In 1911 he was elected as a Social Democrat to the Austrian Parliament and after World War I became a member of the Czechoslovakian National Revolutionary

Assembly. He was one of the founders of the Cooperative Bank of Prague and served as chairman of its board of directors until his death.

JOHANSSON, ALBIN (1886–1968). A cooperative leader in **Sweden**, he began his cooperative work as a shop assistant in the Tanto Cooperative Society, of which he became manager in 1905. In 1907 he joined the **Kooperativa Förbundet (KF)** and served as head of the Credit and Supervising Department until 1915, when he left KF to become manager of the Stockholm Cooperative Society. He returned to KF in 1917 and in 1924 became its managing director. He was the author of the first Swedish manual for **consumer cooperatives** and in 1913 established KFF, an association of cooperative directors, designed to encourage cooperative leadership. He was also an important figure in the formation of the **Nordisk Andelsförbund** and the **International Cooperative Petroleum Association**, which he chaired from its founding in 1946 until 1959. He was for many years a member of the **ICA** Executive Committee and a frequent contributor to the *Review of International Cooperation*.

JORDAN. While the first cooperative started in Jordan in 1922 and there was some activity during the 1930s, it was not until 1952, when **cooperative legislation** was enacted and the Central Union of Cooperatives was established, that a significant effort to organize was undertaken. It was focused principally on the formation of **agricultural cooperatives,** but there was some organization of **worker productive cooperatives** as well. The Jordan Cooperative Organization was established in 1968, replacing the earlier union, and it, along with the Jordan Cooperative Institute, has given a professional cast to the movement's efforts. These efforts have been adversely affected by the continuing tensions between **Israel** and its Arab neighbors. The **ICA Regional Office for Asia and the Pacific** reported that in 1996 there were 699 cooperatives with 72,742 members in the following sectors: agriculture—213 societies/ with 23,041 members; consumer—8/1,200; fisheries—2/60; housing— 145/10,727; multipurpose—181/19,323; savings and credit—13/4,384; worker productive—102/12,507; and others—35/1,500. Cooperative membership was 1.7% of the population.

JÖRGENSEN, SEVERIN (1842–1926). A Danish cooperative pioneer born in Jutland, he was apprenticed at an early age to a grocer and at 24 opened his own grocery. He assisted in the establishment of a cooperative shop in Idestrup and managed it for five years before moving back to Jutland and establishing his base in the Danish consumer movement there. He was instrumental in the foundation in 1888 of a **cooperative wholesale society**, of which he became manager, then chairman when it merged with a similar society in Seeland eight years later. He was active at many levels of the cooperative movement in **Denmark** including the Egg Export Cooperative, the Central Federation of Danish Cooperative Societies, the Cooperative Bank, and the **Nordisk Andelsförbund** (the Scandinavian Cooperative Wholesale Society), one of the earliest efforts at establishing international cooperative trade. He was a member of the **ICA** Central Committee for many years and was one of the first to be elected to the **Committee of Honor of the International Cooperative Alliance**.

JUSTO, JUAN B. A pioneer cooperative leader in **Argentina**, in 1897 he presented the first series of lectures on the cooperative movement in that country. In 1905, in collaboration with **Nicolás Repetto** and others, he established El Hogar Obrero, a consumer, credit and building cooperative, at Buenos Aires. It was entered as No. 1 in the official **register** of cooperatives in Argentina.

K

KAGAWA, TOYOHIKO (1888–1960). An educator, social reformer, labor and cooperative leader in **Japan** who left a family of wealth and influence to live and serve the poor of the Kobe slums. As a converted Christian he considered cooperative organizations the natural expression of his religion's "brotherhood economics," the title of one of his books. Among his cooperative organizational activities were an eating cooperative in Kobe in 1912, a cooperative food store in Osaka, a toothbrush **production cooperative**, a chicken raising cooperative, **credit unions** and medical cooperatives. In 1946 he joined in the postwar organization of the Japan Federation of Cooperatives. He studied in the **United States** and traveled to many parts of the world, speaking to large and enthusiastic audiences who responded to his message that they should consider cooperatives as a positive way of dealing with socio-economic problems and developing a more ethical economic order. Kagawa set forth seven basic values, for each of which a particular type of cooperative was needed. The values and the correlative types of cooperatives were (1) life itself (insurance), (2) labor (production), (3) exchange (marketing),

(4) growth (credit), (5) selection (mutual aid), (6) order (utility), and (7) purpose (consumer).

KAMINSKI, JAN (1922–). A Polish cooperative leader who began his work with the Polish **agricultural cooperatives** in 1946. He held a number of posts and in 1971 was elected president of this sector of Polish cooperatives. He served for many years on the presidium of the Supreme Cooperative Council in **Poland** and in May 1976 was elected its president. He held a number of government posts and served in the Polish Parliament. In 1971, he became a member of the Central Committee of the **ICA** and in 1979 was elected to its Executive Committee, on which he served for 10 years.

KAPLAN, JACOB M. (1892–1987). An American businessman who owned the Welch Grape Juice Company, which he was persuaded to sell to the grape growers who were his suppliers. They established a cooperative to take over its ownership and in turn built it into one of the largest grape growing, processing and marketing businesses in the world. Kaplan retained an interest in the cooperative form of enterprise and later established the Kaplan Fund to provide financing of cooperative housing programs for the low-income elderly. He was inducted into the U.S. **Cooperative Hall of Fame** in 1985.

KAROLYI, COUNT ALEXANDER (1831–1906). A cooperative pioneer in **Hungary** who provided significant leadership in the organization of the agricultural sector of Hungarian cooperatives, holding that cooperatives represented the only way in which small holders in agriculture, using land reform measures and **agricultural credit**, could compete with large, rich agricultural interests. He was the organizer in 1898 of the Hangya cooperatives and provided leadership in other sectors, striving to create a viable movement in the difficult conditions at the close of World War I.

KARPELES, BONE (1868–1938). A cooperator in **Austria**, he was among the founders and organizers of the Austrian Cooperative Wholesale Society and of the Vorwarts Consumer Society in Vienna. He organized the cooperative bakers and flour mill cooperative, Hammerbrotwerke, in the Vienna suburb of Schwechat and was an active participant in the Central Union of Austrian Consumer Cooperatives.

KARVE, D. G. (1898–1967). An economist, administrator, author and cooperative leader in **India,** he was introduced to cooperatives while a student, through the works of **Charles Gide.** He served in a number of academic posts, in national and international agricultural economics associations and in local and national government agencies. He came to view cooperatives as the best way to achieve maximum prosperity with minimum social conflict, particularly in **developing countries.** He served for a period as chair of the **ICA** Principles Commission, resulting in a report that was unanimously adopted by the 23rd Congress of the ICA at Vienna in 1966. He was chairman of the Advisory Council of the **ICA Regional Office** in New Delhi.

KASCH, A. (1871–?). Born in Schleswig-Holstein, **Germany,** he was an editor of labor journals, a freelance journalist and a militant cooperator, becoming director of publications for the German Central Cooperative Union at Hamburg. From 1925 to 1930 he served on the **ICA** Central Committee, including two years on its Executive Committee.

KAUFMANN, HEINRICH (1864–1928). A teacher, author and leader of the German **consumer cooperative** movement, he was active in the German Central Union of Distributive Societies, becoming its general secretary in 1903. His cooperative interests also included the fields of insurance, pension funds and education systems.

KAZAKHSTAN. One of the newly independent states that were formerly part of the **Union of Soviet Socialist Republics.** Its cooperatives are organized in a similar way to those **consumer cooperatives** that made up **Centrosoyus** in the USSR. They are multipurpose organizations that engage in production as well as consumer activities and are operators of various consumer services. The longterm structure for other sectors of cooperative activity in the future remains to be worked out. A **cooperative law** was passed in 1990 granting cooperatives independence from the state. A 1998 **ICA** report to the European Commission reported that in 1996 there were 1,309 consumer cooperatives with a membership of 3,700,000, representing 21.9% of the population.

KAZAN, ABRAHAM E. (1889–1971). Born in **Russia,** he came to the **United States** in 1904 and in the 1920s became the manager of a **credit union** for members of the Amalgamated Clothing Workers Union. A group of credit union families joined together to form Amalgamated Houses, a **housing cooperative**, the first of a number of such enterprises. They ultimately came to provide housing for more than 100,000 people and earned Kazan the title of "father of U.S. housing cooperatives." He helped establish and became president of the United Housing Foundation, which brought together cooperatives, trade unions, civic and fraternal organizations and others to sponsor and build moderate-income cooperative housing. Among them was Coop City, a "new town" within New York City that ultimately became the largest cooperative housing development in the world. He was inducted into the U.S. **Cooperative Hall of Fame** in 1976.

KEEN, GEORGE (1869–1953). Born in England, he moved to **Canada** in 1904. There he pursued his view that cooperatives were the way to achieve greater equity in the benefits of the Industrial Revolution. He became president of the Brantford, Ontario, Cooperative Association and was among the founders in 1909 of the **Cooperative Union of Canada**. Keen became secretary-treasurer of the new organization, a position he held until 1946, and was the editor of *Canadian Cooperator*, the publication of the Union, from its inception until 1947. He was the author of study materials on cooperatives for the Workers Education Association of Ontario and for the **Antigonish Movement** in Nova Scotia, and he broadcast a weekly program on cooperatives on radio station WCLF in Chicago.

KELLEY, OLIVER HUDSON (1826–1913). An American cooperative pioneer and founder with six other government employees in 1866 of the **National Grange of the Patrons of Husbandry** (popularly known as the Grange) of which he became the first national secretary, serving in that position until 1878. The periodic economic distress of the latter part of the 19th century led him and other Grange leadership to conclude that cooperatives were the principal vehicle to which farmers could turn as a group to help ameliorate their economic and social difficulties. The principles of cooperative enterprise were soon embodied formally in the Grange's Declaration of Purposes. The growth and success of the Grange was largely attributed to Kelley's exceptional organizing ability. Kelley is regarded as among those who contributed significantly to the early phases of agricultural cooperation in America.

KENYA. Cooperatives in Kenya (then the Kenya Colony) were initially a phenomenon of the European planters, the first organizational manifestation of which was the Kenya Farmers' Association, established in 1919. In 1924 the Kenya Cooperative Dairymen's Union was established and in 1931 the first **cooperative legislation** passed. The Kenya Cooperative Creameries was established in the same year, and several years later (1937) the Kenya Planters' Cooperative Union came into being, rounding out the network of European cooperative involvement and control. The first **indigenous** African **cooperative societies** were established in 1945. They grew slowly in the years leading up to independence in 1963, when "Africanization" of the cooperative structure began. The Kenya National Federation of Cooperatives was established in 1964, followed by a new Cooperative Societies Act in 1966, the Cooperative College in 1967, and the Cooperative Bank in 1968. Responses to new economic opportunities opened up by such cooperative structures led to a rapid growth of the movement, sometimes outstripping its capacity to be effectively managed, but grow it did and diversify as well. **Credit unions**, first established in 1964 and encouraged by a promotional committee from 1965, quickly became the second main cooperative sector after agriculture. There were 639 registered cooperatives in 1963; by the end of 1973 these had increased to 2,184 and had a membership of more than 620,000. While not trouble-free, and supervised by an often heavy-handed government bureaucratic structure, the Kenya movement has continued to grow and diversify, moving into consumer, fisheries, housing and industrial production, and service activities. In 1994 the **ICA Regional Office for East, Central and Southern Africa** reported that there were 5,691 cooperatives registered in Kenya with a membership of 2,641,000 in the following sectors: agriculture—2,430 cooperatives/with 1,484,000 members; consumer—127/21,000; fisheries—66/15,000; housing—227/47,000; savings and credit—2,470/1,027,000; and worker productive—86/31,000; and others—285/17,000. Cooperative membership was 9.9% of the population. ICA reported that in 1996 the total cooperative membership in Kenya was 2,700,430 (10% of the population).

KERINEC, ROGER (1921–1998). A French **consumer cooperative** leader who was president of the French National Federation of Consumer Cooperatives (FNCC) from 1973 to 1983. He was named a vice president of the **ICA** in 1972 and subsequently served as ICA president for the period 1975–84.

KF. *See* KOOPERATIVA FÖRBUNDET.

KIBBUTZ. An Israeli collective agricultural settlement in which there is collective ownership of assets and labor is communal. The more highly developed kibbutzim include small-scale industrial activity among their operations.

KING, WILLIAM (1786–1865). A British medical doctor regarded as one of the early theorists in the British cooperative tradition, he organized the first **consumer cooperative**, the Cooperative Trading Association, in Brighton in 1828. He thought of the small food store as an effective organizational vehicle for practicing economic democracy and a basis for training in the spirit of cooperation. In this regard he was a precursor of the **Rochdale Pioneers**. King became convinced that cooperatives should be not only an economic vehicle but also a structure through which persons of modest means could open themselves to wider education and culture. To help implement these views he was instrumental in organizing infants' schools for children, the British School of Industry and the Mechanics Institute. In 1828 he established the first cooperative newspaper, *The Cooperator*, which widely disseminated his views regarding cooperation until it ceased publication in 1830.

KINGSLEY, CHARLES (1819–1875). A British clergyman, author, professor of modern history at Cambridge University and Chaplain to Queen Victoria, he was awed by the accomplishments of the Industrial Revolution and appalled by its consequences for the masses of workers who became slaves of its machines and of manufacturers newly liberated by a capitalist creed that glorified greed and economic aggrandizement. Kingsley's answer was to preach the gospel of Christian Socialism, hoping thereby to temper the greed of manufacturers and get them to act more humanely toward their workers, and to summon the downtrodden to claim their rights as human beings. The doctrine and potential of cooperation, he held, were a large part of the answer to these hopes, bolstered by the organization of trade unions and other workers' and farmers' groups. Kingsley foresaw the general expansion of democracy in all segments of society and a time when the majority would equally share the privileges of the economic minority.

KIRIBATI. The initial development of cooperatives in Kiribati took place in the period between 1951 when a Cooperative Societies Ordinance was adopted, 1956 when the first cooperative was organized, and 1966 when the Gilbert and Ellice Islands Cooperative Federation was established.

The division of the Colony of the Gilbert and Ellice Islands in 1975 produced Kiribati (Gilbert Islands), independent in 1979, and Tuvalu (Ellice Islands), independent in 1978. Much of the existing cooperative structure was in Kiribati and has further developed since independence. The **ILO** *Directory* (**1988**) listed 3 **agricultural cooperatives** with 577 members, 25 consumer societies with 23,395 members, 1 savings and credit society with 219 members and 1 **school cooperative** (membership not identified). The **consumer cooperatives** collectively constituted the largest economic enterprise in the country. The 30 cooperatives with 24,191 members in 1984 involved 39.5% of the population.

KLIMOV, ALEXANDER (1914–1979). A Russian educator and cooperative activist after World War II, he was for 35 years active in **Centrosoyus**, the consumer cooperative organization in the **Union of Soviet Socialist Republics**, rising to the position of its director. He was a fighter for his vision of social progress and for world **peace** and worked to define a basis for cooperators from different socio-economic systems working together. He was a regular participant in **ICA** affairs beginning in 1945 and was elected a vice president in 1960. He was highly regarded in the Communist Party and by the Soviet State and was the recipient of a number of honors reflecting this fact.

KNAPP, JOSEPH G. (1901–1983). A student of cooperation, researcher, academician, cooperative organizer and government official, he was the first administrator of the Cooperative Service in the **United States** Department of Agriculture, serving from 1953 until his retirement in 1966. He was the author of three books describing the history and leadership of U.S. cooperatives, books that are regarded as classics in their field: *Rise of American Cooperative Enterprise (1620–1920)*, *Advance of American Cooperative Experience (1920–1945)*, and *Great American Cooperators*. He was inducted into the U.S. **Cooperative Hall of Fame** in 1979.

KOOPERATIVA FÖRBUNDET (KF). The Cooperative Union and Wholesale Society of Swedish Consumer Cooperatives, referred to as KF, was founded in 1899, initially as an educational body. In 1904 it expanded into wholesale production and distribution and subsequently into other important economic and promotional activities, including a program of assistance to cooperatives in **developing countries**. It developed an impressive record of success in breaking monopolies in **Sweden**

that restricted access to reasonably priced consumer goods. Representatives of KF have played important roles in the **ICA** with two of them, **Karl Daniel Mauritz Bonow** and **Lars Marcus**, serving extended periods as presidents.

KOREA, DEMOCRATIC PEOPLE'S REPUBLIC OF. While the two Koreas share a common heritage of indigenous cooperation dating back to early periods of their history and shared a common experience of Japanese annexation during which some elements of cooperation were developed, the two countries have taken radically different paths in the post–World War II period. The Democratic People's Republic of Korea has largely emulated Soviet experience, utilizing cooperatives principally for the delivery of consumer goods and services. However, little has been written about the cooperative movement, and details of its development are sketchy. The **ILO** *Directory* (**1988**) indicated that in 1985 there were 3,524 cooperatives with a membership of 1,600,000 (7.9% of the population).

KOREA, REPUBLIC OF. While there were traditional modes of cooperation reaching far back into Korean history and there were some cooperative development activities during the period of Japan's annexation of Korea (1910–45), modern cooperation dates from 1945 and the close of World War II. It was the period during which the country was officially partitioned into north and south as a condition of the armistice ending the Korean War.

By the 1950s an Agricultural Cooperative Law had been enacted in the south and a national cooperative structure for agriculture developed, partially built around a network of earlier agricultural associations. The first **credit unions** had also been developed, encouraged by Catholic missionaries. The decade of the 1960s was a time of rapid growth and diversification of cooperatives. In 1961 the National Agricultural Cooperative Federation was organized, followed by national **federations** for **fishery cooperatives** and credit unions. A national cooperative training center opened in 1962, the first of a network of such institutions that now serves the four major cooperative sectors of agriculture, fisheries, livestock, and savings and credit.

By 1983, the **ILO** *Directory* (**1988**) reported, there were 1,473 agricultural (mainly multipurpose) cooperatives with 2,099,720 members; 1,138 credit societies (credit unions and agricultural banking) with 833,173 members; 72 fishery cooperatives with 137,038 members; and

126 other cooperatives with a combined membership of 76,071. Ten years later, in 1993, the **ICA Regional Office for Asia and the Pacific** reported the presence of 4,905 cooperatives with 10,076,674 members (22.1% of the population) in the following sectors: agriculture—186 cooperatives/with a membership of 270,000; fisheries—78/153,856; multipurpose—1,441/2,027,818; and savings and credit—3,200/7,625,000. The most recent statistics are for 1997. They report the presence of 5,886 cooperatives with a membership of 19,802,406 in the following sectors: agriculture—1,332 cooperatives/with 2,010,000 members; credit and savings/banks—4,409/16,866,489; fisheries—1,719/164,192; forestry—143/500,000; and insurance—3/416,917. Cooperative members were 43.5 of the population.

KORP, ANDREAS (died 1983). A **consumer cooperative** leader in **Austria** who started his cooperative career as assistant secretary of the Union of Consumer Societies for Styria and Carinthia. He served as director of the district union headquartered in Graz before being appointed in 1933 to the board of the Austrian Cooperative Wholesale Society where he remained even during the period of Nazi domination of his country. He was named Minister of State for Food in the postwar Social Democratic government. In 1955 he was named director general of the Austrian Union of Consumer Cooperatives. He served on the **ICA** Central Committee from 1934 to 1938 and again from 1944 to 1971.

KROPOTKIN, PRINCE PETER ALEXEYEVICH (1842–1921). A Russian theorist of anarchism, he gave up career and social position to pursue the course of a revolutionary. Imprisoned in Siberia and later in France, expelled from Switzerland, he lived much of his life in England where there was greater tolerance of the views he espoused. His writings won international respect, especially his book, *Mutual Aid,* in which he argued that cooperation not competition was the key factor in evolution at all levels. He became an advocate for such **mutual aid** being built into all social and economic institutions. He returned to Russia in 1917 but, disappointed with what he saw, denounced the Bolshevik Revolution and lived in retirement until his death.

KUWAIT. The history of cooperation in Kuwait dates from 1941 when cooperatives were established in educational institutions to provide needed supplies to students. **Consumer cooperatives** date from 1955 when they were established in two government departments, the forerunners of what is now the largest segment of Kuwaiti cooperatives. The Kuwait Constitution of 1962 contained provisions supportive of cooperative development, and by 1972 the Union of Consumer Cooperative Societies had been established as well as a special department in the Ministry of Social Affairs and Labor to supervise cooperatives. The **ILO** *Directory* **(1988)** reported that in 1986 there were 34 cooperatives (1 agricultural, 27 consumer, 4 worker productive and 1 other). The **ICA Regional Office for Asia and the Pacific** reported that in 1992 there were 49 cooperatives with a membership of 177,254. Of these, 42 were consumer cooperatives with 172,630 members. Four agricultural cooperatives were cited with 3,248 members. There were one each of multipurpose, savings and credit, and worker productive cooperatives. Cooperative membership constituted 7.7% of Kuwait's population. The KA membership report for 1996 indicated a total membership of 192,155 (9.9% of the population).

KYRGYZSTAN. Information was unavailable as to the history of the cooperative movement in the country. The **ICA Regional Office for Asia and the Pacific** indicated that in 1993 there were 550 **consumer cooperatives** with 1,069,000 members in Kyrgyzstan, 24.9% of the population. A 1998 **ICA** publication noted for the year 1996 that there had been a sharp reduction in cooperative affiliations to 43 cooperatives and 207,630 members (4.6% of the population).

L

LAAKSO, JALMARI (died 1967). A Finnish cooperative leader, he spent his career in the KK **consumer cooperative** movement (with a particular interest in cooperative housing), serving as deputy director (1943–52) and then director general from 1952 until his retirement in 1961. He was on the **ICA** Central Committee from 1951 to 1962 and was active in the ICA Housing Committee. He was an author of some note on cooperative matters.

LAIDLAW, ALEXANDER FRASER (1908–1980). A Canadian from Nova Scotia, he spent his early career as associate director of the Extension Department at St. Francis Xavier University (famed for its establishment of the **Antigonish Movement** and for work in cooperative promotion) before becoming general secretary of the **Cooperative Union of Canada (CUC)** in 1958. Under his leadership the CUC provided assistance in cooperative formation for low-income people in **Canada** and pioneered the effort for the Canadian movement to do the same in Africa and Asia. He resigned in 1968 to become chairman of the Royal Commission on Cooperatives for Ceylon (**Sri Lanka**). He directed a study for the **ICA**, leading to the publication *Cooperatives in the Year 2000*.

LAIDLER, HARRY WELLINGTON (1884–1970). An American researcher, politician, lecturer on economic and political philosophy, church leader and all-around social activist, he was a member of the Federal Council (now National Council) of Churches Department of Church and Economic Life from 1924 to 1951 and of the Institute for Social Progress from 1933 to 1958. His interest in social movements included cooperatives, and he was a member of the board of directors of **CLUSA** from 1917–20. He was a prolific writer whose work included books and articles on cooperatives.

LAMBERT, PAUL (1912–1977). A cooperative leader in **Belgium**, he was professor of economics at the University of Liège, director of **CIRIEC** and author in 1959 of *La Doctrine coopérative*. In the 1950s he was elected to the board of the Belgian Federation of Socialist Consumer Cooperatives (FEBECOOP), later serving as its president. He was elected to the **ICA** Central Committee in 1962 and to the Executive Committee in 1966. He served in both positions until his death.

LANCASTER, SIR ROBERT (1883–1945). A British cooperative leader, he was most noted for his work with the **English Cooperative Wholesale Society** which he joined as solicitor in 1917, rising to chief executive in 1923. He traveled extensively in his work with the Cooperative Wholesale Society and was active in planning and advocating international structures to support national consumer movements. He was secretary of the International Cooperative Wholesale Society and of the International Cooperative Trading Agency.

LAND O'LAKES INTERNATIONAL DIVISION. Land O'Lakes, one of the largest **agricultural cooperatives** in the **United States**, created an International Division in the early 1980s to carry out international development activities on its own initiative, in addition to its support for the work of **Agricultural Cooperative Development International** and **CLUSA**. It was the first recipient of a grant from **USAID** for use in stimulating direct **movement-to-movement assistance** activities as a supplement to regular government-to-government projects. It provided training and technical assistance primarily in fields related to its corporate experience in the dairy industry.

LAOS. Cooperatives have been a recent development in Laos. The National Cooperative Act was passed in 1973, and in 1978 Agricultural Production Cooperatives (collectives) were proclaimed. The **COPAC** Country Information Note on Laos indicated that there were 2,546 **agricultural cooperatives** with 118,876 members in 1984. In addition, there were 104 **consumer cooperatives** (with an undetermined number of members) and some industrial cooperative activity among weavers and potters. The cooperative effort has struggled with the twists and turns of Laotian politics, military coups and military intrusions from neighboring countries since independence from France in 1953. Cooperative prospects will remain limited until such time as there is an extended period of national stability.

LASSALLE, FERDINAND JOHANN GOTTLIEB (1825–1864). A German lawyer and socialist leader who was among the founders of the first German Social Democratic party. Although influenced by Marx's thinking, he was a believer in the use of state action rather than revolution as the way of revamping society to achieve social equality and justice. He was supportive of cooperatives but viewed **consumer cooperatives** with suspicion, holding that they encouraged individualism and free enterprise, thus hindering the achievement of the socialist state; he saw this type of state as the solution to what he regarded as wage slavery, and the necessary structure for achieving the just distribution to the entire populace of the fruits of an industrial society.

LATIN AMERICAN CONFEDERATION OF CREDIT UNIONS. *See* CONFEDERACIÓN LATINOAMERICANA DE COOPERATIVAS DE AHORRO Y CRÉDITO.

LATVIA. The earliest cooperatives in Latvia date from the latter part of the 19th century, when Latvia was ruled by **Russia**. Early cooperatives developed in patterns similar to those of other European nations. By 1914 and the start of World War I, there were approximately 1,500 cooperatives, about half of which were related to agricultural production of various types; the remainder were consumer, mutual fire insurance, and savings and loan societies. Serious losses were experienced during World War I, but by the end of 1921, and during the first years of national independence, Latvian cooperatives had reestablished themselves to their prewar level and had added new types of cooperatives in the fields of education, housing, labor and production. **Consumer cooperatives** had grown significantly, constituting one-third of all cooperatives in Latvia in 1921. Development continued during the next 20 years, including the establishment of a network of cooperative **unions** reflecting the interests of the various sectors.

In 1940, Latvia was occupied by the **Union of Soviet Socialist Republics,** and the Soviet system of cooperatives was imposed upon the Latvian movement. The Germans occupied the country in 1941 and reestablished the former system; this was again replaced when Russia absorbed Latvia as a republic under the USSR in 1944. All cooperatives save consumer societies were nationalized, and the consumer sector became the focus for almost all cooperative activity during the period up to the reestablishment of independence at the start of the 1990s.

A study by the **ICA** published in 1993 noted that there were 28 large consumer cooperatives with 390,200 members joined in the Latvian Federation of Consumer Societies. The Federation had 10 regional organizations, 3,000 retail outlets, 1,500 public catering establishments, 5 wholesale organizations, production and service agencies, and a structure for cooperative training. The Alliance study also observed that there were new cooperatives in various fields, among the few structures permitted for private services and trade. It further observed that Latvian cooperatives, in contrast to those in **Estonia** and **Lithuania**, had yet to make the transition to real democratic participation and membership control. Membership, nonetheless, continued to grow. In a 1998 membership report of the Alliance it was noted that in 1996 there were 98 cooperatives—agriculture (1), consumer (49), and worker productive (48). Membership figures were available only for the consumer sector, which reported a membership of 305,400 (12.4% of the population). It is estimated that with the additional membership of other sectors the **cooperative penetration** of the Latvian population is 15%.

LAVERGNE, BERNARD (1884–1975). A French cooperator and professor of law, he published in 1908 *Le régime coopératif, étude générale de la coopération de consommation en Europe,* the first of a number of books in which he elaborated cooperative themes. In much of his writing Lavergne protested the tendency toward statism, pointing out that in state industries decisions are made at the top and are passed down step by step to the consumer, whereas in cooperatives decisions work up from the consumer's expressed needs. Lavergne was a close associate of **Charles Gide** and founded with him the important French cooperative journal *Revue des études coopératives*.

LAW. A body of rules governing conduct recognized by the community as binding upon all. In most countries there is a **cooperative law** or laws that specify the structure, work and responsibilities of cooperatives. Other laws may also relate to and cover cooperatives.

LEBANON. The first cooperatives (agricultural) were established in Lebanon in 1937 and the first **cooperative legislation** was enacted in 1941, while the country was still under French rule. A period of slow growth followed, mainly in agriculture, but was augmented in the 1960s by a network of **consumer cooperatives**. A national **federation** was organized in 1968 and new cooperative legislation, reflecting Lebanese conditions and interests, passed. In 1973 the Ministry of Cooperatives and Housing was established, reflecting a growing governmental interest in cooperatives as a way of facilitating Lebanese development. A civil war from 1975 to 1990 introduced a period of unrest, civic division, invasion and destruction that still persists and that has truncated cooperative and other development. The **ILO** *Directory* **(1988)** indicated that in 1984 there were 283 cooperatives with 32,007 members (1.2% of the population). The principal cooperative sectors were in agriculture and consumer supply, with a small number of **housing cooperatives** and savings and credit societies. An **ILO** report from 1993 indicated that the cooperative effort had continued to grow despite complex national conditions, with cooperatives numbering 525 at that time (no data was provided on membership). **Agricultural** and consumer **cooperatives** continue to dominate, but there has been a doubling of the number of housing cooperatives, the emergence of a number of **worker productive cooperatives** and an expansion of savings and credit societies. The percentage of overall **cooperative penetration** remains small.

LEMAIRE, JOSEPH (1882–1966). Born of working-class parents and introduced by his father to the trade union movement and labor party politics, he became a leader of the Belgian and international **insurance cooperative** movement. He dedicated his life's work to the Belgian cooperative insurance society, La Prévoyance sociale, beginning in 1907 as inspector in the province of Liège, rising to director general in 1925. He was chairman of the board of directors at the close of his career. In **Bel-**

gium he was an able and imaginative innovator; his most striking act was to have La Prévoyance sociale commit its profits to the development of social improvements that would benefit the whole society, e.g., health centers, medical clinics, homes for disabled children, health resorts for working people (the first at the Belgian city of Spa), and a university laboratory for viral research. The insurance society became a preeminent social welfare institution in the nation. He was organizer of the **ICA** Insurance Committee in 1922 and served as its secretary for 25 years.

LENIN, VLADIMIR ILYICH (1870–1924). A Russian revolutionary, founder of the Bolshevik (later Communist) Party, leader of the Revolution of 1917 and one of the founders of Soviet Russia. Lenin influenced communism more than anyone other than Karl Marx. He adapted Marxist theory to the realities of a backward Russian economy but had faith that communism was the wave of the future for the world. In 1923 he defined the role of the cooperative movement in the Soviet system, identifying it as one of the legitimate forms of "socialist property." His death only one year later meant that he never had a chance to see the full implication of this contention in practice. There remained contending views within the **Union of Soviet Socialist Republics** as to whether Lenin believed that cooperatives were legitimate per se or only as way stations on the road to a network of comprehensive state enterprises.

LESOTHO. A landlocked country surrounded by South Africa, Lesotho saw its first cooperatives established in 1946, 20 years before it achieved independence from the British. The first **cooperative legislation** (a proclamation) was announced two years later and the position of **Registrar of Cooperatives** established at the same time. Basutoland Cooperative Industries and a banking union were established in the mid-1950s and the first **credit union** formed in 1960. By 1968 a **credit union league** had been founded and the Lesotho Cooperative Handicrafts established. Coop Lesotho, a national **apex cooperative organization**, was formed in 1981. Growth was steady and by 1984, according to the **ILO** *Directory* **(1988)**, there were 259 cooperatives with 53,499 members. In 1994 the **ICA Regional Office for East, Central and Southern Africa** reported that there were 517 cooperatives with a membership of 788,413 in the following sectors: agriculture—328 cooperatives/with 744,490 members; consumer—6/6,510; multipurpose—19/2,040; savings and credit—79/30,919; worker productive—33/1,294; and others—52/3,160. A total of 42.0% of the population were cooperative members in 1994. One interesting feature of cooperatives in Lesotho is the high participation of women, explainable in large part by the fact that more than half of the adult male population works in South Africa in the mines.

LIANG, H. S. A Chinese cooperator who was one of the founders of the Chinese Industrial Cooperatives (CIC) in 1938. The CIC was organized to reestablish factories destroyed by the invading Japanese army, to provide substitutes for goods made abroad, to provide work for refugees and to increase resistance to the Japanese in **China**. The movement was known as INDUSCO in the United States, and its rallying cry was *gung ho*, meaning "working together."

LIBELT, KAROL. A Polish cooperative pioneer who worked to establish **production cooperatives**. In 1868 he published *The Coalition of Labor and Capital.* He is regarded by many as the founder of the cooperative movement in **Poland**.

LIBERIA. The first **cooperative legislation** was passed in 1936 but was not fully implemented until 1970, at which time a Cooperative Division was created within the Ministry of Agriculture to promote cooperative activities (in 1981 it became the Cooperative Development Agency). The first **agricultural cooperatives** were formed in 1970 and the first **credit union** shortly thereafter. By 1972 the credit unions had proliferated enough that the Credit Union National Association was established as a national **federation**. Growth of 20 to 30 new cooperatives per year took place during the 1970s and early 1980s. In 1986 there were 316 societies—230 agricultural, 30 consumer and 56 credit unions, with a total membership of 63,774. By 1990, just before the current civil war began, the Cooperative Development Agency reported that there were 408 cooperatives—325 agricultural, 10 consumer, 68 credit unions, and 5 worker productive—with a combined membership of 85,654. Membership data for the individual sectors was not available, but total cooperative membership represented an estimated 3.4% of the population.

LIBYA. The first Libyan cooperative, Consorzio Agrario Cooperativo, was organized in 1915 during the period in which Italy occupied the coast of Libya (seized in 1911 from the Turkish). Italy formally annexed Libya in 1939, but this was abrogated after World War II. In 1949 the **United Nations** declared Libya an independent state. The first **cooper-**

ative law was enacted in 1956 and the first **agricultural cooperative** started the next year. However, prior to 1970 the growth of cooperatives was extremely modest. A military insurrection in 1969 brought Colonel Muammar al-Quaddafi to power, and his government saw cooperatives as an important instrument for achieving economic and social development. It supported them with enthusiasm and finance, and the number of cooperatives grew rapidly, going from 150 in 1969 to 1,451 in 1979; membership grew from 25,519 to 489,168 (15.9% of the population). (No more recent statistical data could be identified.) In 1979 the cooperative sectors were agriculture—260 cooperatives/with 116,181 members; consumer—1,040/286,987; and housing—151/86,000.

LIECHTENSTEIN. An organization of trading cooperatives was the only cooperative activity in Liechtenstein identified in the **ILO** *Directory* **(1988)**. Information about its history and activity and statistical data were not identified.

LINCOLN, MURRAY (1892–1966). A cooperator in the **United States** who began his career as a county agricultural extension worker in Connecticut. He moved to Ohio where he became executive secretary of the Ohio Farm Bureau Federation. In 1926 he became involved in the formation of Farm Bureau **insurance** operations which later became **Nationwide Insurance** and dedicated much of his career to its advancement. Lincoln was president of Nationwide until his retirement in 1964. He pioneered **rural electric cooperatives** for farmers, was president of **CLUSA** from 1941 to 1965, and was the first president of **CARE (Cooperative for American Relief Everywhere)**, formed in 1945 to provide war relief in Europe. In the **ICA**, where he provided leadership from 1946 to 1957, he was a member of the Central Committee and the Executive Committee and for two years served as a vice president. His autobiography, *Vice-President in Charge of Revolution,* chronicles his cooperative endeavors. Lincoln was inducted into the U.S. **Cooperative Hall of Fame** in 1976.

LINDSTROEM, OLLE (died 1994). Born in Estonia, from where he fled at the age of 16, he had a cooperative career in **Sweden**, concentrating his activities in the **cooperative housing** organization Riksbyggen. He was chairman of the ICA Housing Committee from 1884 to 1992 and an active participant in the Network of Cooperative Development in eastern and central Europe, which **ICA** established to provide advice and counsel to the cooperatives of this area as they adjusted to the changes brought about by the ideological and political changes in their governments after 1989 and 1990. Following his retirement in 1991, Lindstroem committed himself to working for cooperative development in Estonia.

LITHUANIA. The cooperative movement in Lithuania has a long history, the first **consumer cooperative** having been founded in 1869 while Lithuania was part of **Russia**. Consumer cooperatives grew rapidly toward the end of the 19th century, and even though many failed, there was a solid core of successful ones when the Russian Revolution of 1917 took place and when, three years later, Lithuania declared its independence. During this period the Lithuanian Consumers' Cooperative Association was founded. This structure has persisted through the years of Lithuanian independence, the 1940 Russian takeover of the country, the subsequent German invasion, the incorporation of Lithuania into the **Union of Soviet Socialist Republics** and now, again independence. The independence years of the 1920s and 1930s produced a flourishing cooperative movement with **agricultural, producer, consumer, credit** and **insurance cooperatives**. A report in the ILO's *Cooperative Information* in 1939 reported 197 agricultural and rural consumer societies with 21,525 members; 314 credit societies with 117,155 members; 185 dairy societies with 18,372 members; as well as cooperatives in banking, insurance, horticulture, and a large **cooperative wholesale society**. During the Soviet period only the consumer cooperative structure survived and thrived as part of **Centrosoyus** and a centrally planned economy. Its principal role was the supply of consumer goods to rural areas.

With the new independence for Lithuania in 1991, the consumer cooperative structure has been redefined and again made part of the private sector. Many of the anticipated changes in the cooperative system are still to be made, but **housing cooperatives** have begun to function. Agriculture has been privatized and farmer companies have started to form; many expect these to become cooperatives. Based on its history, there are other significant areas of new growth for cooperatives. In 1996, in an **ICA** statistical report, 99 consumer cooperatives were cited with a membership of 246,300, equaling 6.8% of the population.

LIVESTOCK COOPERATIVE. An association of livestock producers whose activities may include the provision of feed and supplies for use by members, breeding and artificial insemination, feed lots, transportation and marketing.

LLOYD, HENRY DEMPREST. American author of *Wealth vs. Commonwealth* and an advocate of profit sharing. He was an American representative at the **ICA** Congress at Delft in 1897.

LONG, CEDRIC (1889–1931). An American clergyman educated at Harvard, he left the ministry to work in the trade union and cooperative movements, becoming the executive secretary of **CLUSA** in 1924, and serving in this position until his early death.

LORBER, JOSEPH. A mid-19th-century cooperative pioneer in **Austria**, he is regarded by many as the father of the cooperative movement in that country. As early as 1847 he was advocating the establishment of cooperative credit associations similar to those formed by **Franz Hermann Schulze-Delitzsch**. In 1851 he helped establish the first Austrian **credit cooperative** at Celsvec (Klagenfurt).

LOVERIDGE, G. B. An education officer for the British **Cooperative Union**, he was recruited by the government of Ceylon (**Sri Lanka**) to examine and make recommendations regarding **cooperative education** and publicity in Ceylon. Subsequently, he was part of a **United Nations** technical assistance program to support cooperatives in that country. Later he worked in similar capacities with a number of countries, as a member of a cooperative unit in the **Overseas Development Administration (ODA)**.

LUBIN, DAVID (1849–1919). American dry-goods merchant and farmer in California, he left these successful business endeavors to move to Rome, Italy, in the early 1900s and in 1905 established the International Institute of Agriculture, forerunner of the **FAO**. His experience with European cooperatives led him to become an active promoter of cooperatives in the **United States,** and he encouraged U.S. president Theodore Roosevelt to support the establishment of cooperative credit societies. Lubin's experience and interests were utilized by a commission that President Roosevelt sent to Europe in 1913 to study the European cooperative experience and determine its relevance for the U.S.

LUDLOW, JOHN MALCOLM (1821–1911). Born in **India**, he studied law in Paris where he became acquainted with the movement to set up cooperative production societies as a way of emancipating the working class. When he returned to England, he was associated with the Christian

Socialists and became a leader in the workers' cooperative movement. He was included among the founders of the Society for Promoting Working Men's Associations, a body that provided much of the impetus for workmen's cooperatives. In 1874 he was appointed Chief Registrar of Friendly and Cooperative Societies, a position he held until 1891. He was among those who worked for the formation of the **ICA** and took part in its first Congress in 1895.

LUTFI, OMAR (1867–1911). A cooperative pioneer in **Egypt** and a political economist, he served as head of the State School of Law at Cairo and later was one of the founders of the New University of Cairo. He visited a number of cooperative systems in Europe, particularly **Switzerland**, and helped define ways in which the **consumer** and **agricultural cooperative** systems he observed there could be relevant to conditions in his own country. He is credited with founding the first **agricultural cooperative** in Egypt in 1908.

LUSTIG, EMIL. A Czechoslovak cooperative leader in the 1930s, he served as chairman of the cooperative **wholesale society**. He was a longtime member of the Executive Committee of the ICA. After the Nazi seizure of his country in 1939 he fled to **Argentina** where he maintained an active cooperative career.

LUXEMBOURG. Agricultural cooperatives, the first of which was established in 1808, have historically been the predominant cooperative sector in Luxembourg. They are currently represented by the Luxembourg Central Agricultural Association but previously had independent cooperative associations. These early cooperatives functioned as general agricultural societies, as well as specialized bodies for agricultural supply and marketing, cattle insurance, dairying and wine production. A home builders' association reflecting cooperative housing interests had its beginnings in 1855, and **Raiffeisen** rural banks date from 1925. A small **consumer cooperative** sector has been formed in more recent years and currently is the predominant cooperative sector in terms of membership. A 1998 **ICA** report to the European Commission cited 63 cooperatives with 17,627 members in the following sectors: agriculture—25 societies/with an undetermined membership; consumer—3/12,000; and savings and credit/banking—35/5,627. Cooperative membership at that time was estimated to be 4.8% of the national population.

LUZZATTI, LUIGI (1841–1927). An Italian economist, financier, law professor, Minister of the Treasury and cooperative leader, he was the originator of a network of people's banks in **Italy**, beginning with the Lombardy People's Bank in Milan, which was established in 1860 when Luzzatti was only 19 years of age. In 1863 he published his first book, *La iffusione del credito e le banche popolari*, spelling out the theory and structure for a network of cooperative banks. In 1867 he began publication of the first Italian cooperative journal, *Cooperazione e Industria*. By the late 1870s Luzzatti was advocating the use of cooperatives as the basis for an Italian wine industry. Early in the 20th century he turned his attention to the issue of **cooperative legislation,** proposing to the government a law that would incorporate and unify the disparate legislative measures that were then accumulating. In 1914 he was the principal founder of the Instituto Nazionale del Credito per la Cooperazione (National Cooperative Credit Institute) and was the principal theorist for the Università Libera della Mutualità Agraria e Cooperazione (Free University of Mutual Agriculture and Cooperation), established in 1922. In 1925 it became the Advanced Institute for Cooperation, forerunner of the present-day Luigi Luzzatti Institute. By 1926 the people's banks had developed to the point where a national association, Ente Nazionale delle Casse Rurali (National Association of Rural Credit Societies), was established at Rome, with Luzzatti named president of its Supreme Council. During the early days of the fascist period in Italy, Luzzatti tried to steer the Italian cooperatives through murky political waters and was criticized by many as being too much of a collaborator with the regime.

M

MABILLEAU, L. (1853–1941). A French cooperator, in 1890 he published *L'Almanach de la coopération française*, included in which is the first mention of **school cooperatives**.

MACCOLL, WILLIAM A. (1909–1989). An American physician and cooperator, he helped create the Group Health Association of America and served on its board of directors from 1950 to 1956. He was part of the group of physicians and consumers, **Grange** members and union officials who negotiated the agreement that established Group Health of Puget Sound in 1946. From 1953 to 1955 Maccoll served as executive director of Group Health and from 1957 to 1965 as chief of their Northgate Medical Center. He became a nationally known expert on cooperative health care and was author of a medical column in the *News Service* from 1951 to 1967. He was author of *Group Practice and Prepayment of Medical Care,* which became the principal guide for such plans as they evolved in the **United States.** He was inducted into the U.S. **Cooperative Hall of Fame** in 1985.

MACDONALD, A. B. (1893–1952). A Nova Scotian by birth, by education (at St. Francis Xavier University) and through cooperation, Angus Bernard MacDonald was associate director of the Extension Division of St. Francis Xavier University (famous for its **cooperative education**) from 1930 to 1944. He subsequently served as the first managing director of the Nova Scotia Credit Union League, before he became general secretary of the **Cooperative Union of Canada (CUC)** in 1945. At the time, the organization was becoming a **federation** of provincial unions and MacDonald was instrumental in ensuring that all types of cooperatives were included in its membership. He was involved in the organization of several **insurance cooperative** associations in **Canada.** He attended the **ICA** Congress in 1946, the first time the CUC had been able to send a representative. He was among the founders of CARE/Canada, served as national chair of UNICEF and was a member of the Canadian Standing Committee on Rural Life.

MACEDONIA. The history of cooperatives in Macedonia is entwined with that of **Greece** and **Yugoslavia,** of which it was a part from 1919 to 1991, when it became an independent state. A General Cooperative Union of Macedonia was established in 1952. No separate statistics were identifiable for the region when it was part of Yugoslavia, nor of its state of development since independence.

MADAGASCAR. Cooperative development began in Madagascar in the 1930s with the issuance of special provisions of the French Cooperative Law dealing with Madagascar and the establishment of the Caisse centrale de crédit agricole, which provided credit for the emerging cooperative structure. One of the unique aspects of this early development, which took place while Madagascar was still a French colony, was the simultaneous organization of cooperatives for Europeans and for the indigenous population. Equally unique was the decision to try to build modern cooperatives on existing self-help groups (*fokolona*).

By 1938, there were 362 agricultural associations with 10,627 members (including 339 indigenous groups with 10,148 members), 51 credit funds with 6,095 members (32 indigenous with 5,636 members) and 5 other cooperative societies with 694 members (4 indigenous with 679 members). Growth was modest in the years before independence in 1960. In that year a cooperative ordinance was enacted, a national cooperative **federation** organized, and a government cooperative department established. A popular military uprising in 1972 and another in 1975, followed by a radical socialist development program that proved unrealistic, difficult economic times, a malaria epidemic and natural disasters have combined to frustrate national development, though cooperatives have maintained a small presence.

In 1990, an **ILO** report identified 905 cooperatives with 71,992 members. However, it noted that of these only 350 with 33,712 members were functioning normally. These included 56 agricultural production societies with 1,796 members: artisans—42/840; fisheries—5/226; rural supply (producer and consumer goods)—222/29,303; and transport societies—25/1,557. The active societies represented 0.28% of the population.

MAGNANI, VALDO (1912–1982). An Italian cooperator who was chairman of the Luzzatti Institute and a member of the Italian Parliament. From 1965 to 1973 he was president of the National Association of Agricultural Cooperatives, leaving that position to become a member of the executive board of the National League of Cooperatives in 1973 and later, in 1977, its president. He was elected to the **ICA** Central Committee in 1972 and to the Executive Committee in 1979. He wanted the ICA to spearhead the idea of cooperatives as the third-sector alternative to **capitalism** and **socialism**.

MAILATH, J. A Hungarian cooperative leader, he was named to the **Committee of Honor of the International Cooperative Alliance**.

MAIRE, MAURICE (1880–1949). A cooperative leader in **Switzerland**, he served as president of the board of administration of the Swiss Consumer Cooperatives from 1939 to 1946. He was concurrently a member of the **ICA** Central and Executive Committees until 1946.

MALAWI. A Cooperative Societies Ordinance for Malawi was enacted in 1946 (then Nyasaland), a revised version in 1960. In between, little happened to stimulate organization. Independence in 1964 came with great hopes, but a government led by Hastings Banda (who declared himself president for life in 1971) had little impact on the lives of the mass of rural agriculturalists eking out an existence as their forebears had. The **credit union movement** got its start in 1972 with the establishment of a Promotion Committee, and **credit unions** have essentially become the **cooperative movement** in Malawi, such as it is. The **ICA Regional Office for East, Central and Southern Africa** in its 1994 report of the statistics of movements in member countries indicated that there were cooperatives in the following sectors: agricultural cooperatives—7/na; consumer cooperative—1/815; credit unions—129/23,709; and multipurpose—3/146. The 140 cooperatives reported a combined membership of 24,670 (0.25% of the population).

MALAYSIA. Cooperatives in Malaysia date from 1920 when the first **cooperative legislation** was enacted and the first cooperatives started. Expansion was slow in rural areas, faster in urban communities. By the mid-1930s there were urban unions of cooperatives at Midlands, Penang and Perak. Immediately before the Japanese occupation during World War II, there were about 850 cooperatives societies—most became dormant during the war. The postwar years brought a new cooperative law, a reorganized governmental cooperative structure, the appointment of a **commissioner** of cooperatives and a revitalized movement. In 1947 there were 878 societies with over 100,000 members. By 1957 and independence the Cooperative Union of Malaysia had been formed, an **insurance cooperative** founded, and a national cooperative housing **federation** organized. In 1958 the Cooperative Central Bank was established. Growth was steady in the ensuing years, reaching 2,967 cooperatives with 477,358 members in 1967. These were supported by 52 secondary-level federations/**unions**. The principal sectoral activities were in agriculture, consumer supply, credit and banking, fisheries and housing. In the 1970s **agricultural** and **fishery cooperatives** were removed from the purview of the cooperative department and placed under the newly established Farmers' Organizations Authority and Fishery Development Authority, a move that has had the effect of restricting overall integration of the cooperative movement. The **ILO *Directory* (1988)** reported 3,446 cooperatives with 2,851,415 members in existence in 1984, with new sectoral activities involving industrial cooperatives and multipurpose societies. An **ICA Regional Office for Asia and the Pacific** report of statistical data for member movements in the region indicated that in 1995 there was a total of 3,554 cooperatives with 4,442,147 members in the following sectors: agriculture—124 cooperatives/with

129,832 members; consumer—915/501,431; housing—83/113,643; insurance—1/281,912; savings and credit/banking—465/1,757,696; school cooperatives—1,155/1,193,333; and worker productive and service—811/444,300. These represented 22.2% of the population.

MALI. While the first cooperative structures in Mali date from 1919, the history of the movement has been one of experimentation with form rather than substantive organization, first by the French colonial administration and then, since independence, by the government and a number of external aid partners. Further, reliable statistics are hard to come by, and they seldom match numbers of cooperative members with numbers of organizations. There has been evidence in recent years that the government acknowledges that a top-down approach to local development has not worked and will not work. Turning the system around is no easy task, impeded by layers of government cooperative bureaucracy. The most optimistic guess about **cooperative penetration**, gleaned from reports of the **ILO, COPAC** and **ICA**, is that less than 1% of the population are cooperative members.

MALTA. Cooperatives were first organized in Malta in 1946 to market fruits and vegetables. Concurrent with these, a Cooperative Societies Ordinance was passed and a government cooperative department established. The Federation of Maltese Cooperatives, established in 1973, is no longer functioning, but there is a Farmers' Central Cooperative acting as a marketing and purchasing agent for eight large **agricultural cooperatives**. Historically, cooperative development has taken place in spurts, 9 societies established in the 1945–47 period, 6 between 1958 and 1965 and 7 since 1983. An **ILO** background report in 1993 identified 21 cooperatives with a total of 3,798 members (1.1% of the population) in the following sectors: agriculture—10 cooperatives/with 1,669 members; consumer—3/1,004; transport—1/270; worker productive—4/284; and others—3/571. A 1996 report of the **ICA** showed an increase in membership to 5,016 (1.3% of the population).

MANAGER. A person employed by a cooperative to work as the executive implementor of its endeavors; sometimes referred to as **secretary/manager, general manager**, or chief executive.

MANNICHE, PETER. Principal of the International Peoples' College in Elsinore, **Denmark**, he emphasized the role of **agricultural cooperatives**, consumer cooperatives and **folk high schools** as structures for use by people in gaining greater control over the economic and social forces that controlled their lives.

MARCUS, LARS (1925–). A Swedish cooperator who served as president of the **ICA** from 1984 to 1995. He was a product of the Swedish **consumer cooperative** movement, beginning his work with Coop Stockholm in 1952 and advancing to its executive management committee in 1965. Since 1975 he has been executive vice president of **Kooperativa Förbundet,** heading its division for information, member education, publishing and international affairs. He became a member of the ICA Central Committee in 1975 and of the Executive Committee in 1980.

MARKETING COOPERATIVE. An association of farmers organized to jointly market their production more efficiently and profitably than can be done individually. These cooperatives also often act as **supply cooperatives** for their members, providing farm inputs and consumer goods. They also often engage in processing, canning, freezing, packaging and storing, as stages of their marketing activity.

MARX, KARL HEINRICH (1818–1883). A German philosopher and economic theorist, he was among the most influential of socialist thinkers. Fleeing Germany after the suppression in 1843 of a newspaper he was editing in Cologne, Marx moved to Paris, then Brussels, and finally to London where he spent most his life as an impoverished theorist. In 1848, with Friedrich Engels, he published the *Communist Manifesto*, in which the social utility of the cooperative movement was acknowledged as one of the vehicles through which a classless society would be achieved.

MATERIALS AND TECHNIQUES FOR COOPERATIVE MANAGEMENT TRAINING (MATCOM). A project of the **ILO** launched in 1978, MATCOM was built on the idea that the benefits of cooperative membership in **developing countries** can be enhanced through improved training programs for staff and **managers** and through the improved efficiency in the operations and services of cooperatives that would result from such training. MATCOM undertook to do this by preparing and distributing materials relevant to the needs of various cooperative sectors, including **agriculture, consumer, credit unions, handicraft** and **worker productive cooperatives**. An interregional program with global coverage, MATCOM produced materials that were adaptable to the differing situations of developing country cooperatives. An essential feature of the MATCOM approach was the introduction and use of participatory learning methods such as group discussions, role playing, case studies and instructor/learner dialogue. MATCOM materials are adaptable to varying national situations and are available in different languages. MATCOM's operations ceased when its grant from the Swedish development agency was exhausted. It has left a legacy of useful cooperative training materials available from the ILO in Geneva.

MAURICE, FREDERICK DENISON. A British professor of theology at King's College, London, he, with **Charles Kingsley** and **John Malcolm Ludlow**, organized the Christian Socialist movement. While not much engaged in the specific work of the cooperative organizational structure, he was a personal and ideological inspiration to many British cooperators of the late 19th and early 20th centuries. He was charged late in life with heresy and removed from his university position, a move that freed his time and interests for other activities, among which was the founding of the Workingmen's College.

MAURITANIA. The establishment of Indigenous Provident Societies in 1926 marks the start of cooperative development in Mauritania. However, serious organizing efforts date from the 1950s and 1960s when **agricultural cooperatives** were formed, **cooperative legislation** passed, and a government structure established to assist and regulate cooperatives, now the Cooperative Division in the Ministry of Rural Development. Agriculture is the principal cooperative sector, with the **ILO** reporting in 1974 that 208 of the 226 cooperatives were in that field. The latest **ICA** report (1985) portrayed a cooperative movement consisting of 1,250 cooperatives with 53,500 members (5.2% of the population). At that time 750 cooperatives with 51,000 members were in agriculture; the balance of 500 (consumer, craftsmen and fisheries) had 2,500 members.

MAURITIUS. A strategically valuable location in the Indian Ocean made Mauritius attractive successively to Portuguese, Dutch, French and British imperial interests. Vestiges of the French presence during the 18th century still remain, but the cooperative traditions of the English have guided the development of the movement. A Cooperative Societies Ordinance was passed in 1913, and the first **credit cooperatives**, serving agriculture, were established that same year. Growth and differentiation of functions characterized the period up to the end of World War II when new **cooperative legislation** was adopted, **fishery cooperatives** initiated, the Cooperative Bank established, and both **agricultural cooperative** and **apex** national **federations** formed. The first **credit union** was organized in 1960, followed by the organization of a national league in 1972. During the same period a Ministry of Cooperatives and Cooperative Development was established, and national federations for pig marketing and for **consumer cooperatives** were initiated. Tea marketing, livestock and housing federations came into being in the 1980s, reflecting the growing importance of these aspects of the economy and the utility of cooperative organizations in support of them. The **ICA Regional Office for East, Central and Southern Africa** reported that in 1994 there were 547 cooperatives with 136,310 members in the following sectors: agriculture—383 cooperatives/with 57,610 members; consumer—57/25,250; housing—8/1,950; savings and credit (credit unions and farm credit)—85/37,300; transport—8/800; worker productive—5/800; and others—1/12,600. They represented 12.4% of the population.

MAXWELL, SIR WILLIAM (1841–1929). A Scottish coach builder and artist of some note, he was a leader of the national and international cooperative movement and an advocate for protective legislation for workers. President of the **Scottish Cooperative Wholesale Society** (1881–1908), he was also active in the **ICA**, serving as its president for the period 1907–21. Maxwell was instrumental in maintaining a sense of internationalism among cooperators whose countries were enemies during World War I and was a major architect of the reunification of the movement following the war. Author of numerous pamphlets on cooperative matters, he also wrote *The History of Cooperation in Scotland.*

MAXWELL-STEIGMAN, DORA (1897–1985). An American social reformer and **credit union** organizer, she helped organize her first credit union at a church in Brooklyn, New York, in 1920, serving as its treasurer until 1930 when she became an organizer for the Credit Union Extension Bureau. She was one of the 33 original signers of the Charter of the **Credit Union National Association** when it was established in 1934; in 1945 she became the head of its Organizational Department. The Dora Maxwell Award was established in her honor, to be given annually to a credit union that has shown outstanding social responsibility for service to its community.

MAY, HENRY J. (1871–1939). General secretary of the **ICA** for the period 1913–39, he was secretary of the Parliamentary Committee of the **Cooperative Union of the U.K.** when he was recruited to serve as ICA's principal staff leader. He was a staunch supporter of the independence of the national cooperative organizations that make up ICA's membership, and on a number of occasions he intervened when these were under political attack within their own countries—most notably in **Austria, Germany, Italy** and **Spain**. May felt that there was an integral relationship between the principles of cooperation and world **peace** and attempted to position ICA to play a role in ameliorating international tensions and rivalries. He was the first ICA staff member to visit **Canada** during the early days of the development of its movement and played a particularly constructive role in drawing all elements of that movement together. An able administrator, May was often applauded for achieving so much in international cooperation with so few resources. He was a prolific writer, much of his work written for inclusion in the ICA *Review of International Cooperation*. This material reflects May's zeal for cooperation, for the international cooperative movement as an instrument of economic and social justice, and for its role in ultimately establishing world peace.

MCINNIS, DUNCAN (1847–1924). A Scottish-born cooperator, he joined the Lincoln Cooperative Society in 1873 and remained a member until his death. In 1886 he was elected a member of the central board of the **Cooperative Union of the U.K.** and from 1898 to 1921 served as a member of the board of the **English Cooperative Wholesale Society**. McInnis was a member of the first Executive Committee of the **ICA** (appointed in 1895) and served in the ICA elected leadership until 1921, for the final year as chairman of the Executive Committee. He was subsequently named to the **Committee of Honor of the International Cooperative Alliance**.

MCPHAIL, ALEXANDER JAMES (1884–1931). A Canadian cooperator, he served as president of Saskatchewan Wheat Pool and later, when it merged with two other pools, as president of the Canadian Wheat Pool. He was widely active in matters dealing with agricultural marketing in **Canada**, and his expertise was called upon by the **United States** Congress when cooperative marketing legislation was being considered there.

MEHTA, VAIKUNTH (1891–1964). Born of a wealthy family, he declined opportunities to engage in lucrative businesses and after his university training became part of the fledgling cooperative movement in **India**. He joined the Bombay State Cooperative Bank in 1910 and became a **manager**, helping to shape the bank into a powerful support system for cooperatives. He served as chairman of a number of institutions, among them the Bombay State Cooperative Union and the Khadi and Village Industries Board, from which emerged some of the earliest Indian industrial cooperatives. Mehta was selected Minister of Finance and Cooperation in the then Bombay State and in that position influenced the direction of cooperative development in the state. **Cooperative education** was a special interest of his and he was a voracious reader and writer. As a testimony to this interest, the Cooperative Management Institute at Pune was named in Mehta's honor.

MELLAERTS, FATHER. A Catholic priest and early Belgian cooperative leader, in 1887 he established the Guilde agricole de Heist-Goor (Heist-Goor Farmers' Guild), the forerunner of the Belgian Boerenbond (Farmers' Organization).

MELMOTH, GRAHAM (1938–). A U.K. cooperative leader of long standing, nearly 25 years with the **English Cooperative Wholesale Society** where he was secretary and then CEO, Melmoth was elected president of **ICA** for the period 1995–97. His important activities included hosting the Centennial Congress of the ICA in Manchester in 1995. Melmoth was elected to the ICA Executive Committee in 1992 and was elected chair of the ICA European Council in 1994.

MEMORIAL SOCIETIES. *See* FUNERAL COOPERATIVES.

MEXICO. The beginning of Mexico's involvement with cooperative forms date from 1839 when a **mutual** savings bank was established in Orizaba. Artisan and **consumer cooperatives** appeared in the 1870s, and the first cooperative legislative provisions were included in the Commercial Code in 1889. The first **agricultural cooperatives** were formed in 1905. The Mexican Revolution of 1910 was followed by land reform programs that reestablished and reinforced the traditional Indian *ejidos* and introduced collective cooperatives with a similar status. The constitution of 1917 gave official status to the cooperative movement, and 10 years later the first national confederation of cooperatives came into being. The period of the Cardenas presidency (1934–40) was a cooperative-friendly period and saw a rapid growth of collective cooperatives that were given legal status as *ejidos*. A national bank for ejidal support was established and a new **cooperative law** enacted. Early in the 1940s a cooperative development bank was organized and the national confederation of cooperatives reconstituted. A confederation of people's banks was formed in 1964, reflecting the growth of the savings and **credit cooperatives**.

Viewed apart from the *ejidos*, which are not regarded by everyone as cooperatives, the movement has had only modest growth and has not yet become an important force in the Mexican economy. In 1988 the "traditional" (non-*ejido*) cooperatives numbered 8,224 with 633,105 members (0.75% of the population). Cooperatives are active in the following sectors: agriculture, consumer, fisheries, housing, savings and credit, transport, and worker productive and service enterprises. Current data on **school cooperatives**, thought to be widespread, was not available. The most recent statistical data on *ejidos*, an **FAO** report in 1980, estimated that there were then 24,000 of them with 2,600,000 members. Were these numbers to be included in cooperative statistics, this would increase to 3.1 the percentage of **cooperative penetration** in the Mexican population.

MICRONESIA. Little information has been generated on the historical development of cooperatives in Micronesia. After World War II, the country was a United Nations Trust Territory, administered by the **United States**. It had an earlier history as a colony of **Spain**, then **Germany**, and a period of control by **Japan**. An **ILO** Memo Report in 1985 indicated that there were 87 registered cooperatives—10 agricultural, 31 consumer, 21 credit unions, and 25 fisheries. No information was included as to numbers of members.

MIDDLE WAY. A term first used in reference to Swedish cooperatives to distinguish a socio-economic system based on cooperation and cooperatives from one based on either capitalist or communist ideology.

MIELCZARSKI, ROMUALD (1871–1926). A pioneer of the cooperative movement in **Poland**, he was an organizer and then president of the Union and Wholesale of Consumer's Cooperative Societies of Poland. Among their other virtues, he regarded cooperatives as the organized power of consumers and as the primary force that could elicit concessions from the **capitalist** system, ultimately replacing it, Mielczarski dreamed, with cooperative economic and political democracy. His essentially socialist vision made him a target of the Czarist government that ruled Poland at the time, and he was first imprisoned and then banished for his views. He spent time in **Germany, Switzerland** and **Belgium** before returning in 1900, only to be imprisoned again and later banished to the Caucasus. At the time of the Revolution of 1905 he returned to Warsaw, where he became a propagandist for and organizer of cooperatives. Mielczarski was elected to the **ICA** Central Committee at the 1921 Basel Congress and served until 1924.

MIGROS. A Swiss **consumer cooperative** organized originally as a joint stock company in 1925 by **Gottlieb Duttweiler.** Its novelty was originally to be found in its method of retail distribution, five mobile vans that carried only six articles: coffee, macaroni, rice, soap, sugar and vegetable cooking fat. Also, its considerably lower price structure, made possible by its limited overhead costs, made it a popular choice. Its novel traveling shops were soon augmented by ordinary shops so that by 1950 there were 77 sales vans and 226 shops. About 1934–35 Duttweiler began to experiment with cooperative forms in some of his new enterprises, the success of which led him and his wife, the sole shareholders of the Migros Joint Stock Companies, into establishing formal cooperatives, which formed a **federation** in 1941. The cooperative, Migros, has continued to expand and, with Coop Switzerland, now controls a major share of the Swiss consumer market. It has remained controversial, with some cooperative purists questioning its origins and conversion.

MILHAUD, EDGARD (1873–1964). Born at Nîmes in **France,** he was one of the early French theorists of cooperation and cooperative organization and was professor of economics at the University of Geneva for 46 years. He believed that cooperatives should not be viewed simply as an economic idea: he regarded cooperative methods and activities as the only way in which an economic system could reconcile freedom and organization. Milhaud also viewed cooperation, by eliminating competition, as the way through which humankind would turn from war and preparation for war to **peace.** During his years in Geneva he concurrently served as director of research for the **ILO,** and his worldwide studies of production provided the bases for the World Economic Conference of 1927, which, among other things, compared cooperative and profit-making methods of distribution. Milhaud founded the journal *Annals of Collective Economy,* and in many articles examined the relationship that did and should exist between the cooperative and public sectors of the economy. His ideas and activity in these areas continue in the international organization **CIRIEC,** which he founded in 1947. He was named to the **Committee of Honor of the International Cooperative Alliance.**

MIRER, G. A. J. (1876–1930). A Dutch cooperative leader, he was president of the Dutch Cooperative Wholesale Society, De Handelskamer, in Rotterdam and was effective in bridging the sectarian differences between the social democratic, Catholic and neutral cooperative movements in the **Netherlands.** He was a member of the International Wholesale Committee of the **ICA** and traveled extensively in Europe and the **United States.**

MITCHELL, JOHN T. W. (1828–1895). A British consumer cooperative leader who was born and lived in **Rochdale** all his life, he became a member of the **Rochdale Society of Equitable Pioneers** in 1853. He was part of the group that organized the North of England Cooperative Wholesale, forerunner of the **English Cooperative Wholesale Society,** of which he became chairman, serving from 1874 to 1895.

MODEL COOPERATIVE SOCIETIES ORDINANCE. A model **cooperative law** that was prepared and distributed in 1946 by the Colonial Office to the British Commonwealth; it led to the adoption of cooperative laws in most British colonies.

MOLDOVA. Moldova became an independent republic in 1991 when the **Union of Soviet Socialist Republics** was disbanded. Prior to that it had been a republic within the USSR and its cooperatives a part of **Centrosoyus,** the Soviet **consumer cooperative** structure. The consumer cooperatives in Moldova have reorganized themselves as a separate movement that in 1996 reported a membership of 595,320 (13.3% of the population) in 149 societies.

MONDRAGON COOPERATIVES. The Cooperative Group of Mondragon is an integrated network of worker-owned industrial and related cooperatives in the Basque Region of **Spain;** in 1990 it included 84 **industrial production,** 8 **agricultural,** 1 **consumer** (with 330 sales points), 17 **housing** and 6 **service cooperatives.** It includes a superstructure that provides constant support in the development of the cooperatives' activities. Included are the Caja Laboral Popular, a worker **cooperative bank** with 189 branches or office; Lagun-Aro, which handles **insurance** and other social security services; and Ikerlan, a technology research center. The Liga de Educación y Cultura (with 45 associated education cooperatives) provides technical and management training as well as general educational and cultural services. Mondragon is seen by many as an alternative way of structuring a modern industrial system, in contrast to that of industrial **capitalism** or state-planned and -controlled enterprise, that may one day be regarded as of similar historical importance as the **Rochdale Pioneers**.

The history of the Mondragon experiment began in 1940 when a recently ordained Catholic priest, **Father José María Arizmendi**-Arrieta, was sent to Mondragon as a counselor for the Catholic Action Group. He organized study groups for young workers but soon realized that their greatest need was for technical training. The result was the establishment in 1943 of the Mondragon Professional College. The first graduates of the college obtained their industrial expert qualifications in 1952 and, after a period of private employment, established in 1956 their own **production cooperative,** ULGOR (named from the initials of the founders' surnames), producing oil stoves and hotplates. Thirty-four years later the 20,157 worker-owners of the 84 Mondragon industrial cooperatives were producing forgings and castings, investment goods, machine tools, intermediate goods and consumer goods and were engaged in construction. Their related networks included 1,000 agricultural members, 150,000 consumer members and 500,000 holders of current accounts in their own savings bank.

MONGOLIA. Little information was available on the cooperative movement in Mongolia, which got its start in 1921 when the first Central People's Cooperative Association was founded at Urga, with assistance from a representative of the Russian **Centrosoyus**. The **ICA Regional Office for Asia and the Pacific** reported that there were 254 consumer cooperatives with 64,200 members in 1992. A subsequent report for 1997 noted 60 agricultural cooperatives with 57 members and 242 consumer cooperatives with 25,000 members. Together they represent 1.0% of the population. For a number of years the government of Mongolia was the initiator in the **United Nations** General Assembly of resolutions supportive of cooperative development, which accompanied the reports of the secretary general on that subject.

MONTSERRAT. At present still a British colony, its first **cooperative legislation** was enacted in 1959, and the first **credit union**, Saint Patrick's, was founded in 1960. The **ILO** *Directory* **(1988)** reported that there were 18 cooperatives in Montserrat with a membership of 1,515 (12.4% of the population). The following sectors were represented: agriculture—3 cooperatives/with 55 members; credit unions—2/1,050; fisheries—1/30; school—10/350; and women—2/30. The 1997 **WOCCU** *Statistical Report* indicated that membership in the one credit union had increased to 4,326. Assuming modest growth in other sectors, the combined **cooperative penetration** at that time was estimated to be 33.8% of the population of 12,800.

MOROCCO. The first of a series of decrees regarding cooperatives was issued in 1922, giving legitimacy to **consumer cooperatives** that were established that year. **Livestock** and **agricultural cooperatives** soon followed, and by 1931 both groups had established national **federations** to represent their interests. The burgeoning Moroccan movement had the distinction in 1932 of receiving the first technical assistance from the **Cooperative Service of the ILO,** provided by **Maurice Colombain**. He returned again in 1937 and is credited with instituting a positive redirection of the movement, moving them into housing and handicraft and providing a rationale for the growing number of cooperative unions in various sectors.

With independence in 1956 and its aftermath came new directions: **school cooperatives**, a government office for the development of cooperatives, decrees extending the cooperative movement to the commercial sector and fisheries, and a decree requiring that cooperatives be established to take over land abandoned by French settlers. During the reign of King Hussan II, starting in 1961, cooperatives have continued to develop and grow, though sectoral **unions** have had limited staying power (usually a sign of weakness in a movement's development). The **ILO** *Directory* **(1988)** listed only two federations, for agricultural cooperatives and cooperative dairies, with no national confederation.

In 1997, the **ICA** reported that in 1995 there were 9,635 cooperatives with a membership of 675,589 in the following sectors: agriculture— 3,474 societies/with 271,739 members; consumer—62/5,802; fisheries—30/839; housing—840/42,484; savings and credit (banks) 23/318,479; worker productive 529/21,027; and others (including school cooperatives)—4,677/15,219. Cooperative membership was 2.5% of the national population.

MOSCOW COOPERATIVE INSTITUTE. The principal cooperative training organization in **Russia** during the period of the **Union of Soviet**

Socialist Republics, it provided training for cooperative leaders from **developing countries**. A number of courses were provided each year in various languages, and developing-country students were also admitted to the five-year course, in Russian, on the economics of cooperation.

MOSHAV. An Israeli cooperative agricultural settlement consisting of families on adjacent land holdings. The families produce individually, but the purchase of supplies, marketing of production and other defined activities are carried out collectively.

MOVEMENT. A collective series of actions and opinions of a group of people and/or organizations aimed at achieving a common purpose, e.g., the cooperative movement.

MOVEMENT-TO-MOVEMENT ASSISTANCE. Technical or financial assistance provided to a cooperative organization or project in a **developing country** by a cooperative organization in an industrialized country without any direct involvement of the governments of the two countries. **Cooperative development organizations** consider this to be a superior form of relationship between cooperative organizations and believe that the provision of assistance in this fashion enhances the development of independence and self-direction by the cooperatives involved.

MOZAMBIQUE. The early history of cooperative development in Mozambique is captured in this quote from the 1987 **COPAC** Country Information Note on cooperatives in Mozambique. It notes simply, "The first cooperatives in Mozambique were established during the colonial time; however, almost all of them were made up of Portuguese immigrants. When the colonial regime in Mozambique collapsed, these cooperatives were closed." The post-independence government adopted a Marxist-Leninist model of development, and any previous cooperative tradition was considered irrelevant. The statistical data in the **ILO** *Directory* **(1988)** for 1985 reflects the decision by the government to establish a distribution network for the country based on **consumer cooperatives** (2,492 societies with 1,120,130 members) and the beginnings of cooperation in the fields of agriculture (569 societies with 49,236 members), fisheries (74 societies with 2,174 members) and craftsmen's productive (137 societies with 2,720 members). The total membership of the movement at that date was 1,174,260 in 3,272 societies (8.5% of the population).

MÜLLER, HANS (1866–1950). A cooperator in **Switzerland**, he was secretary of the Swiss Union of Consumer Cooperatives and represented Swiss cooperatives in the Central Committee of the **ICA**. In 1908 he was named ICA general secretary, serving until 1913, part of the time in London and part in Zurich. During this time he initiated and edited the *International Cooperative Bulletin*, the predecessor of the *Review of International Cooperation*. In later years he was associated with universities in Zurich, Thüringen and Jena.

MULTIPURPOSE COOPERATIVE. An association of cooperators organized to meet several different needs or to provide a mix of needed services; also referred to as a general purpose cooperative.

MUSUNDI, JOHN J. A Kenyan cooperative leader, he was the chief executive of the Kenya National Federation of Cooperatives. In 1972 he was elected to the Executive Committee of the **ICA**.

MUTUAL. An association in which the benefits are given and received equally by two or more persons. In a mutual **insurance** society, for example, **profits** are shared out equally among the policy holders in proportion to the value of their policies. A mutual society is a form of cooperative existing for the benefit of its members, though it does not necessarily apply all the **cooperative principles**.

MUTUAL AID. A theory, posited first by **Peter Kropotkin**, that working together is as innate to human nature as competing. Also the term used to describe the principle of joint assistance manifested in cooperative organizations.

MYANMAR (formerly Burma). Attempts to provide cooperative credit in Burma date back to 1904 when a **cooperative** societies **law** was passed, and the government established a cooperative department to stimulate the formation of voluntary credit organizations. The first cooperatives were organized in 1905 and a provincial bank was set up at Mandalay soon thereafter, followed by others at principal towns. Cooperatives began to develop generally, and by 1927 there were 4,057 with a membership of 92,005. The worldwide depression and then World War II took a drastic toll, however, and it was not until the postwar era that momentum was regained.

By the end of the 1940s, some 2,000 cooperatives had been rejuvenated or started, with a strong emphasis on **consumer cooperatives** among the new. By 1951 development had proceeded sufficiently far to convene a National Cooperative Convention, then to create a National Cooperative Council. Among the Council's plans were those to stimulate the formation of industrial cooperatives, a sector now as large as that of agriculture. An **United Nations/ILO** technical assistance team in the 1950s gave additional stimulus to a movement that has continued to grow. The **ILO** *Directory* **(1988)** reported that there were 20,500 cooperatives with a membership of 6,923,000 (17.5% of the population). The ICA Report Cooperative Statistical Profile by Country (1996) indicated that in 1995 there were 38,320 cooperatives with 3,979,291 members (8.8% of the population) in the following sectors: agriculture—3,389 cooperatives/with 88,875 members; consumer—12,680/3,068,504; fisheries—269/18,570; savings and credit—2,165/371,192; worker productive—1022/57,112; and others—18,695/375,038.

MYRICK, HERBERT (1860–1927). An American editor, publisher and cooperator, he was president of a publishing company that published numerous magazines dealing with farming, including *Farm and Home*. He was an advocate of cooperation as the best way of organizing the agriculture sector and had particular interests in cooperative dairying, procurement and marketing. In 1890 he wrote in 1890 *How to Cooperate*, based in part on his own experience as owner of the 600-acre Wissett Farms. In 1910 he was involved in the organization of the first **credit union** in the **United States**.

N

NAMIBIA. The first semblance of a cooperative like activity in Namibia (then the German Protectorate of South-West Africa) was the establishment in 1913 of a rural credit bank, financed by the German government, to support agricultural development and production activity. Some activity related to South African cooperatives developed during the period in which Namibia was first a League of Nations and later a United Nations Trust Territory, but it involved almost exclusively German and South African settlers. A move on the part of **South Africa** to annex the territory was opposed by the **United Nations,** which established a United Nations Council for Namibia pending the establishment of an independent government. The Council engaged in a variety of nation-developing activities, supported by United Nations and other development agencies. One product of this effort was a **COPAC** Cooperative Information Note on Namibia (1980), exploring various cooperative options that could be developed once independence was achieved. This was further elaborated in 1980 and was part of the background materials available for the ICA Exploratory Mission in 1991, which laid out the framework for cooperative development in the country. This move resulted in a formal policy of a basic cooperative law, appointment of a registrar of cooperatives and general encouragement of cooperative development.

NAMSING, HERMANN (1878–1924). An Estonian cooperative leader and managing director of the Central Society of the Estonian Consumers' Societies, he was a cooperative activist from an early age, serving initially as a journalist and editor of a cooperative journal. With **Estonia's** independence after World War I, he became a leader in the cooperative movement and was instrumental in developing it quickly into the largest economic organization in the country. He was a member of the **ICA** Central Committee at the time of his death.

NATIONAL COOPERATIVE BUSINESS ASSOCIATION (NCBA). The national cooperative **apex organization** in the **United States,** including in its membership all types of cooperative organizations; formerly **CLUSA.**

NATIONAL COUNCIL OF FARMER COOPERATIVES. Organized in 1929, it is a national association in the **United States** of cooperative businesses owned and controlled by farmers. Its membership is made up principally of federated cooperatives serving as central agencies for local cooperatives and state councils of cooperatives. Its affiliates include the Farm Credit Council, **Agricultural Cooperative Development International (ACDI)** and the **American Institute of Cooperation (AIC).**

NATIONAL GRANGE OF THE PATRONS OF HUSBANDRY. A farmer movement in the **United States,** organized in 1867 to improve the social and economic position of farmers. By 1874 it had over 21,000 local chapters, and was known simply as the Grange. The Grange organized local cooperatives based on the **Rochdale Principles** for the supply of farmers' needs and marketing of their produce and was the backbone of the early **agricultural cooperative** movement in the United States. The Grange was among the first organizations in the United States to provide an equal voice and vote for women in its deliberations and operations. Grange policy is established each year through a deliberative process that starts with the local Granges. The motto of the organization is, "In essentials, unity; in non-essentials, liberty; in all things, charity."

NATIONAL RURAL ELECTRIC COOPERATIVE ASSOCIATION (NRECA). Organized in 1942, it represents the rural electric generating and transmission cooperatives that still supply most of the electrical power to the rural areas of the **United States**. It has an international division that assists in the development of electric cooperatives in the developing world, supported by funds from **USAID** as one of the U.S. **cooperative development organizations**.

NATIONWIDE INSURANCE COMPANY. An American **insurance cooperative**, established in the state of Ohio in 1926 as the Farm Bureau Mutual Automobile Insurance Company, added insurance lines for fire and general life as operations soon began to expand beyond Ohio. In 1955, reflecting this growth and spread, it changed its name to Nationwide Insurance, growing in time to become one of the giants of the American insurance industry. Under the initial leadership of **Murray Lincoln,** Nationwide used its financial and human resources to support and influence the development of the American and international cooperative movements. In the latter, Nationwide personnel became active participants in the Insurance Committee of the **ICA** and were particularly important in the work of the **Insurance Development Bureau** that was established to assist cooperative insurance operations in the **developing countries**.

NEALE, EDWARD VANSITTART (1810–1892). A British cooperative leader, he was among the founders of the London Cooperative Society in 1850. In 1853 he founded the Central Cooperative Agency, a forerunner of the **English Cooperative Wholesale Society**. He later served as general secretary of the **Cooperative Union** from 1873 to 1891. With **Edward Owen Greening,** he introduced a resolution at the British Cooperative Congress endorsing the principle of an international cooperative alliance. The resolution was approved. Neale's views on cooperatives were shaped by the social teachings of **François Marie Charles Fourier** and **Robert Owen**, by the Christian doctrine of brotherhood as expounded by **Frederick Denison Maurice**, and by the idealism of Hegel. He held that the rationale for cooperative associations and their unions was deeply embedded in the laws of the universe.

NELDON, N. O. He was a representative of U.S. cooperatives at the founding congress of the **ICA** in 1895.

NEPAL. While there is some mention of cooperatives existing in 1950, the first organized effort at cooperative formation (**credit cooperatives**) took place in 1956, three years after a government Cooperative Development Department was established. The first **legislation** was enacted in 1959. This initial period of cooperative development was animated by government interest and staff, and the results, as with previous international experience, were predictable—poor involvement of people, suspicion as to motives, mistrust and limited success. Several government schemes were tried in the hope of stimulating the development of cooperatives, all with similar results. It was not until the democratic changes of 1990 that a more tempered approach was undertaken. Again the government and its staff took the lead, but now with more attention to their earlier experiences. A high-level Cooperative Development Board was appointed and a new cooperative **act** was adopted in 1992. Steps were taken to revitalize existing societies, and plans developed for a National Cooperative Federation to be built from the bottom up. While longterm results are not yet clear, by 1992 the movement indicated that there were 1,049 cooperatives with 1,480,000 members (7.6% of the population). The **ICA** reported that in 1996 there were 3,208 cooperatives with a membership of 1,050,411 (4.8% of the population) in the following sectors: agriculture (single purpose)—661 societies/with 27,228 members; agriculture (multipurpose)—1,622/971,141; consumer—258/9,106; savings and credit—343/16,041; and others—248/18,895. During this same period **WOCCU** and the Asian Confederation of Credit Unions were assisting in the launching of a **credit union movement** for the country.

NETHERLANDS, THE. The Netherlands was among a small group of European countries that early established a broad-based cooperative movement. Legislation dealing with cooperatives was adopted in 1855 (two years after the **United Kingdom**). The first cooperative (a consumer society) was founded in 1860, precursor of a large and successful network. **Agricultural credit** cooperatives had achieved a sufficient degree of organization by the late 1890s so that a cooperative union of

Raiffeisen-type **credit cooperatives** (predecessor of the current **Rabobank**) had been organized. The importance of the Netherlands cooperatives was attested to in the choice of Delft as the site of the Third Congress of the still new **ICA** in 1897. By this date consumer, credit, dairy, horticultural and marketing societies had been established, followed within 10 years by **unions** for most of these types of cooperatives as well as cooperatives for sugar, soap and fertilizer production, insurance societies, a consumer **cooperative wholesale society** and a **federation** of **housing cooperatives**. This diverse profile of Dutch cooperatives has persisted until the present, surviving and growing through the two world wars and the economic distress of the 1930s. By 1942, 3,406 cooperatives were to be counted in the *Netherlands Register of Trade and Commerce*, 2,444 of them in various aspects of agriculture. By 1947, with postwar adjustment in place, these numbers had increased to 3,755 and 2,818 respectively.

Consolidation, particularly among agricultural societies, has been a major development of the period since then, with the amalgamation of smaller societies into large and sophisticated cooperative enterprises. Some would observe that the Netherlands cooperatives are noteworthy for ignoring the **cooperative principle** of political and religious **neutrality**, with cooperative societies and unions organized under Protestant, Catholic, socialist, and Christian Democratic ideological auspices. Much energy has gone into the tempering of these divisive tendencies within the movement, facilitated by the establishment of a National Cooperative Council. A publication of the Economic and Social Committee of the European Communities in 1986 portrayed a diverse and dynamic movement in agriculture, consumer wholesale and retail supply, credit, housing, insurance and worker productive sectors. While statistical data was incomplete, it reported a total membership in Dutch societies in excess of 2,900,000. In a 1993 EUROSTAT report on European Communities cooperatives it was noted that 4,106 cooperatives then existed. No data, however, was available regarding cooperative membership. Files of the ICA in 1997 showed a movement with 2,492 societies and a combined membership of 6,446,000 (41.1% of the population) in the following sectors: agriculture—271 societies/with a membership of 296,000; consumer—1/70,000; housing—900/1,550,000; pharmacy—50/3,700,000; savings and credit (banks) 970/825,000; worker productive—300/5,000.

NETHERLANDS ANTILLES. A small federation of former Dutch colonies off the northern coast of Venezuela, its cooperative history has been and remains essentially one of **credit unions**. The **ILO** *Directory* **(1988)** indicated that in 1986 there were 43 cooperatives with 12,439 members (6.7% of the population); 35 of the societies were credit unions with 12,400 members. The remainder were 2 agricultural, 1 consumer, and 3 small worker productive cooperatives. WOCCU's *1995 Statistical Report* indicated that in 1994 there were 25 credit unions with a total membership of 16,000. The **International Cooperative Alliance** reported a total membership of 17,000 in 1996. **Cooperative penetration** in that year was estimated to be 8.1% of the population of 209,000.

NETHERLANDS DEVELOPMENT ASSISTANCE. Netherlands assistance to development programs in Third World countries is provided through the Directorate General for International Cooperation, in which some importance is attached to support for cooperatives. Most Dutch assistance to cooperatives is provided through four non-governmental organizations, CEBEMO, ICCO, NOVIB and Stichting Hivos.

NEUTRALITY. The **Rochdale Principle** whereby persons are admitted to cooperative societies without reference to religion, race, gender or politics. Following this principle, a cooperative society should not affiliate itself with any political party, since it represents people who may be members of different parties. This principle does not exclude non-partisan political activity of a type that will benefit an individual cooperative or cooperatives collectively.

NEW HARMONY. A **utopian** cooperative community established in 1825 in the **United States**, in Indiana, by **Robert Owen**.

NEW LANARK ON THE CLYDE. An industrial village in Scotland purchased in 1799 by **Robert Owen,** it provided him with a base for experimenting with improved working conditions for employees and exploring changing personal conditions as a way of achieving the goal of a community built on cooperative ideals. His enterprise was successful, but he came to feel that cooperative communities had to be built anew, unfettered by existing conditions, if they were to achieve his ideal. This conclusion led to his experiments with **utopian** communities in the **United States,** including **New Harmony**.

NEW ZEALAND. The first recorded cooperative activity in New Zealand was the establishment of the New Zealand Farmers' Cooperative

Association in 1881 followed in 1895 by the National Dairy Association. **Cooperative legislation** was enacted in 1908. During the next 10 years a variety of commodity-based **agricultural cooperative** federations were established, and an international agreement for marketing of New Zealand produce had been signed with the Overseas Farmer's Cooperative Federation in London. A national **federation**, the New Zealand Cooperative Alliance, was founded in 1933 and shortly thereafter the New Zealand Cooperative Women's Guild. The New Zealand Credit Union League, a relative newcomer to the cooperative scene in New Zealand, was established in 1961. It reported in 1996 the existence of 115 **credit unions** with 185,374 members (5.2% of the population). Membership data for the entire cooperative movement was unavailable.

NICARAGUA. Cooperative efforts in Nicaragua date from 1914, when the first retail cooperatives were formed and the Commercial Code of the country was amended to include provisions governing them. Growth was not memorable nor was it registered statistically for the ensuing years, and the next notable cooperative events recorded were cooperative-related amendments made to the Labor Code in 1945 and the establishment of collective agrarian cooperatives in 1960. An Agrarian Reform Law in 1963 marked the beginning of official government concern for introducing equity into the land holdings of the country, a contentious issue that persists to the present. The growth of **credit unions** in the country was noted by the establishment of a national **federation** in 1965. A General Cooperative Law was enacted in 1970. The Sandinista Revolution of 1979 introduced a more radical approach to land reform and to peasant empowerment; this persisted until 1990 when the Sandinista government was defeated in national elections. In 1983, 3,475 cooperatives were noted with a membership of over 75,000, approximately 2.2% of the population. The **ICA** reported that in 1991 there were 3,731 cooperatives with a membership of 92,077 (2.4% of the population) in the following sectors: agriculture—3,371 societies/with a membership of 83,106; fisheries—43/na; savings and credit—105/5,596; transport—138/1,600; and worker productive—81/1,775.

NIELSEN, ANDERS (1859–1928). A farmer and cooperative leader in **Denmark,** he was active in his homeland in the formation of butter cooperatives, cooperative import activities, a **cooperative bank** and a national Danish cooperative organization. He served on the **ICA** Central Committee from 1910 to 1928.

NIGER. In Niger the French colonial administration followed the pattern of most French West African countries: the establishment of Native Provident Societies (1910), reorganized first as Mutual Associations for Rural Production (1945) and then as Mutual Associations for Rural Development (1953). Few were notably successful, dominated as they were by government mandates, government officials and government agendas, overlaid by a mistrust of the ability of the "peasants" to handle complex affairs. After independence in 1960 the National Cooperative Union of Niger was established, amid hopes for a more effective effort. A new system, based on *groupements mutualistes* at the village level, was initiated in 1966 and proved to be some improvement. Further reorganization in 1984, including a new cooperative ordinance, provided the basis for recent experience and a growth of *groupements* and cooperatives (10 village *groupements* make up a cooperative). These groups are engaged in multiple activities, rather than being solely marketing organizations for farmers' crops as they had mainly been in the past. By 1976 there were 5,300 *groupements*, growing to 10,628 in 1986. In 1981 there were 771 cooperatives; by 1986, this number had increased to 1,167 with a total individual membership estimated at 531,400 (8.3% of the population). A membership report of the **ICA** stated that cooperative membership had increased to 880,000 in 1996 (9.7% of the population).

NIGERIA. Although there are longstanding cooperation traditions among the ethnic groups that make up the population of Nigeria, and while there were early attempts to organize cooperative-like groups, particularly to service cacao producers, formal cooperation came to Nigeria only in the 1930s. A report in 1933–34 by **C. F. Strickland**, who was experienced in colonial cooperative development, stimulated the first organized nationwide development efforts. A Cooperative Societies Ordinance was passed in 1935, a Cooperative Department established in the national government in 1936, the first **Registrar of Cooperatives** named that year and the first cooperative formally registered in 1937. From the beginning the principal types of cooperatives have been agricultural, the first focusing on cacao production, processing and marketing. An export cooperative association for this product was organized in 1945. Regionalization of the cooperative effort followed in the 1950s, and by the time of independence in 1960 regional **federations** were well established throughout the country. At present there are 19 state federations, mirroring the 19 Nigerian states.

Savings and **credit cooperatives (credit unions)** are numerically and in membership the second largest of the cooperative sectors. They have a national federation as well as state structures through which they associate their activities. **Consumer cooperatives** are the third largest sector and are of long standing in Nigeria. A national **apex** Cooperative Supply Association was established as early as 1940 and a National Cooperative Wholesale Association in 1976 to support the cooperative structure. A network of **cooperative banks** and Cooperative Finance Agencies service the societies' credit needs, and there is a national **insurance cooperative** network. Small groups of fishery and industrial cooperatives round out the picture. Nigeria has yet to establish political and economic stability and has developed a pattern of military "coupocracy" which continues to frustrate achievement of these. Nevertheless, in 1986, the **ILO** *Directory* **(1988)** reported, the cooperative network in Nigeria included 19,802 cooperatives with 1,784,941 members (1.8% of the population) in the following sectors: agriculture—10,799 societies/with 827,342 members; consumer—1,430/287,728; fisheries—251/10,320; housing—1/850; savings and credit—6,958/645,541; worker productive—361/13,140; and others—2/20.

NÎMES, SCHOOL OF. Established in 1886 by **August Fabre** and **Edouard de Boyve** as a local circle of workmen who were anxious to learn and improve themselves and who considered, in tune with the thinking of **François Marie Charles Fourier**, that social conditions would only be ameliorated with the moral and intellectual advancement of the individual. Nîmes became a great intellectual center for the cooperative movement, with economists, sociologists and philanthropists of many nations coming to state their ideas and their theses. **Charles Gide** became associated with the society in its early days and was involved with it and its publications until his death.

NORDISK ANDELSFÖRBUND (NAF). A joint venture **wholesale society** of the Scandinavian **consumer cooperatives** established in 1918, initially involving consumer cooperative organizations in **Denmark**, **Norway** and **Sweden**; later joined by cooperatives in **Finland** and **Iceland**. NAF engages in international and inter-cooperative trading activities, providing a wide range of products to its member organizations as part of the supplies for their national consumer cooperative networks.

NORTH AMERICAN STUDENTS OF COOPERATION (NASCO). Established in 1968, NASCO was an outgrowth of an international effort by Canadian and American **campus cooperatives** to stimulate interest and to provide support for cooperative activity on university campuses in the two countries. It has played a role of increasing importance in providing financial and technical assistance to college-based cooperatives and has been a source of recruitment of young leaders into the cooperative movements of **Canada** and the **United States**.

NORWAY. The initial actions that eventually led to the Norwegian cooperative movement stem from the last half of the 19th century. In 1851 the first cooperative (a consumer society) came into being, a product of a social, semi-revolutionary movement headed by **Marcus Thrane**. In 1856 a cooperative cheese factory became the agriculturalists' first formal cooperative structure. Similar spontaneous local efforts throughout the country characterized the next period, some more successful than others. The latter part of the century saw the establishment of a milk producers' federation in 1881 and the formation in 1895 of the Oslo Cooperative Society, from which much of the energy and enthusiasm of the consumer movement would flow. The Norwegian Consumer Cooperative Union was established in 1906, a year after Norway achieved its independence after 400 years of Danish domination and almost 100 years as a province of **Sweden**. Growth and elaboration of the agricultural and consumer movements continued up to and through World War I, and 1918 saw the formation of both the Agricultural Cooperatives Bank and the **Nordisk Andelsförbund** (NAF) (Nordic Cooperative Wholesale Society), in which the consumer movements in Norway joined with those in Sweden, **Denmark** and later **Finland** and **Iceland** to collectively deal with the growing supply needs of **consumer cooperatives**. The 1920s saw the birth of the Norwegian Cooperative Housing Union, the third important wing of the Norwegian movement, of Samvirke, a national **insurance cooperative** organization, and the beginning, continuing into the 1930s, of a flurry of organization of **agricultural cooperative** unions representing various commodities and functions. National **federations** of fishermen were next to appear in the years leading up to World War II, during which war Norway was occupied by Germany.

In 1945, the Central Federation of Agricultural Cooperatives was formed, composed of 17 national organizations that would help shepherd the agricultural cooperatives through a period of rapid consolidation. In 1981 the Federation became the Division of Agricultural Cooperation of the Norwegian Farmers' Union. This in turn brought an association with the Royal Norwegian Society for Rural Development, in which a Committee for International Cooperative Development was formed that became the structure through which much of Norway's assistance to cooperatives in **developing countries** has taken place. Consumer cooperatives continued their growth and development, consolidating into more logically sized retail units, which in 1956 could boast over 300,000 members. In 1968 these cooperatives formed a **petroleum cooperative** to serve growing automotive needs, and by 1987 their membership had grown to 548,000. Meanwhile **housing cooperatives** flourished, and by 1982 their 675,000 members made them numerically the largest cooperative sector. By 1987 the Norwegian movement represented more than 950 cooperative societies with a combined membership in excess of 1,415,000 members (33.8% of the nation's population). In 1994 the movement totaled 546 cooperatives with a combined membership of 1,531,711 (35.6% of the population). A 1998 report of **ICA** notes that in 1996 there were 4,259 cooperatives with a membership of 1,597,668 in the following sectors: agriculture—96 societies/with 168,244 members; consumer—331/815,000; forestry—na/55,959; housing—3,830/558,485; and insurance—2/na. Cooperative membership was 36.4% of the population.

NOURSE, EDWIN G. (1883–1974). An American economist, he taught at universities in North Dakota, Arkansas and Iowa, during which time he became deeply involved with agriculture and **agricultural cooperatives**, coming to view them as offering the best prospects for improving the economic organization of agriculture. Nourse was also a staunch believer that cooperatives had to be built from the bottom up and could not be imposed arbitrarily. He joined the Economics Institute in Washington, D.C. (later the Brookings Institute) in 1923 and was appointed the first chairman of the Council of Economic Advisors to U.S. president Harry Truman in 1946. He was instrumental in the organization of the **American Institute of Cooperation,** which established an annual award in his name for the best Ph.D. dissertation on cooperatives. Nourse was elected to the U.S. **Cooperative Hall of Fame** in 1976.

NOWELL COMMISSION. The report of the Nowell Commission in the **United Kingdom** in 1938 recommended the establishment of cooperative departments and agricultural **marketing cooperatives** in the British colonies in West Africa.

NYKÖPING, A. D. A Swedish cooperative pioneer, he was active in the establishment of the **consumer** and **worker productive cooperative** movements in **Sweden**.

O

OBISESAN, CHIEF AKINPELU (1887–1963). President of the Cooperative Union of Western Nigeria after a career with the Nigerian Railway and as a farmer, he was a leader in the Gbedun Cooperative Produce Marketing Society, one of the first registered cooperative in **Nigeria**. He served also as president of the Association of Nigerian Cooperative Exporters and of the Cooperative Federation of Nigeria.

ODHE, THORSTEN (1862–1965). A Swedish cooperative leader, he served for 25 years with **Kooperativa Förbundet (KF),** the Swedish **consumer cooperative** federation. KF made him available to serve as the **ICA** representative to the new **United Nations** agencies in 1947, before his selection and service as director of the ICA for the period 1948–51. Returning to **Sweden** he became director of the Swedish Institute for Cooperative Research. He shared the view that cooperatives had a unique opportunity to contribute to the resolution of the world's economic, political and social problems.

OPEN MEMBERSHIP. In the cooperative sense this means that membership in a society is open to all persons who meet the qualifications defined by their **bylaws**. In 1966 the **ICA** adopted **cooperative principles**, among which was one stating: "Membership in a cooperative should be voluntary and available without artificial restriction or any social, political, or religious discrimination to all persons who can make use of its services and who are willing to accept the responsibilities of membership."

OPPENHEIMER, FRANZ (1864–1943). A German cooperative theorist who saw in **communism** the ultimate flowering of the cooperative idea.

OPPOSITION TO COOPERATIVES. From time to time, individuals and special interest groups have expressed antagonism toward and opposition to cooperatives. In some cases this has been because of the economic style of cooperatives and because of hostility toward what opponents regard as a privileged tax position for cooperatives; opponents contended that cooperative **surplus** should be treated the same as any other business **profits**. Major anti-cooperative campaigns were organized in **Japan** in the 1930s by the National Chamber of Commerce and Industry, and in the **United States** in the 1940s under the name of the National Tax Equality Association. Opposition has also come from political conservatives because of the association of many cooperators with egalitarianism and support for democratic participation in the economy of countries, expressed through a **socialist** or social democratic ideology. Opposition to cooperatives in Nazi **Germany**, Fascist **Italy**, and Franco's **Spain** was on such ideological and political grounds. In the immediate postrevolution period of **communism** in **Russia**, cooperatives were opposed as not being socialist enough and were regarded with suspicion as vestiges of capitalist individualism. As some cooperatives in different countries have achieved major success in the business world (some in the United States, for example, are on the Fortune 500 list of the largest American firms), they have been criticized as having lost their unique ideology as cooperatives and become just like profit-oriented enterprises.

ORGANIZATION OF AMERICAN STATES (OAS). Organized in 1948, with roots dating back to the 1890s, it is the oldest of the world's regional intergovernmental organizations. For a period, prior to the emergence of specific national and international development organizations, the OAS provided staff leadership and organizational support for the promotion and development of cooperative organizations in the Americas, and it produced some of the early literature to advance these efforts.

ORGANIZATION OF COOPERATIVES OF THE AMERICAS (OCA). Organized in Montevideo, Uruguay, in 1963 by a group of national cooperative **federations** from the Americas, its affiliates are a diverse mix of cooperatives from 19 countries. Its headquarters are in Bogota, **Colombia**. The OCA's goals are to represent and expand the network of cooperatives in Latin America in matters of education, technical assistance, research and communication. Its programs include seminars, training courses and conferences to discuss major issues affecting the cooperative movement. It publishes a journal, *América Cooperativa.*

ÖRNE, ANDERS (1881–1956). A physician, journalist, and cooperative and political leader in **Sweden**, he was an active advocate of cooperatives' taking an international role in the world economy. In 1919 the Swedish Cooperative Union submitted a memorandum on International Trading and Banking to the **ICA**, largely the work of Örne. Active in the Swedish **consumer cooperative** movement, he was an author of note on cooperative subjects. He was also a member of the ICA Central Committee from 1920 until his death and of the Executive Committee from 1921 to 1927. In Sweden he was elected a Member of the Riksdag (Parliament), where he actively pursued cooperative interests and later was named Minister of Transport and Postmaster General in the Swedish government.

OVERSEAS COOPERATIVE DEVELOPMENT COMMITTEE (OCDC). Established in 1962 by **USAID** as an official Advisory Committee on Overseas Cooperative Development, it provided an arena for early consultation between cooperatives in the **United States** and the U.S. government on program activity after the passage of the **Humphrey Amendment** to the Foreign Assistance Act of 1962. The cooperative representatives, while appreciating their role as advisors on assistance to cooperatives in **developing countries**, decided early on that they preferred not to provide that advice as a part of a formal government structure, and they notified USAID of their intention to continue independently. This has been their role since. Their influence on USAID and on U.S. cooperative interest and involvement in overseas cooperative development has grown over the years. Since the early 1980s the Committee has had full-time staff to assist in its work.

OVERSEAS DEVELOPMENT ADMINISTRATION (ODA). The government agency in the **United Kingdom** responsible for the delivery of assistance to **developing countries**. Support for cooperatives is one of the priority interests of ODA; it is provided in the form of direct funding of developing-country government cooperative initiatives as well as in the form of support for British cooperative development programs operated by the **Cooperative Liaison, Education and Research Unit** of the **Cooperative College, Loughborough,** and the **Plunkett Foundation**. The British Council provides scholarships for the training of cooperative leaders.

OWEN, ROBERT (1771–1858). Welsh born, Owen was a humanist, social reformer, pioneer of universal education and prophet of the cooperative ideal. He left school at age 10 to work for his brother, a saddler in London, and by 14 he had held several other jobs and was in Manchester working as a draper. Four years later, with a loan of £100 from his brother, he was in a short-lived business for himself, and before he was 20 he was managing a yarn-producing enterprise employing 500 people. It was here that Owen first developed the ideas of community in industry that he later applied so successfully at **New Lanark**, as well as his ideas about the effect of environment on character.

New Lanark, the industrial village and mill whose name he made famous, came to fully engage his life and interest in 1799 when he purchased the mill and married his former employer's daughter. He quickly moved to modernize village houses, provided coal and food at low prices, and provided free medical services for workers. Owen reduced working hours, abolished all types of punishment in the factory, and introduced a variety of incentives in their place, including schooling for boys and girls who worked in the mill or were children of mill workers. His radical ideas of how to succeed in a capitalist enterprise while doing good, in what he called "villages of cooperation," were soon attracting the attention of reformers in other parts of Europe as well as in Britain, but they were not always fully shared by those who were partners in his enterprise. In the final arrangement before he left New Lanark, his partnership agreement called for limiting shareholder **profits** to 5%, with all above this invested in efforts to improve the conditions of employees and the community.

Owen's departure from New Lanark in 1825 to establish the utopian community of **New Harmony** in Indiana in the **United States** marked the end of his social reformer period. Henceforth he was an idealist, bent on the complete reconstruction of society based on self-developing communities, motivated by a vision of self-reliance and social harmony deriving from cooperative production and non-competitive living. Four years later New Harmony was a failed experiment, and Owen had returned to Britain homeless and with his personal resources depleted. Undaunted, Owen pursued his dreams, but by 1844 all of his resources had been exhausted in a variety of idealistic schemes and causes. His ideas of cooperatives had on their own caught fire, however, and cooperatives were being formed by the hundreds. Most failed but a few persisted, including one at **Rochdale**, where self-styled Owenites were among the cooperative pioneers. By the time of his death in 1858 the cooperative movement in Britain was fully launched, though in a pattern that Owen did not fully support. Today, were he alive, he would most likely opt for an Israeli **kibbutz** as his model of the cooperative village. Owen was a prolific author, his works including an autobiography, *The Life of Robert Owen Written by Himself.*

P

PAKISTAN. The cooperative movement in Pakistan (then part of **India**) began in 1904 with the establishment of **credit cooperatives** and the passage of the first **cooperative legislation** authorizing such cooperatives. The law was amended in 1912 to give full recognition to all types of cooperative enterprises, and cooperatives grew in the ensuing years as did associated cooperative **unions** in all parts of the country. **Cooperative banks**, the first in Karachi in 1919, were established as a way of facilitating cooperative growth and development.

Agitation for a Muslim state within pre-independence India proved unsuccessful, but with independence in 1947 India was partitioned and Pakistan emerged as a separate country. In 1950, the Pakistan Cooperative Association (now the National Cooperative Union of Pakistan) was formed. During the adjustment to independence, cooperative banks played an important role in ameliorating economic disruptions caused by the movement of large Muslim populations from India into Pakistan and of Hindu populations from Pakistan into India. Also in 1950, the Minister of Cooperation in the Central Government noted that there were 2,100,000 members of cooperatives, mainly in the field of agriculture. The need for additional housing in growing urban areas led to a strong push for cooperative housing estates, and at the present time this part of the movement accounts for nearly one-fourth of the membership in cooperatives in Pakistan.

The *Statistical Profile of Cooperatives in International Cooperative Alliance Member Countries* (1994), published by the **ICA Regional Office for Asia and the Pacific** reported that in 1990 there were 61,931 cooperatives in Pakistan with 3,354,760 members (3.1% of the population). These were structured as follows by sector: agriculture—39,076 cooperatives/with 1,412,790 members; consumer—385/59,713; fisheries—55/8,485; housing—2,016/736,689; insurance—1/na; multipurpose—3,793/237,686; savings and credit—6/43,559; services—1,577/56,513; and others—15,023/799,325. The **ICA** reported that cooperative membership in 1996 was 9,391,926 (7.3% of the population).

PALESTINE (ARAB). A few attempts at cooperative development among Arab communities in Palestine paralleling that of the Jewish population took place early on, including, in 1920, the establishment of the first Arab cooperative at Yafa and the passage of a **cooperative law** by the British administration, mandated by the League of Nations. The first conscientious effort to do so, however, dates from 1933, when the post of **Registrar of Cooperatives** was established by the Palestine Mandate administration and was given special instructions to focus on such development in Arab villages. A special program was developed, focusing on **credit cooperatives,** and by 1935, 14 such cooperatives had been registered with a membership of 3,405. By 1937 this had increased to 121 with 69,371 members. Growth was interrupted by World War II and then by **Israel**'s independence and the first Arab-Israeli war. In 1950 it was reported that only 55 Arab cooperatives were registered in Israel; however, this number grew to 197 in 1972 and encompassed the occupied West Bank.

The several Arab-Israeli wars, along with the occupation of the West Bank by Israel, have disrupted Arab cooperative development, and the Israeli government has not been keen to support and encourage it. In recent years some of the **cooperative development organizations** in the **United States** have organized a special project, funded by **USAID,** to support cooperatives on the West Bank and in Gaza. The **Arab Cooperative Union** (ACU) reported that in 1994 there were 531 cooperatives in Palestine with a membership of 43,117 in the following sectors: agriculture—303 cooperatives/with 18,514 members; consumer—19/2,615; fisheries—27/3,919; housing—103/3,636; multipurpose—19/1,185; services—52/13,248; and worker productive—8/na. A more optimistic estimate was provided in April 1994 by the Agricultural Cooperative Union, based in Nablus—900 cooperatives with a total membership of 160,000. The lack of reliable population data and disagreement as to the definition of territories involved with accuracy make it difficult to determine the exact percentage of penetration of the Arab cooperatives. The existence in ACU of a potential **apex organization** could help ensure that cooperative interests are articulated as Israel and the Arab states argue and the Palestine Authority structures a semblance of a Palestinian state.

PALMER, ROBERT ALEXANDER (LORD RUSHOLME) (1890–1977). A British cooperative official who was from 1930 to 1948 a member of the **ICA** Central and Executive Committees and served as acting president for the period 1940–46 when President **Väinö Tanner** of Finland, because of World War II, was unable to carry out his ICA duties. Palmer was elected ICA president in his own right for the period 1946–48. He began his cooperative association at age 14 and at 21 became a member of the board of directors of the Manchester and Salford Cooperative Societies. He joined the **Cooperative Union** staff, serving later as its general secretary and then as president. A thorough going internationalist, he often commented that "The world is my province."

PANAMA. While legislation in the Commercial Code (1916) and the Labor Code (1947) suggests the existence of cooperatives, the first formal knowledge of them dates from 1954 when a **cooperative law** was enacted and the first official cooperatives were established. Among the earliest were those dealing with savings and credit (the dominant sector in Panama). These had developed sufficiently by 1961 to support a national **credit union** federation. National **federations** for agriculture, fisheries, salt production and transport were established by the mid-1970s, and Panama had become the site of preference for two international cooperative organizations, the **Confederación Latinoamericana de Cooperativas de Ahorro y Crédito (COLAC)** and the **Instituto Cooperativo Interamericano**. In 1980, the government cooperative structure, the Autonomous Cooperative Institute of Panama (IPACOOP), was established. IPACOOP reported that in 1992 there were 327 active cooperatives with a membership of 158,909. By sector they were as follows: consumer—22 societies/with 2,093 members; credit unions—161/128,732; housing—16/2,784; multipurpose (mainly agricultural)—75/18,860; transport—25/3,674; and others—28/2,766. Cooperative membership that year constituted 6.2% of the population.

PAN AMERICAN UNION (PAU). An outgrowth of an international conference of American states held in Washington, D.C., during 1889–90, the PAU was established in 1910 and functioned until 1948 when it became a permanent body of the **Organization of American States (OAS)**, organized that year. In 1970 the OAS charter was amended and the Pan American Union became the Permanent Secretariat for the OAS. Periodic Inter-American Conferences were held by the PAU during the period after 1910, the seventh of which, held in 1933, called for the PAU to provide guidance to and coordinate the development of the cooperative movement in the Western Hemisphere. Among the activities flowing from this resolution was the establishment in 1945 of a Cooperative Service within the PAU, which undertook to provide leadership, coordination and technical assistance to emerging cooperative movements. A number of activities flowed from this organization, including periodic Inter-American Conferences on Cooperation, the first of which was held in Bogota, Colombia, in June 1946. Preparation of technical publications were among its activities, as were programs encouraging **cooperative education** and training. The PAU and its Cooperative Service provided much of the external advice and assistance to fledgling cooperative movements in the early post–World War II years. The emergence of foreign assistance activities on the part of a number of countries in the 1960s and the reorganization of the OAS in 1970 led to this activity becoming a lesser priority of the organization from that time onward.

PANTULU, V. RAMADAS (1873–1944). A cooperative leader in **India**, he was widely known for his work as president of the All-India Cooperative Institutes Association and for his interest and involvement in cooperative training. He edited the *Indian Cooperative Review* from 1935 to 1944. He was active in cooperatives in Madras Province, serving as president of the Madras Provincial Cooperative Union and the Madras Provincial Cooperative Bank. He was a member of the **ICA** Central Committee from 1934 to 1944 and was a frequent contributor of articles on cooperative training to the ***Review of International Cooperation***.

PAPUA NEW GUINEA. Cooperative organizations came upon the scene in Papua New Guinea in 1946, after the end of World War II. In that year, the colonial administration established a Cooperative Section (later the Registry of Cooperative Societies) in the government, which assisted in the formation of the first cooperatives that same year. The initial cooperatives, organized between 1946 and 1950, were mainly multipurpose societies marketing copra and engaging in the supply of retail goods. In 1951 a number of these societies formed district associations, and in 1956 a number of these associations formed the National Federation of Native Associations. By 1967 there were 312 **primary cooperatives** in operation, with a combined membership of 109,488. In 1968 a separate Federation of Cooperative Savings and Credit Societies was formed, and by 1988 it had grown to include 33 **credit unions**. In recent years there has been considerable controversy in government over cooperatives as a type of business organization. In 1991 the Cooperative Registry was abolished and its former staff assigned the responsibility of liquidating the cooperatives. Any future cooperative activity was placed in the purview of the Department of Business Development. In 1994 **WOCCU** indicated that information was unavailable on the status of credit unions in Papua. An **ICA Regional Office for Asia and the Pacific** mission report in February 1995 indicated that all cooperatives had been "de-registered" by the government and were undergoing liquidation. It was the judgment of the ICA regional office staff that there were few immediate prospects for cooperatives in Papua New Guinea.

PARAGUAY. Significant cooperative development in Paraguay came late, only after World War II. Its failure to develop earlier was largely a reflection of conditions in the country resulting from the devastation of war and the reparations paid to **Brazil**, **Argentina**, and **Uruguay** following the conflict with these countries in the period 1865–70. The war resulted in death for half of the Paraguayan population. The first cooperatives and a **cooperative law** date from 1942 and for 30 years there was a slow buildup from this base. A new cooperative law was enacted in 1972 and the National Credit Union League (now CREDICOOP) was established in 1973. **Credit unions** are the principal grouping of cooperatives in terms of membership, but there are sizable numbers of **agricultural** and **worker productive cooperatives** as well. In the 1980s a national **federation** of cooperatives was established. In 1984, the latest date for which comprehensive statistics were available, there were reported to be 281 cooperatives with 52,921 members (1.6% of the population). The **Organization of Cooperatives of the Americas** reported in 1995 that in 1991 there were 258 cooperatives with a membership of 142,936 in the following sectors: agriculture—124 cooperatives/with 42,269 members; consumer—25/11,983; credit unions—83/86,551; housing—1/39; and worker productive—18/2,094. Cooperative membership was 3.3% of the population at that time.

PARENT COOPERATIVE PRESCHOOLS INTERNATIONAL. Founded in 1960 as the American Council of Parent Cooperatives, it changed to its present name in 1964 to reflect the fact that such cooperative groups were being organized in a number of different countries. Its purpose is to encourage, strengthen and expand the **preschool cooperative** movement and to establish standards for such programs. It has offices in **Canada** and the **United States**.

PARETO, VILVREDO (1848–1923). An Italian economist and sociologist who established, with **Léon Walras**, the École de Lausanne in 1896. Among the interests of the school was promotion of cooperative organizations.

PARISIUS, LUDOLF (1827–1900). A German cooperative theorist, largely concerned with the German cooperative movement as shaped by **Franz Hermann Schulze-Delitzsch** and his followers, and with the ways in which **cooperative principles** could be built into German **cooperative law**.

PARKER, FLORENCE E. (1891–1974). A U.S. government official, she spent her career working in Washington, D C., in the Labor Department, in 1946 becoming involved full time with cooperative matters, including compiling statistics and preparing reports on cooperative enterprises. She was a regular participant in the national meetings of **CLUSA** and was briefly a member of its board of directors in 1955. Parker was an observer at the **ICA** congresses in 1948 and 1951. She published innumerable articles dealing with cooperative matters as well as four books, most notably *The First 125 Years: A History of Distributive and Service Cooperatives in the U.S. 1829–1954.*

PATMAN, WRIGHT (1893–1976). A member of the U.S. House of Representatives (Texas), in 1934 he introduced and saw passed legislation authorizing the establishment of **credit unions** in any part of the **United States** and their chartering as federal institutions. To secure a more independent position for credit unions, in 1967 he introduced a bill to establish an independent federal credit union agency, and he saw it become a reality in 1970 as the National Credit Union Administration. During all his years in the Congress Patman was a strong supporter of the **credit union movement** and of the **Credit Union National Association (CUNA)**. The federal credit union whose **common bond** is people working for and dealing with the House of Representatives honored his work by renaming itself the Wright Patman Congressional Credit Union.

PATRONAGE REFUND. One of the original **Rochdale Principles,** whereby a portion of the net savings of a cooperative business is distributed to all patron members in proportion to their purchases.

PATTON, JAMES G. (1903–1985). An American farmer, cooperator and internationalist, he began his cooperative career in the Colorado Farmers' Union, working first with **insurance cooperative** programs. He later became secretary and then president of the Colorado organization. He was elected president of the National **Farmers Union** in 1949 and remained in that position until 1966. Patton was a consultant at the founding meeting of the **FAO,** where he and leaders from a number of other countries made plans for a world farmers' association. This came into being in 1946 as the **International Federation of Agricultural Producers**. His proposals for world food aid programs were a prototype of what emerged in 1954 as the Food for Peace program, now part of **USAID**. Patton served as president of the American Freedom From

Hunger Foundation in the 1960s and after retirement was elected president of the United World Federalists, an organization advocating the formation of an international federation of nations.

PEACE. From the beginning of the modern cooperative era, there has been a belief among most theorists and practitioners of **cooperation** that cooperatives were a means of helping build a socio-economic structure that would lead toward the achievement of a peaceful world. The book, *Cooperative Peace,* by **James Peter Warbasse** is a discussion of this theme. The **ICA** Congress regularly closes its sessions with the adoption of a Peace Resolution articulating the current concerns of cooperators regarding world peace.

PEACE CORPS. Established in 1961 at the urging of President John Kennedy, its purpose is to "promote world peace and friendship, help peoples of other countries in meeting their needs for trained manpower, build a better understanding of the American people on the part of the peoples served, and a better understanding of other people on the part of Americans." In 1977 it was directed to place an emphasis on meeting the basic needs of those living in the poorest areas of the countries in which the Peace Corps operates. Volunteers have from the beginning assisted in projects that promoted the development and operation of cooperatives, acting under the direction of local cooperative officials.

PERU. While the first **cooperative legislation** in Peru dates from 1913 and the first cooperative from 1919, and despite the fact that cooperatives were promoted actively by political parties and trade unions at different times, it was not until the 1960s that active, organized and government-supported cooperative development took place. Since that time, growth has been significant, influenced both positively and negatively by government changes and the policy differences of changing administrations. In recent years the armed political insurrection in the country has been a critical limiting factor in the growth of cooperatives, as has been the rampant inflation which has essentially decapitalized the movement, particularly the **credit unions**. The cooperative movement in Peru has been diverse, with development in a variety of sectors. The **ILO *Directory* (1988)** reported that in 1985 there were 2,655 cooperatives with a membership of 2,057,747 (9.4% of the population) in the following sectors: agriculture—776 cooperatives/with 135,329 members; consumer—193/60,556; fisheries—16/471; housing—575/75,597;

savings and credit—566/1,574,700; transport—101/6,276; worker productive—154/10,728; and others—274/194,090. The financial and political turmoil of the country since then has impacted the cooperative
movement dramatically. The **Organization of Cooperatives of the
Americas** in 1995 reported that the latest statistics for the country
showed 4,130 cooperatives with only 312,360 members (1.4% of the
population). The decline was reflected in all sectors.

PESTALOZZI, JOHANN HEINRICH (1746–1827). Born in a farm
family, raised and educated in Zurich, Pestalozzi first intended to be a
clergyman but later turned to law and then for health reasons returned to
farming. Included in his farming experiments was conversion of his farm
into an education center for Swiss children who were taught agrarian
and home-making skills. Based on these experiences, in 1781 he published a novel, *Leonard and Gertrude*, in which he defined his ideas of
the cooperative ideal. He later became a noted educator and attracted to
his center at Yverdon an international group of people concerned with
the theory of childhood education. His most noted book from this period
was *Gertrude and Her Children*, published in 1801.

PETROLEUM COOPERATIVE. An association of consumers for the
purpose of buying and distributing of gasoline and related petroleum
products on a **patronage refund** and consumer-controlled basis. This
type of cooperative was developed extensively in the American midwest
and in Scandinavia. It is a service that is often now provided through a
multipurpose cooperative.

PFEIFFER, EDUARD VON (1835–1921). After a visit to **Rochdale** in
1862 he became active in the early work of the **consumer cooperative**
movement in **Germany**. He emerged as one of its most important leaders, shaping its development in the period leading up to World War I.

PHALANSTÈRE DE FOURIER. One of the earliest French cooperatives established in 1799 by **François Marie Charles Fourier**. It was
based on Fourier's view that cooperatives should be established as a way
of providing ideal communities where human nature could find its true
expression, uncontaminated by the rest of the world.

**PHILADELPHIA CONTRIBUTIONSHIP FOR THE INSURANCE
OF HOUSES FROM LOSS BY FIRE.** Formed in 1752 with the assis-

tance of **Benjamin Franklin**, who later became one of its directors, it was a cooperative/**mutual insurance** firm which is still in existence under its original name. It is regarded by many as the first American cooperative organization. Its establishment coincided with the establishment of a similar group in London and of **agricultural cooperatives** in **France**. These are regarded as the events from which to date the start, in the 1750s, of the modern cooperative movement.

PHILIPPINES. The formal start of the Philippine cooperative movement dates from 1910, when the first rural cooperatives were organized, followed in 1915 by the passage of the Rural Credit Act, which outlined a legal status for cooperatives. Growth was slow but steady enough to warrant the establishment of a national **federation**, the Cooperative League of the Philippines, in 1937, followed the next year by a national **consumer cooperative** federation. World War II and occupation by the Japanese delayed further development until 1946 when the war ended and independence was achieved. Then began a large-scale development of cooperatives that has continued to the present day. Government began to take an activist role in the 1960s, seeing a government-directed cooperative movement as a potential force for national development. As in other **developing countries** this proved to be a mixed blessing, and the movement is still trying to establish its own independent identity and agenda. The **ICA Regional Office for Asia and the Pacific** reported that in 1991 there were 13,346 cooperatives with a membership of 9,738,505 with **agricultural cooperatives** being the dominant form in numbers and membership. The cooperative profile by sector was as follows: agriculture—9,391 societies/with 7,733,875 members; consumer—366/105,774; fisheries—286/236,396; housing—3/758; multipurpose—1,533/823,221; savings and credit 1,376/766,520; services—249/71,961; and others—142/na. Cooperative membership that year was over 15.5% of the population.

PLUNKETT FOUNDATION FOR COOPERATIVE STUDIES. Established in 1919 in London as the Horace Plunkett Foundation, later renamed the Plunkett Foundation for Cooperative Studies, it was meant by its founder, **Sir Horace Curzon Plunkett** (then 65 years old), to be a place for pursuing his ideas and plans for cooperative development. He hoped that its library, moved from Dublin, would be used as a research center for those interested in cooperative development internationally. In 1927, five years before the founder's death, the Foundation began publication of a

Year Book of Agricultural Cooperation in the British Empire, which in 1930 became the *Year Book of Agricultural Cooperation,* reflecting a broadening of its geographical coverage. Its scope was further enlarged in 1988 when it became the *Yearbook of Cooperative Enterprise.* The Foundation has been a source of intellectual and technical assistance to emerging cooperative movements throughout the world and its library remains a major reference source for students of cooperation. It is currently located in Oxford, **United Kingdom.**

PLUNKETT, SIR HORACE CURZON (1854–1932). Born of an aristocratic Anglo-Irish family, he was educated at Eton and Oxford. At age 25 he purchased a cattle ranch in the **United States** and spent his next 10 years as a rancher, an experience that greatly influenced his later activities, including a longterm relationship with President Theodore Roosevelt. He returned to Ireland in 1889, where he began to organize **agricultural** (creamery) **cooperatives** and ultimately founded the Irish Agricultural Organizations Society. He was among the early leaders of the move to internationalize the cooperative movement and presented a report on cooperative farming at the organizing meeting of the **ICA** in 1895. He went on to establish the Cooperative Reference Library at Dublin, later transferred to London when the Horace Plunkett Foundation (now the **Plunkett Foundation for Cooperative Studies**) was established in 1919. Based on his experience as a member of Parliament, Plunkett recognized the importance of organizing politically to influence events regarding cooperatives but felt that this should be done without cooperative leaders becoming active politicians. In this regard he was an important shaper of the **cooperative principle** of political neutrality. He was an advisor to the governments of the United States (see his book, *Rural Life Problems of the US*) and **India,** and his ideas on cooperatives have taken root in many parts of the world.

POISSON, ERNEST (1882–1942). A French cooperative leader, he was general secretary of the National Federation of Consumer Cooperatives from 1912 to 1940. He was vice president of the **ICA** from 1921 to 1942 and a member of the ICA Central Committee from 1913 to 1942. Poisson was a staunch advocate of unity among the disparate elements of the cooperative movement and was influential in promoting the idea of an international **cooperative bank,** the inclusion of **agricultural cooperatives** in the ICA and outreach to those trade unions that shared an interest in the promotion of cooperative organizations. He was a prolific author on cooperative matters, his works including *La Republique coopérative*, and an orator of note.

POLAND. The first cooperative in Poland dates from 1816 (an agricultural society), formed at a time when Polish territory was divided between Austria, Prussia and Russia. This division lasted through most of the 19th century but cooperatives developed in each section. There was an increase in cooperative activity dating from the 1860s and, by the time Poland regained its independence after World War I, a basic cooperative infrastructure had already been established involving **agricultural**, **credit** and banking, **consumer**, **dairy** and industrial **cooperatives**. The first **cooperative law** was enacted in 1920 and a State Cooperative Council formed that same year. A **cooperative research** institute, the first in the world, was established in 1921 as was the first Polish **housing cooperative**. The Chief Statistical Office of the government reported in 1924 a total of 14,563 cooperatives in the following sectors: agricultural purchase and sale societies—907; building and lodging societies—676; consumers' societies—5,518; credit societies—5,665; dairies and egg collecting societies—536; raw material purchase societies—381; other purchase or sale societies—362; various other societies—518.

Growth and elaboration of the cooperative movement continued on a path similar to that of other European countries during the interwar period, but with special attention given to cultural cooperatives (arts, music, theater) and cooperatives of disabled persons (mainly war veterans). Polish cooperatives were active in the international cooperative movement and participated in the London Conference of 1945 at which the **ICA** took the lead in reestablishing the cooperative contacts and relationships disrupted by World War II.

The postwar period saw Polish cooperatives reformulated on the model of those in the **Union of Soviet Socialist Republics** with an emphasis on fulfillment of certain economic and social roles defined by the Communist Party and government. A notable Polish exception to this model, however, was the lack of any significant collectivization of agriculture, which remained largely in the hands of private farmers. During the communist period, cooperatives continued to grow in number and influence. By the end of 1988, just prior to the collapse of the communist systems in Eastern Europe, the profile of Polish cooperatives was as follows: agricultural circles—2,006 cooperatives/with 113,200 members; agricultural production—2,086/190,400; agricultural supply/

marketing—1,912/3,531,500 members; consumer—397/2,957,500; dairy—323/1,199,400; disabled—454/233,500; handicraft—562/137,400; horticultural marketing—140/55,519; housing—3,128/3,515,000; industrial—2,461/458,100; savings and credit—1,663/2,566,100; and others—101/11,500. Cooperatives totaled 15,233 cooperatives with 14,969,119 members—39.5% of the Polish population.

The 1990 postcommunist government viewed the cooperative movement with great suspicion, particularly its leadership, seeing it as part of the *nomenclatura* that had managed the former system. Laws were passed abolishing all cooperative structures except the **primary cooperatives** and a truncated Supreme Cooperative Council. Cooperatives were not regarded as important elements in the coming free-market system and would survive or fail based on their ability to compete for member loyalty and their economic viability. By 1992 there had been a significant decline in membership, many cooperatives had proven not viable in the new environment, and the cooperative market share in various sectors had dropped. Positive signs of cooperative persistence were the establishment of new sectoral organizations, the election of new or reaffirmed leadership at the primary level, and cooperators' welcome of an opportunity to be independent organizations with their own agendas. The period of readjustment is still under way. The ICA reported that in 1994 there were 19,186 cooperatives with a membership of 6,092,000 (15.9% of the population). A 1998 ICA report, prepared for the European Union and reflecting 1996 data, noted 13,774 cooperatives in Poland with a membership in excess of 2,584,638. Recent statistics on cooperative membership are too sketchy to establish **cooperative penetration,** except to note that the situation in Poland is still adjusting to the new order.

POLLEY, GERTRUDE (GRACE) F. (1900–1982). She joined the staff of the **ICA** in 1917 as personal secretary to director **Henry J. May** and served in this position until his death in 1939. She then served as acting general secretary of the ICA for the period 1939–47, during which she helped maintain the operation of the organization through the difficult war years. Polley then served as general secretary for the period 1947–63. In 1949 she was made an officer of the Order of the British Empire (OBE), an award given by the British government in recognition of her work with cooperatives. She retired in 1963.

PORTUGAL. While cooperative activity of a rudimentary nature has been identified in Portugal as early as the 1850s, and a commercial code adopted in 1867 makes reference to cooperatives, it was not until 1871 that the first formal cooperative was recognized, and it was not until the 1920s that organized efforts were undertaken to really expand the cooperative effort in an organized fashion, particularly with **consumer cooperatives**. Developments continued at a modest pace, and national sectoral organizations were formed for cooperatives in agriculture, consumer, credit, fisheries, housing, and worker productive sections. The **ILO *Directory* (1988)** reported the existence of 11 such groups. The Antonio Sergio Cooperative Institute reported in 1995 that there were 2,960 **primary**-level **cooperatives** and 25 national and regional **federations** reflecting a combined membership of 2,164,119 (21.9% of the population). A 1998 **ICA** report to the European Union for the year 1996 noted 2,966 cooperatives in Portugal with 2,134,670 members in the following sectors: agriculture—952 societies/with 1,002,170 members; consumer—249/331,600; fisheries—28/na; housing—501/144,300; independent retailers—60/66,000; insurance—1/na; savings and credit/banks—198/351,400; worker productive and services—111/2,700; artisans—48/na; and others—818/236,500. **Cooperative penetration** of the population is estimated to be about the same as in 1995, 21.9%.

POTTER, BEATRICE. *See* WEBB, BEATRICE POTTER.

PRATT, HODGSON (1824–1907). Early British Christian Socialist leader whose interests were international **peace** and justice, labor co-partnership, education, and cooperation. He worked initially in **India** from 1846 to 1863, pursuing these interests. Returning to Britain he organized the Working Men's Club and Institute Movement and, in 1878, the Guild of Cooperators. An associate of **Edward Vansittart Neale**, he contributed to the founding of the **ICA** in 1895 and was named a member of its first Executive Committee. The Hodgson Pratt Memorial, a scholarship named in his honor, is administered by the British **Cooperative Union**.

PRECOOPERATIVE. A society or group is said to be a precooperative when it is organizing itself to become a cooperative or, in some cases, is already functioning as a cooperative but has not yet been officially recognized and registered with the appropriate government agency.

PRESCHOOL COOPERATIVE. A cooperative association established by a group of parents who wish to give their children a positive early childhood education experience and who organize a group to do so, set policies for its functioning, and finance the cost of its operations. In some cases these cooperatives function on a completely volunteer basis; in others, they hire professional staff to handle their programs. In almost all cases parents are expected/required to volunteer a certain amount of time for the implementation of program functions.

PRIMARY COOPERATIVE. A primary cooperative is a society, usually organized at the local level, consisting of individual members. It is the level of cooperation experienced most directly by most members. It contrasts with higher-level cooperative **unions** or **federations** in which the membership is composed of primary cooperatives or, in some cases, of regional groupings of primary societies.

PROCESSING. The act of transforming a commodity into a more finished product, e.g., drying coffee beans, making butter or cheese from milk, thus increasing a commodity's economic value. Certain cooperatives are set up to exclusively carry out processing activities and are clearly identifiable as processing cooperatives. In other cases, processing activity may be only one phase of a cooperative's scope of work.

PRODUCER. A person who makes things or who, in farming, makes things grow; a person who produces things for consumers.

PRODUCTION COOPERATIVE. An association of producers, whether agricultural or industrial. In agriculture, producer cooperatives are composed of individual farmers who produce a particular commodity or commodities but who may purchase needed supplies and inputs and process and market their produce collectively. In the industrial sector, production cooperatives are composed of worker-owners who engage in activity together to produce a commodity or commodities. These are often referred to as **worker productive cooperatives**. In some national cooperative movements, groups of persons are organized to provide needed services of a personal nature (like health care) or of a general social nature (transportation or electricity). Such cooperatives are often accounted for statistically as a subset of production cooperatives. As they become more sizable they may form their own federations and become formally classified as **service cooperatives**. Within the ICA organizational structure these various types of cooperatives are connected through CICOPA, the International Organization of Industrial, Artisanal and Service Producers' Cooperatives.

PRODUCTION CREDIT. Loans made available by banks and/or cooperatives for specific production purposes.

PROFIT. The excess of income over expenditure. In most cooperatives, normal profit is referred to as **"surplus"** and is the source of funds used for **patronage refunds**, which are distributed to a society's members according to their patronage of the cooperative's economic activity.

PROFIT, BARTHÉLMY (1867–1946). The founder of the first **school cooperative** in France in 1919.

PROSTHUMA, DR. F. E. A Dutch cooperative leader who was named to the **Committee of Honor of the International Cooperative Alliance**.

PROUDHON, PIERRE JOSEPH (1809–1865). French journalist, political philosopher and social thinker, he is regarded as the founder of modern anarchism and considered to be one of the earliest **utopian** socialists. He believed a time would come when free voluntary cooperation in all spheres of life would replace the need for legal contracts and elected government. Defining his system as mutualism, he dreamed of the day when a perfect system would exist and the need for money and private property would be done away with, launching an era of a cooperative, socialist society. In 1876 a cooperative society, La Fédération, inspired by Proudhon's ideas, was established at Vienne; it became one of the more important French cooperative societies by 1879.

PUERTO RICO. Puerto Rico was among the earliest of the Caribbean islands to involve itself with cooperatives (only **Trinidad** had an earlier start). The first **cooperative legislation** was enacted and the first cooperatives established in 1920. By 1938, cooperatives had developed to the extent that a national cooperative **congress** was held to help the movement articulate its goals and aspirations. Immediately following World War II, development accelerated. A **cooperative law** was enacted, a national **federation** established and the fledgling **credit union movement**, destined to become the dominant cooperative sector, was initiated, assisted by special legislation and by the formation of a national credit union federation. By 1949, 152 cooperatives were registered. During the 1950s a **cooperative bank** was established, as was a cooperative institute. National federations for **consumer** and **agricultural cooperatives** were formed, as well as an **insurance cooperative**. A governmental Cooperative Development

Administration was established. Cooperatives in most sectors have ebbed in recent years, but the credit union movement has expanded. By 1990 the Cooperative Development Administration reported the existence of 360 cooperatives with 738,967 members (20.5% of the population). Of these, credit unions accounted for 240 of the cooperatives and 678,968 of the membership. **ICA** country files for 1995 recorded 295 cooperatives with 1,028,077 members in the following sectors: agriculture—10 societies/with 25,640 members; consumer—3/19,462; housing—23/4,647; insurance—1/135,350; savings and credit—193/807,306; transport—28/15,038; worker productive—37/20,634; and others (insurance)—1/135,350. Cooperative membership at that time was 27.0% of the population.

PULSFORD, F. E. (1874–1923). A cooperative pioneer in **Australia**, he was the organizer of the first All-Australian Cooperative Consumers' Congress held in 1920 and a director of the New South Wales Cooperative Wholesale Society. He was responsible for the establishment of the *Cooperative News*, an early journal of the Australian cooperative movement.

Q

QATAR. Consumer cooperatives, the only cooperative sector in Qatar, were introduced in 1973 at the same time as a national **cooperative law** was proposed. Growth to date has been slow. The **Arab Cooperative Union** reported that in 1994 there were 10 consumer cooperatives with a total of 4,958 members (1.1% of the country's population).

R

RABAGO, DON DIAZ. In 1883 Don Diaz Rabago began promoting the idea of **Raiffeisen** savings banks for **Spain**.

RABBENO, UGO (1863–1897). An early Italian cooperative leader, in 1886 he published *La cooperazione in Italia*, a study of the cooperative movement in **Italy**, a year after preparing a similar book on cooperatives in England. This was one of the earliest efforts to compare and learn from other national cooperative experiences. He was an influential theorist of the early Italian **production cooperatives** and is regarded by many as the founder of the movement in Italy.

RABOBANK. A Dutch **cooperative bank** established in 1898 as the Cooperatieve Centrale Raiffeisen Bank (Central Cooperative Raiffeisen Bank) at Utrecht. It is now one of the leading international banks.

RADESTOCK, MAX (1854–1913). An early **consumer cooperative** leader in **Germany**, he was president of the Central Union of German Distributive Societies from its establishment until his death. He began his cooperative career in 1885 with the society in Pieschen, near Dresden, serving as its manager from 1889. He served as director of the Union of Saxon Distributive Societies, which led to his activity in the formation of the German central union, for which he drafted the first set of rules. He was elected to the Central Committee of the **ICA**, where he was known for his talent for organization and his practical advice.

RAIFFEISEN, FRIEDRICH WILHELM (1818–1888). Born of a family of modest means in the Westwald, near Bonn, Raiffeisen had a brief military career before turning his efforts to municipal management, serving in turn as mayor of three small villages—Weyerbusch, Flammersfeld and Heddesdorf. In each he established structures that provided him with experiences that went into the foundation of the Raiffeisen movement. In Weyerbusch in 1846 he organized a Bread Committee to combat famine during a period of scarcity, demonstrating the value of **mutual aid** and advancing the idea of food aid to people in serious need. It was the beginning of Raiffeisen's cooperative activity. In 1849 Raiffeisen established the Mutual Aid Association of Flammersfeld, his first credit association, from which the idea of **credit cooperatives** grew. In 1854 a rural credit cooperative was established at Heddesdorf. Building on these experiences Raiffeisen became an evangelist for self-help cooperatives, and his efforts, along with his book *Credit Unions as a Remedy for the Poverty of Rural and Industrial Workers and Artisans*, led to a proliferation of such groups. In 1872 he collected the local credit associations into centralized savings societies and in 1874 united the savings banks into one central grouping. Building on the fact that the membership of the credit societies was almost all related to farming, Raiffeisen turned his attention to broader agricultural issues; this led in 1877 to the formation of a **federation** of **agricultural cooperatives**, a structure that after his death became a central element in the German agricultural cooperative movement. The final link in Raiffeisen's vision of cooperation as a system to connect the grassroots with the world came into being on the

150th anniversary of his birth with the foundation of the **International Raiffeisen Union,** now an important international cooperative structure. Raiffeisen is also regarded as the spiritual father of the modern **credit union movement,** which is associated with **WOCCU.**

RAINBOW FLAG. *See* COOPERATIVE FLAG.

RAITTINEN, PAAVO. A cooperative leader in **Finland,** he was general manager of KANSA, an **insurance cooperative.** He was also active in the work of the **ICA.**

RAMUZ, CHARLES FERDINAND (1878–1947). A Swiss author, in 1936 he established La Guilde du livre at Lausanne. It was the world's first cooperative book club.

RAPACKI, MARIAN (1884–1944). A cooperative leader in **Poland,** he was a teacher, author, publicist, poet and theorist of the Polish movement. He was professor of cooperatives at Commercial High School in Warsaw for many years. He joined Spolem, the Polish **consumer cooperative,** in 1920 editing its journal and directing its educational and **audit** programs. Rapacki was a member of the **ICA** Central Committee from 1924 to 1944. He was killed at the Spolem headquarters by a German bomb during the Warsaw Uprising in September 1944.

REBATE. A term erroneously used to refer to the **patronage refunds** given by a cooperative society to its members from the **surplus** earned through the economic activities of the cooperative.

RECOMMENDATION NO. 77 OF THE INTERNATIONAL LABOUR ORGANIZATION. A policy recommendation adopted at the 26th Session of the International Labour Conference, which emphasizes the importance of developing cooperatives.

RECOMMENDATION NO. 126 OF THE INTERNATIONAL LABOUR ORGANIZATION. A policy recommendation adopted by the 50th Session of the International Labour Conference in 1966, it defined the nature of cooperative organizations, particularly in developing countries, and considered the role of government in promoting the cooperative movement.

REGIONAL COOPERATIVE. Used in two senses by cooperatives: first to denote a cooperative serving members over a large geographical area; alternatively, a secondary-level cooperative in which a number of **primary cooperatives** from a large geographical area join in the membership of a regional cooperative.

REGISTER. An official list of organizations, e.g., a register of cooperative societies.

REGISTERED SOCIETY. A cooperative society that has been recognized as fulfilling all the legal requirements and is entered in the government **register** of cooperatives.

REGISTRAR OF COOPERATIVES. A government official in charge of keeping the **register** of cooperatives, and of deciding if a cooperative shall be entered in it. In many countries the registrar also has important advisory, educational and promotional functions. In some countries the registrar is known as the **commissioner** for cooperatives.

RENNER, KARL (1870–1950). A cooperator, economist, political leader and statesman in **Austria**, he was an active supporter of trade unionism and labor politics as well as cooperatives. He was president of the Austrian Cooperative Union from 1911 to 1934 and served on the **ICA** Central Committee beginning in 1913. The first chancellor of the Austrian Republic after World War I (1919–20), he later served as president of Parliament (1931–33). He was arrested in 1934, along with other socialist cooperative leaders, during the abortive military revolt in Austria that year. The German takeover of Austria in 1938 led to Nazi manipulation and control of the cooperative movement, from which he was excluded. He headed the provisional government of Austria after World War II and served as president from 1945 to 1950.

REPETTO, NICOLÁS. A cooperative pioneer in **Argentina**, in Buenos Aires in 1905 he helped organize El Hogar Obrero, a **consumer**, **credit** and building **cooperative**. It was entered as No. 1 in the **register** of cooperatives of the country.

RESEARCH REGISTER OF STUDIES ON COOPERATIVES IN DEVELOPING COUNTRIES. A register of research activities and selected bibliographical items related to cooperatives in **developing countries**, it was established in 1972 as part of the **Cooperative Development Decade**. It was a project of the **ICA** in collaboration with the Cooperative Research Institutes in **Poland** and **Hungary,** with the support of a network of persons involved in **cooperative research**. In 1974 it published a *Directory of Organizations Engaged in Cooperative Research* and, beginning in 1975, 20 volumes of a *Bulletin*, covering the period 1968–88, containing abstracts of current and planned research projects related to cooperatives in developing countries and a catalogue of published materials dealing with such cooperatives. Material for the bulletins was compiled by the Polish Cooperative Research Institute from materials submitted by an International Advisory Group (later compiled from computer database searches conducted by **COPAC**). The bulletins were published and distributed by the Hungarian Cooperative Research Institute.

RETAILER-OWNED COOPERATIVE. A concept that came into being in the mid-1920s whereby independent retail operators would unite to form a cooperative for the purpose of purchasing, advertising, etc., on a collective basis. In the **United States** it was the forerunner of a type of franchise system in which the franchiser may be a cooperative or may carry out certain functions cooperatively. In Europe there is an extensive network of some 250,000 such shops, which in some countries have formed national **federations** and which are represented at the **European Union** level by a federation of such societies.

REVIEW OF INTERNATIONAL COOPERATION. The official journal of the **ICA**, it began publication in 1908 as the *Correspondence Bulletin of the I.C.A.* under the editorship of Dr. Hans Müller and was prepared and circulated by the ICA Secretariat in English, French and German. In January 1909 it was renamed the *International Cooperative Bulletin* and was published in Zurich. In the autumn of 1913 **Henry May**, then the new ICA general secretary, assumed the editorship, and this continued until his death in 1939. Problems due to World War I caused the German version of the *Bulletin* to be published by the Central Union of Consumers' Societies in Hamburg and the French version by the Swiss Union of Cooperatives in Basel. (Similar publication problems were also a feature of the World War II years.)

In April 1925, the *Bulletin* became the *Review of International Cooperation* and began to regularly include the results of the Alliance's own economic research, as well as reports of important developments within the ICA and its member organizations. The *Review* has remained a principal responsibility of the ICA directors over the years, and only since the editorship of Hans Ohlmann and currently of Mary Treacy has it had a separate editor. The pages of the *Review* contain one of the few continuous records of the historical development of world cooperation and the issues that have confronted it at its various stages of development.

REVUE DES ÉTUDES COOPÉRATIVES. Established in 1921 by **Charles Gide** and **Bernard Lavergne** as an outgrowth of a study group, the International Institute for the Study of Cooperation, it was designed to publish the papers of its members presented at periodic **congresses**. It remains a publisher of important cooperative literature in French.

RILEY, J. NORMAN (1922–1979). A Canadian cooperator, he was assistant director of the **Coady International Institute** and taught there for many years, interacting with future cooperative leaders from Africa, Asia and the Pacific, the Caribbean and Latin America. He was an early supporter and advocate of the African **credit union movement** and its regional confederation, the **African Confederation of Cooperative Savings and Credit Associations (ACCOSCA)** He visited all the national credit union movements that were associated with ACCOSCA, urging credit union leaders to give support to their national movements as well as to ACCOSCA. He died suddenly in Malta while on a cooperative development assignment.

ROBERT, CHARLES (1828–1899). General secretary of the French Cooperative Federation (later the Cooperative Union) from 1889, he was a champion of profit-sharing as the organizing principle for cooperation. He was associated with the Christian Socialist Movement and was an activist in the field of cooperative production. He was among those who founded the **ICA**, drafted its proposed statutes and was active in its early leadership.

ROCHDALE. *See* ROCHDALE SOCIETY OF EQUITABLE PIONEERS.

ROCHDALE PIONEERS. *See* ROCHDALE SOCIETY OF EQUITABLE PIONEERS.

ROCHDALE PRINCIPLES. *See* COOPERATIVE PRINCIPLES.

ROCHDALE SOCIETY OF EQUITABLE PIONEERS. A cooperative, established in the community of Rochdale, near Manchester, **United**

Kingdom, in 1844. Though cooperatives were established earlier, this is often referred to as the first cooperative, and the founding of this society is regarded by many as constituting the event from which the modern cooperative movement and **cooperative principles** have evolved. The 28 Rochdale pioneers were people of limited means who knew unemployment first hand, were veterans of unsuccessful strikes, and had come to view the possibilities of achieving social improvement through legislation as futile, but who rejected violence, direct action and revolution as the answer. With little education and less money, they decided to pool their limited resources and try cooperation. The cumulative result of their actions is now reflected in a diverse, worldwide cooperative movement.

ROCQUIGNY DU FAYEL, HENRI, COMTE DE (1845–1929). A cooperative leader in **France,** he studied law and was a minor official in the government before going to work with the Agricultural Credit Bank, during which time he was an active advocate of trade unionism and of cooperatives of various forms—agricultural, credit and productive. In 1897 he became head of the Agricultural Department of the Musée Social, a position he held until 1915. Attending the 1896 Congress of the **ICA,** he was chosen as a member of its Central Committee; he continued active participation in congresses until 1904. At the Budapest Congress in 1904 he presented a report advocating government aid to cooperative development. This was the first airing of a hotly debated issue that has continued in the cooperative movement to the present day.

RODRIGUES, ROBERTO. An activist in the cooperative movements of **Brazil** and Latin America, he is currently (1999) the president of the ICA, elected in 1997. Previously he served as chair of the ICA's Americas Region and of its Agriculture Committee. A farmer, he became president of his local sugar cane planters' cooperative in 1971. He was executive director of the Organization of Cooperatives of Sao Paulo State and served two terms as president of the Organization of Cooperatives of Brazil.

ROMANIA. The first cooperative in Romania was a credit society founded in 1852. This was followed shortly by craftsmen's cooperatives and other credit societies. A **federation** of **Raiffeisen credit cooperatives** was organized in 1887. Cooperative development proceeded to the point that it was a recognized movement, and Romanian cooperatives were invited to participate in the founding meeting of the **ICA** in London in 1895, where the Romanian delegate was selected to serve on the first ICA Central

Committee. Growth was steady except for the interruption of World War I. In 1924 the following statistics were reported for the non-credit societies: consumer supply and sale societies—2,650 cooperatives/with 231,933 members; forestry societies—922/57,652; and productive societies—314/11,397. All sectors continued to expand in the interwar period, interrupted only by the economic depression of the 1930s.

An attempt was made to revitalize the movement immediately after World War II, but the establishment of a communist government in 1947 meant that the cooperative movement became an integral part of a centrally planned and administered economy. The most radical change came about in the agricultural sector as steps were taken to collectivize it in state farms and collective **production cooperatives**. Together, these came to include 90% of farmland. **Consumer** and producer **cooperatives** were able to maintain some of their original cooperative character but were open to frequent state intervention. The communist system collapsed in 1989–90 and has been followed by a democratization process and the **deofficialization** of the cooperative system. **Agricultural cooperatives** have been almost totally reprivatized, and there has been great reluctance to do anything new labeled "cooperative." The consumer movement and the sector involving worker productive and service functions have recast themselves and maintain a significant member loyalty. An **ICA** report on Romanian cooperatives (1994) stated that there were 4,163 cooperatives with 9,230,000 members (40.1% of the total population). The *1996 Membership Report* of the ICA indicated that cooperative membership at that time had fallen to 6,165,000 (28.5% of the population).

ROMKINS, R. P. A Canadian cooperator, he was one of the leaders involved in the establishment of the **Antigonish Movement** in 1923.

ROULEAU, ALFRED (1915–1985). A French-Canadian cooperative leader, he began his career in the mid-1940s with a **mutual insurance** company; then in 1949 he helped found and became general manager, later president and chief executive officer, of the Desjardins Life Assurance Company, remaining president until 1972. That year he became president of the **Confédération des caisses populaires et d'économie Desjardins de Québec**, a position he held until 1981. He was a member of the Central Committee of the **ICA** and of the board of directors of the **International Raiffeisen Union**. Rouleau was the recipient of the Order of Cooperative Merit from the Canadian Cooperative Council in 1975 and a similar award from the Quebec Cooperative Council in 1976.

ROYAL NORWEGIAN SOCIETY FOR RURAL DEVELOPMENT.
A society operating under the patronage of the Norwegian royal family which is concerned with rural development in **Norway** and in **developing countries**. The later focus, supported by funds from the Norwegian government aid agency, NORAD, is implemented by a Division for International Development Aid, which has a Cooperative Development Committee through which work dealing with cooperatives is planned and coordinated, and which has close relations with the Norwegian cooperative movement. It provides funds to support the work of the **ICA Regional Office in West Africa** and provides project support in a number of other African countries.

RUNDBACK, A. A cooperative pioneer in **Sweden**, in 1867 he established the Vaxjo Domestic Economic Association. He was the author of an *Essay on Consumer Cooperatives.*

RURAL ELECTRIC COOPERATIVES. *See* ELECTRIFICATION COOPERATIVE.

RUSHOLME, LORD. *See* PALMER, ROBERT ALEXANDER.

RUSSELL, GEORGE W. (1867–1935). A cooperator, author and poet in **Ireland** who wrote extensively on cooperative matters under the pseudonym "A.E." He was from 1904 to 1923 the editor of *The Irish Homestead*, the journal of the Irish **agricultural cooperative** movement. He was particularly concerned about the low quality of Irish political and social life and urged the people to refashion their own communities, using cooperatives as the method for improving their economic life.

RUSSELL, MRS. J. M. A British cooperator, she joined the **ICA** in 1966 as secretary for Women and Youth after receiving a diploma from the **Cooperative College in Loughborough**. She provided staff support to the ICA Women's Committee and was responsible for organizing women's conferences as part of the pre-Congress activities at the ICA congresses in Hamburg (1969), Warsaw (1972) and Paris (1976). She was responsible for the work of two officers in New Delhi and Moshi who worked on gender-based programs. She retired from the ICA in 1978.

RUSSIA. The roots of Russian cooperatives date back to 1825 when a group of "Decemberists," who had participated in a revolt against the Czar that year, were exiled and imprisoned in Chita, later Petrovsk, in Siberia. They turned to cooperation as a means of their own and their families' survival. In the process they developed rules of procedure that were very similar to those of **Rochdale. Mutual aid** societies similar to cooperatives emerged in various places during the 1830s, but it was not until the 1860s that formally recognized **cooperatives, consumer** and **agricultural credit,** were established and emulated in different parts of the country. By 1900 there were an estimated 1,000 consumer societies with 250,000 members and 1,500 agricultural credit (multipurpose) societies with 500,000 members. Growth and diversification continued with the formation of the Moscow Union of Consumer societies in 1898 and the first agricultural **credit union** in 1901 at Berdiansk. The first Russian Cooperative Congress was held in Moscow in 1908 and the Moscow Narodny (People's) Bank was established as the central financial institution for cooperatives in 1912. By 1915 the cooperative movement had grown to approximately 35,000 societies and a membership of 12,000,000.

Revolution was to characterize the next phase of cooperative development. Cooperative leaders, who filled 15 of the ministerial and assistant ministerial positions in the Kerensky government, found themselves and the cooperative movement under a cloud of suspicion when the Bolshevik faction won in the civil war and set out to establish a communist state. The communists were initially not sure what to do about cooperatives and so their first moves were to gain control. In 1919 **Centrosoyus** replaced the Moscow Consumer Union, and the Moscow Narodny (People's) Bank was made the cooperative department of the State Bank. Agricultural credit cooperatives were gradually made part of the financing structure for collective farms. Communist officials were placed on the **boards of directors** of key cooperative institutions.

Partly out of ideological considerations and partly out of economic necessity, cooperatives were finally acknowledged as a legitimate form of social property and assigned certain specific tasks, mostly under the umbrella of Centrosoyus as a national consumer cooperative **federation.** Centrosoyus became the Russian member of the **ICA,** now representing the new **Union of Soviet Socialist Republics,** where counterparts to Centrosoyus were being established in the various Soviet republics. While many cooperators outside the USSR fretted, with reason, about the legitimacy of the cooperatives there, Centrosoyus set about building the network of cooperatives and the necessary support structure that would service the vast and diverse nationwide consumer population. Training institutions were established to provide the staff and leadership. Production enterprises were organized and distribution networks formed. By the start of World War II the Centrosoyus network was fully ensconced and it became a pivotal part of the wartime economy.

Following World War II and the rebuilding of the destroyed cooperative infrastructure, Centrosoyus found itself no longer the only national cooperative movement functioning in a Marxist-Leninist environment. It was now joined by cooperative allies in the Eastern European countries, which shared a common ideology, and by a number of cooperative movements in **developing countries,** which were attracted to a socialist path for their development. One of the results of this was a heightened degree of ideological conflict within the international movement, but it was a testimony to cooperative solidarity that these Cold War disputes never precipitated a rupture of cooperative relations. Cooperatives in the USSR continued their growth and elaboration as the principal vehicle for consumer services to the Soviet population, particularly in the rural areas. A broadened network of support organizations, including cooperative institutes and trading organizations, was developed to facilitate their work. In addition, the **Moscow Cooperative Institute** became a major training institution for cooperators from developing countries, providing both long- and short-term training opportunities, particularly for those from countries sharing a common socio-political ideology.

The ideological dissolution of communist control in the USSR beginning in the mid-1980s found Centrosoyus at its pinnacle of development. The 1988 **ILO** *International Directory of Cooperative Organizations* indicated that there were 6,817 cooperative societies in the USSR with 60,100,000 members—21.2% of the population. Since that date, major changes still under way have taken place. Centrosoyus has restructured itself to function apart from government. Cooperative forms have been used by many as a means to exploit the market opportunities presented by the changes, not always to the ideological benefit of cooperatives. In 1995 the cooperative movement in Russia, now separated from its counterparts in a number of the former Soviet republics, reported that there were 4,538 cooperatives with a membership of 11,600,000 (7.8% of the population). The *1996 Membership Report* of the ICA showed a membership increase to 12,578,015 (8.5% of the population). A 1997 statistical profile of the Russian movement, prepared by the ICA, showed a growing diversification in the structure of Russian cooperatives, with a major increase in primary-level societies and with activities in a variety of sectors: agriculture—40,000 societies/with a membership of 300,000; banks—15/500; consumer—3,744/13,712,128; credit unions—40/20,000; and worker productive—10,350/90,000. Movement totals for 1997 were 54,149 cooperatives with 14,122,628 members (9.5% of the national population).

RWANDA. The cooperative effort in Rwanda dates from 1949, when a decree was issued regarding **agricultural cooperatives** and organizing activity in this sector began. The first registered cooperative was formed in 1956, and by 1972 there were 12 cooperatives and 41 **precooperatives** in agriculture. Development diversified into other sectors including fisheries, **housing**, savings and **credit**, and **worker productive cooperatives**. A separate youth cooperative movement has also developed. Currently the dominant portion of the cooperative movement in terms of affiliates and membership is the credit and savings sector (Banques populaires du Rwanda). Statistics on the movement, dating from the mid-1980s, sketchy as they are, indicated that there were 241 cooperatives with 291,368 members, approximately 4.9% of the population, affiliated with cooperatives at that time. The political unrest (long-existing and based on deep ethnic animosities) that exploded again in the early 1990s has periodically disrupted the total society of Rwanda, including the cooperatives. More recent statistics on the cooperative movement were unavailable.

S

SAINT CHRISTOPHER (ST. KITTS)/NEVIS. Cooperative efforts were initiated in 1956 in the then Federation of Saint Kitts/Nevis and Anguilla (**Anguilla** withdrew from the Federation in 1971) with the enactment of a Cooperative Societies Ordinance. The first cooperative, a **credit union**, was organized in 1959. Rules governing cooperatives were issued in 1965 and the cooperative register was opened in 1969. **Cooperative societies** have been organized in agriculture, credit, fisheries and worker productive sectors, with a related movement in the schools. By 1972 there were 8 registered societies. The **ILO** *Directory* (**1988**) indicated that in 1984 there were 33 cooperatives with a membership of 5,108 (10.7% of the population) in the following sectors: agriculture—3 cooperatives/with 44 members; credit unions—3/1,775; fisheries—4/150; worker productive—4/142; and others (mainly school)—19/2,597. The 1997 **WOCCU** *Statistical Report* indicated that credit union membership had increased to 8,689 in 1996. **Cooperative penetration** in the population of 41,369 that year was estimated to be 26.8%.

SAINT LUCIA. Cooperative efforts were formalized in 1946 with the enactment of a Cooperative Societies Ordinance, and they developed gradually with activities involving the agriculture, consumer, **credit union** and fishery sectors. By 1969 there were 14 registered cooperatives with a membership of 1,503. The 9 credit unions accounted for three-fifths of the membership, a ratio that has persisted to the present. The **ILO** *Directory* **(1988)** provided statistics for the year 1984, indicating the existence of 33 cooperative societies with 9,765 members (8.0% of the population) in the following sectors: agriculture—5 cooperatives/with 248 members; consumer—1/430; credit unions—14/7,501; fisheries—9/691; school—1/167; and transport—3/728. The 1997 **WOCCU** *Statistical Report* indicated that 22 credit unions had a combined membership of 23,287. The **cooperative penetration** in that year was estimated to be 16.2% of the population.

SAINT SIEGENS, GEORGE. A cooperative pioneer in **Honduras**, he became an official of the **FAO** in Rome. Following his retirement he authored the 1983 **COPAC** study of cooperative development in Honduras.

SAINT-SIMON, CLAUDE HENRI DE ROUVROY, COMTE DE (1760–1825). A French social philosopher, he envisioned a society organized by scientists and industrialists. He advocated collectivism, a redistribution of wealth to be accomplished primarily by the elimination of inheritance, and the abolition of social distinctions other than those based on one's labor and ability. He was the author of the book *Le Système industriel* and is regarded by many as one of the initiators of the age of cooperative thought and the father of **socialism**.

SAINT VINCENT AND THE GRENADINES. Cooperative legislation enacted in Saint Vincent in 1954 initiated a slow period of cooperative development, with **credit unions** soon becoming the dominant cooperative grouping. The **ILO** *Directory* **(1988)** reported that in 1984 there were 18 cooperatives with a membership of 6,685 (6.4% of the population) as follows: credit unions—6 societies/with 3,857 members; fisheries—2/143; others—10/2,685. **WOCCU** reported in 1997 that the number of credit unions had increased to 9, with a combined membership of 20,109. Total **cooperative penetration** in 1996 was estimated to be 19.4% of a population of 118,344.

SAITO, JIROZAEMON (1909–1998). Mr. Saito served as president of primary-level **fishery cooperatives** for 43 years. He was chair of the **ICA** Fisheries Committee from 1976 to 1992.

SALCIUS, PETRAS. A Lithuanian cooperative leader who was a regular reporter of Lithuanian cooperative activities in the **ICA** *Review of International Cooperation.*

SAMOA (WESTERN). Little information was found on the history of cooperative development in Samoa, except for note of the passage of the first **cooperative legislation** in 1960 and some sketchy details regarding **credit union** development, which began in 1954 when Father **Marion Moses Ganey**, S.J. visited from **Fiji** to establish a pilot project. This was successful enough to lead to the establishment in 1958 of the Credit Union League of Western Samoa. A period of stagnation followed, however, and soon all but one of the credit unions had become inactive. The Credit Union League was reestablished in 1982 and by November of that year 12 credit unions with 820 members were functional, with an additional 11 groups identified as potential. **WOCCU** proposed and was seeking funding for a five-year development program. No more current information was obtainable.

SAUDI ARABIA. The first cooperatives were organized in Saudi Arabia in the villages of Diriyah and Irqah in 1961. The next year, with the adoption of a **cooperative law**, there was a rush of 20 new societies, and growth has been steady since that time. By 1972 there were 55 societies with a membership of 22,325, the predominant types being **multipurpose** and **consumer cooperatives**. By 1994 the movement had grown to include 179 cooperatives with a membership of 54,697 (3.4% of the population) in the following sectors: agriculture—35 cooperatives/with 8,691 members; consumer—9/9,867; fisheries—2/184; multipurpose—128/34,518; and service—5/1,437. In the **ILO** *Directory* **(1988)** there was no indication of any cooperative structure above the **primary** level, independent of the government department that deals with cooperative matters. This is usually an indication that the government is a controlling factor in the cooperative movement.

SAXENA, SUREN (1926–). A cooperative leader in **India**, he served as director of the **ICA Regional Office** and Education Center for South-East Asia for the period 1959–68 and then as director of the **ICA** for the period 1968–81. He migrated to **Canada,** where he established a consulting business in which much of his work dealt with cooperative matters.

SCANDINAVIAN WHOLESALE SOCIETY. *See* NORDISK ANDELSFÖRBUND.

SCHÄR, DR. OSKAR (1846–1924). A lawyer and cooperative leader in **Switzerland,** he was active in the Swiss **consumer cooperative** movement, joining the board of directors of the Swiss Cooperative Union in 1909 and rising to serve as president of its administrative board from 1935 to 1939. He was twice elected a member of the Swiss Parliament, and he was involved in the leadership of the **ICA** for the period 1904–21. Upon his retirement he was named to the **Committee of Honor of the International Cooperative Alliance.**

SCHOOL COOPERATIVE. An association of students of a school who have organized to engage in cooperative activities and to provide training in the **cooperative principles.** Common activities undertaken in such cooperatives include savings and credit, book and school equipment purchases, and canteens. The cooperatives are usually assisted in their activities by one or more teachers or school staff who are experienced cooperators.

SCHOOL OF NÎMES. *See* NÎMES, SCHOOL OF.

SCHULZE-DELITZSCH, FRANZ HERMANN (1808–1883). Lawyer, economist, and politician, he is regarded by many as the father of the German cooperative movement. After legal studies, he returned to his home town of Delitzsch (whose name he annexed to differentiate himself from other Schulzes) and succeeded his father as mayor and hereditary magistrate. From these positions, he came to realize the complexities and difficulties that his countrymen were facing in adjusting to the conditions of the Industrial Revolution. He initially employed traditional social welfare measures to help alleviate the suffering of his fellow citizens but increasingly became convinced that self-help rather than charity was the longterm solution to the problems faced. In 1849 at Delitzsch he established his first **cooperative society** (of carpenters), followed by a second for shoemakers, and a year later his first credit society. In 1853 he published his first book, *Assoziationsbuch für Deutsche Handwerker und Arbeiter,* in which he outlined his own experiences and put forward his model for a new kind of economic development for German artisans and workers.

His ideas spread rapidly and in 1857 he organized the Deutscher Genossenschaftsverband Schulze-Delitzsche (German Schulze-Delitzsche Cooperative Union) at Bonn. By 1864, 400 groups were reported as member societies and in 1865 the first Schultze-Delitzsche Central Cooperative Bank was established at Weimar. Wanting to give formal legal status to his burgeoning movement, Schulze-Delitzsch prepared a draft **cooperative law**, based to some extent on the English law of 1852, and in 1867 he saw such a law passed by the Prussian Parliament in which he was serving. He was working on a similar law relating to industrial cooperatives at the time of his death. The passage of that law soon thereafter was further testimony to the efficacy of his ideas and work. His basic beliefs were that member-patrons of cooperatives should capitalize and control their organizations, that they should accept no charity, public or private, and that cooperative growth should proceed slowly through self-help.

SCOTTISH COOPERATIVE WHOLESALE SOCIETY. *See* COOPERATIVE WHOLESALE SOCIETY, LTD., UNITED KINGDOM.

SECONDARY SOCIETY. A cooperative society whose members are **primary cooperatives** and not individuals. Secondary societies are formed by primary societies to support their efforts, e.g., by joint marketing, processing, bookkeeping, joint purchasing, education and other services.

SECRETARY/MANAGER. A person employed by a cooperative to carry out the dual functions of managing the business affairs of a society and acting as secretary to the board of directors and to other **committees** elected by the members.

SENEGAL. Cooperative activity began in Senegal just prior to World War I, with the establishment of indigenous provident societies in 1910 and the first **consumer cooperative** in 1916 at Dakar (the first such cooperative in West Africa). Growth was very modest until after World War II, when various experiments with rural development structure to encourage cooperatives were undertaken by the French in their West African colonies; some of these proved efficacious in Senegal. **Cooperative legislation** was passed in 1947. A **regional cooperative union** was established at Dakar in 1963; a national Office for Cooperative Development in 1966. By 1972 an **ILO** report indicated the presence of 2,251 cooperative societies, all but 232 in various aspects of agriculture. Developments since that date have continued, but no statistical data for more recent years was available. A **COPAC** study (1985) indicated a total of 1,750 cooperatives; the **ICA Regional Office for West Africa** in 1986 reported that cooperative membership was an estimated 2,300,000 (approximately 34% of the population that year). The **ILO** *Directory* (**1988**) reported a national **federation** established in 1983 and a national **credit union** federation which, according to 1996 **WOCCU** statistics, had not yet shown significant signs of growth and development. The **ICA Regional Office for West Africa** reported that in 1993 there were 2,766 cooperatives with a membership of 2,337,904 (28.0% of the population). Of these cooperatives, 94.7% were in the agricultural sector. Small sectoral activities involving cooperatives were noted involving consumer, fisheries, housing, multipurpose, savings and credit, school and worker productive enterprises.

SERGIO, ANTONIO (1885–1969). A historian, philosopher and cooperative leader in **Portugal**, in 1951 he founded *Boletim Cooperativista*, a cooperative newspaper. The Antonio Sergio Institute, source of much information regarding Portuguese cooperatives, was named in his honor.

SERVICE COOPERATIVE. A cooperative association established to provide specific services to its members. The services provided vary greatly and may include such things as electrical and telephone services, taxi and other transport services, educational and health services, etc. Service cooperatives have been formed to provide specialized services within different cooperative sectors, for example in agriculture, where they have been organized to provide such diverse services as agricultural equipment supply, pesticide programs, crop harvesting, and artificial insemination of livestock. (*See* PRODUCTION COOPERATIVES.)

SERWY, VICTOR (1863–1946). A cooperative leader in **Belgium**, he started his career in 1884 as a teacher in Brussels, working in his spare time as a volunteer in the Belgian Labor Party. His active cooperative involvement began in 1888 when he joined the Executive Committee of the cooperative, Maison du Peuple, in Brussels. Ten years later Serwy became the full-time secretary of the Federation of Cooperative Societies and in 1919 director of the Belgian Cooperative Union. From 1906 to 1935 he edited *La Coopération Belge*. In 1902 he was elected to the **ICA** Central Committee and in 1921 to its Executive Committee, on which he served until his retirement in 1937. He was a staunch believer that cooperatives should be active agents for achieving world **peace**. He completed a five-volume history of the Belgian cooperative movement just prior to his death.

SERWY, WILLY (1891–1974). A cooperative leader in **Belgium** and son of **Victor Serwy**, he worked before World War I with the German **consumer cooperative** movement. After the war he became secretary of the Office coopératif belge, and in 1924 he became secretary of Les Propagateurs de la coopération, where he served for 10 years. In 1935 he became general secretary of the Société générale coopérative, directing its non-commercial activities. He was subsequently general secretary of the Belgian Socialist Federation of Consumer Cooperatives (FEBECOOP). He was elected to the **ICA** Central Committee in 1945 and the Executive Committee in 1946, serving on both until his retirement in 1973.

SEYCHELLES. Cooperative development started in the Seychelles in 1960, with the passage of a cooperative societies ordinance and the establishment of the first coconut producers' cooperative. In 1965 a national cooperative **union** was established. By 1973 there were 12 cooperatives with a combined membership of 1,012 (3.8% of the population) in the following sectors: agriculture—8 societies/with 448 members; consumer—2/168; credit union—1/374; and worker productive—1/22. No more recent comprehensive statistics were available. **WOCCU** reported that in 1996 the one **credit union** had grown to 8,516 members. Assuming modest growth for other types of cooperatives (to a total of approximately 9,282), **cooperative penetration** that year was estimated to be 12.0% of the population.

SHADID, MICHAEL (1882–1966). Lebanese born, he migrated to the **United States** and in 1907 earned a medical degree. He established his medical practice in Elk City, Oklahoma, and set out with others to demonstrate that cooperative principles could be applicable to health care. Over the opposition of other medical professionals, they established in 1929 the Farmers' Union Community Hospital Association, the first cooperative hospital in the United States; a prepaid health plan, owned by the people of the community, was included. Shadid traveled extensively in the United States describing the Oklahoma association and urging others to emulate it. In 1946 he was elected the first president of the Cooperative Health Federation of America. His autobiography, *A Doctor for the People,* portrays his life and dreams for cooperative health care. He was inducted into the U.S. **Cooperative Hall of Fame** in 1981.

SHARE. A contribution to or a part owned of something, like capital. In a cooperative, the shares are amounts of money contributed by each member to the capital of the society. A modest interest is usually paid annually on the shares, which are normally refunded if a member leaves the society.

SHILLITO, JOHN (1832–1915). Born of simple working folk in Halifax, Yorkshire, he was a skilled knitter of stockings by the age of 6, then a worker in cottage industry and at 8 a full-time farmer with his father. His formal schooling had been completed by age 6 but he became a lifelong, self-taught learner. In these ways, Shillito was like many of the early British cooperative leaders—hardy, self-made, inquiring, intent on transforming the economic system to make it responsive to all rather than only to those of wealth and privilege. He became a natural scientist, geologist and physical geographer and was eventually elected a Fellow of the Royal Geographical Society. His cooperative career began in 1861 in the Halifax Industrial Cooperative Society, and within a short period he had emerged among its leaders. Within 10 years Shillito was elected to a seat on the board of the **English Cooperative Wholesale Society,** of which he became the president in 1895, serving in that capacity for 20 years. He was a longtime member of the Central Committee of the **ICA.**

SHIPE, J. ORRIN (1912–1989). A **credit union** leader in the **United States,** he began this work in 1934 at age 21, when he helped organize a credit union at the Buffalo Insurance Company where he was employed. By 1939, when he joined the **Credit Union National Association (CUNA)** as a field representative, he had already been treasurer and president of his credit union, organized dozens of other credit unions, been president of the Buffalo, New York, chapter and director of the New York Credit Union League. He was the first educational director of CUNA and editor of *Bridge,* the forerunner of the *Credit Union Magazine.* He rose through a number of positions in CUNA and **CUNA Mutual Insurance Society,** becoming assistant managing director in 1956 and managing director in 1963, a position he held until 1971. He was also the first managing director of **WOCCU.** Following his retirement he became president of the Arizona Credit Union League and acted as a national and international consultant for the **credit union movement** until his death.

SIDOROV, NIKOLAI. A Soviet cooperative leader, he was elected vice president of the **ICA** in 1946.

SIERRA LEONE. While the **English Cooperative Wholesale Society** had export operations in Sierra Leone as early as 1914, the first local **cooperative society** was established only in 1936, followed in 1939 by the passage of a cooperative societies ordinance. New activity was modest until the first consumer society was organized in 1947 and rural cooperatives came into being in 1950. The first women's cooperative in the country, the Freetown Women Traders' Cooperative Society, was organized in 1954. Agricultural producers' cooperatives had expanded to the extent that they justified the establishment of a marketing **federation** in 1960. Independence came in 1961. A cooperative development bank was established in 1971, coincident with the holding of the first National Cooperative Congress. The **ILO** has reported that at that time there were 600 **credit unions**, 279 marketing societies and 71 other cooperatives, a total of 950. Membership was approximately 48,000. Development of the cooperative movement in recent years has been adversely influenced by economic instability and political unrest. In 1988 the **ICA Regional Office for West Africa** reported that in 1986 there were 1,084 cooperatives with a membership of 83,061 (2.2% of the population). **Agricultural cooperatives** and **credit unions** dominated the membership, with small numbers of **consumer**, fisheries, and **worker productive cooperatives**. The lack of more recent statistics is partly a reflection of the civil unrest that has plagued the country in recent years.

SILIN, VILIS (died 1935). A Latvian farmer and cooperative leader who was president of the Council of the Cooperative Congress of **Latvia**. He served on the **ICA** Central Committee from 1924 until his death.

SINGAPORE. The cooperative movement started in Singapore in 1925 with the establishment of a **credit cooperative** to serve members of the civil service. Others followed, and in 1929 the cooperative consultant **C. F. Strickland** was invited to study the local cooperative movement and to make recommendations about its development. Partly in response to his study the Singapore Cooperative Union was established in 1933, but development of new societies was only sporadic until after World War II.

In 1948 a **housing cooperative** was formed and a cooperative societies ordinance enacted. An **agricultural cooperative union** and a **cooperative bank** soon followed. With independence in 1966, a Cooperative Development Division was established in the Ministry of Social Affairs, and with the joint interest of cooperatives and the government, development accelerated. A 1994 report of the **ICA Regional Office for Asia and the Pacific** cited statistics for the movement in Singapore in 1993 indicating 70 cooperatives with a membership of 740,217 (25.9% of the population). A 1996 report by the **ICA** headquarters noted that there were 64 cooperatives with 971,257 members in the following sectors: consumer—2 societies/with 366,603 members; housing—2/354; insurance—1/517,972; savings and credit—35/65,596; and others—24/20,732. Cooperative membership that year was 27.3% of the population. More than half of this membership, however, is that of one **insurance cooperative** whose policy holders, presumably, may have membership in other cooperatives as well.

SLOVAKIA. The early stages of cooperative development in Slovakia took place during the period up to 1918, when Slovakia was part of **Hungary** in the Austro-Hungarian Empire. Early cooperative developments in Hungary were reflected in Slovakia (*See* HUNGARY). In 1918, Slovakia achieved independence as part of a federated **Czechoslovakia** and, from 1918 through 1992, its cooperative experience was concurrent with or paralleled that of Czechoslovakia. In December 1992 Slovakia again became a separate nation.

The first cooperative, a savings and credit society for farmers, was established in Slovakia in 1845 in the village of Sobotiste. The first **cooperative law** was enacted in 1873 and applied to all of Hungary. By that date more than 40 self-help food associations existed in Slovakia, predecessors of the future **consumer cooperatives**. By the turn of the century there were also the beginnings of housing societies and of artisan cooperatives. When Slovakia combined with Bohemia and Moravia to form the new nation of Czechoslovakia in 1918, the cooperative traditions of the different areas were joined and development in all areas accelerated at a rapid pace. By 1922 there were 5,839 **agricultural cooperatives** in the country. The interwar years saw a slower but steady growth and diversification of cooperatives in the Slovakian portion of the country, with significant activity in the agriculture, consumer, housing, and worker productive sectors.

World War II was a disruptive period for cooperatives, and the early postwar efforts to reestablish the prewar movement were aborted by the establishment of a communist government in 1948, a government that had a different ideological role in mind for cooperatives as part of a socialist economy. The existing sectoral movements were reorganized, new leadership named, and new unions established for the two socialist republics, Czech and Slovak. Growth of the cooperative movement continued, even though cooperatives were sometimes an imposed rather than a democratically chosen structure. By 1989, just prior to the collapse of the communist regime, there were 865 cooperatives in Slovakia with 1,766,606 members (20.6% of the population) in the following sectors: agriculture—635 societies/with 392,000 members; consumer—37/969,266; housing—80/352,600; and worker productive—113/52,740.

Since 1989, Slovak cooperatives, along with those of other Eastern Europe states, have undergone a transition to democracy and a market economy. Not easy in itself, this was made even more complicated by the division of Czechoslovakia into two separate nations at the end of 1992. The 1995 membership report of the **ICA** reflected some of these changes within Slovakia—a number of new cooperatives and a reduction in overall membership. In 1995, there were 1,328 cooperatives with a combined membership of 1,425,917 (28.0% of the population). A 1996 statistical report of ICA reflected more of the results of the transition—1,108 cooperatives with a membership of 782,966 in the following sectors: agriculture—757 societies/with 126,000 members; consumer—40/220,604; health—1/320,413; housing—130/98,387; insurance—1/na; and worker productive—170/17,562. Cooperative membership was now only 14.6% of the population.

SLOVENIA. The first cooperative in Slovenia, then part of the Austro-Hungarian Empire, was a **credit cooperative** established in Ljubljana in 1851. A **union** of such cooperatives was organized in 1883 and a general cooperative union in 1899; it was reorganized in 1907. A **cooperative bank** was established at Ljubljana in 1920, a year after the formation of the Kingdom of Serbs, Croats and Slovenes that in 1929 became **Yugoslavia**. The history of cooperative development in Slovenia was bound up with that of Yugoslavia until Slovenia declared its independence in 1991. A 1998 **ICA** report indicated that in 1996 there were 174 cooperatives with 220,334+ members in the following sectors: agriculture—107 societies/with 20,354 members; banking—1/na; credit unions—62/200,000; forestry—2/na; insurance—1/na; and others—1/na. Cooperative membership was estimated to be 12.3% of the population.

SMABY, ARTHUR J. (1908–1972). A cooperative leader in the **United States**, soon after his graduation from college he became manager of Tri-County Cooperative Oil Association in Minnesota and then joined Midland Cooperative where he had a 32-year career, including 25 years (1939–64) as general manager. He joined the board of directors of **CLUSA** in 1943 and served as its chairman from 1953 to 1955 and as a trustee of the CLUSA Fund for International Cooperative Development. Smaby was also a trustee of the **American Institute of Cooperation** for a number of years. He was inducted into the U.S. **Cooperative Hall of Fame** in 1978.

SMITH, L. O. (1836–1913). A cooperative pioneer in **Sweden**, he started the Ring Movement in 1878, an effort to amalgamate the early **consumer cooperatives**. The movement expanded to include some 500 affiliated organizations before disbanding around 1890.

SOCIAL AUDIT. The practice among a growing number of cooperatives to report to their membership on the impact of their endeavors on society in general, in addition to reporting on the specific economic benefit for members. Areas of focus of social audits have included such things as environmental impact, education of consumers, community needs such as housing, day care and cultural facilities, problems of the aged and disabled, poverty and large disparities in income.

SOCIALISM. An economy in which the major production and distribution organizations are owned by the state and are part of a centralized planning process aimed at more equitably sharing the goods and services and other benefits of the activity of that economy. Particular qualifying adjectives have been applied to socialism to differentiate particular emphases of socialist individuals and groups: these include terms such as democratic, Christian, Marxist, or cooperative. In the last-mentioned case, cooperatives rather than state bureaucracies are proposed as the collective form for social ownership of the means of production and distribution.

SOCIÉTÉ COOPÉRATIVE DE DÉVELOPPEMENT INTERNATIONAL (SOCODEVI). SOCODEVI is a Canadian **cooperative development organization** founded by a number of French-speaking Canadian cooperative organizations. It conducts programs of development education in **Canada** and provides short- and long-term technical assistance to cooperatives in **developing countries,** utilizing funds made available by the **Canadian International Development Agency**.

SOCIÉTÉ DE DÉVELOPPEMENT INTERNATIONAL DES-JARDINS (SDID). Part of the **Desjardins Group**, it was established in 1970 to support cooperatives in **developing countries**. Its primary efforts have been in **credit cooperative** development but it has assisted other types of cooperatives in Africa, Latin America and the Caribbean. It is the recipient of funds from the **Canadian International Development Agency,** which it combines with funds from French-speaking Canadian cooperatives to implement its projects.

SOCIETY. A group formed to pursue common interests or objectives. In cooperative circles it refers to the cooperative itself, and the terms "cooperative" and "society" are used interchangeably.

SOLOMON ISLANDS. Cooperatives first came into being in the Solomon Islands after the passage of a cooperative societies act in 1953 and the establishment of a cooperative department in the government in 1957. Growth was rather rapid, and an **ILO** report noted that there were 221 societies with 16,064 members by 1979, 70% of which were **multipurpose cooperatives** engaging in marketing produce and providing consumer services. The **ILO** *Directory* **(1988)**, citing information for 1983, indicated that there were at that time 280 cooperatives. More recently, an **ICA Regional Office for Asia and the Pacific** report noted that in 1995 there were 85 cooperatives with 14,935 members (4.0% of the population).

SOMALIA. The first cooperatives in Somalia (two agricultural societies) were established in 1950 in what was then Italian Somaliland. Some growth took place in the ensuing years, during which the British and Italian sections of the country merged and independence was achieved in 1960. The first **cooperative legislation** was passed in 1969. It was not until the 1970s, however, and with active governmental involvement that growth took place, encouraged by a new **cooperative law** enacted in 1973. A national cooperative **union**, Union of the Somali Cooperative Movement, was established in 1978, made up of 7 national sectoral organizations. It was unique in that, in addition to being the **apex cooperative organization**, it was assigned by law those responsibilities usually assumed by a government cooperative department. The **ILO** *Directory* **(1988)** indicated that in 1984 there were 760 cooperatives with a total membership of 91,622 (1.4% of the national population). By sectors they were as follows: agriculture—496 societies/with 55,036 members;

consumer—70/9,059; fisheries—23/2,892; livestock, forestry and incense—83/10,448; transport—33/5,887; and worker productive—55/8,300. In 1994 the **Arab Cooperative Union** reported that there were 813 cooperatives with 92,600 members (0.96% of the population). The dissolution of the Somalian government in 1992 and the civil war in the country have affected the cooperative movement as they have affected everything else in the country. The future of the cooperative movement awaits the return of a stable civil society.

SONNE, HANS CHRISTIAN (1817–1880). A Danish pastor, he is regarded as the father of the cooperative movement in **Denmark**. In 1866, adapting the **Rochdale Principles** to Danish conditions, he established the first Danish **consumer cooperative** at Thisted. In 1871 he was part of the group that formed a joint buying structure that was the forerunner of the Danish Cooperative Wholesale Society.

SONNICHSEN, ALBERT (1878–1931). An early **consumer cooperative** leader in the **United States**, he saw cooperatives as an alternative to socialism. He helped form the Cooperative Propaganda Publishing Association, which later became the Consumers' Cooperative Publishing Association and then the Consumers' Cooperative Union. He edited and published *The Cooperative Consumer* from 1914 to 1918. Sonnichsen was instrumental in the organization of a meeting in 1916 at the home of **James and Agnes Warbasse,** from which emerged **CLUSA**, now the **National Cooperative Business Association**. His book *Consumers' Cooperation*, published in 1918, was an important contribution to the philosophy and operation of American cooperatives.

SOUSA BRANDAO. A Portuguese cooperative pioneer, he established the Center for the Progress of the Working Classes, publicized the ideas of **François Marie Charles Fourier**, and delineated the **cooperative principles** that guided the development of the **movement** in **Portugal**.

SOUTH AFRICA. In 1902, the Boers Farmers' Cooperative was established in South Africa, the first cooperative in the country and the first in all sub-Saharan Africa. Further development was slow, but by 1919 there had been enough to warrant the establishment of the Federated Farmers' Cooperative Association (again, the first of its type in sub-Saharan Africa) and a year later the Overseas Farmer's Cooperative Federation, which concluded agreements to ship agricultural produce to the **English Co-**

operative **Wholesale Society**. In 1922 the first **cooperative law** was passed. Modest growth has characterized cooperatives since then for both "Natives" and "Europeans" though, as in other things, the benefits have not flowed equally to the two groups. In the mid-1930s the ILO's *Cooperative Information* carried two articles on South Africa's cooperatives. The first reported the beginnings of **credit, consumer** and **agricultural cooperatives** among the "Natives"; the second reported on the fuller development that had taken place among the "Europeans": 272 societies with 84,815 members. Cooperatives were engaged in consumer supply, crop insurance, marketing, manufacturing, supply, and services. By 1947 cooperatives ("Native" and "European" together) had increased in number and membership, to 376 cooperatives (including 3 cooperative farms) with 254,153 members. Specific note was made of the spread of the movement among "non-Europeans." Modest growth continued, and the movement further developed through the 1970s with the formation of sectoral **unions**. At that point information available on developments among cooperatives diminished, reflecting the worldwide campaign mounted against apartheid in South Africa. A 1995 **ILO** report, *Privatization of Cooperative Services in East and Southern Africa*, reported the presence of 618 societies, 41 unions and 318,378 members, still less than 1% of the total population of the country. A 1997 report of the **ICA** reporting for 1992 showed 461 cooperatives with 310,192 members (0.76% of the population) in the following sectors: agriculture—248 societies/with 167,580 members; savings and credit—10/2,067; and trading—203/140,545.

Small as the cooperative movement has been, it will have to go through some dramatic changes in structure and control. Commercial agriculture in South Africa, as in Zimbabwe, has been and still is the province of the whites. The blacks seek land reform and land distribution and are disdainful of existing land ownership and control patterns. Trading, the other major cooperative sector, presents easier opportunities for change and integrated action. **Credit unions** were introduced first in Cape Town through integrated church structures where they had initial success prior to the elimination of apartheid. They are minuscule in penetration of the population, only 0.02% now, but have aspirations to become a national movement.

SOUTHERN, ROBERT. A British cooperator, he worked for most of his career in the **consumer cooperative** movement in the **United Kingdom**, beginning in 1929 when he became an assistant to **Robert Palmer** at the

English Cooperative Wholesale Society. He became acting general manager before Palmer's retirement and was named general manager in 1951. He became a member of the **ICA** Central and Executive Committees in 1948.

SPAIN. While the first Spanish cooperative, an association of stock breeders, was established in 1838, it was **worker productive** and **consumer** rather than **agricultural cooperatives** that were to be the principal early cooperative structures in Spain. All these types emerged from groups with strong socialist orientations. The first **cooperative legislation** dates from 1885 when a special section of the Commercial Code was enacted to deal with the emerging cooperatives. **Regional cooperative** structures, an important feature of Spanish cooperation to this day, emerged first in Catalonia in 1898 and were soon found in diverse sectors—agriculture, consumer, credit, housing and industrial production. The first national **congress** of cooperatives took place in 1913 and reflected the growing national character of the movement. However, in its deliberations the congress brought to public light sectarian and political differences that reflected the different sectoral and regional structures. A national cooperative **federation** was formed in 1928 and represented Spanish cooperatives in the **ICA** until the time of the Spanish Revolution.

After Franco's victory, the national federation was replaced in 1942 by a new governmental structure. The new government also declared illegal and liquidated the existing sectoral and regional cooperative federation structures, then representing about 2,200 cooperative societies. While politically constrained (many cooperative leaders left the country in fear of their lives), cooperatives continued to grow and diversify under the Franco regime. An **ILO** report (1972) noted the existence of 14,984 societies in 1971 with a membership in excess of 2.6 million (approximately 8.5% of the population). With the death of Franco in 1975, the dictatorship collapsed and with it, eventually, the imposed cooperative structure.

Regional multisectoral federations have again emerged as important elements in the cooperative movement. These have been accompanied by new or revived national sectoral federations representing cooperatives in the following sectors: agriculture, consumer, credit, fisheries, food retailing, housing and worker productive. More recently, the Spanish Confederation of Cooperatives was formed as the national **apex cooperative organization**. A European Community publication in 1986 reported 25,868 cooperatives with 3,864,182 members (10.0% of the population).

A 1998 statistical summary of ICA member countries notes that in 1996 there were 23,481 cooperatives in Spain with a membership of 4,336,502 in the following sectors: agriculture—4,350 societies/with 950,000 members; banking—96/905,473; consumer—381/806,387; fisheries—178/12,443; health—3/186,942; housing—3,378/1,255,961; independent retailers—na/2,674; insurance—1/na; transport—396/4,710; worker productive—13,101/163,952; and others—1,597/47,960. Cooperative membership at that time was 11.1% of the national population.

Several distinctive elements of the Spanish cooperatives should be noted: the **Mondragon** industrial cooperatives in the Basque country (a highly successful network of **worker productive cooperatives**), 300 or so cooperative schools, a national system of pharmacy cooperatives, and a national network of **health cooperatives**. Each of these has made unique contributions to the Spanish and worldwide cooperative experience.

SPAR. A retail store network in Europe organized in 1932 by shop owners who wished to establish a cooperative wholesale supply system for their shops. The **ILO** *Directory* **(1988)** noted that the network at that time encompassed 247,000 shops which were represented by an European Community cooperative organization, the Union of Retailer-owned Wholesalers in Foodstuffs, based in Brussels.

SPRUDZ, ALEKSANDRS. A Canadian cooperator, he was active in the formation of cooperatives for indigenous peoples in the north of **Canada** and was the author of a major work on cooperatives in developing areas.

SRI LANKA (formerly Ceylon). Confronted with the dual problems of perpetual rural indebtedness and a growing need to mediate the conflict between plantation and small-holder-based agriculture, in 1909 the colonial administration of what was then Ceylon initiated a study of ways to resolve these. One of the study's proposals, for legislation that would circumvent rural usurers and enhance the economic position of small farmers, resulted in the enactment of the Cooperative Credit Societies Act of 1911. This law provided the basis for organizing **credit cooperatives**, which began immediately after its enactment. These were the focus of most cooperative development activity until the passage of a broader **cooperative law** in 1921. Progress in expanding the cooperative movement, however, was slow, and by 1926 only 315 societies had been organized and registered. Growth and diversification of cooperatives later began to accelerate, however, and by the time of World War II and then independence in 1948 the cooperative movement was established in a variety of diverse sectors including agricultural marketing, banking, consumers, cooperative agricultural estates, credit, dairying, fisheries, hospitals, housing, labor societies and **school cooperatives**.

The government mechanisms designed to assist and supervise cooperatives had similarly grown, and the earlier well-articulated plans to **deofficialize** the cooperative structure and make it dependent on its own efforts and resources rather than those of government fell by the wayside. First reduced during World War II when cooperative structures were created to handle distribution of food and other consumer goods, cooperative independence gave way to a Sri Lanka government decision to use cooperatives to achieve a variety of development tasks, whether or not the cooperatives agreed, and whether or not they had the needed capacity. Each cooperative shortfall in accomplishment brought further governmental planning and involvement, and strengthened a government-cooperative relationship that is still a brake on independent cooperative development. The movement, however, has continued to grow, most notably in recent years in the **credit union** sector, which has vigorously defended its independence from governmental control. An **ICA Regional Office for Asia and the Pacific** statistical survey of member movements reported that in 1992 there were 10,964 cooperatives with 4,434,200 members in Sri Lanka (24.6% of the nation's population) in the following sectors: agriculture—578 societies/with 87,500 members; consumer—1,456/295,600; fisheries—845/92,300; multipurpose—292/2,604,200; savings and credit—6,940/730,100; services—96/452,100; worker productive—373/75,700; and others—384/96,700. In 1996 the Sri Lanka movement reported a membership totaling 4,549,800 (24.5% of the national population).

STANDIGER, FRANZ (1849–1922). An academic, author and official in the **consumer cooperative** movement in **Germany**, he was one of Germany's most esteemed champions and promoters of the cooperative movement of his day. His books, *Ethics and Politics* and *Ethics and Socialism,* brought him into contact with the cooperative movement, and he immersed himself in it, preparing studies of the British and other national consumer movements. Standiger was the author of numerous texts used in cooperative training and was a frequent contributor to the journal of the German consumer movement.

STANTON, BERYLE (1909–1983). A cooperative journalist in the **United States**, she was editor for many years of the *News for Farmer Cooperatives*, published by the Farmers Cooperative Service of the United States Department of Agriculture, where she was head of the information department. Stanton was secretary and a board member of the Cooperative Editorial Association and in 1966 received the organization's Klinefelter Award for outstanding contributions to cooperative journalism. Following her retirement from government service, she edited the *Yearbook* of the **American Institute of Cooperation**.

STATISTICS ON THE COOPERATIVE MOVEMENT. A major bit of unfinished business in the world cooperative movement is the preparation and availability of reliable statistics. At present, these are not routinely collected and published in but a few countries. In several countries where data is systematically collected, the systems used are not integrated with one another and do not allow for reliable summaries or comparisons. Where data is collected and summarized by registrars of cooperatives, it is often of questionable reliability because of large numbers of registered but now inactive societies still carried on the books. No international organization collecting socio-economic data includes the world's cooperatives in their purview.

The existence of this problem through the entire 20th century has been lamented by everyone trying to comprehend the cooperative movement in its entirety. A few efforts have been made to deal with it in pieces, fewer involving the whole. **ICA**, at the international and some regional levels, has developed systems that are generally accurate for their member organizations. **WOCCU** has done similarly. Both organizations can provide a reasonably good statistical profile of their member organizations and of the larger picture that they collectively represent.

The member organizations of **COPAC** have been considering the problem and have sought an answer using the statistics-gathering arm of the United Nations. Two ICA regional offices—for Asia and the Pacific and for Europe—have attempted to be more comprehensive in their coverage, including in their country data nonmember cooperative organizations, and in their regional data countries that may not be affiliated internationally. Such efforts should be applauded and encouraged. It is unlikely that statistics-gathering agencies will take on the cooperative statistics problem on their own, nor is it wise to do so. The most positive effort to date has been that of the ICA's European region in collaboration with and assisted financially by the Commission of the European

Communities. Much of the data in this book for European countries came from this source.

STEWART, SIR ROBERT (1860–1937). Born in Glasgow, Scotland, he started his cooperative activity as a carpenter in the Shieldhall Factories of the **Scottish Cooperative Wholesale Society**, where he became an active trade unionist. For 15 years he was president of the Kinning Park Cooperative Society and from 1908 until 1932 he was president of the Scottish Cooperative Wholesale Society. Stewart was active in the Central Committee of the **ICA** from 1921 to 1934 and served as chairman of the International Cooperative Wholesale Society from 1929 to 1934.

STOKDYK, ELLIS A. (1897–1945). An academic and cooperative leader in the **United States**, he was a cooperative activist in Wisconsin, Kansas and California, to which last-mentioned state he moved in 1929 to teach and do research at the University of California. With the establishment of the **Farm Credit System**, he was named president of the Berkeley Bank for Cooperatives, serving for 12 years until his early death. Stokdyk was a principal proponent of the idea that cooperatives should buy out the U.S. government contribution to the Farm Credit System, thus making it truly a cooperative-owned financial institution, a step that was achieved later.

STRICKLAND, C. F. A British cooperator and colonial administrator, he served for a number of years in **India** promoting the cooperative movement. In 1925 he advised on cooperative development in Ceylon (**Sri Lanka**) with **William Campbell**. In 1928, after extensive study in **Nigeria**, he recommended the introduction of cooperative societies. In 1929 Strickland visited **Singapore,** where he studied the local cooperative movement and made recommendations regarding its future course. During the 1930s his assignments took him to **Palestine**, Tanganyika (**Tanzania**), and the **Cameroons,** and he helped define the future developments of cooperative movements in those countries.

STUDENT COOPERATIVE. *See* SCHOOL COOPERATIVE.

SUDAN. Although there were some experiments with **credit** and **irrigation cooperatives** in the 1930s, it was not until 1947 that the first successful **agricultural cooperatives** were established, almost concurrent with the passage of the first **cooperative legislation** in 1948. In 1953 a national cooperative **union** was established at Khartoum, based on the growing co-operative effort around the country. A Sudan Wholesale Cooperative Society was established in 1962, reflecting the need to supply a growing number of **consumer cooperatives**. In that same year the **ILO** reported the presence of 720 cooperatives in the country. Growth has continued over the years despite a seemingly endless civil war in the south of the country, military coups, various attempts to apply Islamic law to all facets of national life, and a deteriorating economy. By 1970 the ILO reported that there were 1,053 cooperatives with 204,000 members, and in 1983 6,156 with 1,720,673 members. The cumulative political, economic and military disruption of recent years makes it difficult to obtain reliable information on cooperative development in Sudan. However, the **Arab Cooperative Union** reported the existence of 9,848 cooperatives in 1994 with 1,535,131 members (5.4% of the population) in the following sectors: agriculture, consumer, fisheries, industrial, multipurpose and services.

SUN YAT-SEN (1866–1925). A Chinese revolutionary and statesman, he is regarded by many as the ideological father of modern **China**. Influenced by **Karl Marx** and Henry George, in 1894 he organized in a movement in opposition to the Manchu government. Exiled in 1895, he formulated the principles of democracy, nationalism and **socialism** which were the ideological underpinnings of the Kuomintang, the party he founded and led. In 1911 the Manchus were overthrown and Sun Yat-Sen became the first president of China. He resigned in 1912, but not before issuing directives that effectively launched the Chinese cooperative movement.

SUPERVISION. The act of checking or overseeing work being done by others: e.g., a cooperative may be kept under close supervision by government officials before it is decided that it may be registered; or, if a society has been identified as having financial or other difficulties that may jeopardize its operation, it may be given closer supervision.

SUPPLY COOPERATIVE. An association of farmers who pool their resources to buy needed input supplies such as seed, fertilizer, petroleum and farming equipment. By purchasing together, they obtain the savings of volume purchases and can better guarantee the quality of the products. Supply cooperatives range in size from small, informal buying groups to large regional associations and have affiliated in some instances with other cooperatives to own phosphate deposits, fertilizer plants, refineries and other similar facilities.

SURINAME. Agricultural **mutual aid** societies were the cooperative form to first appear in Suriname in 1920. These groups over the years have become agricultural supply and marketing societies. **Cooperative legislation** was enacted in 1944. Savings and **credit cooperatives**, in the form of **credit unions**, were introduced in the late 1950s and a national **credit union league** established in 1962. A government cooperative service came into being in 1959. An **ILO** mission in 1989 reported the presence of 107 cooperatives with an estimated 13,000 members (3.3% of the population). No information was provided regarding membership by sector, but it is known that credit unions are predominant in terms of number of societies and membership size. **WOCCU** reported in 1997 that in 1996 there were 21 credit unions with 8,722 members. Overall **cooperative penetration** of the nation's 423,000 population in 1996 was estimated to be 3.4%.

SURPLUS. The amount left over in a cooperative after all items of expenditure have been met. From the surplus, the cooperative will designate money for investments, reserves, education and other purposes; a part of the surplus will usually be set aside for a **patronage refund** and as a dividend to be paid on **shares**.

SURRIDGE, B. J. A British cooperative advisor, he served as a registrar of cooperative societies in **Cyprus** from 1934 to 1943, as cooperative advisor to the government of **Iraq** in 1946–47, and as advisor on cooperatives to the British government from 1947 until his retirement. He was vice chairman and a trustee of the **Plunkett Foundation for Cooperative Studies** and is widely known for his *Manual of Cooperative Law and Practice,* written jointly with **Margaret Digby**.

SUTER, ANTON (1863–1942). A Swiss cooperator, he served on the **ICA** Central Committee for 17 years and on the Executive Committee from 1921 to 1927.

SWAZILAND. The first **cooperative legislation** (Proclamation No. 8 of 1931) and the first cooperative, the Swaziland Cooperative Tobacco Company, established the same year, effectively represented the cooperative effort in the country until 1963–64. In that two-year period a **registrar of cooperatives** was appointed, the first **agricultural cooperatives** formed, a new Cooperative Proclamation, No. 28, issued, and the Central Cooperative Union established. From then on, growth has been slow, steady and modest overall—28 societies in 1970, 132 in 1980 and 171 in 1993. The predominant types by sector are agriculture (mainly tobacco and cotton, which have marketing **federations** that sell the majority of these crops) and **credit unions** (which predominate in size of membership). A 1994 report of the **ICA Regional Office for East, Central and Southern Africa** reported 171 cooperatives with 16,430 members in 1993 (2.2% of the population) as follows: agriculture—115 societies/with 4,000 members; consumer—4/200; credit union—46/12,000; industrial—1/30; multipurpose—3/150; and transport 2/50. The **ICA** reported membership totaling 17,430 in 1996, 1.7% of the population.

SWEDEN. The cooperative developments in the first half of the 19th century in Sweden and in other European countries that led to the modern cooperative movement were in large part adaptations of traditional **mutual aid** arrangements already existing among farmers and villagers. They were organizational responses to the gradual breakdown of an agrarian system based on subsistence farming, barter and small-scale production. In urban areas, cooperatives were a response to the transition from a mercantile guild system of production by a skilled few for a small urban elite, to one based on the exploitation of a large new urban workforce to meet an emerging industrial order. The response of many farmers and workers alike was to organize institutions to help buffer themselves against debilitating conditions in their work and provide a way of collectively responding to the needs of daily living.

The first **agricultural cooperative**, a wholesale purchasing society, was established in Sweden by farmers in 1850 in Örsundsbro; it was designed to provide a way of making group purchases of agricultural inputs and consumer goods. In Stockholm in 1852, associations of tailors and typographers were organized to work together as an alternative method of production to those of individual entrepreneurs; this presaged some 50 or so **worker productive cooperatives** that emerged in the next 25 years. "Food associations," established at the same time, were precursors to the 400 or so consumer retail societies (including one still in existence at Trollhättan) that emerged during the same period as a way of meeting daily consumer needs and obtaining access to the products of an industrialized economy. Passage of the Freedom of Commerce Law in 1864 and of specific **cooperative legislation** in 1895 established the legal position of cooperative societies. By the end of the century a central cooperative **union** of farmers in the south of Sweden had been formed. **Kooperativa Förbundet (KF)**, a **consumer cooperative** union and

wholesale society, had been organized and the first cooperative dairies, housing societies, and savings and **credit cooperatives** established.

The first half of the 20th century saw rapid growth and expansion of cooperatives. By 1910 there were 5,100 societies, by 1936 14,700, by 1950 34,600. Cooperatives also extended into new areas of activity— banking, crafts and trades, child care, fisheries, horticulture, recreation and transport. National **federations** reflecting these were formed. Folksam, now a world-renowned **insurance cooperative** structure, came into being. Cooperative structures for travel services and provision of petroleum products were initiated. By mid-century, cooperation and self-help were deeply embedded in Swedish life and economy, and much of the cooperative history of recent years reflects this and the experience of the cooperative movement in dealing with its established status.

The continued shift of population from rural to urban areas was reflected in agricultural consolidation among farmers and in their supporting organizational infrastructure. The number of farming units decreased; the organizations supporting them consolidated. Farming became big business. KF and its supporting organizations and industries diversified. The extensive network of small consumer shops consolidated into larger, more complex units and increased in economic and social sophistication. Economic problems and occasional faulty investment decisions were accommodated. Growth and market penetration continued.

By 1988 when the **ICA** decided for the third time to hold its congress in Sweden (previous occasions were in 1927 and 1957), the cooperative movement was solidly in place, facing its changing environment and problems. A 1988 publication, *The Cooperative Movement in Sweden— Past, Present—the Future*, portrayed the scene that year in the various cooperative sectors. In agriculture there were 1,050,000 members in 630 societies with 16 supporting business organizations. KF and its consumer network was present, with 137 societies, 1,807 retail outlets and 2,013,254 members, augmented by membership in **petroleum cooperatives**, insurance, housing and new endeavors such as funeral and burial services. More than half the Swedish population had become members of cooperative societies. In 1998, an ICA report to the European Commission reported that the Swedish movement had 15,106 cooperatives with a membership of 4,779,540+ (some membership figures were incomplete) in the following sectors: agriculture—84 societies/with 200,000 members; banking—10/82,000; consumer—513/3,845,000; forestry— 26/90,000; housing—11,942/560,240; independent retailers—na/2,300; insurance—1/na; social care—877/na; transport—272/na; utilities—

117/na; worker productive—152/na; and others—1,112/na. Cooperative membership was 53.7% of the national population.

Moving beyond their own borders, Swedish cooperatives for more than 30 years have provided active support to cooperatives in the **developing countries** through the **Swedish Cooperative Center**. In addition to country-specific or regional cooperative development projects, Swedish cooperatives have actively supported an expanding network of ICA regional offices. This has provided regional mechanisms through which the varied national and sectoral parts of the growing world cooperative movement may collaborate.

SWEDISH COOPERATIVE CENTER (SCC). The Swedish cooperative movement's organization for building development assistance, it works closely with the **Swedish International Development Authority,** which covers about 70% of the SCC costs for projects or other cooperative activities. A major portion of SCC support is for **ICA** regional office programs and for the Nordic Project in East Africa, but its cooperative interests have found expression in numerous parts of the world.

SWEDISH INTERNATIONAL DEVELOPMENT AUTHORITY (SIDA). The agency within the government of Sweden that supports financial and technical development efforts in Third World countries. Cooperatives are an aid priority in SIDA, with support being delivered through grants to the **Swedish Cooperative Center**, through assistance to the **ICA** in its headquarters and regional office operations, and through support for cooperative development efforts undertaken by **United Nations** agencies.

SWITZERLAND. Cooperation in Switzerland started, as in other countries, with propagandists promoting the idea. The book *Leonard and Gertrude*, published in serialized fashion by the noted educator **Johann Heinrich Pestalozzi** in 1781–87, provided an ideological backdrop to Swiss cooperative thinking and efforts. Their ideas materialized first as cheesemakers' societies in Bern and Fribourg in 1816. A bakers' cooperative in Geneva (1837), a **consumer cooperative** (1850), the first **agricultural cooperative** established at Schwanden (1860), and the establishment of the Swiss Popular Bank in Bern (1869) were further steps leading to an acceleration of cooperative activity. By the end of the 19th century, initial **cooperative legislation** had been enacted, **federations** of agricultural cooperatives had been established in several regions of the country, the Swiss Union of Consumer Cooperatives had been organized and the Swiss credit cooperative movement, modeled on the **Raiffeisen** experience in **Germany**, initiated.

These activities were expanded and elaborated in the first half of the 20th century, augmented by new cooperative activity in the fields of housing, insurance, pharmacy and production (both by artisans and within the consumer movement). By 1922, there were 11,408 cooperatives. In 1921 a Guilde des coopératrices (Women's Cooperative Guild) was formed to represent women's interest in and support for the cooperative movement. In 1925, **Migros**, because of its conversion from a private business into a cooperative, became a controversial part of Swiss cooperative history, emerging in subsequent years as a second major consumer cooperative structure rivaling Coop Schweiz. In 1927 the Central Cooperative Bank was launched. Growth in the number of cooperatives, though not in membership, had leveled off by 1941 when 11,570 cooperatives were reported by Swiss cooperators. Since that date, consolidation has been a hallmark of the movement with a reduction in the number of farmer organizations and a consolidation of consumer cooperatives in which small shops have been merged into larger and more complex retail outlets. A 1998 **ICA** report to the European Commission noted that in 1996 there were 1,651 cooperatives with a membership of 3,657,155 in the following sectors: agriculture—656 societies/with 120,176 members; banking—964/654,979; consumer—29/2,882,000; and insurance—2/na. Cooperative membership in 1996 was 50.1% of national population.

SYRIA. Although Syria is an agricultural society, and its first cooperative was established in 1943, it was not until after World War II and the achievement of independence from France in 1946 that cooperative development became a serious concern. The first **cooperative law** was enacted in 1950, with periodic modifications in subsequent years, and a cooperative department was established to provide governmental leadership. An Agrarian Reform Law (1958) forecast the establishment of the network of **agricultural cooperatives** which has since taken place. In 1961 a union of **housing cooperatives** came into being to provide leadership to that sector of cooperative development. **Consumer cooperatives** became the focus for the provision of goods and services to the general populace. **Production cooperatives** on a modest scale reflected the government's interest in worker-owned and -controlled enterprises as an expression of its socialist ideology. By 1994, the **Arab**

Cooperative Union reported, the four sectors of Syrian cooperation had developed as follows: agriculture—4,468 societies/with 563,467 members; consumer—117/483,825; housing—1,200/300,000; and worker productive—311/94,191. A total of 6,096 societies were noted with a membership of 1,441,483 (10.5% of the total population). The **ILO** *Directory* **(1988)** listed only cooperative structures related to various governmental departments. This is usually an indication that an independent cooperative infrastructure had yet to materialize.

T

TAIWAN. Two strains of cooperative development experience are reflected in Taiwanese history. The first reflects the period of Japanese control of the island from 1895 to the end of World War II; the second, that of the Nationalist Chinese who moved to the island when a communist government was established on the mainland in 1949. During the Japanese period, modest development of cooperatives took place, with the first society started in 1912. A **cooperative law** was enacted in 1913, another in 1934. There was a measure of development of **agricultural cooperatives**, enough to warrant the establishment of the Taiwan Provincial Farmers' Association in 1937. During the war years no significant development occurred. With the establishment in Taiwan of the Republic of China, a cooperative system based on a mainland experience dating from the 1920s was introduced (*see* CHINA). In 1949 the Cooperative League of the Republic of China was reestablished, followed by **consumer cooperatives** designed to assist government officials, teachers and students. Collective farming, primarily involving war veterans and their families, was introduced to accelerate agricultural development. Cooperative training was formalized in 1953 with the opening of a Cooperative Correspondence School and a Department of Cooperatives at the Chung-hsing University. A new cooperative law followed in 1957 and gave additional impetus, principally to agricultural and consumer cooperative development. The Credit Union League of China was established in 1968, representing the development of that fledgling sector as a supplement to an already existing **credit cooperative** network based on a **Schulze-Delitzsch** model. A report in the 1970 edition of the ILO's *Cooperative Information* indicated that there were then 2,701 cooperatives of many types (including 59 **federations**) with a combined membership of 1,493,521. By 1984, the **ILO** *Directory* **(1988)** reported, there had been an increase to 4,375 cooperatives with a membership of 2,710,198 (13.9% of the population) in the following sectors: agriculture—407 societies/with 297,010 members; consumer—3,355/1,662,569; savings and credit—335/711,105; worker productive—51/7,216; and others—227/32,298.

TAJIKISTAN. During the period that Tajikistan was part of the **Union of Soviet Socialist Republics**, the cooperatives of the area were part of the **Centrosoyus consumer cooperative** system. Since independence was declared, the cooperatives have not yet been able to reestablish themselves as an independent economic factor. This has been largely due to political insurrections that have so far negated any group's claims of political legitimacy. This struggle must be resolved before there can be a redefined role for cooperatives.

TAKKI, JUNO KRISTIAN (died 1968). A cooperative, educational and political leader in **Finland**, he began his work with cooperatives at an early age, working at the Cooperative Union from 1918 to 1922 before becoming a teacher and later head of the KK Cooperative School. He served as administrative director of OTK from 1942 to 1952 and as managing director from 1952 to 1966. Takki was a member of the Finnish Parliament from 1945 to 1952 and again from 1966 to 1968, when he was appointed minister of trade and supply. He was a member of the **ICA** Central Committee from 1952 to 1966.

TANNER, VÄINÖ ALFRED (1881–1966). A Finnish cooperative leader and founder of SOK, a **consumer cooperative** organization in **Finland**, he served in a number of prominent political positions, including president and prime minister of Finland. Tanner became a member of the **ICA** Central Committee in 1910 and was elected to serve as its president from 1927 to 1945. Because of political problems associated with his and Finland's participation in World War II, he was effectively precluded from functioning as ICA president for the period 1940–45. In 1946 he was convicted as a "war criminal" for his role in Finland's wartime government and was imprisoned until 1949 when he returned to a leadership role in the Elanto Cooperative in Helsinki, where he had earlier served for 31 years as managing director. Tanner was a staunch advocate of the view that cooperatives should keep themselves free of governmental interference.

TANZANIA. The establishment of the Kilimanjaro Native Planters' Association in 1925 marked the beginning of modern cooperation in what was then Tanganyika. It was followed by the enactment of a cooperative societies ordinance in 1932, which set the stage for the establishment of coffee and tobacco **production cooperatives** and related **unions** and the beginnings of **regional cooperative federations,** which expanded in number up to the time of independence in 1961. The Cooperative Union of Tanzania came into being in 1961, and a **Cooperative College** was established at Moshi in 1963, an institution that has effectively trained several generations of cooperative leaders and officials in the movement and the government.

The government of Tanzania under Julius Nyerere opted for a socialist path to the country's development, to be based on a structured network of *ujaama* **villages,** which were to be organized and function as cooperatives. This was seen as a way of building a national grassroots cooperative spirit from the bottom up (though directed from the top), which was also to be the basic production structure for the economy. Above the village level, the supply and marketing functions of existing cooperative federations (which were abolished) were assumed by state supply and trading organizations. The country was effectively organized into villages by the latter part of the 1970s, achieving to a significant degree the drawing together of a widely dispersed population. The expectations for cooperative villages, however, were never widely realized, and the limited achievement of that part of the vision was acknowledged in the early 1980s. Legislation was passed at that time authorizing establishment of **primary cooperatives** separate from the village governments, reinstituting cooperative unions and authorizing a new national cooperative organization to be built on the new network of cooperatives.

Nyerere retired as president in 1985, and with his departure came the acknowledgment that the organizational arrangements that had been part of the *ujaama* vision had proven unrealistic. Since then, the movement has been reconstituting itself. The **ICA Regional Office for East, Central and Southern Africa** reported in 1994 that there were 8,909 cooperatives in Tanzania with 1,351,018 members (5.0% of the population). An **ILO** report in 1995 covering several countries in East and Southern Africa lists Tanzania as having 4,316 cooperatives with 526,475 members. These divergent statistics suggest that there are probably large numbers of inactive cooperatives reflected in official figures.

TAXATION OF COOPERATIVES. Traditionally, cooperatives have requested or been given an exemption from taxation on the assumption that they do not make a **profit,** returning any **surplus** generated in their operation to their members. It is generally regarded as legitimate to tax the income of any profit-making subsidiaries of a cooperative that have been set up as part of expanded operations and go beyond its basic purpose as established in the **bylaws**.

TELEPHONE COOPERATIVE. A cooperative association established to provide telephone service to its members. Such associations are usually fairly small in membership and are found mostly in rural areas.

TERTIARY SOCIETY. A **federation** of district or regional societies which are themselves secondary-level societies. A tertiary society may be the **apex organization** in the national structure of a particular type of cooperative. It may also refer to the apex cooperative that represents all cooperative interests in a country.

THAILAND. With the passage in 1916 of amendments to the Associations Law acknowledging cooperatives, the appointment the same year of Prince Bidyalongkorn as the first **registrar of cooperatives** and the establishment of the first **Raiffeisen**-style **agricultural credit cooperative** in 1917, the **cooperative movement** in Thailand was effectively launched. Limited to credit cooperatives in its early years (there were 150 by 1931), it was not until 1932 that the movement began to diversify and its growth to accelerate. By 1940 there were 1,874 societies, 87 of which were noncredit. By 1944 there were 4,747, including 189 noncredit societies active in several sectors: 69 consumer societies, 44 colonization cooperatives, 14 land purchase and improvement societies and 52 marketing groups. These have generally remained the sectoral activities of cooperatives in Thailand, supplemented by a small number of **fishery cooperatives** and a network of **service cooperatives**. The Cooperative League of Thailand was established in 1948 (reconstituted in 1968) and serves as the national **apex cooperative organization**. In 1972 the Cooperative Promotion Department was established as a way of unifying governmental services dealing with cooperatives. The **ICA Regional Office for Asia and the Pacific** reported that in 1993 there were 3,744 cooperatives with a combined membership of 5,843,961 (9.8% of the population) in the following sectors: agriculture—2,071 societies/with 3,397,098 members; consumer—351/687,078; fisheries—46/8,030; savings and credit—966/1,648,561; and services—310/103,194.

THOMAS, ALBERT (1878–1932). A French cooperative leader, active in the **ICA** from 1910 until his death, he was the first director of the **ILO**.

One of his earliest actions in this position was to establish the **Cooperative Service** in the ILO structure, to ensure cooperative development integral to the concerns of the organization. He held that the cooperative movement was a means of substituting group action for the scattered activities of individual producers and consumers confronting the organized economic forces of society. Recognizing the importance of an integrated cooperative movement, he served, while ILO director, as chairman of a joint committee of agricultural producers and **consumer cooperative** organizations, which explored areas of common economic and social interest.

THOMPSON, WILLIAM (1755–1833). An early cooperative theorist and activist, he was described by a biographer as Britain's pioneer socialist, feminist and cooperator.

THORDARSON, BRUCE (1944–). A Canadian, he has been director (now director general) of the **ICA** since its 29th Congress in Stockholm in July 1988. He joined the ICA in November 1985 as associate director and director of development.

Before joining the ICA, Thordarson was executive director of the **Cooperative Union of Canada** (now the **Canadian Cooperative Association**.) Earlier, he served as director of government affairs of the **Canadian Cooperative Credit Society**.

A native of Saskatoon, Canada, Thordarson holds a bachelor of arts degree in history and political science and a master of arts degree in international affairs.

THRANE, MARCUS. The founder of the first **consumer cooperative** established in **Norway** in 1851. He was the leader of a semirevolutionary social movement advocating the formation of workers' cooperative organizations.

TOAD LANE. A side street in **Rochdale** on which the first cooperative store was established by the **Rochdale pioneers** on December 21, 1844. The store had very modest beginnings with a starting inventory of 6 sacks of flour, 20 pounds of butter, 50 pounds of sugar, 1 sack of oatmeal and 24 candles. The building is now a cooperative museum.

TOGO. Cooperative legislation passed in 1931 and the establishment that year of the first agricultural **production** (cacao) **cooperative** at Sokodé mark the beginnings of a slowly growing cooperative development in Togo. The 1950s were a period of diversification, with initial efforts to establish **consumer**, **credit** and **fishery cooperatives**, but the principal development remained in agriculture until recent years, when there has been a significant development of **credit unions**. The **ILO** *Directory* **(1988)** provided the latest comprehensive statistics on the movement in Togo. It reported that in 1984–85 there were 910 cooperatives with a membership of 58,410 (1.9% of the population) in the following sectors: agriculture—753 societies (some **precooperatives**)/with 39,810 members; consumer 10/1,500; credit unions 103/11,160; fisheries 14/190; transport—1/60; worker productive—3/100; and others—26/5,590. **WOCCU** indicated in its 1997 *Statistical Report* that the Togo credit union movement then had 86,402 members in 186 societies, 1.9% of the population.

TOLSTOY, COUNT LEO NIKOLEYEVICH (1828–1910). A Russian novelist, late in life he embraced an ascetic Christian anarchism. Shortly before his death he published a "Letter about Cooperation," in which he described how cooperative organizations fitted into his vision of a future society.

TOMLINSON, ANNIE BAMFORD (died 1933). A leader in the British Cooperative Women's Guild, she was for many years the editor of the Women's Pages of the *Coop News,* published by the **Cooperative Union of the U.K.** She frequently attended **ICA** congresses and helped organize branches of the **International Cooperative Women's Guild** in other countries.

TOMPKINS, FATHER JAMES J. (JIMMY) (1870–1953). A Canadian clergyman, academic and cooperative leader, he was a pioneer in developing cooperatives in Nova Scotia, **Canada**. With his cousin, **M. M. Coady,** and **A. B. MacDonald,** he was instrumental in establishing the **Antigonish Movement**, a community development organization utilizing cooperatives, designed to help low-income farmers, fishermen and others achieve a measure of economic security and independence. He was a leader of a group that developed housing in Tompkinsville, a new city, established in 1939, built by the Reserve Mines, Nova Scotia, City Housing Cooperative and named in honor of Father Tompkins.

TONGA. The first cooperative in Tonga was organized in 1964, but it was not until the passage of the Cooperative Societies Act of 1973 that a cooperative sector of the nation's economy could be identified. A national **federation**, the Tonga Cooperative Federation, came into existence in 1977, and growth in the number of cooperatives has been steady. Seventy-five cooperatives, mainly multipurpose consumer societies, existed in 1983, plus 55 credit unions. (No data was available as to membership.) An **ICA Regional Office for Asia and the Pacific** Mission Report in 1995 mentioned 122 cooperatives with 6,679 members (4.9% of the population).

TOPSHEE, REV. GEORGE (1916–1984). A native of Nova Scotia, he was educated at St. Francis Xavier University, to which he returned after his ordination to become director of the University Extension Department in 1969 and later director of the **Coady International Institute**. He helped organize an Extension Department in **Lesotho**. He was honored by the establishment of the Topshee Memorial Fund, which provides for an annual conference on contemporary socio-economic issues.

TORTOLA. Tortola is the principal island of the British Virgin Island group. The **ILO** *Directory* (**1988**) listed 2 cooperatives in Tortola with 86 members in 1986, 1 credit union with 74 members, and 1 fishery society with 12. In its 1997 membership report, **WOCCU** reported that the one credit union had increased its membership to 220. **Cooperative penetration** that year was estimated to be 1.2% of Tortola's population.

TOTOMIANTS, VAKHAN (1875–1964). A professor at the University of Tiflis, Georgia, an early cooperative advocate and general secretary in 1908 of the Russian National Committee for the Propagation of Cooperation, Totomiants came to the cooperative movement while a student in Switzerland where he became involved in leadership of **consumer cooperatives**. His early studies were augmented later by studies of cooperation in Brussels, Berlin and Paris. Totomiants was involved in the early organization of Russian cooperatives including the Moscow Narodny (People's) Bank. His cooperative career was dealt a serious blow in 1917 when he suddenly lost his eyesight. He sought treatment in Western Europe, where he spent most of the rest of his life teaching and writing about cooperatives.

TRANSPORT COOPERATIVE. An association of people who have joined together to cooperatively provide transport services, among which are those designed to facilitate the movement of goods between producers and consumers and those, such as taxis and buses, that provide transport for individuals.

TRINIDAD AND TOBAGO. Cooperative development in Trinidad and Tobago dates from 1916, when an **agricultural credit** ordinance was enacted and the first cooperatives of this type began to operate. Growth of these and other cooperatives was slow, but by 1941 the movement had become extensive enough to warrant the establishment of the Federation of Agricultural, Fishing and Other Cooperatives, followed in 1947 by a national **credit union** federation. In 1972 the emerging **consumer cooperatives** federated nationally. The Cipriani Labor College, established in 1973, provides a regular curriculum of cooperative training in addition to its training for the trade union movement. The **ILO** *Directory* **(1988)** reported that in 1985 there were 694 cooperatives with a membership of 212,321 (17.7% of the population). A total of 231 credit unions made up 53% of the cooperatives and 89% of the membership. The remainder were in **agricultural**, consumer, fisheries and other societies. There was also a network of 256 youth cooperatives with a membership of 15,638. In 1996, **WOCCU** indicated that the credit unions in Trinidad and Tobago had consolidated into 101 societies with a membership of 336,102. While detailed statistics were not available for all sectors, overall **cooperative penetration** for 1996 was an estimated 29.7%.

TUNISIA. With the first **agricultural cooperative** established in 1905 and a **cooperative law** enacted two years later, the movement in Tunisia started only slowly growing. A central agricultural **wholesale cooperative** was functioning in 1912, followed soon thereafter by an agricultural mechanization cooperative, cooperative grain elevators and, in 1932, a **federation** of cooperative wine cellars. During the late 1930s and the 1940s the movement diversified with cooperatives for consumers, fisheries and handicrafts. A solid base had been established by the time of independence in 1959, but changing governments and governmental policies, including a period of collectivization in the 1960s, have taken their toll on the societies and on the supporting network of federations that had emerged to support them. The **ILO** *Directory* **(1988)**, reporting for the year 1985, indicated that there were 352 cooperatives with 81,195 members (1.1% of the population) and that, except for a national federation of cooperatives, there was only one remaining higher-level federation (of wine producers). No more recent statistical data could be identified.

TURKEY. A stirring of cooperative activity, mainly related to **agricultural credit,** can be traced to the period 1863–99, but it lacked staying power, even when reinforced by the passage of the first **cooperative law** in 1867 and the establishment of the Agricultural Bank in 1888. Another effort, early in the 20th century, revolved around fig producers and resulted in a fig producers' union in 1914. Some regard this as the real beginning of the cooperative movement.

The first concerted cooperative development effort came with the establishment of the Turkish Republic under **Kemal Ataturk** in 1923. Ataturk saw cooperatives as one of the ways of modernizing Turkish society so as to broadly distribute the economic benefits and encourage democratic participation. A number of cooperative laws were passed embodying these ideas but, detrimentally, they built in an ongoing role for government as guide to the movement. Cooperative unions based on agricultural commodities and/or regions proliferated, reflecting the growing number of cooperative societies. By the time of Ataturk's death in 1938 the movement was well established. In 1944 the first National Cooperative Congress was held, providing the movement with a chance to more independently articulate and plan for its continued development. An article in the ILO's *Cooperative Information* reported that in 1944 Turkey had the following cooperative profile: agricultural credit and marketing—605 societies; consumer—65; handicraft—125; housing—46; and others—2. Membership data was not included.

World War II and the postwar period saw Turkey move to orient itself more toward Europe. One of the results of this has been a mutual sharing of Western Europe's cooperative experience with that of the indigenous Turkish movement as it grew and elaborated its activities. A 1996 **ICA** report to the European Commission indicated that there were then 50,150 cooperatives with a combined membership of 8,081,100 in the following sectors: agriculture—6,627 societies/with 3,001,556 members; consumer—2,077/457,045; credit unions—3,319/2,570,831; fisheries—313/15,783; housing—33,376—1,655,853; independent retailers—124/8,968; insurance—1,215; social care—3/983; transport—2,184/104,070; worker productives—1,887/248,575; and others—239/16,221. Cooperative membership included 12.9% of the population.

TURKMENISTAN. A historical review of cooperative development in Turkmenistan, apart from that of its place in **Centrosoyus** in the former **Union of Soviet Socialist Republics,** was not available. An **ICA Regional Office for Asia and the Pacific** report on cooperative membership in **ICA** member countries indicated that there were 250 **consumer cooperatives** in Turkmenistan in 1992 with 885,000 members (23.7% of the population). The ICA membership report for 1996 reported a membership that year of 738,000 (17.8% of the population).

TUVALU. A cooperative societies ordinance, based on the British model, was adopted in 1951, the first cooperative formed in 1956, and a cooperative **federation** established in 1966 while the present Tuvalu was part of the Gilbert and Ellice Islands. The two sets of islands, with two quite culturally different racial populations, were administered together by the British as a bureaucratic convenience. With the separation of the two in 1975 (the Gilbert Islands became **Kiribati**), Tuvalu set its own cooperative course, centered mainly around the Tuvalu Cooperative Society, which functions on all eight islands of the country. In 1986 it had 3,456 members, 40.1% of the nation's population of 8,500. A copra marketing society, with 640 members, handled that product from all the islands. A solar electric cooperative was established in 1984 and had an early membership of 158. Two additional cooperatives are located on the island of Vaitupu.

TWEEDALE, ANN (1800–1850). The only woman reported as among the original 28 members of the **Rochdale Society of Equitable Pioneers**.

U

UGANDA. The first recorded cooperative (for agricultural marketing) was established in 1913, a prelude to a sporadic effort to form indigenous African organizations to better serve producer needs. It was followed by the establishment of a planters' association in 1920 and the formation of the Uganda Growers' Cooperative Union in 1935. A study by **William Campbell** in 1944 documented the potential for cooperative development, and legislation to assist in that regard was passed in 1946. In 1948 the first **consumer** and **dairy cooperatives** were formed. A Cooperative Development Council was established in 1953, a forerunner of the Uganda Cooperative Alliance formed in 1961. A **cooperative bank** came on the scene in 1964, followed by the Consumer Cooperative Wholesale Society in 1965 and national **federations** for handicrafts and **credit unions** in 1971. Twenty-five years of development, however, were placed in serious jeopardy by the 1971 coup, the subsequent genocidal regime of Idi Amin Dada and a war with Tanzania. Various military coups and rampaging inflation marked most of the 1980s, and the cooperative movement has been trying to reestablish the foundations of its earlier years. The **ICA** reported in 1998 that in 1995 there were 3,131 cooperatives in Uganda with a membership of 637,015 in the following sectors: agriculture—2,663 societies/with 574,701 members; consumer—37/2,467; credit unions—284/48,667; fisheries—30/2,402; housing—5/163; transport—47/4,088; worker productives—37/2,122; and others—28/2,405. Cooperative membership that year was 3.2% of the population.

UJAAMA **VILLAGES.** A system of cooperative villages intended to be the basis for the socialist economic development of **Tanzania**. Each village, to be established by drawing together the dispersed population into groups, was to function as a cooperative organization. The system was successful as a way of drawing together the population, but the proposed cooperative mode of organizing the villages proved unsuccessful. In 1981, without rejecting the *ujaama* ideology, legislation was passed reestablishing a more typical form of cooperative organization for Tanzania, with **primary cooperatives** in villages, regional **federations**, and a national confederation.

UKRAINE. The **ILO** *Directory* **(1988)** stated that in 1987, while still part of the **Union of Soviet Socialist Republics**, the Ukraine reported a central **consumer cooperative** organization, consisting of 1,273 cooperatives organized into 254 district and 25 regional unions with a membership of 13,086,900 (25.3% of the population), affiliated with **Centrosoyus**. Since the dissolution of the USSR and the attempts to **de-officialize** the cooperative movements in its former republics and other countries, these groups have taken steps to reorganize and to adapt themselves to a different social reality. The adjustment has taken its toll almost everywhere. In the Ukraine this has meant a change from a single sectoral organization to a multipurpose national cooperative **federation**. A statistical report by the **ICA** to the European Union in 1998, covering 1996, showed a cooperative movement of 4,717 societies with 6,189,815+ members (membership figures for all sectors were not always available) in the following sectors: agriculture—74 societies/with (na) members; consumer—1,956/6,172,135; credit unions—52/17,680; housing—1,072/na; transport—150/na; and others—619/na. Cooperative membership that year was equivalent to at least 12.2% of the national population.

The Ukrainian cooperative movement has a rich and varied past, most of which developed in the mid-1800s while the Ukraine was part of Russia and Poland. Greater independence and varied sectoral activity developed in the western (largely Polish) portion of the Ukraine. In the east, the Russian government was suspicious of cooperatives as a potential political opposition and was reluctant to encourage them. Independent cooperative forces in the Ukraine were essentially eliminated under the post–World War I Soviet government, which opted for a single consumer cooperative structure. After World War II the Ukraine cooperators were fully integrated into the Centrosoyus structures. Since the collapse of the Soviet Union, new manifestations of old cooperative traditions are reasserting themselves, but with yet unclear results.

UNDP. *See* UNITED NATIONS DEVELOPMENT PROGRAM.

UNESCO. *See* UNITED NATIONS EDUCATIONAL, SCIENTIFIC AND CULTURAL ORGANIZATION.

UNION. In cooperative terms, a union is an organization at a regional or national level of a group of cooperatives, not individuals. Unions normally do business on behalf of their member cooperatives and often provide educational, promotional and advisory services. A major exception to this definition is found in the term **credit union**, which refers to a type of savings and credit society at the primary level.

UNION OF SOVIET SOCIALIST REPUBLICS. *See* RUSSIA.

UNITED ARAB EMIRATES (UAE). Established as a nation in 1971 through the federation of seven small emirates on the Persian Gulf between Oman and Qatar, UAE cooperative activity has been almost exclusively in **consumer cooperatives**, the first of which was established in Dubai in 1972. **Cooperative legislation** was passed in 1976 to facilitate their development. By 1984 there were 12 cooperatives with a membership of 4,346. The **Arab Cooperative Union** reported that in 1994 there were 53 consumer societies with 8,603 members (0.57% of the population).

UNITED KINGDOM. Organized cooperation in the United Kingdom dates from the early 1750s and is associated with the establishment in London of a **mutual** fire **insurance** society. This was followed in the 1760s by the organization of weavers into cooperatives and the establishment of collective mills in England and Scotland. The 1770s saw the emergence of joint building societies, cooperative-like organizations that attempted to deal with the appalling housing conditions brought on by rapid rural to urban migration. This decade also saw the formation of the first tailors' cooperative, precursor of the worker productive movement. By the end of the century, **Robert Owen** had emerged as an important figure in the fledgling cooperative movement, establishing **New Lanark on the Clyde** in 1799 as a model of industrial cooperation.

In the early 1800s there were various experiments with shops organized along cooperative lines, culminating in the 1820s with the organization of the first formal **consumer cooperative** in Brighton by Dr. **William King**, also known for his establishment of *The Cooperator*, the first cooperative newspaper. By 1830, the **ILO** *Cooperative Chronology* indicates, there were 300 cooperative societies and 12 cooperative newspapers officially registered. In the following year the first U.K. Cooperative Congress was held in Manchester. The establishment of the **Rochdale Society of Equitable Pioneers** in 1844, therefore, while widely regarded as inaugurating the modern cooperative movement, was preceded in the U.K. and elsewhere by almost 100 years of cooperative thinking and experimentation, of which the Rochdale society was a product.

The period from Rochdale to World War I was a time of dramatic development and growth. Action was taken by the government, establishing the position of registrar of cooperatives in 1846, followed by the **Industrial and Provident Societies Act of 1852** (the first **cooperative legislation** in the world), which was amended in 1862 to allow for the formation of cooperative **unions**. The first cooperative in Wales, for miners, was formed in 1859. New sectoral cooperatives made their appearance, including **worker productive** (1850), consumer **wholesale societies** (1862, 1863), **insurance** (1867), **agricultural** (1867), banking (1868, 1872, 1876), building societies (1884), and **housing cooperatives** (1900). **Cooperative federations/**unions and other support groups were formed, among them the Cooperative Union at Manchester (1869), a production federation (1882), and agricultural (1901) and fishery (1914) federations. Cooperative Women's Guilds for England and Wales (1884) and Scotland (1892) and an Advisory Education Committee (forerunner of the **Cooperative College, Loughborough**) were established. The annual **congresses** of the U.K. cooperative movement took on an increasingly international cast when, as a solidarity gesture, foreign cooperators were invited to attend as observers. The London Congress of 1869 initiated this process, and by 1886 **Edouard de Boyve**, a

French cooperator, would urge the internationalization process by his proposal for the formation of an international cooperative federation, an important step leading to the establishment of the **ICA** in 1895.

The years between the two world wars were a time of building and institutionalization of the many steps that had been initiated in earlier years. In 1919 the Cooperative College at Loughborough was established, as was the **Cooperative Party**, designed to more aggressively pursue cooperative political and economic interests. The production activities of the consumer movement expanded, the English and Scottish cooperative wholesale organizations merged, and attention was given to making cooperative facilities more easily and readily available to the public. Agricultural cooperatives expanded their work, with the establishment of the Welsh Agricultural Cooperative Association and a Cooperative Committee within the National Farmers Union. The Horace Plunkett Foundation, established in London in 1919 (later the **Plunkett Foundation for Cooperative Studies**), became a principal instrument for agricultural cooperative information and activity, beginning publication in 1926 of its *Year Book of Agricultural Cooperatives*. In 1920 the Overseas Farmer' Cooperative Association was established to facilitate relations and trade with cooperatives in **Australia, New Zealand** and **South Africa**. Deepening the involvement of younger cooperators was also an important theme. The first International Cooperative Summer School was held in 1921, the National Guild of Cooperators was established in 1926, as was the Woodcraft Folk, which focused on cooperative activities for children. In 1941 the National Federation of Young Cooperators was formed.

In the immediate post–World War II period, cooperatives were mainly concerned with reconstruction and with reestablishing their networks in the peacetime economy of the country. Consumer shops were rebuilt, production enterprises restored, housing construction undertaken, and agriculture restructured and reorganized to reflect the continued rural to urban migration and the increased sophistication of agricultural production. Consumer cooperatives were confronted with increasingly sophisticated competition, which necessitated a rethinking of established ways of operating. Small local shops were supplemented and often replaced by more modern supermarkets and these in turn by regional hypermarkets that were akin to department stores in the scope of their operations. Cooperative housing, mainly in London and the northwest of **England**, continued to expand, becoming the second largest cooperative sector in terms of membership. With assistance from the U.S. **credit union move-**

ment and **WOCCU**, a credit union structure was established; by 1994 it had grown to 340 **credit unions** with 135,000 members. **Production co-operatives** remained a small active sector of the movement.

Cooperatives in the U.K. turned a portion of their attention to assisting nascent movements in **developing countries,** led by the **Plunkett Foundation** and the **Cooperative Liaison, Education and Research Unit** of the Cooperative College. The government's **Overseas Development Administration** employed cooperative specialists to assist in the design of cooperative projects and in their implementation. The Cooperative Bank and the Cooperative Insurance Society of the U.K. provided leadership in their sectors of the international movement and in assistance programs in developing countries. The different national sectoral organizations joined in the growing European movement reflected by the network of European Community cooperative organizations. At the Centennial meeting of the ICA in 1995 the world movement selected a U.K. cooperator, **Graham Melmoth,** as its new president.

In the mid-1980s, the U.K. cooperatives reported a total of 3,638 societies with a membership of 9,322,446 (16.5% of the population) in the following sectors: agriculture, consumers, fisheries, housing, savings and credit, and worker productive. A report of the chief registrar for 1995 to 1996 showed a total of 10,656 cooperatives with more than 9,652,000 members (membership figures were incomplete) in the following sectors: agriculture—980 societies/with 262,000 members; banking—1/na; consumer—266/5,917,000; credit unions—531/182,000; fisheries—80/4,000; housing—4,041/173,000; insurance 1/na; services—1,088/544,000; worker productive—1,088/1,544,000; and others—3,667/2,590,000. Cooperative membership in 1996 was equivalent to 16.6% of the population.

UNITED NATIONS (UN). The UN was established in 1945 to "maintain international peace and security; to develop friendly relations among nations; to cooperate internationally in solving international economic, social, cultural and humanitarian problems and in promoting respect for human rights and fundamental freedoms; and to be a center for harmonizing the actions of nations in attaining these common ends."

The **ICA** was among the non-governmental organizations represented by observers at the San Francisco Conference during which the UN charter was adopted. Early on, the ICA was accorded official observer status in UN deliberations, a role later accorded also to **WOCCU.** From its inception the UN has been supportive of the cooperative movement, structuring program activity through the Department of International

Economic and Social Affairs and its Center for Social Development and Humanitarian Affairs. The UN secretary general has been called upon by UN member states to submit periodic reports on the status of cooperatives worldwide. The UN is one of the seven member organizations making up **COPAC**, the function of which is the promotion of and assistance to cooperatives in **developing countries**.

UNITED NATIONS CENTER FOR HUMAN SETTLEMENTS— HABITAT. The specialized agency within the **United Nations** system that focuses on housing conditions and needs. Its housing interests have included cooperative housing, where the private collective approach of cooperatives to the problem of the unavailability or inadequacy of housing is viewed as an alternative to other types of public ownership.

UNITED NATIONS DEVELOPMENT FUND FOR WOMEN (UNIFEM). A special program of the **United Nations** that grew out of activities initiated by the United Nations Decade For Women. Becoming operational in 1978, it was designed to support innovative and experimental programs that benefit both rural and urban women, particularly in **developing countries**. While cooperatives were not singled out for special emphasis, they soon became a focus for support as an institutional structure around which economic development for women could logically be organized. UNIFEM provided a grant to **COPAC** in 1983 to survey the extent of, and difficulties encountered in organizing, cooperatives for women. This resulted in the COPAC/UNIFEM publication *Women in Cooperatives,* prepared by Susan Dean.

UNITED NATIONS DEVELOPMENT PROGRAM (UNDP). The specialized organ within the **United Nations** system that concerns itself with the economic and social development of **developing countries**. It has supported, through grants and loans, the development of cooperative organizations in these countries. At times such programs are directly implemented by UNDP, but in most cases they have been implemented by the **FAO**, the **ILO** and, on a lesser scale, **UNIDO,** with UNDP financing.

UNITED NATIONS EDUCATIONAL, SCIENTIFIC AND CULTURAL ORGANIZATION (UNESCO). A specialized agency of the **United Nations** whose program interests have included consideration of the role of cooperatives as educational institutions in providing literacy training and basic education for their membership. UNESCO has at times provided grants for cooperative leaders participating in training programs.

UNITED NATIONS INDUSTRIAL DEVELOPMENT ORGANIZA-TION (UNIDO). The specialized agency within the **United Nations** system that has concerned itself with encouraging industrialization as a critical step in the economic advancement of **developing countries**, as it had earlier been in the emergence of the now industrialized countries. UNIDO has developed and financed projects involving the formation of **production cooperatives** and has explored, in conjunction with the **ICA**, the role of cooperatives in industrial development.

UNITED STATES. The beginning of the cooperative movement in the United States of America is generally associated with the establishment of the **Philadelphia Contributionship for the Insurance of Homes from Loss of Fire,** formed by **Benjamin Franklin** and his colleagues in the early 1750s. It grew out of an earlier move to organize their community against fire hazards. Philadelphia was also the site for the first organization of an **agricultural cooperative** society in 1785, the Philadelphia Society for Promoting Agriculture. Other developments of cooperative organizations were sporadic and isolated, but by the time of the founding of the **Rochdale Society** in England in 1844, the following had been organized: the first agricultural **production cooperative** (a cooperative cheese factory, established in South Trenton, New Jersey, in 1810); the first **consumer cooperative**, established by **William Bryn** in New York City in 1830; and the cooperative communities organized at **New Harmony**, Indiana, by **Robert Owen** in 1825 and at **Brook Farm**, near Boston, in 1841. Both of these communities were short-lived **utopian** experiments. The cooperative movement in the United States by the end of its first hundred years had seen much experimentation but was still a movement of only modest proportions.

As if to give credence to the designation of the Rochdale Society's founding as the start of the modern cooperative movement, cooperative activities accelerated in the U.S. at the same time. Hardly a year went by between 1845 and the end of World War I (1918) without some event important enough to register itself in the various chronologies of this period of cooperative history. Successful agricultural cooperatives for supply, processing and marketing sprang up in various parts of the country—in Massachusetts, Connecticut, New York and New Jersey in the northeast; in Maryland, Pennsylvania and West Virginia in the mid-Atlantic region; in Ohio, Illinois, Iowa, Wisconsin and Minnesota in the midwest; in Texas, Arkansas, Louisiana and Kentucky in the south; and in California on the then-faraway west coast. **Federations** of cooperatives for producers of commodities including citrus and other fruits, cranberries, grain, milk products and tobacco emerged on a regional basis and later as national groups. General promotion of agricultural cooperatives and their interests was undertaken on a nationwide basis by the **National Grange of the Patrons of Husbandry** (founded in 1867), the Farmers Alliance (1874), the National **Farmers Union** (1902), and the American **Farm Bureau Federation** (1919), each with its network of state and local organizations.

The planned organization of consumer cooperatives, beyond the continued formation of individual societies by local groups, came to the fore in this period in such diverse places as Boston (1845), in Utah among the Mormons (1868), in the New England Cooperative Association (1880), in a Retailers' Cooperative of a hundred grocers in Philadelphia (1888), among the Patrons of Industry (1889) in the midwest, the Nelson Cooperative Stores (1892) in New Orleans and Saint Louis, the Rochdale Wholesale Society in San Francisco (1900), the Kansas State Cooperative Association (1901), and on the Pacific coast (1913). Also noteworthy was the promotion of consumer cooperatives by trade union organizations, e.g., the Sovereigns of Industry, Knights of Labor, and United Mine Workers, which saw them as fellow workers for a better world and as a way of assisting trade union members to improve their lot. The first **student cooperative** stores were organized at the University of Tennessee and at Harvard College. A national voice for consumer cooperatives struggled into existence, first as the Cooperative Union of America (1895) (the first U.S. member of the **ICA**), then as the Cooperative League (1909) and finally as the **Cooperative League of the U.S.A** (1916). It has now become the **National Cooperative Business Association** and is more broadly representative of all cooperative sectors.

Other notable cooperative activity included producer and **service cooperatives**: first among tailors in Boston (1849), then cheese producers in New York (1856), a shipyard in Baltimore (1865), the Philadelphia Industrial Cooperative Association (1874), and **telephone cooperatives**, the first of which was established in 1893. The first **irrigation cooperative** was organized in Tulare, California. Cooperative banking became important in Philadelphia, included the first **cooperative bank** for African Americans. The first **housing cooperative**, the Finnish Home Building Association, was established in 1918, and the first **funeral cooperative** was established by miners in Illinois in 1915. The first **credit unions** were established in New England in 1909, encouraged by Boston entrepreneur **Edward Filene** in collaboration with Canadian cooperator **Alphonse Desjardins**. **Cooperative legislation** was adopted, first in

Michigan in 1865, then in New York (1867) and Pennsylvania (1887). National legislation affecting cooperatives included the Sherman Anti-Trust Act (1890), the Clayton Anti-Trust Act (1914), and the Federal Farm Loan Act (1916) establishing the forerunner of the present cooperative **Farm Credit System**. Important publications of this period included the *History of Cooperation in the United States*, published by Johns Hopkins University in 1888, and **Herbert Myrick's** *How to Cooperate* (1891). By the close of World War I, cooperatives were an established fact in the United States.

The period between the end of World War I and the outbreak of World War II was one of continued growth and challenge, as the U.S. cooperative movement moved toward becoming numerically one of the largest in the world. Agricultural cooperatives reached a peak of over 12,000 societies in the early 1930s and were organized into state, regional and national commodity federations and geographical groupings. Large **regional cooperatives** for supply, processing and marketing increased in number. The **American Institute of Cooperation**, largely reflecting agricultural cooperative interests, was organized in 1925 and launched its annual national institute and annual publication, *American Cooperation*. The **National Council of Farmer Cooperatives**, first organized as the National Chamber of Agricultural Cooperatives, was established in 1929 and remains the main voice of farmer cooperatives in the United States. Credit unions, hardly of note in 1919, had grown to a total of 8,683 in 1945 with nearly 3,000,000 members, supported by the **Credit Union National Association (CUNA)** established in 1934, **CUNA Mutual Insurance** and CUNA Supply.

CLUSA held its first national convention in 1918 and undertook to rally the disparate consumer cooperative organizations that were its principal focus in the early years. It encouraged cooperative consumer stores and other consumer services, supported by organized labor, which found the economic conditions of its members being threatened by postwar inflation. Edward Filene, in addition to his promotion and financing of credit unions, poured a large amount of money into encouraging consumer cooperatives through the Filene Goodwill Fund, the Twentieth Century Fund and the Consumer Distribution Corporation, the latter giving grants for consumer cooperative development. Consumer cooperative associations in 1945 numbered 7,600 with a combined membership of 2,610,000. **Petroleum cooperatives** emerged in the 1920s to service the growing automobile-owning population and an increasingly mechanized agriculture. By 1945 there were 1,500 such associations with over

900,000 members. What would become the **Nationwide Insurance Company** was established in 1926 and was joined in 1934 by a second company, Mutual Service Insurance. These and 2,000 other smaller cooperative insurance associations had 10,550,000 policy holders in 1945. **Rural electric cooperatives** were first formed in the mid-1930s and in 1942 established their own organization, **NRECA**, which by 1945 reported a membership of 850 associations with 1,150,000 members. Closely related cooperative telephone associations had grown to 5,000 mainly small systems serving 330,000 members in 1945. **Health** service **cooperatives**, appearing first as a cooperative hospital in 1929, had grown into the Group Health Federation in 1939, supported by a Bureau of Cooperative Medicine in CLUSA. By 1945, there were 75 such groups with 150,000 members, the prototypes of the current **HMOs** in the United States.

A growing government interest in cooperatives at the national and state levels reflected itself in an increasing body of cooperative legislation. At the national level, the **Capper-Volstead Act of 1922** was followed by the Agricultural Credit Act of 1923, the Cooperative Marketing Act of 1926, the Farm Credit Act of 1933, the **Federal Credit Union Act of 1934**, and the Rural Electrification Act of 1936. At the state level, there were many reflections of these laws, and credit union advocates included in their strategy of development the enactment of state credit union laws, to add to their legitimacy.

Other groups were joining in the push for cooperatives. Both the National Catholic Conference and the National Council of Churches launched organizations in 1937 to encourage the membership of their churches to establish, become members of, and support cooperatives. In 1944, 11 international **unions** established the Council for Cooperative Development to promote cooperatives among their members. During the depression of the 1930s, the U.S. government included in its economic recovery activities a number of which encouraged self-help cooperatives. Among these projects, in New York City, was the **Cooperative Project** of the Works Progress Administration (WPA), which employed several hundred people to research and publish material about all aspects of cooperative development. Among their unachieved plans was the proposed publication of an *Encyclopedia of Cooperatives*.

The period since 1945–46 has seen significant changes in the profile of the U.S. cooperative movement. Agricultural cooperatives reached their zenith in the early 1950s with 10,179 cooperatives operating with a combined membership of 7,732,000. Thereafter, a combination of events, including continued rural to urban migration, an increased cost of farming (particularly for small operators), the consolidation of smaller cooperatives into larger units, and the continued evolution of regional and then interregional organizations all contributed to a decline in the number of societies and in membership. By 1984 they had declined to approximately 6,000 cooperatives with 5,000,000 members. Throughout the period, the Farm Credit System moved ahead, repaying the final portion of the original government investment made at its foundation. With some stress and further government assistance, it has now restructured itself and adapted to the changing agricultural scene, and it is successfully operating in a more integrated and international fashion.

Consumer cooperatives saw a new surge of activity and interest in the immediate post–World War II period, but soon even the larger established consumer stores, faced with a growing competitive environment and a decline in member loyalty, were in difficulty. Smaller societies closed down and larger ones tried to keep up with sophisticated new supermarket chains. On the positive side there was the growth of a new wave consumer movement focusing on non-traditional and more ideological approaches. Some specialized services, such as recreational supplies, expanded their market. The long-sought consumer cooperative bank was voted into existence by the United States Congress in 1978 and has been the source of renewed encouragement and finance for the consumer movement. However, consumer cooperatives, which numbered 9,100 in 1945 with 3,500,000 members, had declined to 5,030 societies with 1,500,000 members by 1984. CLUSA, which started as a largely consumer cooperative movement in 1916, completed its transformation to a more inclusive perspective when it changed its name in 1985 to the **National Cooperative Business Association**.

The growth side of the American movement during the period was most dramatic among credit unions, which numbered 8,842 with 2,838,000 members in 1945. By 1984 they numbered 19,200 with a membership of 48,500,000. In 1994, reflecting a move to consolidate smaller units, there were 11,140 with a membership of 66,340,012. The **credit union movement** evolved into an international movement, first by including Canadian credit unions, later those from other Western Hemisphere countries, in their activities and support system. In 1970 the **World Council of Credit Unions (WOCCU)** was organized, with its headquarters in Madison, Wisconsin, the home of the U.S. movement.

Insurance cooperatives and rural electric cooperatives have both shown substantial growth, with numbers of societies remaining steady but membership increasing substantially. Insurance societies increased only from 2,000 to 2,034 between 1945 and 1984, but their number of policy holders increased from 1,550,000 to 18,600,000. Rural electric cooperatives increased from 850 to 936 during the same period but membership increased significantly from 1,150,000 to 8,972,500. Housing cooperatives, minuscule at 60 societies with 3,000 members in 1945 had grown to 1,500 societies with 620,000 members in 1984, but growth has slowed in recent years. Telephone cooperatives have declined dramatically in number, from 5,000 in 1945 to 256 in 1984, but membership has increased significantly from 300,000 to 1,575,000.

A notable development of this recent period was the move of U.S. cooperative organizations into active support of the development of cooperatives in the Third World. While such attention was not new for some parts of the cooperative movement (for example, CUNA had had a long-standing involvement in credit union development in different parts of the world, as did CLUSA through its cooperative associations in the ICA), a new general concern for the development of these areas and the move of the United States government to provide assistance led to an acceleration of this type of activity. The United States Congress adopted the **Humphrey Amendment** to the Foreign Assistance Act in 1962, calling upon **USAID** to support cooperative development and to utilize the expertise of U.S. cooperative organizations in doing so. This resulted in the designation of six **cooperative development organizations—Agricultural Cooperative Development International, Cooperative Housing Foundation**, the Credit Union National Association, the National Rural Electric Cooperative Association, the Cooperative League of the USA (now the National Cooperative Business Association) and **Volunteers in Overseas Cooperative Assistance**—all of which have had active programs since that date, largely supported by USAID funds. It also led the American cooperatives to form a coordinating mechanism for this work, the **Overseas Cooperative Development Committee**, which for a time acted as an official advisory committee to USAID.

In 1998, the U.S. cooperative movement remains, in terms of membership, one of the world's largest, exceeded only by those of **China** and **India**. The country files of the ICA in 1997 offer the following profile of American cooperatives in 1995: 27,599 societies with 150,692,000 members in the following sectors: agriculture—4,244 cooperatives/with 4,000,000 members; child care—650/50,000; consumer—350/324,000; health care—11/1,600,000; banking—90/na; credit unions—12,560/ 67,500,000; housing—6,450/1,018,000; insurance—1,800/50,000,000;

rural electric—1,290/26,200,000; and worker productive—154/na. (There are also known to be a small number of **fishery cooperatives**, a network of telephone cooperatives, and assorted other cooperatives that were not enumerated.) Cooperative membership that year was equivalent to 56.7% of the population.

In 1990, the Cooperative Alumni Association, 250 Rainbow Lane, Richmond, Kentucky 40475 (mainly retired "veterans" of the U.S. cooperative movement), published, with support from 17 national cooperative organizations, the *Cooperative/Credit Union Dictionary and Reference*, a comprehensive 410-page book providing information on the history, development and current situation of cooperatives, mainly in the United States and **Canada**. It was a valuable resource for the author of this book and is highly recommended to those who would like to review the North American cooperative movement in fuller detail.

UNITED STATES AGENCY FOR INTERNATIONAL DEVELOPMENT (USAID). The international development organization of the **United States** government, established by the Foreign Assistance Act. Since 1962, after passage of the **Humphrey Amendment**, USAID has provided funds to a group of U.S. cooperative organizations for assistance to cooperatives in **developing countries**. Administering this program is a Coordinator of Cooperative Development.

UNIVERSITY CENTER FOR COOPERATIVES, UNIVERSITY OF WISCONSIN. Mindful of a long history of education and research on-cooperatives, the University of Wisconsin was chosen in 1962 by **USAID** and U.S. cooperative officials as the site for international cooperative training in the **United States**. The intent was to help implement the **Humphrey Amendment** to the United States Foreign Assistance Act. With grant assistance through the 1960s, an international program was developed, providing introductory and advanced courses for cooperators from the developing world. In 1972, when USAID funding ended, the international and domestic training and research efforts were combined into the University Center for Cooperatives. *See also* INTERNATIONAL COOPERATIVE TRAINING CENTER.

URUGUAY. The cooperative movement in Uruguay started with the establishment of the first **agricultural cooperatives** in 1909, and an **agricultural credit** law of 1912 provided the first legislative backdrop for cooperatives. Growth was steady in the 1920–40 period with the establishment of cooperatives in a variety of sectors: banking, consumer, dairy and transport. In the period 1954–64, sectors arrived at a strength which made appropriate the establishment of national **federations**, for agriculture and livestock, **consumer** and **worker productive cooperatives**. Also established (1961) was a national **apex organization**, the Uruguayan Cooperative Center. **Credit** (1964), **housing** (1966) and **school** (1969) **cooperatives** were part of the next wave of cooperative activity, soon supported by their own national federations. Growth was steady, with some consolidation of smaller societies into larger units. The **ILO** *Directory* (**1988**) reported that Uruguay in 1984 had 860 cooperatives with 494,248 members. Growth continued, and the **Organization of Cooperatives of the Americas** reported that in 1991 there were 740 societies with 586,395 members (18.9% of the population) in the following sectors: agriculture—189 societies/with 48,846 members; consumer—53/237,098; credit unions—48/279,684; housing—308/12,586; and worker productive—142/8,191. The membership report of the **ICA** in 1996 gave a total of 844,651 members (26.1% of the population).

USAID. *See* UNITED STATES AGENCY FOR INTERNATIONAL DEVELOPMENT.

UTILITY COOPERATIVES. Associations formed to provide, on a cooperative basis, basic public utilities such as electricity, telephone service, water supply and sewage services where such services are not readily available to all or are only available at prohibitive cost.

UTOPIANS, THE. A term used to describe some of the early pioneers of cooperative thought and action, during the period starting in the mid-1700s, who believed in the innate goodness of human nature. While they varied in emphasis, they generally agreed in the belief that this innate goodness is corrupted by evil societies. They believed that the creation of soundly conceived and executed cooperative communities would provide the environment in which humans could and would achieve their ideal selves.

UZBEKISTAN. The first **consumer cooperatives** in Uzbekistan were established in 1893 at Tashkent, Samarkand and Bokhara. Information on this earlier cooperative movement is sketchy. During the period of the **Union of Soviet Socialist Republics,** cooperatives in Uzbekistan were part of the **Centrosoyus** network. Since Uzbekistan became an independent state in 1991, the movement has been reconstituting itself as an economic organization independent of state control. Local cooperatives are members of 84 district societies affiliated with 13 **regional cooperative unions**. The activities of the cooperatives are mainly retail and wholesale trade of food and non-food items through more than 19,000 shops. The cooperatives also provide public catering for schools, cafes, workplace dining rooms and restaurants and engage in a wide range of food processing. The **ICA Regional Office for Asia and the Pacific** reported in 1992 that there were 2,770 consumer cooperatives with a membership of 3,640,243 (16.7% of the population). The *ICA News* reported in 1993 that the movement then had 385 societies with a membership of 4 million (18.2% of the population).

V

VAIKUNTH MEHTA NATIONAL INSTITUTE OF COOPERATIVE MANAGEMENT. Established at Poona, **India**, in 1947, and named in honor of Indian cooperative pioneer **Vaikunth Mehta**, the Institute offers about 50 management courses a year for senior officers employed in cooperative institutions and government cooperative departments. It offers a 38-week core course in cooperative business management.

VAILLANCOURT, CYRILLE (1892–1969). A French Canadian cooperator, educator and politician, he was on the staff of the Quebec Department of Agriculture from 1915 to 1934 and held, concurrently, leadership positions from 1924 to 1969 in the **Caisse populaire de Lévis,** Union régionale de Québec, Fédération de Québec des unions régionales des caisses populaires Desjardins, and Société d'assurance des caisses populaires. Vaillancourt was a part-time lecturer in cooperation at Laval University from 1934 to 1937 and was a member of the Canadian Senate from 1944 to 1969.

VALKO, LASZLO (1907–1982). An American academic and cooperative theorist, he was a professor in the external department of Washington State University where he wrote extensively on cooperative subjects. He is widely recognized for his work in the field of **cooperative law** and for his books and articles dealing with the international cooperative movement.

VANUATU. Formerly the New Hebrides. Vanuatu's cooperative history began in 1962 with the passage of the Joint Native Cooperative Societies

Act, and its first cooperative, a transport society, was established in 1967. Few other details of the cooperative movement's development are known, except that there is at present a Vanuatu Cooperative Federation and that an **ICA Regional Office for Asia and the Pacific** Mission Report indicated that there were 94 cooperative societies with a membership of 5,203 (3.0% of the population) in 1994.

VÅR GÅRD. A cooperative training center organized by **Kooperativa Förbundet** in 1924 at Saltsjöbaden, near Stockholm, **Sweden.** It was designed to provide short-term training for cooperative employees, committee members and education workers. In recent years it has provided training to cooperators from **developing countries,** and its facilities have been used for international cooperative meetings.

VASENIUS, HUGO (1886–?). A Finnish cooperator, he was a leader of the Neutral Cooperative Movement (SOK), which he joined in 1908, serving in important management positions before his selection as managing director in 1921. He served for a period of time in the Finnish government, dealing with matters of food distribution, and he was also vice chairman of the **Nordisk Andelsförbund.**

VENEZUELA. While Venezuela's first cooperative (a savings and building society) dates from 1903 and the first of several legislative attempts to deal with cooperatives was enacted in 1910, little of the early effort to build a cooperative movement has persisted. The **ILO** *Directory* **(1988)** reported that in 1983–85 there were 561 societies with 136,360 members (0.79% of the population), making Venezuela one of the least "cooperativized" among countries of similar size and economic development. The *Directory* notes the existence of a national confederation which has existed since 1963, but no reference is made to national **federations** by sector, although a number of these were established in 1964 or earlier for **agriculture, consumer, credit, housing, transport,** and **worker productive cooperatives.** The **Organization of Cooperatives of the Americas** reported that in 1991 there were 791 cooperatives with a total of 202,812 members (1.0% of the population) in the following sectors: agriculture—9 societies/with 824 members; consumer—28/2,194; education—1/438; housing—31/1,897; insurance—160/69,941; multipurpose—215/94,920; savings and credit—65/24,798; and worker productive and services—282/7,800.

VENTOSA Y ROIG, JUAN (1883–1961). A leader of the cooperative movement in Catalonia and in all of **Spain**, he was president of the Catalonian Cooperative Federation, president of the Spanish Cooperative Federation, and a member of the **ICA** Executive Committee. In exile after the Spanish Civil War, he lived and worked in Latin America and authored important books on cooperatives, including works on cooperatives and the state, **school cooperatives** and **cooperative education**.

VERGNANINI, ANTONIO (1861–1934). An Italian poet, idealist and non-Marxist Christian socialist, he was general secretary and president of the Italian League of Cooperatives from 1912 until 1924 when the organization was banned by the Fascist government. He had ongoing ideological and political conflicts with the government, while continuing to edit the journal *La Cooperazione Italiana*. Vergnanini represented Italian cooperatives in the **ICA** Central Committee until 1924.

VIETNAM. Cooperative activity in Vietnam was encouraged by the French colonial administration, which issued an order in 1909 applying to Vietnam the French legislation regarding **agricultural credit** societies. The first of these was established in 1912, followed by others in subsequent years. In 1934 the first cooperative of agricultural producers was established, and the number of such cooperatives grew until the occupation by Japan during World War II. Independence was declared in 1945, but conflict continued with French colonial forces until their defeat in 1954. The **United States** entered the conflict shortly thereafter in collaboration with a South Vietnam regime, and the next 20 years were a period of conflict in which cooperatives played minor roles, with both northern and southern regimes pursuing armed conflict and ideological ends related to their respective visions of the future. The defeat of the American and South Vietnamese military forces by the North ushered in a period of common ideology regarding cooperatives that persists today. The national government decided early that small and medium-sized cooperatives could play a key role in national development and were to be encouraged. There was also to be a continuing role for collective farming, which had been initiated earlier. The **ICA Regional Office for Asia and the Pacific** reported that in 1992 there were 42,500 cooperative societies with a membership of 20,000,000 (28.9% of the population). The report noted cooperatives of two types—16,341 agricultural societies with 6,158,000 members and 26,159 multipurpose societies with 13,842,000 members.

VIGANO, F. An Italian cooperative pioneer, in 1864 he helped establish the first Italian **consumer cooperative** at Como.

VIVES DEL SOLAR, FERNANDO. A Chilean Jesuit priest who in the 1920s and 1930s organized **consumer, credit** and **housing cooperatives**. He regarded cooperatives as effective means of helping to achieve a Christian society.

VOLSTEAD, ANDREW J. (1861–1947). A member of the United States House of Representatives from Minnesota, he was cosponsor with **Alfred Capper** of the **Capper-Volstead Cooperative Marketing Act of 1922,** which affirmed that farmers could join together in associations to market their production, exempt from anti-trust laws. This legislation and Volstead's continuing interest in cooperative matters were the basis for his induction into the U.S. **Cooperative Hall of Fame** in 1979.

VOLUNTARY SERVICE OVERSEAS (VSO). A volunteer agency in the **United Kingdom** sponsoring the service of British volunteers in **developing countries**. Consistent with the interest of the British government and the British cooperative movement, many VSO volunteers have assisted in cooperative development projects.

VOLUNTEER ASSISTANCE TO COOPERATIVE DEVELOPMENT. While volunteer service has been and remains a core activity in cooperatives, a unique aspect of assistance to cooperatives in **developing countries** has been the assignment of volunteers by international agencies to assist, on a long-term basis, in the development of cooperatives and cooperative movements in these countries. The 1989 edition of the **COPAC** *Directory of Agencies Assisting Cooperatives in Developing Countries* lists 44 such agencies from 21 countries. Among those with longstanding programs providing significant numbers of volunteers in diverse countries are the United Nations Volunteers, **CUSO (Canada), Voluntary Service Overseas (United Kingdom), the Peace Corps (United States),** and **Volunteers in Overseas Cooperative Assistance** (U.S.).

VOLUNTEERS IN OVERSEAS COOPERATIVE ASSISTANCE (VOCA). Established in 1970 at the initiative of the **cooperative development organizations** in the **United States** and **USAID**, VOCA, on request, has provided short-term volunteer technical assistance to cooperatives in **developing countries,** utilizing the services of experienced active and retired cooperators from the American cooperative movement. Its funding has come principally from an annual grant from USAID.

VON ELM, ADOLPH (1857–1916). A German cooperative leader, he was active initially with agricultural **production cooperatives,** where he became aware that successfully organized production must depend equally on well-organized consumption, a reality that brought him into the orbit of the Central Union of German **distributive societies,** the chairmanship of which he held at the time of his death. Von Elm was also active in cooperative **insurance** affairs as director of the Trade Union and Cooperative Insurance Society. Elected to the Central Committee of the **ICA** in 1909, he served there until his death in 1916.

VON KOCH. In 1898 in **Sweden,** Von Koch published *The Workers' Cooperative Movement,* spelling out the importance of cooperatives to the working class. In 1904, **Kooperativa Förbundet** began publication of a magazine, *Kooperatören,* with Von Koch as the first editor.

VOORHIS, JEREMIAH (JERRY) (1901–1984). An American educator, politician, and cooperative leader, he was for 20 years (1947–67) executive director/president of **CLUSA.** Early in his career (1928–38) he was director of a home for orphan boys in Wyoming and later, while teaching American history at Pomona College in California, of the Voorhis School for Boys. Elected to the **United States** Congress in 1936, he served for 10 years, actively involving himself in legislation affecting cooperatives, before his defeat in 1946 by Richard Nixon. While head of CLUSA, he was instrumental in the formation of the Group Health Association and helped shape the early history and future of **HMOs** in the U.S. He was active in the Cooperative Foundation, the National Association of Housing Cooperatives, and associations of cooperative educators and editors. He was one of the founders of the **Organization of Cooperatives of the Americas** and served for almost 20 years on the Central Committee of the **ICA.** On his death he was eulogized by many who shared his belief that cooperatives were a way of improving the lot of the poor and powerless.

VUKOVICH, DR. ANDREAS. A 20th-century Austrian **consumer cooperative** leader, he served for 32 years as head of the Austrian Cooperative Union, Konsumverband, helping to rebuild the Austrian movement after two world wars. He was a longtime member of the **ICA** Central Committee.

W

WALRAS, LÉON (1834–1910). A Swiss neoclassical economist who with **Vilfredo Pareto** established the Ecôle de Lausanne. He was author in 1865 of *Les Associations populaires*.

WARBASSE, AGNES DYER (1877–1945). An American cooperator, she was an ardent advocate of the vote for women and a supporter of social reform. She worked with her husband, **James Peter Warbasse**, in the organization of a national cooperative organization in the **United States;** the meetings out of which it grew in 1916 were held in their home. She acted as a volunteer secretary of **CLUSA** from its founding in 1916 through 1928. Agnes Warbasse was a delegate to **ICA** congresses in Basel, Ghent and Vienna and was the author of books and articles on cooperative subjects. She was one of the founders of the New School for Social Research.

WARBASSE, JAMES PETER (1866–1957). An American physician and cooperative leader, he was the first president of **CLUSA**, serving in that capacity for 25 years. He was elected to the Central Committee of the **ICA** in 1930 and thereafter was a frequent contributor to the *Review of International Cooperation*. In 1956 his autobiography, in which he spelled out the life experiences that shaped his thinking and action, was published. James Warbasse developed a profound skepticism of statism and of government's tendency to spread and spread. He was a vigorous exponent of the view that self-help was the key to sound economic development and warned cooperators against relying on a benevolent state.

WATKINS, WILLIAM P. (1893–1995). An English cooperator, he served as the director of the **ICA** for the period 1951–63. Born in Plymouth, England, he was introduced to cooperatives by his father and attended his first cooperative course at age 12. At 16 he spent time in Paris studying the French **consumer** and **production cooperatives**. Following World War I Watkins took up a career in the cooperative movement, becoming a tutor at the **Cooperative College, Loughborough**, in 1920. In 1929 he joined the ICA staff, with responsibility for the preparation of publications on cooperative matters and organizing the annual ICA-sponsored International Cooperative School. In 1939 he joined the staff of the cooperative Sunday newspaper *Reynolds News*, and from 1946 to 1950 was an advisor on cooperation to the British military governor in

Germany. Watkins authored the book *The International Cooperative Alliance 1895–1970*, a history of the first 75 years of the ICA.

WAWRZYNIAK, REV. PETER. A cleric and early pioneer of the **cooperative movement** in **Poland**, he became a director of the Polish Cooperative Union in 1892 and dedicated much of his life to strengthening and expanding the scope and discipline of the Polish cooperatives, particularly in Posen and Western Prussia. Joining the Polish Union at a time when it was stagnating from lack of vision, discipline and solidarity, he led it to assume a role in auditing the records of local societies, introduced training programs to improve management, and helped develop a vision of what the Polish cooperatives could become. Wawrzyniak was instrumental in grouping small societies into central cooperative societies and was a key actor in the formation of an early **cooperative bank**. He was a model for the role of a number of Catholic clergy who, following papal leadership and encyclicals, saw in cooperatives an economic model for the expression of Catholic social principles.

WEBB, BEATRICE POTTER (1858–1943). A British sociologist who left a life of wealth and comfort to live and work among the poor and to act as a publicist of their misery. In 1899 she began an intensive study of the cooperative movement and in the process met her husband, **Sidney Webb**. Their marriage began a lifelong and famous partnership in causes dealing with cooperatives, trade unionism, and Fabian **socialism**. In 1920 the Webbs became involved with the London School of Economics and their work, particularly in its social science department, contributed greatly to the establishment of the school's worldwide reputation. Beatrice Webb was the author of a number of books dealing with cooperatives, including *The Cooperative Movement in Great Britain* and *The Discovery of the Consumer.*

WEBB, SIDNEY JAMES (1869–1942). A British intellectual and political leader, he was active in the Fabian socialist movement all his adult life as one of their most prolific and convincing writers and speakers. He was convinced that political democracy would achieve only limited ends unless it was accompanied by economic democracy, and he believed that cooperatives, trade unions and the Labour Party were the instruments needed to achieve economic democracy. Webb was a member of the London City Council for many years, the articulator in 1918 of an early Labour Party program, and a labour member of Parliament from 1922 to

1928. He became a member of the House of Lords in 1929. With his wife, **Beatrice Potter Webb**, he was an important figure in the development of the London School of Economics as a world-recognized institution.

WEBER, MAX (1897–1974). A Swiss cooperator, he had an early career as head of the Economic Section of the Federation of Swiss Trade Unions and later as president of the Building and Woodworkers' Union. He joined the board of the Swiss Union of Cooperatives (VSK) in 1944 and was elected chairman in 1946. He was also president of the Central Cooperative Bank and taught Social Policy and Cooperation at the University of Bern. Weber was elected to the **ICA** Central Committee in 1946 and served on its Executive Committee from 1948 to 1951.

WEGNER, HERBERT GAIRD (1929–1987). A **credit union** leader in the **United States**, he emerged in the leadership of the **credit union movement** as director of **CUNA's** Latin American Regional Office in **Panama** from 1963 to 1971. He and his staff were instrumental in starting new credit union movements and strengthening existing ones in South and Central America. Their work also laid the ground for the **Confederación Latinoamericana de Cooperativas de Ahorro y Crédito (COLAC)** (Latin American Confederation of Savings and Credit Cooperatives). In 1971 Wegner became the managing director of both CUNA and **WOCCU**. He was instrumental in directing the U.S. credit union movement into the era of electronic fund transactions and undertook an aggressive publicity campaign on behalf of credit unions. After leaving CUNA, he was an international development consultant and later served as Coordinator for Cooperative Development for **USAID**, overseeing the Agency's work with U.S. **cooperative development organizations**.

WHOLESALE COOPERATIVES. An important supply function of **consumer cooperatives,** which a group of consumer societies join together to form a cooperative to produce or purchase items at wholesale prices; these are then provided to individual cooperatives for resale at retail prices. The **surplus** generated in these operations is distributed to the member cooperatives or retained for expansion of the business of the wholesale society.

WHOLESALE SOCIETIES. *See* WHOLESALE COOPERATIVES.

WILLIAMS, ANEURIN (1859–1924). A British cooperative and political leader, he was a longtime member of the **ICA** Central and Executive Committees, beginning in 1907. He was chairman of the Executive Committee from 1908 (a year after the Cremona Congress) until his retirement. This was a key time in the early shaping of the program of the Alliance. Williams participated in the first ICA Congress in 1895, representing the Labour Association, that group of **production cooperatives** that would later become the Labour Co-Partnership Association. The association actively advocated the principle of profit-sharing with employees of **cooperative societies**, a principle that was hotly debated in the early years of the ICA. Williams was elected a member of Parliament in the **United Kingdom**; he served there for many years and took a keen interest in international affairs, supporting various measures to relieve the situation of refugees in a number of countries. His wider interests included urban beautification and proportional representation in legislative bodies.

WOCCU. *See* WORLD COUNCIL OF CREDIT UNIONS.

WOLFF, HENRY W. (1840–1930). A British-born cooperator, he was educated at Bonn and Heidelberg Universities. He helped establish credit societies in **Ireland** in 1894 and had an active interest and involvement with cooperatives in **India**. He was the convener of the conference at which the **ICA** was established in 1895 and exercised considerable influence due to his extensive contacts with European cooperative leaders. Wolff served as the first ICA president from 1895 to 1907. In 1921 he was named to the **Committee of Honor of the International Cooperative Alliance,** in recognition of his work with national movements and the ICA.

WOLLEMBORG, LEONE (1859–1932). An Italian cooperative pioneer, he was an associate of **Luigi Luzzatti.** In 1883 in Padua he established the first Italian credit society, patterned on the **Raiffeisen** model. It and its counterparts in other communities became an important arm of the cooperative movement in **Italy**. In 1883 he also established the first Italian cooperative publication, *La Cooperazione Rurale.*

WOODCOCK, LESLIE E. (1893–1974). An American cooperator, he was active in the cooperative movement for more than 50 years, starting as one of the founders of Consumer Cooperative Services, a chain of cooperative cafeterias in New York City for which he served as secretary from 1921 to 1930. In 1925 he was involved in what ultimately became

Eastern Cooperatives, of which he became general manager. Woodcock was a director of the **Nationwide Insurance Company** and of National Cooperatives. He was a member of the board of **CLUSA**, serving as its treasurer from 1939 to 1946. He was associated for a time with the Russell Sage Foundation and in his later years served as a representative of the **ICA** to the **United Nations** in New York. He was named to the U.S. **Cooperative Hall of Fame** in 1980.

WORKER PRODUCTIVE COOPERATIVE. *See* PRODUCTION COOPERATIVE.

WORLD BANK. Formally the International Bank for Reconstruction and Development, the World Bank is a specialized agency of the **United Nations,** organized in 1945. It lends money to its member states to support investment, trade and development programs. In 1989 the **COPAC** *Directory of Agencies Assisting Cooperatives in Developing Countries* indicated that a "recent internal study of Bank-assisted projects showed that almost half of their agriculture and rural development projects had cooperative components to them."

WORLD COUNCIL OF CREDIT UNIONS (WOCCU). The world **apex organization** of the **credit union movement,** established in 1970. It was an outgrowth of the **credit cooperative** activity generated first in Germany by **Friedrich Wilhelm Raiffeisen** and **Herman Schultze-Delitzsch** in the 1850s, which spread in several forms throughout Europe and in **Canada** at the turn of the 20th century through the vision and work of **Alphonse Desjardins**. Credit cooperatives appeared in **India** in 1900 and had developed sufficiently by 1907 to impress upon **Edward Filene**, an American visitor to that country, that there was potential for such organizations in the **United States**. With Filene's energy and financial resources, combined with the efforts of **Roy Bergengren** and others, the American credit union movement was launched, with the establishment of the first U.S. **credit union** in 1909, growing gradually into what became the **Credit Union National Association (CUNA)** in 1934. By the end of World War II and in the early postwar years, a number of fledgling credit union movements had begun in **developing countries** as well as in **Japan** and **Australia**.

These, and Bergengren's and others' dreams of a world movement, led CUNA to establish, in 1954, the World Extension Division to assist emerging national movements and to stimulate others. By 1964 these efforts had proven productive enough that CUNA changed its name to CUNA International and established a structure for the participation of a growing number of multinational associates. After extended discussion of the ways in which an international movement might be structured to allow maximum autonomy for all in a united effort, the WOCCU was voted into existence in 1970. It was structured to give prominent roles to regional confederations of credit unions that had already been formed in the Caribbean, Africa and Latin America (soon joined by the Asian Confederation), allied with established national movements. Its first managing director was a Jamaican, Paddy Bailey.

In the early 1980s the development arm of the American movement, CUNA Global Projects, headed by Paul Hebert, was merged with the World Council, and an expanded technical assistance effort in the developing world was undertaken. Concurrently, relationships were established with credit cooperative structures in Europe and elsewhere through participation in the **International Liaison Committee on Cooperative Thrift and Credit (CLICEC)**; through this WOCCU has participated in the organization of a series of international conferences dealing with cooperative savings and credit. WOCCU has attracted into its membership the Confédération nationale du crédit mutuel of **France**, the International Cooperative Banking Association of the **ICA** and the **International Raiffeisen Union**. WOCCU in turn became a member of IRU. New national credit union structures in **Poland**, **Russia** and the **Ukraine** have further extended its international outreach. In 1998 WOCCU reported that its membership the previous year included 34,212 credit unions in more than 80 countries, representing 95,489,858 individual members.

WORLD FOOD PROGRAM (WFP). A program of the **United Nations**, headquartered in Rome at the **FAO**, it is designed to provide food assistance to low-income, food-deficit countries. It makes considerable quantities of food assistance available for food-for-work projects, some of which involve cooperatives. A 1986 program survey indicated that in June 1986 the WFP was supporting 140 such cooperative projects, 43 in Africa, 17 in Asia, 3 in the Caribbean, 35 in Latin America, 39 in North Africa/Near East and 3 in Europe.

WORLEY, J. J. (1887–1944). A British cooperative official who was secretary of the British Cooperative Productive Federation from 1922 until his death. He was an orator of note, an effective propagandist and an active lecturer on cooperative subjects. He served on the **ICA** Central Committee from 1921 to 1944.

WWW.COOP.ORG. *See* INTERNET.

Y

YAFFE, E. An Israeli cooperative pioneer who in 1919 published *The Foundation of Moshavei Ovdim,* outlining the rules of the *moshav* cooperative settlement movement in **Israel**.

YEAR BOOK OF AGRICULTURAL COOPERATION. An annual publication since 1927 of the Horace Plunkett Foundation (renamed the **Plunkett Foundation for Cooperative Studies**), its original title was the *Year Book of Agricultural Cooperation in the British Empire.* Its title was changed to the above in 1932 to provide for consideration of the growing worldwide cooperative movement. In 1988, its scope was further enlarged to include all sectors of the cooperative movement, and it was accordingly renamed the *Yearbook of Cooperative Enterprise.* It has been an important source of information regarding cooperatives and their development in all parts of the world, including compilations of important bibliographical references.

YEMEN. Yemen was united as one country in 1990 after a long history of division (the north supported by **Saudi Arabia**, the south by Britain and, after independence, by a Yemeni Marxist regime). Evolving cooperative efforts have occurred in both areas, dating from the mid-1950s. In both areas there have been **cooperative laws,** and **agricultural cooperatives** have been the predominate sector. An **ILO** appraisal team visited the country shortly after the 1990 merger and found the cooperative structure shown in the following table. There were a total of 258 cooperatives having 212,545 members (2.2% of the population).

	North		South		Total	
	Coops	Members	Coops	Members	Coops	Members
Agriculture	112	25,216	58	54,900	170	80,116
Consumer	7	25,207	34	84,131	41	109,338
Fisheries	5	3,113	12	11,546	17	14,659
Handicraft	17	699	8	742	25	1,441
Housing	5	6,991	—	—	5	6,991
Total	146	61,226	112	151,319	258	212,545

YUGOSLAVIA. Created in 1918 as the Kingdom of the Serbs Croats and Slovenes, renamed Yugoslavia in 1929, and proclaimed a federated republic with a communist government after World War II. The federation split up in 1991 with **Slovenia, Croatia, Bosnia-Herzegovina** and

Macedonia declaring themselves independent. The beginnings of the cooperative movement date to 1870 when the first **handicraft** and **consumer cooperatives** were established at Belgrade. The first **Raiffeisen credit cooperative** was founded in Belgrade, Serbia, in 1894 and in the following year the General Union of Serbian Agricultural Cooperatives, also in Belgrade. In 1919 a Federation of Cooperative Unions was established, drawing together the nascent movements in the various territories making up the new nation. From that date until 1991 the movement, like the country, was federated, with cooperative organizations for agriculture, consumers, credit, fisheries, health care and livestock. A cooperative health care movement was begun in 1921 by **Michael Avramovitch**. The first federal **cooperative legislation** was enacted in 1925, but it was replaced in 1946 by constitutional provisions and basic legislation regarding cooperatives reflecting the new government and modeled to a degree on the experience of the **Union of Soviet Socialist Republics**. After the country's split with the USSR, the Yugoslav government placed great emphasis on workers' self-management as an organizing principle for the economy, and the cooperative movement adopted this as well. In the **ILO** *Directory* **(1988)** the only listing of cooperative organizations for Yugoslavia was the Cooperative Union of Yugoslavia, with 1,506,000 individual members in 1985 (6.5% of the population). No comprehensive statistical data on cooperatives in post-1991 Yugoslavia was available.

Z

ZAHRADNIK, JINDRICH. An electrical engineer, technologist, government official and cooperator, he was elected president of the Central Cooperative Council of **Czechoslovakia** beginning in 1981, and he also served on the **ICA** Central and Executive Committees from that date. Prior to that, in 1971, he had become a member of Parliament and was named deputy prime minister of the Czechoslovak government, having major responsibilities dealing with science and technology, national wage policy and the environment. Zahradnik played a major role in starting an ideological transition of the cooperative movement in Czechoslovakia, which preceded the changes produced by the collapse of the communist systems in Eastern and Central Europe in 1989–90.

ZAIRE (now the Democratic Republic of Congo). Although cooperative rules were issued as early as 1921 and the first **cooperative** organized in 1923, cooperative development moved only slowly in the then Belgian

Congo. Colonial government frustration with the process was evident in 1939 when cooperative societies were transformed into Rural Provident Associations, patterned after similar groups in French colonial territories. A 1948 study of the problems of cooperatives offered hope for a better future for them, but it resulted in little tangible or lasting change. New decrees were issued proclaiming the formation of small farmer cooperative associations; these were soon reformed into Rural Development Mutual Societies. In the 1960s, after independence, a national cooperative **federation** was established (no longer in existence) and a national office formed in the government for **agricultural cooperatives**. Political turmoil followed independence, and the government was seized in 1965 by Mobutu Sese Seko, who remained in power until 1997. By most accounts, Mobutu used his office to create a vast realm of personal wealth. There have been few significant cooperative developments since 1965, and it has proven impossible to obtain any semblance of usable statistics about the cooperative movement, if such a movement even exists. The **ILO** made note of this fact in 1972 and again in its *International Directory of Cooperative Organizations* in 1988. **WOCCU** (and CUNA Global Projects before it), which has been encouraging a fledgling **credit union movement** in Zaire, has been unable to provide statistics on that activity for many years.

ZAMBIA. The first cooperative society (for colonists) was established in then Northern Rhodesia in 1914, but it was not until 1930 that a Cooperative Societies Ordinance was passed and, two years later, the first attempts made to establish cooperatives for the indigenous population. In 1938 one of the pioneer Zambian cooperatives, a tobacco growers' society, was established at Petauke. Development of other societies was slow but steady, and by 1951 there were 97 cooperatives with 15,500 members. The 1950s were a period of continued growth and the establishment of provincial cooperative **unions**.

In 1961, there were seven of these, and their affiliated cooperatives had grown to 228 with 36,413 members. The next significant growth period was after independence in 1964; the number of cooperatives doubled in the year following that event. By the end of the decade, the cooperative movement reported 1,121 societies and a membership of 44,670. By then, building societies and **credit unions** had been established and were supported by national **federations**. In 1973 the Zambia Cooperative Federation was formed and a Cooperative Training Center, forerunner of the present Cooperative College, established.

In the mid-1970s a decision was made to form cooperatives that could meet a variety of the different member needs, and thus **multipurpose cooperatives,** now the dominant cooperative sector, began to appear. From that time, growth has been steady as the movement has expanded and diversified to meet some of the nation's development needs. In 1993, the **ICA Regional Office for East, Central and Southern Africa** reported, there were 1,805 cooperatives in Zambia with a membership of 814,000 (9.4% of the population) in the following sectors: agriculture— 36 societies/with 12,000 members; consumer—170/16,000; fisheries 10/1,000; multipurpose—804/437,000; savings and credit 265/44,000; school—126/28,000; marketing—65/7,000; ward cooperatives—249/ 249,000; and others—80/20,000.

ZICHY, COUNT ALADÁR. In 1897 in **Hungary,** he established the Union of Christian Cooperative Societies and served as its president until 1916 when the organization amalgamated with the Hangya cooperatives. He was elected president of Hangya in 1925, a position from which he retired in 1934.

ZIMBABWE. The formal cooperative experience in Zimbabwe began in 1902 (then Southern Rhodesia) with the establishment of a Civil Service Association serving employees of the colonial administration. This was followed in 1909 by an **agricultural cooperative** societies law, designed to give a legal foundation to the expanding development of farms by European colonists. This group was the focus of almost all cooperative activity in the then Southern Rhodesia, and by the time of independence in 1980 some 5,000 of these farmers were producing about 80% of Zimbabwe's agricultural products on its best land. In 1956 a Cooperative Societies Act was passed, with the goal of encouraging and assisting **indigenous** farmer **cooperatives.** Progress in this regard was slow, with only 21 societies developed by 1960. Ten years later the number had grown to 283 and at independence in 1980 to 374 with over 40,000 members, supported by a network of 13 cooperative **unions** established between 1966 and 1975.

With independence and government priority given to cooperative development, the number of cooperatives grew rapidly to 1,892 by 1990, and the cooperative sector diversified into **housing, credit** and **worker production cooperatives.** A membership report of the **ICA** for 1995 indicated that there were 2,410 cooperatives with 272,144 members (2.4% of the population) in the following sectors: agriculture—1,483 societies/

with 201,522 members; credit unions—57/38,427; housing—50/2,997; worker productive—220/18,198; and others—600/11,000. The settler cooperatives (now cooperative companies) remain a contentious issue. Many people who had struggled in the independence movement had expected widespread expropriation of these lands, which would then be made available to the indigenous population. This has not yet taken place. There is some indication that the indigenous and settler systems have begun to relate, and that the technical experience and expertise of the latter sector may come to benefit more and more from the farming community of the country.

ZLATARIC, BRANKO. An active cooperator in **Yugoslavia**, he was an official in the Serbian and Croatian cooperative movements after World War II as well as a government official. From 1964 to 1970 he was Secretary for Agriculture in the **ICA**, a position he returned to in 1978 after a period of work in the field of cooperatives with the **FAO** in Rome.

Appendix 1
Year First Cooperatives Established

These tables indicate the year when the first known cooperative organization was organized in each country. The information is presented first
worldwide and chronologically starting with the year 1750, then by regional groupings:

- Worldwide
- Europe/North America
- Africa
- Asia/Pacific
- Caribbean
- Latin America
- North Africa/Near East

YEAR FIRST COOPERATIVES ESTABLISHED WORLDWIDE

1750	France, United Kingdom, United States
1780	Greece
1794	Austria
1806	Italy
1808	Luxembourg
1816	Poland, Switzerland
1825	Russia
1838	Spain
1839	Mexico
1843	Japan
1844	Iceland
1845	Germany, Slovakia
1847	Brazil
1848	Belgium
1850	Hungary, Sweden
1851	Denmark, Norway, Slovenia

1852	Czech Republic, Romania
1859	Australia, Ireland
1860	Latvia, Netherlands
1861	Canada
1863	Bulgaria, Turkey
1869	Lithuania
1870	Finland, Yugoslavia
1871	Portugal
1875	Argentina
1876	Honduras
1878	Israel (Palestine)
1881	New Zealand
1893	Uzbekistan
1898	Estonia
1900	India
1901	Algeria
1902	South Africa, Zimbabwe
1903	Venezuela
1904	Chile, Pakistan
1905	Bangladesh, Myanmar, Tunisia
1906	Guatemala, Sri Lanka
1907	Korea
1908	Egypt, Indonesia, Kenya
1909	Cyprus, Uruguay
1910	Niger, Philippines
1912	China, El Salvador, Taiwan, Vietnam
1913	Mauritius, Namibia, Uganda
1914	Nicaragua, Zambia
1915	Libya
1916	Colombia, Senegal, Trinidad & Tobago
1917	Thailand
1919	Ecuador, Mali, Peru
1920	Costa Rica, Malaysia, Puerto Rico, Suriname
1921	Burundi, Mongolia
1922	Jordan, Morocco
1923	Zaire
1924	Cameroon
1925	Singapore, Tanzania
1926	Congo, Iran, Mauritania
1927	Martinique
1928	Ghana
1929	Réunion

1930	Iraq, Jamaica, Nigeria
1931	Burkina Faso, Guinea, Madagascar, Swaziland, Togo
1932	Côte d'Ivoire, Guadeloupe
1933	Guyana, Palestine (Arab)
1936	Sierra Leone
1937	Haiti, Lebanon
1939	Bolivia
1940	Barbados, Saint Vincent and the Grenadines
1941	Kuwait
1942	Paraguay
1943	Belize, Syria
1945	Ethiopia, Fiji
1946	Albania, Bahamas, Dominica, Dominican Republic, Lesotho, Malta, Papua New Guinea, Saint Lucia
1947	Benin, Hong Kong, Sudan
1949	Chad
1950	Gambia, Nepal, Solomon Islands, Somalia
1951	Cuba
1954	Cambodia, Panama, Samoa
1955	Cook Islands
1956	Kiribati, Rwanda, Tuvalu
1958	Antigua, Grenada, Yemen
1959	Anguilla, Saint Christopher (St. Kitts)/Nevis
1960	Micronesia, Montserrat
1961	Central African Republic, Gabon, Saudi Arabia, Seychelles
1964	Botswana, Tonga
1965	Afghanistan
1967	Vanuatu
1969	Bermuda
1970	Liberia
1971	Guinea-Bissau
1972	Cayman Islands, United Arab Emirates
1973	Qatar
1975	Brunei
1978	Laos
1984	Tortola

Unknown: Angola, Armenia, Azerbaijan, Bahrain, Belarus, Bosnia-Herzegovina, Cape Verde, Croatia, Georgia, Kazakhstan, Kyrgyzstan, Latvia, Liechtenstein, Macedonia, Malawi, Moldova, Mozambique, Netherlands Antilles, Turkmenistan, Ukraine

YEAR FIRST COOPERATIVES ESTABLISHED IN EUROPE/NORTH AMERICA

1750	France, United Kingdom, United States
1780	Greece
1794	Austria
1806	Italy
1808	Luxembourg
1816	Poland, Switzerland
1825	Russia
1838	Spain
1843	Japan
1844	Iceland
1845	Germany, Slovakia
1848	Belgium
1850	Hungary, Sweden
1851	Denmark, Norway, Slovenia
1852	Czech Republic, Romania
1859	Australia, Ireland
1860	Latvia, Netherlands
1861	Canada
1863	Bulgaria, Turkey
1869	Lithuania
1870	Finland, Yugoslavia
1871	Portugal
1881	New Zealand
1893	Uzbekistan
1898	Estonia
1902	South Africa
1909	Cyprus
1946	Albania, Malta

NA: Azerbaijan, Belarus, Bosnia-Herzegovina, Croatia, Georgia, Liechtenstein, Moldova, Ukraine

YEAR FIRST COOPERATIVES ESTABLISHED IN AFRICA

1902	South Africa
1908	Kenya
1910	Niger
1913	Mauritius, Namibia, Uganda
1914	Zambia
1916	Senegal

1919	Mali
1921	Burundi
1923	Zaire
1924	Cameroon
1925	Tanzania
1926	Congo, Mauritania
1928	Ghana
1930	Nigeria
1931	Burkina Faso, Guinea, Madagascar, Swaziland, Togo
1932	Côte d'Ivoire
1936	Sierra Leone
1945	Ethiopia
1946	Lesotho, Malawi
1947	Benin, Sudan
1949	Chad
1950	Gambia, Somalia
1956	Rwanda
1961	Central African Republic, Gabon, Seychelles
1964	Botswana
1970	Liberia
1971	Guinea-Bissau

NA: Angola, Cape Verde, Malawi, Mozambique

YEAR FIRST COOPERATIVES ESTABLISHED IN ASIA/PACIFIC

1843	Japan
1849	Australia
1881	New Zealand
1893	Uzbekistan
1900	India
1904	Pakistan
1905	Bangladesh, Myanmar
1906	Sri Lanka
1907	Korea
1908	Indonesia
1910	Philippines
1912	China, Taiwan, Vietnam
1917	Thailand
1920	Malaysia
1921	Mongolia
1925	Singapore
1945	Fiji

1946	Papua New Guinea
1947	Hong Kong
1950	Nepal, Solomon Islands
1954	Cambodia, Samoa
1955	Cook Islands
1956	Kiribati, Tuvalu
1960	Micronesia
1964	Tonga
1967	Vanuatu
1975	Brunei
1978	Laos

NA: Kazakhstan, Kyrgyzstan, Tajikistan, Turkmenistan

YEAR FIRST COOPERATIVES ESTABLISHED IN THE CARIBBEAN

1916	Trinidad and Tobago
1920	Puerto Rico, Suriname
1927	Martinique
1930	Jamaica
1932	Guadeloupe
1933	Guyana
1937	Haiti
1940	Barbados, Saint Vincent and the Grenadines
1943	Belize
1946	Bahamas, Dominica, Saint Lucia
1958	Antigua and Barbuda, Grenada
1959	Anguilla, Saint Christopher (St. Kitts)/Nevis
1960	Montserrat
1969	Bermuda
1972	Cayman Islands
1984	Tortola

NA: Netherlands Antilles

YEAR FIRST COOPERATIVES ESTABLISHED IN LATIN AMERICA

1839	Mexico
1847	Brazil
1875	Argentina
1876	Honduras
1903	Venezuela

1904   Chile
1906   Guatemala
1909   Uruguay
1912   El Salvador
1914   Nicaragua
1916   Colombia
1919   Ecuador, Peru
1920   Costa Rica, Puerto Rico
1939   Bolivia
1942   Paraguay
1946   Dominican Republic
1951   Cuba
1954   Panama

YEAR FIRST COOPERATIVES ESTABLISHED IN NORTH AFRICA/NEAR EAST

1878   Israel (Palestine)
1901   Algeria
1905   Tunisia
1908   Egypt
1915   Libya
1922   Jordan, Morocco
1926   Iran
1930   Iraq
1933   Palestine (Arab)
1937   Lebanon
1941   Kuwait
1943   Syria
1958   Yemen
1961   Saudi Arabia
1965   Afghanistan
1972   United Arab Emirates
1973   Qatar

NA: Bahrain

Appendix 2
Types of Cooperatives by Country

These tables indicate the various major types of cooperatives that have been identified as operating in each country. They are identified as follows:

AGR	Agricultural Cooperatives
CON	Consumer Cooperatives
FIN	Financial Cooperatives
FSH	Fisheries Cooperatives
HSG	Housing Cooperatives
INS	Insurance Cooperatives
MUL	Multipurpose Cooperatives
PRO	Worker Productive Cooperatives
OTH	Other Types of Cooperatives

The information is presented by region as follows:

2A	Europe/North America
2B	Africa
2C	Asia/Pacific
2D	Caribbean
2E	Latin America
2F	North Africa/Near East

The designation NA is used in instances where data was unavailable for a country.

TYPES OF COOPERATIVES IN EUROPE/NORTH AMERICA

	AGR	CON	FIN	FSH	HSG	INS	MUL	PRO	OTH
Albania (NA)									
Armenia	x	x		x				x	x
Austria	x	x	x		x	x		x	x
Azerbaijan		x							
Belarus		x							
Belgium	x	x	x			x	x		x
Bosnia-Herzegovina	x								
Bulgaria	x	x				x		x	
Canada	x	x	x	x	x	x		x	x
Croatia	x		x	x	x				
Cyprus	x	x	x		x	x	x	x	x
Czech Republic	x	x			x			x	
Denmark	x	x	x	x	x	x		x	x
Estonia		x							
Finland	x	x	x		x	x		x	x
France	x	x	x	x	x	x		x	x
Georgia		x							
Germany	x	x	x		x	x			x
Greece	x	x				x			x
Hungary	x	x	x	x	x		x	x	
Iceland	x	x	x			x	x	x	
Ireland	x		x		x	x			x
Italy	x	x	x	x	x	x	x	x	x
Latvia	x	x						x	
Liechtenstein (NA)									
Lithuania		x			x				
Luxembourg	x	x	x		x	x			
Macedonia (NA)									

	AGR	CON	FIN	FSH	HSG	INS	MUL	PRO	OTH
Malta	x	x						x	x
Moldova		x							
Netherlands	x	x	x		x	x		x	x
Norway	x	x	x	x	x	x			x
Poland	x	x	x		x	x		x	x
Portugal	x	x	x	x	x			x	x
Romania		x	x					x	
Russia		x	x						
Slovakia	x	x			x	x		x	
Slovenia			x				x		x
Spain	x	x	x	x	x	x		x	x
Sweden	x	x	x	x	x	x		x	x
Switzerland	x	x	x			x		x	
Turkey	x	x	x	x	x			x	x
Ukraine		x	x		x			x	x
United Kingdom	x	x	x		x	x			x
United States	x	x	x	x	x	x		x	x
Yugoslavia	x	x	x	x					x

TYPES OF COOPERATIVES IN AFRICA

	AGR	CON	FIN	FSH	HSG	INS	MUL	PRO	OTH
Angola	x	x							
Benin	x	x	x	x	x			x	x
Botswana	x	x	x			x	x	x	
Burkina Faso	x	x					x	x	
Burundi	x			x				x	
Cameroon	x	x	x	x	x	x		x	x
Cape Verde	x	x	x	x			x	x	x
Cent. Afr. Rep.	x	x	x	x				x	

	AGR	CON	FIN	FSH	HSG	INS	MUL	PRO	OTH
Chad	x	x		x				x	
Congo	x	x		x				x	
Côte d'Ivoire	x		x	x				x	
Ethiopia	x	x	x		x			x	
Gabon	x								
Gambia	x	x	x						
Ghana	x	x	x	x	x	x	x	x	
Guinea	x				x			x	
Guinea-Bissau	x							x	
Kenya	x	x	x	x	x	x		x	x
Lesotho	x	x	x				x	x	x
Liberia	x	x	x					x	
Madagascar	x	x		x				x	x
Malawi	x	x	x				x		
Mali	x	x		x				x	
Mauritania	x	x		x				x	
Mauritius	x	x	x	x	x			x	
Mozambique	x	x	x	x				x	
Namibia	x								
Niger			x				x		x
Nigeria	x	x	x	x	x	x		x	x
Rwanda	x		x	x	x			x	x
Senegal	x	x	x	x	x		x	x	x
Seychelles	x	x	x					x	
Sierra Leone	x	x	x	x				x	x
Somalia	x	x		x	x			x	
South Africa	x		x						
Sudan	x	x		x		x	x	x	
Swaziland	x	x	x				x	x	

	AGR	CON	FIN	FSH	HSG	INS	MUL	PRO	OTH
Tanzania	x	x	x	x	x			x	
Togo	x	x	x	x				x	x
Uganda	x	x	x	x	x	x		x	x
Zaire		x	x					x	
Zambia	x	x	x	x		x	x		x
Zimbabwe	x	x	x	x			x	x	x

TYPES OF COOPERATIVES IN ASIA/PACIFIC

	AGR	CON	FIN	FSH	HSG	INS	MUL	PRO	OTH
Australia	x	x	x	x	x		x		x
Bangladesh	x		x	x	x		x	x	x
Brunei (NA)									
Cambodia (NA)									
China						x	x		
Cook Islands (NA)									
Fiji	x	x	x	x	x		x	x	x
Hong Kong	x		x						
India	x	x	x	x	x		x	x	x
Indonesia	x	x	x	x		x	x	x	x
Japan	x	x	x	x	x	x		x	x
Kazakhstan		x							
Kiribati	x	x	x						x
Korea (PDR)		x							
Korea (Rep)	x		x	x		x	x		x
Kyrgyzstan		x							
Laos	x	x						x	
Malaysia	x	x	x	x	x	x	x	x	x

	AGR	CON	FIN	FSH	HSG	INS	MUL	PRO	OTH
Micronesia	x	x	x	x					
Mongolia	x	x							
Myanmar	x	x	x					x	x
Nepal	x	x	x				x	x	x
New Zealand	x		x						
Pakistan	x	x	x	x	x	x	x	x	x
Papua New Guinea (NA)									
Philippines	x	x	x	x	x	x	x	x	x
Samoa (NA)									
Singapore		x	x		x	x	x	x	x
Solomon Islands	x	x	x	x	x		x	x	x
Sri Lanka	x	x	x	x			x	x	x
Taiwan	x	x	x					x	x
Tajikistan (NA)									
Thailand	x	x	x	x				x	
Tonga		x	x				x	x	x
Turkmenistan		x							
Tuvalu	x						x	x	x
Uzbekistan		x							
Vanuatu		x						x	
Vietnam	x						x		

TYPES OF COOPERATIVES IN THE CARIBBEAN

	AGR	CON	FIN	FSH	HSG	INS	MUL	PRO	OTH
Anguilla		x	x					x	x
Antigua & Barbuda	x	x	x					x	x
Bahamas	x	x	x	x	x			x	x
Barbados	x	x	x	x		x		x	

	AGR	CON	FIN	FSH	HSG	INS	MUL	PRO	OTH
Belize	x	x	x	x				x	x
Bermuda		x	x					x	
Cayman Islands			x						
Dominica	x	x	x	x				x	x
Grenada	x		x	x				x	x
Guadeloupe	x		x					x	x
Guyana	x	x	x	x	x			x	x
Haiti (NA)									
Jamaica	x	x	x	x	x	x		x	x
Montserrat	x		x	x					x
Neth. Antilles	x	x	x			x		x	
Saint Christopher/ Nevis	x		x	x				x	x
Saint Lucia	x	x	x	x				x	x
Saint Vincent			x	x					x
Suriname	x		x	x			x		x
Tortola			x	x					
Trinidad & Tobago	x	x	x	x		x			x

TYPES OF COOPERATIVES IN LATIN AMERICA

	AGR	CON	FIN	FSH	HSG	INS	MUL	PRO	OTH
Argentina	x	x	x		x	x		x	x
Bolivia	x	x	x	x	x	x		x	x
Brazil	x	x	x		x			x	x
Chile	x	x	x	x	x		x	x	x
Colombia	x	x	x		x	x		x	x
Costa Rica	x	x	x		x	x	x	x	x
Cuba	x								

	AGR	CON	FIN	FSH	HSG	INS	MUL	PRO	OTH
Dominican Republic	x	x	x	x	x	x	x	x	
Ecuador	x	x	x			x		x	
El Salvador	x		x	x		x			x
Guatemala	x	x	x	x	x	x		x	x
Honduras	x	x	x	x	x	x	x	x	x
Mexico	x	x	x	x	x			x	x
Nicaragua	x	x	x	x	x			x	x
Panama		x	x		x	x	x	x	x
Paraguay	x	x	x					x	x
Peru	x	x	x	x	x	x		x	x
Puerto Rico	x	x	x		x	x		x	x
Uruguay	x	x	x		x	x		x	
Venezuela	x	x	x	x	x			x	x

TYPES OF COOPERATIVES IN NORTH AFRICA/NEAR EAST

	AGR	CON	FIN	FSH	HSG	INS	MUL	PRO	OTH
Afghanistan	x	x						x	
Algeria	x	x	x		x			x	
Bahrain	x	x		x			x		
Egypt	x	x		x	x			x	
Iran	x	x	x		x		x	x	x
Iraq	x	x	x		x			x	x
Israel	x	x	x		x	x	x	x	x
Jordan	x	x	x	x	x		x	x	x
Kuwait	x	x	x				x	x	
Lebanon	x	x	x		x			x	x
Libya	x	x			x				

	AGR	CON	FIN	FSH	HSG	INS	MUL	PRO	OTH
Morocco	x	x	x	x	x		x	x	x
Palestine (Arab)	x	x		x	x		x	x	
Qatar		x							
Saudi Arabia	x	x		x			x	x	
Syria	x	x			x			x	
Tunisia	x		x			x			x
Un. Arab Emirates		x							
Yemen	x	x		x	x			x	

Appendix 3
Basic Data on Cooperatives by Country

These tables provide basic information about cooperatives in individual countries, arranged by the following categories:

First Cooperative.   Year in which the first established and formally acknowledged cooperative was identified in this country.

First Cooperative Law.   Year in which the first cooperative legislation was enacted in this country.

Statistics.   Most recent summary statistics regarding total number of cooperatives and total number of members identified in this country (abbreviated date of information).

Penetration.   The percentage of the total national population that were members of cooperatives at the time data was gathered.

They are presented regionally as follows:

- Europe/North America
- Africa
- Asia/Pacific
- Caribbean
- Latin America
- North Africa/Near East

BASIC COOPERATIVE DATA FOR EUROPE/NORTH AMERICA

Country	First Coop.	First Coop. Law	Statistics Number Coops(yr)	Statistics Number Members	Penetration
Albania	1946	na	na	na	na
Armenia	na	na	5,725(96)	571,065	16.5
Austria	1794	1873	1,485(96)	3,839,376	47.4
Azerbaijan	na	na	79(96)	660,000	9.0

Country	First Coop.	First Coop. Law	Statistics		
			Number Coops(yr)	Number Members	Penetration
Belarus	na	na	147(96)	1,927,100	18.5
Belgium	1848	1873	1,553(96)	3,597,262	35.4
Bosnia-Herzegovina	na	na	70(96)	na	na
Bulgaria	1863	1907	4,814(96)	1,213,000	14.0
Canada	1861	1949	7,870(96)	14,518,682	50.4
Croatia	na	na	1,211(96)	na	na
Cyprus-Greek	1909	1914	690(96)	515,352	69.2
Cyprus-Turkish	1909	1914	272(94)	28,227	21.1
Czech Republic	1852	1873	2,185(96)	1,381,583	13.4
Denmark	1851	na	1,445(98)	1,797,067	34.2
Estonia	1898	1917	30(96)	53,528	3.7
Finland	1870	1901	1,664(98)	2,337,374	45.8
France	1750	1887	23,573(96)	17,485,573	30.1
Georgia	1919	na	105(96)	200,000	3.8
Germany	1845	1867	10,320(96)	22,322,050	27.9
Greece	1780	1914	6,970(96)	1,043,381	9.9
Hungary	1850	1875	3,497(96)	3,013,000	29.6
Iceland	1844	1937	43(87)	46,804	20.0
Ireland	1859	1893	723(96)	2,123,576	59.5
Italy	1806	1886	39,025(96)	7,624,430	13.3
Latvia	1860	na	98(96)	305,400	15.0
Liechtenstein (na)					
Lithuania	1869	1917	99(96)	246,300	6.8
Luxembourg	1808	1884	63(98)	17,627	4.8
Macedonia (na)					
Malta	1946	1946	21(96)	5,016	1.3
Moldova	na	na	149(96)	595,320	13.3
Netherlands	1860	1855	2,492(97)	6,446,000	41.1
Norway	1851	1935	4,259(96)	1,597,668	36.4
Poland	1816	1920	13,774(96)	2,584,638+	na
Portugal	1871	1867	2,966(96)	2,134,670	21.9
Romania	1852	1903	na(96)	6,165,000	28.5
Russia	1825	1907	54,149(97)	14,122,628	9.5
Slovakia	1845	1873	1,108(96)	782,966	14.6
Slovenia	1851	na	174(96)	220,334	12.3
Spain	1838	1885	23,481(96)	4,336,502	11.1
Sweden	1850	1895	15,106(98)	4,779,540	53.7
Switzerland	1816	1881	1,651(96)	3,657,155	50.1

Country	First Coop.	First Coop. Law	Statistics		Penetration
			Number Coops(yr)	Number Members	
Turkey	1863	1867	50,150(98)	8,081,100	12.9
Ukraine	na	na	4,717(96)	6,189,815	12.2
United Kingdom	1750	1852	10,656(96)	9,652,000	16.6
United States	1750	1865	27,599(95)	150,692,000	56.7
Yugoslavia	1870	1925	1(88)	1,506,000	6.5

BASIC COOPERATIVE DATA FOR AFRICA

Country	First Coop.	First Coop. Law	Statistics		Penetration
			Number Coops(yr)	Number Members	
Angola	na	1975	940(79)	440,000	5.8
Benin	1947	1947	2,100(98)	191,000	3.3
Botswana	1964	1910	180(96)	77,736	5.3
Burkina Faso	1931	1947	160(88)	61,345	0.78
Burundi	1921	1921	207(88)	48,751	1.04
Cameroon	1924	1935	404(85)	na	na
Cape Verde	na	na	216(88)	20,165	4.5
Cent. African Rep.	1961	1947	29(85)	30,488	1.2
Chad	1949	1947	32(86)	3,600	0.07
Congo	1926	1947	841(81)	20,908	1.8
Cote d'Ivoire	1932	1947	3,342(96)	213,405	1.4
Ethiopia	1945	1960	4,274(94)	5,122,856	8.9
Gabon	1961	1946	40(84)	1,142	0.11
Gambia	1950	1951	na(96)	100,000	8.3
Ghana	1928	1931	8,085(86)	3,500,000	27.6
Guinea	1931	1947	104(89)	4,323	0.06
Guinea-Bissau	1971	1971	11(86)	326	0.03
Kenya	1908	1931	5,691(94/6)	2,700,430	10.0
Lesotho	1946	1948	517(94)	788,413	42.0
Liberia	1970	1936	408(90)	85,654	3.4
Madagascar	1931	1931	350(90)	33,712	0.28
Malawi	na	1946	140(94)	24,670	0.25
Mali	1919	1947	na	na	na
Mauritania	1926	1947	1,250(85)	53,500	5.2
Mauritius	1913	1913	547(94)	136,310	12.4

Country	First Coop.	First Coop. Law	Statistics		
			Number Coops(yr)	Number Members	Penetration
Mozambique	na	na	3,272(85)	1,174,260	8.5
Namibia	1913	na	na	na	na
Niger	1910	1947	1,167(92)	880,000	9.7
Nigeria	1930	1925	19,802(86)	1,784,941	1.8
Rwanda	1956	1949	241(86)	291,368	4.9
Senegal	1916	1947	2,766(93)	2,337,904	28.0
Seychelles	1961	1960	14(96)	9,282	12.0
Sierra Leone	1936	1939	1,084(86)	83,061	2.2
Somalia	1950	1969	813(94)	92,600	0.96
South Africa	1902	1922	461(92)	310,192	0.76
Sudan	1947	1948	9,848(94)	1,535,131	5.4
Swaziland	1931	1931	171(94)	17,430	1.7
Tanzania	1925	1932	8,909(94)	1,351,018	5.0
Togo	1931	1931	910(85)	58,410	1.9
Uganda	1913	1946	3,131(95)	637,015	3.2
Zaire	1923	1921	na	na	na
Zambia	1914	1930	1,805(93)	814,000	9.4
Zimbabwe	1902	1956	2,410(95)	272,144	2.4

BASIC COOPERATIVE DATA FOR ASIA/PACIFIC

Country	First Coop.	First Coop. Law	Statistics		
			Number Coops(yr)	Number Members	Penetration
Australia	1849	1881	9,232(92)	2,880,810	14.8
Bangladesh	1905	1904	130,022(94)	7,476,967	6.1
Brunei	1975	1975	100(96)	na	na
Cambodia	1954	1957	700(74)	430,000	7.7
China	1912	1928	32,000(92)	160,000,000	13.8
Cook Islands	1955	1953	54(72)	4,750	22.3
Fiji	1945	1947	532(96)	28,961	3.7
Hong Kong	1947	1947	204(84)	34,436	1.1
India	1900	1904	446,784(95)	182,921,000	19.7
Indonesia	1908	1915	32,249(92)	35,715,623	19.2
Japan	1843	1900	9,688(93)	57,527,085	45.9
Kazakhstan	na	na	1,309(96)	3,700,000	21.9
Kiribati	1956	1951	30(84)	24,191	39.5

Country	First Coop.	First Coop. Law	Statistics		
			Number Coops(yr)	Number Members	Penetration
Korea (PDR)	1907	na	3,524(85)	1,600,000	7.9
Korea (Rep.)	1907	1957	7,606(97)	19,957,598	43.4
Kyrgyzstan	na	na	43(96)	207,630	4.6
Laos	1978	1973	2,650(84)	na	na
Malaysia	1920	1920	3,554(95)	4,442,147	22.2
Micronesia	1960	1963	87(85)	na	na
Mongolia	1921	na	302(97)	25,057	1.0
Myanmar	1905	1904	38,220(95)	3,979,291	8.8
Nepal	1950	1959	3,208(96)	1,050,411	4.8
New Zealand	1881	1908	na	na	na
Pakistan	1904	1904	na(96)	9,391,926	7.3
Papua New Guinea	1946	1951	na	na	na
Philippines	1910	1915	13,346(91)	9,738,505	15.5
Samoa	1954	1960	na	na	na
Singapore	1925	1948	64(96)	971,257	27.3
Solomon Islands	1950	1953	85(95)	14,935	4.0
Sri Lanka	1906	1911	10,904(92/6)	4,549,800	24.5
Taiwan	1912	1913	4,375(84)	2,710,198	13.9
Tajikistan (na)					
Thailand	1917	1916	3,744(93)	5,843,961	9.8
Tonga	1964	1973	122(95)	6,679	4.9
Turkmenistan	na	na	250(92/6)	738,000	17.8
Tuvalu	1956	1951	5(86)	3,456	40.1
Uzbekistan	1893	na	385(93)	4,000,000	18.2
Vanuatu	1967	1962	94(94)	5,203	3.0
Vietnam	1912	1909	42,500(92)	20,000,000	28.9

BASIC COOPERATIVE DATA FOR THE CARIBBEAN

Country	First Coop.	First Coop. Law	Statistics		
			Number Coops(yr)	Number Members	Penetration
Anguilla	1959	1956	6(85)	na	na
Antigua and Barbuda*	1958	1958	10(96)	12,854	19.6

Country	First Coop.	First Coop. Law	Statistics		
			Number Coops(yr)	Number Members	Penetration
Bahamas*	1946	1974	30(82/96)	29,531	11.4
Barbados*	1940	1949	60(86/96)	24,758	9.6
Belize	1943	1948	155(88/96)	34,518	10.7
Bermuda	1969	na	3(86/96)	4,847	7.8
Cayman Islands	1972	na	1(96)	3,823	10.5
Dominica*	1946	1950	53(87/96)	65,180	78.6
Grenada*	1958	1955	36(87/96)	18,344	19.3
Guadeloupe	1932	1947	na	na	na
Guyana	1933	1948	1,505(85)	165,797	17.5
Haiti	1937	1939	300(90)	100,000	1.45
Jamaica*	1930	1949	225(86/96)	656,221	25.3
Martinique	1927	1947	na	na	na
Montserrat*	1960	1959	17(87/96)	4,326	33.8
Neth. Antilles	na	na	na(96)	17,000	8.1
St. Christopher/ Nevis*	1959	1956	33(84/96)	12,092	29.2
Saint Lucia*	1946	1946	34(84/96)	25,575	16.2
Saint Vincent*	1940	1954	22(84/96)	22,993	19.4
Suriname*	1920	1944	67(89/96)	14,382	1.6
Tortola *	1984	na	2(86/96)	233	1.6
Trinidad and Tobago*	1916	1919	333(85/96)	397,734	29.7

* The penetration percentages for these countries are extrapolations based on recent statistics maintained by WOCCU on credit union membership, combined with projections from the most recent data available (in many cases quite dated) for other types of cooperatives in the country. In each country the credit union membership constitutes the vast majority of total cooperative membership.

BASIC COOPERATIVE DATA FOR LATIN AMERICA

Country	First Coop.	First Coop. Law	Statistics		
			Number Coops(yr)	Number Members	Penetration
Argentina	1875	1905	8,142(91)	9,103,269	27.8
Bolivia	1939	1939	4,121(91)	447,490	6.4
Brazil	1847	1903	5,399(98)	3,741,667	2.3

Country	First Coop.	First Coop. Law	Statistics		Penetration
			Number Coops(yr)	Number Members	
Chile	1904	1924	1,960(91)	581,593	4.3
Colombia	1916	1918	1,936(96)	4,818,250	13.1
Costa Rica	1920	1925	359(92)	293,608	9.5
Cuba	1951	1960	na	na	na
Dominican Republic	1946	1952	238(88)	157,993	2.0
Ecuador	1919	1937	6,048(87)	898,295	9.02
El Salvador	1912	1905	1,039(93)	124,512	2.3
Guatemala	1906	1903	1,174(97)	277,134	2.9
Honduras	1876	1936	na(98)	225,000	4.0
Mexico	1839	1889	8,224(88)	633,105	0.75
Nicaragua	1914	1914	3,731(91)	92,137	2.4
Panama	1954	1916	327(92)	158,909	6.2
Paraguay	1942	1942	258(91)	142,936	3.3
Peru	1919	1913	4,130(95)	312,360	1.4
Puerto Rico	1920	1920	295(95)	1,028,077	27.0
Uruguay	1909	1912	740(91)	586,395	18.9
Venezuela	1903	1910	791(91)	202,812	1.0

BASIC COOPERATIVE DATA FOR NORTH AFRICA/NEAR EAST

Country	First Coop.	First Coop. Law	Statistics		Penetration
			Number Coops(yr)	Number Members	
Afghanistan	1965	1968	671(86)	147,600	0.9
Algeria	1901	1893	na	na	na
Bahrain	na	na	17(94)	8,218	1.5
Egypt	1908	1923	18,165(94)	11,466,200	20.3
Iran	1926	1952	35,085(97)	9,240,120	14.0
Iraq	1930	1944	2,600(92)	1,200,000	6.5
Israel	1878	1920	2,677(94)	1,877,276	38.3
Jordan	1922	1952	699(96)	72,722	1.7
Kuwait	1941	1962	49(92)	177,254	7.7
Lebanon	1937	1941	283(84)	32,007	1.2
Libya	1915	1956	1,451(79)	489,168	15.9
Morocco	1922	1922	9,635(95)	675,589	2.5

Country	First Coop.	First Coop. Law	Statistics		
			Number Coops(yr)	Number Members	Penetration
Palestine (Arab)	1933	1920	531(94)	43,117	na
Qatar	1973	1973	10(94)	4,958	1.1
Saudi Arabia	1961	1962	179(94)	54,697	3.4
Syria	1943	1950	6,096(94)	1,441,483	10.5
Tunisia	1905	1907	352(85)	81,195	1.1
United Arab Emirates	1972	1976	53(94)	8,603	0.3
Yemen	1958	1961	258(90)	212,545	2.2

Bibliography

CONTENTS

I. Introduction   450

II. General Reference Resources   451
     A. Cooperative Bibliographies
     B. Cooperative Dictionaries/Lexicons
     C. Cooperative Manuals
     D. Cooperative Directories
     E. Cooperative Biography

III. Cooperative Theory and Practice   456
     A. Literature by or about 19th-Century Theorists
     B. 20th-Century Theory and Practice
        1. Theories of Cooperation
           a. General Theories
           b. Religious Bases of Cooperation
           c. Sociobiology and Cooperation
           d. Human Solidarity as the Basis for Cooperation (Utilitarianism, Humanism)
           e. Cooperation, Mutualism and the Social Economy
           f. Socialism and Cooperation
           g. Cooperation and Marxism
           h. Rochdale Principles of Cooperation
        2. Reformulating Cooperative Principles
        3. Organizing Cooperation
        4. Cooperation and Society
           a. Cooperation as Economic Democracy
           b. Cooperation and Economic Development
           c. Cooperation and the Poor
           d. Cooperation and Peace
           e. Social Impacts of Cooperation
           f. Cooperation as the Basis for a Future Society
        5. Economics of Cooperation

6. Cooperation—Comparisons with Other Socio-Economic Systems
7. Cooperation and Competition
8. Nurturing Cooperation
9. Cooperation in Developing Countries

IV. Types of Cooperatives   489
  A. Agricultural Cooperatives
    1. Agricultural Cooperatives—Bibliographies
    2. Agricultural Cooperatives—Early Experience—Through World War I (1919)
    3. Agricultural Cooperatives—Theory and Practice
    4. Agricultural Cooperatives in Europe
    5. Agricultural Cooperatives in North America
    6. Agricultural Cooperatives in Developing Countries
  B. Dairy Cooperatives
  C. Agricultural Credit Cooperatives
  D. Marketing Cooperatives
  E. Communal Settlements
    1. Theory and Practice—General
      a. Communes
      b. Group Farming
    2. China—Communes
    3. Israel—Kibbutz and Moshav
      a. Kibbutz
      b. Moshav
    4. Mexico—Ejidos
    5. Soviet Union—Collective Farms
    6. Tanzania—Ujamaa Villages
    7. United States
    8. Other Countries
  F. Consumer Cooperatives
    1. Consumer Cooperatives—Early Experience—Through World War I (1919)
    2. Consumer Cooperatives—Theory and Practice
    3. Consumer Cooperatives—Organization and Management
    4. Consumer Cooperatives in Europe
    5. Consumer Cooperatives in North America
    6. Consumer Cooperatives in Developing Countries
    7. Consumer Cooperatives—"New Wave Coops"
  G. Financial Cooperatives
    1. Cooperative Banks

    2. Savings and Credit Cooperatives
    3. Credit Unions
       a. Credit Union History and Theory
       b. Credit Union Operations/Management
       c. Credit Unions in Canada
       d. Credit Unions in Canada—Desjardins Movement
       e. Credit Unions in the United States
       f. Credit Unions—Other Countries
H. Fisheries Cooperatives
 I. Forestry Cooperatives
 J. Housing Cooperatives
    1. Housing Cooperatives—Theory and Practice
    2. Housing Cooperatives—Operations and Management
    3. Housing Cooperatives in Europe
    4. Housing Cooperatives in North America
    5. Housing Cooperatives in Developing Countries
K. Industrial Cooperatives
    1. Industrial Cooperatives—Early Experience—Through World War I (1919)
    2. Industrial Cooperatives—1920 to 1995
       a. Industrial Cooperatives—Theory and History
       b. Industrial Cooperatives—Operations and Management
       c. Industrial Cooperatives—National Experiences
          (1) Industrial Cooperatives in Europe
          (2) Mondragon Cooperatives in Spain
          (3) Industrial Cooperatives in North America
          (4) Industrial Cooperatives in Developing Countries
    3. Handicraft Cooperatives
    4. Disabled Persons' Cooperatives
    5. Public Utilities/Services Cooperatives
       a. Electricity Cooperatives
       b. Irrigation Cooperatives
       c. Telephone Cooperatives
    6. Services Cooperatives
       a. Health Care Cooperatives
       b. Cooperative Nurseries/Preschools
       c. Funeral/Memorial Cooperatives
       d. Petroleum Cooperatives
       e. Transport Cooperatives
L. Insurance Cooperatives

M. Multipurpose Cooperatives
N. School and Youth Cooperatives
   1. School Cooperatives—Theory and Practice
   2. School Cooperatives—Operation and Management
   3. School Cooperatives—Curriculum Materials
   4. School Cooperatives—National Experiences
   5. Youth Cooperatives
V. Cooperative Functions and Activities   557
A. Administration and Finance in Cooperatives
   1. Operation and Management of Cooperatives
     a. General Works
     b. Operational Manuals
   2. Cooperative Finance
     a. Financing Cooperatives
     b. Financial Controls
   3. Membership Participation and Control
   4. Cooperatives as Employers
B. Cooperative Education and Training
   1. Cooperative Education and Training—Theory and History
   2. Cooperative Education and Training—Organization and Management
   3. Cooperative Education and Training—Types of Training
     a. Cooperative Leadership
     b. Cooperative Members
     c. Cooperative Employees
     d. General Public
   4. Cooperative Education and Training—Facilities
     a. Cooperative Training Centers
     b. Colleges and Universities
   5. Cooperative Education and Training—Curriculum Materials
   6. Cooperative Education and Training—Some National Experiences
C. Cooperative Communications
D. Women in Cooperatives
   1. Women in Cooperatives—Historical Developments
   2. Women in Cooperatives—General Literature
   3. Women in Cooperatives—Some National Experiences
   4. Women in Cooperatives—Integration versus Separation
E. Trade Unions and Cooperatives
F. Research and Evaluation in Cooperatives

     1. Research on Cooperatives
     2. Evaluation of Cooperatives
VI. Cooperatives and the State   577
   A. Cooperatives and the State—General Literature
   B. De-officialization of Cooperatives
   C. Cooperative Legislation/Law
     1. Cooperative Law—Early Literature—Through World War I (1919)
     2. Cooperative Law—Literature—1920 to 1995
VII. Cooperative Experience and/or Histories   581
   A. Precooperative Traditions
   B. Histories of Early Cooperative Activity
   C. General Cooperative Histories—20th Century
     1. Cooperative Histories—Published 1900 to 1950
     2. Cooperative Histories—Published 1951 to 1995
   D. Regional Cooperative Experience
     1. Cooperative Experience—Europe
     2. Cooperative Experience—Eastern Europe
     3. Cooperative Experience—North America
     4. Cooperative Experience—Developing Countries
       a. Cooperative Experience—Developing Countries—General
       b. Cooperative Experience—Africa
       c. Cooperative Experience—Asia/Pacific
       d. Cooperative Experience—Caribbean
       e. Cooperative Experience—Latin America
       f. Cooperative Experience—Near East and North Africa
     5. Assistance to Cooperatives in Developing Countries
VIII. International Cooperative Organizations   603
   A. International Cooperative Alliance
   B. International Raiffeisen Union
   C. World Council of Credit Unions
IX. The United Nations System and Cooperatives   604
   A. United Nations Secretary General's Reports
   B. United Nations Secretariat
   C. United Nations Regional Economic Commissions
     1. Economic Commission for Africa
     2. Economic Commission for Asia and the Pacific
     3. Economic Commission for Latin America and the Caribbean
   D. Food and Agriculture Organization (FAO)

E. International Labour Office (ILO)
F. United Nations Center for Human Settlements (HABITAT)
G. United Nations Development Program (UNDP)
H. United Nations Educational, Scientific and Cultural Organization (UNESCO)
I. United Nations Fund for Women (UNIFEM)
J. United Nations Industrial Development Organization (UNIDO)
K. United Nations Conference on Trade and Development (UNCTAD)/General Agreement on Tariffs and Trade (GATT)

I. INTRODUCTION

Few, save the most avid of cooperators, are aware of the extensiveness of the literature that has been produced on cooperatives and their development. There are a few inclusive collections around the world, but mostly the literature is diffused and found in special collections at universities and cooperative institutions with a research interest. Bits and pieces will be found in small libraries of cooperative organizations, and many cooperators will have their own selected sources dealing with cooperative theory and practice or other topics of local or personal interest.

Attempts have been made over the years to collect and publish references to the literature, the first by the ICA in its 1906 publication *International Cooperative Bibliography,* London: P. S. King and Son, prepared in English, French and German. The next major undertaking was the publication by the ILO of a special *Bibliography* supplement to its journal, *Cooperative Information*, in 1973, and additions in subsequent years. This series undertook to catalogue all books it could identify that had been written about cooperatives from 1813 to 1975.

Efforts to keep abreast of important new cooperative literature have been undertaken by the editors of the ICA *Review of International Cooperation* and the Plunkett Foundation *Year Book of Agricultural Cooperation,* both of which at different times have included bibliographical citations in their publications. A similar effort regarding literature relating to cooperatives in developing countries, the ICA-sponsored *Research Register of Studies on Cooperatives in Developing Countries and Selected Bibliography, Volumes 1–20,* covered literature produced during the period 1968–1988.

The principal library collections that the author had access to and found useful were those of the ICA and the ILO in Geneva, the FAO in Rome and the United States Library of Congress in Washington, D.C. In addition, Alina Pawlowska, documentation officer of the ICA in Geneva, was an important personal source, making fully available her paper and electronic files so that ICA sources would be well represented. Similar sources would have no doubt been identified in other national libraries and in the libraries of a number of cooperative educational and research institutions, had there been an opportunity to make a personal worldwide survey.

Confronted with the volume of information available and the limitation of space in this publication, certain choices had to be made regarding what to include. First, I decided that, with a few exceptions, only references to books and other free standing publications would be included. This required the exclusion of an extensive and valuable literature published as articles in journals and periodicals. I acknowledge that not all that is important to be said about cooperatives is found in books!

Cooperative literature appears in many languages, all important. The most extensive productions, however, have been in English, French, German and Spanish. These were, therefore, the main language sources I chose for this bibliography. I acknowledge that, because of this choice, important literature in Arabic, Chinese, Italian, Japanese, Polish, Portuguese, Russian, Swedish and a number of other languages in both industrialized and developing countries is not included. In the era of computers, hopefully, someone someday will be able to include a more comprehensive listing.

While an attempt is made to present a worldwide vision of cooperatives in this publication, English-language sources predominate. This is in practical recognition of the fact that the publisher is located in the United States, the text is in English, and the book will tend to be more readily available and usable where English is spoken or is a working language. It is not meant to imply that cooperative visions occur or cooperative work is best done in any one language.

A number of acronyms and abbreviations are used in the bibliography as a way of saving space. A list of these is found at the front of the book.

II. GENERAL REFERENCE RESOURCES

II. A. Cooperative Bibliographies

Annotated Bibliography of Literature Produced by the Cooperative Movements in South-East Asia. New Delhi: ICA, ROECSEA, 1964.

Baden, Anne Laura, compiler. *Cooperation in the United States and Foreign Countries.* Washington, D.C.: Library of Congress, Division of Bibliography, 1943.

Une bibliographie de la coopération dans le Pacifique sud. Noumea, New Caledonia: South Pacific Commission, 1953.

Bibliography of Canadian Writings on Cooperation 1900–1950. Ottawa: CUC, 1960.

Bibliography on Cooperation. New Delhi: NCUI, Committee for Cooperative Training, 1963.

Bibliography on Cooperation and Social and Economic Development. Madison: University of Wisconsin, International Cooperative Training Center, 1964.

Bibliography on Cooperatives. Georgetown, Guyana: Public Free Library, 1971.

Bibliography. Survey of Cooperative Literature From 1813 to 1973—List of Written Works on Cooperation. Cooperative Information 1973, Supplement 1. Geneva: ILO, 1973. Five Additions to this publication were issued as follows: 1st Addition, *Cooperative Information,* ILO, Geneva (2, 1973): 101 ff; 2nd Addition, *Cooperative Information,* ILO, Geneva (1, 1974): 105–148; 3rd Addition, *Cooperative Information,* ILO, Geneva (2, 1974): 117–158; 4th Addition, *Cooperative Information,* ILO, Geneva (1, 1975): 125–155; 5th Addition, *Cooperative Information,* ILO, Geneva (3, 1975): 155–207.

Bibliothekskatalog der Genossenschaftsliteratur der Deutschen Genossenschaftskasse. Frankfurt: Deutsche Genossenschaftskasse, 1971.

Bolaños V., Rafael Angel, eds. *Bibliografía sobre cooperativismo disponible en Costa Rica.* Rodrigo Facio City University: Universidad de Costa Rica, Vicerectoría de Investigación, Instituto de Investigaciones Sociales, 1985.

Books on the Cooperative Movement. Jerusalem: Hebrew University. Jewish National and University Library, 1954.

Casselman, Paul. *Cooperation.* Ottawa: Université d'Ottawa, Centre social, 1953.

Cooperation. New York: Russell Sage Foundation Library, 1921.

Cooperatives and International Development: An Annotated Bibliography. Saskatoon: Cooperative College of Canada, 1985.

Les coopératives: bibliographie. Abidjan, Côte d'Ivoire: INADES-documentation, 1983.

Cooperativismo: bibliografía. Mexico City: Centro de Documentación Laboral, 1982.

Deschenes, Gaston. *Le mouvement coopératif québecois: guide bibliographique.* Montreal: Editions du jour, 1980.

Dix ans de documentation intercoopérative (1972–1982). Paris: Service de documentation intercoopérative, 1982.

Dunne, Janeen. *Cooperatives, An Annotated Bibliography.* Cape Town: South African Labor and Development Research Unit, 1991.

Exposición universitaria del libro cooperativo: Catálogo de la II. La Plata, Argentina: Universidad Nacional, Instituto de Estudios Cooperativos, 1964.

Films on Cooperation: An Annotated Bibliography of Cooperative Films. New Delhi: ICA, ROECSEA, 1975.

Gascon, H. *Bibliografía hispánica de cooperación y cooperativas.* Madrid: Editorial de Historia, 1960.

Genossenschaftliche Bibliographie selbständiger Werke in deutscher Sprache. Frankfurt: Deutsche Genossenschaftskasse, 1957.

A Guide to Publications on Cooperatives. Saskatoon: Cooperative College of Canada, 1974.

Gyllstrom, Bjorn, and Hans Holmen. *Bibliography on Cooperatives and Development.* Lund, Sweden: University of Lund, 1985.

Hill, Patricia M., Maryjean McGrath, and Elena Reyes. *Cooperative Bibliography: An Annotated Guide to Works in English About Cooperatives and Cooperation.* Madison: University of Wisconsin, University Center for Cooperatives, 1981.

ICA. *International Cooperative Bibliography.* London: P. S. King and Son, 1906. (Also in French and German.)

ICA, ROAP, Publications—Part 1 (microform). New Delhi: Library of Congress, 1993; Washington, D.C.: Library of Congress Photoduplication Service, 1993.

ICA, ROECSEA, Library Catalogue of Collection 1960–1976. New Delhi: ICA, ROECSEA, 1978.

International Working Party of Cooperative Librarians and Documentation Officers. *Basic Books on Cooperative Movements.* London: ICA, 1976. (Also in French and German.)

Lamming, Anne. *Select International Cooperative Bibliography.* London: ICA, 1970.

Maggiolo, V. Lorenzo, and Augusto M. Celis. *Bibliografía sobre cooperativas.* Valencia, Venezuela: Ediciones de la Universidad de Carabobo, 1968.

Periodicals and Journals of Historical and Cooperative Interest Contained In The Library of the Cooperative Union Ltd., Manchester. Manchester: Coop Union, 1975.

Plunkett Foundation for Cooperative Studies. *Year Book of Agricultural Cooperation.* Oxford: Blackwell. (Published annually from 1927 through 1986; in 1987 renamed *Yearbook of Cooperative Enterprise*—each *Year Book* contains a selected bibliography covering a variety of cooperative subjects.)

Research Register of Studies on Cooperatives in Developing Countries and Selected Bibliography, Volumes 1–20. Geneva: ICA (in collaboration with the Polish and Hungarian Cooperative Research Institutes), 1975–1988. (Includes literature published 1968–1988.)

Sager, Tore. *Bibliography of Cooperative Economics, 1920–1975: Books and Articles in English, French, German, and Scandinavian.* Monticello, Ill.: Vance Bibliographies, 1979.

Saskatchewan. Department of Cooperation and Cooperative Development. *Bibliography of Canadian Writings on Cooperation 1900–1950.* Ottawa: CUC, 1960.

Select Bibliography on Cooperation. London: Plunkett, 1954.

Select Bibliography on Cooperation. Rome: FAO, 1957.

Selected International Cooperative Bibliography. London: ICA, 1970.

Serugendo, Emmanuel. *Le mouvement coopératif.* Butare, Rwanda: Université du Rwanda, Campus universitaire de Butare, Bibliothèque Centrale, 1988.

Studies of the Cooperative Project. New York: WPA, Division of Study of Cooperation, Project #465-97-3-18, Bibliographies and Indices of Special Subjects, 1938–1942.

United States. Agricultural Adjustment Administration. *Sources of Information Regarding Cooperatives*. Washington, D.C.: GPO, 1935.

Verzeichnis der genossenschaftlichen Literatur der Schweiz: Zusammengestellt auf Veranlassung des internationalen Genossenschaftsbundes. Basel: VSK, 1904.

II. B. Cooperative Dictionaries/Lexicons

Badawi, Ahmad Zaki. *Mu'jam al-mustalahat al-tijariyah wa-al-ta'awuniyah, Inkilizi-Arabi-Faransi. (A Dictionary of Commerce and Cooperatives, English-Arab-French)*. Beirut: Dar al-Nahdah al-Arabiyah, 1984. (Arabic)

Bänsch, Axel. *Genossenschaftliches Wörterbuch*. Bern: H. Lang, 1972.

Bogardus, Emory S. *Dictionary of Cooperation, Including Encyclopedic Materials*. New York: CLUSA, 1948.

Bottini, E. *Terminología cooperativa*. Buenos Aires: Asociación pro Instituto de Estudios Cooperativos, 1961.

A Cooperator's Dictionary. Nairobi: Cooperative College of Kenya, 1972.

Dulfer, E., ed. *International Handbook of Cooperative Organizations*. Göttingen, Germany: Vandenhoeck and Ruprecht, [n.d.].

Glossaire coopératif (allemand, français, anglais, espagnol). Bonn: Freier Ausschuss der Deutschen Genossenschaftsverbände, 1965.

Gyula, Ferenczy. *Otnyelvu ipari szovetkezeti szotar: magyar, angol, nemet, francia, orosz*. Budapest: Ipari Szovetkezetek Orsazagos Tanacsa Oktatasi Kozpont, 1977. (Hungarian)

Henriques. *Kamus koperasi lima bahasa. (Cooperative Dictionary in 5 Languages: Indonesian, English, Dutch, German, and French.)* Bandung, Indonesia: Angkasa, 1993. (Indonesian)

International Cooperative Alliance. *Vocabulary of Cooperative Terms*. London: ICA, 1974.

Lamming, Anne, ed. *A Cooperator's Dictionary: A Basic List of Cooperative and Commercial Terms for Use at Primary Level in Developing Countries*. London: ICA, CEMAS, 1977.

Mändle, Eduard, and Hans-Werner Winter, eds. *Handwörterbuch des Genossenschaftswesens*. Wiesbaden, Germany: Deutscher Genossenschafts-Verlag, 1980.

McLanahan, Jack and Connie, eds. *Cooperative/Credit Union Dictionary and Reference (including encyclopedic materials)*. Richmond, Ky.: Cooperative Alumni Association, 1990.

Olivera, Julio. *Diccionario de Economía y cooperativismo*. Buenos Aires: COGTAL, 1970.

Osuustoimintaan liittyviä sanoja ja mimityksiä (Vocabulaire coopératif finois, suédois, anglais, français, allemand). Helsinki: Kesutusosuukuntien Keskusliitto, 1971. (Finnish)

Pinho Diva, Benevides. *Dicionário de cooperativismo*. Sao Paulo: E. Dotto Garcia, 1961. (Portuguese)

Sources of Cooperative Information. Geneva: ICA, CEMAS, 1985.
Totomiants, Vakhan, and Robert Schloesser. *Internationales Handwörterbuch des Genossenschaftswesens.* Berlin: Stuppe und Winckler, 1928.

II. C. Cooperative Manuals

Alanne, Veino. *Manual for Cooperative Directors.* Superior, Wis.: Cooperative Publishing Association, 1938.
Hall, F. *Handbook for Members of Cooperative Committees.* Manchester: Coop Union, 1928.
Kellershals, W., and C. Kamp. *Manual for Cooperative Libraries and Documentation Services.* London: ICA, 1968. (Also in German.)
Totomiants, Vakhan. *Manuel abrégé de la coopération.* Bucharest: Banque centrale coopérative, 1937.

II. D. Cooperative Directories

Baulier, Françoise, and Anne Lamming. *Directory of Cooperative Libraries and Documentation Services.* London: ICA, 1974.
Bayley, J. E. *Directory of Cooperative Research and Education in the UK, Ireland and Europe.* Oxford: Plunkett, 1981.
Cooperative Education Directory: Directory of Cooperative Colleges, Training Centers and University Institutes. London: ICA, 1972.
Cooperative Information—1975, Supplement No. 3. Directory of Cooperative Organizations: Africa South of the Sahara. Geneva: ILO, 1975.
Cooperative Trade Directory for South-East Asia. New Delhi: ICA, ROECSEA, 1967.
Directory of Agencies Assisting Cooperatives in Developing Countries. Rome: COPAC, 1993. (Issued periodically.)
Directory of Cooperative Organizations in South-East Asia. New Delhi: ICA, ROECSEA, 1966. (Issued periodically.)
Dülfer, Eberhard. *Training Facilities for Cooperative Personnel in African Countries.* Rome: FAO, 1971.
International Directory of Cooperative Organizations. 13th Edition, Geneva: ILO, 1988. (12th Edition, 1971; 11th Edition, 1958; 10th Edition, 1939; 9th Edition, 1936; 8th Edition, 1933; 7th Edition, 1929; 6th Edition, 1927; 5th Edition, 1925; 4th Edition, 1924; 3rd Edition, 1923; 2nd Edition, 1922; 1st Edition, 1920—"Répertoire international des coopératives.")

II. E. Cooperative Biography

Evans, J. N. *Great Figures in the Labor Movement.* Oxford: Pergamon Press, 1965.
Garnett, R. G. *William Pare Cooperator and Social Reformer.* Coop Union, Education Department: Loughborough, U.K., 1973.

Homage à Edgard Milhaud (1873–1964). CIRIEC: Liège, 1964.

Knapp, Joseph G., et al. *Great American Cooperators: Bibliographical Sketches of 101 Major Pioneers in Cooperative Development.* Washington, D.C.: AIC, 1967.

Protagonists and Figures of Catholic Cooperation, 1893–1963. Edizioni di Casse Rurali ed Artigiane: Rome, [n.d.].

Thompson, David J. *Weavers of Dreams—Founders of the Modern Cooperative Movement.* Davis, Calif.: Center for Cooperatives, University of California, 1994.

A Tribute to Bernard Lavergne, 5th December 1972. Brussels: CIRIEC, 1972.

Webb, C. *Lives of Great Men and Women: A Short Biography of Some Heroes and Friends of Cooperation.* Manchester: Coop Union, 1911.

III. COOPERATIVE THEORY AND PRACTICE

III. A. Literature by or about 19th-Century Theorists

Blanc, Louis, 1811–1882

Blanc, Louis. *Organisation du travail.* Paris: Bureau de la Société de l'industrie fraternelle, 1848.

—— ——. *Organisation der Arbeit.* Berlin: R. L. Prager, 1899.

—— ——. *Organization of Work.* Cincinnati, Ohio: University Press, 1911.

Keller, Paul. *Louis Blanc und die Revolution von 1848.* Zurich: Girsberger, 1926.

Laurens, E. *Louis Blanc.* Paris: Rousseau, 1908.

Loubère, Leo A. *Louis Blanc: His Life and His Contribution to the Rise of French Jacobin-Socialism.* Evanston, Ill.: Northwestern University Press, 1961; reissued, Westport, Conn.: Greenwood Press, 1980.

Buchez, Philippe Joseph Benjamin, 1796–1865

Cuvillier, A. *Une des premières coopératives de production: L'Association buchézienne des bijouteries en Doré (1834–1873).* Paris: Rivière, 1933.

Desroche, Henri. *La tradition buchézienne. Enquête sur la proprieté collective dans l'histoire du socialisme coopératif.* Paris: BECC, 1957.

Geissberger, Werner P. *Philippe Joseph Benjamin Buchez, Theoritiker einer christlichen Sozialökonomie und Pionier der Produktiv-genossenschaften.* Winterthur, Switzerland: P. G. Keller, 1956.

Isambert, François A. *Politique, religion et science de l'homme chez Philippe Buchez.* Paris: Cujas, 1967.

Petri, Barbara P. *The Historical Thought of P. J. B. Buchez.* Washington, D.C.: Catholic University of America Press, 1958.

Cabet, Etienne, 1788–1856

Cabet, Etienne. *Oeuvres d'Etienne Cabet.* Paris: Anthropos, 1970.

————. *Voyage en Icaris*. Paris: Bureau du populaire, 1848; reissued, Clifton, N.J.: A. M. Kelley, 1973.

————. *Travels in Icaria*. Macomb: Western Illinois University, 1985.

Prudhommeaux, J. *Icarie et son fondateur Etienne Cabet*. Paris: Cornély, 1907; reissued, Philadelphia: Porcupine Press, 1972.

Crüger, Hans, 1859–1927

Crüger, Hans. *Einführung in das deutsche Genossenschaftswesen*. Berlin: Guttentag, 1907.

————. *Grundriss des deutschen Genossenschaftswesens*. Leipzig: Gloeckner, 1908.

————. *Der heutige Stand des deutschen Genossenschaftswesens*. Berlin: L. Simion, 1898.

————. *Der Internationale Genossenschafts-Kongress in Paris im Jahre 1900*. Berlin: Guttentag, 1901.

Crüger, Hans, and H. Jäger, eds. *Rohstoffgenossenschaften der Handwerker und Anleitung zur Buchführung einer Rohstoffgenossenschaft*. Berlin: Guttentag, 1896.

de Boyve, Edouard, 1840–1923

de Boyve, Edouard. *Histoire de la coopération à Nîmes et son influence sur le mouvement coopératif en France*. Paris: [n.p.], 1889.

————. *Histoire et préliminaires du premier Congrès de sociétés coopératives de France à Paris en 1885*. Paris: Alcan, 1921.

Fourier, François Marie Charles, 1772–1837

Bebel, August. *Charles Fourier*. Stuttgart: Dietz, 1890; reissued, Frankfurt-am-Main: Röderberg-Verlag, 1978.

Bo, Giuseppe Del. *Charles Fourier e la Scuola Societaria, 1801–1922*. Milan: Feltrinelli, 1957.

Considérant, Victor. *Exposition abrégée du système phalanstérien de Fourier*. Paris: Librairie sociétaire, 1846.

Desroche, Henri. *Fouriérisme écrit et fouriérisme pratiqué*. Paris: Éditions de minuit, 1957.

Fourier, Charles. *Le nouveau monde industriel et sociétaire*. Paris: Bossange, 1829; reissued, Paris: Flammarion, 1973.

————. *Selections From the Works of Fourier*. New York: Gordon Press, 1972.

————. *Social Science: The Theory of the Universal Unity*. New York: American News Company, 1900.

————. *Théorie de l'unité universelle*. Paris: [n.p.], 1834.

————. *Théorie des quatre mouvements et des destinées générales*. Lyon: [n.p.], 1808; reissued, Paris: J.-J. Pauvert, 1967; Vienna: Europa Verlag, 1966 (German); Cambridge, U.K. and New York: Cambridge University Press, 1996 (English).

————. *The Utopian Vision of Charles Fourier: Selected Texts on Work, Love, and Passionate Attraction.* Columbia: University of Missouri Press, 1983.

Gide, Charles. *Fourier, précurseur de la coopération and Revue des études coopération.* Paris: Association pour l'enseignement de la coopération, 1927.

Institut français de la coopération. *Homage à Charles Fourier, 1772–1837.* Paris: Institut français de la coopération, 1972.

Poisson, E. *Fourier.* Paris: Librairie F. Alan, 1932.

Riasanovsky, Nicholas V. *The Teaching of Charles Fourier.* Berkeley: University of California Press, 1969.

Schérer, Rene. *Charles Fourier: ou, la contestation globale,* Paris: Seghers, 1970.

Garrido Tortosa, Fernando, 1821–1883

Garrido Tortosa, F. *La cooperación, estudio teorético-prá ctico.* Barcelona: Consejo de Ciento, 1879.

————. *El trabajador asociado.* Bilbao: Zero, 1873.

Gide, Charles, 1847–1932

Desroches, Henri. *Charles Gide (1847–1932): Trois étapes d'une créativité: Coopérative, sociale, universitaire.* Paris: Coopérative d'information et d'édition mutualiste, 1982.

Díaz Arana, Juan J. *Un economista, Charles Gide maestro de la cooperación.* Buenos Aires: Federación Argentina de Cooperativas de Consumo, 1947.

Gide, Charles. *Almanach de la coopération française.* Paris: Union coopérative des sociétés française de consommation, 1896.

————. *Les associations coopératives agricoles.* Paris: Association pour l'enseignement de la coopération, 1928.

————. *Les colonies communistes et coopératives.* Paris: Association pour l'enseignement de la coopération, 1928.

————. *Communist and Cooperative Colonies.* New York: Crowell, 1930; reissued, New York: AMS Press, 1974.

————. *Consumers' Cooperative Societies.* Manchester: Coop Union, 1921; London: T. F. Unwin, 1921; New York: A. A. Knopf, 1921; reissued, New York: Haskell House, 1971.

————. *La coopération.* Paris: Larose, 1900.

————. *La coopération à l'école primaire.* Paris: FNCC, 1927.

————. *La coopération à l'étranger, Angleterre et Russie.* Paris: [n.p.], 1926.

————. *La coopération dans les pays latins.* Paris: Association pour l'enseignement de la coopération, 1925.

————. *Les coopératives de construction.* Paris: Association pour l'enseignement de la coopération, 1924.

————. *Cooperativismo.* Buenos Aires: Federación Argentina de Cooperativas de Consumo, 1944.

————. *L'école de Nîmes.* Paris: PUF, 1947.

————. *Le juste prix.* Paris: PUF, 1922; reissued, 1941.

————. *Die Konsumgenossenschaftsbewegung in Frankreich und in den Vereinigten Staaten von Amerika.* Munich and Leipzig: Duncker und Humblot, 1924.

————. *Der Kooperativismus.* Halberstadt: H. Meyer, 1929.

————. *La lutte contre la cherté et la coopération.* Paris: Association pour l'enseignement de la coopération, 1925.

————. *Principes d'économie politique.* Paris: Sirey, 1931.

————. *Profit dans les coopératives.* Paris: Association pour l'enseignement de la coopération, 1923.

————. *Le programme coopératiste.* Paris: Association pour l'enseignement de la coopération, 1924.

————. *La question du logement et la coopération.* Paris: Association pour l'enseignement de la coopération, 1923.

————. *Las sociedades cooperativas de consumo.* Mexico: Talleres Gráficos de la Nación, 1924.

————. *Les sociétés coopératives de consommation.* Paris: Sirey, 1904; reissued, Paris: L. Tenin, 1917.

————. *La solidarité.* Paris: PUF, 1932.

Gide, Charles, and Charles Rist. *Histoire des doctrines économiques depuis les physiocrates jusqu'à nos jours.* Paris: Sirez, 1909.

————. *A History of Economic Doctrines From the Time of the Physiocrats to the Present Day.* Boston: D. C. Heath, 2nd English edition, 1948.

Lavondès. A. *Charles Gide: Un apôtre de la coopération.* Uzès, France: La Capitelle, 1953.

Miyajima, T. *Souvenirs sur Charles Gide, 1847–1932.* Paris: Sirey, 1933.

Walter, Karl, ed. *Cooperation and Charles Gide.* London: P. S. King and Son, 1933.

Gierke, Otto Friedrich von, 1841–1921

Gierke, Otto F. von. *Associations and Law: The Classical and Early Christian Stages.* Toronto and Buffalo: University of Toronto Press, 1977.

————. *Das deutsche Genossenschaftsrecht, 1868–1913.* Berlin: Weidmann, 1868–1913; reissued, Graz: Akademische Druck und Verlagsanstalt, 1954.

————. *Die Genossenschaftstheorie und die deutsche Rechtsprechung.* Berlin: Weidmann, 1887.

Lewis, John D. *The genossenschaft-theory of Otto von Gierke.* Madison: University of Wisconsin, 1935.

Mogi, Sobei. *Otto von Gierke, His Political Teaching and Jurisprudence.* London: P. S. King and Son, 1932.

Spindler, Helga. *Von der Genossenschaft zur Betriebsgemeinschaft: Kritische Darstellung der Sozialrechtslehre Otto von Gierkes.* Frankfurt: Lang, 1982.

Greening, Edward Owen, 1836–1923

Crimes, Tom. *Edward Owen Greening: A Maker of Modern Cooperation.* London: T. F. Unwin, 1924.

Greening, Edward Owen. *Memories of Robert Owen and the Cooperative Pioneers.* Manchester: Coop Union, 1925.

Holyoake, George Jacob, 1817–1906

Blaszak, Barbara J. *George Jacob Holyoake (1817–1906) and the Development of the British Cooperative Movement.* Lewiston, N.Y.: Edwin Mellen Press, 1988.

George Jacob Holyoake: Checklist of Books, Pamphlets, Press-cuttings and MSS in the Library of the Cooperative Union. Manchester: Coop Union, 1975.

Goss, Charles W. *A Descriptive Bibliography of the Writings of George Jacob Holyoake with a Brief Sketch of His Life.* London: Crowther and Goodman, 1908.

Grugel, Lee E. *George Jacob Holyoake: A Study in the Evolution of a Victorian Radical.* Philadelphia: Porcupine Press, 1976.

Holyoake, George J. *Among the Americans,* and *A Stranger in America.* Westport, Conn.: Greenwood Press, 1970 (reprint of the 1881 edition).

———. *The Cooperative Movement Today.* London: Methuen, 1896.

———. *Histoire de la coopération à Rochdale.* Paris: Librairie universelle, 1888.

———. *Histoire des équitable pionniers de Rochdale.* Nîmes: Bibliothèque de l'émancipation, 1890.

———. *The History of Cooperation.* London: T. F. Unwin, 1908.

———. *The History of Cooperation in England: Its Literature and Its Advocates.* London: Trübner, 1875–1879; reprinted, New York: AMS Press, 1971.

———. *Manual of Cooperation, Being an Epitome of Holyoake's "History of Cooperation."* New York: J. B. Alden, 1885; reissued, New York: Consumer's Publishing Association, 1969.

———. *Moral Errors Which Endanger the Permanence of Cooperative Societies.* Boston: Boston Labor Reform Association, 1864.

———. *Partnerships of Industry: A Statement of the Cooperative Case Divested of Sentimentality.* London: Austin, 1865.

———. *Self-Help by the People, a History of Cooperation in Rochdale.* London: S. Sonnenschein, 1893; New York: C. Scribner's Sons, 1893.

———. *Self Help a Hundred Years Ago.* London: S. Sonnenschein, 1891.

———. *Sixty Years of an Agitator's Life.* London: T. F. Unwin, 1906; reissued, New York: Garland, 1984.

McCabe, J. *Life and Letters of George Jacob Holyoake.* London: Watts, 1922.

Schloesser, Robert, ed. *Holyoakes Geschichte der Rochdaler Pioniere.* Cologne: Gepagverlag, 1928.

Huber, Victor Aimé, 1800–1869

Elvers, Rudolf. *Victor Aimé Huber: Sein Werden und Wirken.* Bremen: C. E. Müller, 1872.

Faust, E. *Victor Aimé Huber, Ein Bahnbreher der Genossenschafts-idee.* Hamburg: Verlag der Konsumgenossenschaften, 1952.

Huber, Victor. *Soziale Fragen.* Nordhausen, Germany: Förstermann, 1863.

————. *Die genossenschaftliche Selbsthilfe der arbeitenden Klassen.* Elberfeld, Germany: Friedrichs, 1865.

King, William, 1786–1865

Dent, J. *The Cooperative Ideals of Dr. William King.* Manchester: Coop Union, 1921.

Mercer, Thomas W. *Cooperation's Prophets. The Life and Letters of Doctor William King of Brighton.* Manchester: Coop Union, 1947.

————, ed. *Dr. William King and the Cooperator, 1828–1830.* Manchester: Coop Union, 1922.

Lassalle, Ferdinand Johan Gottlieb, 1825–1864

Bernstein, Edouard. *Ferdinand Lassalle as a Social Reformer.* London: S. Sonnenschein, 1893; reissued, Westport, Conn.: Greenwood Press, 1969; St. Clair Shores, Mich.: Scholarly Press, 1970.

Brandes, Georg M. C. *Ferdinand Lassalle.* Leipzig: Barsdorf, 1889; reissued, New York: Bernard G. Richards, 1925; Westport, Conn.: Greenwood Press, 1970.

Lassalle, Ferdinand. *Ferdinand Lassalle's Reden und Schriften.* Berlin: Verlag der Expedition des "Vorwärts," 1892–1893; reissued, Munich: Deutscher Taschenbuch Verlag, 1970; Leipzig: P. Reclam, 1987.

Luzzatti, Luigi, 1841–1927

Luzzatti, Luigi. *La diffusione del credito delle banche popolari.* Milan: [n.p.], 1863. (Italian)

Parrillo, Francesco, ed. *Attualita di Luigi Luzzatti.* Milan: Giuffrè, 1964. (Italian)

Myrick, Herbert, 1860–1927

Myrick, Herbert. *Cooperative Finance.* New York: Orange Judd, 1912.

————. *How To Cooperate. The Full Fruits of Labor to Producer, Honest Value to Consumer, Just Return to Capital, Prosperity to All. A Manual for Cooperators.* New York: Orange Judd, 1891.

Neale, Edward Vansittart, 1810–1892

Backstrom, Philip N. *Christian Socialism and Cooperation in Victorian England: Edward Vansittart Neale and the Cooperative Movement.* London: Croom Helm, 1974.

Hughes, Thomas, and E. V. Neale, eds. *Foundations: A Study in the Ethics and Economics of the Cooperative Movement.* Manchester: Coop Union, 1916.

————. *A Manual for Cooperators*. Manchester: Coop Union, 1881.

Pitman, H. *Memorial of Edward Vansittart Neale*. Manchester: Coop Union, 1894.

Oppenheimer, Franz, 1864–1943

Oppenheimer, Franz. *Les coopératives de mise en valeur: Essai de dépassement du communisme par la solution du problème coopératif et de la question agraire*. Leipzig: [n.p.], 1896.

————. *Die Siedlungsgenossenschaft. Versuch einer positiven Überwindung des Kommunismus durch Lösung des Genossenschafts-problems und der Agrarfrage*. Berlin: Vita, 1896.

————. *Die soziale Bedeutung der Genossenschaft*. Berlin: [n.p.], 1899.

Owen, Robert, 1771–1858

A Bibliography of Robert Owen, the Socialist, 1771–1858. Aberystwyth, U.K.: National Library of Wales, 1925.

Booth, A. *Robert Owen, The Founder of Socialism in England*. London: Trübner, 1869.

Butt, John. *Robert Owen, Prince of Cotton Spinners*. London: David and Charles, 1970.

Cem, Joad. *Robert Owen, Idealist*. London: Fabian Society, 1917.

Cole, G. D. H. *Robert Owen*. London: Benn, 1925; 3rd edition, Hamden, Conn.: Archon Books, 1966.

Cole, Margaret. *Robert Owen of New Lanark*. New York and Oxford: Oxford University Press, 1953.

Desroche, Henri, A. Lon and D. Rocher. "Owénisme et utopies françaises." *Communautés*, Paris 30 (1971).

Dolleans, Edouard. *Robert Owen (1771–1859)*. Paris: G. Bellais, 1905.

Garnett, R. *Cooperation and the Owenite Socialist Communities in Britain, 1825–1945*. Manchester: Manchester University Press, 1972.

Goto, Shigeru. *Robert Owen, 1771–1858, A New Bibliographical Study*. Osaka: Osaka Shoka Daigaku, 1932.

Harrison, J. F. C. *Robert Owen and the Owenites in Britain and in America*. London: Routledge and Kegan Paul, 1969.

Harvey, Rowland. *Robert Owen, Social Idealist*. Berkeley: University of California Press, 1949.

Holyoake, George J. *Life and Last Days of Robert Owen of New Lanark*. London: Watts, 1859.

Hutchison, B. L. *Robert Owen, Social Reformer*. London: Fabian Society, 1918.

Morton, A. L. *The Life and Ideas of Robert Owen*. London: Lawrence and Wishart, 1962.

Motherwell and Orbison. The First Owenite Attempts at Cooperative Communities. 1822–1825. New York: Arno Press, 1972.

Owen, Robert. *Essays on the Formation of the Human Character.* Manchester: A. Heywood, 1837.

———. *Esquisse du système d'éducation suivie dans les écoles de New Lanark.* Paris: Lugan, 1825.

———. *The Future of the Human Race.* London: E. Wilson, 1853.

———. *The Inauguration of the Millennium, May 14th, 1855.* London: J. Clayton and Son, 1855.

———. *The Life of Robert Owen Written by Himself.* London: E. Wilson, 1857–1858; reissued, London: C. Knight, 1971.

———. *A New View of Society.* London: Everyman's, 1813; reissued, Oxford and New York: Woodstock Books, 1991.

———. *Report to the County of Lanark, of a Plan for Relieving Public Distress, and Removing Discontent, by Giving Permanent, Productive Employment to the Poor and Working Classes.* Glasgow: Wardlaw and Cunninghame, 1821.

———. *Robert Owen in the United States.* New York: Humanities Press, 1970.

———. *Robert Owen's Journal. Explanatory of the Means to Well-Place and Well-Feed, Well-Clothe, Well-Lodge, Well-Employ, Well-Educate, Well-Govern, and Cordially Unite, the Population of the World.* London: [n.p.], 1850.

Owenism and the Working Class: Six Pamphlets and Four Broadsides, 1821–1834. New York: Arno Press, 1972.

Packard, F. *A Life of Robert Owen.* Philadelphia: A. B. Lippincott, 1868.

Podmore, Frank. *Robert Owen, A Biography.* New York: A. M. Kelley, 1968.

Pollard, Sidney, and John Salt, eds. *Robert Owen, Prophet of the Poor.* London: Macmillan, 1971; Lewisburg, Pa.: Bucknell University Press, 1971.

Rey, J. *Lettres sur le système de la coopération mutuelle et de la communauté de tous les biens d'après le plan de M. Owen.* Paris: A. Santelet, 1828.

Robert Owen and His Relevance to Our Times. Manchester: Coop Union, 1971.

Thomas, Albert. *Quelques notes sur Robert Owen et la législation internationale du travail.* Strasbourg, France: Istra, 1924.

Parisius, Ludolf, 1827–1900

Parisius, L. *Die Genossenschaftsgesetze im Deutschen Reiche.* Berlin: Guttentag, 1876.

———. *Doktor L. Glackmeyer in Hannover und sein Kampf gegen die Organisation und die Grundlehren von Schulze-Delitzsch.* Berlin: Guttentag, 1894.

———, ed. *Das Reichsgesetz, betreffend die erwerbs-und wirtschaftsgenossenschaften.* Berlin: W. de Gruyter, 1943.

———. *Schulze-Delitzsch und Alwin Sörgel. Beitrage zur Geschichte der deutschen Genossenschaftsbewegung.* Berlin: Guttentag, 1899.

Pfeiffer, Eduard von, 1835–1921

Bittel, Karl. *Eduard Pfeiffer und die deutsche Konsumgenossen-schaftsbewegung.* Munich and Leipzig: Duncker und Humblot, 1915.

Pfeiffer, Eduard. *A propos du principe coopératif: Qu'est la condition du travailleur et que peut-elle devenir?*. Leipzig: [n.p.], 1863.

———. *Des sociétés coopératives de consommation*. Valence, France: Imprimerie Jules Céas et fils, 1867.

Plunkett, Horace Curzon, Sir, 1854–1932

Anderson, Robert A. *With Plunkett in Ireland: The Coop Organizer's Story*. Blackrock, Ireland: Irish Academic Press, 1983.

Keating, Carla, ed. *Plunkett and Cooperatives: Past, Present and Future*. Cork, Ireland: University College, Bank of Ireland Centre for Cooperative Studies, 1983.

Metcalf, Rupert. *England and Sir Horace Plunkett*. London: G. Howe, 1933.

West, Trevor. *Horace Plunkett: Cooperation and Politics: An Irish Biography*. Gerrards Cross, U.K.: C. Smythe, 1986; Washington, D.C.: Catholic University of America, 1986.

Rabbeno, Ugo, 1863–1897

Basevi, A. *Ugo Rabbeno*. Rome: La rivista della cooperazione, 1953. (Italian)

Rabbeno, Ugo. *La cooperazione in Inghilterra*. Milan: Fratelli Dumolard, 1885. (Italian)

———. *La Cooperazione in Italia, saggio di sociologia economica*. Milan: Fratelli Dumolard, 1886. (Italian)

———. *La società cooperative di produzione*. Milan: Fratelli Dumolard, 1889; reissued, Milan: Lega Nazionale delle Cooperative, 1915. (Italian)

Raiffeisen, Friedrich Wilhelm, 1818–1888

Bauert-Keetmann, Ingrid. *Raiffeisen—Verwirklichung einer Idee*. Tübingen: Wunderlich, 1970.

Braumann, Franz. *Frédéric-Guillaume Raiffeisen, 1888–1988: Car j'ai eu faim*. Strasbourg, France: Coprur, 1988.

Fassbender, Martin. *Friedrich Wilhelm Raiffeisen in seinem Leben, Denken und Wirken*. Berlin: P. Parey, 1902.

Glackmeyer, L. *Die Creditvereine nach Schulze-Delitzsch und die Darlehnskassen nach Raiffeisen*. Hanover: C. Meyer, 1887.

Henzler, Reinhold, Hrsg. *F. W. Raiffeisen zum Gedächtnis*. Neuwied am Rhein: Genossenschaftsdruckerei Raiffeisen, 1938.

Hüttl, Ludwig. *Friedrich Wilhelm Raiffeisen, Leben und Werk: Eine Biographie*. Munich: Bayerischer Raiffeisenverband, 1988.

Koch, Walter. *Der Genossenschaftsgedanke F. W. Raiffeisen als Kooperationsmodell in der modernen Industriegesellschaft*. Würzburg: Creator, 1991.

————, ed. *F. W. Raiffeisen: Dokumente und Briefe, 1818–1888.* Vienna: Österreichischer Agrarverlag, 1988.

Lubin, David. *Frederick William Raiffeisen.* Washington, D.C.: GPO, 1913.

A Man Conquers Poverty—The Story of Wilhelm Raiffeisen. Madison, Wis.: CUNA, 1963.

Maxeiner, Rudolf, Gunther Aschoff, and Herbert Wendt, eds. *Raiffeisen: Der Mann, die Idee und das Werk.* Wiesbaden: Deutscher Genossenschafts-Verlag, 1988.

Raiffeisen, Friedrich W. *Die Darlehnskassen-Vereine.* Neuwied, Germany: [n.p.], 1866; reissued, Neuwied, Germany: Verlag der Raiffeisen-druckerei, 1966.

Richter, H. F. W. *Raiffeisen und die Entwicklung seiner Genossenschaftsidee.* Nurenberg: [n.p.], 1965.

Schmidt, F. *Die Genossenschafts-Systeme Schulze-Delitzsch und Raiffeisen.* Vienna: Hölder, 1889.

Schuster, Leo, ed. *Raiffeisen: Idee und Verwirklichung.* Bern: P. Haupt, 1979.

Sellmann-Eggebert, Erich L. *Friedrich Wilhelm Raiffeisen.* Stuttgart: W. Kohlhammer, 1928.

Siepmann, Heinzfried. *Brüder und Genossen: Ansätze für einen genossenschaftlichen Gemeindeaufbau.* Cologne: Rheinland-Verlag, 1987; Bonn: R. Habelt, 1987.

Stadelmann, Franz J. *Frédéric Guillaume Raiffeisen, sa vie et son oeuvre.* Saint Gallen, Switzerland: Union suisse des caisses de crédit mutuel, 1930.

Valko, Laszlo. *Raiffeisen, Father of Agricultural Credit Cooperatives.* Pullman: Washington State University, 1968.

Rocquigny du Fayel, Henri, comte de, 1845–1929

Rocquigny du Fayel, Henri, comte de. *La coopération de production dans l'agriculture.* Paris: Guillaumin, 1896.

————. *Les syndicats agricoles et leurs oeuvres.* Paris: Colin, 1900.

Schulze-Delitzsch, Hermann, 1808–1883

Aldenhoff, Rita. *Schulze-Delitzsch: Ein Beitrag zur Geschichte des Liberalismus zwischen Revolution und Reichsgründung.* Baden-Baden, Germany: Nomos, 1984.

Bernstein, Aaron D. *Schulze-Delitzsch. Leben und Wirken.* Berlin: M. Bading. 1890.

Boettcher, Erik, ed. *Die Genossenschaftsidee im Widerstreit der Meinungen: Das Vermächtnis von Hermann Schulze-Delitzsch aus der Sicht von Wissenschaft, Praxis und Politik.* Münster: Institut für Genossenschaftswesen der Westfälischen Wilhelms-Universität, 1984.

Conze, Werner. *Möglichkeiten und Grenzen der liberalen Arbeiterbewegung in Deutschland: Das Beispiel Schulze-Delitzsch.* Heidelberg: C. Winter, 1965.

Faust, Helmut. *Schulze-Delitzsch und sein genossenschaftliches Werk.* Marburg, Germany: Simons, 1949.

Finck, Richard. *Das Schulze-Delitzsch Genossenschaftswesen und die modernen genossenschaftlichen Entwicklungstendenzen.* Jena, Germany: G. Fischer, 1909.

Glackemeyer, L. *Die Kreditvereine nach Schulze-Delitzsch und die Darlehnskassen nach Raiffeisen.* Hanover: Meyer, 1887.

Heuss, Theodor. *Schulze-Delitzsch: Leistung und Vermachtnis.* Tübingen: Rainer Wunderlich, 1956.

Klein, Wolfgang. *Schulze-Delitzsch Kampf um die Anerkennung der Erwerbs-und Wirtschaftsgenossenschaft als Rechtssubjekt vor dem Hintergrund der politischen Verhältnisse in Preussen mit einer vergleichenden Darstellung der englischen und französischen Entwicklung.* Heidelberg: [n.p.], 1972.

Lassalle, Ferdinand J. G. *Herr Bastiat-Schulze von Delitzsch, der ökonomische, Julian oder: Kapital und Arbeit.* Berlin: R. Schlingmann, 1864.

Quincy, Samuel M. *The People's Banks of Germany: Their Organization Under the Recent Law.* Boston: Little, Brown, 1870.

Schmidt, F. *Die Genossenschafts-Systeme von Schulze-Delitzsch und Raiffeisen.* Vienna: Hölder, 1889.

Schulze-Delitzsch, 1808–1958: Festschrift zur 150. Wiederkehr seines Geburtstages. Bonn: Deutscher Genossenschaftsverband, 1958.

Schulze-Delitzsch, Hermann. *Die arbeitenden Klassen und das Assoziationswesen in Deutschland als Programm zu einem deutschen Kongress.* Leipzig: G. Mayer, 1858.

———. *Assoziationsbuch für deutsche Handwerker und Arbeiter.* Leipzig: E. Keil, 1853.

———. *Cours d'économie politique à l'usage des ouvriers et des artisans.* Paris: Guillaumin, 1874.

———. *Die Entwicklung des Genossenschaftswesens in Deutschland.* Berlin: Janke, 1870.

———. *Die Genossenschaften in einzelnen Gewerbszweigen.* Leipzig: E. Keil, 1873.

———. *Die Gesetzebung über die privatrechtliche Stellung der Erwerbs-.und Wirtschaftsgenossenschaften mit besonderer Rücksicht auf die Haftpflicht bei kommerziellen Gesellschaften.* Berlin: F. A. Herbig, 1869.

———. *Material zur Revision des Genossenschaftsgesetzes.* Leipzig: E. Keil, 1883.

———. *Vorschuss-.und Kreditvereine als Volksbanken.* Leipzig: E. Keil, 1855; reissued, Berlin: Guttentag, 1915.

Thorwart, Friedrich, ed. *Hermann Schulze-Delitzsch's Schriften und Reden.* Berlin: Guttentag, 1913.

Thompson, William, 1755–1833

Pankhurst, R. *William Thompson 1755–1833, Britain's Pioneer Socialist, Feminist and Cooperator.* London: [n.p.], 1954.

Thompson, W. *An Inquiry into the Principles of the Distribution of Wealth Most Conducive to Human Happiness.* London: W. S. Orr, 1850; reissued, New York: A. Kelley, 1963; New York: B. Franklin, 1968.

————. *Practical Directions for the Speedy and Economical Establishment of Communities on the Principles of Mutual Cooperation.* London: [n.p.], 1830.

Walras, Léon, 1834–1910

Boson, Marcel. *La pensée sociale et coopérative de Léon Walras.* Paris: Institut des études coopératives, 1963.

Walras, Léon. *Les associations populaires de consommation, de production et de crédit.* Paris: Dentu, 1865; reissued, Rome: Bizzarri, 1969.

————. *Études d'économie sociale appliquée.* Lausanne: F. Rouge et cie, 1898; reissued, Rome: Bizzarri, 1969.

Others (Single Publications)

Acland, Arthur Herbert Dyke, Sir. *Working Men Cooperators: What They Have Done, and What They Are Doing.* London and New York: Cassell, 1889.

Ameline H. *Les institutions ouvrières au XIXe siècle.* Paris: Pedrone, 1866.

Apostol, P. *Das Artjel.* Stuttgart: Cotta, 1898.

Les associations ouvrières de production. Paris: Office du travail, 1897.

Baernreither, Josef M. *English Associations of Working Men.* Detroit: Gale Research, 1966.

Baker, F. *First Lecture on Cooperation.* London: Bolton Chronicle, 1830.

Barnard, Charles. *Cooperation as a Business.* New York: Putnam, 1881.

Bertrand, Louis. *La coopération.* Brussels: Rosez, 1898.

Birnbaum, K. *Das Genossenschaftsprinzip in Anwendung und Anwendbarkeit der Landwirtschaft.* Leipzig: Weissbach, 1870.

Bonnemère, E. *Histoire de l'association agricole et solution pratique.* Paris: Dusacq, 1850.

Cavare, P. *Étude sur les associations coopératives, précédée d'un examen du contrat de société de droit romain.* Paris: Parent, 1867.

Ertl, Moriz, and Stefan Licht. *Das landwirtschaftliche Genossenschaftswesen in Deutschland.* Vienna: Manz, 1899.

First Community of Mutual Cooperation. London: London Cooperative Society, 1825.

Goldschmidt, L. *Erwerbs-und Wirtschaftsgenossenschaften.* Stuttgart: Enke, 1882.

Hantschke, H. *Die Gewerblichen Produktivgenossenschaften in Deutschland.* Berlin: Gertz, 1894.

Hennell, H. *An Outline of the Various Social Systems and Communities Which Have Been Founded on the Principle of Cooperation.* London: [n.p.], 1844.

History of Cooperation in the United States. Baltimore: Johns Hopkins University, 1888; reissued, New York: Johnson Press, 1973.

Jäger, E. *Das Genossenschaftswesen und die Reform des Genossenschaftsgesetzes.* Berlin: Verlag der Germania, 1884.

Knittel, A. *Beiträge zur Geschichte des deutschen Genossenschaftswesen*. Freiburg, Germany: [n.p.], 1895.

Kraus, T. *Die Solidarhaft bei den Erwerbs-und Wirtschaftgenossenschaften*. Bonn: Strauss, 1878.

Kudelka, T. *Das landwirtschaftliche Genossenschaftswesen in Frankreich*. Berlin: Puttkammer, 1899.

Lagasse, C. *Les sociétés coopératives*. Paris: [n.p.], 1887.

Malherbe, G. *Les fromageries ou fruitières coopératives*. Brussels: Schopers, 1899.

Meyenschein, A. *Die ländlichen Genossenschaften im Regierungsbezirk Kassel: Die Raiffeisenschen Genossenschaften*. Kassel, Germany: [n.p.], 1899.

Moreau, J. *Le salaire et les associations coopératives, suivi d'une description du Familistère de Guise*. Paris: Guillaumin, 1866.

Nadaud, M. *Les sociétés ouvrières*. Paris: Librairie démocratique, 1873.

Pankhurst, Richard. *The Saint Simonians, Mill and Carlyle*. London: Sidwick and Jackson, 1957; reissued, Norwood, Pa.: Norwood Editions, 1976.

Pedregal y Canedo. *Sociedades cooperativas*. Madrid: [n.p.], 1884.

Pelletier, E. *Du mouvement coopératif international, étude théorique et pratique sur les différentes formes de l'association*. Paris: Guillaumin et Dentu, 1867.

Pestalozzi, J. *Léonard et Gertrude*. Leipzig: Brockaus, 1888; New York: Gordon Press, 1977.

Piernas Hurtado, J. *El movimiento cooperativo*. Madrid: Tipografía G. Hernandez, 1890.

Polo de Bernabé. *Las sociedades cooperativas*. Madrid: [n.p.], 1867.

Pröbst, F. *Die Grundlehren der deutschen Genossenschaften*. Munich: [n.p.], 1875.

Rayneri, August. *Le crédit agricole par association coopérative*. Paris: Guillermin, 1896.

Real, R. *Sociedades cooperativas*. Buenos Aires: Schürer Stolle, 1900.

Retzbach, A. *Die Handwerker und die Kreditgenossenschaften*. Freiburg, Germany: [n.p.], 1899.

Rosenthal, J. *Die Kredit-Erwerbs- und Wirtschaftsgenossenschaften*. Berlin: Barth und Fritze, 1871.

Rosin, Heinrich. *Das Recht der öffentlichen Genossenschaft*. Freiburg, Germany: Möhr, 1886.

Say, L. *Des sociétés de coopération et de leur constitution légale*. Paris: Rivière, 1865.

Stross, E. *Das österreichische Genossenschaftsrecht*. Vienna: Perles, 1887.

von Broich, F. *Sozialreform und Genossenschaftswesen*. Berlin: [n.p.], 1890.

von Löw, K. *Über die Markgenossenschaften*. Heidelberg: Möhr, 1829.

von Sicherer, H. *Die Genossenschaftsgesetzgebung in Deutschland*. Erlangen, Germany: [n.p.], 1872.

Zeidler, H. *Geschichte des deutschen Genossenschaftswesen der Neuzeit*. Leipzig: Duncker und Humblot, 1893.

III. B. 20th-Century Theory and Practice

III. B. 1. Theories of Cooperation

III. B. 1. a. General Theories

Andreou, Paris, ed. *Cooperative Institutions and Economic Development in Developed and Developing Nations: Selected International Readings in the Economics, Marketing, and Management of Cooperative Institutions and Their Role in Economic Development.* Nairobi: East African Literature Bureau, 1977.

Anthology of Cooperative Thought. New Delhi: NCUI, 1975.

Balbi de Gonzalo, Nidia, and Dante Cracogna. *Introducción al cooperativismo.* Buenos Aires: Intercoop. 1985.

Bedi, Raghubans D. *Theory, History and Practice of Cooperation.* Meerut, India: International Publishing House, 1961.

Birchall, Johnston. *Coop: The People's Business.* Manchester and New York: Manchester University Press, 1994.

Blais, P. *L'esprit coopératif.* Quebec: Service social économique, 1952.

Boettcher, Erik. *Theorie and Praxis der Kooperation.* Münster: Institut für Genossenschaftswesen, 1972.

Bonilla, F. *Cooperativismo.* Lima: Editorial Mercurio, 1970.

Bottomley, Trevor. *Introduction to Cooperatives: A Programmed Learning Text.* London: Intermediate Technology Publications, 1979; republished 1987.

Briscoe, Bob, et al. *The Cooperative Idea.* Cork, Ireland: University College, Bank of Ireland Centre for Cooperative Studies, 1982.

de Brouckere, Louis. *La coopération, ses origines, sa nature, ses grandes fonctions.* Brussels: [n.p.], 1926.

Campbell, Wallace, and Richard Giles. *Helping People Help Themselves.* Washington, D.C.: Public Affairs Institute, 1950.

Casselman, Paul. *Coopération.* Ottawa: Université d'Ottawa, Centre social, 1953.

Chama, Maynard M. *Booklet on Basic Cooperative Information.* Lusaka, Zambia: Cooperative College, 1982.

Chamorro Turrez, Eduardo. *Introducción al cooperativismo.* Madrid: Editorial ZYX, 1968.

Cooperation, An Interdisciplinary Approach. Poona, India: Mehta, 1969.

Craig, John G. *The Nature of Cooperation.* Montreal and New York: Black Rose Books, 1993.

Daniels, John. *Cooperation, the American Way.* New York: Covici, 1938.

Dessauer, Friedrich. *Kooperative Wirtschaft.* Bonn: F. Cohen, 1929.

Durrell, F. *Cooperation: Its Essence and Background.* Boston: Bruce Humphries, 1936.

Effective Self Help, Moving Ahead With Coops. Chicago: CLUSA, 1966.

Eldridge, Seba. *Development of Collective Enterprise. Dynamics of an Emergent Economy.* Lawrence: University of Kansas Press, 1943.

Enriquez, C. G. *Structure and Functions of Cooperatives*. Antigonish, Nova Scotia: Coady, 1983.

Fabra Ribas, Antonio. *La cooperación*. Caracas: Editorial Bolívar, 1943; Medellín, Colombia: Imprenta Universidad, 1945.

Fowler, B. *The Cooperative Challenge*. Boston: Brown, 1947.

Goslin, R. *Cooperatives*. New York: Foreign Policy Association, 1937.

Greer, Paul. *Cooperatives*. New York: Harper, 1955.

Guerrero Palacio de Burgos, M. *Cooperativismo y cooperativas*. Bogota: Editorial El Voto Nacional, 1963.

Hammerschmid, A. *Beiträge zur Theorie des Genossenschaftswesens*. Vienna: Ostern-Wirtschaftsverlag, 1937.

Harper, R. K. *Cooperative Origins and Primary Philosophy*. Manila: Bureau of Public Schools, 1958.

Hertzler, Joyce. *History of Utopian Thought*. New York: Macmillan, 1926.

Higgins, J. *Cooperation*. Panmur, New Zealand: Griffin Press, 1947.

Jacob, Eduard. *Volkswirtschaftliche Theorie der Genossenschaften*. Berlin: W. Kohlhammer, 1913.

Justo, Juan B. *Cooperación libre*. Buenos Aires: La Vanguardia, 1938.

———. *Obras completas*. Buenos Aires: La Vanguardia, 1929.

Keleher, James F. *A Philosophy of Cooperation*. Mineola, N.Y.: Davenport Press, 1948.

Klimis, A. *Les coopératives*. Athens, Greece: [n.p.], 1946.

Kress, Andrew. *Introduction to the Cooperative Movement*. New York and London: Harper, 1941.

Kulkarni, K. R. *Theory and Practice of Cooperation in India and Abroad*. Bombay: Cooperators Book Depot, 1955.

Laidlaw, A. F. *Cooperatives in the Year 2000*. [n.l.]: ICA, 1980.

Lambert, Paul. *Studies in the Social Philosophy of Cooperation*. Manchester: Coop Union, 1963; Chicago: CLUSA, 1963.

Lasserre, George. *La coopération*. Paris: PUF, 1958.

Lavergne, B. *L'ordre coopératif*. Paris: Alcan, 1926.

McGrath, M. J. *Cooperativas prosperas*. Mexico City: Editorial Roble, 1972.

Métellus, Champagne. *La doctrine coopérative*. Port-au-Prince, Haiti: Imprimerie la palange, 1984.

Meyer, E. *Genossenschaften*. Munich: Beck'scherVerlag, 1956.

Miller, R. *A Conservative Looks at Cooperatives*. Athens: Ohio University, 1964.

Müller, Hugo. *Genossenschaft*. Vienna: Österreich Agrarrel, 1972.

O'Neill, A. *Cuerpo y alma del cooperativismo*. Santurce, Puerto Rico: Artce, 1958.

Panzoni, E. *Cooperativismo: función, doctrina e historia*. Buenos Aires: Asociación Pro-Instituto de Estudios Cooperativos, 1958.

———. *Naturaleza del sistema cooperativo*. Buenos Aires: Instituto Nacional de Tecnología Agropecuaria, 1962.

Parrilla Bonilla, Antulio. *Cooperativismo*. San Juan, Puerto Rico: Editorial Universitaria, Universidad de Puerto Rico, 1971.

Perez Baró, Albert. *Cooperativismo.* Barcelona: Ediciones 62, 1987.

Plunkett Foundation. *The World of Cooperative Enterprise.* Oxford: Plunkett, published annually.

Rauter, A. E. *Der Dritte Weg.* Vienna: Konsumverband, [n.d.].

Rodriguez Rosa, Antonio. *La revolución sin sangre: El cooperativismo.* Mexico City: B. Costa-Amic, 1964.

Ross, John E. *Cooperative Plenty.* St. Louis, Mo., and London: B. Herder, 1941.

Roy, E. P. *Cooperatives: Development, Principles and Management.* Danville, Ill.: Interstate Printers and Publishers, 1981.

Sanchez, A. V., et al. *Cooperatives: A Direction for Progress.* Quezon City, Philippines: Asia Pillar Publications, 1975.

Saxena, K. K. *Evolution of Cooperative Thought.* Bombay: Samaiya Publications, 1974.

Seraphim, Hans J. *Die genossenschaftliche Gesinnung und das moderne Genossenschaftswesen.* Karlsruhe, Germany: C. F. Müller, 1956.

Serwy, Victor. *La coopération.* Gand, Belgium: Société coopérative Volksdrukkerij, 1910.

Solís, Marcial. *El cooperativismo, el cambio y el desarrollo.* Tegucigalpa, Honduras: Editorial Universitario, 1986.

Totomiants, Vakhan F., ed. *Anthologie des Genossenschaftswesens, mit einem Vorwort von Charles Gide und einem Schlusswort von Werner Sombart.* Berlin: R. L. Prager, 1922.

Uribe Garzón, Carlos. *Bases del cooperativismo.* Medellín, Colombia: Editorial Granamericana, 1965.

Valko, Laszlo. *Essays on Modern Cooperation.* Pullman: Washington State University Press, 1964.

———. *Estudios cooperativos.* Pullman: Washington State University Press, 1963.

Veerashingham, V. *Practice and Philosophy of Cooperation.* Colombo: Times of Ceylon, 1949.

Verhagen, Koenraad. *Cooperation for Survival.* Amsterdam: ICA/Royal Tropical Institute, 1984.

Voorhis, Jerry. *Cooperativas: desarrollo, función y futuro.* Mexico City: Editorial Pax, 1970.

Warbasse, James P. *The Cooperative Way.* Chicago: CLUSA, 1946; New York: Barnes and Noble, 1946.

———. *El sistemo cooperativo.* Buenos Aires: Editorial America Lee, 1946.

Ziegenfuss, W. *Die Genossenschaften.* Berlin: De Gruyter, 1948.

III. B. 1. b. Religious Bases of Cooperation

Bosson, Marcel. *La pensée et l'action coopérative des "socialistes chrétiens" en Angleterre.* Basel: USC, 1957.

Catholic Churchmen and Cooperatives. Huntington, Ind.: Our Sunday Visitor, 1944.

Coady, M. M. *Cooperation and Religion.* Chicago: CLUSA, 1939.

Coutinho, Boavida. *Cooperations the Key to Progress.* Rome: Gregorian University Press, 1972.

La Empresa artesana y cooperativa a la luz de la doctrina social católica. Madrid: Centro de Estudios Sociales de la Santa Cruz del Valle de los Caidos, 1963.

La encíclica Mater et Magistra y las cooperativas. Madrid: Servicio de Información y Publicaciones Sindicales, 1962.

Fabra Ribas, Antonio. *Los católicos de las Américas y la cooperación.* Monterey, Mexico: Instituto Tecnológico, 1950.

————. *Las modernas corrientes económicas y las enseñanzas de Santo Tomás de Aquino.* Medellín, Colombia: [n.p.], 1944.

Kagawa, Toyohiko. *Brotherhood Economics.* New York and London: Harper and Brothers, 1936.

Landis, Benson Y. *Bethlehem and Rochdale.* Chicago: CLUSA, 1944.

Moore, William H. *Religion and the Consumers' Cooperative Movement.* Chicago: University of Chicago, 1940.

Morgan, John M. *The Christian Commonwealth.* London: Longman, Brown, Green and Longmans, 1849.

Niemeyer, Mary Fredericus, Sister. *The One and the Many in the Social Order According to Saint Thomas Aquinas.* Washington, D.C.: Catholic University of America Press, 1951.

Schmiedeler, Edgar. *Cooperation, a Christian Mode in Industry.* Ozone Park, N.Y.: Catholic Literary Guild, 1941.

Steel, Pablo. *Cooperativismo.* Trujillo, Dominican Republic: Arzobispado do Santo Domingo, 1954.

Tagore, Rabindranath. *The Cooperative Principle.* Calcutta: Visva-Bharati, 1963.

Tete, Peter. *A Missionary Social Worker in India: J. B. Hoffmann, the Chota Nagpur Tenancy Act and the Catholic Cooperatives, 1893–1928.* Rome: Università Gregoriana Editrice, 1984.

Thurman, Howard. *The Search for Common Ground: An Inquiry Into the Basis of Man's Experience of Community.* New York: Harper and Row, 1971; reissued, Richmond, Ind.: Friends United Press, 1986.

Ward, Leo R. *United for Freedom; Cooperation and Christian Democracy.* Milwaukee: Bruce, 1945.

III. B. 1. c. Sociobiology and Cooperation

Albrecht, G. *Die soziale Funktion des Genossenschaftswesens.* Berlin: Humblot, 1965.

Argyle, Michael. *Cooperation, the Basis of Sociability.* London and New York: Routledge, 1991.

Axelrod, Robert M. *The Evolution of Cooperation.* London and New York: Penguin Books, 1990.

Badcock, Christopher R. *Evolution and Individual Behavior: An Introduction to Human Sociobiology.* Oxford and Cambridge, Mass.: B. Blackwell, 1991.

Barnes, Lemuel C. *Cooperation: the Master Key in Universal Problems.* New York: Schulte Press, 1939.

Boswell, Jonathan. *Community and the Economy: The Theory of Public Cooperation.* London and New York: Routledge, 1990.

Brown, David W. *When Strangers Cooperate: Using Social Conventions to Govern Ourselves.* New York: Free Press, 1995.

Casti, John L., and Anders Karlqvist, eds. *Cooperation and Conflict in General Evolutionary Processes.* New York: Wiley, 1995.

Derlega, Valerian J., and Janusz Grzelak, eds. *Cooperation and Helping Behavior: Theories and Research.* New York: Academic Press, 1982.

Earley, Joseph E., ed. *Individuality and Cooperative Action.* Washington, D.C.: Georgetown University Press, 1991.

Hewetson, John. *Mutual Aid and Social Evolution; Mutual Aid and the Social Significance of Darwinism.* London: Freedom Press, 1946.

Huxley, Thomas H. *The Struggle for Existence.* New York: Garland Publishers (reissue), 1972.

Infield, Henrik F. *The Sociological Study of Cooperation: An Outline.* Loughborough, U.K.: Coop Union, Education Department, 1956.

———. *Utopia and Experiment: Essays in the Sociology of Cooperation.* New York: F. A. Praeger, 1955; reissued, Port Washington, New York: Kennikat Press, 1971.

Kramer, Wendell B., ed. *Choose Life: Survival Through Cooperation.* Sacramento, Calif.: Third Wave Association, 1984.

Kropotkin, Peter. *Mutual Aid, a Factor of Evolution.* New York: McClure, Phillips and Company, 1902; reissued, London: Heinemann, 1915; New York: A. A. Knopf, 1925; New York: New York University Press, 1972; N.Y.: Garland Publishers, 1972; London: Freedom Press, 1987.

Mansbridge, Jane J., ed. *Beyond Self-Interest.* Chicago: University of Chicago Press, 1990.

Mattessich, Paul W., and Barbara Monsey. *Collaboration—What Makes It Work: A Review of Research Literature on Factors Influencing Successful Collaboration.* St. Paul, Minn.: Amherst H. Wilder Foundation, 1992.

Montagu, Ashley. *The Direction of Human Development.* New York: Harper, 1955; reissued, New York: Hawthorn Books, 1970.

———. *On Being Human.* New York: Hawthorn Books, 2nd edition, 1967.

Soli, George. *Homo Sapiens: Evolve or Perish.* Solvang, Calif.: Engel-Pavin Associates, 1987.

Van der Dennen, J., and V. Falger, eds. *Sociobiology and Conflict: Evolutionary Perspectives on Competition, Cooperation, Violence and Warfare.* London and New York: Chapman and Hall, 1990.

Wallas, Graham. *Our Social Heritage.* New Haven: Yale University Press, 1921; reissued, Freeport, N. Y.: Books for Libraries Press, 1972.

III. B. 1. d. Human Solidarity as the Basis for Cooperation (Utilitarianism, Humanism)

Ankerl, Géza. *Towards a Social Contract on a World-Wide Scale: Solidarity Contracts.* Geneva: International Institute for Labor Studies, 1980.

Baldwin, Peter. *The Politics of Social Solidarity: Class Bases of the European Welfare State, 1875–1975.* Cambridge, U.K. and New York: Cambridge University Press, 1990.

Danziger, Sheldon, and Robert Haveman. *An Economic Concept of Solidarity: Its Application to Poverty and Income Distribution Policy in the United States.* Geneva: International Institute for Labor Studies, 1978.

Loewy, Erich H. *Freedom and Community: The Ethics of Interdependence.* Albany: State University of New York Press, 1993.

Regan, Donald. *Utilitarianism and Cooperation.* Oxford: Clarendon Press, 1980; New York: Oxford University Press, 1980.

Wrong, Dennis H. *The Problem of Order: What Unites and Divides Society.* New York: Free Press, 1994; Toronto: Maxwell Macmillan Canada, 1994; New York: Maxwell Macmillan International, 1994.

III. B. 1. e. Cooperation, Mutualism and the Social Economy

Annals of Collective Economy. Geneva and Brussels: 6 (January–December 1925).

Bennet, Jean. *Biographies de personnalités mutualistes: XIXe–XXe siècles.* Paris: Mutualité française, 1987.

Congreso sobre el Cooperativismo y la Economia Social en el Mundo, 1987, Universidad de Deusto. Gasteiz, Spain: Eusko Jaurlaritzaren Argitalpen-Zerbitzu Nagusia, 1988.

Desroche, Henri. *Histoires d'économies sociales: D'un tiers état aux tiers secteurs, 1791–1991.* Paris: Syros/Alternatives, 1991.

———. *Pour un traite d'économie social.* Paris: Coopérative d'information et d'édition mutualiste, 1983.

Desroche, Henri, and M. Rubel. *Associationisme de 1848.* Paris: BECC, 1959.

Economic and Social Consultative Assembly. *The Cooperative, Mutual and Non-Profit Sector and Its Organizations.* Luxembourg: European Communities, Economic and Social Committee, 1986.

Gueslin, Andre. *L'invention de l'économie sociale: Le XIXe siècle français.* Paris: Economica, 1987.

Heflebower, Richard B. *Cooperatives and Mutuals in the Market System.* Madison: University of Wisconsin Press, 1980.

Lavielle, Romain. *Histoire de la Mutualité.* Paris: Hachette, 1964.

Parsons, Frank. *The Philosophy of Mutualism.* Boston: Arena Publishing, 1894.

Rocard, Michel, et al. *Économie sociale et cycle de vie des institutions.* Paris: Economia, 1983.

Swartz, Clarence L. *What Is Mutualism?* New York: Vanguard Press, 1927; reissued, Indore City, India: Modern Publishers, 1945.

III. B. 1. f. Socialism and Cooperation

Backstrom, Philip N. *Christian Socialism and Cooperation in Victorian England: Edward Vansittart Neale and the Cooperative Movement.* London: Croom Helm, 1974.

Derrick, Paul. *A Cooperative Approach to Socialism.* London: National Labour Press for the Socialist Christian League, 1956.

Dorrien, Gary J. *The Democratic Socialist Vision.* Totowa, N. J.: Rowman and Littlefield, 1986.

Laski, Harold J. *The Spirit of Cooperation.* Manchester: Coop Union, 1936.

Lauzel, Maurice. *Manuel du coopérateur socialiste.* Paris: G. Bellais, 1900.

Lavergne, B. *Le socialisme coopératif.* Paris: PUF, 1955.

Metha, V. L. *Towards a Cooperative Socialist Commonwealth.* Bombay: Cooperative Union, 1965.

Muckle, F. *Die grossen Sozialisten: Owen, Fourier, Proudhon, Saint-Simon, Pecqueur, Buchez, Blanc, Rodbertus, Weitling, Marx, Lassalle.* Berlin and Leipzig: Teubner, 1920.

Poisson, Ernest. *Socialisme et coopération. Socialisme politique, socialisme des producteurs, socialisme des consommateurs.* Paris: Rieder, 1922.

Woolf, Leonard S. *Fabian Essays on Cooperation.* London: Fabian Society, 1923.

———. *Socialism and Cooperation.* London: L. Parsons, 1921.

III. B. 1. g. Cooperation and Marxism

La conception soviétique de la coopération. Brussels: Société générale coopérative, 1958.

Klimov, Aleksandr P. *Cooperative Democracy Today. Address and Report at the 24th Congress of the ICA on the Theory and Practice of Cooperatives of the Socialist Countries, Hamburg, September, 1969.* Moscow: Novosti Press Agency Publishing House, 1969.

Lenin, Vladimir. *On Cooperation.* Moscow: Novosti Press Agency Publishing House, 1970; Berlin: Allgemeiner Genossenschaftsverlag, 1925 (German); Rome: Edizioni Rinascita, 1949 (Italian).

Partito comunista italiano. *I comunisti e la cooperazione: Storia documentaria. 1945–1980.* Bari, Italy: De Donato, 1981. (Italian)

Salute to the Coops, 1844–1944: Centenary Tribute to the Cooperative Movement by the Communist Party. London: Communist Party of Great Britain, 1944.

III. B. 1. h. Rochdale Principles of Cooperation

Alvarez Palacios, Fernando. *Los Justos Pioneros de Rochdale: aproximación al moderno cooperativismo democrático.* Seville: Federación Regional de Cooperativas Andaluzas, 1979.

Bórea, Domingo. *Tratado de cooperación.* Buenos Aires: Imprenta Gadola, 1927.

Brown, Henry. *The Rochdale Pioneers.* Manchester: Coop Union, 1944.

Brown, William H. *Rochdale Pioneers: The Story of the Toad Lane Store, 1844, and the Origin of the Cooperative Union, 1869.* Manchester: Coop Union, 1931.

Cole, G. D. H. *A Century of Cooperation.* Manchester: Coop Union, 1945.

Davidovic, George. *Reformulation of the Cooperative Principles: A Commentary on the Guiding Principles of Cooperative Organization, With an Analysis of Canadian Views on the Rochdale Principles.* Ottawa: CUC, 1966.

Flanagan, Desmond. *The Cooperative Movement's First 100 Years.* London: Pilot Press, 1944.

Handschin, Hans. *Die Grundsätze der redlichen Pioniere von Rochdale.* Basel: Buchdruckerei, 1944.

———. *Les principes de Rochdale et le coopérativisme.* Basel: Bibliothèque coopérative populaire, 1938.

Hasselmann, Erwin. *Die Rochdaler Grundsätze im Wandel der Zeit.* Frankfurt: Deutsche Genossenschaftskasse, 1968.

Holyoake, George J. *Histoire des équitables pionniers de Rochdale.* Nîmes: Bibliothèque de l'émancipation, 1890.

———. *Holyoake's Geschichte der Rochdaler Pioniere.* Cologne: Gepagverlag, 1928.

———. *Self-Help by the People, a History of Cooperation in Rochdale.* London: S. Sonnenschein, 1893; New York: C. Scribner's Sons, 1893.

Hommage à la mémoire des pionniers de Rochdale. Basel: Coopérateur suisse, 1944.

Peach, Lawrence du Garde. *Cooperative Centenary.* Manchester: Coop Union, 1944.

Reeves, Joseph. *A Century of Rochdale Cooperation, 1844–1944.* London: Lawrence and Wishart, 1944.

Rivera Campos, Julian. *El secreto de Rochdale; nueva filosofía de la vida.* Buenos Aires: Intercoop, 1961.

The Rochdale Equitable Pioneer's Society: An Illustrated Souvenir. Manchester: Coop Union, 1967.

Schloesser, Robert. *Die berühmten Grundsätze der Rochdaler Pioniere nebst Originalstatuten.* Cologne: Gepagverlag, 1927.

Serwy, Victor. *Le centenaire des équitables pionniers de Rochdale.* Brussels: Les Propagateurs de la coopération, 1946.

Valko, Laszlo. *The Rochdale Principles Today.* Pullman: Washington State University Press, 1966.

III. B. 2. Reformulating Cooperative Principles

Barve, Sadashiv G. *The Cooperative Principle: Purpose and Potential.* Bombay: Bombay Gandhi Smarak Nidhi, 1967.

Bhat, P., and P. Khanti. *Cooperative Principles and History.* Bangalore, India: Mysore State Cooperative Union, 1971.

Bogardus, Emory. *Principles of Cooperation.* Chicago: CLUSA, 1952; 2nd edition, 1958; 3rd edition, 1964.

Book, Sven Ake. *Cooperative Values in a Changing World.* Geneva: ICA, 1992.

Cooperative Principles and the By-Laws. A Study Guide Related to the By-Laws of a Primary Cooperative Society. Baghdad: Institute of Cooperation and Agricultural Extension, 1969.

Cooperative Principles in the Modern World: Essays Contributed in Memory of Arnold Bonner. Loughborough, U.K.: Coop Union, Education Department, 1967.

Davidovic, George. *Reformulation of the Cooperative Principles: A Commentary on the Guiding Principles of Cooperative Organizations, With an Analysis of Canadian Views on the Rochdale Principles.* Ottawa: CUC, 1966.

Desroches, Henri. *Principes rochdaliens? Lesquels?* Paris: BECC, 1962.

Dubhashi, P. R. *Principles and Philosophy of Cooperation.* Poona, India: Mehta, 1970.

Erdman, Henry E., and James M. Tinley. *The Principles of Cooperation and Their Relation to Success or Failure.* Berkeley: University of California, Division of Agricultural Sciences, 1957.

Fabra Ribas, Antonio. *La neutralidad política y religiosa en el movimiento cooperativo.* San José, Costa Rica: [n.p.], 1948.

Fisher, John W. *The Principles of Cooperation and the Principles of Cooperative Organization.* Chicago: American Institute of Agriculture, 1923.

Harris, Thomas D. *Cooperative Principles: Their Practice, Problems and Potential in Canada.* Winnipeg: University of Manitoba, 1968.

Karve, D. *Cooperation: Principles and Substance.* Poona: Gokhale Institute of Politics and Economics, 1968; Bombay and New York: Asia Publishing House, 1968.

———. *Reformulation of Cooperative Principles.* Bombay: Bombay Gandhi Smarak Nidhi, 1967.

Lockward, G. *Los siete principios cooperativos.* Trujillo, Dominican Republic: Editorial del Caribe, 1957.

MacPherson, Ian. *Cooperative Principles for the 21st Century.* Geneva: ICA, 1995.

Mladenatz, Gromoslav. *Histoire des doctrines coopératives.* Paris: PUF, 1933; also Mexico City: Editorial America, 1944 (Spanish).

Münkner, Hans H. *Cooperative Principles and Cooperative Law.* Marburg, Germany: Institut für Genossenschaftswesen in Entwicklungsländern, 1974.

Nast, A. *Principes coopératifs.* Paris: Rivière, 1949.

Nuevos enfoques de los principios cooperativos en el mundo. Rosario, Argentina: Ediciones Instituto, 1967.

Orne, Anders E. *Cooperative Ideals and Problems.* Manchester: Coop Union, 1937.

Les principes coopératifs hier, aujourd'hui, demain: colloque, Liège, Mars, 1966. Paris: Institut des études coopératives, 1967.

The Present Application of the Rochdale Principles of Cooperation. London: ICA, 1937; also ICA Studies and Reports, London, 1964.

Puri, S. S. *Ends and Means of Cooperative Development.* New Delhi: NCUI, 1979.

Report of the ICA Commission on Cooperative Principles. London: ICA, 1971.

Report of the ICA Commission on Cooperative Principles. Geneva: ICA, CEMAS, 1986.

Tufts, James H. *The Ethics of Cooperation.* Boston and New York: Houghton Mifflin, 1918.

Valko, Laszlo. *The Rochdale Principles Today.* Pullman: Washington State University Press, 1966.

Van der Post, A. *The Principles of Cooperation.* Pretoria: Government Printer, 1930.

Watkins, William P. *Cooperative Principles: Today and Tomorrow.* Manchester: Holyoake Books, 1986.

Weeraman, P. E. *The Cooperative Principles.* New Delhi: ICA, ROECSEA, 1973.

III. B. 3. Organizing Cooperation

Acevedo Ardila, Mario. *Régimen de sociedades cooperativas.* Bogota: Editorial Centro, 1940.

Campo Redundo, L. *Asociaciones cooperativas; fundamentos, constitución, legalización, registro, funcionamiento, peligros, secretos del triunfo.* Madrid: Bergua, 1932.

Casselman, Paul. *The Cooperative Movement and Some of Its Problems.* New York: Philosophical Library, 1952.

Cerda y Richart, Baldomero. *El régimen cooperativo.* Barcelona: Bosch, 1959.

Conference on Cooperative Thought and Practice, Cooperative College of Canada, 1977. Saskatoon: Cooperative College of Canada, 1978.

Craig, John G. *Locally Owned Multinational Enterprises: International Cooperation Between Cooperatives.* Downsville, Canada: York University, Department of Sociology, 1974.

Davidovic, George. *The Structure of Cooperative Unions and Central Cooperative Organizations in Various Countries: Great Britain, Finland, Norway, Sweden, Switzerland, United States.* Ottawa: CUC, 1965.

Dechant, Josef. *Untersuchungen zur Theorie der Gesamtorganisation des Genossenschaftswesens.* Erlangen, Germany: Forschungsinstitut für das Genossenschaftswesen, 1970.

Desroche, Henri. *Le développement intercoopératif, ses modèles et ses combinations.* Sherbrooke, Quebec: Librairie de la Cité Universitaire, 1969.

——. *Planification et volontariat dans le développement coopératif.* Paris: Mouton, 1963.

——. *Le projet coopératif. Son utopie et sa pratique. Ses appareils et ses réseaux. Ses espérances et ses déconvenues.* Paris: Éditions Économie et Humanisme, Les Éditions ouvrieres, 1976.

Digby, Margaret. *Cooperation: What It Means and How It Works.* London and New York: Longmans, Green, 1947.

——. *Cooperatives.* London: Overseas Development Institute, 1963.

Fabra Ribas, Antonio. *El ABC de la cooperación.* Albacete, Spain: [n.p.], 1932.

Goel, Brij Bhushan. *Cooperative Management and Administration: Organization and Working of an Apex Federation.* New Delhi: Deep and Deep, 1984.

Grünfeld, Ernst. *Handbuch des Genossenschaftswesens.* Halberstadt, Germany: Meyer, 1928.

Hazela, T. N. *Principles, Problems and Practice of Cooperation.* Agra, India: Shiva Lal Agarwala, 1973.

Hettlage, Robert. *Genossenchaftstheorie und Partizipations-diskussion.* Göttingen, Germany: Vandenhoeck and Ruprecht, 1987.

Holyoake, George J. *Manual of Cooperation.* New York: J. B. Alden, 1885.

Hughes, Thomas, and Edward Vansittart Neale, eds. *A Manual for Cooperators.* London: Macmillan, 1881.

Institut für Genossenschaftswesen. *Planning in Cooperation.* Göttingen, Germany: Vandenhoek and Ruprecht, 1967.

An Introduction to Cooperative Practice. Geneva: ILO, 1952. (Also in Spanish.)

Klein, F. *Aktuelle Probleme des Genossenschaftswesens.* Göttingen, Germany: Vandenhoeck and Ruprecht, 1957.

Lasserre, Georges. *Des obstacles au développement du mouvement coopératif.* Paris: Sirey, 1927.

Lavergne, B. *Les régies coopératives.* Paris: Alcan, 1927.

Lynip, Ryllis. *Cooperatives.* New York: Foreign Policy Association, 1937.

Mathema, Cain. *Cooperatives, What About Them?* Harare, Zimbabwe: Kingstons, 1988.

Myrick, Herbert. *How To Cooperate. The Full Fruits of Labor to Producer, Honest Value to Consumer, Just Return to Capital, Prosperity to All. A Manual for Co-operators.* New York: O. Judd, 1891.

Pfüller, R. *Der Genossenschaftsverband, Grundlagen, Entwicklung, Probleme, Tendenzen.* Göttingen, Germany: Vandenhoeck and Ruprecht, 1964.

Power, Richard A. *The Cooperative Primer.* Viroqua, Wis.: R. A. Power, 1939.

Richardson, G. *A.B.C. of Cooperatives.* Toronto: Longman, 1940.

Robinson, E. L. *A Common Sense Cooperative System.* Cave Mills, Tenn.: Coming Nation Printers, 1896.

Roy, Ewell P. *Cooperatives: Development, Principles, and Management.* Danville, Ill.: Interstate Printers and Publishers, 1981.

Rozy, Henri. *Étude sur les sociétés coopératives et leur constitution légale.* Paris: Guillaumin, 1866.

Saint Siegens R, Jorge. *Manual de texto sobre cooperativas.* Tegucigalpa, Honduras: Talleres Tipográficos Nacionales, 1952.

Skar, J., et al. *Cooperative Systems Development: Proceedings from an International Conference at the University of Stockholm, June, 1981.* Stockholm: Stockholms Universitet, Foretagsekonomiska Institutionen, 1982.

Sommerhoff, Walter. *Tres Congresos Internacionales: doctrina, estructura, planificación y financiamiento cooperativo.* Santiago: SODIMAC, 1968.

Vela Sastre, Jaime. *Manual de organización y funciones para las cooperativas.* Lima: Centro de Estudios y Promoción del Desarrollo, 1975.

Warbasse, James P. *Problems of Cooperation. A Study of the Deficiencies of Cooperative Method of Economic Organization and the Difficulties in the Way of Expansion.* New York: Island Press, 1942.

Watkins, William P. *School of Democracy.* Manchester: Coop Union, 1951.

Why Cooperatives Succeed and Fail. Washington, D.C.: Overseas Cooperative Development Committee, 1985.

Why Coops? What Are They? How Do They Work? Madison, Wis.: United States Armed Forces Institute, 1944.

III. B. 4. Cooperation and Society

III. B. 4. a. Cooperation as Economic Democracy

Bárdos-Feltoronyi, Nicolas, et al. *Coopération: Défis pour une démocratie économique.* Brussels: Evo, 1993.

Bowen, Eugene R. *A Charter of Economic Freedom.* Chicago: CLUSA, 1944.

———. *A Cooperative Economic Democracy.* Chicago and New York: CLUSA, 1944.

Coady, M. M. *Masters of Their Own Destiny.* New York: Harper, 1939.

Colombain, Maurice. *Le mouvement coopératif dans un régime démocratique.* Quebec: [n.p.], 1943.

Landis, Benson. *A Cooperative Economy, A Study of a Democratic Economic Movement.* New York: Harper, 1943.

Lasserre, Georges. *L'expérience coopérative de démocratie économique.* Paris: FNCC, 1957.

Plumb, Glenn E., and William G. Roylance. *Industrial Democracy: A Plan For Its Achievement.* New York: B. W. Huebsch, 1923.

Poisson, Ernest. *Démocratie et coopération.* Paris: PUF, 1932.

Voorhis, Horace J. (Jerry). *The Morale of Democracy: Three Addresses on the Twenty-Fifth Anniversary of the Cooperative League of the U.S.A.* New York: Greystone Press, 1941.

Warbasse, James P. *Cooperative Democracy Through Voluntary Association of the People as Consumers.* New York: Harper, 1947.

———. *Democracia cooperativa.* Buenos Aires: Editorial Atalaya, 1945.

———. *Genossenschaftliche Demokratie.* Hamburg: Verlags-gesellschaft deutscher Konsumvereine, 1926.

Watkins, W. *School of Democracy.* Manchester: Coop Union, 1951.

III. B. 4. b. Cooperation and Economic Development

Bodenstedt, A. A., ed. *Self-Help: Instrument or Objective in Rural Development.* Saarbrücken, Germany: Verlag der SSIP-Schriften Breitenbach, 1976.

Bowen, Eugene R. *The Cooperative Road to Abundance.* New York: H. Schuman, 1953.

———. *Cooperation Between Producers and Consumers.* New York and Chicago: CLUSA, 1939.

Coady, M. M. *Las cooperativas como método de desarrollo de regiones y comunidades.* Washington, D.C.: Unión Panamericana, 1964.

Craig, John G. *Multinational Cooperatives: An Alternative for World Development.* Saskatoon, Saskatchewan: Western Producer Prairie Books, 1976.

Konopnicki, M., and Gaston Vendewalle, eds. *Cooperation as an Instrument for Rural Development: Papers From an International Conference, Ghent University, Belgium, September, 1976.* London: ICA, 1978.

Léon Alvarado, Manuel. *Genossenschaften als Träger der Diffusion von Innovationen.* Tübingen: Mohr, 1980.

Levi, Yair, and Howard Litwin, eds. *Community and Cooperatives in Participatory Development.* Aldershot, U. K. and Brookfield, Vt.: Gower, 1986.

Moller, Edwin A. *El cooperativismo como proceso de cambio.* La Paz, Bolivia: Editorial los Amigos del Libro, 1986.

Panzoni, E. *Cooperativismo, desarrollo y tendencias actuales.* Santa Fe, Argentina: Editorial Belgrano, 1966.

Peck, Bradford. *The World, A Department Store.* Lewiston, Me.: B. Peck, 1900; reissued, New York: Arno Press, 1971.

The Role of Cooperation in Rural Development. Tel Aviv: CIRCOM, 1965.

Role of Cooperation in Social and Economic Development. New Delhi: ICA, ROECSEA, [n.d.]; reissued, New York, Bombay and London: Asia Publishing House, 1966.

Solis, Marcial. *El cooperativismo, el cambio y el desarrollo.* Tegucigalpa, Honduras: Editorial Universitaria, 1986.

Thordarson, Bruce. *Banking on the Grass Roots—Cooperatives in Global Development.* Ottawa: North-South Institute, 1990.

III. B. 4. c. Cooperation and the Poor

Agrawal, Govind R., and Neeru Shrestha, eds. *Cooperative Development and Basic Needs.* Katmandu, Nepal: Tribhuvan University, 1985.

Bellamy, Edward. *How to Employ the Unemployed in Mutual Maintenance.* Boston: [n.p.], 1893.

Doyle, Marion Wade. *A Guide for a Self-Help Exchange.* Washington, D.C.: Washington Self-Help Exchange, 1943.

Hoyland, J. *Digging for a New England; The Cooperative Farm for the Unemployed.* London: Cape, 1936.

Kerr, Clark. *Productive Enterprises of the Unemployed, 1931–1938.* Berkeley: University of California Press, 1939.

Machima, Pradit, and Daman Prakash. *Cooperatives for Development of the Rural Poor.* Dacca, Bangladesh: Center on Integrated Rural Development for Asia and the Pacific, 1987.

Mercer, Thomas W. *Towards the Cooperative Commonwealth. Why Poverty in the Midst of Plenty?* Manchester: Cooperative Press, 1936.

Münkner, Hans H. *Annotated Bibliography on Cooperatives and Rural Poverty.* Rome: COPAC, 1978.

————. *Short Analytical Review of Research Results on Cooperatives and Rural Poverty and Indications of Priorities for the Future Research on Cooperatives and Rural Poverty.* Rome: COPAC, 1978.

Report of an Experts' Consultation on Cooperatives and the Poor, Cooperative College, Loughborough, U.K., July, 1977. London: ICA, Studies and Reports, 1978.

Report on Symposium: Cooperatives Against Rural Poverty. Rome: COPAC, 1978.

Rutzebeck, Hjalmar. *Reciprocal Economy: Self-Help, Cooperative Technique and Management.* Santa Barbara, Calif.: J. F. Rowny Press, 3rd edition, 1935.

Self-Help Cooperatives: An Introductory Study. Washington, D.C.: Federal Emergency Relief Administration, 1935.

Self-Help Program of the Federal Emergency Relief Administration. Summary of Federal Aid to Self-Help Cooperatives in the United States, July 1, 1933— December 31, 1935. Washington, D.C.: Federal Emergency Relief Administration, Division of Self-Help Cooperatives, 1936.

United States. Federal Emergency Relief Administration. *Cooperative Self-Help.* Richmond Va.: Printed by the Citizens' Service Exchange, a Self-Help Cooperative, 1934.

III. B. 4. d. Cooperation and Peace

Carpenter, Julius H. *Peace Through Cooperation.* New York and London: Harper and Brothers, 1944.

Carter, G. R. *Cooperation and the Great War.* London: P. S. King and Son, 1915.

Johansson, H. C. *International Cooperation and Peace.* Chicago: CLUSA, 1957.

Kagawa, Toyohiko. *Proposals for World Peace Based on International Cooperatives.* [n.l.]: [n.p.], 1937.

Warbasse, James P. *Cooperation as a Way of Peace.* New York and London: Harper and Brothers, 1939.

————. *Cooperative Peace.* Superior, Wis.: Cooperative Publishing Association, 1950.

III. B. 4. e. Social Impacts of Cooperation

Arnold, Joseph I. *Cooperative Citizenship.* Evanston, Ill., and Philadelphia: Row, Peterson, 1933.

Coady, M. M. *The Social Significance of the Cooperative Movement.* Antigonish: St. Francis Xavier University, 1945.

The Cooperative Movement and Better Nutrition: Standard Definitions of Foodstuffs, Education of Producers and Consumers. Geneva: ILO, 1937.

Fowler, Bertram B. *The Cooperative Challenge.* Boston: Little, Brown, 1947.

Gide, Charles. *Le juste prix, leçons professées au College de France.* Paris: PUF, 1941.

May, Henry J. Foundation. *Social Aspects of Cooperation.* London: ICA, 1950.

Pick, F. *Cooperation and Human Rights.* Manchester: Coop Union, 1949.

Sinha, B. P. *Cooperation: Instrument for Socio-Economic Justice.* Bombay: Himalaya Publishing House, 1992.

Worley, J. *Social Philosophy of Cooperation.* Manchester: Coop Union, 1942.

III. B. 4. f. Cooperation as the Basis for a Future Society

Angevine, Erma. *In League With The Future.* Chicago: CLUSA, 1959.

Angueira Miranda, Miguel. *Carácter revolucionario del cooperativismo.* Buenos Aires: Intercoop, 1960.

———. *Hacia la comunidad cooperativa libre.* Buenos Aires: Intercoop, 1975.

Bishop, Claire H. *All Things Common.* New York: Harper, 1950.

Bossle, Lothar, ed. *Die Zukunft der Genossenschaften im 21. Jahrhundert: Zur Erinnerung an Friedrich W. Raiffeisen und Georg Heim.* Würzberg, Germany: Creator, 1989.

Davidovic, George. *Towards a Cooperative World, Economically, Socially and Politically.* Antigonish: Coady International Institute, 1967.

———. *Vers un monde coopératif.* Ottawa: Éditions du jour, 1975.

Dey, Surendra K. *Sahakari Samaj: The Cooperative Commonwealth.* New York and Bombay: Asia Publishing House, 1967.

Eddy, George Sherwood. *Creative Pioneers: Building a New Society Through Adventurous Vocations and Avocations: The Political Movement, the Cooperative Movement, Race Relations and Socialized Religion.* New York: Association Press, 1937.

Fabra Rivas, Antonio. *Hacia un nuevo orden económico.* Medellín, Colombia: [n.p.], 1943.

Goodenough, Ward H. *Cooperation in Change.* New York: Russell Sage Foundation, 1963.

Knight, H. V. *The Consumers Awaken: The Challenge of Cooperation.* Jamestown: Farmers' Union Cooperative Education Service, 1939.

Laidlaw, Alexander F. *Cooperatives in the Year 2000: A Paper Prepared for the 27th Congress of the International Cooperative Alliance, Moscow, October, 1980.* London: ICA, 1980.

Lasker, Emanuel. *The Community of the Future.* New York: M. J. Bernin, 1940.

Mercer, Thomas W. *Towards the Cooperative Commonwealth.* Manchester: Cooperative Press, 1936.

Mooney, George S. *Cooperatives Today and Tomorrow.* Montreal: Montreal Survey on Cooperation, 1938.

Parnell, Edgar. *Reinventing the Cooperative: Enterprises for the 21st Century.* Oxford: Plunkett, 1995.

Poisson, Ernest. *La république coopérative.* Paris: Bernard Grasset, 1920.

———. *The Cooperative Republic.* Manchester: Coop Union, 1925.

Ross, John E. *Cooperative Plenty.* London and St. Louis: B. Herder, 1941.

Taimni, K. K. *Cooperative Development: The Next Phase.* New Delhi: ICA/Domus Trust, 1993.

Voorhis, Horace Jeremiah (Jerry). *The Cooperatives Look Ahead*. New York: Public Affairs, 1952.

Wallace, Henry Agard. *Cooperation: The Dominant Economic Idea of the Future*. New York: CLUSA, 1936.

III. B. 5. Economics of Cooperation

Abrahamsen, Martin A. *Cooperative Business Enterprise*. New York: McGraw-Hill, 1976.

Almarcha Hernandez, Luis. *La cooperación como sistema económico-social*. Madrid: Obra Sindical Cooperación, 1945; 4th edition, León: Centro de Estudios e Investigación San Isidoro, 1970.

Angers, François A. *La coopération: De la réalité à la théorie économique*. Montreal: Fides, 1974.

Baarda, James R. *Cooperative Principles and Statutes: Legal Descriptions of Unique Enterprises*. Washington, D.C.: USDA, FCS, 1986.

Baker, Jacob. *Cooperative Enterprise*. New York: Vanguard, 1937.

Barnard, Charles. *Cooperation As A Business*. New York: G. P. Putnam's Sons, 1881.

Bunn, Harriet F. *Cooperative Life and Business*. Milwaukee, Wis.: E. M. Hale, 1936.

Dufour, A. L. *La place des coopératives dans l'économie*. Dijon: Imprimerie Jobard, 1942.

Emelianoff, Ivan V. *Economic Theory of Cooperation*. Washington, D.C.: Edward Bross, 1942.

Faucher, Albert. *L'entreprise coopérative*. Quebec: Éditions du cap diamant, 1944.

Fernández, Joaquín. *Economía para cooperativas*. Barcelona: Ediciones Ceac, 1983.

Gide, Charles. *Cours d'économie politique*. Paris: Recueil Sirey, 1913.

Harper, R. *Economics of Cooperation*. Manila: Bureau of Public Schools, 1958.

Ihimodu, Ifeyori I. *Cooperative Economics: A Concise Analysis in Theory and Applications*. Kaduna, Nigeria: Nigerian Agricultural and Cooperative Bank, 1988; Ilorin, Nigeria: Department of Economics, University of Ilorin, 1988.

Kaarlehto, P. *On the Economic Nature of Cooperation*. Stockholm: Alinquist and Wicksells, 1956.

Kennedy, Liam, ed. *Economic Theory of Cooperative Enterprises: Selected Readings*. Oxford: Plunkett, 1983.

Knapp, Joseph G. *Farmers in Business: Studies in Cooperative Enterprise*. Washington, D.C.: AIC, 1963.

Landis, Benson Y. *A Cooperative Economy*. New York and London: Harper and Brothers, 1943.

Lasserre, Georges. *Les éntreprises coopératives*. Paris: PUF, 1977.

Leclercq, Robert. *La position du mouvement coopératif devant l'évolution économique*. Paris: FNCC, 1955.

Louis, Dieter. *Zu einer allgemeinen Théorie der ökonomischen Kooperation: Verhaltenstheoret. Grundlegung der wirtschaftlichen Zusammenarbeit.* Göttingen, Germany: Vandenhoeck and Ruprecht, 1979.

Odhe, Thorsten. *The Place of Cooperation in the World Economy.* London: ICA, 1947.

Perrault, P. T. *Application des théories de la firme et de quelques notions modernes à l'étude de l'entreprise coopérative.* Sherbrooke, Quebec: Librairie de la Cité Universitaire, 1972.

Pichette, Claude, and Jean C. Mailhot. *Analyse microéconomique et coopérative.* Sherbrooke, Quebec: Librairie de la Cité Universitaire, 1972.

Ross, John E. *Cooperative Plenty.* St. Louis and London: B. Herder, 1941.

Warbasse, James P. *Problems of Cooperation: A Study of the Deficiencies of the Cooperative Method of Economic Organization and the Difficulties in the Way of Its Expansion.* New York: Island Press, 1942.

III. B. 6. Cooperation—Comparisons with Other Socio-Economic Systems

Almarcha Hernández, Luis. *El capitalismo y el comunismo y la cooperación.* Madrid: Unión Nacional de Cooperativas del Campo, 1947.

Bessaignet, Pierre. *Coopération et capitalisme d'état.* Paris: PUF, 1953.

Boettcher, Erik. *Die Genossenschaft in der Marktwirtschaft: Einzelwirtschaftliche Théorie der Genossenschaften.* Tübingen: Mohr, 1980.

Bowen, Eugene R. *The Cooperative Road to Abundance: The Alternative to Monopolism and Communism.* New York: Schumann, 1953.

Buber, Martin. *Caminos de Utopia.* Mexico City: Fondo de Cultura Económica, 1955.

———. *Paths in Utopia.* London: Routledge and Kegan Paul, 1949; New York: Macmillan, 1950; reissued, Boston: Beacon Press, 1985; New York: Collier Books, 1986.

———. *Pfade in Utopia: Uber Gemeinschaft und deren Verwirklichung.* Heidelberg: L. Schneider, 1985.

Childs, Marquis. *Sweden, The Middle Way.* London: Faber, 1936; New Haven: Yale University Press, 1936; reissued, New Haven: Yale University Press, 1980.

Clay, Henry. *Cooperation and Private Enterprise.* London: E. Benn, 1928.

Compart, Eddo. *Kapitalistische Entwicklungswege bei der Genossenschaft.* Frankfurt: Haag and Herchen, 1977.

Davis, Jerome. *Contemporary Social Movements.* New York and London: Century, 1930.

de Drimer, Alicia, and B. de Drimer, eds. *Relaciones entre el cooperativismo y otras doctrinas o movimientos de carácter económico social.* Buenos Aires: Intercoop, 1970.

Does the Cooperative Movement Offer a Meeting Ground Between Socialism and Capitalism? Brisbane: Australian Broadcasting Commission, 1946.

Économie privée et socialisme coopératif. Lausanne: Schweizerischer Gewerbe-verband, 1950.

Fauquet, Georges. *Le secteur coopératif.* Paris: Imprimerie coopérative ouvrière, 1935; reissued, Paris: PUF, 1942.

Galofré, E. *La empresa cooperativa. Un tipo de empresa no-capitalista.* Santiago: Universidad Católica de Chile, 1973.

Heflebower, Richard B. *Cooperatives and Mutuals in the Market System.* Madison: University of Wisconsin Press, 1980.

Herzog, Louis. *Democracy's Answer to Communism Through Group Enterprise.* New York: William-Frederick Press, 1955.

Hobley, L. F. *Working-Class and Democratic Movements.* Glasgow: Blackie, 1970.

Kress, Andrew. *Capitalism, Cooperation, Communism.* Washington, D.C.: Rans-dell, 1932.

Kummer, Karl. *Der dritte Weg: Grundsätzliche und praktische Vorschläge für eine Sozialreform.* Vienna: [n.p.], 1949.

Laidler, Harry. *Social Economic Movements, an Historical and Comparative Survey of Socialism, Communism, Cooperation and Utopianism.* London: Routledge and Kegan Paul, 1949.

Lewis, John S. *Fairer Shares: A Possible Advance in Civilization and Perhaps the Only Alternative to Communism.* London: Staples Press, 1954.

Longden, Fred. *Cooperative Politics Inside Capitalist Society.* Birmingham, U.K.: Cornish Brothers, 1941.

Loucks, William N. *Comparative Economic Systems: Capitalism, Communism, Fascism, Socialism, Cooperation.* New York and London: Harper and Brothers, 1938.

Mansilla, M. A. *Postulados y principios cooperativos y sus diferencias y aproximaciones con otros sistemas.* Bogota: Universidad de Santo Tomás, 1971.

Miller, Raymond W. *A Conservative Looks at Cooperatives.* Athens: Ohio University Press, 1964.

Outrequin, Philippe, Anne Potier, and Patrice Sauvage. *Les entreprises alternatives.* Paris: Syros, 1986.

Torres y Torres Lara, Carlos. *Cooperativismo, el modelo alternativo: Estudio sobre su ideología, instituciones y técnicas.* Lima: Universidad de Lima, 1983.

Totomiants, Vakhan F. *The Place of Cooperation Among Other Social Movements.* Manchester: Coop Union, 1923.

Valko, Laszlo. *Cooperative Ideas in the Eastern and Western Worlds.* Pullman: Washington State University Press, 1951.

Zimand, Savel. *Modern Social Movements: Descriptive Summaries and Bibliographies.* New York: H. W. Wilson, 1921; reissued, New York: Revisionist Press, 1972.

III. B. 7. Cooperation and Competition

Colman, Andrew M, ed. *Cooperation and Competition in Humans and Animals.* Wokingham, U. K.: Van Nostrand Reinhold, 1982.

Combs, Allan, ed. *Cooperation: Beyond the Age of Competition.* Philadelphia: Gordon and Breach, 1992.

Jorge, Antonio. *Competition, Cooperation, Efficiency, and Social Organization: Introduction to a Political Economy.* Rutherford, N. J.: Fairleigh Dickinson University Press, 1978.

Kohn, Alfie. *No Contest: The Case Against Competition.* Boston: Houghton Mifflin, 1992.

Lazo, Hector. *Controlled Competition: Corporate Chains, Cartels and Cooperatives.* Washington, D.C.: Cooperative Food Distributors of America, 1939.

Memorandum on Research in Competition and Cooperation. New York: Social Science Research Council, 1937.

Olson, M. *The Logic of Collective Action.* Cambridge: Harvard University Press, 1965.

III. B. 8. Nurturing Cooperation

Goley, Elaine P. *Learn the Value of Cooperation.* Vero Beach, Fla.: Rourke Enterprises, 1988.

Honig, Alice S., and Donna S. Wittmer. *Prosocial Development in Children: Caring, Helping, and Cooperating: A Bibliographic Resource Guide.* New York: Garland Publishers, 1992.

Orlick, Terry. *The Cooperative Sports and Games Book: Challenge Without Competition.* New York: Pantheon Books, 1978.

Orlick, Terry, and Cal Botterill. *Every Kid Can Win.* Chicago: Nelson-Hall, 1975.

———. *The Second Cooperative Sports and Games Book.* New York: Pantheon Books, 1982.

———. *Winning Through Cooperation: Competitive Insanity, Cooperative Alternatives.* Washington, D.C.: Acropolis Books, 1978.

Riehecky, Janet. *Cooperation.* Chicago: Child's World/Children's Press, 1990.

Sobel, Jeffrey. *Everybody Wins II: 1,000 Non-Competitive Games.* Martinsville, Ind.: American Camping Association, 1994.

Wrightsman, Lawrence, John O'Connor, and Norma J. Baker. *Cooperation and Competition: Readings on Mixed-Motive Games.* Belmont, Calif.: Brooks/Cole Publishing, 1972.

III. B. 9. Cooperation in Developing Countries

Araneta, T. C. A. *Cooperatives: A Strategy for Development.* Quezon City: Filipino Publishing, 1973.

Bakken, Henry H. *Basic Concepts, Principles and Practice of Cooperation.* Madison, Wis.: Mimir Publishers, 1963.

Benecke, Dieter W. *Cooperation and Development: Role of Cooperative Societies in Developing Countries.* Mainz: Hase and Köhler, 1982; Santiago: Nueva Universidad, 1973 (Spanish).

————— *Las cooperativas. Una herramienta para perfeccionar la competencia en los países en vias de desarrollo.* Santiago: Universidad Católica de Chile, 1973.

Bognár, J. *Problem of the Economic Growth in the Developing Countries and Role of the Cooperatives in Their National Economy.* Budapest: Federation of Hungarian Cooperatives, 1964.

Campbell, W. *Cooperation for Economically Underdeveloped Countries.* Washington, D.C.: League of Nations, 1938.

Carello, L. A. *Cooperativismo y desarrollo.* Buenos Aires: Intercoop, 1979.

Coopération et développement, éléments bibliographiques. Paris: Centre de recherches coopératives, 1964.

Cooperative Movement and Social Justice. New Delhi: NCUI, 1976.

Desroche, Henri. *Coopération et développement: Mouvements coopératifs et stratégie du développement.* Paris: PUF, 1964.

—————. *Promotion of Cooperatives in Developing Countries.* Strasbourg, France: Council of Europe, Third Seminar on International Voluntary Service, Cooperation in Economic and Social Development, 1968.

La encíclica Mater et Magistra y las cooperativas. Madrid: Servicio de Información y Publicaciones Sindicales, 1962.

Enriquez, C. G. *Cooperatives and Development.* Antigonish, Nova Scotia, Antigonish: Coady International Institute, 1986.

Farizov, I. O. *Rural Cooperation in the Developing Countries.* Moscow: Kolos, 1973. (Also in French, German and Russian.)

Garcia, Quintin. *Cooperativismo y desarrollo.* Madrid: Marsiega, 1974.

Ghaussy, Abdul G. *Das Genossenschaftswesen in den Entwicklungs-ländern.* Freiburg, Germany: Rombach, 1964.

ICA Policy for Cooperative Development. Geneva: ICA, 1983.

ICA. *Role of Cooperation in Social and Economic Development: Proceedings of a Regional Conference, Tokyo, April, 1964.* Bombay and New York: Asia Publishing House, 1966.

Kuhn, Johannes. *Die Genossenschaft: Eine anpassungsfähige Form der Selbstorganisation ländlicher Gruppen.* Marburg, Germany: Institut für Kooperation in Entwicklungsländern, 1981.

McGrath, Mary Jean, ed. *Guidelines for Cooperatives in Developing Economies: A Book of Readings.* Madison: University of Wisconsin, International Cooperative Training Center, 1969.

Münkner, Hans. *Genossenschaftsförderung in Entwicklungsländern.* Marburg, Germany: Deutsche Stiftung für Entwicklungsländer, 1964.

Niefeldt-Schoenbeck, W. *Möglichkeiten des Einsatzes von Genossenschaften als Mittel der Wachstumspolitik in Entwicklungsländern.* Bonn: Landwirtschaftliche Fakultät, 1976.

Le rôle des coopératives dans le développement économique et social des pays en voie de développement. Geneva: BIT, 1965 (also in English).

Sieber, L. *Cooperatives and Development.* Prague: Central Cooperative Council, 1981.

Trappe, Paul. *Warum Genossenschaften in Entwicklungsländern.* Neuwied and Berlin: Luchterhand, 1966.

Van Dooren, P. J. *Cooperatives for Developing Countries: Objectives, Policies and Practices.* Oxford: Plunkett, 1982.

Verhagen, Koenraad. *Cooperation for Survival.* [n.l.]: ICA-Royal Tropical Institute, 1984.

Wörz, J. *Cooperation as an Instrument for Rural Development in the Third World.* Witzenhausen: University of Witzenhausen, 1984.

Youngjohn, B. A. *Cooperatives in Development.* London: [n.p.], 1977.

IV. TYPES OF COOPERATIVES

IV. A. Agricultural Cooperatives

IV. A. 1. Agricultural Cooperatives—Bibliographies

Agricultural Cooperation: Annotated Bibliography. Rome: FAO, 1971. (Also in French and Spanish.)

Agricultural Cooperatives: Annotated Bibliography. Paris: Organization for Economic Cooperation and Development, Development Center, 1971.

Bibliographie de l'entreprise coopérative agricole. Paris: Centre national de la coopération agricole, 1971.

Davis, Elizabeth G. *Bibliography on Cooperation in Agriculture.* Washington, D.C.: National Agricultural Library, Library List No. 41, 1954.

Houee, Paul. *Coopération et organisation agricole française: Bibliographie 1864–1966.* Paris: Cujas, 1969.

Nielander, William A. *A Selected and Annotated Bibliography of Literature on Farmer Cooperatives.* Austin: University of Texas, 1947.

Publications and Documents of FAO on Agricultural Cooperation. Rome: FAO, 1968.

Tschiersch, Joachim E. *Cooperation in Agricultural Production: A Selective Bibliography.* Saarbrücken: Verlag der SSIP-Schriften, 1974.

IV. A. 2. Agricultural Cooperatives—Early Experience— Through World War I (1919)

American Commission for the Study of the Application of the Cooperative System to Agricultural Production, Distribution, and Finance in European Countries: Report. Washington, D.C.: GPO, 1913.

Austin, Charles B. *Cooperation in Agriculture.* Austin: University of Texas, 1914.

Barrett, Charles. *The Mission, History and Times of the Farmers Union.* Nashville, Tenn.: Marshall and Bruce, 1909.

Blanc, Rene. *Les sociétés coopératives agricoles en France.* Montpellier: Firminet, 1912.

Bonnemere, E. *Histoire de l'association agricole et solution pratique.* Paris: Dusacq, 1850.

Bussen, F. *Landwirtschaftliches Genossenschaftswesen.* Hanover: Jänecke, 1909.

Coulter, T. L. *Cooperation Among Farmers, the Keystone of Rural Prosperity.* New York: Young Farmers' Library, 1917.

Desbons, G. *La crise agricole et le remède coopératif.* Montpellier: Firmin et Montane, 1917; also Zaragoza: Imprenta del Hospicio Provincial, 1919 (Spanish).

Girola, C. *Las cooperativas agrícolas en Argentina.* Buenos Aires: [n.p.], 1913.

Hays, Willet M. *Cooperation in Agriculture.* Washington, D.C.: GPO, 1910.

Hertel, H. *Cooperation in Danish Agriculture.* London: Longman, 1918.

Kohl, M. *Das landwirtschaftliche Genossenschaftswesen des Grossherzogstums—1875–1925.* Luxembourg: Worré-Martens, 1925.

Lecolle, Gabriel. *Les associations agricoles, syndicats, coopératives, mutualités.* Paris: J. B. Bailliere et fils, 1912.

Lucas, C. *Des coopératives agricoles en France.* Bordeaux: Cadoret, 1908.

Malherbe, G. *Les fromageries ou fruitières coopératives.* Brussels: Schopers, 1899.

Milliot, L. *L'association agricole chez les Musulmans du Maghreb.* Paris: Rousseau, 1911.

Molins, J. *La asociación y cooperación agrícolas.* Barcelona: Estudio Social, 1912.

Monographs on Agricultural Cooperation in Various Countries. Rome: International Institute of Agriculture, 1915. (Also in French.)

Neuman, C. *Das landwirtschaftliche Genossenschaftswesen in Deutschland.* Stuttgart: Ulmer, 1901.

Plunkett, Horace. *The Rural Life Problems of the United States.* New York: Macmillan, 1910.

Poe, Clarence. *How Farmers Cooperate and Double Profits.* New York: Judd, 1915.

Powell, George H. *Cooperation in Agriculture.* New York: Macmillan, 1913.

Radford, George. *Agricultural Cooperation.* London: P. S. King and Son, 1909.

———. *Agricultural Cooperation and Organization.* London and New York: Hodder and Stoughton, 1917.

Sherlock, C. C. *The Modern Farm Cooperative Movement.* Des Moines, Iowa: Homestead, 1922.

Smith-Gordon, and E. P. Lionel. *Cooperation for Farmers.* London: Williams and Norgate, 1918.

Wolff, Henry W. *Cooperation in Agriculture.* London: P. S. King and Son, 1912.

IV. A. 3. Agricultural Cooperatives—Theory and Practice

Abrahamsen, Martin A., and Claude L. Scroggs. *Agricultural Cooperation: Selected Readings.* Minneapolis: University of Minnesota Press, 1957.

Análisis económico y sociológico del cooperativismo agrícola. Madrid: Confederación Española de Cajas de Ahorro, 1972.

Bakht, Z. *Agricultural Cooperatives as a Strategy for Economic Development.* Ithaca, N.Y.: Cornell University, 1978.

Bastros, Norena. *Étude comparative des modèles de groupements agricoles dans cinq pays du Bassin Méditerranéen: Algérie, Espagne, Israël, Italie, Yougoslavie.* Paris: Université de Paris, 1971; Madrid: Editorial Tecnos, 1974 (Spanish).

Beal, G. *The Roots of Participation in Farmer Cooperatives.* Ames: Iowa State University, 1954.

Bergmann, Theodor, and Takekazu B. Ogura. *Cooperation in World Agriculture— Experiences, Problems and Perspectives.* Tokyo: Food and Agriculture Policy Research Center, 1985.

Black, John D. *Research in Agricultural Cooperation.* New York: Social Science Research Council, 1933.

Boulet, D. *Éléments pour une théorie de l'entreprise coopérative agricole.* Montpellier: Institut national de recherche agronomique, 1972.

Buberstein, G. *Die Bauerngenossenschaften.* Berlin: Bauernverlag, 1937.

Cobia, David W., ed. *Cooperatives in Agriculture.* Englewood Cliffs, N.J.: Prentice-Hall, 1989.

del Arco Alvarez, J. L. *Análisis económico y sociologico de cooperativismo agrícola.* Madrid: Asociación de Estudios Cooperativos, 1972.

Digby, Margaret. *Agricultural Cooperation in the Commonwealth.* Oxford: Blackwell, 1970.

———. *Cooperatives and Land Use.* Rome: FAO, 1957. (Also in French.)

Farm Security Administration. *Managing the Small Farmers' Cooperative.* Washington, D.C.: GPO, 1940.

Filley, Horace C. *Cooperation in Agriculture.* New York: J. Wiley and Sons, 1929.

Gardner, Chastina, ed. *Cooperation in Agriculture.* Washington, D.C.: GPO, 1927; revised, 1931, 1936.

Gide, Charles. *Les associations coopératives agricoles.* Paris: Association pour l'enseignement de la coopération, 1928.

Gimeno, José M. *Socialismo y agricultura: reforma agraria y otros aspectos en Unión Soviética, China, Yugoslavia, Cuba, Argelia, Israel, Bulgaria, Vietnam, Polonia, Albania, Corea, República Democrática Alemana, Rumania, Hungría, Checoslovaquia, República Arabe Unida, Chile, e información básica sobre diversos aspectos estructurales en el agro uruguayo.* Montevideo, Uruguay: Fundación de Cultura Universitaria, 1984.

Gupta, V. K., and V. R. Gaikwad. *A Guide to Management of Small Farmer's Cooperatives.* Rome: FAO, 1982.

History of Agricultural Cooperatives. Tokyo: Central Union of Agricultural Cooperatives, 1965.

Hodgkin, C. *Business Interests and Social Ideals in Farmers' Cooperatives.* Chicago: CLUSA, 1955.

Jaggi, E. *Die landwirtschaftlichen Genossenschaften und Vereine.* Frauenfeld, Germany: Verlag Huber, 1972.

Kirsch, Ottfried C. *Vertical Cooperation Among Agricultural Producers in Western Europe and in Developing Countries.* Saarbrücken, Germany: Verlag der SSIP-Schriften Breitenbach, 1976.

Kobke, Uwe. *Landwirtschaftliche Kooperation in Theorie und Praxis.* Stuttgart: Ulmer, 1972.

La coopération agricole. Rome: Institut international d'Agriculture, 1932.

Lanneau, G. *Agriculture et coopération. Étude psycho-sociologique de la coopération agricole.* Paris: Centre de recherches coopératives, 1969.

Lidoff, Lorraine, and Susan Abbott. *Promoting Self-Help Ventures in Food Production and Distribution.* Washington, D.C.: National Council on the Aging, 1983.

Malgras, D. *Coopération en agriculture.* Abidjan, Côte d'Ivoire: INADES, 1968.

McBride, Glynn. *Agricultural Cooperatives: Their Why and Their How.* Westport, Conn.: AVI Publishing, 1986.

Ministère de l'agriculture. *Guide pratique de la coopération agricole.* Paris: Imprimerie nationale, 1954.

Mischler, Raymond J., H. H. Hulbert, and Samuel Sanders. *Organizing a Farmer Cooperative.* Washington, D.C.: GPO, 1957.

Le mouvement coopératif agricole et ses possibilités de développement. Melun, France: Maison centrale, 1937.

Nourse, Edwin G. *The Legal Status of Agricultural Cooperation.* New York: Macmillan, 1928.

Olsen, H. *Some Principles and Practices of Farmer Cooperatives.* Danville, Ill.: Interstate Printers, 1961.

Plunkett Foundation for Cooperative Studies. *Year Book of Agricultural Cooperation.* Oxford: Blackwell, (published annually beginning in 1927).

Poitevin, J. *La coopération agricole.* Paris: Dalloz, 1971.

Present Situation, Problems and Future Tasks of Agricultural Cooperatives. New Delhi: ICA, ROAP, 1990.

Rashad, I. *Agricultural Cooperation.* Baghdad: Bulaq, 1935.

Report of the Open World Conference on the Role of Agricultural Cooperatives in Economic and Social Development. London: ICA, 1972.

Rosier, B. *Structures agricoles et développement économique.* Paris: Mouton, 1968.

Rozier, Jean. *Les coopératives agricoles.* Paris: Librairie technique, 1962.

Rural Progress Through Cooperatives: The Place of Cooperative Associations in Agricultural Development. New York: United Nations, Department of Economic Affairs, 1954.

Sanders, Samuel D. *Organizing a Farmers' Cooperative.* Washington, D.C.: GPO, 1945.

Sargent, Malcolm. *Agricultural Cooperation.* Aldershot, U.K.: Gower, 1982.

Sauvage, A. *L'option coopérative en agriculture.* Paris: Synercau, 1972.

Shah, Tushaar. *Making Farmers' Cooperatives Work: Design, Governance and Management.* New Delhi and Thousand Oaks, Calif.: Sage Publications, 1995.

Smith, Louis P. *The Evolution of Agricultural Cooperation.* Oxford: Blackwell, 1961.

Srivastava, S. *Agricultural Economics and Cooperatives.* New Delhi: Chand, 1970.

Temas de cooperación agrícola. Madrid: Unión Nacional de Cooperativas del Campo, 1951.

Urrutia, H. E. *El sector agrario y el rol de las cooperativas.* Santiago: Universidad Católica de Chile, 1976.

Wad, J. *Agrarian Policies and Problems in Communist and Non-Communist Countries.* Seattle: University of Washington Press, 1967.

IV. A. 4. Agricultural Cooperatives in Europe

Agricultural Cooperative Organizations in Denmark, the Irish Republic and Norway. London: Central Council for Agricultural and Horticultural Cooperation, 1972.

Agricultural Cooperative Organizations in the E.E.C. London: Central Council for Agricultural and Horticultural Cooperation, 1970.

Broadbent, K. P., et al. *Agricultural Cooperatives in Europe.* Slough, U.K.: Commonwealth Agricultural Bureau, 1976.

Deutsche Gesellschaft für Agrarrecht. *Kooperation in der Landwirtschaft.* Berlin and Bonn: Landschriften-Verlag, 1970.

Elsworth, R. *The Story of Farmers' Cooperatives.* Washington, D.C.: USDA, FCS, 1954.

Financial Structure of Farmer Cooperatives. Washington, D.C.: USDA, FCS, 1970.

Gide, Pierre. *Les coopératives agricoles dans le Marché Commun.* Paris: Dictionnaires A. Joly, 1969.

Heckman, J., and J. Wheeler. *Agricultural Cooperation in Europe.* Washington, D.C.: USDA, FCS, 1955.

Hunacek, Zdenek. *Rechtliche Aspekte der Kooperation in der Landwirtschaft der Sowjetunion unter Berücksichtigung der Entwicklung in der DDR und CSSR.* Berlin: In Kommission bei Duncker and Humblot, 1980.

Hunek, Tadeusz, et al. *Reorienting the Cooperative Structure in Selected Eastern European Countries. Summary of Case Studies.* Rome: FAO, 1994.

Just, Flemming, ed. *Cooperatives and Farmers' Unions in Western Europe: Collaboration and Tensions.* Esbjerg, Denmark: South Jutland University Press, 1990.

Korcini, Donika, et al. *Reorienting the Cooperative Structure in Selected Eastern European Countries. Report of the Workshop, Godollo, Hungary, June, 1992.* Rome: FAO, 1994.

———. *Strengthening and Developing Voluntary Farmers' Organizations in Eastern and Central Europe. Report of the Workshop, Sofia, Bulgaria, September, 1993.* Rome: FAO, 1994.

Lockhart, Jacques, et al. *Agricultural Cooperation in the European Economic Community.* Brussels: European Economic Community, 1967. (Also in French.)

Pearson, Raymond A. *Agricultural Organizations in European Countries.* Albany, N.Y.: J. B. Lyon, 1914.

Sanders, Irwin T. *Collectivization of Agriculture in Eastern Europe.* Lexington: University of Kentucky Press, 1958.

Schulze-Hagen, Bernhard. *Die landwirtschaftlichen Zusammenschlüsse nach deutschem und europaischem Wettbewerbsrecht.* Cologne, Berlin, Bonn and Munich: Heymann, 1977.

Siulemezov, Stoian. *The Role of Agricultural Cooperatives in the Economic and Social Development of the Socialist Countries.* Sofia: Central Cooperative Union, 1973.

Todev, Tode, and Johann Brazda. *Landwirtschaftliche Produktionsgenossenschaften in Mittel- und Osteuropa: Vergangenheit, Gegenwart, Zukunft.* Göttingen, Germany: Vandenhoeck and Ruprecht, 1994.

IV. A. 5. Agricultural Cooperatives in North America

Abrahamsen, Martin A. *Agricultural Cooperation in the United States.* Oxford: Plunkett, 1980.

American Cooperation 1950. A Mid-Century Look at Farmer Cooperatives. Washington, D.C.: AIC, 1950.

Christensen, C. *Farmers' Cooperative Associations in the United States.* Washington, D.C.: GPO, 1929.

Commission royale d'enquete sur l'agriculture au Québec. *Les coopératives agricoles et les plans conjoints au Québec.* Quebec: Imprimeur de la reine, 1968.

Elisseieff, Katharina. *Die Getreideabsatzgenossenschaften in Nordamerika.* Neuwied, Germany: Verlag der Raiffeisendruckerei, 1951.

Ewing, J. M. *Agricultural Cooperation in Canada 1969.* Ontario, Canada: National Advisory Service, 1970.

Fay, Charles R. *Agricultural Cooperation in the Canadian West.* London: P. S. King and Son, 1925.

Fetrow, Ward, and R. Elsworth. *Agricultural Cooperation in the United States.* Washington, D.C.: USDA, FCS, 1947.

French, Charles, et al. *Survival Strategies for Agricultural Cooperatives.* Ames: Iowa State University Press, 1980.

Gorst, S. *The Structure of Agricultural Cooperation in the USA.* London: Plunkett, 1957.

Kaufmann, Hans. *Der kanadische Weizenpool.* Berlin and Vienna: Industrieverlag Spaeth and Linde, 1932.

Klohn, Werner. *Die Farmer-Genossenschaften in den USA.* Vechta, Germany: Vechtaer Druckerei and Verlag, 1990.

Mackintosh, William A. *Agricultural Cooperation in Western Canada.* Toronto: Ryerson Press, 1924.

Rasmussen, Wayne David. *Farmers, Cooperatives, and USDA: A History of Agricultural Cooperative Service.* Washington, D.C.: USDA, 1991.

Scherer, Bruno. *Das landwirtschaftliche Genossenschaftswesen und landwirtschaftlichen Verwertungsgenossenschaften in Kanada.* Münster: Landwirtschaftsverlag, 1955.

Sexton, Richard J., and Julie Iskow. *Factors Critical to the Success or Failure of Emerging (U.S.) Agricultural Cooperatives.* Davis: University of California, 1988.

Shereff, Henry D., et al. *Agricultural Cooperatives (Law and Legislation), 1979.* New York: Practicing Law Institute, 1979.

IV. A. 6. Agricultural Cooperatives in Developing Countries

Agricultural Cooperatives in Asia and the Pacific: Report of APO Multi-Country Study Mission, June, 1989. Tokyo: Asian Productivity Organization, 1991.

Anschel, Kurt R., Russell H. Brannon, and Eldon D. Smith, eds. *Agricultural Cooperatives and Markets in Developing Countries.* New York: Praeger, 1969.

Armbruster, Paul G. *Finanzielle Infrastruktur und organische Entwicklung durch Genossenschaften in ländlichen Raumen der Dritten Welt.* Göttingen, Germany: Vandenhoeck and Ruprecht, 1990.

Atlas de la mutualité agricole en Afrique du Nord. Algiers: Caisse centrale de reassurance de mutuelles, 1947.

Belloncle, Guy. *Le crédit agricole dans les pays d'Afrique d'expression française au sud du Sahara.* Rome: FAO, 1968.

Berthelot, J. *Criteria and Methods of Evaluating the Efficiency of Agricultural Cooperatives in Developing Countries.* Ann Arbor: University of Michigan, 1973.

Braverman, Avishay, et al. *Promoting Rural Cooperatives in Developing Countries: The Case of Sub-Saharan Africa.* Washington, D.C.: World Bank, 1991.

Cliffe, Lionel. *Experiences of Agricultural and Rural Cooperatives in Socialist Countries in Africa.* Rome: FAO, 1985.

Comte, Bernard. *Développement rural et coopération agricole en Afrique tropicale.* Fribourg, Switzerland: Éditeurs universitaires, 1968.

Coopération agricole et développement rural. Actes du colloque international de Tel Aviv, Israel, mars, 1965. Paris/La Haye: Mouton, 1967.

Las cooperativas en el desarrollo rural. San José, Costa Rica: ACI, ORCC, 1992.

Las cooperativas y los pequeños productores como agentes de desarrollo. San José, Costa Rica: ACI, ORCC, 1993.

Cooperativismo y desarrollo rural: La experiencia latinoamericana. Quito: Ediciones de la Pontificia Universidad Católica del Ecuador, 1985.

DeGraft-Johnson, John C. *African Experiment: Cooperative Agriculture and Banking in British West Africa.* London: Watts, 1958.

Delion, Jean. *Animation coopérative et développement melanesien.* Paris: PUF, 1984.

Dubell, Folke. *Cooperative Development: Methods of Starting and Reorganizing Agricultural Cooperative Societies in a Developing Country.* Linkoping, Sweden: Education and Research Consultant, 1981.

Dülfer, Eberhard. *Operational Efficiency of Agricultural Cooperatives in Developing Countries.* Rome: FAO, 1974.

Fledderjohn, David, and Bartlett Harvey. *Building Small Farmer Cooperatives: A Central American Experience.* Washington, D.C.: ACDI, 1990.

Garcia, Antonio. *Cooperación agraria y estrategias de desarrollo.* Mexico City: Siglo Veintiuno Editores, 1976.

————. *Las cooperativas agrarias en el desarrollo de América Latina.* Bogota: Ediciones Colatina, 1976.

Laidlaw, A. F. *Mobilization of Human Resources for Rural Development Through Agricultural Cooperatives.* Rome: FAO, 1973.

Lamming, G. N. *Promotion of Small Farmers' Cooperatives in Asia.* Rome: FAO, 1980.

Madane, Madhav V. *Long Term Agricultural Development Program Through Agricultural Cooperatives and Technical Assistance.* New Delhi: ICA, ROECSEA, 1974.

Maldini, Eduardo, Alvaro Ramos, and Carlos Vasallo. *Contribución del sistema de cooperativas agrarias al desarrollo rural.* Montevideo, Uruguay: Universidad de la República, 1987.

McGrath, M. J., ed. *Cooperatives, Small Farmers and Rural Development.* Madison: University of Wisconsin, Center for Cooperatives, 1978.

Mendoza, Eugenio V. *Agricultural Cooperation in Developing Countries: A Management Approach.* Quezon City, Philippines: Bustamente Press, 1980.

Michalski, Klaus J. *Landwirtschafliche Genossenschaften in afro-asiatischen Entwicklungsländern.* Berlin: Akademie Verlag, 1973.

Milliot, L. *L'association agricole chez les musulmans du Maghreb (Maroc, Algerie, Tunisie).* Paris: A. Rousseau, 1912.

Newiger, Nikolaus. *The Role of New Forms of Cooperation in Agricultural Development in Developing Countries.* Rome: FAO, 1970.

Odhe, T. *Agricultural Cooperation and Developing Countries.* Stockholm: KF, 1966.

Okouin Akiyo, Jean Marie. *La coopération en Afrique: bilan et prespectives.* Sherbrooke, Quebec: Université de Sherbrooke, 1974.

Ortiz Villacis, Marcelo. *Aspectos del problema agrario latino-americano y la organización cooperativa.* Quito: Editorial Casa de la Cultura Ecuatoriana, 1968.

Powell, Jane S. *Agricultural Cooperatives in Latin America.* Washington, D.C.: Pan American Union, 1942.

Present Situation, Problems and Future Tasks of Agricultural Cooperatives: Study Reports from Bangladesh, India, Malaysia, Philippines and Sri Lanka. New Delhi: ICA, ROAP, 1990.

Rana, J. M. *Education for Agricultural Cooperatives in South-East Asia.* New Delhi: ICA, ROECSEA, 1971.

Regional Seminar on Cooperatives in Agriculture: An Integrated Approach, Tokyo, 1967: Report. New Delhi: ICA, ROECSEA, 1967.

The Role of Agricultural Cooperatives in Development Strategies: A Cooperative Workshop held in Accra, Ghana, March, 1974. Washington, D.C.: ACDI, 1974.

San Martin G., Orlando, Wim Dierckxsens, and Jorge Vargas Roldan. *Cooperativismo centroamericano en cifras: Con énfasis en sector agropecuario.* San José, Costa Rica: CCC-CA, 1992.

Statistical Information on Agriculture and Agricultural Cooperatives in South-East Asia, 1978. New Delhi: ICA, ROECSEA, 1978.

Taimni, K. K., ed. *Asia's Rural Cooperatives*. Boulder, Colo.: Westview Press, 1994.

Tenaw, Shimelles, and Sini Cedercreutz, eds. *Seminar Report on Rural Development and the Challenges to Cooperative Movements in Developing Countries, May, 1992, Helsinki*. Helsinki: Yliopistopaino, 1992.

Treydte, Klaus-Peter, and Wolfgang Ule, eds. *Agriculture in the Near East: Organizational Patterns and Socio-Economic Development*. Bonn-Bad Godesberg: Verlag Neue Gesellschaft, 1973.

Turtiainen, Turto, and J. D. Von Pischke. *Investment and Finance in Agricultural Service Cooperatives*. Washington, D.C.: World Bank, 1986.

Watkins, W. P., ed. *The Role of Agricultural Cooperatives in Economic and Social Development: Report of the Open World Conference, Rome, May, 1972*. London: ICA, 1973.

Weber, Wilhelm. *Absatzgenossenschaften in Entwicklungsländern*. Marburg, Germany: Euckerdruck, 1966.

Wong, John, ed. *Group Farming in Asia: Experience and Potentials*. Singapore: Singapore University Press, 1979.

Worsley, Peter, and Ann Allen, eds. *Two Blades of Grass: Rural Cooperatives in Agricultural Modernization*. Manchester: Manchester University Press, 1971.

Worz, Johannes, ed. *Witzenhauser Hochschulwoche (11th, 1981, University of Kassel). Cooperation as an Instrument for Rural Development in the Third World*. Witzenhausen, Germany: Selbstverlag des Verbandes der Tropenlandwirte Witzenhausen, 1984.

IV. B. Dairy Cooperatives

Abdel-Khalik, A. R. Z. *The Production and Distribution of Milk and Dairy Products in Egypt: Towards a Cooperative System*. Stockholm: Stockholms Universitet, 1981.

Alderman, Harold, George Mergos, and Roger Slade. *Coooperatives and the Commercialization of Milk Production in India: A Literature Review*. Washington, D.C.: International Food Policy Research Institute, 1987.

The Anand Dairy Cooperatives in India—A Cooperative Success Story. Rome: COPAC, 1984.

Bartlett, Roland W. *Cooperation in Marketing Dairy Products*. Springfield, Ill., and Baltimore: C. C. Thomas, 1931.

Bluhm, Franz. *Die Milchwirtschaft und das Molkereiwesen in Pommern unter besonderer Berüucksichtigung der Genossenschafts-molkereien*. Cologne: Bohlau, 1988.

Buteyo, G. Wafula. *Kenya's Experience in Rural Dairy Development, Education, and Training*. Nairobi: Ministry of Livestock Development, 1980.

Le coopérateur laitier. Conseil de la coopération laitière du Quebec, 1989 (periodical).

Depetris de Guiguet, Edith, ed. *Situación y desafíos del cooperativismo lechero argentino*. Santa Fe, Argentina: Universidad Nacional del Litoral, Centro de Publicaciones, 1995.

Empson, J. *International Study of Dairy Cooperatives. Country Case Studies.* [n.1.]: International Dairy Federation, Bulletin No. 155, 1983.

George, Shanti. *A Matter of People: Cooperative Dairying in India and Zimbabwe.* New Delhi and New York: Oxford University Press, 1994.

Halse, M. *India Case Study on Dairy Development.* Rome: FAO, 1977.

Jenkins, T. N. *The Financing of German Dairy Cooperatives: An Empirical Investigation.* Aberystwyth, U.K.: University College of Wales, 1984.

Jul, M. *The Place of Dairying in Development.* Dublin: Boole Press, 1983.

Kamath, M. V. *Management Kurien-Style: The Story of the White Revolution.* Delhi: Konark Publishers, 1989.

Kislev, Y., M. Meisels, and S. Amir. *Dairy Industry of Israel. Development of Animal Production Systems.* New York: Elsevier Science Publishers, 1984.

Kulandaiswamy, V. *Cooperative Dairying in India.* Coimbatore, India: Rainbow Publications, 1982.

Mbaja, G. O., and J. De Graaff. *Marketing Development Project: Milk Marketing and Pricing in Kenya. The Role of Cooperatives.* Rome: FAO, 1978.

Mertin, R. G. *Guide to Milk Procurement Through Village Dairy Cooperative Societies.* Canberra: Australian Development Assistance Bureau, 1977.

Mascarenhas, R. C. *A Strategy for Rural Development: Dairy Cooperatives in India.* New Delhi and Newbury Park, Calif.: Sage Publications, 1988.

Mergos, George, and Roger Slade. *Dairy Development and Milk Cooperatives. The Effects of a Dairy Project in India.* Washington, D.C.: World Bank, 1987.

Operation Flood. Anand: National Dairy Development Board, 1972.

Participation of Women in Dairy Development in South Asia. Bangkok: UN, Economic and Social Commission for Asia and the Pacific, 1981.

Ram, Jawana. *Management of Dairy Enterprises.* Jaipur, India: Kuber Associates and Publishers, 1987.

Regional Seminar on "The Development of Dairy Cooperatives in South-East Asia," Anand, February, 1975—Conference Documents. New Delhi: ICA, ROECSEA, 1975.

Replication of Anand Pattern Milk Producer's Cooperatives. Anand, India: National Dairy Development Board, 1977.

Robotka, Frank. *Cooperative Creameries in the United States.* Washington, D.C.: Pan American Union, 1940.

Shah, Dilip R. *Dairy Cooperativization, An Instrument of Social Change.* Jaipur, India: Rawat Publications, 1992.

Singh, S., and P. L. Kelley. *Amul: An Experiment in Rural Economic Development.* New Delhi: Macmillan, 1981.

Somjee, Geeta, and A. H. Somjee. *Reaching Out to the Poor: The Unfinished Rural Revolution.* Basingstoke, U.K.: Macmillan, 1989.

Spatz, Karen J, and Eric Brainich. *Exporting, An Avenue for Dairy Cooperatives.* Washington, D.C.: USDA, FCS, 1990.

Stafford, Thomas H., and James B. Roof. *Marketing Operations of Dairy Cooperatives.* Washington, D.C.: USDA, FCS, 1984.

Stimulating Milk Marketing and Dairy Development—Operation Flood. Project Findings and Recommendations. Rome: FAO, 1979.

Tereshtenko, Valery. *Cooperative Dairying: A Bibliography of The Cooperative Project.* New York: WPA, 1940.

Welden, William C. *Lecherias cooperativas.* Washington, D.C.: Unión Panamericana, 1940.

————. *Organizing Fluid-Milk Marketing Cooperatives in the United States.* Washington, D.C.: Pan American Union, 1939.

IV. C. Agricultural Credit Cooperatives

Agricultural Cooperative Credit in South-East Asia. New Delhi: ICA, ROECSEA, 1967; London: Asia Publishing House, 1968.

Agricultural Credit Through Cooperatives and Other Institutions. Rome: FAO, 1965.

Cooperative Credit for Agricultural Development. Third Asian Conference on Agricultural Credit and Cooperatives. New Delhi: ICA, ROECSEA, 1977.

Degon, M. *Le crédit agricole.* Paris: Sirey, 1939.

de Roda y Jimenez, R. *El crédito agrícola cooperativo.* Barcelona: Salvat, 1932.

Effectiveness of Cooperative Credit for Agricultural Production. New Delhi: National Council of Applied Economic Research, 1972.

Erdman, H., and G. Larsen. *Revolving Finance in Agricultural Cooperatives.* Madison, Wis.: Mimir Publishers, 1965.

Financial Structure of Farmer Cooperatives. Washington, D.C.: USDA, FCS, 1970.

Financing Agricultural Cooperatives. London: Maxwell Stamp Associates, 1967.

Ghosh, E. H. *The Theory of Cooperative Credit.* Calcutta: Auddy, 1915.

Herrick, M. *Rural Credits: Land and Cooperative.* New York: Appleton, 1914.

Leseanu, N. *La structure et l'organisation de la coopération de crédit en Roumanie.* Paris: PUF, 1933.

Marsan, J. *Le crédit mutualiste dans l'agriculture d'Outre-Mer.* Paris: Caisse centrale de coopération économique, 1963.

Mendieta y Nuñez, L. *El crédito agrario en México: Origen, evolución, estado actual, crítica del sistema cooperativo.* Mexico City: Impresa Mundial, 1933.

Misra, J. P. *Principles of Organization of Agricultural Cooperative Credit Societies in India.* Bhagalpur, India: United Press, 1932.

Morman, J. *Farm Credit in the United States and Canada.* New York: Macmillan, 1924.

Peters, E. T. *Cooperative Credit Associations in Certain European Countries and their Relations to Agricultural Interests.* Washington, D.C.: GPO, 1915.

Pickett, Liam P. *Management of Cooperative Credit.* Geneva: ILO, 1975.

Rayneri, Auguste. *Le crédit agricole par association coopérative.* Paris: Guillermin, 1896.

Sparks, S. *History and Theory of Agricultural Credit in the United States.* New York: Cromwell, 1932.

Strickland, C. F. *Rural Finance and Cooperation.* Shanghai: Chung Hwa Books, 1937.

Von Pischke, J. D., Dale W. Adams, and G. Donald. *Rural Financial Markets in Developing Countries: Their Use and Abuse.* Baltimore: Johns Hopkins University Press, 1983.

Wolff, H. W. *Cooperative Credit for the United States.* New York: Sturgis and Walton, 1917.

The Zimbabwe Project and Collective Cooperatives: Rural Credit and the Revolving Loan Fund. Harare, Zimbabwe: The Project, 1988.

IV. D. Marketing Cooperatives

Africa-Asia Rural Reconstruction Organization. *Business Practice of Cooperative Marketing.* Tokyo: RECA, 1970.

Andreou, Paris. *Agricultural Development and Cooperative Marketing in Cyprus: Some Lessons for Developing Countries.* Nairobi: East African Literature Bureau, 1977.

Anschel, K., R. Brannon, and E. Smith. *Agricultural Cooperatives and Markets in Developing Countries.* New York: Praeger, 1969.

Bakken, Henry H., and M. Schaars. *The Economics of Cooperative Marketing.* New York: McGraw Hill, 1937.

Bernotavicz, John W., Gordon E. Stein, and Freda D. Bernotavicz. *How to Organize Agricultural Marketing Cooperatives: A Handbook.* Augusta: Maine State Planning Office, 1985.

Blankertz, Donald F. *Marketing Cooperatives.* New York: Ronald Press, 1940.

Bourgeois, E. *La coopérative agricole face aux problèmes de commercialisation.* Paris: Cujas, 1967.

Chang, L. R. *The Marketing Organization in Agricultural Cooperative Business.* Athens: University of Georgia, 1972.

Comish, N. *Cooperative Marketing of Agricultural Products.* New York: Appleton, 1929.

Digby, Margaret, and R. H. Gretton. *Cooperative Marketing for Agricultural Producers.* Rome: FAO, 1952.

Federal Trade Commission. *Cooperative Marketing.* New York: Arno Press, 1975.

Feingold, Jo. *Commodity Marketing through Cooperatives—Some Experiences from Africa and Asia and Some Lessons for the Future.* Rome: COPAC, 1984.

Fetrow, W. *Cooperative Marketing of Agricultural Products.* Washington, D.C.: FCA, 1936.

Fippin, Elmer O. *First Principles of Cooperation in Buying and Selling in Agriculture.* Richmond, Va.: Garrett and Masssie, 1934.

Frankel, Sally H. *Cooperation and Competition in the Marketing of Maize in South Africa.* London: P. S. King and Son, 1926.

Goel, Brij Bhushan. *Management of Marketing Cooperatives.* New Delhi: Deep and Deep Publications, 1991.

Jessness, Oscar B. *The Cooperative Marketing of Farm Products.* Philadelphia and London: J. B. Lippincott, 1923.

Knapp, J. *A Cooperative Marketing Manual.* Raleigh, N.C.: Agricultural Station, 1930.

Lele, Uma J., and Robert E. Christiansen. *Markets, Marketing Boards, and Cooperatives in Africa: Issues in Adjustment Policy.* Washington, D.C.: World Bank, 1989.

Losada, Carlos, and Ferran Maruny. *Marketing para cooperativas.* Barcelona: Ediciones Ceac, 1981.

McKay, Andrew W. *Practical Cooperative Marketing.* New York: J. Wiley and Sons, 1928; London: Chapman and Hall, 1928.

Mears, Eliot G., and Mathew O. Tobriner. *Principles and Practices of Cooperative Marketing.* Boston: Ginn, 1926.

Muntjewerff, C. A. *Produce Marketing Cooperatives in West Africa.* Leiden, Netherlands: African Studies Center, 1982.

Murphy, M. *Cooperative Marketing of Agricultural Products.* Cork, Ireland: Cork University Press, 1928.

Nourse, Edwin G. *The Philosophy of Cooperative Marketing.* Washington, D.C.: Pan American Union, 1936.

Raval, D. S. *A Comparative Study of Cooperative Marketing of Agricultural Produce in India and the United States.* Washington, D.C.: George Washington University, 1972.

Survey of Agricultural Cooperative Marketing Projects in South-East Asia. New Delhi: ICA, ROECSEA, 1973.

Wertime, Mary Beth. *Food Crop Marketing and Women's Cooperatives in the North West Province, Republic of Cameroon: A Peace Corps Study.* Yaoundé, Cameroon: United States Peace Corps, 1987.

IV. E. Communal Settlements

IV. E. 1. Theory and Practice—General

IV. E. 1. a. Communes

Abrams, Philip, Andrew McCulloch, Sheila Abrams and Pat Gore. *Communes, Sociology, and Society.* Cambridge, U.K., and New York: Cambridge University Press, 1976.

Apsler, Alfred. *Communes Through the Ages: The Search for Utopia.* New York: J. Messner, 1974.

Armytage, W. *Heavens Below: Utopian Experiments in England 1560–1960.* London: Routledge and Kegan Paul, 1961.

Bennett, J. W. *Hutterian Brethren: The Agricultural Economy and Social Organization of a Communal People.* Stanford, Calif.: Stanford University Press, 1967.

Carandell, José Maria. *Las comunas*. Barcelona: Tusquest, 1972.

Derda, Hans-Jurgen. *Vita communis: Studien zur Geschichte einer Lebensform in Mittelalter und Neuzeit*. Cologne: Bohlau, 1992.

Gorni, Yosef, Yaacov Oved, and Idit Paz, eds. *Communal Life: An International Perspective*. Ramat-Efal, Israel: Yad Tabenkin, 1987; New Brunswick, N.J.: Transaction Books, 1987.

Hall, Lynn. *Too Near the Sun*. Chicago: Follett Publishing Company, 1970.

Infield, Henrik. *The American Intentional Communities, Study in Sociology of Co-operation*. Glen Gardner, N.J.: Glen Gardner Press, 1956.

———. *Communidades cooperativas: sociología de la cooperación*. Buenos Aires: Intercoop, 1972.

———. *Cooperative Communities at Work*. New York: Dryden Press, 1945.

———. *Coopératives communautaires et sociologie experimentale*. Paris: Éditions de minuit, 1955.

———. *Utopia and Experiment: Essays in the Sociology of Cooperation*. New York: Praeger, 1955.

Infield, Henrik, and J. Maier. *Cooperative Group Living*. New York: Harry Koosis, 1950.

International Conference on Kibbutz and Communes. *Kibbutz and Communes, Past and Future: International Conference, Yad Tabenkin, May, 1985. Abstracts of the Lectures*. Ramat-Efal, Israel: Yad Tabenkin, 1985.

Kanter, Rosabeth M., ed. *Communes: Creating and Managing the Collective Life*. New York: Harper and Row, 1973.

Melnyk, George. *The Search for Community: From Utopia to a Cooperative Society*. Montreal and Buffalo: Black Rose Books, 1985.

Moffat, G. *A History of Intentional Community; Community Heritage in Western Civilization*. Toronto: Alternate Society, 1971.

Ozinga, James. *The Recurring Dream of Equality: Communal Sharing and Communism Throughout History*. Lanham, Md.: University Press of America, 1995.

Poulton, Robert, and Robin Cohen. *Contemporary Communes, A Bibliographical and Interpretative Essay*. Birmingham, U.K.: University of Birmingham, 1977.

Rexroth, Kenneth. *Communalism: From Its Origins to the Twentieth Century*. New York: Seabury Press, 1974; London: Owen, 1975.

Shenker, Barry. *Intentional Communities: Ideology and Alienation in Communal Societies*. London and Boston: Routledge and Kegan Paul, 1986.

Spagnoletti, Cheryl D., and Jeremy Johnson, eds. *Alternative Lifestyles: A Selective Bibliography*. Adelaide: South Australian Housing Trust, 1978.

Ungers, Liselotte. *Kommunen in der Neuen Welt, 1740–1971*. Cologne: Kiepenheuer and Witsch, 1972.

IV. E. 1. b. Group Farming

Bellas, J. *Industrial Democracy and the Worker-Owned Farm*. London: Pall Mall Press, 1972.

Cliff, T. *Marxism and Collectivization of Agriculture*. London: Socialists Unlimited, 1980.

Cooperative and Commune: Group Farming in the Economic Development of Agriculture. Proceedings of a Conference on Group Farming. Madison: University of Wisconsin Press, 1977.

Domar, Evsey D. *On Collective Farms and Producer Cooperatives*. Santa Monica, Calif.: Rand Corporation, 1965.

Eaton, J. N. *Research Guide on Cooperative Group Farming*. New York: H. W. Wilson, 1942.

Francisco, R. A., B. A. Laird, and R. D. Laird, eds. *The Political Economy of Collectivized Agriculture. A Comparative Study of Communist and Non-communist Systems*. New York: Pergamon Press, 1979.

Galeski, B. *The Prospects for Collective Farming*. Madison: University of Wisconsin, Land Tenure Center, 1973.

Group Farming. Paris: Organization for Economic Cooperation and Development, 1972.

Gide, Charles. *Communist and Cooperative Colonies*. New York: AMS Press, 1974.

Karpinski, V. *What Are Collective Farms?* London: Lindsay Drummond, 1944.

Murry, J. M. *Community Farm*. London: Peter Nevil, 1952.

Nash, June, Jorge Dandler, and Nicholas Hopkins, eds. *Popular Participation in Social Change: Cooperatives, Collectives and Nationalized Industry*. The Hague: Mouton, 1976.

Nauta, Paul. *El colectivismo agrario*. Buenos Aires: Ediciones Forum, 1975.

Newiger, Nicholas. *Village Settlement Schemes, the Problems of Cooperative Farming*. Rome: FAO, 1965.

Roussel, M., and R. Peyat. *Action en commun des agriculteurs*. Paris: Baillière, 1966.

Wong, J., ed. *Group Farming in Asia: Experiences and Potentials*. Singapore: Singapore University Press, 1979.

IV. E. 2. China—Communes

Breth, R. M. *Mao's China: A Study of Socialist Economic Development*. Melbourne: Longman Cheshire, 1977.

Burki, S. *A Study of Chinese Communes*. Cambridge: Harvard University, 1969.

Domes, J. *Socialism in the Chinese Countryside, Rural Societal Policies in the People's Republic of China—1949–1979*. London: C. Hurst, 1980; Montreal: McGill-Queen's University Press, 1980

Durau, Joachim. *Arbeitskooperation in der chinesischen Landwirtschaft*. Bochum, Germany: Brockmayer, 1983.

Dutt, G. *Rural Communes of China*. London: Asia Publishing House, 1967.

Engelborghs-Bertels, M. *La Chine rurale des villages aux communes populaires*. Brussels: Université de Bruxelles, 1974.

Mao Tse Tung. *The Question of Agricultural Cooperation*. Beijing: Foreign Language Press, 1956.

Myrdal, J. *Report from a Chinese Village.* New York: Pantheon Books, 1965.

Smith, A. H. *Village Life in China, a Study in Sociology.* New York: Haskell House, 1968.

Yamamoto, Hideao. *Development of Agriculture Collectivization in China.* Tokyo: National Research Institute of Agriculture, 1961.

IV. E. 3. Israel—Kibbutz and Moshav

IV. E. 3. a. Kibbutz

Barkai, H. *Growth Patterns of the Kibbutz Economy.* Amsterdam, New York and Oxford: North Holland Publishing, 1977.

Ben-Rafael, E., Maurice Konopnicki, and P. Rambaud. *Le kibbutz.* Paris: PUF, 1983.

Bentwich, N. *A New Way of Life, the Collective Settlement of Israel.* London: Shindler and Golomb, 1949.

Blasi, Joseph R. *The Quality of Life in a Kibbutz Cooperative Community.* Cambridge, Mass.: Institute for Cooperative Community, 1978; New York: Givat Chaviva Educational Foundation, 1978.

Bockenheimer, P. *Struktur und Entwicklung ausgewahlter Kibbutze in Israel.* Giessen, Germany: Universität Giessen, 1978.

Brun, Marcel B. *Der Kibbutz: Die Verwirklichung einer Illusion?* Zurich: Verlag Der Scheideweg, 1950.

Castelotte Lopez, Jesus. *Socialismo agrario en Israel.* Madrid: Editorial ZYX, 1965.

Cohen, Erik. *Bibliography of the Kibbutz.* Tel Aviv: Giv'at-Haviva, 1964.

———. *Rules of Life in Kibbutz Society.* Tel Aviv: Hoza'at Hakibbutz Ham Uchad, 1960.

Cohen, R. *Principles of Kibbutz Economy.* Tel Aviv: Hoza'at Hakkibutz Ham Uchad, 1946.

Darin, Haim. *Der Kibbutz. Die Neue Gesellschaft in Israel.* Stuttgart: Klett, 1967.

Desroche, Henri. *Au pays du kibboutz: essai sur le secteur coopératif israélien.* Basel: USC, 1960.

Fishman, A. *The Religious Kibbutz Movement: The Revival of the Jewish Religious Community.* Jerusalem: Religious Section of the Youth and Hehalutz Department of the Zionist Organization, 1957.

Habonim, I. *Kibbutz, a New Society? An Anthology.* Tel Aviv: Private Printer, 1971.

Hartog, A. *The Kvutzah and Related Forms of Settlement.* New York: Cooperative Group Living Anthology, 1950.

Horigan, Francis D. *The Israeli Kibbutz: Psychiatric, Psychological, and Social Studies With Emphasis on Family Life and Family Structure: A Survey of Literature.* Bethesda, Md.: National Institutes of Health, 1962.

Infield, Henrik. *Cooperative Group Living in Palestine.* London: K. Paul, Trench, Trübner, 1946.

Kanovsky, Eliyahu. *The Economy of the Israeli Kibbutz.* Cambridge: Harvard University Press, 1966.

Leon, D. *The Kibbutz, a New Way of Life.* Oxford: Pergamon Press, 1969.

Liegle, Ludwig. *Familie und Kollektiv im Kibbutz.* Weinheim, Berlin and Basel: Beltz, 1971.

Malraux, Clara. *Civilisation du kibboutz.* Geneva: Éditions Gonthier, 1964.

Meier-Cronemeyer, Hermann. *Kibbuzim—Geschichte, Geist und Gestalt.* Hanover: Verlag für Literatur, 1969.

Menendez, Ivan. *El kibbutz de Israel.* Mexico City: B. Costa-Amic, 1971.

Muller, Leopoldo. *Los hijos del kibutz.* Buenos Aires: Paidos, 1973.

Pallman, M. *Der Kibbutz.* Tübingen: Mohr, 1966.

Paz, Yehuda, ed. *The Kibbutz.* Jerusalem and London: Weidenfeld and Nicolson, 1973; New York: New York Times Quadrangle Books, 1973.

Pearlman, Moshe. *Collective Adventure; An Informal Account of the Communal Settlements of Palestine.* London: Heinemann, 1938.

Rabin, A. I. *Kibbutz Studies: A Digest of Books and Articles on the Kibbutz by Social Scientists, Educators and Others.* East Lansing: Michigan State University Press, 1971.

Rosner, M. *The Kibbutz as a Way of Life in Modern Society.* Tel Aviv: Givat Haviva, 1972.

Rozenkier, B. *Les différences entre les générations dans le domaine des valeurs kibboutziques.* Paris: École pratique des hautes études, 1974.

Samuel, Edwin. *Les colonies collectivistes de Palestine.* Jerusalem: R. Mass, 1946.

Shatil, J. E. *Bibliography of Studies of Rural Cooperation in Israel.* Tel Aviv: Ministry of Labor, 1965.

———. *L'économie collective du Kibboutz israélien.* Paris: Éditions de minuit, 1960.

Shur, Shimon. *Kibbutz Bibliography (On the base of E. Cohen's Bibliography of the Kibbutz).* Tel Aviv: Council for Higher Education of the Federation of Kibbutz Movements, 1971.

Spiro, Melford. *Children of the Kibbutz.* New York: Schocken Books, 1965.

———. *Kibbutz, Venture in Utopia.* New York: Schocken Books, 1963.

Westerlind, P. B. *From Farm to Factory: The Economic Development of the Kibbutz.* Santa Barbara: University of California, 1978.

IV. E. 3. b. Moshav

Abarbanel, J. S. *The Cooperative Farmer and the Welfare State—Economic Change in an Israeli Moshav.* Manchester: Manchester University Press, 1974.

Assaf, A. *The Worker's Moshav in Israel.* Tel Aviv: Am Oved Publishing House, 1954.

Desroche, Henri. *Opération moshav: d'un développement des villages à une villagisation du développement.* Paris: Cujas, 1971.

Klayman, M. *The Moshav in Israel.* New York: Praeger, 1970.

Meyer, E. *Der Moshav (1948–1963).* Tübingen: Mohr, 1968.

Rubin, J. *Les chemins du moshav.* Tel Aviv: Mouvement des Moshavims, 1964.

Schwartz, Moshe, Susan Lees and Gideon Kressel, eds. *Rural Cooperatives in Socialist Utopia: Thirty Years of Moshav Development in Israel.* Westport, Conn.: Praeger, 1995.

Zussman, Pinchas. *Individual Behavior and Social Choice in a Cooperative Settlement: The Theory and Practice of the Israeli Moshav.* Jerusalem: Magnes Press, Hebrew University, 1988.

IV. E. 4. Mexico—Ejidos

Alarcón Rodriguez, Salvador. *El ejido y su industrialización.* Mexico City: [n.p.], 1954

Baring-Gould, M. D. *Agricultural and Community Development in Mexican Ejidos: Relatives in Conflict.* Ithaca, N.Y.: Cornell University, 1974.

Desroche, Henri, et al. *Les ejidos mexicains.* Paris: Éditions de minuit, 1956.

Directorio de Ejidos de Comunidades Agrarias. V censo ejidal, 1970. Mexico City: Dirección General de Estadística, 1972.

Les ejidos mexicains. Paris: Entente communautaire BECC, 1956.

Fernandez y Fernandez, Ramon. *Cooperación agrícola y organización economica del ejido.* Mexico City: Secretaria de Educación Publica, 1973.

Garizurieta, C. *Realidad del ejido.* Mexico City: Editorial Dialectica, 1938.

Gomez Saldana, Jorge R. *La organización del ejido en sus formas individual y colectiva.* Mexico City: [n.p.], 1960.

Infield, Henrik, and Koka Frier. *People in Ejidos: A Visit to the Cooperative Farms of Mexico.* New York: Praeger, 1954.

Kelley, J. C. *Political Structure and Conflict in a Mexican Ejido.* New York: Columbia University, 1974.

Leyva Velazquez, Gabriel. *El ejido.* Mexico City: [n.p.], 1946.

Markiewicz, Dana. *Ejido Organization in Mexico, 1934–1976.* Los Angeles: University of California, UCLA Latin American Center Publications, 1980.

Palomo Valencia, F. *Historia del ejido actual.* Mexico City: Editorial América, 1959.

Primer censo ejidal, 1935. Mexico City: Dirección General de Estadistica, 1937–1938.

Segundo censo ejidal de los Estados Unidos Mexicanos, 1940; Resumen general. Mexico City: Dirección General de Estadística, 1940.

Simpson, E. *The Ejido, Mexico's Way Out.* Chapel Hill: University of North Carolina Press, 1937.

Stavenhagen, R. *Land Reform and Institutional Alternatives in Agriculture: The Case of Mexican Ejidos.* Vienna: Vienna Institute for Development, 1973.

Venebra Vargas, Roman. *El cooperativismo como base de la organización ejidal.* Mexico City: Universidad Nacional, 1942.

IV. E. 5. Soviet Union—Collective Farms

Belov, F. *The History of a Soviet Collective Farm.* New York: Praeger, 1955.

Dumont, Rene. *Sovkoze, kolkhoze ou le problématique communisme.* Paris: Éditions du seuil, 1964.

Klimenko, Fedor N. *The Kolkhoz (Collective Farm).* Moscow: Foreign Language Publishing House, 1939.

Laird, R., and B. Laird. *Soviet Communism and Agrarian Revolution.* Harmondsworth, U.K.: Penguin Books, 1970.

Nacou, D. *Du kolkhoze au sovkhoze.* Paris: Éditions de minuit, 1958.

Nove, Alec. *The Evolution of Soviet Collective Farms.* Oxford: St. Antony's College, 1957.

Pershin, P. *Leninism on the Agrarian-Peasant Question.* Moscow: Novosti Press, 1970.

Stalin, Joseph. *Building Collective Farms.* London: Modern Books, 1931.

Stuart, R. C. *The Collective Farm in Soviet Agriculture.* Lexington: Heath, 1972.

Wesson, Robert G. *Soviet Communes.* New Brunswick, N.J.: Rutgers University Press, 1963.

IV. E. 6. Tanzania—Ujamaa Villages

Baldus, R. D. *Zur operationell Effizienz der Ujamaa Kooperative Tansanias.* Marburg, Germany: Universität Marburg, Marburger Schriften zum Genossenschaftswesen, 1976.

Cedillo, V. G. *Rural Development Through Ujamaa: A Tanzania Case Report.* Vienna: Vienna Institute for Development, Occasional Paper 73/11, 1973.

Coulson, Andrew, ed. *African Socialism in Practice: The Tanzanian Experience.* Nottingham, U.K.: Spokesman, 1979.

de Vries, J. *Agricultural Extension and the Development of Ujamaa Villages in Tanzania: Towards a Dialogical Agricultural Extension Model.* Madison: University of Wisconsin, 1978.

Fortmann, L. *Ujamaa Villages. Tanzania's Experience With Agrarian Socialism.* Rome: FAO, WCARRD Meeting Papers, 1979.

Freyhold, Michaela von. *Ujamaa Villages in Tanzania: Analysis of a Social Experiment.* New York: Monthly Review Press, 1979.

Hess, O. *Tanzania: Ujamaa and Development.* Ithaca, N.Y.: Cornell University, Department of Agricultural Economics, 1976.

Hyden, Goran. *Beyond Ujamaa in Tanzania: Underdevelopment and an Uncaptured Peasantry.* London: Heinemann, 1980.

Kayombo, E. O., et al. *A Collection of Essays on Ujamaa Villages.* Dar-es-Salaam: University of Dar-es-Salaam, 1971.

McHenry, Dean E. *Tanzania's Ujamaa Villages; The Implementation of a Rural Development Strategy.* Berkeley: University of California, Institute of International Studies, 1979.

Mwoleka, Christopher, and Joseph Healey, eds. *Ujamaa and Christian Communities.* Eldoret, Kenya: Gaba Publications, 1976.

Ndissi, C. *Ujamaa Villages as a Collective Development Strategy in Tanzania's Economic Development.* Ann Arbor: University of Michigan, 1976.

Putterman, L. G. *Is a Democratic Collective Agriculture Possible? Theoretical Considerations and Evidence From Tanzania.* Providence, R.I.: Brown University, Department of Economics, Working Paper 80-18, 1980.

Ujamaa in Tanzania. London: Commonwealth Institute, 1978.

Urfer, S. *Ujamaa, espoir du socialisme africain en Tanzanie.* Paris: Aubier-Montaigne, 1971.

von Freyhold, M. *Ujamaa Villages in Tanzania: Analysis of a Social Experiment.* London: Heinemann Educational, 1979; New York: Monthly Review Press, 1979.

IV. E. 7. United States

Berry, Brian. *America's Utopian Experiments: Communal Havens From Long-Wave Crises.* Hanover, N.H.: Dartmouth College, University Press of New England, 1992.

Bestor, Arthur. *Backwoods Utopias: The Sectarian and Owenite Phases of Communitarian Socialism in America, 1663–1829.* Philadelphia: University of Pennsylvania, 1950.

Case, John, and Rosemary Taylor, eds. *Coops, Communes and Collectives: Experiments in Social Change in the 1960s and 1970s.* New York: Pantheon Books, 1979.

Cohen, Daniel. *Not of the World: A History of the Commune in America.* Chicago: Follett, 1973.

Curl, John. *History of Work Cooperation in America: Cooperatives, Cooperative Movements, Collectivity, and Communalism from Early America to the Present.* Berkeley: Homeward Press, 1980.

Dare, Philip N. *American Communes to 1860: Bibliography.* New York: Garland Publications, 1990

Fogarty, Robert S. *All Things New: American Communes and Utopian Movements, 1860–1914.* Chicago: University of Chicago Press, 1990.

———. *Dictionary of American Communal and Utopian History.* Westport, Conn.: Greenwood Press, 1980.

Guarneri, Carl. *The Utopian Alternative: Fourierism in Nineteenth Century America.* Ithaca, N.Y.: Cornell University Press, 1991.

Infield, Henrik. *The American Intentional Communities: Study in the Sociology of Cooperation.* Glen Gardner, N.J.: Glen Gardner Community Press, 1955.

James, Henry Ammon. *Communism in America.* New York: H. Holt, 1879; reissued, New York: Arno Press, 1977.

Kanter, Rosabeth M. *Commitment and Community: Communes and Utopias in Sociological Perspective.* Cambridge: Harvard University Press, 1972.

Kephart, William M., and William W. Zellner. *Extraordinary Groups: An Examination of Unconventional Life-Styles.* New York: St. Martin's Press, 1994.

Kesten, Seymour R. *Utopian Episodes: Daily Life in Experimental Colonies Dedicated to Changing the World.* Syracuse, N.Y.: Syracuse University Press, 1993.

Miller, Timothy. *American Communes, 1860–1960: A Bibliography.* New York: Garland Publications, 1990.

Minturn, Leigh, Mary Ann West, and Christopher Peterson. *American Communal Societies—Theory and Ethnography: A Selected, Annotated Bibliography.* Monticello, Ill.: Vance Bibliographies, 1981.

Moment, Gairdner B., and Otto F. Kraushaar. *Utopias, the American Experience.* Metuchen, N.J.: Scarecrow Press, 1980.

Motherwell and Orbiston: The First Owenite Attempts at Cooperative Communities: Three Pamphlets, 1822–1825. New York: Arno Press, 1972.

Nordhoff, Charles. *The Communistic Societies of the United States.* New York: Harper, 1875; reissued as: *American Utopias.* Stockbridge, Mass.: Berkshire House, 1993.

Spann, Edward K. *Brotherly Tomorrows: Movements for a Cooperative Society in America, 1820–1920.* New York: Columbia University Press, 1989.

IV. E. 8. Other Countries

Abrams, Philip, Andrew McCulloch, Sheila Abrams, and Pat Gore. *Communes, Sociology and Society (Great Britain).* Cambridge, U.K., and New York: Cambridge University Press, 1976.

Arecchi, Alberto, and M. Arkoun. *Villages socialistes en Afrique: Somalie, Tanzanie, Mozambique, Algérie.* Dakar: Environement africain, Serie études et recherches, No. 76, 1982.

Bastos Norena, E. *Agricultura socializada; Experiencias actuales en: Israel, Yugoslavia, Argelia, Italia y España.* Madrid: Editorial Tecnos, 1974.

Bouvier, C. *La collectivisation de l'agriculture, URSS, Chine, Démocraties populaires.* Paris: A. Colin, 1958.

Carter, Novia. *Something of Promise: The Canadian Communes.* Ottawa: Canadian Council on Social Development, 1974.

Chilivumbo, Alifeyo. *Communal Agrarian Cooperative Societies: An Experiment in Rural Socialism (Zambia).* Lusaka, Zambia: National Commission for Development Planning, 1986.

Douard, Georges. *Du Kohlhoze au kibboutz.* Paris: Plon, 1961.

Garnett, Ronald G. *Cooperation and the Owenite Socialist Communities in Britain, 1825–45.* Manchester: Manchester University Press, 1972.

Goyal, S. *Some Aspects of Cooperative Farming in India.* London: Asia Publishing House, 1966.

Hardy, Dennis. *Alternative Communities in Nineteenth Century England.* London, New York: Longman, 1979.

Hewlett, Robert, and John Markie. "Cooperative Farming as an Instrument of Rural Development: Examples from China, Vietnam, Tanzania and India." *Land Reform, Land Settlement and Cooperatives,* Rome (2, 1976): 41–54.

Houtart, F., and G. Lemercinier. *Hai Van: Life in a Vietnamese Commune.* London: Zed Books, 1984.

Jackson, D. R. *The Communal Cooperative Experience: An Example From El Salvador.* Madison: University of Wisconsin, 1980.

Laxminarayan, H., and K. Kanungo. *Glimpses of Cooperative Farming in India.* Bombay: Asia Publishing House, 1967.

Leal Luque, Judith. *Instituciones agrarias: Union Sovietica, China, Israel, México: Estudio Comparativo.* Mexico City: Ediciones Oasis, 1967.

McHenry, Dean E. "The Ujamaa Village in Tanzania: Comparison with Chinese, Soviet and Mexican Experiences in Collectivization." *Comparative Studies in Society and History* (New York) 18 (3, 1976): 347–370.

Muya, M. S. R. *Strategies for Integrated Village Development: A Study of the Kibbutzim in Israel, Communes in China and Ujamaa Villages in Tanzania.* Loughborough, U.K.: Cooperative College, 1979.

Newiger, Nikolaus. *Cooperative Farming in Kenya and Tanzania.* Munich: Weltforum Verlag, 1967.

Report on the FAO Regional Seminar on Cooperative Farming for Asia and the Far East, New Delhi, May, 1966. Rome: FAO, 1967.

Rizov, A., and M. Alexieva. *Organization and Management of Cooperative Farms in Bulgaria.* Sofia: Sofia Press, 1968.

Zavidov, R. *L'expérience israélienne du développement des villages coopératifs dans les pays neufs.* Paris: Centre de recherches coopératives, 1974.

IV. F. Consumer Cooperatives

IV. F. 1. Consumer Cooperatives—Early Experience— Through World War I (1919)

Bexell, John A. *A Survey of Typical Cooperative Stores in the United States.* Washington, D.C.: GPO, 1916.

Bittel, K. *Eduard Pfeiffer und seine Bedeutung für die deutsche Konsumgenossenschaftsbewegung.* Hamburg: VDK, 1915.

Cassau, T. *Die Konsumvereinsbewegung in Grossbritannien.* Leipzig: Duncker and Humblot, 1915.

Correard, J. *Les coopératives de consommation en France et à l'étranger.* Paris: Lethielleux, 1908.

Gide, Charles. *Les sociétés coopératives de consommation.* Paris: Sirey, 1910.

Girard, J. *Vers la solidarité par les sociétés coopératives de consommation.* Paris: Jouve, 1904.

Göhre, P. *Die deutschen Arbeiter-Konsumvereine.* Berlin: Buchhandlung Vorwärts, 1910.

Nicholson, I. *Die Geschichte der Konsumvereine in England.* Basel: Verlag der Schweizer Konsumvereine, 1904.

Redfern, Percy. *The Story of the CWS.* Manchester: Cooperative Wholesale Society, 1913.

Richter, Eugen. *Cooperative Stores, Their History, Organization, and Management.* New York: Leypoldt and Holt, 1867.

Sonnischen, Albert. *Consumers' Cooperation.* New York: Macmillan, 1919.

Vicent, P. *Cooperativas de consumo, de crédito y de producción*. Valencia, Spain: Tipografía Ortega, 1905.

IV. F. 2. Consumer Cooperatives—Theory and Practice

Alanne, V. *Fundamentals of Consumer Cooperation*. Superior, Wis.: Cooperative Publishing Association, 1946.

Bowen, Eugene R. *The Cooperative Organization of Consumers*. Chicago: CLUSA, 1957.

Brainerd, John G., ed. *Consumers' Cooperation*. Philadelphia: American Academy of Political and Social Science, 1937.

Brazda, Johann, and Robert Schediwy. *Consumer Cooperatives in a Changing World* (2 volumes). Geneva: ICA, 1989.

Building a Better World by Consumer Cooperation. Chicago: CLUSA, 1944.

Bussière, Eugène. *Coopératives de consommation*. Quebec: Université de Laval, 1949.

Consumer Cooperatives. Washington, D.C.: National Education Association, 1940.

Consumers' Cooperation. New York: Russell Sage Foundation, 1935.

Consumers' Cooperative Societies. Washington, D.C.: Bureau of Foreign and Domestic Commerce, 1936.

The Consumers' Cooperative Societies in 1919. Geneva: ILO, 1920.

Cooperativas de consumo. Lima: Sección tecnica de propaganda agropecuaria, 1943.

Cowling, E. *A Short Introduction to Consumer's Cooperation*. Chicago: CLUSA, 1948.

Defosse, Gaston. *La coopération de consommation, théorie et technique*. Paris: PUF, 1942.

Emerson, H. *Cooperation, the Hope of the Consumers*. New York: Macmillan, 1919.

Gide, Charles. *Consumers' Cooperative Societies*. Manchester: Coop Union, 1921; reissued, New York: Haskell House Publishers, 1971.

ICA. *Readings in Consumer Cooperation*. New York: Asia Publishing House, 1972.

Jacobson, Dorothy H. *Our Interests as Consumers*. New York and London: Harper and Brothers, 1941.

Johnsen, Julia E., Jasber Garland, and Charles Phillips. *Consumers' Cooperatives*. New York: H. W. Wilson, 1936.

Kellen, H. M. *The Decline and Rise of the Consumer: A Philosophy of Consumer Cooperation*. New York: D. Appleton-Century, 1936.

Lacroix, J. *Types de groupements coopératifs de consommation*. Paris: BECC, 1951.

Laidlaw, A. F. *The Consumer Cooperative Movement: Problems of Education and Culture*. New York: Warbasse Memorial Library Association, 1962.

Laidler, Harry, and Wallace Campbell. *Consumers' Cooperation, a Social Interpretation*. New York: League for Industrial Democracy, 1937.

———. *The Consumer Cooperative Movement*. New York: League for Industrial Democracy, 1940.

Landis, Benson Y. *Bethlehem and Rochdale. The Churches and Consumer Cooperation 1844–1944.* Chicago: CLUSA, 1944.

Lincoln, Murray D. *Objectives of Consumers' Cooperation.* New York: National Cooperatives, 1947.

Perez Baro, A. *Los consumidores y el cooperativismo.* Barcelona: Cooperativa Paz y Justicia, 1969.

Schmeideler, Edgar. *Consumers' Cooperatives.* New York: Paulist Press, 1937.

Sood, P. S. *Economics and Methods of Consumers' Cooperation.* New Delhi: Beecham Press, 1949.

Sorenson, H. *The Consumer Movement, What It Is and What It Means.* New York and London: Harper and Brothers, 1941.

Totomiants, Vakhan. *Konsumentenorganisation, Theorie, Geschichte und Praxis der Konsumgenossenschaften.* Berlin: [n.p.], 1929.

Valdivieso, C. *Cooperativas de consumo. Un instrumento eficaz para la defensa del consumidor.* Santiago: Universidad Católica de Chile, 1973.

Walker, W. *The Consumers' Movement.* Manchester: Coop Union, 1950.

Warbasse, James P. *Consumer Cooperation and the Society of the Future.* New York: Consumers' Cooperative Publishing Association, 1970.

———. *What Is Cooperation? A Discussion of the Consumers' Cooperative Movement, Its Principles, Methods and Accomplishments.* New York: Vanguard Press, 1927; reissued, Indore, India: Modern Publishers, 1947; New York: Gordon Press, 1980.

Ward, L. *Ourselves: The Story of Consumer Free Enterprise.* New York and London: Harper, 1945; Washington, D.C.: CLUSA, 1945.

Webb, Beatrice Potter. *The Discovery of the Consumer.* London: E. Benn, 1928; reissued, Chicago: CLUSA, 1947.

Webb, Sidney J., and Beatrice Potter. *The Consumers' Cooperative Movement.* London and New York: Longman, Green, 1921.

IV. F. 3. Consumer Cooperatives—Organization and Management

Basic Economics of a Consumer Cooperative: A Learning Element for Staff of Consumer Cooperatives. Geneva: ILO, Matcom, 1979.

Bonow, Mauritz. *The Cooperative Movement and the Protection of the Consumer.* Geneva: ILO, 1960.

Burley, O. E. *The Consumers' Cooperatives as a Distributive Agency.* New York: McGraw-Hill, 1939.

Chávez Nuñez, Fernando. *Organización y administración de las cooperativas de consumo.* Washington, D.C.: Unión Panamericana, 1950.

Consumer Cooperative Leadership. Boston: Edward A. Filene Good Will Fund, 1945.

Consumer Cooperative Trading and Finance. Stockholm: KF, 1970.

Failor, C. W. *Consumers' Cooperatives and their Workers.* Chicago: Science Research Associate Publications, 1939.

Haberle, H. *Die Grosshandelsorganisationen der Einzelhändler Kesko (Finland) und Edeka (Deutschland).* Düsseldorf: Triltisch, 1960.

Hedberg, A. *International Wholesale Cooperation, Ideas and Proposals.* Stockholm: KF, 1925; Manchester: National Cooperative Publishing Society, 1925.

Hough, John. *Cooperative Retailing, 1914–1945.* London: ICA, 1949.

How to Start and Run a Cooperative Store on the Rochdale Plan. New York: CLUSA, 1920.

Lasserre, Georges. *Le secteur coopératif et la protection des consommateurs.* Paris: FNCC, 1958.

Lazo, Hector. *Retailer Cooperatives: How to Run Them.* New York and London: Harper and Brothers, 1937.

Lopez, S. L. *Las cooperativas de consumo en relación con la producción y el crédito agrícola.* Mexico City: Fondo de Garantía y Fomento para la Agricultura, Ganaderia y Avicultura, 1970.

Luck, J. M. *The War on Malnutrition and Poverty, the Role of Consumer Cooperatives.* New York: Harper, 1946.

Manager's Manual for Cooperative Stores. Boston: Edward A. Filene Good Will Fund, 1945.

O'Leary, E. *Cooperative Wholesaling in Grocery Distribution.* Columbus: Ohio State University, 1942.

Parker, Florence E. *Organization and Management of Consumers' Cooperatives.* Washington, D.C.: GPO, 1951.

Radetzki, M. *Economics of Consumer Cooperatives.* New Delhi: ICA, ROECSEA, 1965; reissued, Bangkok: Thammasat University Press, 1976.

Staermose, R. *Management of Urban Cooperative Consumers Society.* Lahore, Pakistan: Cooperative Institute of Management, 1964.

Taimni, K. K. *Studies in Retailing, Consumer Cooperation and Public Distribution System.* Poona, India: Harshad Prakashan, 1975.

Trainer's Manual: Staff Training for Consumer Cooperatives. Geneva: ILO, Matcom, 1979.

Turner, H. H. *Case Studies of Consumers' Cooperatives.* New York: Columbia University Press, 1941.

Wieting, G. M. *How to Teach Consumers' Cooperation.* New York and London: Harper and Brothers, 1942.

IV. F. 4. Consumer Cooperatives in Europe

Freitag, F. O. *Aus der Praxis der konsumgenossenschaftlichen Wirtschaftsdemokratie Bundesrepublik Deutschland-Schweden-Schweiz.* Basel: COOP, 1969.

Fuchs, C. *Die Konsumvereinsbewegung in den einzelnen Ländern.* Munich: Duncker and Humblot, 1923.

Furlough, Ellen. *Consumer Cooperation in France: The Politics of Consumption, 1834–1930.* Ithaca, N.Y., and London: Cornell University Press, 1991.

Goedhart, G. J. D. C. *Die konsumvereine in Holland, Japan, Österreich und der Schweiz.* Munich and Leipzig: Duncker and Humblot, 1923.

Kaufmann, H. *Kurzer Abriss der Geschichte des Zentralverbandes deutscher Konsumvereine.* Hamburg: Deutscher Konsumverein, 1928.

Kinloch, James, and John Butt. *History of the Scottish CWS.* Manchester, U.K., Cooperative Wholesale Society, 1981.

Lavergne, B. *Le régime coopératif, étude générale de la coopération de consommation en Europe.* Paris: Rousseau, 1908.

League of Nations. *Results of Certain of the Enquiries for Instituting a Comparison Between the Retail Prices in Private Trade and Those of Distributive Cooperative Societies.* Geneva: ILO, International Economic Conference, 1927.

Ralph Nader Task Force on European Cooperatives. *Making Change? Learning from Europe's Cooperatives.* Washington, D.C.: Center for Study of Responsive Law, 1985.

Richardson, William (Sir). *The CWS in War and Peace, 1938–1978.* Manchester: Cooperative Wholesale Society, 1977.

Ruwwe, H. F. *Die Stellung der Konsumgenossenschaften im Sozialismus Osteuropas.* Tübingen: Mohr, 1972.

Totomiants, Vakhan. *Die Konsumvereine in Russland.* Munich: Duncker and Humblot, 1922.

IV. F. 5. Consumer Cooperatives in North America

Bolles, J. K. *The People's Business. The Progress of Consumers' Cooperatives in America.* New York: Harper, 1942.

Bowen, E. R. *American Answer: Consumer Cooperation.* Chicago: CLUSA, 1960.

Bryngelson, L. *A Survey of Consumers' Cooperatives in the United States.* New York: Columbia University, 1941.

Consumer Cooperatives in America. Chicago and New York: CLUSA, 1942.

Fowler, Bertram B. *Consumer Cooperation in America.* New York: Vanguard Press, 1936.

Keen, G. *The Organization of a Consumer's Cooperative.* Brandford, Ontario, Canada: CUC, 1938.

Kerinec, Roger. *Les coopératives de consommation aux USA.* Paris: PUF, 1948.

Laidlaw, A. F. *The Consumer Cooperative Movement: Problems of Education and Culture.* New York: Warbasse Memorial Library Association, 1962.

Neptune, Robert. *California's Uncommon Markets. The Story of the Consumer Cooperatives 1935–1971.* Richmond, Calif.: Associated Cooperatives, 1971.

Schmaltz, C. *Operating Results of Consumers' Cooperatives in the United States.* Cambridge, Mass.: Harvard University Press, 1937.

United States Bureau of Labor Statistics. *Organization and Management of Consumers' Cooperative Associations and Clubs (with model by-laws).* Washington, D.C.: GPO, 1934.

IV. F. 6. Consumer Cooperatives in Developing Countries

Alon, S. *Consumers' Cooperatives.* Tel Aviv: Afro-Asian Institute for Cooperatives, 1962.

Anangisye, E. M. *Cooperative Shops in Africa.* London: Trans-Africa, 1977.

Consumer Cooperation in South-East Asia. New Delhi: ICA, ROECSEA, 1976.

Les coopératives de consommation dans la stratégie du développement. Paris: École Pratique des Hautes Études, 1964.

Doing Business With Consumer Cooperative of America. San José, Costa Rica: ICA ROAM, 1998.

Doing Business with Healthcare Cooperatives in the Americas. San José, Costa Rica: ICA ROAM, 1997.

Jara, J. C. de la, P. Klemann, and E. Rusch, et al. *Las cooperativas de consumo latinoamericanas. Su problemática económica y perspectiva como factores aceleradores de desarrollo.* Santiago: Interamerican Cooperative Conference, 1972.

Kerbs, H. *Consumer Cooperatives and Developing Countries.* Bonn: Friedrich Ebert Foundation, 1968.

Open Asian Conference on Consumer Cooperation, October 23–25, 1976, Kuala Lumpur: Consumer Cooperation in South-East Asia. New Delhi: ICA, ROECSEA, 1976.

An Overview of Consumer Cooperation in Asia. New Delhi: ICA, ROAP, 1989.

Report on Development of Consumer Cooperatives—Problems and Methods. Stockholm: SCC, 1979.

Report on ICA/SCC Pro-Seminars in Botswana and Nigeria, 1978–79, on Consumer Cooperative Development. Stockholm: SCC, 1979.

IV. F. 7. Consumer Cooperatives—"New Wave Coops"

Coop Handbook Collective. *The Food Coop Handbook: How to Bypass Supermarkets to Control the Quality and Price of Your Food.* Boston: Houghton Mifflin, 1975.

Cox, Craig. *Storefront Revolution: Food Coops and the Counterculture.* New Brunswick, N.J.: Rutgers University Press, 1994.

Freundlich, Paul, Chris Collins, and Mikki Wenig. *A Guide to Cooperative Alternatives.* New Haven, Conn.: Community Publications Cooperative, 1979.

Guthrie, Brian, et al. *The Bulk Buy Book: A Comprehensive Guide to Buying in Bulk With Other People.* London: National Consumer Council, 1978.

Ronco, William C. *Food Coops: An Alternative to Shopping in Supermarkets.* Boston: Beacon Press, 1974.

Stern, Gloria. *How To Start Your Own Food Coop (With a Little Help From Your Friends): A Guide to Wholesale Buying.* New York: Walker, 1974.

Vellela, Tony. *Food Coops for Small Groups.* New York: Workman Publishing, 1975.
Wickstrom, Lois. *The Food Conspiracy Cookbook: How to Start a Neighborhood Buying Club and Eat Cheaply.* San Francisco: 101 Productions, 1974.

IV. G. Financial Cooperatives

IV. G. 1. Cooperative Banks

Alila, Patrick O., and Gerrishon K. Ikiara. *Cooperative Banking in Kenya: Twenty-five years in the Development of the National Economy.* Nairobi: Cooperative Bank of Kenya, 1993.
Arndt, Ernst H. D. *People's Banks in South Africa.* Pretoria: J. H. De Bussy, 1940.
Barou, Noah. *Cooperative Banking.* London: P. S. King and Son, 1931.
Baumann, Horst, and Lorenz Falkenstein. *Die Volksbanken und Raiffeisenbanken.* Frankfurt: Knapp, 1976.
Bergengren, Roy. *Cooperative Banking.* New York: Macmillan, 1923.
Bisotra, Rattan L. *Agricultural Development Through Cooperative Banks.* New Delhi: Deep and Deep Publications, 1994.
Castro Nue, Juan Carlos. *Historia de los bancos cooperativos en el Perú (1867–1978).* Lima: Editorial Carpentier, 1979.
Choubey, B. N. *Principles and Practice of Cooperative Banking in India.* London: Asia Publishing House, 1968.
Le crédit mutuel. Paris: Dunod, 1967.
Davenport, D. H. *The Cooperative Banks of Massachusetts.* Boston: Harvard University, 1938.
Fagneux, Louis. *La caisse de crédit Raiffeisen. Le raiffeisenisme en France et à l'étranger.* Paris: A. Leclerc, 1908.
Giles, Richard Y. *Credit for the Millions.* New York: Harper, 1951.
Gueslin, Andre. *Le crédit mutuel: De la caisse rurale à la banque sociale.* Strasbourg: Éditions Coprur, 1982.
Hesselbach, W. *Gemeinwirtschaftsbanken in Entwicklungsländern.* Mannheim: Bank für Gemeinwirtschaft Aktiongesellschaft, 1972.
Illan, J. M. *Hacia una sociedad cooperativa por medio de la banca cooperativa.* Buenos Aires: Intercoop, 1970.
Laud, G. *Cooperative Banking in India.* Calcutta: Cooperative Book Depot, 1956.
Millan, S. *Banco cooperativo.* Santiago: Editorial Jurídica, 1967.
Nikkiran, S. *Cooperative Banking in India.* Coimbatore, India: Rainbow Publications, 1980.
Ojo, Ade T., and Wole Adewunmi. *Cooperative Banking in Nigeria: Evolution, Structure and Operations.* Lagos: University of Lagos Press, 1980.
Plessis, Jacques. *Cinquante années de marche en avant (Banques populaires, 1917–1967).* Paris: O. G. P. Conseil, 1967.
Profil des institutions bancaires coopératives dans le monde. Montreal: École de gestion coopérative. 1998.

Report to the Government of Gambia on Cooperative Banking. Geneva: ILO, 1964.

Report to the Government of Malaysia on Cooperative Banking. Geneva: ILO, 1961.

Report to the Government of the Republic of Sierra Leone on Cooperative Banking, Finance and Credit. Geneva: ILO, 1973.

Roquelpo, Jean A. *Le crédit mutuel.* Paris: Librairie générale de droit et de jurisprudence, 1951.

Second Report to the Government of Gambia on Cooperative Banking. Geneva: ILO, 1965.

Sherman, F. *Modern Story of Mutual Savings Banks.* New York: Little and Yves, 1934.

Sie helfen sich selbst. Bonn: Deutscher Raiffeisenverband, 1962.

Tucker, D. *The Evolution of People's Bank.* New York: Columbia University Press, 1922; reissued, New York: AMS Press, 1967.

Weitz, Josef H. *Der Bankenmarkt in Spanien unter besonderer Berücksichtigung des Genossenschaftssektors.* Frankfurt and New York: P. Lang, 1993.

Welfing, Weldon. *Mutual Savings Banks, the Evolution of a Financial Industry.* Cleveland, Ohio: Press of Case Western Reserve University, 1968.

Wolff, H. *Cooperative Banking.* London: P. S. King and Son, 1907.

———. *Cooperative Credit Banks.* London: P. S. King and Son, 1898.

———. *A People's Bank Manual.* London: P. S. King and Son, 1895.

———. *People's Banks: A Record of Social and Economic Success.* London: P. S. King and Son, 1919.

IV. G. 2. Savings and Credit Cooperatives

Aredo, Dejene. *The Informal and Semi-Formal Financial Sectors in Ethiopia: A Study of Iqqub, Iddir, and Savings and Credit Cooperatives.* Nairobi: African Economic Research Consortium, 1993.

Aznar Sánchez, J. *Cooperativas de crédito.* Madrid: Universidad Maria Cristina, 1970.

Bayon y Marime, I. *Régimen jurídico de las cooperativas, estudio especial sobre las cooperativas de crédito.* Madrid: Editorial Anaya, 1970.

Bergengren, Roy. *Note on Cooperative Credit.* Geneva: ILO, 1943.

Bialik, Manoah L. *The Cooperative Credit Movement in Palestine.* Ann Arbor, Mich.: Edwards Brothers, 1940.

Brown, Mary Wilcox. *The Development of Thrift.* New York: Macmillan, 1899.

Chichosz, Janusz. *Savings and Credit Cooperatives in Poland.* Warsaw: Publishing House of the Central Agricultural Union of "Peasant Self-Aid" Cooperatives, 1972.

Community Credit Mechanisms: Training Module. Nairobi: HABITAT, 1989.

Cooperative Credit. New York: Russell Sage Foundation Library, 1914.

Ditron Diaz, R. *Unidos contra la usura en las cooperativas de crédito.* Santo Domingo, Dominican Republic: Editorial Itesa, 1964.

Dourakis, V. *Épargne et développement dans les pays sousdéveloppés.* Paris: Université de Paris, 1972.

Garcia Ruiz, Camilo. *Análisis de los resultados en uniones de crédito.* Mexico City: [n.p.], 1953.

Gentil, Dominique, and Yves Fournier. *Coopératives d'épargne et crédit et voies alternatives au financement du développement rural en Afrique "francophone."* Paris: Caisse centrale de coopération économique, 1988.

Ghosh, Henry H. *Theory of Cooperative Credit.* Calcutta: R. Cambray, 1914.

Gorst, Sheila. *Cooperative Credit for Producers and Consumers.* Oxford: Blackwell, 1962.

Group Based Savings and Credit for the Rural Poor. Geneva: ILO, 1984.

Huppi, Monika, and Gershon Feder. *The Role of Groups and Credit Cooperatives in Rural Lending.* Washington, D.C.: World Bank, 1989.

International Liaison Committee on Cooperative Thrift and Credit. *Democracy and Efficiency in Thrift and Credit Cooperatives: Report of the 3rd International Conference on Cooperative Thrift and Credit, London, June, 1974.* London: ICA, 1975.

Jones, Robert C. *Cooperativas de crédito en los Estados Unidos.* Washington, D.C.: Unión Panamericana, 1944.

Liang, C. C. *Mobilization of Rural Savings with Special Reference to the Far East.* New York: UN, Economic Commission for Asia, 1951.

Matos, Carlos M. *Normas de funcionamiento para cooperativas de crédito.* San Juan, Puerto Rico: Departamento de Agricultura y Comercio, 1954.

Nweze, Noble J. *The Role of Women's Traditional Savings and Credit Cooperatives in Small-Farm Development.* Morrilton, Ark.: Winrock International Institute for Agricultural Development, 1990.

Pickett, Liam P. *Management of Cooperative Credit.* Geneva: ILO, 1975.

The Program of Possible and Potential Activities by Credit Cooperatives in Latin America. Bonn: Friedrich Ebert Foundation, 1968.

Punia, K. R. *Administration of Credit Cooperatives.* New Delhi: Deep and Deep Publications, 1989.

Report of the Open Asian Conference on Cooperative Credit and Financial Management, November, 1976, Madras, India. New Delhi: ICA, ROECSEA, 1976.

Report on the Regional Seminar on Cooperative Credit, Tokyo, April 1973. New Delhi: ICA, ROECSEA, 1973.

Schujman, L. *El cooperativismo de crédito, sus proyecciones económicas y sociales.* Buenos Aires: Instituto Movilizador de Fondo Cooperativo, 1966.

Second International Conference on Cooperative Thrift and Credit. Paris: Caisse centrale de crédit coopératif, 1972.

Venkatappiah, B. *Regional Report on Training Facilities for Personnel of Credit Cooperatives and Agricultural Banks.* (Nepal, Bangladesh, Sri Lanka, India) Rome: FAO, 1979.

Vienney, H. D., et al. *Épargne et crédit en développement coopératif.* Paris: Union du crédit coopératif, 1970.

IV. G. 3. Credit Unions

IV. G. 3. a. Credit Union History and Theory

Bergengren, Roy. *Credit Unions, Their Operation and Value.* New York: American Management Association, 1926.

Boyle, George. *The Poor Man's Prayer: The Story of Credit Union Beginnings.* Baltimore: Helicon Press, 1962.

Brann, E., ed. *You . . . and Credit Union History.* Madison, Wis.: CUNA International, 1970.

Bros, Peter K. *The Credit Union: Its Position in the Consumer Financial Marketplace.* Springfield, Va.: Financial Book Partners, 1989.

Chávez Nuñez, Fernando, and Carlos Matos. *Cooperativas de Ahorro y Crédito.* Washington, D.C.: Unión Panamericana, 1947.

Community-Based Finance Institutions: The Role of Cooperatives and Credit Unions in Mobilizing Finance for the Improvement of Low-Income Human Settlements. Nairobi: HABITAT, 1984.

Croteau, John T. *The Economics of the Credit Union.* Detroit: Wayne State University Press, 1963.

Davis, R. W. *Comparative Digest of Credit Union Acts.* Madison, Wis.: CUNA, 1966.

Dublin, Jack. *Credit Unions: Theory and Practice.* Detroit: Wayne State University, 1966; reissued, 1971.

Feldman, Stephen, ed. *Credit Unions.* Hempstead, N.Y.: Hofstra University, 1974.

Flannery, John B. *Reflection: An Examination of Credit Union Philosophy and Principles.* Walled Lake, Mich.: [n.p.], 1965.

Francis, Kent W. *Credit Unions Are People.* Madison, Wis.: CUNA International, 1969.

Giles, R. *Credit for the Millions.* New York: Harper, 1951.

The Great Credit Union Story. Madison, Wis.: CUNA, 1965.

Great Moments in Credit Union History. Madison, Wis.: CUNA Mutual, 1963.

Kusi, A. M. *The Economic Power of Cooperatives in Developing Countries and Credit Unions in Capital Formation Within the Cooperative System.* Legon, Ghana: University of Ghana, Institute of Adult Education, 1974.

Lee, Pamela, ed. *Introduction to Credit Unions.* Madison, Wis.: CUNA, 1981; Dubuque, Iowa: Kendall/Hunt, 1981; 4th edition, 1990.

MacIssac, J. *The Credit Union.* Antigonish: St. Francis Xavier University, 1956.

McLanahan, Jack and Connie, eds. *Cooperative/Credit Union Dictionary and Reference (including encyclopedic materials).* Richmond, Ky.: Cooperative Alumni Association, 1990.

McLane, C. *Credit Union Bibliography.* Washington, D.C.: Riverford Publishing, 1936.

Mitchell, Humfrey. *People's Banks in North America. A Survey of the Desjardins System of Cooperative Banks in Canada and Their Adoption in the United States.* Washington, D.C.: GPO, 1914.

Moodey, J. Carroll, and Gilbert Fite. *The Credit Union Movement: Origins and Development, 1850–1970.* Lincoln: University of Nebraska Press, 1971; Madison, Wis.: CUNA, 1971; reissued, Dubuque, Iowa: Kendall/Hunt, 1984.

Neifeld, M. *Cooperative Consumer Credit, with Special Reference to Credit Unions.* New York: Harper, 1936.

O'Hara, Frank. *Credit Unions.* New York: Paulist Press, 1937.

Polner, W., and M. Dean. *Credit Union Bibliography.* Madison, Wis.: CUNA, 1973.

Prindle, T. R. *It's Not Just Money.* Madison, Wis.: CUNA, 1967.

Pursell, A. *Keys to Effective Rural Credit Unions.* Washington, D.C.: USDA, 1961.

Robinson, Ceretha F. *Credit and the War on Poverty: An Analysis of the Credit Union Programs of the Office of Economic Opportunity.* Chicago: Woodstock Institute, 1993.

Russell, E. *All About Credit Unions.* St. John, New Brunswick: Department of Natural Resources, 1945.

Stewart, Maxwell S. *Credit Unions—Self-Help Family Finance.* New York: Public Affairs Committee, 1955.

———. *Credit Unions—The People's Banks.* New York: Public Affairs Committee, 1944.

Tholin, Kathryn, and Jean Pogge. *Banking Services for the Poor: Community Development Credit Unions.* Chicago: Woodstock Institute, 1991.

Valle Pastora, Alfonso. *Las cooperativas de ahorro y crédito y la usura.* León, Nicaragua: Editorial Hospicio, 1970.

Voorhis, Jerry. *Credit Unions.* Chicago: CLUSA, 1965.

———. *Credit Unions, Basic Cooperatives.* Chicago: CLUSA, 1959.

Whitney, Edson L. *Cooperative Credit Societies (Credit Unions) in America and in Foreign Countries.* Washington, D.C.: GPO, 1922.

Wilson, Charles M. *Common Sense Credit: Credit Unions Come of Age.* New York: Devin-Adair, 1962.

Witzeling, Ruth. *People, Not Profit: The Story of the Credit Union Movement.* Madison, Wis.: CUNA, 1993; Dubuque, Iowa: Kendall/Hunt, 1993.

IV. G. 3. b. Credit Union Operations/Management

Arneil, S. F. *Forming and Running a Credit Union.* Adelaide, Australia: Rigby, 1971.

———. *Secrets of the Board Room: The Credit Union Director in the Eighties.* Sydney: Alternative Publications Cooperative, 1980.

Audits of Credit Unions. New York: American Institute of Certified Public Accountants, Credit Union Committee, 1986.

Burger, Albert E., and Tina Dacin. *Field of Membership: An Evolving Concept.* Madison, Wis.: Filene Research Institute, 1992.

Burger, Altert E., and Gregory J. Lypny. *Taxation of Credit Unions.* Madison, Wis.: Filene Research Institute, 1991.

Butler, Paul D. *Credit Union Board of Directors Handbook.* Madison, Wis.: CUNA, 1990; Dubuque, Iowa: Kendall/Hunt, 1990.

Bylaws Manual for Federal Credit Unions. Washington, D.C.: National Association of Federal Credit Unions, 1985; reissued, 1992.

Cameron, Archie. *Credit Union Personnel Management.* Madison, Wis.: CUNA, 1981; Dubuque, Iowa: Kendall/Hunt, 1981.

———. *Credit Union Salary Administration.* Madison, Wis.: CUNA, 1982; Dubuque, Iowa: Kendall/Hunt, 1982.

Cargill, Thomas F. *Recent Research on Credit Unions: A Survey.* Reno: University of Nevada, Bureau of Business and Economic Research, 1976.

Cook, Jeff. *A Collective Concern: Setting Policies and Procedures for Credit Union Collections.* Madison, Wis.: Credit Union Executives Society, 1993.

———. *Credit Union Mergers: A Professional Analysis and Real-Life Examples.* Madison, Wis.: Credit Union Executives Society, 1994.

Credit Union Accounting. Madison, Wis.: CUNA, 1986; Dubuque, Iowa: Kendall/Hunt, 1986; reissued, 1990.

Credit Union Compliance Manual. Redmond: Washington State Credit Union League, 1990.

A Credit Union Handbook. Cincinnati, Ohio: Associated Kemba Credit Unions, 1935.

Ellsworth, Pat. *You—The Credit Union Member.* Longview, Wash.: Key Word, 1976.

Facts About Credit Unions. Washington, D.C.: National Association of Federal Credit Unions, 1991.

Financial Reporting for Credit Unions. Toronto: Canadian Institute of Chartered Accountants, 1984.

Fortin, Karen. *Introduction to Financial Accounting.* Madison, Wis.: CUNA, 1981; Dubuque, Iowa: Kendall/Hunt, 1981.

Fountain, Wendell V. *The Credit Union Director: Roles, Duties, and Responsibilities.* Jacksonville, Fla.: FAI Publishers, 1994.

Francis, Kent W., and Ray P. Bauschke. *Credit Union Directors: A Focus on Power.* Madison, Wis.: CUNA, 1971.

———. *Credit Union Dynamics: How to Make Your Credit Union "Go."* Madison, Wis.: CUNA International, 1968.

Gastonguay, Denis J. and Mary Ann Strom. *Credit Union Operations.* Madison, Wis.: CUNA, 1981; Dubuque, Iowa: Kendall/Hunt, 1981.

Giacomino, Don E. *Accounting for Management Decision Making.* Madison, Wis.: CUNA, 1981; Dubuque, Iowa: Kendall/Hunt, 1981.

Guiltinan, Joseph P. *Pricing Credit Union Products and Services.* Madison, Wis.: CUNA, 1985; Dubuque, Iowa: Kendall/Hunt, 1985.

Ham, Arthur H. *A Credit Union Primer.* New York: Russell Sage Foundation, 1930.

Hoyle: Glenn C. *Supervisory Committee: Duties and Responsibilities.* Madison, Wis.: CUNA, 1980; Dubuque, Iowa: Kendall/Hunt, 1980.

Huber, A. *Credit Union Handbook.* Manila: National Cooperative Corporation, 1948.

Hunt, John. *Credit Union Administration: An Introduction.* Port-of-Spain, Trinidad: Coopers and Lybrand, 1989.

Introducing Total Quality Management: A Credit Union Reader. Madison, Wis.: CUNA, 1994; Dubuque, Iowa: Kendall/Hunt, 1994.

Itkin, Donald. *50 Successful Ideas for Marketing Credit Union Loans.* Madison, Wis.: CUNA, 1993; Dubuque, Iowa: Kendall/Hunt, 1993.

Jerving, Jim. *The Central Finance Facility: A Guide to Development and Operations.* Madison, Wis.: WOCCU, 1987.

———. *Financial Management for Credit Union Managers and Directors.* Madison, Wis.: WOCCU, 1989; 2nd edition, 1994.

Kamstra, Clare, ed. *Credit Union Accounting.* Madison, Wis.: CUNA, 1983; Dubuque, Iowa: Kendall/Hunt, 2nd edition, 1983.

Kibirige, E. *Human Development Through Credit Unions: A Guide for Credit Union Promoters.* Nairobi: ACCOSCA, 1980.

Knight, Henry, and Wayne Peasgood. *Credit Union Performance Improvement: Practical Ideas for Directors and Managers.* Chicago: Probus Publishing, 1989.

Mapother, William R. *Winning Bankruptcy Strategies for Credit Unions.* Louisville, Ky.: Creditors' Law Center, 1986.

Marthinuss, George, and Larry L. Perry. *Credit Union Audit Manual.* New York: American Institute of Certified Public Accountants (looseleaf), 1992– .

The Model Credit Union Act and Commentary. Madison, Wis.: CUNA, Governmental Affairs Division, 1979.

Sanfilippo, Barbara. *Five-Star Service Solutions: Winning Ideas for Achieving Exceptional Service in Today's Financial Institutions.* Naperville, Ill.: Financial Sourcebooks, 1990.

Sauber, Mary Anne. *Credit Union Loan Professional Handbook.* Madison, Wis.: CUNA, 1991; Dubuque, Iowa: Kendall/Hunt, 1991.

Schroeder, Dennis. *Membership Promotion.* Madison, Wis.: CUNA, 1988; Dubuque, Iowa: Kendall/Hunt, 1988.

Seibert, Paul. *Credit Union Facility Planning: From Strategy to Reality.* Madison, Wis.: Credit Union Executives Society, 1994.

Staats, William F. *Key Concepts of Financial Management for Credit Unions.* San Antonio, Tex.: Council for Professional Education, 1989.

Stevenson, Richard A. *Asset-Liability Management.* Madison, Wis.: CUNA, 1984; Dubuque, Iowa: Kendall/Hunt, 1984; 2nd edition, 1994.

Tenenbaum, David. *Involving Credit Union Volunteers.* Madison, Wis.: WOCCU, 1988.

Warfel, George. *Credit Union Financial Management.* Madison: CUNA, 1981; Dubuque, Iowa: Kendall/Hunt, 1981; revised edition,1984.

White, Phillip D. *Pricing Credit Union Services: Issues and Strategies.* Madison, Wis.: CUNA, 1992; Dubuque, Iowa: Kendall/Hunt, 1992.

Witzeling, Ruth. *Risk Management and Insurance: A Credit Union Perspective.* Dubuque, Iowa: Kendall/Hunt, 1993.

IV. G. 3. c. Credit Unions in Canada

Arnason, B. N. *History, Philosophy and Development of the Credit Union Movement in Saskatchewan.* Regina: Credit Union League of Saskatchewan, 1959.

Clements, M. *By Their Bootstraps, a History of the Credit Union Movement in Saskatchewan.* Toronto: Clarke, Irwin, 1965.

Kenyon, Ron. *To the Credit of the People.* Toronto: Ontario Credit Union League, 1976.

Mercure, Gilles. *Credit Unions and Caisses Populaires.* Ottawa: Royal Commission on Banking and Finance, 1962.

O'Meara, J. E. *Credit Unions in Canada.* Ottawa: Department of Agriculture, 1945.

Purden, Christine. *Agents for Change: Credit Unions in Saskatchewan.* Regina: Credit Union Central (Saskatchewan), 1980.

IV. G. 3. d. Credit Unions in Canada—Desjardins Movement

Boyle, Georges. *The Poor Man's Prayer: The Story of Alphonse Desjardins.* Montreal: Palm Publishers, 1962.

Bussière, Eugène. *Caisses populaires.* Quebec: Université de Laval, 1949.

Charron, Paul Emile. *Les caisses populaires Desjardins.* Montreal: UCC, 1953.

Credit Unions = Caisses populaires, d'épargne et de crédit. Ottawa: Dominion Bureau of Statistics, 1966–1982 (annual).

Desjardins, Alphonse. *The Cooperative Peoples Bank.* New York: Russell Sage Foundation, 1914.

Faucher, A. *Alphonse Desjardins.* Quebec: Université de Laval, 1948. Grondin, P. *Catéchisme des caisses populaires Desjardins.* Sherbrooke, Quebec: Le Messager, 1961.

Lamarche, Jacques. *Alphonse Desjardins, un homme au service des autres.* Montreal: Éditions du jour, 1977.

———. *Les Caisses populaires.* Montreal: Éditions Lidec, 1967.

———. *Cyrille Vaillancourt: Homme d'action, homme d'unité, coopérateur émérité (1892–1969).* Montreal: Éditions du jour, 1979.

———. *Le mouvement Desjardins. Les bâtisseurs du 20ᵉ siècle.* Lévis: Éditions Lidec, 1962.

———. *La saga des caisses populaires.* Montreal: Éditions à presse, 1985.

Mitchell, Humfrey. *People's Banks in North America. A Survey of the Desjardins System of Cooperative Banks in Canada and Their Adoption in the United States.* Washington, D.C.: GPO, 1914.

Réflexion faite: L'institut coopératif Desjardins cinq ans après. Lévis: Institut coopératif Desjardins, 1968.

Revision de la loi sur les banques: Mémoire soumis par la Fédération de Québec des caisses populaires Desjardins. Quebec: Fédération de Québec des caisses populaires Desjardins, 1975.

Roy, Yves. *Alphonse Desjardins et les caisses populaires, 1854–1920.* Montreal: Fides, 1964.

———. *Alphonse Desjardins, 1900–1920: Les caisses populaires.* Quebec: Fédération de Québec des caisses populaires Desjardins, 1975.

Rudin, Ronald. *In Whose Interest? Quebec's Caisses Populaires, 1900–1945*. Montreal and Buffalo: McGill-Queen's University Press, 1990.

Tremblay, R. *Le mouvement coopératif Desjardins*. Lévis: Fédération des caisses populaires Desjardins, 1969.

Vachon, Stanislas. *Alphonse Desjardins, fondateur des caisses populaires*. Charlesbourg, Quebec: [n.p.], 1962.

Vaillancourt, Cyrille, and A. Faucher. *Alphonse Desjardins, pionnier de la coopération d'épargne et de crédit en Amérique*. Lévis: Le quotidien, 1950.

IV. G. 3. e. Credit Unions in the United States

Bergengren, Roy F. *Credit Union, North America*. New York: Southern Publishers, 1940.

———. *Crusade, the Fight for Economic Democracy in North America, 1921–1945*. New York: Exposition Press, 1952.

———. *CUNA Emerges*. Madison, Wis.: CUNA, 1936.

———. *I Speak for Joe Doakes*. New York: Harper, 1945.

———. *Note on Cooperative Credit*. Geneva: ILO, 1943

———. *The Place of Cooperatives in Postwar Society: the Credit Union Ideas*. New York: Institute of Postwar Reconstruction, 1944.

———. *Soul, a Fourth Credit Union Book*. Madison, Wis.: Cantwell Press, 1938.

———. *The War and After, a Sixth Credit Union Book*. Madison, Wis.: Straus, 1942.

Bils, Charles F. *What the Courts Hold on Credit Unions: Briefs of Significant Court Decisions Involving Credit Unions, Their Practices and Usages, 1937–1976*. Madison, Wis.: CUNA, 1976.

Brixner, V. *Credit Unions in den USA*. Frankfurt: Fritz Knapp Verlag, 1971.

Clark, Lincoln H. *Credit Unions in the United States*. Chicago: [n.p.], 1940.

The Credit Union Industry: Trends, Structure, and Competitiveness: A Study Prepared for the American Bankers Association Under the Direction of the Secura Group. Washington, D.C.: American Bankers Association, 1989.

Credit Union Law Service (looseleaf). New York: M. Bender, 1984.

Croteau, John T. *A National Central Credit Union Society and the Liquidity Problem of the Credit Union Movement*. Madison, Wis.: CUNA. 1960.

———. *The Federal Credit Union, Policy and Practice*. New York: Harper, 1956.

Crow, W., and S. Chucker. *The Federal Credit Union*. New York: Oriom Press, 1935.

Federal National Mortgage Association. *Credit Unions: Expanding Opportunities in the Secondary Mortgage Market*. Washington, D.C.: Fannie Mae, Customer Education Group, 1991.

Golembe, Carter H. Associates. *State Supervision of Credit Unions: Analysis and Comment: A Study*. Madison, Wis.: CUNA, 1973.

Isbister, John. *Thin Cats: The Community Development Credit Union Movement in the United States*. Davis: University of California, Center for Cooperatives, 1994.

Jerving, Jim. *Changing Youth: Starting a Youth Credit Union and Learning Center: A Case Study of the D. Edward Wells Youth Credit Union.* Dubuque, Iowa: Kendall/Hunt, 1993.

Legislative History of the Federal Credit Union Act: A Study of the Historical Development, 1934–1974, of the Statute Governing Federal Credit Unions. Washington, D.C.: CUNA, Governmental Affairs Division, 1975.

Melford, Donald J. *The Federal Income Tax Exemption of Credit Unions: A Historical, Competitive, and Legal Analysis.* Washington, D.C.: Defense Credit Union Council, 1981.

Moen, R. *Rural Credit Unions in the United States.* Raleigh, N. C.: [n.p.], 1931.

NAFCU's Compliance Guide for Credit Unions (looseleaf). Austin, Tex.: Sheshunoff Information Services, 1994– .

Orchard, C., C. Hyland, and C. Clarke. *CUNA Mutual and the Credit Union Movement.* Madison, Wis.: CUNA, 1963.

Pugh, Olin S., and F. Jerry Ingram. *Credit Unions: A Movement Becomes an Industry.* Reston, Va.: Reston Publishing, 1984.

Ricke, Keith G. *Credit Union Membership Study, 1986.* St. Paul, Minn.: Concepts in Marketing Research, 1987.

Taxation of Banks and Thrift Institutions: Prepared by the Staff of the Joint Committee on Taxation (of the U. S. Congress). Washington, D.C.: GPO, 1983.

Tenenbaum, Shelly. *A Credit to Their Community: Jewish Loan Societies in the United States, 1880–1945.* Detroit: Wayne State University Press, 1993.

United States. Congress. House. Committee on Banking, Finance, and Urban Affairs. Subcommittee on General Oversight and Investigations. *Issues Concerning the Failure of Federally Insured Federal Credit Unions.* Washington, D.C.: GPO, 1989.

United States. Congress. Senate. Committee on Banking and Currency. Subcommittee on Financial Institutions. *Federal Share Insurance for Credit Unions.* Washington, D.C.: GPO, 1970.

United States. General Accounting Office. *Progress Being Made and Difficulties Being Encountered by Credit Unions Serving Low-Income Persons.* Washington, D.C.: General Accounting Office, 1971.

Woods, W. *Rural Credit Unions of the United States.* Washington, D.C.: USDA, FCS, 1965.

IV. G. 3. f. Credit Unions—Other Countries

Amit, H. R., and Norman Riley. *Report of the Proceedings: Fourth Annual Credit Union Seminar, February 1976, Sponsored by the Liberian Credit Union National Association.* Antigonish: Coady International Institute, 1976.

Blondel, Eaulin. *Credit Unions, Cooperatives, Trade Unions, and Friendly Societies in Barbados: A Directory.* St. Augustine, Trinidad: E. A. Blondel, 1986.

Cazares, José L. *Cooperativas de ahorro y crédito: Ley 10.761, Decreto-ley 15.322, Ley 16.327.* Montevideo, Uruguay: Fundación de Cultura Universitaria, 1993.

Cooperative Housing Foundation. *Financing Housing Through Savings and Credit Cooperative Societies in Kenya.* Washington, D.C.: USAID, Office of Housing and Urban Development, 1989.

Crapp, Harvey R., and Michael T. Skully. *Credit Unions in Australia: Development, Operations and Future.* Lindfield, New South Wales: Kuring-gai College of Advanced Education, Center for Management Studies, 1983.

Credit Union National Council. *Credit Union Movement in Rhodesia (Zimbabwe)—Annual Conference Report 1968.* Harare, Zimbabwe: Chishawasha Mission Press, 1969.

Credit Union Seminar Report, Trinidad and Tobago. May 1978. Antigonish: Coady International Institute and Cooperative Credit Union League of Trinidad and Tobago, 1978.

Culloty, A. T. *Nora Herlihy: Irish Credit Union Pioneer.* Dublin: Irish League of Credit Unions, 1990.

Da Ros, Giuseppina. *El cooperativismo de ahorro y crédito en el Ecuador.* Quito: Pontificia Universidad Católica del Ecuador, 1985.

Davis, Robert W., and Alfredo Lanza, eds. *International Digest of Laws Governing Credit Unions: A Reference Guide to the Laws Under Which Credit Unions Are Organized and Operate in Various Countries and Jurisdictions Throughout the World.* Madison, Wis.: WOCCU, 1993.

Dublin, Jack, and Selma Dublin. *Credit Unions in a Changing World: The Tanzania-Kenya Experience.* Detroit: Wayne State University Press, 1983.

Dublin, Jack, David P. Harmon, and Mebratu Tsegaye. *Mid-Term Evaluation of the Malawi Union of Savings and Credit Cooperatives Project (612-0205).* Lilongwe: USAID/Malawi, 1983.

Gentile, Dominique, and Yves Fournier. *Coopératives d'épargne et crédit et voies alternatives au financement du développement rural en Afrique "francophone."* Paris: Caisse centrale de coopération économique, 1988.

A Glimpse Into the Asian Credit Union Movement: A Compilation of the Histories of Credit Unions in Six Asian Countries. Seoul: Asian Confederation of Credit Unions, 1981.

Göricke F. V., and O. C. Kirsch. *Spar- und Darlehensgenossenschaften in ausgewählten Ländern Ostafrikas—Äthiopien, Kenia, Tansania, Sambia.* Heidelberg: Forschungsstelle für Internationale Agrarentwicklung, 1976.

Kirsch, O. C., and F. V. Goricke. *Scope and Impact of the Credit Union Movement in Selected African Countries.* Mainz: Hase and Koehler Verlag, English Series No. 3, 1977.

Kirsch, O. C., and D. Kroker. *Spar- und Darlehensgenossenschaften in ausgewählten Ländern Westafrikas—Kamerun, Ghana.* Heidelberg: Forschungsstelle für Internationale Agrarentwicklung, 1975.

Labonte, Roger. *Notre caisses populaire, coopératives d'épargne et de prêts.* Port-au-Prince, Haiti: La phalange, 1959.

Lafonj, M. *Introduction to the Japanese Credit Union Movement.* Tokyo: Sophia University, 1972.

Lamothe, Camille. *Une étape de l'évolution coopérative dans de domaine de l'épargne et du crédit.* Port-au-Prince, Haiti: H. Deschamps, 1958.

Münkner, Hans H., ed. *Credit Union Development in Africa.* Mainz: Hase and Koehler, English Series No. 4, 1978.

Nouvelle stratégie de développement des COOPEC au Zaire. Kinshasa, Zaire: USAID/Kinshasa, 1991; Madison, Wis.: WOCCU, 1991.

Quinn, Anthony P. *Credit Unions in Ireland.* Dublin: Oak Tree Press, 1994.

Report of the Eighth African Conference on Mobilization of Local Savings and Annual General Meeting of the Board of Directors of the African Cooperative Savings and Credit Association, August, 1970, Buea, Cameroon. Madison, Wis.: CUNA International, World Extension Department, 1970.

Report of the Ninth African Conference on the Mobilization of Local Savings and Annual General Meeting of ACCOSCA, August, 1971, Addis Ababa, Ethiopia. Madison, Wis.: WOCCU, 1972.

Report of the Seventh African Conference on the Mobilization of Local Savings and the First Annual General Meeting of ACCOSCA, August 1969, Accra, Ghana. Madison, Wis.: CUNA International, World Extension Department, 1969.

Reynolds, Norman. *The Credit Union Movement in Zimbabwe: A Diagnostic Study (prepared for the Self-Help Development Foundation).* Harare, Zimbabwe: Southern Africa Foundation for Economic Research, 1988.

Runcie, Neil, ed. *Credit Unions in the South Pacific: Australia, Fiji, New Zealand, Papua and New Guinea.* London: University of London Press, 1969.

Sarwe, Patrick N. W. *Report on the Credit Union Seminar Held at the Ghana Institute of Management, Accra, Ghana, July 1977.* Yaoundé, Cameroon: Sarwe, 1977.

A Short Introduction to the Cooperative Savings and Credit Societies and Tanzania Rural Savings and Credit Scheme. Dar-es-Salaam: Office of the Prime Minister, 1977.

Songsore, Jacob. *Cooperative Credit Unions as Instruments of Regional Development: The Example of N. W. Ghana.* Swansea, U.K.: University of Swansea, Centre for Development Studies, 1983.

Towards Design of a Mission Strategy for Development of Zaire's Savings and Credit Cooperative Movement. Kinshasa, Zaire: USAID/Zaire, 1990.

IV. H. Fisheries Cooperatives

Berube, L. *Fishery Cooperatives in North America.* Rome: FAO, 1959.

Chávez Perez, Silvestre. *Manuel de cooperativas pesqueras.* Washington, D.C.: Unión Panamericana, 1961.

Clement, Wallace. *The Struggle to Organize: Resistance in Canada's Fishery.* Toronto: McClelland and Stewart, 1986.

Les coopératives de pêcheurs. Rome: FAO, 1971.

Les coopératives de pêcheurs au Québec. Montreal: Pêcheurs unis du Québec, 1959.

Delforge, Guy. *Les pêcheurs face à la coopérative: enquête sociale.* Port-Louis, Mauritius: Institut pour le développement et le progrès, 1972.

Digby, Margaret. *Cooperation for Fishermen.* Rome: FAO, 1961; London: ICA, 1961.

———. *Organization of Fishermen's Cooperatives.* Oxford: Plunkett, 1973.

Eddiwan. *The Bank for Fishermen's Cooperatives.* Bangkok: IPFC, 1959.

Fisheries Cooperative Symposium: Proceedings, University of Washington, Seattle, February, 1975. Corvallis: Oregon State University Extension Service, 1976.

Fisheries Cooperatives in Korea. Seoul: National Federation of Fisheries Cooperatives, 1981.

Fishermen's Cooperatives in Canada. Ottawa: CUC, 1962.

Fishermen's Cooperatives in Selected Countries in Europe. Rome: FAO, 1966.

The Fishing Industry in Cuba. Havana: Instituto Nacional de la Pesca, 1967.

Forms of Cooperation in the Fishing Industry: Denmark, Ireland, United Kingdom. Brussels: Directorate General for Agriculture of the Commission of the European Communities, 1976.

Garland, William R., and Phillip F. Brown. *Fishery Cooperatives.* Washington, D.C.: USDA, FCS, 1985.

Groot, Emile. *Las cooperativas pesqueras en México.* Mexico City: Instituto Nacional de Estudios de Trabajo, 1982.

Habibullah, M., and Mahbub Ahmed. *Management Constraints of Cooperatives.* Dacca, Bangladesh: University of Dacca, 1986.

Hill, A. V. *Tides of Change. A Story of Fishermen's Cooperatives in British Columbia.* Prince Rupert, British Columbia: Fishermen's Cooperative Association, 1967.

Larocque, Paul. *Pêche et coopération au Québec.* Montreal: Éditions du jour, 1978.

Leblanc, A. *The Cooperative Work of United Maritime Fishermen Ltd.* Rome: FAO, 1970.

Lefebvre, A. *La coopération maritime chez les pêcheurs.* Algiers: Carbonel, 1932.

MacNeil, R. J. *United Maritime Fishermen.* Antigonish: St. Francis Xavier University, 1945.

Magnus, Albrecht. *Landwirtschafts- und Fischereigenossenschaften im heutigen Japan.* Hamburg: Institut für Asienkunde, 1970.

Manual on Fishermen's Cooperatives. Rome: FAO, 1971.

Möller, Hans. *Fischereigenossenschaftswesen und Fischwirtschaft in Deutschland und anderen europäischen Fischereiländern.* Düsseldorf: Triltisch, 1959.

Nociones basicas sobre cooperativismo pesquero. Mexico City: Secretaria de Pesca, 1985.

Nordset, Arne, and Aslak Aasbo. *Cooperation Among Fishermen in Norway.* Bergen: J. Griegs Boktrykkeri, 1959.

Pollnac, Richard B. *Evaluating the Potential of Fishermen's Organizations in Developing Countries.* Kingston: University of Rhode Island, 1988.

———. *Socio-cultural Aspects of Developing Small-Scale Fisheries: Delivering Services to the Poor.* Washington, D.C.: World Bank, 1981.

Ponnathurai, K. S. *Report on Cooperative Fishery Movement in Bangladesh.* New Delhi: ICA, ROECSEA, 1975.

Ponnathurai, K. S., and A. W. Viddiyasekera. *Theory and Practice of Accounting in Fishery Cooperative Societies.* New Delhi: ICA, ROECSEA, 1977.

Report of the FAO Training Center in Fishery Cooperatives and Administration: Sydney, N.S.W. and Adelaide, South Australia, 1957–1958. Rome: FAO, 1958.

Report of the First Open World Conference on Cooperative Fisheries, Tokyo, September/October, 1975: Theme, Modernization of Fisheries and the Rational Utilization of Resources: The Role of Cooperatives. London: ICA, 1976.

Report on Credit for Artisanal Fishermen in South East Asia. Rome: FAO Fisheries Reports No. 122, 1972.

Sánchez Blanco, Jeronimo. *Historia del crédito social pesquero: 1900–1985.* Madrid: Ministerio de Agricultura, Pesca y Alimentación, 1992.

Small-Scale Fisheries Cooperatives—Some Lessons for the Future. Rome: COPAC, Occasional Paper No. 2, 1984.

Szczepanik, E. *The Economic Role of Middlemen and Cooperatives in Indo-Pacific Fisheries.* Rome: FAO, 1960.

———. *Fishermen's Cooperatives in the Indo-Pacific Region.* Rome: FAO, 1958.

Women in Development Through Fishery Coops in Asia: Report of the Joint ICA-CCA-SDID Planning Mission on Bangladesh, India, and Philippines. New Delhi: ICA, ROAP, 1990.

Worker's Cooperative Productive and Artisanal Societies in the Fishing Industry in Canada, France, Israel, Italy, Japan and Mexico. London: ICA, 1959.

IV. I. Forestry Cooperatives

Benecke, Dieter W. *El sistema cooperativo en América Latina y su aplicación en el sector forestal.* Santiago: Universidad Católica de Chile, 1973.

Brandl, H. *Organisatorische Gestaltungsprobleme in Forstwirtschaftlichen Zusammenschlüssen.* Freiburg, Germany: Forstliche Versuchs- und Forschungsanstalt Baden-Württemberg, 1977.

Christiansen, P. H. *Las cooperativas forestales a nivel communitario. Estudio de tres casos: México, Guatemala, Honduras.* Rome: FAO, 1979.

Le coopérateur forestier. Quebec: Éditions forestières, [n.d.](periodical).

Cooperative Marketing of Forest Products: A Bibliography. Washington, D.C.: U.S. Forest Service, 1939.

Coopératives ouvrières de production, coopératives forestieres, coopératives industrielles: France, Espagne, "Mondragon." Quebec: Ministère des consommateurs, coopératives et institutions financières, 1979.

Curtis, Albert B. *White Pines and Fires: Cooperative Forestry in Idaho.* Moscow: University Press of Idaho, 1983.

Dempsey, Gilbert P. *Forest Cooperatives: A Bibliography.* Upper Darby, Pa.: Northeastern Forest Experiment Station, 1967.

Dempsey, Gilbert P., and Clyde B. Markeson. *Guidelines for Establishing Forestry Cooperatives.* Upper Darby, Pa.: Northeastern Forest Experiment Station, 1969.

Digby, Margaret, and T. E. Edwardson. *Organization of Forestry Cooperatives.* Oxford: Plunkett, 1976.

Dubey, Sumati N., and Ratna Murdia. *Organization and Administration of Forest Laborers Cooperatives in Maharashtra.* Bombay: Tata Institute of Social Sciences, 1977.

Hartzell, Hal. *Birth of a Cooperative: Hoedads, Inc., a Worker Owned Forest Labor Coop.* Eugene, Ore.: Hulogos'i, 1987.

Hederstrom, T. *Las cooperativas forestales como sistema para crear fuentes de trabajo y mejores posibilidades de desarrollo forestal.* Rome: FAO, 1976.

———. *Desarrollo del movimiento cooperativa forestal—Guatemala.* Rome: FAO, 1977.

Kissin, I. *Cooperation in Forestry.* Oxford: Imperial Forestry Bureau, 1944.

Milk, R. *Marketing Forest Products Cooperatively in the United States, Canada and Europe.* Knoxville: University of Tennessee, 1941.

Muranjan, S. W. *Exploitation of Forests Through Forest Labor Cooperatives.* Poona, India: Gokhale Institute of Politics and Economics, 1972.

Scharf, E. *Forest Cooperation in Saskatchewan.* Regina: Cooperative Union of Saskatchewan, 1969.

Solin, L. *A Study of Farm Woodland Cooperatives in the United States.* Syracuse: New York State College of Forestry, 1940.

Tree Growers' Cooperatives: Papers Presented at the National Seminar on Tree Growers' Cooperatives, Indian Institute of Rural Management, Anand, India, October, 1991. New Delhi: ISO/Swedforest, 1993.

IV. J. Housing Cooperatives

IV. J. 1. Housing Cooperatives—Theory and Practice

Bellman, H. *The Building Societies Movement.* London: Methuen, 1927.

Benecke, Dieter W. *Algunos aspectos de las cooperativas de vivienda.* Santiago: Universidad Católica de Chile, Instituto de Cooperativismo, 1968.

A Bibliography on Housing Built or Managed Cooperatively (Denmark, France, Great Britain, Holland, Norway, Sweden, Switzerland, and USA). New York: Housing and Home Finance Agency, 1950.

Burr, P. C. *Las cooperativas de vivienda.* Santiago: Editorial Universitaría, 1958.

Cahill, William D. *Cooperative Housing: A Selective and Partially Annotated Bibliography.* Monticello, Ill.: Vance Bibliographies, 1979.

Carvallo Hederra, Sergio. *Cooperativas de habitación.* Washington, D.C.: Unión Panamericana, 1952.

Clurman, David, F. Scott Jackson, and Edna L. Hebard. *Condominiums and Cooperatives.* New York: Wiley, 1984.

Cooperative Housing. Berlin: ICA Housing Committee, 1980; 2nd Revised Edition, Stockholm: 1987.

Cooperative Housing. Bombay: Reserve Bank of India, 1950.

Cooperative Housing. New Delhi: ICA, ROECSEA, 1966.

Cooperative Housing. Stockholm: Riksförbund, 1952.

Danenberg, Elsie F. *Get Your Own Home the Cooperative Way.* New York: Greenberg, 1949.

del Giudice, J. C. *Vivienda y cooperativismo.* Buenos Aires: Intercoop, 1959.

Digby, Margaret. *Cooperative Housing.* Oxford: Plunkett, 1978.

Dodge, J. Robert. *Cooperative Housing.* Washington: USAID, 1971.

Dwyer, Marie. *Cooperative Housing: Beyond Buying or Renting: A Discussion of Cooperative Housing Overseas and the Implications of This Form of Housing for New Zealand.* Auckland, New Zealand: Auckland Regional Authority, 1981.

Fernandez Diaz, J. *Régimen Cooperativo de Vivienda.* Rosario, Argentina: Editorial Ciencia, 1957.

Fischer, R. *Desarrollo de la comunidad y cooperativas de vivienda.* Santiago: [n.p.], 1970.

Fischer, R., E. Rusch, and C. Villarroel. *Función de las cooperativas de vivienda en el desarrollo de la comunidad.* Santiago: [n.p.], 1971.

Gide, Charles. *Les coopératives de construction.* Paris: Association pour l'enseignement de la coopération, 1924.

———. *La question du logement et la coopération.* Paris: Association pour l'enseignement de la coopération, 1923.

Gray, Alison, and Judith Davey. *Prospects for Cooperative Housing in New Zealand.* Wellington, New Zealand: National Housing Commission. 1983.

Hands, John. *Housing Cooperatives.* London: Society for Cooperative Dwellings, 1975.

Housing: A Cooperative Approach. London: Cooperative Party, 1959.

Housing and Community Facilities in Integrated Rural Development: A Cooperative Approach. Washington, D.C.: FCH, 1976.

ICA. *Readings in Cooperative Housing.* Bombay: Allied Publishers, 1973.

Kaplan de Drimer, Alicia. *Cooperativas de vivienda: Caracteres, sistemas, proyecto de ley, estatutos.* Buenos Aires: Bibliografica Omeba, 1961.

Leduc, Murielle. *Les coopératives d'habitation: Nouvelles experiences et perspectives de développement.* Montreal: Éditions du jour, 1978.

Liblit, Jerome, ed. *Housing, the Cooperative Way: Selected Readings.* New York: Twayne, 1964.

McCafferty, Paul, and David Riley. *A Study of Cooperative Housing.* London: H.M.S.O., 1989.

McCamant, Kathryn, Charles Durrett, and Ellen Hertzman. *Cohousing: A Contemporary Approach to Housing Ourselves.* Berkeley: Ten Speed Press, 1993.

Meister, Albert. *Coopération d'habitation et sociologie voisinage.* Paris: Éditions de minuit, 1957.

Moe, Christine E. *Housing Cooperatives.* Monticello, Ill.: Vance Bibliographies, 1980.

Novy, Klaus. *Genossenschafts-Bewegung: Zur Geschichte und Zukunft der Wohnreform.* Berlin: Transit, 1983.

Organización de los Estados Americanos. *Cooperativas de vivienda.* Washington, D.C.: Unión Panamericana, 1962.

Ospina, Jose. *Housing Ourselves.* London: H. Shipman, 1987.

Paredes Revelo, B. A. *Defensa de la vivienda cooperativa.* Bogota: Editorial Herrera, 1972.

Pearson, Lynn F. *The Architectural and Social History of Cooperative Living.* Dover, N.H.: Longwood Academic, 1987.

Rippert, Stephan K. *Die Rechtsstellung des Mitgliedes in der Wohnungsbaugenossenschaft.* Wiesbaden: WDS Sofortdruck, 1993.

Rossi Rubattino, A. *La Sociedad Cooperativa de Viviendas.* Santiago: Cámara Chilena de la Construcción, 1958.

Ruiz Lujan, S. *Housing Cooperatives.* Geneva: ILO, 1964.

Scholz, Thomas. *Genossenschaftlicher Wohnungsbau: Politik, Recht, Geschichte.* Stuttgart: IRB-Literaturauslese, 1988.

Seminar on Housing and Urban Management Through Cooperatives, Ankara, September, 1987. Ankara: Kent Koop and ICA, 1987.

Seminario Regional sobre Cooperativas de Vivienda. Washington, D.C.: Unión Panamericana, 1963.

Sullivan, D. G. *Cooperative Housing and Community Development.* London: Pall Mall Press, 1972.

Teodosio, Virginia A., Melisa R. Serrano, and Danilo A. Silvestre, eds. *Housing Cooperativism and Society.* Quezon City, Philippines: UP Employees Housing Cooperative, 1991.

Ubhayaker, N. *A Primer of Cooperative Housing.* Bombay: Bombay Cooperative Housing Federation, 1953.

United States. Congress. House. Committee on Banking and Currency. *Cooperative Housing Abroad.* Washington, D.C.: GPO, 1950

Vollmer-Ruprecht, Guenther. *Coopératives de construction d'habitation, un moyen d'entraide.* Bonn: Friedrich-Ebert-Stiftung, 1968.

IV. J. 2. Housing Cooperatives—Operations and Management

Andrews, Howard F., and Helen J. Breslauer. *Cooperative Housing Project: An Overview of a Case Study, Methods and Findings.* Toronto: University of Toronto, Centre for Urban and Community Studies, 1976.

———. *User Satisfaction and Participation: Preliminary Findings From a Case Study of Cooperative Housing.* Toronto: University of Toronto, Centre for Urban Community Studies, 1976.

Brandwein, Nancy, Jill MacNeice, and Peter Spiers. *The Group House Handbook.* Washington, D.C.: Acropolis Books, 1982.

Cooperative Housing: A Handbook for Effective Operations. Ann Arbor, Mich.: Midwest Association of Housing Cooperatives, 1977.

Coughlan, William, and Monte Franke. *Going Coop: The Complete Guide to Buying and Owning Your Own Apartment.* Boston: Beacon Press, 1983.

del Giudice, J. C. *Financiación cooperativa de vivienda.* Buenos Aires: Intercoop, 1965.

Emery, R. *Ingredients for a Successful Self Sustaining Cooperative Housing Program.* Washington, D.C.: FCH, 1965.

Hodgson, L. *Building Societies: Origins, Methods and Principles.* London: Long, 1929.

Jara, J. C. de la, and E. Galofré. *Rol de la administración en las cooperativas de vivienda.* Santiago: [n.p.], 1971.

MacIntyre, J. D. *Cooperative Housing Handbook.* Sydney, Nova Scotia: St. Francis Xavier University, 1970.

Naik, D. D. *Practices of Housing Cooperatives.* Bombay: Bombay Law House, 1972.

Scheidt, A. *Handbuch für Baugenossenschaften.* Berlin: Guttentag, 1913.

Verhagen, Frans C. *Energy in Cooperative Housing: A Selected Socio-Technical Bibliography.* Monticello, Ill.: Vance Bibliographies, 1984.

Volunteer Leadership in Cooperative Housing. New York: Play Schools Association, 1960.

IV. J. 3. Housing Cooperatives in Europe

Arndt, Michael, and Holger Rogall. *Berliner Wohnungsbau-genossenschaften: Eine exemplarische Bestandsaufnahme und analytische Beschreibung der Merkmale des genossenschaftlichen Wohnens in der Gegenwart.* Berlin: Verlag A. Spitz, 1987.

Ashworth, H. *Housing Finance in Western Europe.* London: ICA, 1955.

Batikent: New Settlement Project. Ankara: Kent-Koop, 1983.

Clapham, David, and Keith Kintrea. *Housing Cooperatives in Britain: Achievements and Prospects.* Harlow, U.K.: Longman, 1992.

Cooperative Housing Societies in the Federal Republic of Germany. Cologne: Universität Köln, 1961.

Cupal, Wilhelm. *Die gemeinnützige Wohnungswirtschaft Österreichs von 1955–1967: unter bes. Beachtung ihrer Struktur. Wirtschaftlichkeit und Eigenkapitalausstattung.* Göttingen, Germany: Vandenhoeck and Ruprecht, 1976.

Eppich, E. *Das deutsche Baugenossenschaftswesen.* Berlin: Puttkammer, 1913.

Financiación de la construcción de viviendas sociales en Europa. Madrid: Ministerio de la Vivienda, 1969.

Gesamtverband gemeinnütziger Wohnungsunternehmen. *Die Wohnungsbaugenossenschaften in der Bundesrepublik Deutschland.* Hamburg: Hammonia-Verlag, 1969.

Greve, John. *Voluntary Housing in Scandinavia: A Study of Denmark, Norway and Sweden.* Birmingham, U.K.: University of Birmingham, Centre for Urban and Regional Studies, 1971.

Housing Through HSB Cooperation: Information on Membership and Residence. Stockholm: HSB Riksförbund, 1966.

Papillon, M. *Les sociétés coopératives d'habitation à bon marché.* Paris: PUF, 1929.

Patera, Mario. *Genossenschaftsentwicklung im österreichischen Wohnungsbau.* Frankfurt and New York: Campus, 1987.

————. *Die Zukunft von Wohnbaugenossenschaften: Das Beispiel Österreich.* Frankfurt and New York: Campus, 1994.

Polkowski, Dieter, and Thomas Rolf. *Öffentlich kontrollierte Träger von Mietwohnungen in Grossbritannien.* Oldenburg, Germany: Bibliotheks- and Informationssystem der Universität Oldenburg, 1987.

Sayin, Erol, Cihan Altinoz, and Tugyan Dinc. *Batikent Housing Savings Bank.* Ankara: Kent-Koop Union of Batikent Housing Construction Cooperatives, 1985.

Segunda Asemblea Nacional de Cooperativas de Viviendas, Madrid, Junio, 1966. Madrid: [n.p.], 1966.

Tucker, Vincent, ed. *Cooperative Housing in Ireland.* Cork, Ireland: Bank of Ireland Center for Cooperative Studies, University College, 1982.

Vossberg, W. *Die deutsche Baugenossenschaftsbewegung.* Berlin: Unger, 1906.

IV. J. 4. Housing Cooperatives in North America

Bodfish, H. *History of Building and Loan Associations in the USA.* New York: Doubleday, 1931.

CHF Research. Ottawa: Cooperative Housing Foundation (occasional).

Collin, Jean-Pierre. *La cité coopérative canadienne-française: Saint-Leonard-de-Port-Maurice, 1955–1963.* Montreal: INRS-Urbanisation, 1986; Sillery, Quebec: Presses de l'Université de Québec. 1986.

Cochran, Clay L. *Cooperative Self-Help Housing in Nova Scotia.* Washington, D.C.: International Self-Help Housing Association, 1968.

The Conversion of Rental Housing to Condominiums and Cooperatives: Annotated Bibliography. Washington, D.C.: Department of Housing and Urban Development, 1980.

Cooper, Matthew, and Margaret Critchlow. *New Neighbors: A Case Study of Cooperative Housing in Toronto.* Toronto and Buffalo: University of Toronto Press, 1992.

Les coopératives d'habitation au Québec. Montreal: Conseil de la coopération du Québec, 1968.

Directory of Housing Cooperatives. Ottawa: Cooperative Housing Foundation, 1978.

Laben, J. *Steps to Cooperative Housing in Nova Scotia.* Antigonish: St. Francis Xavier University, 1958.

Laidlaw, Alexander F. *Housing You Can Afford.* Toronto: Green Tree Publishing Company, 1977.

Landman, Ruth H. *Creating Community in the City: Cooperatives and Community Gardens in Washington, D.C.* Westport, Conn.: Bergin and Garvey, 1993.

Leavitt, Jacqueline, and Susan Saegert. *From Abandonment to Hope: Community Households in Harlem.* New York: Columbia University Press, 1990.

Midmore, J. F. *Report on Cooperative Housing.* Ottawa: CUC, 1962.

Preston, Caroline E. *Some Psychological and Sociological Implications of the Cooperative Housing Movement on the Campuses of Colleges and Universities.* Boulder: University of Colorado, 1942.

Proceedings, 2nd National Conference on Cooperative Housing, Washington, D.C., March, 1959. Washington, D.C.: CLUSA, 1959.

Rapport du comité d'étude pour promouvoir le développement des coopératives d'habitation au Québec. Quebec: Conseil de la coopération du Québec, 1976.

Rohe, William M. *Housing Cooperatives: A Feasible Alternative to Public Housing?* Washington, D.C.: Fannie Mae, 1993.

30 Years of Amalgamated Cooperative Housing 1927–1957. New York: Amalgamated Housing Corporation, 1958.

Vienney, Claude, et al. *Analyse socio-économique comparée des coopératives d'habitation en France et au Québec: rapport de recherche.* Chicoutimi, Quebec: Groupe de recherche et d'intervention regionales, Université du Québec à Chicoutimi, 1985.

IV. J. 5. Housing Cooperatives in Developing Countries

Chávez, Daniel. *FUCVAM, la historia viva: testimonios de organización y lucha: el cooperativismo de vivienda por ayuda mutua en el Uruguay.* Montevideo, Uruguay: FUCVAM, 1990.

Community-Based Finance Institutions: The Role of Cooperatives and Credit Unions in Mobilizing Finance for the Improvement of Low-Income Human Settlements. Nairobi: HABITAT, 1984.

Las cooperativas como método de desarrollo de regiones y communidades. Washington, D.C.: Unión Panamericana, 1964.

Cooperative Housing: An Answer to Housing Problems in West Pakistan. Lahore, Pakistan: Communications and Works Department, 1970.

Cooperative Housing and the Minimum Shelter Approach in Latin America. Washington, D.C.: FCH, 1972.

Cooperative Housing: Experiences of Mutual Self-Help. Nairobi: HABITAT, 1989.

Cooperative Housing for Africa. Meeting on Technical and Social Problems of Urbanization, Addis Ababa, January, 1969. New York: ECOSOC, 1969.

Dass, G. S. *Housing Cooperatives in Malaysia.* Petaling Jaya: Malaysian Cooperative Printing Press Society, 1971.

Dubey, Sumati N., and Ratna Murdia. *Organization and Administration of Cooperative Housing Schemes for the Backward Classes in Maharashtra and Andhra Pradesh.* Bombay: Tata Institute of Social Sciences, 1977.

Foundation for Cooperative Housing. *A Report on Cooperative Housing and Related Activities in Cameroon, Gabon, Kenya, Libya, Nyasaland (Malawi), Sudan.* Washington, D.C.: USAID, 1963.

Gatabaki-Kumau, Rose. *Cooperative Housing Development in Kenya: A Socio-Economic Appraisal.* Nairobi: University of Nairobi, Housing Research and Development Unit, 1985.

Gunawardana, H. P. Lionel, and D. D. Naik. *Status of Cooperative and Rural Housing Programs in Bangladesh Today.* New Delhi: ICA, ROECSEA, 1973.

Hakim, Besim S. *Cooperative Housing, Baghdad, Iraq.* Cambridge, Mass.: Harvard University Library of the Graduate School of Design, 1973.

Herrera, R. Guillermo. *Las cooperativas de vivienda en Colombia.* Bogota: Universidad Santo Tomás de Aquino, 1975.

Housing the Campesino: A Case Study of Cooperative Housing in Rural Panama. Washington, D.C.: FCH, 1966.

Johnson, Byron L. *Cooperative Housing Possibilities in Afghanistan, Ethiopia, India, Iran, Pakistan, Philippines, Taiwan, Thailand.* Washington, D.C.: USAID, 1964.

Kateregga, J. K., et al. *Non-Conventional Approaches to Financing Low-Cost Housing Schemes in Kenya: A Study.* Nairobi: University of Nairobi, 1983.

Keulder, Christiaan. *Urban Women and Self-Help Housing in Namibia: A Case Study of Saamstaan Housing Cooperative.* Windhoek, Namibia: Namibian Economic Policy Research Unit, 1994.

Khan, Kahsan U. *Cooperative House Building Societies: An Evaluation of the Selected Cooperative House Building Societies at Lahore.* Lahore, Pakistan: Directorate of Physical Planning, 1973.

Lewin, A. C. *Housing Cooperatives in Developing Countries: A Manual for Self-Help in Low Cost Housing Schemes.* Chichester, U.K., and New York: Intermediate Technology Publications, J. Wiley, 1981.

Muller, M. S. *Housing Cooperative Societies in Kenya: Performance and Potential.* Nairobi: University of Nairobi, Housing Research and Development Unit, 1978.

National Cooperative Housing Union (NACHU): A Project Document for Cooperative Housing with Special Emphasis on Low Income Families in Kenya. Nairobi: Ministry of Cooperative Development, 1981.

National Workshop on Housing Cooperatives in Kenya Held at the Cooperative College of Kenya, April, 1988. Nairobi: National Cooperative Housing Union, 1990.

Ndatulu, T. S. and H. B. Makileo. *Housing Cooperatives in Tanzania.* Dar-es-Salaam: Building Research Unit, 1989.

NGOs and Shelter. Nairobi: Mazingira Institute, 1986.

Nicolich, Gustavo, and Herbert Porro. *Viviendas en el Uruguay: plan nacional, cooperativas.* Montevideo, Uruguay: [n.p.], 1974.

A Program: Ingredients for a Successful Self Sustaining Cooperative Housing Program: A Study Prepared for the Agency for International Development, 1966. Washington, D.C.: FCH, 1966.

Rapport au gouvernement de la Republique Arabe Syrienne sur les coopératives d'habitation. Geneva: BIT, 1970.

Report: National Seminar on the Development of Housing Cooperatives in Ceylon, Colombo, 1971. Colombo: Cooperative Federation of Ceylon, 1972; New Delhi: ICA, ROECSEA, 1972.

Report of the Regional Seminar on Cooperative Housing, Kuala Lumpur, November/December, 1964. New Delhi: ICA, ROECSEA, 1966.

Report: Regional Seminar on the Development of Housing Cooperatives in South-East Asia, Malaysia, 1970. New Delhi: ICA, ROECSEA, 1970.

Zimbabwe National Workshop on Construction and Housing Cooperatives, Harare, July, 1987. Harare, Zimbabwe: Ministry of Community and Cooperative Development, 1988; Nairobi: Mazingira Institute, 1988.

IV. K. Industrial Cooperatives

IV. K. 1. Industrial Cooperatives—Early Experience— Through World War I (1919)

Baernreither, J. *English Associations of Working Men.* Detroit, Mich.: Gale Research, 1889.

Barre, R. *Discours et écrits sur la coopération de production.* Paris: Association "Le Papier," 1900.

Chagot, J. *Les associations ouvrières de production dans l'industrie.* Paris: Pedone, 1904.

Cochut, A. *Les associations ouvrières.* Paris: [n.p.], 1851.

Crüger, Hans. *Grundlehren und Erfahrungen der Handwerksgenossen-schaften.* Berlin: Guttentag, 1910.

Cuvillier, A. *Une des premières coopératives de production: L'association buchézienne des bijouteries en Doré (1834–1873).* Paris: Rivière, 1933.

Dallet, G. *Twenty Years of Co-partnership at Guise.* London: Labour Co-partnership Association, 1908.

Direction du travail. *Les associations ouvrières de production.* Paris: Imprimerie nationale, 1897.

Dubreuil, H. *La coopérative de main-d'oeuvre.* Paris: Grasset, 1915.

Du Roure, H. *La première coopérative de production.* Paris: Le Sillon, 1906.

Eisenberg, Christine: *Frühe Arbeiterbewegung und Genossenschaften: Theorie und Praxis der Produktivgenossenschaften in der deutschen Sozialdemokratie und den Gewerkschaften der 1860er/1870er Jahre.* Bonn: Verlag Neue Gesellschaft, 1985.

Gabriel, H. *Die gewerblichen Genossenschaften.* Vienna: Manz, 1905.

Gabriel, R. *Des sociétés coopératives de production: difficultés d'ordre économique et juridique.* Paris: C. Crès, 1910.

Geissberger, W. P. *Buchez, Theoritiker einer christlichen Sozialökonomie und Pionier der Produktivgenossenschaften.* Winterthur, Switzerland: Keller, 1956.

Hantschke, H. *Die Gewerblichen Produktivgenossenschaften in Deutschland.* Berlin: Gertz, 1894.

Huber, V. *Die genossenschaftliche Selbsthilfe der arbeitenden Klassen.* Elberfeld, Germany: Friedrichs, 1865.

Jones, Benjamin. *Cooperative Production.* Oxford: Clarendon Press, 1894.

Justo, Juan B. *Cooperación obrera.* Buenos Aires: La Vanguardia, 1906.
Michell, H. *Profit Sharing and Producer's Cooperation in Canada.* Kingston, Canada: Jackson Press, 1918.
Monographies de coopératives de production, 1906–1910. Paris: Le Sillon, 1910.
Nadaud, M. *Les sociétés ouvrières.* Paris: Librairie démocratique, 1873.
Office du Travail. *Les associations ouvrières de production.* Paris: Imprimerie nationale, 1897.
Pragier, A. *Die Produktivgenossenchaften der schweizerischen Arbeiter.* Zurich and Leipzig: Rascher, 1913.
Schulze-Delitzsch, H. *Assoziationsbuch für deutsche Handwerker und Arbeiter.* Leipzig: [n.p.], 1853.
Ventosa i Roig, Joan. *Las cooperativas obreras.* Barcelona: [n.p.], 1918.
Webb, Catherine, ed. *Industrial Cooperation: The Story of Peaceful Revolution.* Manchester: Coop Union, 1904; reissued, 1921.

IV. K. 2. Industrial Cooperatives—1920 to 1995

IV. K. 2. a. Industrial Cooperatives—Theory and History

Alvarado-Greenwood, William, et al. *Organizing Production Cooperatives: A Strategy for Community Economic Development.* Berkeley: National Economic Development Law Center, 1978.
Anderson, Albert. *Entwicklung der Produktionsgenossenschaften des Handwerks und die Rolle ihres genossenschaftlichen Eigentums.* Berlin: Verlag Die Wirtschaft, 1961.
Aranzadi, Dionisio. *Cooperativismo industrial como sistema, empresa y experiencia.* Bilbao: Publicaciones de las Universidad de Deusto, 1976.
Bridault, Alain, et Dominique Ouellet. *Revue critique de la littérature en français sur la coopération ouvrière de production dans les pays industrialisés, 1975–1983.* Sherbrooke, Quebec: Université de Sherbrooke, Institut de recherche et d'enseignement pour les coopératives, 1983.
Brous, Ira, et al. *Democracy in the Workplace: Readings on the Implementation of Self-Management in America.* Washington, D.C.: Strongforce, 1977.
Centre coopératif de recherche en politique sociale. *Les coopératives ouvrières de production et la lutte des travailleurs.* Montreal: La centrale de l'enseignement du Québec, 1975.
Cerda y Richart, Baldomero. *Cooperativas de producción y trabajo.* Barcelona: Bosch, 1937.
Clayre, Alasdair, ed. *The Political Economy of Cooperation and Participation: A Third Sector.* Oxford and New York: Oxford University Press, 1980.
Coates, K., and W. Williams. *How and Why Industry Must be Democratised.* Nottingham, U.K.: Institute of Workers' Control, 1969.
———, et al. *The New Worker Cooperatives.* Nottingham, U.K.: Spokesman Books for the Institute for Workers' Control, 1976.

Cooperativas de trabajo: algunos elementos para su analisis. Buenos Aires: PRONATASS, 1994.

Del Río, Jorge. *Las cooperativas de trabajo.* Buenos Aires: Librería Juridica, 1954; reissued, Buenos Aires: Intercoop, 1962.

Demoustier, Daniele, and Bertrand Beley. *Les coopératives ouvrières de production.* Paris: Éditions la découverte, 1984.

Derrick, P., and J. F. Phipps. *Co-ownership, Cooperation and Control, an Industrial Objective.* London: Longman, 1969.

Employment Creation and Utilization of Labor Potential Through Cooperatives in Rural Areas. Geneva: ILO, 1974.

Gomez Calcerrada, José L. *La cooperativa de trabajo.* Barcelona: Ediciones Ceac, 1983.

Grafe, Friederike. *Das Mitglied in der Produktivgenossenschaft im Spannungsfeld zwischen Arbeitsrecht und Gesellschaftsrecht: eine Untersuchung am Beispiel der Produktionsgenossenschaft des Handwerks.* Frankfurt and New York: P. Lang, 1995.

Greenberg, Edward S. *Workplace Democracy: The Political Effects of Participation.* Ithaca, N.Y.: Cornell University Press, 1986.

Gregory, P. *Socialist and Non-Socialist Industrialization Patterns.* London: Pall Mall Press, 1971.

Halstead, R. *The Producer's Place in Society.* Manchester: Coop Union, 1921.

Hernandez, V. G. *Introducción a la teoría de producciones cooperativas.* Zaragoza, Spain: Escuela de Gerentes Cooperativos, 1969.

History of the Development of Industrial Cooperative Societies. Tokyo: Ienohikari Publishing Corporation, 1966.

Hutt, Jennifer. *Work Cooperatives.* Wellington, New Zealand: Ministry of Recreation and Sport, 1978.

International Cooperative Alliance. *Documents of the Ssecond World Conference on Industrial Worker Cooperatives "For a Democratic Industrial Revolution; Worker Cooperatives on the Horizon of the Third Millenary," Warsaw, 1983.* [n.l.]: CICOPA, 1983.

————. *The Future of Participative and Democratic Enterprises. Third World Conference of CICOPA, Paris, 1988.* [n.l.]: ICA. 1988.

————. *Industrial Co-operation: A Bibliography.* London: CICOPA, 1978.

————. *Proceedings of International Seminar on "The Contribution of Work Cooperatives to the Rural Development," Florence, 1982.* Rome: CICOPA, 1982.

Jansson, Sune, and Ann-Britt Hellmark, eds. *Labor-Owned Firms and Workers' Cooperatives.* Aldershot, U.K., and Brookfield, Vt.: Gower, 1986.

Jaramillo Machinandiarena, Ana. *Gestión cooperativa en la producción.* Mexico City: Instituto Nacional de Estudios del Trabajo, 1982.

Klatzman, Joseph, Benjamin Y. Ilan, and Yair Levi. *The Role of Group Action in the Industrialization of Rural Areas.* New York: Praeger, 1971.

Larionova, M. *Producers' Cooperatives.* Moscow: Progress Publishers (occasional).

Lindenfeld, Frank, and Joyce Rothschild-Whitt, eds. *Workplace Democracy and Social Change*. Boston: Porter Sargent Publishers, 1982.

Linehan, Mary, and Vincent Tucker, eds. *Workers' Cooperatives: Potential and Problems*. Cork, Ireland: University College, Bank of Ireland Centre for Cooperative Studies, 1983; Dublin: Irish Academic Press, 1983.

Louis, Raymond. *Labor Cooperatives: Retrospect and Prospects*. Geneva: ILO, 1983. (Also in French.)

Mellor, Mary, Jane Hannah, and John Stirling. *Worker Cooperatives in Theory and Practice*. Milton Keynes, United Kingdom and Philadelphia: Open University Press, 1988.

Morgaut, Marc. *Coopératives artisanales*. Paris: Nouvelle edition, 1942.

Müller, Birgit. *Toward an Alternative Culture of Work: Political Idealism and Economic Practices in West Berlin Collective Enterprises*. Boulder, Colo.: Westview Press, 1991.

Müller, P. *Die Genossenschaften in Handwerk*. Zurich: Leemann, 1932.

Nash, June, Jorge Dandler, and Nicholas S. Hopkins. *Popular Participation in Social Change: Cooperatives, Collectives, and Nationalized Industry*. The Hague: Mouton, 1976.

Nature and Role of Industrial Cooperatives in Industrial Development. Vienna: UNIDO, 1969.

Norrung, Per, Jens Kjeldsen, and Martin Schultz. *The Producing Commune*. Ålborg, Denmark: Forlaget Alfuff, 1985.

Oakeshott, Robert. *The Case for Workers' Coops*. London and Boston: Routledge and Kegan Paul, 1978.

O'Connor, Robert, and Philip Kelly. *A Study of Industrial Workers' Cooperatives*. Dublin: Economic and Social Research Institute, 1980.

Pandey, B. D. *Select Bibliography on Worker's Productive and Industrial Cooperatives*. New Delhi: ICA, ROECSEA, 1973.

Perroux, F. *Industrie et création collective*. Paris: PUF, 1964.

Place of Cooperatives in Industrial Development. Madras: Tamil Nadu Cooperative Union, 1970.

Prychitko, David L., and Jaroslav Vanek. *Producer Cooperatives and Labor-Managed System*. Cheltenham, U.K., and Brookfield, Vt.: Edward Elgar, 1995.

Riaza Ballesteros, J. *Cooperativas de producción, experiencias y futuro*. Barcelona: Editorial Deusto, 1967.

Rojas Coria, R. *Las sociedades cooperativas de productores*. Mexico City: Editorial Promesa, 1943.

Sanz Lamora, Lorenzo. *Cooperativas de trabajo asociado*. Madrid: Subdirección Técnica de la Obra Sindical de Cooperación, 1971.

Schmiedeler E. *Cooperation, a Christian Mode in Industry*. New York: Catholic Literacy Guild, 1941.

Schütte, H. *Die Rolle der Genossenschaften bei der Industrialisierung*. Hanover: Verlag für Literatur und Zeitgeschehen, 1971.

Themistocli, K. *Industrial Cooperation: A Bibliography.* Rome: International Committee of Workers' Cooperative Productive and Artisanal Societies (CICOPA), 1978.

Thornley, Jennifer. *Workers' Cooperatives: Jobs and Dreams.* London and Exeter, N.H.: Heinemann Educational, 1981.

Treacy, Mary, and Lajos Varadi, eds. *Cooperatives Today; Selected Essays from Various Fields of Cooperative Activities.* [n.l.]: ICA, 1986.

Valdes Dal-Re, Fernando. *Las cooperativas de producción: un estudio sobre el trabajo asociado.* Madrid: Montecorvo, 1975.

Vandervelde, Emile. *Le collectivisme et l'évolution industrielle.* Paris: Rieder, 1921.

Vanek, J. *Cooperative of Work at the Crossroads of History.* Ithaca, N.Y.: Cornell Self-Management Research Cooperative, 1978.

Vienney, C. *Utilization de principes coopératifs dans les entreprises gérées par leurs propres travailleurs.* Geneva: BIT, 1975.

Wisman, Jon, ed. *Worker Empowerment: The Struggle for Workplace Democracy.* New York: Bootstrap Press, 1991.

Woolf, Leonard. *Cooperation and the Future of Industry.* London: G. Allen and Unwin, 1920.

Worker's Cooperatives: A GMBATU View. Oxford: General, Municipal, Boilermakers, and Allied Trades Union, 1986; New York: Pergamon Press, 1986.

Wright, D. H. *Cooperatives and Community: The Theory and Practice of Producer Cooperatives.* London: Bedford Square Press, 1979.

IV. K. 2. b. Industrial Cooperatives—Operations and Management

Adams, Frank T. *Putting Democracy to Work: A Practical Guide for Starting Worker-Owned Businesses.* Eugene, Ore.: Hulogos'i Communications, 1987.

Adams, Frank T., and Gary B. Hansen. *Putting Democracy to Work: A Practical Guide for Starting and Managing Worker-Owned Businesses.* San Francisco: Barrett-Koehler Publishers, 1992; Eugene, Ore.: Hulogos'i Communications, 1992.

Aid to Industrial Cooperatives. New Delhi: Ministry of Commerce and Industry, 1962.

Cooperativas de producción, organización y dirección: documento de los participantes. Mexico City: Instituto Nacional de Estudios del Trabajo, 1981.

Cornforth, Chris, et al. *Developing Successful Worker Cooperatives.* London and Newbury Park, Calif.: Sage Publications, 1988.

Étude comparée de législation concernant les coopératives de travailleurs. Geneva: BIT, 1975.

Honigsberg, Peter J., Bernard Kamoroff, and Jim Beatty. *We Own It: Starting and Managing Coops, Collectives and Employee-Owned Ventures.* Laytonville, Calif.: Bell Springs Publishers, 1982.

Mwabuki, Joseph. *Breaking the Chains: A Handbook for Industrial Cooperatives.* Harare, Zimbabwe: ZIMFEP, 1985.

No Bosses Here: A Manual on Working Collectively. Cambridge, Mass.: Vocations for Social Change, 1976.

Pearce, John. *Running Your Own Cooperative: A Guide to the Setting Up of Worker and Community Owned Enterprises.* London: Kogan Page, 1984.

Perthuis, R. *Guide de la constitution et du fonctionnement juridique des sociétés coopératives ouvrières de production.* Paris: CGSCOP, 1971.

Pillai, Mecheril V. N. *Handbook of Industrial Cooperation.* New Delhi: Committee for Cooperative Training, 1971.

Preparación, evaluación and administración de proyectos agroindustriales. San José, Costa Rica: CCC-CA, 1992.

Rojos Torrecilla, Eduardo, and Isabel Vidal Martinez. *Medidas de apoyo de las empresas de trabajo asociado.* Madrid: Ministerio de Trabajo y Seguridad Social, 1988.

Rosner, Menahem. *The Structural Conditions of Self-Management: The Case of Kibbutz Industry.* Haifa: University of Haifa Institute for Study and Research of the Kibbutz and the Cooperative Idea, 1982.

Rosner, Menahem, and Arnold S. Tannenbaum. *Ownership and Alienation in Kibbutz Factories.* Haifa: University of Haifa Institute for Study and Research of the Kibbutz and the Cooperative Idea, 1983.

Saglio, Janet H., and J. Richard Hackman. *The Design of Governance Systems for Small Worker Cooperatives.* Somerville, Mass.: Industrial Cooperative Association, 1982.

Shah, D. A., and V. Rao. *How to Form an Industrial Cooperative and Run It Successfully.* Bombay: Khadi and Village Industries Commission, 1970.

Stephen, Frank H. *The Economic Analysis of Producers' Cooperatives.* New York: St. Martin's Press, 1984.

Tayler, John B. *Organization of Industrial Cooperatives.* Bombay: Industrial Cooperative Library, 1947; reissued, New Delhi: NCUI, 1964.

Tsuchiya, T. *A Study on the Difference Between Urban and Rural Industrial Cooperative Societies.* Tokyo: Tokyo University Press, 1933.

Van Buiren, Shirley. *The Quantitative and Qualitative Significance of the Emergence of Local Initiatives for Employment Creation.* Luxembourg: Office for Official Publications of the European Communities, 1986.

IV. K. 2. c. Industrial Cooperatives—National Experiences

IV. K. 2. c. (1). Industrial Cooperatives in Europe

Die Arbeiterproduktiv und Handwerkergenossenschaften im Baugewerbe in Frankreich, Grossbritannien, Israel, Italien, Schweiz, Tchechoslowakien. Rome: ACI, Comité Auxiliaire des SCOP, 1957.

Bernstein, H., and J. Bernstein. *Industrial Democracy in Twelve Nations.* Washington, D.C.: GPO, 1979.

Chataignier, Alain, Monique Fabian, and Marie-Francoise Lefilleul. *Portraits de S.C.O.P.: Pratiques coopératives et innovations sociales.* Paris: Syros, 1984.

The Cooperative Workers' Productive Societies of Great Britain. Leicester, U.K.: Cooperative Productive Federation, 1947.

Desroche, Henri, A. Meister, J. Gaumont, and E. Poulat. *Études sur la tradition française de l'association ouvrière.* Paris: Éditions de menthe, 1956.

Fischer, Herbert. *Ergebnisse britischer Genossenschaften in der Bekleidungsindustrie.* Halberstadt: H. Meyer, 1929.

Forms of Organization, Type of Employment, Working Conditions and Industrial Relations in Cooperatives or Any Collectiveness or Other Self-Managing Structures of the EEC. Luxembourg: Office for Official Publications of the European Communities, 1986.

Holmstrom, Mark. *Industrial Democracy in Italy: Workers' Coops and the Self-Management Debate.* Aldershot, U.K., and Brookfield, Vt.: Avebury, 1989.

Jirik, Stanislav. *Czechoslovak Producer Cooperatives.* Prague: Central Cooperative Council, 1966.

Newnham, Rosemary. *Community Enterprise: British Potential and American Experience.* Reading, U.K.: School of Planning Studies, 1980.

Prospects for Workers' Cooperatives in Europe. Luxembourg: Office for Official Publications of the European Communities, 1984.

Sibille, Hugues. *Worker Cooperatives in France: A Report.* Melbourne, Australia: Department of Employment and Industrial Affairs, 1982.

Stoephasius, H.-Peter von. *Zusammenarbeit von Unternehmen, europaweit: Leitfaden für Kooperation nach dem EG-Wettbewerbsrecht.* Bonn: Economica, 1992.

Uca, Mehmet Nezir. *Worker's Participation and Self-Management in Turkey: An Evaluation of Attempts and Experiences.* The Hague: Institute of Social Studies, 1983.

Van Buiren, Shirley. *New Information Technologies and Small Scale Job Creation: The Alternative Economy and Job Creation in the USA With Policy Recommendations Applicable to the European Context: Final Report.* Luxembourg: Office for Official Publications of the European Communities, 1984.

IV. K. 2. c. (2). Mondragon Cooperatives in Spain

Arizmendi, José Maria. *Experiencias sobre una forma cooperativa, Mondragon.* Madrid: Estudios Cooperativas, 1966.

Bradley, Keith, and Alan Gelb. *Cooperation at Work: The Mondragon Experience.* London and Exeter, N.H.: Heinemann Educational, 1983.

Coopératives ouvrières de production, coopératives forestières, coopératives industrielles: France, Espagne, "Mondragon." Quebec: Ministère des consommateurs, coopératives et institutions financières, 1979.

Garcia, Quentin. *Les Coopératives industrielles de Mondragon.* Paris: Les éditions ouvrières, 1970.

Hacker, Sally. *Pleasure, Power, and Technology: Some Tales of Gender, Engineering and the Cooperative Workplace.* Boston: Unwin Hyman, 1989.

Kasmir, Sharryn. *The Myth of Mondragon: Cooperatives, Politics, and Working-Class: Life in a Basque Town.* Albany: State University of New York Press, 1996.

Larranaga, Jesus. *Don José Maria Arizmendi-Arrieta (1915–1976) y la experiencia cooperativa de Mondragon.* Mondragon, Guipúzcoa, Spain: Caja Laboral Popular, 1981.

Letona Arrieta, José. *Mondragon, sus calles.* San Sebastián, Spain: Caja de Ahorros Provincial de Guipúzcoa, 1975.

Monzon Campos, José L. *Cooperativas de trabajo asociado: el caso valenciano.* Valencia: Escuela Universitaria de Estudios Empresariales de la Universidad de Valencia, 1984.

Thomas, Hank, and Chris Logan. *Mondragon: An Economic Analysis.* London and Boston: G. Allen and Unwin, 1982.

Whyte, William F., and Kathleen King Whyte. *Making Mondragon: The Growth and Dynamics of the Worker Cooperative Complex.* Ithaca, N.Y.: ILR Press, 1988; 2nd edition, 1991.

Worker-Owners, the Mondragon Achievement: The Caja Laboral Popular and the Mondragon Cooperatives in the Basque Provinces of Spain: A Report. London: Anglo-German Foundation for the Study of Industrial Society, 1977.

IV. K. 2. c. (3). Industrial Cooperatives in North America

Bellas, Carl J. *Industrial Democracy and the Worker-Owned Firm: A Study of Twenty-One Plywood Companies in the Pacific Northwest.* New York: Praeger, 1972.

Berman, K. V. *Worker Owned Plywood Companies, An Economic Analysis.* Pullman: Washington State University, 1967.

Curl, John. *History of Work Cooperation in America: Cooperatives, Cooperative Movements, Collectivity and Communalism from Early America to the Present.* Berkeley: Homeward Press, 1980.

Derber, M. *The American Idea of Industrial Democracy, 1865–1965.* Urbana: University of Illinois Press, 1970.

Hetherington, John A. C. *Mutual and Cooperative Enterprises: An Analysis of Customer-Owned Firms in the United States.* Charlottesville: University of Virginia Press, 1991.

Jackall, Robert, and Henry M. Levin. *Worker Cooperatives in America.* Berkeley: University of California Press, 1984.

Newnham, Rosemary. *Community Enterprise: British Potential and American Experience.* Reading, U.K.: School of Planning Studies, 1980.

Panunzio, C. *Self-Help Cooperatives in Los Angeles.* Berkeley: University of California Press, 1939.

Tracy, John A. *A Performance Analysis of Cooperative Wholesalers Owned by Member Retail Hardware Stores.* Boulder: University of Colorado, 1982.

Van Buiren, Shirley. *New Information Technologies and Small Scale Job Creation: The Alternative Economy and Job Creation in USA With Policy Recommendations Applicable to the European Context: Final Report.* Luxembourg: Office for Official Publications of the European Communities, 1984.

IV. K. 2. c. (4). Industrial Cooperatives in Developing Countries

Abell, Peter. *Establishing Support Systems for Industrial Cooperatives: Case Studies From the Third World.* Aldershot, U.K.: Avebury, 1988; Brookfield, Vt.: Gower Publishing, 1988.

Abell, Peter, and Nicholas Mahoney. *Small-Scale Industrial Producer Cooperatives in Developing Countries.* Delhi: Oxford University Press, 1988.

Alley, Rewi. *Two Years of Indusco.* Hong Kong: Chinese Industrial Cooperatives, Hong Kong Organizing Committee, 1940.

Alurralde Anaya, A. *Cooperativas mineras en Bolivia.* La Paz: Editorial Don Bosco, 1973.

Benecke, Dieter W. *Las Cooperativas de producción artesanal en Chile.* Santiago: Universidad Católica de Chile, 1969.

Bergmann, Theodor. *Funktionen und Wirkungsgrenzen von Produktions-genossenschaften in Entwicklungländern.* Frankfurt: Euopäische Verlagsanstalt, 1967.

Brahme, Sulabha. *Producers' Cooperatives: Experience and Lessons From India.* The Hague: Institute of Social Studies, 1984.

Chinese Industrial Cooperatives. Hong Kong: Hong Kong and Shanghai Promotion Committee, 1940.

La coopération de production et l'industrialisation du tiers monde. Paris: CGSCOP, 1962.

Dadson, J. A. *Production Cooperatives and Rural Development in Ghana.* Addis Ababa: Economic Commission for Africa, 1985.

Green, Thuso J. *Report on a Survey of Primary Producer Cooperatives, Village Development Councils, and Other Organizations.* Maseru, Lesotho: Sechaba Consultants, 1990.

Huq, M. Ameerul. *Five Years of a Workmen's Cooperative.* Comilla, Bangladesh: Pakistan Academy for Rural Development, 1965.

Huq, M. Nurul. *Comilla Khaddar: A Case-Study of an Artisan Cooperative Society.* Comilla, Bangladesh: Bangladesh Academy for Rural Development, 1973.

Icheboudéne, L. *Armée et développement, les coopératives industrielles de l'armée en Algérie.* Paris: Centre de recherches coopératives, 1974.

Industrial Cooperative Banks in India. New Delhi: NCUI, 1965.

Kowalak, T. *Cooperatives in the Industrial Development of the Third World.* Warsaw: Spóldzielczy Kwartalnik Naukowy, 1972.

Magana Castro, Rogelio. *Cooperativas industriales en la industria mediana y pequeña en México.* Mexico City: Fundación Friedrich Ebert, 1989.

Mehta, S. C. *Industrial Cooperatives in India.* Delhi: Atma Ram, 1975.

Población, empleo y cooperación en América Latina. San José, Costa Rica: OIT, Oficina área en San José, 1976.

Policies and Measures to Promote Industrial Cooperatives in Africa. New York: UNIDO, 1985.

Poluha, Eva. *Central Planning and Local Reality: The Case of a Producer's Cooperative in Ethiopia.* Stockholm: University of Stockholm, 1989.

Rana, J. M. *Cooperation and Small Industries in South-East Asia.* New Delhi: ICA, ROECSEA, 1965.

Rayudu, C. S. *Industrial Cooperatives: A Regional Synthesis to Andhra Pradesh.* New Delhi: Northern Book Center, 1992.

Small Industries Extension Training Institute. *Case Studies on Industrial Cooperatives.* New Delhi: NCUI, 1972.

Snow, H. *China Builds for Democracy: A Story of Cooperative Industry.* New York: Modern Age Books, 1941.

Stolz, Martin. *Der genossenschaftliche Bergbau in Bolivien: Analyse seiner Funktionsweise und seines Entwicklungsbeitrages.* Münster: Institut für Genossenschaftswesen der Westfälischen Wilhelms-Universität, 1984.

Yoshida, Masao. *Rural Industrialization in Tanzania: A Case Study of Ten Cooperative Enterprises.* Dar-es-Salaam: University of Dar-es-Salaam, Economic Research Bureau, 1980.

Zapata Cusicanqui, Carlos. *Las cooperativas artesanales de Bolivia.* La Paz: Universidad Católica Boliviana, Departamento de Estudios Cooperativos, 1978.

IV. K. 3. Handicraft Cooperatives

Arterburn, Y. J. *The Loom of Independence: Silkweaving Cooperatives in Kanchipuram.* New Delhi: Hindustan Publishing Company, 1982.

Bayer, V. *Folkart Production in the Czechoslovak Cooperative Movement.* Prague: Central Cooperative Council, 1967.

Brabec, Barbara. *A Treasure Trove of Crafts Marketing Success Secrets.* Naperville, Ill.: B. Brabec Productions, 1986.

Holz, Loretta. *Make It and Sell It: A Young People's Guide to Marketing Crafts.* New York: Scribner, 1978.

ILO and UNDP Inter-regional Seminar on the Organization and Development of Work Cooperatives in the Field of Folk and Artistic Handicrafts and Cottage Industry, Poland, September, 1977. Geneva: ILO, 1978.

Koll, M. *Crafts and Cooperation in Western Nigeria—A Sociological Contribution to Indigenous Economics.* Düsseldorf: Bertelsmann University, 1969.

Rapport au Gouvernement du Royaume du Maroc sur l'artisanat. Rabat, Morocco: ILO and UNDP, 1983.

Report on a Cooptrade Short-term Consultancy in Product Adaptation, Management and Export Techniques Regarding Handicrafts Produced by the Cooperative Members' Housewives Projects, Yasothorn, Thailand, 1992. Geneva: ILO, 1993.

Report to the Government of the Yemen Arab Republic on a National Plan for Cooperative Assistance to the Handicraft Trades of the Yemen Arab Republic. Geneva: ILO, 1979.

IV. K. 4. Disabled Persons' Cooperatives

Cooperatives for the Disabled, Organization and Development: Proceedings, Conclusions and Recommendations of a Seminar on the Organization and Development of Cooperatives for Disabled Persons, Warsaw, Poland, October, 1977. Geneva: ILO, 1978.

Futro, Aleksander. *Invalids' Cooperatives in Poland.* Warsaw: Publishing House of the Central Agricultural Union of Cooperatives, 1964.

Gudmundsson, Johann. *Cooperatives of Disabled Persons. A Guide for Promotion and Organization.* Rome: COPAC, 1984.

Hashemite Kingdom of Jordan: Vocational Rehabilitation of the Disabled: Project Findings and Recommendations. Geneva: ILO, 1979.

Hübner, A., and K. Roger. *Finanzierung einkommenschaffender Vorhaben für benachteiligte Gruppen in Entwicklungsländern. Untersuchung zum Konzept der ökumenischen Entwicklungs-genossenschaft.* Heidelberg: Arbeitsgemeinschaft Planungsforschung GmbH, 1977.

Invalid's Cooperative Union. *Invalid's Cooperatives in People's Poland 1949–1979.* Warsaw: Publishing House of the Central Agricultural Union of Peasant Self-Aid Cooperatives, 1980.

Iran—Vocational Rehabilitation of the Disabled: Project Findings and Recommendations. Geneva: ILO, 1977.

Morris, Alfred. *New Horizons for the Disabled.* London: Cooperative Party, 1980.

Mrowczynski, Boleslaw. *With Heart and Hand.* Warsaw: Union of Cooperatives of Invalids, 1959.

Proceedings, Conclusions and Recommendations of the Regional Seminar on the Organization and Development of Disabled Persons' Cooperatives, Warsaw, September/October, 1974. Geneva: ILO, 1974.

Report on the ILO/SIDA African Regional Seminar on the Organization of Cooperatives for Handicapped Persons, Teheran, June, 1978. Geneva: ILO, 1978.

Sikking, Maggi. *Coops With a Difference: Worker Coops for People With Special Needs.* London: ICOM Co-Publications, 1986.

Skop, Otakar. *Invalids' Cooperatives in Czechoslovakia.* Prague: Svepomoc, 1981.

Tyl, R., M. Zeimmer, and B. Holatkova. *Disabled Persons' Cooperatives in Czechoslovakia.* Prague: Central Cooperative Council, 1968.

IV. K. 5. Public Utilities/Services Cooperatives

de Brouckere, Louis. *La coopération et l'état dans l'organisation des services publics.* Brussels: Les Propagateurs de la coopération, 1937.

Mack, Stephen F. *Organizing for Cooperative Water Resources Development in Alaska.* Anchorage: Department of Natural Resources, 1980.

Orr, Fay. *Harvesting the Flame: The History of Alberta's Rural Natural Gas Cooperatives.* Edmonton, Alberta: Reidmore Books, 1989.

Reid, Crowther, and Partners. *Guidelines for Action Towards More Efficient Operation of Gas Cooperatives.* Edmonton, Alberta: Ernst and Ernst Chartered Accountants, [n.d.] (looseleaf for updating).

IV. K. 5. a. Electricity Cooperatives

Arana, J. J. *Las cooperativas de electricidad.* Buenos Aires: [n.p.], 1942.

Carvallo Hederra, Sergio. *Las cooperativas de electrificación en Chile.* Washington, D.C.: Unión Panamericana, 1950.

Childs, Marquis. *Farmers Take a Hand: The Electric Power Revolution in Rural America.* New York: Doubleday, 1952.

Cooper, D. H. *Rural Electric Facts, American Success Story.* Washington, D.C.: National Rural Electric Cooperative Association, 1970.

Las cooperativas de electrificación en Argentina, Chile y Estado Unidos. Washington, D.C.: Organización de Estados Americanos, 1972.

Coyle, D. C. *Electric Power on the Farm.* Washington, D.C.: GPO, 1936.

Cruzat, G. *Las cooperativas de electrificación rural en Chile.* Santiago: Universidad Católica de Chile, Instituto de Cooperativismo, Serie Estudios No. 4, 1969.

Del Rio, J. *Cooperativas de electricidad y usinas populares.* Buenos Aires: La Electricultura Argentina, 1940.

Denton, F. H. *Lighting up the Countryside. The Story of Electric Cooperatives in the Philippines.* Manila: Development Academy of the Philippines, 1979.

Diaz Arana, Juan J. *Las cooperativas de electricidad.* Buenos Aires: Talleres Gráficos "Radio Revista," 1942.

Doyle, Jack, et al. *Lines Across the Land: Rural Electric Cooperatives, the Changing Politics of Energy in Rural America: With Case Studies of Rural Electric Cooperatives in 14 States.* Washington, D.C.: Rural Land and Energy Project, Environmental Policy Institute, 1979.

Electricidad en el campo. Santiago: Empresa Nacional de Electricidad, 1950.

Ellis, Clyde. *A Giant Step.* Washington, D.C.: National Rural Electric Cooperative Association, 1966.

Hoffmann, G. *Die ländlichen Elektrizitätsgenossenschaften in den USA.* Düsseldorf: Triltisch, 1954.

Jaramillo, Baltazar V. *Las cooperativas eléctricas.* Buenos Aires: Universidad de Buenos Aires, 1939.

Martinez Civelli, A. *La electrificación de la Argentina y la cooperación.* Buenos Aires: Federación Argentina de Cooperativas de Electrificación, 1946.

El movimiento cooperativo electrico Argentino. Buenos Aires: Intercoop, 1972.

Patel, S. M., V. K. Gupta, and K. B. Kothari. *Rural Electric Cooperative: Kodinar.* Ahmedabad: Indian Institute of Management, 1968.

Rall, U. *Cooperative Rural Electrification in the United States.* Washington, D.C.: Pan American Union, 1940.

Ross, J. E. *Cooperative Rural Electrification, Case Studies in Latin America.* New York: Praeger, 1972.

Rural Electrification Administration. *Telling the Coop Story, An Educational Handbook for Rural Electric Coops.* Washington, D.C.: GPO, 1949.

Saunders, J., J. M. Davis, G. C. Moses, and J. E. Ross. *Rural Electrification and Development: Social and Economic Impact in Costa Rica and Colombia.* Boulder, Colo.: Westview Press, 1978.

Schmidt, Walter G. *Rural Electric and Supply Cooperatives Were My Concern: An Autobiography.* Kansas City, Mo.: WL-Pan Press, 1987.

Sen, L. L. *Rural Electrification in Indonesia: Current and Future Perspectives.* Cambridge, Mass.: Harvard University, Institute for International Development, 1982.

Slattery, H. *Rural America Lights Up.* Washington, D.C.: National Home Library, 1940.

Wasserman, G., and A. Davenport. *Power to the People: Rural Electrification Sector—Summary Report.* Washington, D.C.: USAID, 1983.

IV. K. 5. b. Irrigation Cooperatives

Boutaout, A. *Action coopérative: ses agences et ses acteurs dans le périmètre irrigué du Haouz (Maroc).* Paris: École des haute études en sciences sociales, 1979.

Hutchins, W. *Organization and Operation of Cooperative Irrigation Companies.* Washington, D.C.: FCA, 1936.

McKone, C. E. *Katilu Cooperative Society and Farmer Participation in the Irrigation Scheme Management.* Rome: FAO, 1983.

Pant, Niranjan, and R. K. Verma. *Farmers' Organization and Irrigation Management.* New Delhi: Asish Publishing House, 1983.

Qadir, S. A., B. M. Chowdhury, J. P. Emmert, and R. N. Dey. *Productivity and Equity in IRDP Irrigation Schemes.* Honolulu: East-West Center, Resource Systems Institute, 1978.

Siy, R. Y. *Rural Organizations for Community Resource Management: Indigenous Irrigation Systems in the Northern Philippines.* Ithaca, N.Y.: Cornell University, 1982.

IV. K. 5. c. Telephone Cooperatives

Allred, C. *Rural Cooperative Telephones in Tennessee.* Knoxville, Tenn.: Agricultural Station, 1937.

Ascheri, Edmundo. *Apuntes para la historia del cooperativismo telefónico.* Rosario, Argentina: Ediciones Instituto, 1966.

IV. K. 6. Service Cooperatives

IV. K. 6. a. Health Care Cooperatives

Akin, J. S., D. K. Guilkey, D. C. Griffin, and B. M. Popkin. *The Demand for Primary Health Services in the Third World.* Towota, N.J.: Rowman and Allanheld, 1985.

Alonso Soto, Francisco. *La Alternativa del Cooperativismo Sanitario.* Madrid: Gabinete de Estudios y Promoción del Cooperativismo Sanitario, 1987.

Basu, S. *The Place of the Calcutta Central Cooperative Anti-Malaria and Public Health Society in Rural Development.* Calcutta: Central Cooperative Anti-Malaria and Public Health Society, 1955.

Body of Policy. A Statement of Principles and Objectives for Member Plans. St. Paul, Minn.: Cooperative Health Federation of America, 1949.

Bureau of Cooperative Medicine. *The Vital Importance and Function of Cooperative Health Associations.* Chicago: CLUSA, 1937.

Centrale agricole des coopératives "Entraide Paysanne." *Les coopératives de santé en Pologne.* Warsaw: Conseil coopératif suprême, 1965.

Chang, W. *Cooperative Medical Service Is Fine: How the Rural Cooperative Medical System Works in Changwei Prefecture, Shantung Province.* Beijing: Foreign Languages Press, 1978.

Colombain, M. *L'hygiène rurale et les coopératives sanitaires en Yougoslavie.* Geneva: BIT, 1935.

Cooperative Enterprise in the Health and Social Care Sectors—A Global Survey. New York: United Nations, 1997.

Cooperative Medical Programs. New York: National Industrial Conference Board, 1953.

Cooperativismo Sanitario. Barcelona: Cianófilo, 1986.

Del Alamo y Mahou, J. G. *Estudio juridico del cooperativismo sanitario.* Madrid: Gabinete de Estudios y Promocion del Cooperativismo Sanitario, 1988.

Forbes, J. *Las cooperativas de servicios médicos.* San Juan, Puerto Rico: OCA, 1971.

Frizzi, A. *Rumbos cooperativos.* Buenos Aires: Cooperativa Salud Pública, 1946.

Goldman, F. *Voluntary Medical Care Insurance in the USA.* New York: Columbia University Press, 1948.

Handbook: Cooperative Health Association. Salt Lake City: Utah WPA, 1939.

Hanse, H. R. *Laws Affecting Group Health Plans.* Des Moines: Iowa Law Review, 1950.

Health Cooperatives. Bombay: Reserve Bank of India, 1949.

Hunt, G. H., and M. S. Goldstein. *Medical Group Practices in the USA.* Washington, D.C.: Public Health Service, 1951.

Johnston, Helen L. *Rural Health Cooperatives.* Washington, D.C.: FCA and U.S. Public Health Service, 1950.

Konstantinovitch, B. *Principles of Rural Hygiene and Health Cooperatives.* Belgrade: Union of Health Cooperatives, 1931.

Lewis, R. *How to Organize a Health Cooperative.* St. Paul, Minn.: Health Center Committee, 1948.

Rothenberg, R., and K. Pickard. *Group Medicine and Health Insurance in Action.* New York: Crown Publishers, 1949.

Rovira Forns, Joan, and Isabel Vidal Martínez. *Posibilidades de desarrollo del co-operativismo en el sector sanitario español.* Madrid: Gabinete de Estudios y Promoción del Cooperativismo Sanitario, 1987.

Sanidad y Cooperativismo. Zaragoza: Editorial CENEC, 1983.

Shadid, Michael A. *Crusading Doctor: My Fight for Cooperative Medicine.* Norman: University of Oklahoma Press, 1992.

———. *A Doctor for the People, Autobiography of the Founder of America's First Cooperative Hospital.* New York: Vanguard Press, 1949.

Sistema público de seguridad social y cogestión sanitaria cooperativa. Barcelona: Gabinete de Estudios y Promoción del Cooperativismo Sanitario, 1988.

Tereshtenko, Valery. *The Problems of Cooperative Medicine (Bibliography).* New York: WPA, 1940.

United States. Congress. Senate. Committee on Labor and Human Resources. *Health Insurance Purchasing Cooperative Act: To Promote the Use of State-Coordinated Health Insurance Buying Programs and Assist States in Establishing Health Insurance Purchasing Cooperatives, Through Which Small Employers May Purchase Health Insurance.* Washington, D.C.: GPO, 1992.

Warbasse, J. *Cooperative Medicine.* New York: CLUSA, 3rd edition, 1942.

IV. K. 6. b. Cooperative Nurseries/Preschools

Cooperative Nursery Schools. Wheaton, Md.: Montgomery County Council of Cooperative Nursery Schools, 1960.

IV. K. 6. c. Funeral/Memorial Cooperatives

Myers, J. *Cooperative Funeral Associations.* New York: CLUSA, 1946.

IV. K. 6. d. Petroleum Cooperatives

Cooperative Expansion in the Petroleum Industry. Chicago: National Tax Equality Association, 1944.

Cooperatives in the Petroleum Industry. New York: Petroleum Industry Research Foundation, 1947.

Erickson, Stanford G., and David W. Cobia. *Cooperatives in North Dakota Petroleum Markets.* Fargo: North Dakota State University, 1972.

Gessner, A. *Integrated Petroleum Operations Through Farmer Cooperatives 1950–1957.* Washington, D.C.: USDA, FCS, 1959.

Mather, James W. *Petroleum Operations of Farmer Cooperatives.* Washington, D.C.: FCA, 1951.

Oil Cooperatives in Wisconsin. Madison: Wisconsin Committee on Cooperatives, 1934.

Organization and Management of Cooperative Gasoline and Oil Associations (with model bylaws). Washington, D.C.: GPO, 1934.

IV. K. 6. e. Transport Cooperatives

Ahmad, R. *Transport Management in the Marketing Cooperatives.* Bamenda, Cameroon: National Center for the Development of Cooperative Enterprises, 1976.

Canals y Contreras, Norberto. *Organización y funcionamiento de las sociedades cooperativas de auto-transportes.* Mexico City: [n.p.], 1936.

Dick, H. M. *Cooperative Transport Management.* Edinburgh: Wilson, 1960.

Eaton, Richard J., ed. *Transport Management in Cooperative Movement.* Loughborough, U.K.: Coop Union, Education Department, 1967.

Frank, W. *Estudio de depósito para las cooperativas de transporte en Bogota.* Bogota: Universidad de Santo Tomás, Instituto de Educación e Investigación Cooperativa, 1972.

Hallin, W. *Cooperatives, Tourism and Transport.* Folkestone, U.K.: CARL, 1967.

———. *Principles and Features of Transport, Tourism, Labor, Power, Agriculture, and Their Application in Ireland and Elsewhere.* Dublin: C.A.R.E., 1967.

Hove, A. *Bus Services in Israel, Cooperative Form, Monopolistic Structure, Public Control.* Jerusalem: Ministry of Labor, 1951.

Kirugi, S. *Transport Activities in Marketing Cooperatives With Special Reference to Kenya.* Loughborough, U.K.: University of Loughborough, 1975.

Prat Samper, M. *Las cooperativas de transportes de casa y su influencia en la economía nacional.* Havana: Tomaye, 1948.

Technical Memorandum to the Government of the Gambia on Cooperative Transport and Management. Geneva: ILO, 1982.

Die Transportgenossenschaften und Hilfsgenossenschaften des Transportgewerbes in Frankreich, Israel, Italien, Westdeutschland. Rome: ACI, Comité Auxiliare des SCOP, 1957.

Vijayakumar, K. C. *Management of Cooperative Sector: With Special Reference to Transport Cooperatives.* Jaipur, India: Printwell, 1991.

IV. L. Insurance Cooperatives

Apelqvist, S. *Transcending Old Boundaries; Views on International Cooperative Insurance.* Stockholm: Folksam, 1964.

L'Assurance mutuelle. Quebec: Conseil supérieur de la coopération, 1942.

Atlas de la mutualité agricole en Afrique du nord, assurances, crédit, coopération, 1907–1947. Algiers: Caisse centrale de réassurance des mutuelles agricoles de l'Afrique du nord, 1947.

Bainbridge, John. *Biography of an Idea: The Story of Mutual Fire and Casualty Insurance.* New York: Doubleday, 1952.

Barou, Noah. *Cooperative Insurance.* London: P. S. King and Son, 1936.

Blanchoin, A. *L'assurance mutuelle agricole.* Paris: Librairie technique et économique, 1935.

Bubolz, G. *Farmers' Mutual Windstorm Insurance Companies.* Washington, D.C.: FCA, Cooperative Division, 1938.

Bucht, O. *Folket-Samarbete: The Insurance Societies of Swedish Cooperation.* Stockholm: Folksam, 1947.

Caceres Ugarte, M. *Las sociedades de socorros mutuos ante la legislación chilena.* Santiago: Imp. Cervantes, 1938.

A Century of Cooperative Insurance, 1867–1967. Manchester: Cooperative Insurance Society, 1967.

Doss, B. *People Working Together. The Story of the Nationwide Insurance Company.* New York: Newcomen Society, 1968.

Gallo Prot, A. *Cooperativas de seguros, sus principios doctrinarios, económicos, técnicos y legales.* Buenos Aires: Cooperativa Patronal de Seguros, 1954.

Garnett, Ronald. *A Century of Cooperative Insurance.* London: Allen and Unwin, 1968.

Neb, D. P. *Social Insurance Through Cooperatives—A Study of Social Insurance Schemes in Cooperatives in Indore City.* New Delhi: ICA, ROECSEA, 1975.

Niwata, Noriaki. *The Theory of Insurance and Social Security in Japan.* Tokyo: Insurance Institute of the Keio University, 1986.

Report on the Regional Seminar on Cooperative Insurance and Promotion of Savings, Tokyo, September, 1976. New Delhi: ICA, ROECSEA, 1976.

Valdren, V. N. *Farmers' Mutual Fire Insurance in the United States.* Chicago: University of Chicago Press, 1924.

Worldwide Cooperative Insurance. Manchester: International Cooperative Insurance Federation, 1983.

IV. M. Multipurpose Cooperatives

Favzi, R. A. *The Place of Multipurpose Cooperatives in Integrated Rural Development.* Loughborough, U.K.: University of Loughborough, 1974.

Gunawardana, H. P. Lionel. *Report of the Regional Seminar on Management of Agricultural Cooperatives with Special Reference to Multipurpose Cooperatives, Tokyo, 1977.* New Delhi: ICA, ROECSEA, 1978.

Igben, M. S. *Achieving Integrated Rural Development in Nigeria Through Multipurpose Cooperatives.* Ibadan, Nigeria: University of Benin, 1980.

Rana, J. M. *Multipurpose Cooperative Societies in South-East Asia.* New Delhi: ICA, ROECSEA, 1972.

Rao, K. V. *The Multipurpose Cooperative Society.* Moti Katra, Agra, India: Banwari Lal Jain, 1949.

Report of the Regional Seminar on Multipurpose Cooperative Societies with Special Reference to Japan, Tokyo, May/June, 1972. New Delhi: ICA, ROECSEA, 1973.

Strengthening the Performance of the Multipurpose Cooperative Societies Through Apex Organizations. Colombo: Cooperative Management Services Center, 1973.

IV. N. School and Youth Cooperatives

IV. N. 1. School Cooperatives—Theory and Practice

Cattier, F. and L. *Ce qu'il faut savoir de la coopération scolaire.* Paris: Éditions elcé, 1945.

Colombain, Maurice. *La valeur éducative des coopératives scolaires.* Basel: USC, 1941.

Cooperatives in School and Community. New York: Columbia University, 1947.

Daude-Bancel, A. *Le cooperativisme devant les écoles sociales.* Paris: Bibliothèque artistique et littéraire, 1897.

Delom, B. *El cooperativismo en las escuelas.* Buenos Aires: Federación Argentina de Cooperativas de Consumo, 1947.

Drimer, A. K., and B. Drimer. *Las cooperativas escolares.* Buenos Aires: Intercoop, 1987.

Freinet, C. *La coopération à l'école moderne.* Paris: Éditions de l'imprimerie à l'école, 1946.

Gide, Charles. *La coopération à l'école primaire.* Paris: FNCC, 1927.

Gomez Uria, M. *Cooperativas escolares en el mundo.* Cordóba, Argentina: La Falda, 1964.

Hernandez Ruiz, Santiago. *Cooperativas escolares.* Bogota: Cundinamarca, 1936.

Kaplan de Drimer, Alicia, and Bernardo de Drimer. *Cooperativas escolares.* Buenos Aires: Federación Argentina de Cooperativas de Consumo, 1966; Buenos Aires: Intercoop, 1971.

Lockward, S., and George A. *Cooperativas escolares.* Santo Domingo: Editorial Educativa Dominicana, 1974.

Marchand, M. *La escuela y el cooperativismo.* Rio Piedras: Universidad de Puerto Rico, Instituto de Cooperativismo, 1961.

Moreno Avendano, J. *Cooperativas de educación.* Bogota: Ediciones Tercer Mundo, 1973.

Office central de la coopération à l'école. *La coopération scolaire. Textes officiels et règlements.* Paris: Institut pédagogique national, 1964.

———. *La coopération scolaire.* Paris: Institut pédagogique national, 1968.

Papadimitriou, M. *Pédagogie de la coopération scolaire.* Paris: PUF, 1960.

Profit, Barthélemy. *La coopération à l'école primaire.* Paris: Delagrave, 1934.

———. *L'éducation mutuelle à l'école.* Amay, Belgium: Centrale du PES de Belgique, 1938.

Ratier, H., and E. Bottini. *El cooperativismo en la escuela primaria.* Buenos Aires: Intercoop, 1967.

Saint Aubert, J. de. *La coopération scolaire, ses buts et ses moyens.* Paris: FNCC, 1953.

Santiago, H. R. *Cooperativas escolares.* Madrid: Aguilar, 1965.

Tirado Benedi, Domingo. *Cooperativas, talleres, huertos y granjas escolares.* Mexico City: Editorial Atlante, Serie Pedagógica, 1940.

Torres Franco, L. *Las cooperativas en las escuelas primarias.* Mexico City: Escuela Normal Las Rosas, 1967.

Torres Murga, M. *Cooperativas escolares en la enseñanza primaria.* Lima: Pontificia Universidad Católica, 1969.

Vuillet, J. *La coopération à l'école.* Paris: PUF, 1968; Paris: Office central de la coopération à l'école, 1970.

Zaragoza Alvado, F. *La mutualidad escolar.* Madrid: Editorial Morata, 1947.

IV. N. 2. School Cooperatives—Operation and Management

Ballesteros, Antonio. *Cómo se organiza la cooperación en la escuela primaria.* Mexico City: E.D.I.A.P.S.A., 1940.

Becerra, Jesus Maria. *Educación y código cooperativo.* Bogota: Librería Stella, 1962.

Development of College Consumer Cooperatives, Cafeterias and Common Kitchen Centers. Geneva: ILO, 1980.

Harper, R. *The Role of Public School Teachers in Cooperation Through Education.* Manila: Bureau of Public Schools, 1958.

Ventosa y Roig, Joan. *Elementos de cooperación escolar.* Mexico City: Editorial Educación, 1955.

IV. N. 3. School Cooperatives—Curriculum Materials

Chiasson, Remi J., ed. *Cooperation, the Key to Better Communities: A handbook on the philosophy, history, and development of cooperative organizations in Nova Scotia for use in the schools of the Province at the grade eight to twelve level.* Antigonish: St. Francis Xavier University, 1961.

Cyr, Frank W., and James H. Tipton. *What High Schools Are Teaching About Cooperatives.* New York: Columbia University, Teachers College, 1945.

Freinet, C. *Naissance d'une pédagogie populaire. Historique de la coopération de l'enseignement laïque.* Cannes: Éditions de l'école moderne, 1949.

———. *Les techniques Freinet et l'école moderne.* Paris: Colin, 1964.

Nicholson, Isa. *Our Story, A History of the Cooperative Movement for Young People.* Manchester: Coop Union, 1921.

Prevot, G. *La coopération scolaire et sa pédagogie.* Paris: Éditions ESF, 1972.

Réforme de l'enseignement et pédagogie coopérative. Paris: Institut des études coopératives, 1968.

Vasquez, A., and E. Oury. *De la classe coopérative à la pédagogie institutionnelle.* Paris: Maspero, 1971.

IV. N. 4. School Cooperatives—National Experiences

Badano, A., and T. Chianelli. *Legislación argentina sobre la enseñanza del cooperativismo en la escuela.* Buenos Aires: Círculo de Estudios Cooperativistas, 1961.

Boos, C. *Origines et développement de la coopération scolaire en France*. Paris: Institut des études coopératives, 1968.

Les coopératives scolaires en Pologne. Warsaw: Conseil coopératif suprême, 1969.

Corrie, M. B. *Cooperative Education in Schools with Reference to a Curriculum for Jamaica*. Loughborough, U.K.: Cooperative College, 1979.

Espindola, Hugo D., et al. *Entre muchos: cinco años del Programa Jóvenes de las Cooperativas, 1986–1991*. Montevideo, Uruguay: CAF-PRODECO, Foro Juvenil, 1991.

Gouzil and Pigeon. *Barthélemy Profit et la coopération scolaire française, anthologie*. Paris: Office de la coopération à l'école, 1970.

Guide de la coopérative scolaire en Republique populaire du Benin. Cotonou: Ministère des enseignments maternel et de base, 1980.

Harper, R. *Mechanics of Teaching Cooperation to Young People*. Manila: Bureau of Public Schools, 1958.

International Cooperative Alliance. *Anthology of Cooperative Experiences in the European Schools*. Rome: CENSCOOP, 1995.

Lacoursière, C. *Histoire des coopératives étudiantes du Québec*. Quebec: Ministère de l'Éducation, 1971.

El movimiento cooperativo escolar en México. Mexico City: Universidad Autonoma, 1944.

Parker, Florence E. *Student Cooperatives in the United States, 1941*. Washington, D.C.: GPO, 1943.

Piotrowski, Franciszek. *School Cooperatives in Poland*. Warsaw: Supreme Cooperative Council, 1969.

Profil des coopératives du milieu scolaire de 1986 à 1990. Quebec: Gouvernement du Québec, 1993.

Robin, L. *La coopération scolaire française des républiques d'enfants*. Bordeaux: Éditions Taffard, 1938.

IV. N. 5. Youth Cooperatives

Cowling, E. *Facing the Sunrise: Youth and the Cooperative Movement*. Chicago: CLUSA, 1936.

Juventud y cooperativas. San José, Costa Rica: Centro de Estudios Democraticos de América Latina, 1970.

Lebeau, O., and J. Heckman. *Cooperative Business Training for Farm Youth*. Washington, D.C.: USDA, FCS, 1953.

Nigro, J. *La conquista del niño para la acción cooperativa*. Buenos Aires: Tandil, 1947.

"Report of a Regional Seminar on Youth and Cooperatives, Kuala Lumpur, March–June, 1983." *Regional Bulletin*, New Delhi, ICA, ROECSEA, 23 (3, 1983).

Schnabl, L. *Youth Work Within the Swedish Cooperative Movement*. Stockholm: KF, 1964.

Sinha, B. K. *Cooperative Youth Movement in Europe.* London: Brockley Cooperative Youth Club, 1957.

Skrubeltrang, F. *The Danish Folk High School.* Copenhagen: Danske Selskab, 1947.

Twiff, H. *Junior Cooperatives and Their Organization.* Manchester: Coop Union, 1934.

Uganda Young Farmers Cooperative Project—Summary Description. Rome: FAO Paper RU/Misc./69/19, 1969.

Young Cooperator. London: Federation of Young Cooperators, 1958 (periodical).

Youth and Cooperatives. Washington, D.C.: AIC, 1954.

V. COOPERATIVE FUNCTIONS AND ACTIVITIES

V. A. Administration and Finance in Cooperatives

V. A. 1. Operation and Management of Cooperatives

V. A. 1. a. General Works

Administration et technique. Paris: Coopération agricole, 1964.

Ahmad, R. *Cooperative Management Problems and Solutions/Guidelines.* Bamenda, Cameroon: National Centre for the Development of Cooperative Enterprises, 1974.

Bussière, Eugène. *Organisation administrative et financière des coopératives.* Quebec: Université de Laval, 1949.

Cerda y Richart, Baldomero. *El régimen cooperativo, administración y contabilidad.* Barcelona: Bosch, 1959.

Conceptos generales sobre administración de empresas cooperativas. Mexico City: Confederación Nacional Cooperativa de la República Mexicana, 1979.

Cooperative Management and Administration. Geneva: ILO, 1960; reissued, 1988.

Cooperative Management for the 1970s. London: ICA, 1970.

Dechant, J. *Untersuchungen zur Theorie der Gesamtorganisation des Genossenschaftwesens.* Erlangen, Germany: Forschungsinstitut für Genossenschaftswesens, 1970.

Democratic Management and Economic Efficiency in Rural Cooperative Communities: Second World Congress of Rural Sociology, Enschede, Netherlands, 1968. Tel Aviv: CIRCOM, 1969.

Diaz Boza, J. *Organización y administración de cooperativas.* Lima: Empresa Periodistica Nacional, 1966.

Dinesh, C. *Cooperative Leadership and Management, an Empirical Approach.* Poona, India: Mehta, 1970.

Fledderjohn, H. C. *The Management of Cooperatives. Guidelines for Cooperatives in Developing Economies.* Madison: University of Wisconsin, 1969.

Goel, S. L., and Brij Bhushan Goel. *Principles, Problems and Prospects of Cooperative Administration.* New Delhi: Sterling, 1979.

Kamat, G. S. *New Dimensions of Cooperative Management*. Bombay: Himalaya Publishing House, 1978.

Kranz, W. *Das Management der Unternehmensgruppe Konsum*. Münster: Universität Münster, 1968.

Laflamme, Marcel, and Andre Roy. *L'Administration et le développement coopératif*. Montreal: Éditions du jour, 1978.

Laflamme, Marcel, et al. *La gestion moderne des coopératives*. Chicoutimi, Quebec: G. Morin, 1981.

Louis, R. *Organisation et fonctionnement administratif des coopératives*. Geneva: ILO, 1976.

Meng, S., and R. Alley. *Cooperative Management*. Bombay: Industrial Cooperative Library, 1948.

Rana, J. M., and H. Lamm, eds. *Cooperative Management; Recommendations Made by the Regional Seminar on Cooperative Management, The Philippines, January 10–30, 1973*. New Delhi: ICA, ROECSEA, 1973.

Readings in Cooperative Management. New Delhi: ICA, ROECSEA, 1977.

Relato del seminario internacional sobre administración y contabilidad cooperativa. Geneva: OIT, 1975.

Report of the Open Asia Conference on Cooperative Management, Manila, Philippines, 1975. New Delhi: ICA, ROECSEA, 1976.

Stephenson, Thomas E. *Management in Cooperative Societies*. London: Heinemann, 1963.

Svozil, Z. *Psychology and Sociology Applied to the Management of Cooperatives*. Prague: Central Cooperative Council, 1984.

Taimni, K. K. *Cooperative Organization and Management*. New Delhi: W.A.F.M. Farmers' Welfare Trust Society, 1976.

———. *Managing the Cooperative Enterprise*. Calcutta: Minerva Associates, [n.d.].

V. A. 1. b. Operational Manuals

Ciurrana Fernandez, J. M. *Las cooperativas en la práctica*. Barcelona: Bosch, 1970.

Gachanja, Chris. *How to Make By-Laws*. Marburg, Germany: Institute for Cooperation in Developing Countries, 1989.

Guía de sociedades cooperativas. La Plata, Argentina: Ministerio de Asuntos Exteriores, 1956.

Gutmann, Rudolph, et al. *The Organization and Management of Cooperative Societies; Manual for Cooperative Officials*. Berlin: Verlag Verband Deutscher Konsumgenossenschaften, 1967.

Jacques, J. *Manual on Cooperative Management*. Manchester: Coop Union, 1969.

Kerr, William H., and George A. Nahstoll. *Cooperative Organization Business Methods*. Washington, D.C.: GPO, 1915.

Lamming, G. N. *Cooperative Sector "Idea Book" for Cooperative Administration and Management*. Rome: FAO, 1971.

Management Education and Training in India. Poona, India: Mehta, 1970.

Mejia Scarneo, Julio. *Manual de cooperativas, sus fundamentos y técnica de organización y administración*. Lima: [n.p.], 1956.

———. *Manual de organización y administración de empresas cooperativas*. Washington, D.C.: Unión Panamericana, 1956.

Moirano, Armando A. *Organización de las sociedades cooperativas, constitución, administración, fiscalización, contabilidad*. Buenos Aires: El Ateneo, 1950.

Rikken, Gerard R. *People Oriented Development Workers: Case Studies in Cooperative Management*. Malate, Philippines: Asian Social Institute in Cooperation with Misereor, 1994.

Rutzebeck, H. *Reciprocal Economy: Self-Help Cooperative Technique and Management*. Santa Barbara, Calif.: Rowny Press, 1935.

Taimni, K. K. *Professionalization of Management in Cooperatives*. Poona, India: Mehta, 1973.

V. A. 2. Cooperative Finance

V. A. 2. a. Financing Cooperatives

de Brouckere, Louis. *Les finances coopératives*. Brussels: Les propagateurs de la coopération, 1928.

Helm, F. C. *The Economics of Cooperative Enterprise*. London: University of London Press, 1968.

Hildebrand, K. *Die Finanzierung eingetragener Genossenschaften*. Berlin: De Gruyter, 1921.

International Financing of Cooperative Enterprise in Developing Countries. Geneva: ILO, 1974. (A joint publication of the FAO, ICA and ILO.)

Maddock, W. J. *Financing Cooperatives in Developing Countries. Guidelines for Cooperatives in Developing Economies*. Madison: University of Wisconsin, 1969.

Mehta, V. *Studies in Cooperative Finance*. Poona, India: Aryabhusham Press, 1927.

Myrick, Herbert. *Cooperative Finance*. New York: Orange Judd, 1912.

SIDEFCOOP. *Financiamiento cooperativo*. Santiago: SODIMAC, 1968.

Sommerhoff, Walter R. *Financiamiento cooperativo*. Buenos Aires: Intercoop, 1972.

———. *La inflación y el cooperativismo*. Buenos Aires: Intercoop, 1978.

Tronet B., and N. Stolpe. *Financing of Cooperative Activities*. Stockholm: KF, 1966.

United States Congress. House of Representatives. Committee on Ways and Means. *Tax Treatment of Earnings of Cooperatives*. Washington, D.C.: GPO, 1960.

Valck, W. J. *El problema de financiamiento de las cooperativas*. Santiago: Universidad Católica de Chile, 1969.

V. A. 2. b. Financial Controls

Banarjea, D. K. *Cooperative Bookkeeping and Accounts*. New Delhi: Committee for Cooperative Training, NCUI, 1974.

Bastaros, J. *Técnica del control económico en las cooperativas*. Zaragoza: Escuela de Gerentes Cooperativos, 1965.

Buscemi, Oscar A. *Manual de contabilidad elemental para cooperativas.* Washington, D.C.: Organización de los Estados Americanos, 1958; reprinted, 1979.
Cooperative Bookkeeping. [n.l.]: ICA-CEMAS, 1987.
How to Read a Balance Sheet. An ILO Programmed Book. Geneva: ILO, 1985.
Laurinkari, Juhani, ed. *The International Cooperative Movement—Changes in Economic and Social Policy.* [n.l.]: ICA, 1988.
Manual de auditoría para cooperativas de tipo medio. Washington, D.C.: Organización de los Estados Americanos, 1979.
Manual de contabilidad elemental para cooperativas. Washington, D.C.: Unión Panamericana, 1958.
Staermose, R. *Cooperative Bookkeeping as Introduction to Management.* Lahore, Pakistan: West Pakistan Cooperative Union, 1964.

V. A. 3. Membership Participation and Control

Béland, Claude. *Les Assemblées délibérantes dans les coopératives.* Quebec: Éditeurs Robel, 1971.
Initiation à la pratique de la coopération. Geneva: BIT, 1952.
Krishnaswami, O. R. *Cooperative Democracy in Action.* Bombay: Somaiya Publications, 1976.
Yeo, Peter, et al. *The Work of a Cooperative Committee: A Programmed Learning Text.* London: Intermediate Technology Publications (for CEMAS), 1978.

V. A. 4. Cooperatives as Employers

The Cooperative Consumers' Societies and the Working Conditions of Cooperative Employees. Amsterdam: International Federation of Commercial, Clerical and Technical Employees, 1939.
Cooperative Employee Training. New Delhi: ICA, ROECSEA, 1966.
Miller, Glenn W. *Labor Policies of Consumers' Cooperatives in Great Britain and the United States.* Urbana, Ill.: [n.p.], 1939.
Rhodes, G. W. *Cooperative Labor Relations 1900–1952.* Loughborough, U.K.: Coop Union, 1952.
Taimni, K. K. *Industrial Relations in Cooperative Sector—Field Studies.* Poona, India: Mehta, 1972.
Walford, A. S. *Handbook for Cooperative Personnel.* Oxford: Plunkett, 1977.

V. B. Cooperative Education and Training

V. B. 1. Cooperative Education and Training—Theory and History

Batarinyebwa, Pius K., and Charles Kabuga. *Cooperative Education: Yesterday, Today and Tomorrow.* Kampala: Uganda Cooperative Alliance, 1992.
Benecke, Dieter W. *La educación. Su importancia para el desarrollo y la integración de las cooperativas.* Santiago: Universidad Católica de Chile, 1973.

Blais, P. *Education Through Cooperation.* Quebec: Service Social Économique, 1952.

Bonow, Mauritz. *The Importance of Cooperative Education.* New Delhi: ICA, ROECSEA, 1971.

Bussière, Eugène. *L'éducation coopérative.* Quebec: Université de Laval, 1949.

Cooperative Education. Bombay: Reserve Bank of India, 1951.

Cooperative Education. New Delhi: ICA, ROECSEA, 1969.

Education and Voluntary Movements. New Delhi: ICA, ROECSEA, 1965.

L'éducation dans le mouvement coopératif. Quebec: Conseil supérieur de la coopération du Québec, 1942.

Hatta, Mohammad. *Education by Cooperation.* Jakarta: Ministry of Information, 1956.

Marshall, Robert. *Cooperative Education.* London: London Cooperative Society, 1948.

Mungai, Joseph M., and Florence M. Asila, eds. *Cooperative Education for Enhanced Growth and Development.* Nairobi: Friedrich Ebert Foundation, 1988.

Report of the International Conference on Cooperative Education. New Delhi: ICA, ROECSEA, 1969.

Report of an International Conference of Cooperative Education Leaders. (Cosponsored by ICA and UNESCO). London: ICA, 1970.

Report of an International Symposium on Cooperative Education for Developing Countries: Education and Training for Progress and Development. Prague: Central Cooperative Council, 1984.

Srivastava, N. P. *Education for Cooperatives.* New Delhi: Atma Ram, India, 1971; Lucknow, India: Atsukh Rai Lane, 1971.

Tereshtenko, Valery. *A Bibliographical Review of the Literature on Cooperative Education.* New York: WPA, 1941.

Twigg, H. *An Outline of the History of Cooperative Education.* Manchester: Coop Union, 1924.

Uribe Garzon, C. *Cooperación y educación cooperativa.* Bogota: Facultad de Derecho, 1950.

Warbasse, James P. *Cooperative Education.* New York: Cooperative League of America, 1920; reissued, Chicago: CLUSA, 1948.

Widhe, E. *International Cooperative Education.* Stockholm: Union of Swedish Cooperative Women's Guilds, 1948.

ïeo, Peter H. *The Needs of Cooperatives in Less Developed Countries for Education and Training.* Loughborough, U.K.: Loughborough University of Technology and International Cooperative Training Centre, 1974.

V. B. 2. Cooperative Education and Training— Organization and Management

Bibangambah, J., and E. Onega, eds. *An Integrated Approach to Cooperative Mobilization and Education.* Kampala: Uganda Cooperative Alliance, 1990.

Chávez Nuñez, Fernando. *Manual de educación cooperativa*. Washington, D.C.: Unión Panamericana, 1958.

Chianelli and E. Olivier. *La ley nacional de educación cooperativa*. Buenos Aires: CECBA, 1967.

Cooperative Education, a Handbook of Practical Guidance for Cooperative Educationists. Loughborough, U.K.: Coop Union, 1961.

Cooperative Education Center. *Handbook on Cooperative Education*. Arusha: Tanzania Litho, 1970.

Cooperative Education Directory. London: ICA, CEMAS, 1979.

Hutchinson, C. R. *Cooperative Education and Training in Developing Countries. Guidelines for Cooperatives in Developing Economies*. Madison: University of Wisconsin, Center for Cooperatives, 1969.

Lebeau, O. *Educational Practices of Farmer Cooperatives*. Washington, D.C.: FCA, 1950.

Manual de educación cooperativa. Washington, D.C.: Unión Panamericana, 1958.

Mshiu, Sam. *Organization and Management of Field Education: A Manual for Cooperative Field Educators*. Geneva: ICA, CEMAS, 1982.

Necesidades básicas, tecnología y cooperación. San José, Costa Rica: OIT, 1976.

Nuevas proyecciones de la educatión en los procesos cooperativos y/o asociativos. San José, Costa Rica: OIT, 1976.

Organization, Methods and Contents of Cooperative Education and Training. Stockholm: SCC, 1970.

Russell, Ralph. *Educational Methods for Promoting Cooperation*. Washington, D.C.: Pan American Union, 1938. (Also in Spanish)

Watkins, W. *Organization of Cooperative Education*. London: ICA, 1937.

Worldwide Training of Cooperative Experts. London: ICA, 1970.

V. B. 3. Cooperative Education and Training—Types of Training

V. B. 3. a. Cooperative Leadership

Coutinho, Boavida. *Cooperation the Key to Progress, a Guide for Cooperative Leaders*. Rome: Gregorian University, 1972.

Digby, Margaret. *Members, Committees and Staff*. London: Plunkett, 1959.

Wiseman, B.L. *Accounting for Successful Business*. Oxford: Plunkett, 1988.

Yeo, P. *The Work of a Cooperative Committee: A Programmed Learning Text*. London: Intermediate Technology Publications, 1978.

V. B. 3. b. Cooperative Members

Colombain, Maurice. *Las cooperativas y la educación fundamental*. Paris: UNESCO, 1950.

———. *Les coopératives et l'éducation de base*. Paris: UNESCO, 1950.

Coutinho, Boavida. *El progreso comunitario a través de la educación de los adultos y de las cooperativas*. Rome: CISIC Institutum Sociologia Pastoralis, 1965.

Experts' Consultation on Cooperative Member Education, April 15–29, 1979, Trincomalee, Sri Lanka: Report and Papers. New Delhi: ICA, ROECSEA, 1980.

Le mouvement coopératif et l'éducation des adultes. Montreal: Conseil de la coopération du Québec, 1969; Montreal: Institut canadien d'éducation des adultes, 1970.

Report of the ICA Seminar on Functional Literacy and Cooperatives, Ibadan, Nigeria, February 1975. London: ICA, 1975.

Report of the Regional Seminar on Cooperative Member Education and Member Communication, Tokyo, April, 1974. New Delhi: ICA, ROECSEA, 1974.

Rouillard, H. *Pioneers in Adult Education.* Toronto: Nelson and Sons, 1952.

Watkins, W. P. *Adult Education for Cooperators.* London: London Cooperative Societies' Joint Education Committee, [n.d.].

V. B. 3. c. Cooperative Employees

Cooperative Employee Training. New Delhi: ICA, ROECSEA, 1966.

Landesberg, H. *La formation des cadres, un des éléments fondamentaux du développement de la coopération.* Warsaw: Conseil coopératif suprême, 1964.

Verhagen, Koenrad C. W. *A Regional Survey of High Level Manpower Training Needs.* Moshi, Tanzania: ICA, ROECSA, 1975.

V. B. 3. d. General Public

Bralich, J. *El cooperativismo como método de educación social.* Buenos Aires: Intercoop, 1963.

Laidlaw, A. *La formation et la vulgarisation en matière de coopération.* Rome: FAO, 1962. (Also in English.)

———. *Training and Extension in the Cooperative Movement. A Guide for Fieldmen and Extension Workers.* Rome: FAO, Economic and Social Development Series, No. 11, 1978.

V. B. 4. Cooperative Education and Training—Facilities

V. B. 4. a. Cooperative Training Centers

Directory of Agencies Assisting Cooperatives in Developing Countries. Section VII. Cooperative Training Courses Available to Students from Developing Countries Outside Their Own Countries. Rome: COPAC, 1993.

Godbour, Léopold. *École populaire de coopération.* Quebec: Conseil supérieur de la coopération, 1944.

Moreno Avendano, José. *Cooperativas de educación (colegios cooperativos); una nueva dimensión educativa para el cambio en las países del tercer mundo: planeación, organización, operación, control.* Bogota: Ediciones Tercer Mundo, 1973.

Regional Conference of Principals and Teachers of National Cooperative Training Institutions, Djakarta, June, 1974. New Delhi: ICA, ROECSEA, 1974.

Repetto, N. *Escuela de la cooperación, Cursos.* Buenos Aires: Federación Nacional de Cooperativas de Consumo, 1938.

Serwy, V. *Les institutions d'enseignement coopératif.* Brussels: Les propagateurs de la coopération, 1946.

V. B. 4. b. Colleges and Universities

Benecke, Dieter W. *Estudio de factibilidad: carrera cooperativista en la Universidad Nacional Autónoma de Honduras.* Santiago: [n.p.], 1972.

Davidovic, G. *University Teaching of Cooperation in Various Countries: A Survey and Analysis.* Ottawa: CUC, 1967.

V. B. 5. Cooperative Education and Training—Curriculum Materials

Bogardus, Emery. *Problems of Cooperation, A Discussion Group Guide.* Chicago: CLUSA, 1960.

Botham, Cecil N. *Audio-visual Aids for Cooperative Education and Training.* Rome: FAO, 1967. (Also in French.)

Bottomley, Trevor. *An Introduction to Cooperatives. A Programmed Learning Text.* London: Intermediate Technology Publications, 1979.

Colombain, Maurice. *La coopération. Cours d'éducation ouvrière.* Geneva: BIT, 1956.

(Cooperativas) ¿Qué es? ¿Cómo funciona? Madrid: Instituto de Estudios Sindicales, Sociales y Cooperativas, 1965.

Cusin, A. *Curso de enseñanza cooperativa.* Havana: Talleres del Diario de la Marina, 1950.

Desroche, Henri. *Le projet coopératif: son utopie et sa pratique; ses appareils et ses reseaux; ses espérances et des déconvenues.* Paris: Économie et humanisme, 1976.

Fernandez, J. M. *Curso de cooperación.* Barcelona: Casa Editorial, 1969.

Hwang Kyung, K. *Confidence in You: A Korean Teacher Talks About Cooperatives and Some "Main Points" for Rural Cooperative Teachers.* Seoul: Ministry of Agriculture, 1957.

Rojas Coria, R. *Introducción al estudio de cooperativismo.* Mexico City: Fondo de Cultura, 1961.

Rossi Chavarria, J. *Curso de Cooperativas.* San José, Costa Rica: Editorial Aurora Social, 1949.

Watkins, W. P. *Cooperative Storekeeping—A Syllabus for Discussion Groups.* Manchester: Coop Union, 1944.

Wieting, Maurice. *The Progress of Cooperatives, with Aids for Teachers.* New York: Harper, 1952.

V. B. 6. Cooperative Education and Training—
Some National Experiences

Chávez Nuñez, Fernando. *La educación cooperativa en América Latina.* Washington, D.C.: Unión Panamericana, 1962.

Cheneau. *L'enseignement de la coopération en France et en Angleterre.* Paris: PUF, 1925.

Cooperative Education and Training in Latin America. Geneva: ILO, 1977.

Cooperative Education in India, an Approach. New Delhi: ICA, ROECSEA, 1962.

Hoque, F. *A Comparative Analysis of Cooperative Training Programs in India, Tanzania and Bangladesh.* Loughborough, U.K.: Cooperative College, 1979.

Interim Report to the Government of the Union of Burma on Cooperative Education. Geneva: ILO, 1963.

Rana, J. M., and V. N. Pandya. *ICA-NCUI Cooperative Education Field Project, Indore District, India: A Report.* New Delhi: ICA, ROECSEA, 1975.

Report on the Proceedings of the ICA/UNESCO Conference of African Cooperative Education Leaders. Moshi, Tanzania: ICA, ROECSA, 1973.

Report to the Government of Gambia on Cooperative Education and Training. Geneva: ILO, 1969.

Report to the Government of Kenya on Cooperative Education and Training. Geneva: ILO, 1970.

Report to the Government of Malawi on Cooperative Education and Training. Geneva: ILO, 1966.

Report to the Government of Pakistan on Cooperative Education. Geneva: ILO, 1966.

Report to the Government of the Philippines on Cooperative Education. Geneva: ILO, 1966.

Report to the Government of the Union of Burma on Cooperative Education and Training. Geneva: ILO, 1967.

Report to the Government of Zambia on Cooperative Education. Geneva: ILO, 1973.

Survey of Cooperative Education in East and Central Africa. Moshi, Tanzania: ICA, ROECSA, 1970.

Vir, D. *Cooperative Member Education in South-East Asia.* New Delhi: ICA, ROECSEA, 1972.

V. C. Cooperative Communications

Directory of Cooperative Press in South-East Asia. New Delhi: ICA, ROECSEA, 1969.

International Directory of the Cooperative Press. London, Zurich: ICA, 1909, 1990. (Reissued irregularly, most recently in 1990.)

V. D. Women in Cooperatives

V. D. 1. Women in Cooperatives—Historical Developments

Buchan, A. *History of the Scottish Cooperative Women's Guild 1892–1913*. Glasgow: Scottish Cooperative Wholesale Society, 1913.

Chmielewski, Wendy, Louis J. Kern, and Marlyn Klee-Hartzell. *Women in Spiritual and Communitarian Societies in the United States*. Syracuse, N.Y.: Syracuse University Press, 1993.

Cooperative Women in Agriculture. London: International Cooperative Women's Guild, 1951.

Davies, Margaret L., ed. *Life As We Have Known It, by Cooperative Working Women*. London: Hogarth Press, 1931; reprinted, London: Virago, 1977.

————. *The Women's Cooperative Guild, 1883–1904*. Kirkby Lonsdale, U.K.: Women's Cooperative Guild, 1904.

Die Gewerkschaft der Hausfrauen. Vienna: Verband Deutsch-österreichischer Konsumvereine, 1928.

Enfield, H. *The Legal Position of Women in Cooperative Societies*. London: International Cooperative Women's Guild, 1930.

Freundlich, Emmy. *Housewives Build a New World*. London: International Cooperative Women's Guild, 1935.

Gaffin, Jean, and David Thomas. *Caring and Sharing: The Centenary History of the Cooperative Women's Guild*. Manchester: Coop Union, 1983.

Gerlach, K. *Die Frau und das Genossenschaftswesen*. Jena, Germany: Fischer, 1918.

Hardstaff, A. *The Rights of Women in Cooperative Societies*. London: International Cooperative Women's Guild, 1930.

International Cooperative Alliance ROAP. *Report of the ICA ROAP Sub-Regional Workshops on Gender Integration in Cooperatives*. New Delhi: ROAP, 1996.

International Labor Office. *Women at Work. ILO: Women's Participation in Cooperatives*. Geneva: ILO, 1987.

The International Woman Cooperator. London: International Cooperative Women's Guild, [n.d.] (periodical).

Kluge, Arnd H. *Frauen und Genossenschaften in Deutschland: von der Mitte des 19. Jahrhunderts bis zur Gegenwart*. Marburg, Germany: Institut für Genossenschaftswesen an der Philipps-Universität, 1992.

Kolmerten, Carol A. *Women in Utopia: The Ideology of Gender in the American Owenite Communities*. Bloomington: Indiana University Press, 1990.

Men and Women Who Have Made History. Loughborough, U.K.: Coop Union, 1956.

Mrskova, A. *How the Cooperative Movement Can Help the Peasant Women*. London: International Cooperative Women's Guild, 1951.

L'organisation des ménagères dans le mouvement coopératif. Liège: Guilde des coopératrices, 1935.

Plunkett, Horace. *The United Irishwomen; Their Place, Work and Ideals.* Dublin: Maunsel, 1911.

Report of the Committee, 1937–46. London: International Cooperative Women's Guild, 1947.

Riedl, Emmy. *Position of Women in the Cooperative Movement.* London: International Cooperative Women's Guild, 1951.

Schloesser, R. *Die Frauenfrage in der Genossenschaftsbewegung.* Düsseldorf: Verlag der Konsumvereine, 1922.

Taylor, Barbara. *Eve and the New Jerusalem: Socialism and Feminism in the Nineteenth Century.* London: Virago Press, 1983; reissued, Cambridge, Mass.: Harvard University Press, 1993.

Twenty-one Years, 1907–1928. Belfast: Irish Cooperative Women's Guild, 1928.

Webb, C. *The Woman With the Basket: The History of the Women's Cooperative Guild, 1883–1927.* London: Women's Cooperative Guild, 1927.

V. D. 2. Women in Cooperatives—General Literature

Anderson, Walfred A. *Farm Cooperatives and Farm Women.* Ithaca, N.Y.: Cornell University Agricultural Experiment Station, 1945.

Centre for Research on European Women. *The Viability of Employment Initiatives Involving Women.* Luxembourg: Office for Official Publications of the European Communities, 1986.

D'Cruz, M. *Key to Household Economy.* New Delhi: ICA, ROECSEA, 1972.

Dean, Susan. *Women in Cooperatives.* Rome: COPAC, 1985. (Includes a 56-page bibliography.)

Dixon, R. B. *Rural Women at Work; Strategies for Development in South Asia.* Baltimore: Johns Hopkins University Press, 1978.

Garcia, Ana Isabel, ed. *Hacia la concertación de géneros en el cooperativismo centroamericano: Mujer y participación social.* San José, Costa Rica: CCC-CA, 1992.

Guerrero de Burgos, M. *Cooperativismo y cambio social: Un programa para la mujer.* Bogota: ASCOOP, 1972.

Hacker, Sally. *Pleasure, Power and Technology: Some Tales of Gender, Engineering, and the Cooperative Workplace.* Boston: Unwin Hyman, 1989.

International Cooperative Alliance ROAM. *Bases para la elaboracion de una estrategia de genero en cooperativas en las Americas.* San José, Costa Rica: ICA, ROAM, 1996.

———. *Hacia la concertacion de generos en el movimiento cooperativo.* San José, Costa Rica: ICA, ROAM, 1992.

——— ROAP. *Cooperative Leadership Training for Women. Report of the Preparatory Regional Workshop, Kuala Lumpur, 1997.* New Delhi: ROAP, 1998.

———. *Gender Planning in Cooperatives.* New Delhi: ICA, ROAP, 1993.

———. *Strategy for Cooperative Development in Vietnam—A Workshop Report.* New Delhi: ROAP, 1995.

International Labour Office. *Gender Awareness and Planning Manual for Training of Trainers, Project Planners and Implementors in the Cooperative Sector.* Jakarta: ILO, 1993.

International Women's Rights Action Watch. *Assessing the Status of Women.* New York: IWRAW, 1988.

Knapp, Joseph. *Women and Cooperatives.* Washington, D.C.: USDA, FCS, 1965.

Lamming, G. N. *Women in Agricultural Cooperatives: Constraints and Limitations to Full Participation.* Rome: FAO, 1983.

Lebeau, O. *How Women Help Their Farmer Cooperatives.* Washington, D.C.: USDA, FCS, 1956.

Mavrogiannis, Dionysos. *L'intégration des femmes aux coopératives.* Geneva: BIT, 1986.

McCarthy, F. E. *Pilot Project in Population Planning and Rural Women's Cooperatives: Third Report, 1976–1977.* Dacca, Bangladesh: Integrated Rural Development Programme, 1978.

New Types of Employment Initiatives Especially As Relating to Women. Luxembourg: Office for Official Publication of the European Communities, 1984.

Orientation Seminar for Participants of the 7th International Seminar for Women on "Leadership Through Education," New Delhi, March/April, 1976. New Delhi: ICA, ROECSEA, 1976.

La participación de la mujer en la organización campesina. Un estudio de casos propiciado por CAMPOCOOP (Confederación Nacional de Federaciones de Cooperativas Campesinas, Chile). Santiago: CAMPOCOOP, 1980.

"Proceedings of a Regional Workshop for Women Cooperative Leaders, Sri Lanka, July, 1982." *Regional Bulletin,* New Delhi, ICA, ROECSEA, 22 (4, 1982).

Raj, M. K. *Approaches to Self-Reliance for Women: Some Urban Models.* Bombay: Shreemati Nathibai Damodar Thackersey Women's University, Research Unit on Women's Studies, 1980.

Rapport du séminaire sur la femme et les coopératives, Yaoundé, novembre, 1977. Addis Ababa: Commission économique pour l'Afrique, 1978.

Rapport du séminaire sur la formation des femmes en matière de coopérative villageoise, Kabala, Mali, mai, 1980. Addis Ababa: La Commission économique pour l'Afrique, 1981.

Report of a Seminar for Women on the Role of Women in Cooperatives, Ibadan, January, 1972 (co-sponsored by ICA and the Cooperative Union of Western Nigeria). Ibadan, Nigeria: Cooperative Union of Western Nigeria, 1972.

Report of the Proceedings of the Regional Women Cooperators' Seminar, Kampala, Uganda, January, 1974. Moshi, Tanzania: ICA, ROECSA, 1974.

Report of the Regional Conference on "The Role Of Women in Cooperative Development," Kuala Lumpur, July, 1975. New Delhi: ICA, ROECSEA, 1975.

Report of the Workshop on the Participation of Women in Development Through Cooperatives With Special Emphasis on Handicrafts and Small-Scale Industries, Khartoum, October, 1979. Addis Ababa: Economic Commission for Africa, 1980.

Report on a Cooptrade Short-term Consultancy in Product Adaptation, Management and Export Techniques Regarding Handicrafts Produced by the Cooperative Members' Housewives Projects, Yasothorn, Thailand, 1982. Geneva: ILO, 1983.

Savoye, M. *Women's Cooperative Participation and Fight Against Rural Poverty.* Rome: COPAC, 1978.

Schmucker, Lee W. *Women in Credit Unions. The Untapped Resource.* Madison, Wis.: ACCOSCA and WOCCU, 1993.

Some Guidelines for Cooperative Women's Education and Representation. Colombo: Cooperative Management Services Center, 1977.

Tice, Karin E. *Kuna Crafts (Panama), Gender, and the Global Economy.* Austin: University of Texas Press, 1995.

Women in Cooperatives: Report of the Kenya NGO Sub-Committee Workshop held at the Cooperative College of Kenya, Nairobi, June 1984. Nairobi: Kenya NGO Organizing Committee, Forum '85 of the World Conference of the U.N. Decade for Women, 1985.

V. D. 3. Women in Cooperatives—Some National Experiences

Boresova, M. *Women in the Czechoslovak Cooperative Movement.* Prague: Central Cooperative Council, 1966.

Bulumulla, Jayantha C. T. *Women's Consumer Education and Information Through Cooperatives in Sri Lanka. An Experience in Enhancing Women's Involvement in Cooperative Activity.* New Delhi: ICA, ROAP, [n.d.].

Calivari, M. N. M. "Participación de la mujer en la actividad cooperativa" (Argentina). *Revista de la Cooperation*, Buenos Aires, Argentina, (1/2 1977): 147–168.

Cardona, A. A., and E. R. Alvarado. *Participación de la mujer en el proceso de desarrollo agrícola en organizaciónes cooperativas—La experiencia en Honduras.* Rome: FAO, 1980.

Centro de Investigaciones y Estudios de la Reforma Agraria. *La mujer en las cooperativas agropecuarias en Nicaragua.* Managua: MIDINRA, 1984.

Collège coopératif Rhône-Alpes (C.C.R.A.). *Femmes coopératives et développements.* Lyon: Université coopérative internationale, 1985.

Dean, Susan. *Women in Cooperatives in Central America.* Rome: COPAC, 1987.

Denisse, C., and M. J. Doucet. *Production agricole des femmes et les conditions de leur intégration dans les coopératives du Niger.* Paris: Institut de recherches et d'applications des méthodes de développement, 1979.

Directory of Women's Cooperatives in India. New Delhi: Centre for Womens' Development Studies, 1982.

Enquête effectuée auprès de groupements féminins, mars-juin 1985. Kigali, Rwanda: Centre de formation et de recherche coopératives, 1985.

Halatuituia, L., S. N. Latu, and M. L. Moimoi. "Women's Cooperatives in Tonga." *Pacific Perspectives* (Suva) 2 (2, 1982): 13–17.

Herath, W.U. *An Overview of Gender Integration and Women in Cooperative Development in Asia and the Pacific.* New Delhi: ROAP, 1992.

Ijere, Martin O. *Women in Nigerian Cooperatives.* Enugu, Nigeria: Acena Publishers, 1991.

ICA ROAM. *La mujer cooperativista y su realidad inmediata.* San José, Costa Rica: ICA, ROAM, [n.d.].

———. *Muyer y cooperativismo. Aportes en el proceso de integracion de la muyer.* San José, Costa Rica: ICA, ROAM, 1991.

———. *Gender Integration in Cooperatives.* New Delhi: ICA, ROAP, 1992. (Country studies: *Afghanistan.* Azizy, Fahima; *Bangladesh.* Kabir, Mabud Fatima; *Indonesia.* Berninghaussent, J., Dr.; *Fiji.* Vuluvano, M.; *India.* Rikhy, Gurveen; *Iran.* Saleh, Maryam K.; *Japan.* Yamauchi, Akiko; *Korea DPR.* Ok, Gung Jong; *Malaysia.* Baheran, Rahaiah; *Pakistan.* Kazi, S.; *Sri Lanka.* Rupasinghe, Chandra; *Thailand.* Supakivilekagarn, Pailin.)

———. *Housewives in Consumer Coops. The Report of the ICA Regional Follow-up Workshop on Housewives' Involvement in Consumer Cooperatives, Osaka.* New Delhi: ICA, ROAP, 1989.

———. *Rural Women Leadership Development in Agricultural Cooperatives in Asia. Reports of Seminars.* New Delhi: ICA, ROAP, 1995, 1996, 1997, 1998.

———. *Women in Development Through Fishery Cooperatives in Asia.* New Delhi: ICA, ROAP, 1990.

Involvement of Women in Cooperatives and Other Self-Help Organs in English-Speaking Africa. Rome: FAO, 1975.

Karaki, N. *Les associations féminines au Liban.* Paris: Collège coopératif, 1975.

Klingshirn, A. *Report of a UNFPA/FAO Study Mission on the Involvement of Women in Cooperatives Connected with Food Production and Distribution and Related Population Activities in Zaire and Ghana, October–December, 1976.* Rome: FAO, 1977.

Mavrogiannis, D. *Women's Involvement in Thrift and Credit Cooperatives in Selected Asian Countries.* Geneva: ILO, 1991.

Mayoux, L. *All Are Not Equal—African Women in Cooperatives. Report of a Conference Held at the Institute for African Alternatives, 10–11 September 1988.* London: IFAA, 1988.

Meghji, Zakia, Ramadhan Meghi, and Clement Kwayu. *The Woman Cooperator and Development: Experiences from Eastern, Central and Southern Africa.* Nairobi: Maarifa Publishers, 1985.

Milimo, M. M. *Chikuni Fruit and Vegetable Producers' Cooperative Society, Zambia.* Geneva: ILO/WEP, 1984.

Mora A., Jorge A. *FECOPA R.L. y la mujer campesina.* San José, Costa Rica: Federación de Cooperativas Campesinas de Producción Agropecuaria y Servicios Múltiples, 1985.

La mujer en las cooperativas agropecuarias en Nicaragua. Managua: Centro de Investigaciones y Estudios de la Reforma Agraria, 1984.

Mutiso, Roberta. *Poverty, Women, and Cooperatives in Kenya.* East Lansing: Michigan State University, Women in International Development, 1987.

Nevo, Naomi, and David Solomonica. *Ideological Change of Rural Women's Role and Status: A Case Study of Family Based Cooperative Villages in Israel.* East Lansing: Michigan State University, Office of Women in International Development (16, 1983).

Nkebukwa, Anna K., ed. *Proceedings of the Seminar on Women's Involvement in Cooperatives in Tanzania, Dar-es-Salaam, April, 1987.* Dar-es-Salaam: University of Dar-es-Salaam, 1989.

Opondo, Diane. *Women and Cooperatives: Egypt, the Libyan Arab Jamahiriya and the Sudan.* Addis Ababa: UN, Economic Commission for Africa, 1980.

Osuntogun, A., and A. Akinbode. *The Involvement of Women in Rural Cooperatives in Nigeria and Population Education.* Rome: FAO, 1980.

Outline of the Agricultural Cooperative Women's Bureau (1948–1957). Tokyo: National Agricultural Cooperative Women's Council, 1957.

Rao, H. R. S. *The Functioning of Andhra Pradesh Women's Cooperatives Finance Corporation and the Impact of the Scheme Financed By It.* New Delhi: Indian Council of Social Science Research, 1982.

Report of the Third ICA/Japan Training Course for Rural Women Leaders of Agricultural Cooperatives in Asia, June/July, 1993, Tokyo. New Delhi: ICA, ROAP, 1993.

Richards, M. *La femme batanga dans la société kribienne (Zaire).* Paris: Centre de recherches coopératives, 1969.

Sawekema, Monde Caroline, ed. *Report on the Preparatory Workshop for Conducting an Action Research on the Position of Women in the Cooperative Movement, Lusaka, October, 1980.* Lusaka: Zambia Cooperative Federation, 1987.

Sjernstedt, D. C. M. "Successful Women's Projects: The Case of Mupona Multi-Purpose Cooperative Society, Zambia." In *Rural Development and Women: Lessons From the Field,* Geneva: ILO, 2 (1985): 89–98.

Tiger, L., and J. Sheper. *Women in Kibbutz.* New York: Harcourt, Brace, Jovanovich, 1975.

Wachtel, Eleanor, and Andy Wachtel. *Women's Cooperative Enterprise in Nakuru.* Nairobi: Nairobi University, Institute for Development Studies, 1977.

Wertime, Mary Beth. *Foodcrop Marketing and Women's Cooperatives in the North West Province, Republic of Cameroon, A Peace Corps Study.* Yaoundé: United States Peace Corps, 1987.

Wojciechowska, J. *La femme dans les coopératives en Pologne.* Warsaw: Conseil coopératif suprême, 1963.

Women of Kibwezi: A Case Study of the Kibwezi Women's Integrated Rural Development Program. Nairobi: HABITAT, 1990.

Women's Cooperatives in Gujarat. Ahmedabad, India: Gujarat State Cooperative Union, 1976.

Yanat, H. *Travail communautaire avec les femmes algériennes.* Paris: College coopératif, 1975.

V. D. 4. Women in Cooperatives—Integration versus Separation

Bruce, J. *Market Women's Cooperatives: Giving Women Credit.* Washington, D.C.: Seeds, 1980.

Cooperatives for Female Ex-combatants. Geneva: ILO/WEP, 1984.

Caughman, Susan. *Women at Work in Mali: The Case of the Markala Cooperative.* Boston: Boston University, African Studies Center, 1981.

Caughman, Susan, and M. N. Thiam. *The Markala Cooperative (in Mali): A New Approach to Traditional Economic Roles.* Washington, D.C.: Seeds, Number 5, 1982.

Descarreaux, Rachel, and Dominique Ouellet. *Le fonctionnement collectif dans deux entreprises crées par des femmes.* Sherbrooke, Quebec: Institut de recherche et d'enseignement pour les coopératives de l'Université de Sherbrooke, 1986.

Education and Information Through Cooperatives in Sri Lanka: An Experience in Enhancing Women's Involvement in Cooperative Activity. New Delhi: ICA, ROECSEA, 1984.

Gender Integration in Cooperatives: Report of the ICA/SCC/NCC Regional Consultation in Colombo, 27 April–2 May, 1993. New Delhi: ICA, ROAP, 1993.

Illo, Jeanne F., and Cecile C. Uy. *Members But Not Leaders: Finding a Niche for Women in Cooperatives: The NATCCO Enhancement of Women's Involvement in Cooperatives Project.* Manila: Ateneo de Manila University, Institute of Philippine Culture, 1992.

Ladipo, P. "Developing Women's Cooperatives: An Experiment in Rural Nigeria." *Journal of Development Studies* 17 (3, 1981): 123–136.

Lin, T. Y. *The Kubang Pasu Timur Women's Multipurpose Cooperative, Malaysia.* Geneva: ILO/WEP, 1984.

Okonkwo, John N. P. *Better Life for Rural Women Cooperatives.* Enugu, Nigeria: Cooperative Publishers, 1989.

St. Martin, Nicole, Jasmine Godbout, and Dominique Ouellet. *L'autogestion au féminin: La création de coopératives de travail par des femmes.* Sherbrooke, Quebec: Institut de recherche et d'enseignement pour les coopératives de l'Université de Sherbrooke, 1991.

V. E. Trade Unions and Cooperatives

América Latina: sindicatos y cooperativas. San José, Costa Rica: CEDAL, 1970.

Bupette, F. *Coopération et syndicalisme.* Paris: Imp. Réaumur, 1969.

Caribbean Regional Seminar on the Trade Unions and Cooperatives in Workers' Education, November/December, 1972. Geneva: ILO, 1974.

Clerc, Charles. *Les syndicats professionels dans leurs rapports avec les sociétés coopératives.* Paris: E. Larose, 1910.

Cole, G. D. H. *Coops and Labour.* London: London Cooperative Society, 1945.

Collaboration Between Trade Unions and Cooperatives in Developing Countries: A Survey. London: ICA, 1975.

Colombain, Maurice. *Cooperation, A Workers' Education Manual.* Geneva: ILO, 1956.

The Cooperative Movement and Trade Unions. Stockholm: KF, 1971.

Cooperativismo y sindicalismo: protagonistas del cambio social. San José, Costa Rica: CCC-CA, 1991.

Curso-seminario Latinoamericano de cooperativismo en el movimiento de los trabajadores. Caracas: Universidad do los Trabajadores de América Latina, 1975.

Eger, Akiva. *The Role of Labor and Cooperation in the Development of Young States.* Tel Aviv: Afro-Asian Institute for Labor Studies and Cooperation, 1965.

Estudios sindicales y cooperativos. Madrid: Instituto de Estudios Sindicales, Sociales y Cooperativos, 1972.

Evans, J. N. *Great Figures in the Labor Movement.* Oxford: Pergamon Press, 1965.

Fabra Ribas, Antonio. *Los sindicatos y las cooperativas.* Popayán, Colombia: [n.p.], 1944.

Levi, Y. *Trade Unions and Cooperatives: Common Roots and Relationships in Past and Present Times.* Tel Aviv: Afro-Asian Institute for Cooperative and Labor Studies, 1971.

Michel, J. *Syndicalisme et coopératives de consommation en Alsace.* Paris: Institut des études coopératives, 1970.

Mutschles, C. *Coopératives et syndicats.* Paris: Rivière, 1913.

Myers, J. *Labor and Cooperatives.* Chicago: CLUSA, 1943; reissued, Washington, D.C.: CLUSA, 1949.

Odubandjo, M. *Cooperative Guide for Trade Unions.* New York: African-American Labor Center, 1972.

Quelch, H. *Trade Unionism, Cooperation, and Social Democracy.* London: Twentieth Century Press, 189– .

Report of Asia Regional Seminar on Trade Unions and Cooperatives, Singapore, October, 1970. Geneva: ILO, 1972.

Report of the ILO/DANIDA Regional Seminar on Trade Unions and Cooperatives in Workers' Education, Ankara, March, 1973. Geneva: ILO, 1973.

Report of the Seminar on Trade Unions and Cooperatives in Africa, Nairobi, August, 1969. Geneva: ILO, 1969.

Report on the South East Asia Sub-Regional Seminar on Trade Union Cooperative Activities, Manila, October, 1979. Geneva: ILO, 1980.

Rodríguez Vargas, Francisco, and Antoine Antoni. *Cooperativismo y sindicalismo.* Bogota: Ediciones Colatina, 1979.

Séminaire BIT/DANIDA "Syndicalisme et coopératives," Lomé, Togo, January, 1976: Rapport. Geneva: BIT, 1976.

Sindicatos y Cooperativas. San José, Costa Rica: Centro de Estudios Democráticos de América Latina, 1971.

Solasse, B. *Syndicalisme, consommation et société de consommation.* Ottawa: Task Force on Labor Relations, 1970.

Stolpe, H. *The Cooperative Movement and the Trade Unions.* Stockholm: KF, 1971.

Le syndicalisme paysan en République Arabe Syrienne. Damascus: Office arabe de presses et de documentation, 1969.

Trade Union and Cooperative in a One Party State—Tanzania. London: Acland Travelling Scholarship Trust, 1972.

Trade Unions and Cooperatives. New Delhi: ICA, ROECSEA, 1966.

Trade Unions and Cooperatives in the Development of Asia. Bonn-Bad Godesberg: Friedrich Ebert Foundation, [n.d.].

V. F. Research and Evaluation in Cooperatives

V. F. 1. Research on Cooperatives

Bayley, J. E. *Directory of Cooperative Research and Education in the UK, Ireland and Europe.* Oxford: Plunkett, 1981.

Blümle, Ernst-Bernd, and Peter Schwarz, eds. *Erwartungen der Genossenschaftspraxis an die Wissenschaft: Tagungsbericht der IX. internationalen genossenschaftswissenschaftlichen Tagung 1978 in Freiburg, Schweiz.* Göttingen, Germany: Vandenhoeck and Ruprecht, 1979.

Boettcher, Erik, ed. *Die Genossenschaft im Wettbewerb der Ideen: eine europaische Herausforderung: Bericht der XI. Internationalen Genossenschaftswissenschaftlichen Tagung 1985 in Münster.* Tübingen: Mohr, 1985.

Boettcher, Erik, and H. Westermann. *Genossenschaften—Demokratie und Wettbewerb: Verhandlungsberichte und Diskussionsergebnisse der VII. Internationalen Genossenschaftswissenschaftlichen Tagung, Münster, 1972.* Tübingen: Mohr, 1972.

Bridault, Alain, and Dominique Oullet. *Analytical Inventory of Canadian University Research on Cooperatives: 1970–1985.* Montreal: Interuniversity Center, 1987. (Also in French.)

Cooperative Research and Planning. Proceedings of the ICA Regional Conference on Cooperative Research and Planning, Arusha, April, 1974. Moshi, Tanzania: ICA, ROECSA, 1974.

Cooperative Research Perspectives in East and Central Africa. Papers and Proceedings of the 2nd ICA Regional Cooperative Research and Planning Conference, Lusaka, April, 1977. Moshi, Tanzania: ICA, ROECSA, 1977.

Dülfer, Eberhard, ed. *Zur Krise der Genossenschaften in der Entwicklungspolitik.* Göttingen, Germany: Vandenhoeck and Ruprecht, 1975.

Forschungsinstitut für Genossenschaftswesen an der Universität- Wien. *Neuere Tendenzen im Genossenschaftswesen.* Göttingen, Germany: Vandenhoeck and Ruprecht, 1966.

Hartmann, Rudolph. *Importance morale et économique de la coopération en l'heure actuelle.* Munich: Congrès international de la recherche scientifique, 1957.

Hirschfeld, A. *Recherche coopérative et développement.* Paris: Institut français de la coopération, 1972.

Institut de recherches coopératives, Marburg, Germany. *Problèmes internationaux de la coopération.* Göttingen, Germany: Vandenhoeck and Ruprecht, 1960.

Institut für Genossenschaftswesen, Universität Hamburg. *Fifth International Conference on Cooperative Science, Hamburg, 1966. Theme: Planning in Cooperation.* Göttingen, Germany: Vandenhoeck and Ruprecht, 1967.

International Conference on Cooperative Science. *The Cooperative and the State.* Göttingen, Germany: Vandenhoeck and Ruprecht, 1965.

———. *The Cooperative Movement Today: Its Cultural, Social and Economic Position.* Göttingen, Germany: Vandenhoeck and Ruprecht, 1964.

International Cooperative Alliance. *Directory of Organizations Engaged in Cooperative Research.* London: ICA, 1973.

International Seminar on Research Sponsored by Developed Countries Relating to Cooperatives in Developing Countries. Warsaw: Polish Cooperative Research Institute and Hungarian Cooperative Research Institute, 1972; London: ICA, 1972.

Die internationale Genossenschaftsbewegung. Ihr Wachstum, ihre Struktur und ihre zukünftigen Möglichkeiten. Frankfurt: Deutsche Genossenschaftskasse, 1969.

Internationale Genossenschaftswissenschaftliche Tagung. *Die kulturelle, soziale und ökonomische Lage des Genossenschafts-wesens in der Gegenwart.* Göttingen, Germany: Vandenhoeck and Ruprecht, 1959.

Internationale Professoren-Konferenz des Genossenschaftswesens Freidorf bei Basel, 1952. *Aktuelle Genossenschaftsprobleme.* Bern: A. Franke, 1953.

Kimble, Helen, ed. *Second Cooperative Research Seminar, Wolfson College, Oxford, September, 1977.* Oxford: Plunkett, 1978.

Meister, A. *Quelques aspects méthodologiques de la recherche sociologique dans les associations volontaires et les groupements coopératifs.* Paris: BECC, 1962.

Münkner, Hans. *Short Analytical Review of Research Results on "Cooperatives and Rural Poverty" and Indication of Priorities for Future Research.* Rome, COPAC, 1978.

Research in Cooperation (in India)—A Review. Poona, India: Mehta, 1975.

Research Register of Studies on Cooperatives in Developing Countries and Selected Bibliography, Volumes 1–20. Geneva: ICA, 1975–1988. (A project of ICA in collaboration with the Cooperative Research Institute, Warsaw and Cooperative Research Institute, Budapest.)

Rural Cooperatives As Agents of Change: A Research Report and a Debate. Geneva: UNRISID, 1975.

Schultz, D. *VIII. Internationale genossenschaftswissenschaftliche Tagung 1975 in Darmstadt.* Darmstadt, Germany: Zeitschrift für das Gesamte Genossenschaftswesen, 1978.

Schuman, H. *Economic Development and Individual Change, the Comilla Experiment.* Cambridge, Mass.: Harvard University, 1967.

Sixth International Conference on Cooperative Science, Giessen 1969—Cooperatives in Economic Growth. Göttingen, Germany: Vandenhoeck and Ruprecht, 1969.

Verhagen, Koenrad C. W. *Cooperation for Survival—An Analysis of an Experiment in Participatory Research and Planning with Small Farmers in Sri Lanka and Thailand.* Wageningen, Netherlands: Royal Tropical Institute, 1984.

———. *The Organization of Production and Utilization of Cooperative Research.* Moshi, Tanzania: ICA, ROECSA, 1974.

V. F. 2. Evaluation of Cooperatives

Apthorpe, R., and D. Gasper. *Public Policy Evaluation, Meta-evaluation, and Essentialism: The Case of Rural Cooperatives.* The Hague: Institute of Social Studies, 1979.

Auto-évaluation des activités du centre IWACU: 1984–1990. Kigali, Rwanda: Centre de formation et de recherche coopératives (Rwanda), 1991.

Berthelot, J. *Criteria and Methods of Evaluating the Efficiency of Agricultural Cooperatives in Developing Countries.* Ann Arbor: University of Michigan, Center of Research on Economic Development, 1973.

Cooperative Program Note: Rural Cooperatives—Some Lessons and Suggestions from a UNDP Evaluation Study. Rome: COPAC, 1983.

Desroche, Henri. "Types de valeurs en evaluations coopératives." *Revue des études coopératives, 1980* (Paris) 202 (1980): 23–58.

Dülfer, Eberhard. *Guide to Evaluation of Cooperative Organizations in Developing Countries.* Rome: FAO, 1981.

———. *Leitfaden für die Evaluierung kooperativer Organisationen in Entwicklungsländern.* Göttingen, Germany: Vandenhoeck and Ruprecht, 1979.

Efficiency in the Performance of Cooperatives. Uppsala, Sweden: Scandinavian Institute of African Studies, 1973.

Hanel, A. *Report on the Introduction of the Tripartite Approach of Evaluating Cooperative Organizations with Particular Reference to Member Participation in Indonesia and of a Manual for the Evaluations of KUDs (Indonesian Farm Cooperatives).* Rome: FAO, 1982.

Hanel, A., and J. O. Mueller. *Improving the Methodology of Evaluating the Development of Rural Cooperatives in Developing Countries. Case Study—Iran.* Rome: FAO, 1978.

Kuhn, J., and H. Stoffregen. *How to Measure the Efficiency of Agricultural Cooperatives in Developing Countries—Kenya.* Rome: FAO, 1975.

Liboreiro, E. S. *Metodologia tentativa para la evaluación de empresas comunitarias campesinas (América Latina).* Bogota: IICA, 1976.

Report on the Expert Consultation on Improving the Methodology of Evaluation of Rural Cooperatives in Developing Countries. Rome: FAO, 1976.

Skillicorn, M. *The Measurement of Efficiency in Cooperative Retailing.* Loughborough, U.K.: Coop Union, 1958.

Widstrand, C. G., et al. *Seminar on Efficiency in the Performance of Cooperatives, Langata, Kenya, November, 1971.* Uppsala, Sweden: Scandinavian Institute of African Studies, 1972.

VI. COOPERATIVES AND THE STATE

VI. A. Cooperatives and the State—General Literature

Benecke, Dieter W., ed. *Las cooperativas y el estado, sus relaciones en el proceso de desarrollo.* Santiago: Instituto de Cooperativismo, 1970.

Capek, M. *Cooperatives and the State. Mutual Relations in Countries with Different Social Systems.* Prague: Central Cooperative Council, 1960.

Las cooperativas y el estado. Santiago: Instituto Chileno de Educación Cooperativa. 1970.

Cooperative Organization and the Intervention of Public Authorities in the Economic Field. Geneva: ILO, 1939.

Cooperatives and Government. Rome: COPAC, 1984.

Cooperatives and the State: A Report of the Discussions Held at the Meeting of the ICA Central Committee, 11–13 September 1978, Copenhagen, Denmark. London: ICA, 1980.

Cooperative Values and Relations between Cooperatives and the State. Working Papers of a Seminar in New Delhi, October 3–6, 1989. New Delhi: ICA, ROAP, 1990.

Daniel, A. *The Israeli Case With Regard to Interrelations Between the Government and the Cooperative Movement.* Tel Aviv: CIRCOM, 1974.

Germann, R. E. *Verwaltung und Einheitspartei in Tunesien unter besonderer Berücksichtigung des Genossenschaftswesens.* Zurich: Europa-Verlag, 1968.

Gyllstrom, Bjorn. *State Administered Rural Change: Agricultural Cooperatives in Kenya.* London and New York: Routledge, 1991.

Gyllstrom, Bjorn, and Franz-Michael Rundquist, eds. *State, Cooperatives, and Rural Change.* Lund, Sweden: Lund University Press, 1989.

Hanel, A. *State-Sponsored Cooperatives and Self-Reliance: Some Aspects of the Reorganization of Officialized Cooperative Structures With Regard to Africa.* Marburg, Germany: Institute for Cooperation in Developing Countries, 1989.

Holmen, Hans. *State, Cooperatives, and Development in Africa.* Uppsala, Sweden: Scandinavian Institute of African Studies, 1990.

ICA/ILO. *State and Cooperative Development.* Bombay: Allied Publishers, 1971.

International Conference on Cooperative Science. *The Cooperative and the State.* Göttingen, Germany: Vandenhoeck and Ruprecht, 1965.

Kramarovsky, Y. *Cooperatives and the State.* Moscow: Centrosoyus, 1969.

Londoño, C. M. *El estado y la acción politica del cooperativismo.* Bogota: Universidad Santo Tomás de Aquino, 1974.

———. *El movimiento cooperativo y el estado.* Buenos Aires: Intercoop, 1976.

Luz Filho, F. *El cooperativismo y el estado.* Buenos Aires: Intercoop, 1961.

Mars, L. *The Village and the State. Administration, Ethnicity and Politics in an Israeli Cooperative Village.* Farnborough, U.K.: Gower Publishing, 1980.

Parikh, G. O. *State and Cooperative Development in India with Special Reference to Cooperative Credit.* Tel Aviv: CIRCOM 1974.

Pastrana Polanco, Raul. *El estado y la cooperación.* Bogota: Editorial Alfa, 1955.
Rana, J. M. *Forms of Government Aid and Cooperative Democracy in South-East Asia.* New Delhi: ICA, ROECSEA, 1974.
Report on an International Symposium on Dynamics Between Agricultural Cooperatives and the Government. Tel Aviv: CIRCOM, 1974.
St. Siegens, George, and P. Pouros. *Les coopératives agricoles et le soutien de l'état dans les pays en voie de développement.* Rome: FAO, 1964.
Stanis, V. F., G. B. Khromushin, and V. P. Mozolin. *The Role of the State in Socio-Economic Reforms in Developing Countries.* Moscow: Progress Publishers, 1976.
State and Cooperative Development. New Delhi: ICA, ROECSEA, 1971; Bombay: Allied Publishers, 1971.
Vainstock, A. *El estado, la empresa y las sociedades cooperativas.* Buenos Aires: Intercoop, 1960.
Valko, Laszlo. *Economic Status of Cooperatives in Relation to the State.* Washington, D.C.: AIC, 1963.
Youngjohn, B. *Cooperation and the State, 1814–1914.* Loughborough, U.K.: Coop Union, Education Department, 1954.

VI. B. De-officialization of Cooperatives

Don, Y. *De-officializing Cooperatives: A Model for Policy Optimization.* Tel Aviv: CIRCOM, 1974.
Dublin, Jack. *Theoretical and Practical Issues in the Weaning Processes of Cooperatives.* Tel Aviv: CIRCOM, 1974.
Gentil, Dominique. *Les Mouvements coopératifs en Afrique de l'Ouest: Interventions de l'état ou organisations paysannes?* Paris: L'Harmattan, 1986.
Hanel, A. "Conditions for the Selected Problems of Deofficialization of Rural Cooperatives in Developing Countries—The Lessening of State Administrative Control." In *Cooperation as an Instrument for Rural Development,* M. Konopnicki and G. Vandewalle, eds. London: ICA, 1978.
———. *State Sponsored Cooperatives and Self-Reliance.* Marburg, Germany: Institute for Cooperation in Developing Countries, 1989.
Levi, Y. *The Cooperative Dilemma in Rural Developing Areas: Development "From Below" or "From Above."* Tel Aviv: CIRCOM, 1974.
Parnell, Edgar. *Movement to Movement Aid.* Rome: COPAC, 1983.
Report of the Seminar on the Role of Government in Promoting the Cooperative Movement in Developing Countries, Moscow, May, 1987. Vienna: UN Office at Vienna. 1987.

VI. C. Cooperative Legislation/Law

VI. C. 1. Cooperative Law—Early Literature—Through World War I (1919)

Deumer, R. *Das Recht der eingetragenen Genossenschaften.* Leipzig: Duncker and Humblot, 1912.

Gierke, Otto von. *Das deutsche Genossenschaftsrecht, 1868–1913.* Berlin: Weidmann, 1913.

———. *Die Genossenschaftstheorie und die deutsche Rechts-sprechung.* Berlin: Weidmann, 1887.

Kaff, S. *Aus dem Reich der britischen Genossenschaften.* Vienna: Druck und Verlag, 1909.

Kleine, F. *Rechtssprechung im Genossenschaftswesen.* Berlin: De Gruyter, 1919.

Nast, A. *Principes coopératifs et exposition synthétique de la législation.* Paris: Rivière, 1919.

———. *Le régime juridique des coopératives.* Paris: Jouve, 1919.

Rosin, H. *Das Recht der öffentlichen Genossenschaft.* Freiburg, Germany: Möhr, 1886.

Say, L. *Des sociétés de coopération et de leur constitution légale.* Paris: Rivière, 1865.

Scholz, E. *Rechtsbuch für Genossenschaften.* Berlin: Guttentag, 1908.

Stross, E. *Das österreichische Genossenschaftsrecht.* Vienna: Perles, 1887.

VI. C. 2. Cooperative Law—Literature—1920 to 1995

Alon, S. *Cooperative Legislation with Reference to Existing Laws in Various Countries.* Tel Aviv: Afro-Asian Institute for Cooperation, 1968.

Beuthien, Volker. *Genossensschaftsrecht—woher?, wohin? 100 Jahre Genossenschaftsgesetz 1889—1989.* Göttingen, Germany: Vandenhoeck and Ruprecht, 1989.

Calvert, H. *The Law and Principles of Cooperation.* Calcutta: Thacker, 1959.

Cardoso, M. *Bases para el derecho cooperativo americano.* Washington, D.C.: Unión Panamericana, 1950.

Casselman, Paul. *Cooperatives and Taxation.* Ottawa: University of Ottawa, 1945.

Chávez Nuñez, Fernando. *Estudio comparativo de la legislación cooperativa de América.* Washington, D.C.: Unión Panamericana, 1957.

Cooperative Legislation for Afro-Asian Countries, Guidelines and Model Bill. New Delhi: Afro-Asian Rural Reconstruction Organization, 1966.

Cooperative Legislation in Central and Eastern Europe Countries. Geneva: ILO and ICA, 1991.

Cooperatives and Federal Regulations: Proceedings of the Third National Symposium on Cooperatives and the Law, May 4–6, 1976, Madison, Wisconsin. Madison: University of Wisconsin, University Center for Cooperatives, 1976.

Coutant, Lucien. *L'évolution du droit coopératif de ses origines à 1950.* Reims: Matot-Braine, 1950.

Cracogna, Dante. *Comentarios a la ley de cooperativas.* Buenos Aires: Intercoop, 1985.

Daly Guevarra, J. *Derecho cooperativo.* Caracas: Universidad de Venezuela, 1967.

Davidovic, G. *The Law Position of Cooperatives in Various Countries.* Ottawa: CUC, 1963.

Digby, Margaret. *Digest of Cooperative Law at Home and Abroad.* London: Plunkett, 1933; London: P. S. King and Son, 1933.

Ebbert, K. *Genossenschaftsrecht auf internationaler Ebene.* Marburg, Germany: Philipps-Universität, Institut für Genossenschaftswesen, 1966.

Evans, F., and E. Stockdyk. *Laws of Agricultural Cooperative Marketing.* Rochester, N.Y.: Lawyers' Cooperative Publishing Company, 1937.

Fernández, S., S. Pérez, y M. Rebeco. *Derecho cooperativo.* Santiago: Editorial Quilantal, 1971.

Fuchs, C. *Genossenschaftsrecht und Genossenschaftswesen.* Leipzig: Gloekner, 1928.

Hulbert, Lyman S. *Legal Phases of Cooperative Associations.* Washington, D.C.: GPO, 1942.

International Cooperative Alliance—ROAP. *Cooperative Legislation in Asia—a Study. Parts One and Two.* New Delhi: ICA, ROAP, 1991.

Irrizarry, M., et al. *Aspectos legales del cooperativismo.* Río Piedras, Puerto Rico: Editorial Universitaria, 1965.

Jenkins, D. *Law for Cooperatives.* Oxford: Blackwell, 1958.

Jensen, A. *Cooperative Corporate Association Law.* Washington, D.C.: AIC, 1950.

Legislación básica sobre cooperativas. Madrid: Editorial Segura, 1991.

Legislación cooperativa—Informe del primer taller regional de legislación. San José, Costa Rica: Confederacion de Cooperativas del Caribe, 1989.

Leiserson, S. *La cooperación, su régimen jurídico.* Buenos Aires: Impresora Argentina, 1927.

Luis y Navas, J. *Derecho de cooperativas.* Barcelona: Bosch, 1972.

Lockhardt, J. *Étude comparative du droit de la coopération agricole en Europe.* Brugg, Switzerland: Publications de la CEA, 1963.

Louis, Raymond. *La législation coopérative dans les pays en voie de développement.* Geneva: BIT, 1975.

Mavrogiannis, D. *USSR, Consultancy on Cooperative Legislation.* Geneva: ILO, 1988.

McAuslan, J. P. "Cooperatives and the Law in East Africa." In *Cooperatives and Rural Development in East Africa,* C. C. Widstrand, ed., 81–120. Uppsala, Sweden: Scandinavian Institute of African Studies, 1970.

Münkner, Hans H. *Comparative Study of Cooperative Law in Africa.* Marburg, Germany: Marburg Consult for Self-Help Promotion, 1989.

———. *Cooperative Law in the Federal Republic of Germany.* Marburg, Germany: Institute for Cooperation in Developing Countries, 1989.

———. *Cooperative Principles and Cooperative Law.* Marburg, Germany: Institut für Genossenschaftswesen in Entwicklungsländern, 1974.

———. *The Legal Status of Pre-Cooperatives.* Bonn/Bad Godesberg: Friedrich Ebert Foundation, 1979.

———. *New Trends in Cooperative Law of English Speaking Countries of Africa.* Marburg, Germany: Philipps-Universität, Institute for Cooperation in Developing Countries, 1974.

———. *Six Lectures on Cooperative Law.* Bonn: Friedrich Ebert Foundation, 1978.

Nast, A. *Code de la coopération.* Paris: Sirey, 1928.

Nourse, E. G. *The Legal Status of Agricultural Cooperation.* New York: Macmillan, 1927.

Packel, Israel. *The Law of the Organization and Operation of Cooperatives.* Albany, N.Y.: Bender, 1947.

Scott, S. *European Post-war Cooperative Legislation.* London: Plunkett, 1954.

Sharma, B. D. *Company Law and Cooperative Law: A Comparative Study.* New Delhi: NCUI, 1983.

Sullivan, J. M. *Abstract of Cooperative Legislation in Canada.* Ottawa: Department of Agriculture, 1966.

Surridge, Brewster J., and Margaret Digby. *A Manual of Cooperative Law and Practice.* Cambridge, U.K.: Heffer and Sons, 1958.

Tereshtenko, Valery. *Bibliographical Review of the Literature on Legal Phases of Cooperation.* New York: WPA, 1941.

Torres Lara, C. *Legislación de cooperativas.* Lima.

Valko, Laszlo. *The Cooperative Law in Asia.* Pullman: Washington State University, 1969.

———. *The First Cooperative Law.* Pullman: Washington State University, 1952.

———. *International Handbook of Cooperative Legislation.* Pullman: Washington State University, 1954.

Villalón Galdames, A. *Bibliografía jurídica de América Latina 1810–1965.* Santiago: Editorial Jurídica de Chile, 1966.

Weeraman, P. E. *The Effect of Cooperative Law on the Autonomy of Cooperatives in South-East Asia.* New Delhi: ICA, ROECSEA, 1974.

———. *A Model Cooperative Law.* New Delhi: ICA, ROECSEA, 1971.

———. *The Role of Law in Cooperative Development.* New Delhi: ICA, ROECSEA, 1971.

Weeraman, P.E., and R. C. Dwivedi. *Indian Cooperative Law vis-à-vis Cooperative Principles.* New Delhi: ICA, ROECSEA, 1986.

Yeo, Peter. *Cooperative Law in Practice: A Handbook of Legislation for Cooperative Development.* Oxford: Plunkett Foundation and Holyoake Books, 1989.

VII. COOPERATIVE EXPERIENCE AND/OR HISTORIES

VII. A. Precooperative Traditions

Castro-Pozzo, H. *Del ayllu al cooperativismo socialista.* Lima: Librería J. Mejía Baca, 1936.

Gosselin, G. *Développement et tradition dans les sociétés rurales africaines.* Geneva: BIT, 1970.

Guevara, L. *Granjas comunales indígenas.* Lima: Empresa Periodísticas, 1945.

Matos, J. *Las actuales comunidades indígenas.* Lima: Universidad de San Marcos, 1958.

Urquidi, A. *Las comunidades indígenas en Bolivia.* Cochabamba: Editorial Los Amigos del Libro, 1971.

VII. B. Histories of Early Cooperative Activity

Barou, Noah. *World Cooperation, 1844–1944.* London: Gollancz, 1944.
Cole, G. D. H. *A Century of Cooperation.* Manchester: Coop Union, 1944.
Flanagan, Desmond. *The Cooperative Movement's First 100 Years.* London: Pilot Press, 1944.
Holyoake, George J. *The History of Cooperation.* London: T. F. Unwin, 1908.
Knapp, Martin A. *The Advent of Cooperation.* Philadelphia: International Printing Company, 1912.
Malherbe, G. *Les fromageries ou fruitères coopératives.* Brussels: Schopers, 1899.
Milliot, L. *L'association agricole chez les Musulmans du Maghreb.* Paris: Rousseau, 1911.
Pelletier, E. *Du mouvement coopératif international, étude théorique et pratique sur les différentes formes de l'association.* Paris: Guillaumin et Dentu, 1867.
Rochdale Pioneers Museum, Toad Lane. Manchester: Holyoake Books, 1990.
Schärr., J. F. *Genossenschaftliche Reden und Schriften—Pioniere und Theoretiker des Genossenschaftswesens.* Basel: VSK, 1920.
Walras, Leon. *Les associations populaires de consommation, de production et de crédit.* Paris: Dentu, 1865; reissued, Rome: Bizzarri, 1969.
Webb, Beatrice Potter. *The Cooperative Movement in Great Britain.* London: S. Sonnenschein, 1893; reissued, Brookfield, Vt.: Gower, 1987.

VII. C. General Cooperative Histories—20th Century

VII. C. 1. Cooperative Histories—Published 1900 to 1950

Cerda y Richart, Baldomero. *Resumen histórico del movimiento cooperativo mundial.* Barcelona: [n.p.], 1942.
Cole, G. D. H. *A Century of Cooperation.* Manchester: Coop Union, 1944.
Cramois, A. *La coopération agricole dans les colonies françaises.* Paris: Fédération nationale de la mutualité, 1932.
Edwards, Gladys Talbott. *The Second Hundred Years of Cooperatives.* Denver: Farmers' Educational and Cooperative Union of America, 1947.
Fabian Colonial Bureau. *Cooperation in the Colonies.* London: Allen and Unwin, 1945.
Fay, Charles R. *Cooperation at Home and Abroad.* London: P. S. King and Son, 1908; New York: Macmillan, 1908; Revised, 3rd edition, 1925; Revised, 4th edition, 1936.
———. *Cooperation at Home and Abroad, A Description and Analysis (1908–1938).* London: P. S. King and Son, 1939.

———. *Cooperation at Home and Abroad: A Description and Analysis.* London and New York: Staples Press, 1948.

Flanagan, Desmond. *The Cooperative Movement's First 100 Years.* London: Pilot Press, 1944.

Gaumont, J. *Histoire abrégée de la coopération en France et à l'étranger.* Paris: Rieder, 1921.

Gould, Frederick J. *Working Together: Cooperation Through the Ages.* Manchester: Coop Union, 1931.

Lavergne, B. *Le progrès des coopératives de consommation en Europe (1900–1910).* Paris: Larose, 1911.

———. *Le régime coopératif, étude générale de la coopération de consommation en Europe.* Paris: A. Rousseau, 1908.

Miller, Allen D. *The Cooperative Movement: Today and Tomorrow.* London: Hogarth Press, 1936.

Palmer, R. *World Cooperation: A Record of International Cooperative Relations.* Manchester: Coop Union, 1937.

Smith-Gordon, L. *Cooperation in Many Lands.* Manchester: Coop Union, 1919.

Tardy, L., and Maurice Colombain. *La coopération dans les colonies.* Paris: FNCC, 1931.

Totomiants, Vakhan. *La coopération mondiale, histoire, organisation et principes.* Villeneuve St. Georges, France: Imprimerie Coopérative l'union typographie, 1923.

Warbasse, Agnes D. *The Story of Cooperation.* New York: CLUSA, 3rd edition, 1921.

VII. C. 2. Cooperative Histories—Published 1951 to 1995

Back, J. M. *The Cooperative Movement Today: Its Cultural, Social and Economic Position.* Göttingen, Germany: Vandenhoek and Ruprecht, 1961.

Bedi, Raghubans D. *Theory, History and Practice of Cooperation,* Meerut, India: International Publishing House, 1966.

Birchall, Johnston. *The International Cooperative Movement.* Manchester: Manchester University Press, 1997.

Bogardus, Emory S. *History of Cooperation, for Discussion Circles.* Chicago: CLUSA, 2nd edition, 1955.

Developments and Trends in the World Cooperative Movement. Geneva: ILO, 1962.

Digby, Margaret. *The World Cooperative Movement.* London: Hutchinson University Library, 1948; reissued, 1965.

Gaudibert, Jean Claude. *L'hydre aux oeufs d'or: Les choix solidaristes en France et dans le monde.* Paris: Godin, 1980.

Gaumont, J. *125 ans d'histoire coopérative.* Paris: [n.p.], 1960.

Hasselmann, Erwin. *Die internationale Genossenschaftbewegung (1947–1951).* Hamburg: Deutsche Konsumgenossenschaften, 1951.

International Cooperation 1949–1957, Reports on 74 Cooperative Organizations in 38 Countries. London: ICA, 1961.

Martínez, B. and Juan Ramón. *Historia del movimiento cooperativo.* Tegucigalpa, Honduras: Instituto de Formación e Investigación Cooperativista, 1976.

Modern Cooperatives and Traditional Rural Societies: Notes and Opinions by a Group of Experts. Tel Aviv: CIRCOM, 1968.

OIT, Comité de Correspondencia de la Cooperación. *Aspectos del cooperativismo mundial.* Bogota: Imprenta Nacional, 1954.

Preuss, Walter. *Modern Trends in the World Cooperative Movement.* Tel Aviv: Institute for Labor Studies and Cooperation, 1960.

Rhodes, Rita. *The International Cooperative Alliance in War and Peace 1910–1950.* Geneva: ICA, 1995.

Ritter, U. *Comunidades indigenas y cooperativismo en el Perú.* Bilbao: Ediciones Deusto, 1965.

Roy, Ewell P. *Cooperatives Today and Tomorrow.* Danville, Ill.: Interstate Printers, 2nd edition, 1969.

Saxena, K. K. *Evolution of Cooperative Thought.* Bombay: Somaiya Publications, 1974.

Seibel, H. D., and A. Massing. *Traditional Organizations and Economic Development: Studies of Indigenous Cooperatives in Liberia.* New York: Praeger, 1974.

Soldevilla y Villar, Antonio D. *El movimiento cooperativista mundial—Sus orígenes, desarrollo y problemática actual.* Valladolid: Talleres Graficos Seres, 1973.

Spaull, Hebe. *The Cooperative Movement in the World Today.* London: Barrie and Rockliff, 1965.

Stettner, Leonora. *Cooperation Today.* Manchester: Coop Union, 1969.

Texier, J. M. *Formas no convencionales de cooperación.* Bogota: Fundación para la Capacitación e Investigación Aplicada a la Reforma Agraria, 1970.

Watkins, W. P. *International Cooperation, 1937–1949.* London: ICA, 1953.

———. *Die internationale Genossenschaftsbewegung.* Frankfurt: Deutsche Genossenschaftskasse, 1970.

Wieting, Maurice. *The Progress of Cooperatives.* New York: Harper, 1952.

VII. D. Regional Cooperative Experience

VII. D. 1. Cooperative Experience—Europe

Agricultural Cooperative Organizations in the EEC. London: Central Council for Agricultural and Horticultural Cooperation, 1970.

Commission des Communautés. *Instruments financiers spécifiques pour les entreprises d'économie sociale: Titres subordonnés et fonds européen: Rapport final.* Luxembourg: Office des publications officielles des Communautés européenes, 1993.

La coopération agricole dans la Communauté économique européenne. Brussels: COGECA, 1967.

La coopération agricole française et quelques aspects des coopératives agricoles dans les pays de la CEE. Paris: Confédération française de la coopération agricole, 1971.

Cooperative Action in Rural Development. European Conference on Rural Life, Geneva, 1939. Geneva: ILO, 1939.

Cooperative Organizations and Post-War Relief. Montreal: ILO, 1943.

Correard, J. *Les coopératives de consommation en France et à l'étranger.* Paris: Lethielleux, 1908.

Cowden, Howard. *A Trip to Cooperative Europe.* North Kansas City, Mo.: Consumers Cooperative Association, 1934.

Crews, Cecil R., ed. *Europe's Coops as We Saw Them.* Chicago: CLUSA, 1947.

Études monographiques sur la coopération agricole dans quelques pays. Rome: Institut international d'agriculture, 1911. (Also in English.)

A European Challenge. Tübingen: AGI, 1985.

Fagneux, Louis. *La caisse de crédit Raiffeisen. Le raiffeisenisme en France et à l'étranger.* Paris: A Leclerc, 1908.

Faust, Helmut. *Geschichte der Genossenschaftsbewegung: Ursprung und Aufbruch der Genossenschaftsbewegung in England, Frankreich und Deutschland sowie weitere Entwicklung im deutsch Sprachraum.* Frankfurt: Knapp, 1977.

Gide, Charles. *La coopération dans les pays latins.* Paris: Association pour l'enseignement de la coopération, 1925.

Gustav, Theo. *Die Eigenarten der Entstehung der modernen Genossenschaftsbewegungen in Deutschland, England und Frankreich.* Coblenz: Krabbensche Buchdruckerei, 1940.

Halbert, Leroy A., Henryk J. Szoszkies, and Valery Tereshtenko. *Task of the Cooperatives in Post-War Relief and Reconstruction.* Washington, D.C.: CLUSA, 1943.

Hanel, A. *Die Einkaufsgenossenschaften des Handwerks in den Ländern der Europäischen Wirtschaftsgemeinschaft.* Marburg, Germany: Universität Marburg, Institut für Genossenschaftswesen, 1962.

Heckman, J., and J. Wheeler. *Agricultural Cooperation in Europe.* Washington, D.C.: USDA, 1955.

———, and Anna Wheeler. *Agricultural Cooperation in Western Europe: The Benelux Countries.* Washington, D.C.: USDA, FCS, 1954.

The Impact of the European Union's Enlargement on Cooperatives (Studies and Reports No. 31). Geneva: ICA, 1998.

Instituto Italiano di Studi Cooperativi "Luigi Luzzatti." *La Législation en vigeur dans les pays de la Communauté Européenne en matière d'entreprises coopératives, dans la perspective du marché commun.* Luxembourg: Office des publications officielles des Communautés européennes, 1993.

International Cooperative Reconstruction Conference, Washington, D.C., 1944. Coops Plan for the Post-War World. Chicago and New York. CLUSA, 1944.

Leclerc, Andre. *Les Doctrines coopératives en Europe et au Canada: Naissance, évolution et interrelations.* Sherbrooke, Quebec: IRECUS, 1982.

Lockhardt, J. *Étude comparative du droit de la coopération en Europe.* Brugg, Switzerland: Publications de la Confédération européenne de l'agriculture, 1963.
————. *Agricultural Cooperation in the European Economic Community.* Brussels: European Economic Community, 1967.
Möller, H. *Fischereigenossenschaftswesen und Fischwirtschaft in Deutschland und anderen europäischen Fischereiländern.* Düsseldorf: Triltisch, 1959.
Müller, Julius O. *Voraussetzungen und Verfahrensweisen bei der Errichtung von Genossenschaften in Europa vor 1900: Analyse der Strategien des Genossenschaftsaufbaus in dem Frühstadien der industriewirtschaftlichen Entwicklung.* Göttingen, Germany: Vandenhoeck and Ruprecht, 1976.
Norema-Bastos, E. *Étude comparative des modèles de groupements agricoles dans cinq pays du bassin méditerranéen: Algérie, Espagne, Israel, Italie et Yougoslavie.* Paris: CIHEAM, Options Mediterranées, 1971.
Parker, Florence E. *Cooperative Associations in Europe and Their Possibilities for Post-War Reconstruction.* Washington, D.C.: Department of Labor, 1944.
————. *Cooperatives in Post-War Europe.* Washington, D.C.: GPO, 1948.
Parrao, O. *Aspectos del movimiento cooperativo: Estudios y observaciones de un viaje por América y Europa.* Santiago: Imp. Cultura, 1938.
Peters, E. T. *Cooperative Credit Associations in Certain European Countries and Their Relations to Agricultural Interests.* Washington, D.C.: GPO, 1915.
Plunkett Foundation. *Agricultural Cooperatives in Europe.* Slough, U.K.: Commonwealth Agricultural Bureau, 1976.
Pudor, H. *Das landwirtschaftliche Genossenschaftswesen im Ausland.* Leipzig: Dietrich, 1904.
Rapport du conseil supérieur de la coopération—Le mouvement coopératif dans l'union européenne. Brussels: Ministère de l'emploi et de la solidarité, 1998.
Report of the Inquiry on Cooperative Enterprise in Europe, 1937. Washington, D.C.: GPO, 1937.
Reus, A. *Influencia de la cooperación en la cuestión social europea.* Toledo: Vinda, 1918.
Rhyn, A. *Cooperative Systems in Scandinavia and the Baltic States.* Washington, D.C.: Bureau of Foreign Commerce, 1936.
Richter, Oswald. *Die Einkaufsgenossenschaften des selbständigen Einzelhandels in den Ländern der Europaischen Wirtschafts-gemeinschaft.* Marburg, Germany: Universität Marburg, Institut für Genossenschaftswesen, 1962.
Riddell, Glenn E. *Buying and Selling by Cooperatives in Europe.* Washington, D.C.: GPO, 1950.
Roure i Gavines, J. *Cooperative Structure in the European Economic Community.* Barcelona: Fundacio Roca Galès, 1987.
Strickland, C. *Studies in European Cooperation.* Lahore, Pakistan: GPO, 1922–1925.
Tereshtenko, Valery. *Cooperatives and the Problem of Post-War Relief and Rehabilitation.* Washington, D.C.: USDA, 1943.
Villeneuve, J. G. de *Les coopératives dans le marché commun: études comparées, régime juridique, fiscal, social et financier.* Paris: Dictionnaires A. Joly, 1970.

Watkins, W. *Cooperation in the European Market Economies.* London: ICA, 1967.

VII. D. 2. Cooperative Experience—Eastern Europe

Balawyder, Aloysius, ed. *Cooperative Movements in Eastern Europe: Proceedings of the Stephen B. Roman Symposium, St. Francis Xavier University, Antigonish, Nova Scotia, October, 1978.* Montclair, N.J.: Allanhead, Osmun, 1980.

Cusin, Alexander C. *The International Cooperative Federations Union With a Project for a Uniform Cooperative Organization in a Federated Eastern Europe.* New York: Mid-European Studies Center of the National Committee for a Free Europe, 1953.

International Conference on Cooperative Property and Privatization. Geneva: ICA, 1993.

Klimov, Aleksandr P. *La démocratie coopérative aujourd'hui.* Moscow: Éditions de l'agence de presse Novosti, 1970.

Ruwwe, Hans-Friedrich. *Die Stellung der Konsumgenossenschaften im Sozialismus Osteuropas.* Tübingen: Mohr, 1972.

Seraphim, Peter H. *Das Genossenschaftswesen in Osteuropa.* Neuwied: Verlag der Raiffeisendruckerei, 1951.

Studies and Reports: Cooperatives in Eastern and Central Europe. Geneva: ICA, 1992–1994. A series including the following: Juhasz, Janos. *Hungary.* 1992; Kowalak, Tadeusz. *Poland.* 1993; Ahnlund, Mats. *Estonia, Latvia & Lithuania.* 1993; Sozánski, Gabriella. *Romania.* 1994; Bosiak, V., E. Jergová, V. Majerník, and F. Manda. *Slovakia.* 1994; Mavrogiannis, Dionysos. *Bulgaria.* 1994.

VII. D. 3. Cooperative Experience—North America

Banks for Cooperatives, A Quarter Century of Progress. Washington, D.C.: FCA, 1960.

Daniels, John. *American Cooperatives, Yesterday, Today, Tomorrow.* New York: New Leader Publishing Association, 1945.

Derber, M. *The American Idea of Industrial Democracy, 1865–1965.* Urbana: University of Illinois Press, 1970.

Fulton, Murray E., ed. *Cooperative Organizations and Canadian Society: Popular Institutions and the Dilemmas of Change.* Toronto and Buffalo: University of Toronto Press, 1990.

Good, William C. *Farmer Citizen: My Fifty Years in the Canadian Farmers' Movement.* Toronto: Ryerson Press, 1958.

History of Cooperation in the United States. Baltimore: Johns Hopkins University, 1888; reprinted, New York: Johnson Reprint Corporation, 1973.

Holman, Charles. *American Cooperation.* Washington, D.C.: AIC, 1926 (published annually).

Knapp, Joseph G. *The Advance of American Cooperative Enterprise.* Danville, Ill.: Interstate Publishers, 1972.

————. *The Rise of American Cooperative Enterprise, 1620–1920.* Danville, Ill.: Interstate Printers, 1969.

Lipset, S. *Agrarian Socialism, the Cooperative Commonwealth Federation in Saskatchewan. A Study in Political Sociology.* New York: Doubleday, 1950.

MacPherson, Ian. *Building and Protecting the Cooperative Movement: A Brief History of the Cooperative Union of Canada, 1909–1984.* Ottawa: CUC, 1984.

————. *The Cooperative Movement on the Prairies, 1900–1955.* Ottawa: Canadian Historical Association, 1979.

Parker, Florence E. *Cooperative Movement in the United States in 1925 (Other Than Agricultural).* Washington, D.C.: GPO, 1927.

Patterns and Trends of Canadian Cooperative Development. Downsville, Ontario, Canada: Cooperative Future Directions Project, 1982.

Thompson, Rollie. *People Do It All the Time: How Community-Based Enterprises Across Canada Are Successfully Meeting the Needs of Their Communities.* Toronto: Macmillan Canada, 1976.

Voorhis, Horace Jeremiah (Jerry). *American Cooperatives; Where They Come From, What They Do, Where They Are Going.* New York: Harper, 1961; reprinted, Westport, Conn.: Greenwood Press, 1973.

Wood, L. A. *A History of Farmers' Movements in Canada.* Toronto: Ryerson Press, 1924.

VII. D. 4. Cooperative Experience—Developing Countries

VII. D. 4. a. Cooperative Experience—Developing Countries—General

Barratt, Neal. *The Cooperative Model as an Instrument in the Community Economic Development Process.* Grahamstown, South Africa: Rhodes University, Institute of Social and Economic Research, 1989.

Benecke, Dieter W. *Kooperation und Wachstum in Entwicklungsländern.* Tübingen: Mohr, 1972.

Campbell, William K. H. *Practical Cooperation in Asia and Africa.* Cambridge, U.K.: W. Heffer, 1951.

Carroll, T. F., et al. *A Review of Rural Cooperation in Developing Areas: Papers on Latin America, Asia and Africa.* Geneva: UNRISID, 1969.

The Changing Pattern of Cooperative Development. Report of a Symposium, Wageningen, March 1977. Rome: COPAC, 1977.

Chinchankar, P. Y., and M. V. Namjoshi. *Cooperation and the Dynamics of Change.* Bombay: Somaiya Publications, 1977.

Colloque international de Tel-Aviv. *Coopération en agriculture et développement rural.* Paris: Mouton, 1965.

La coopération de production et l'industrialisation du Tiers monde. Paris: CGSCOP, 1962.

Cooperation in the Developing Countries. Loughborough, U.K.: Coop Union, Education Department, 1966.

Cooperation in the United Kingdom Dependencies. London: Central Office of Information, 1961.

Cooperative Development Decade 1971–1980. London: ICA, 1972.

The Cooperative Network in Developing Countries. A Statistical Picture. Rome: COPAC, 1984.

Cooperative Thrift, Credit and Marketing in Economically Underdeveloped Countries. Rome: FAO, 1953.

Cooperatives and Cooperative Problems in Developing Countries. Stockholm: SCC, 1963.

Cooperatives as Institutions for Development of the Rural Poor. Dacca, Bangladesh: Center on Integrated Rural Development for Asia and the Pacific (CIRDAP), Study Series Number 86, 1986.

Digby, Margaret. *Cooperatives.* London: Overseas Development Institute, 1963.

Dülfer, Eberhard. *Zur Krise der Genossenschaften in der Entwicklungspolitik.* Göttingen, Germany: Vandenhoeck and Ruprecht, 1975.

Engelmann, Konrad. *Building Cooperative Movements in Developing Countries: The Sociological and Psychological Aspects.* New York: Praeger, 1968; Frankfurt: Deutsche Genossenschaftskasse, 1966 (German).

Fabian Society, Colonial Bureau. *Cooperation in the Colonies.* London: G. Allen and Unwin, 1945.

Farmer Cooperatives in Developing Countries. Washington, D.C.: Advisory Committee on Overseas Cooperative Development, 1971.

Gorst, Sheila. *Cooperative Organization in Tropical Countries.* Oxford: Blackwell, 1959.

Hubert-Valleroux, Paul. *Les associations coopératives en France et à l'étranger.* Paris: Guillaumin, 1884.

International Cooperative Seminar, 43rd, Dresden, September, 1975. *Technical Assistance for Cooperatives in Developing Countries, Need and Response.* London: ICA, 1976.

Klower, Gerd G. *Genossenschaften in Entwicklungsländern: Genese, Innovation und Diffusion: Ein Beitrag zur Entwicklungspolitik.* Göttingen, Germany: O. Schwartz, 1981.

Konopnicki, Maurice, and G. Vandewalle, eds. *Cooperation as an Instrument for Rural Development. Papers from an International Conference Organized at Ghent University, Belgium, September, 1976.* London: ICA, 1978.

Konrad-Adenauer-Stiftung. *Genossenschaftsprobleme in Deutschland und in den Entwicklungsländern.* Mainz: Hase and Koehler, 1969.

Krebs, H. *Consumer Cooperatives and Developing Countries.* Bonn: Friedrich Ebert Foundation, 1968.

Levi, Y. *The Cooperative Dilemma in Rural Developing Areas: Development "From Below" or "From Above."* Tel Aviv: CIRCOM, 1974.

Mamoria, C. B., and Rameshwar Saxena. *Cooperation in Foreign Lands.* Allahabad, India: Kitab Mahal, 1963.

Modern Cooperatives and Traditional Rural Societies. Tel Aviv: CIRCOM, 1968.

Le mouvement coopératif en territoires tropicaux arriérés. Deuxième symposium international d'économie rural tropicale, 1952. Leiden: Universitaire Piers Leiden, 1953.

Mouvements coopératifs en Afrique noire et à Madagascar. Paris: Institut français d'action coopérative, Collège coopératif, 1964.

Nicholson, M. *Cooperation in the British Colonies.* Manchester: Coop Union, 1953.

Petersen, Günter. *Genossenschaften in Britisch-Indien und Tropisch-Afrika.* Hamburg: Hansischer Gildenverlag, 1939.

Taimni, K. K. *Consumers' Cooperatives in Third World Strategy for Development.* Poona, India: Harshad Prakashan, 1978.

Talek Biki, F. *The Idea of Cooperation and Cooperative Experience in Developing Countries.* Teheran: Teheran University, 1970.

United Kingdom Parliament. Advisory Committee on Cooperatives. *Cooperatives Overseas: Report.* London: H. M. S. O., 1964.

United States. General Accounting Office. *AID Must Consider Social Factors in Establishing Cooperatives in Developing Countries.* Washington, D.C.: GPO, 1980.

Viswanathan, M. *Cooperation in Foreign Countries.* Madras: Asoka Publications, 1950.

Ward, G. H. *The Structure and Organization of Cooperatives in Developing Nations.* Madison: University of Wisconsin, 1969.

Webster, F. H., and B. J. Surridge. *Cooperative Thrift, Credit, Marketing and Supply in Developing Countries.* Rome: FAO, 1977.

Why Cooperatives Succeed . . . and Fail. Washington, D.C.: Overseas Cooperative Development Committee, 1985.

Zavidov, R. *L'expérience israélienne du développement des villages coopératifs dans les pays neufs.* Paris: Centre de recherches coopératives, 1974.

VII. D. 4. b. Cooperative Experience—Africa

Aldington, T. J. *Report to the Governments of Kenya, Tanzania and Uganda on Agricultural Cooperation in the East African Community.* Rome: FAO, 1974.

Anangisye, E. M. *Cooperative Shops in Africa.* London: Transafrica, 1977.

Apeadu, Kwafo. *The Cooperative Movement (in West Africa).* London: Bureau of Current Affairs, 1951.

Apthorpe, Raymond. *Peasants and Planistrators and Rural Cooperatives in Eastern Africa—1960–1970.* Norwich, U.K.: University of East Anglia, 1975.

———. *Rural Cooperatives and Planned Change in Africa—An Analytical Overview.* Geneva: UNRISID, 1972.

Belloncle, Guy. *Coopératives et développement en Afrique noire sahelienne.* Sherbrooke, Quebec: Université de Sherbrooke, 1978.

Belloncle, Guy, and Dominique Gentil. *Policies and Structures for Cooperative Promotion in Sahelian Africa (Mali, Niger, Senegal, Upper Volta).* Rome: COPAC, 1983.

Boyer, M. *Les sociétés indigènes de prévoyance, de secours et de prêt mutuels agricoles en Afrique occidentale française.* [n.l.]: Domat-Montchretien, 1935.

Buckley, et al. *Die Genossenschaftsbewegung in Afrika.* Bonn: Friedrich-Ebert-Stiftung, 1965.

Campbell, W. H. *Practical Cooperation in Asia and Africa.* Cambridge, U.K.: Heffer and Sons, 1951.

Cave, Roy C. *Cooperative Development and Outlook in East and Central Africa.* San Francisco: San Francisco State College, Consumer Research Institute, 1961.

Compte rendu séminaire de l'ACI sur les unions coopératives, Abidjan, March, 1979. Moshi, Tanzania: ICA, ROECSA, 1979.

Comte, Bernard. *Développement rural et coopération en Afrique tropicale.* Fribourg, Switzerland: Éditions universitaires, 1968.

La Coopération en Afrique. Abidjan: Office national de la promotion rurale, 1979.

Cooperative Marketing Development in Africa. Three Case Studies from Nigeria, the Sudan and Tanzania. Oxford: Plunkett, 1976.

The Cooperative Movement in Africa. New York: UN, Economic Commission for Africa, 1962.

Cooperative Movements in Afro-Asian Countries. New Delhi: Afro-Asian Rural Reconstruction Organization, 1969.

Les coopératives: Bibliographie. Abidjan: INADES-documentation, 1980–1983.

Les coopératives en Afrique: symposium, Mai 1977, Université de Sherbrooke. Sherbrooke, Quebec: CEDEC, 1977.

Cramois, A. *La coopération agricole dans les colonies françaises.* Paris: Fédération nationale de la mutualité, 1932.

Crellin, G. F. *The Development of Intra-African Trade Through Cooperatives: A Preliminary Study.* Paris: International Federation of Agricultural Producers, 1969.

Degraft-Johnson, T. C. *African Experiment: Cooperative Agriculture and Banking in British West Africa.* London: Watts, 1958.

Derman, W. *Cooperatives, Initiative, Participation and Socio-Economic Change in the Sahel.* Ann Arbor: University of Michigan, 1978.

Dia, Mamadou. *Contribution à l'étude du mouvement coopératif en Afrique noire.* Paris: Présence africaine, 1958.

Directory of Cooperative Organizations—Africa, South of the Sahara. Geneva: ILO, 1975.

Étude socio-économique. Quelques données sur le mouvement coopératif dans le bassin du Fleuve Sénégal (Sénégal, Mali, Mauritanie). Dakar: Organisation pour la mise en valeur du Fleuve Sénégal, 1978.

Favier, J. *Effets et rôles de la formule coopérative dans le procéssus de développement en Afrique noire francophone.* Grenoble: Institut d'études politiques, 1969.

Fischer, P. H. *Genossenschaften in Westafrika: Dahomey, Elfenbeinküste, Niger, Obervolta.* Marburg, Germany: Institut für Genossenschafswesen in Entwicklungsländern der Universität Marburg, 1970.

Frank, M. *Cooperative Land Settlements in Israel and Their Relevance to African Countries.* Tübingen: Mohr, 1968.

Die Genossenschaftsbewegung in Afrika. Bonn: Friedrich-Ebert-Stiftung, 1965.

Genossenschaftswesen in Afrika: Jüngste Entwicklung, 1966–80: Kurzbibliographie. Hamburg: Institut für Afrika-Kunde im Verband der Stiftung Deutsches Ubersee-Institut, Dokumentations-Leitstelle Afrika, 1981.

Gentil, Dominique. *Les mouvements coopératifs en Afrique de l'Ouest.* Paris: L'Harmattan, 1986.

———. *Les pratiques coopératives en milieu rural africain.* Sherbrooke, Quebec: CEDEC, 1979.

Gosselin, G. *Développement et traditions dans les sociétés rurales africaines.* Geneva: BIT, 1970.

Guidelines for the Implementation of the Regional Cooperative Development Decade, 1985–1995. Moshi, Tanzania: ICA, ROECSA, 1984.

Hedlund, Hans, ed. *Cooperatives Revisited.* Uppsala, Sweden: Scandinavian Institute of African Studies, 1988.

Holman, Hans. *State, Cooperatives and Development in Africa.* Uppsala, Sweden: Scandinavian Institute of African Studies, 1990.

Hyden, Goran. *Efficiency Versus Distribution in East African Cooperatives: A Study in Organizational Conflicts.* Nairobi: East African Literature Bureau, 1973.

Inter-African Conference on Cooperative Societies: Report. London: [n.p.], 1959.

Jucker-Fleetwood, E. *Money and Finance in Africa.* New York: Praeger, 1965.

Kane, P., ed. *Symposium 6 mai 1977: Les coopératives en Afrique.* Sherbrooke, Quebec: Université de Sherbrooke, Institut de recherche et d'enseignement pour les coopératives, 1977.

Lamb, G. B. *Public Policy, Cooperative Organization and Agricultural Development in East Africa.* Brighton, U.K.: Institute of Development Studies, University of Sussex, 1973.

Le Floch, Georges, Henri Desroche, et al. *Mouvements coopératifs en Afrique noire (Cameroun, Côte d'Ivoire, Mali, Congo, Rwanda, Dahomey) et à Madagascar: Bilan et perspectives.* Paris: Bureau pour le développement de la production agricole, 1964.

Maslennikov, Vladimir P. *The Cooperative Movement in Asia and Africa: Problems and Prospects.* Moscow: Progress Publishers, 1990.

Millette, M. *Problèmes de commerce coopératif international de produits agricoles en Afrique francophone.* Sherbrooke, Quebec: Université de Sherbrooke, Centre d'études en économie coopérative. 1975.

Münkner, Hans H. *Challenges Facing ACCOSCA in the Second Decade.* Marburg, Germany: Institute for Cooperation in Developing Countries, 1979.

———. *Comparative Study of Cooperative Law in Africa: Six Country Reports (Burkina Faso, Ghana, Ivory Coast, Nigeria, Senegal, Tanzania) and General Report.* Marburg, Germany: Marburg Consult for Self-Help Promotion, 1989.

———. *Die Organisation der eingetragenen Genossenschaften in den um der englischen Rechtskreis gehörenden Ländern Schwarzafrikas.* Marburg, Germany: Institut für Genossenschaftswesen in Entwicklungsländern der Philipps-Universität, 1971.

Münkner, Hans H., and E. Shah. *Creating a Favourable Climate and Conditions for Cooperative Development in Africa.* Geneva: ILO, Enterprise and Cooperative Development Department, 1993.

N'Guyen Manh Tu. *La coopération en Afrique Occidentale.* Abidjan: CENAPEC, 1973.

Owen, Ferris, and Felix Rondeau. *Cooperatives in West Africa.* Chicago: CLUSA, 1966.

Petersen, G. *Genossenschaften in Britisch-Indien und Tropisch-Afrika.* Hamburg: Hansischer Gildenval, 1939.

Report of a Regional Workshop on Agrarian Transformation in Centrally Planned Economies in Africa. Rome: FAO, 1984.

Report of the FAO/ILO/IFAP ad hoc Consultation of Experts on Problems of Agricultural Cooperatives and Other Agricultural Associations in Countries of Africa South of Sahara, Niamey, Niger, December, 1967. Rome: FAO, 1967.

Report on the Expert Consultation on Cooperatives and Other Farmers' Organizations in Agrarian Reform Areas in Africa and the Near East, Cairo, December, 1972. Rome: FAO, 1972.

Review of and Strategies for Cooperative Development in East, Central and Southern Africa: Proceedings of the First African Ministerial Cooperative Conference, Gaborone, Botswana, May, 1984. Moshi, Tanzania: ICA, ROECSA, 1984.

Riley, Norman, and H. R. Amit, eds. *West African Seminar, February, 1975: Report of Proceedings.* Antigonish: Coady International Institute, 1975.

Schmandt, M. *Les coopératives de crédit appliquées à l'agriculture en Afrique.* Paris: Mouton, 1963.

Schumacher, C. *Les coopératives, clé de la prospérité; un guide pour l'Afrique.* Brussels: Les Cahiers africains, 1970.

Search for New Lines of Action and Strategies for Cooperative Development Specific to West Africa—various country reports. Abidjan: ICA ROWA, 1986.

Seibel, H. Dieter, and Michael Koll. *Einheimische Genossenschaften in Afrika: Formen wirtschaftlicher Zusammenarbeit bei westafrikanischen Stämmen.* Freiburg, Germany: Bertelsmann Universitätverlag, 1968. (Introduction also in English and French.)

Strickland, C. F. *Cooperation for Africa,* London: Oxford University Press; reissued 1963.

Tardy, L., and M. Colombain. *La coopération dans les colonies.* Paris: FNCC, 1931.

Taylor, David R. F., and Fiona Mackenzie, eds. *Development From Within: Survival in Rural Africa.* London and New York: Routledge, 1992.

Trappe, Paul. *Die Entwicklungsfunktion des Genossenschaftswesens am Beispiel ostafrikanischer Stämme.* Neuwied, Germany: Luchterhand, 1966.

Widstrand, Carl G., ed. *Cooperatives and Rural Development in East Africa.* Uppsala, Sweden: Scandinavian Institute of African Studies, 1970; New York: Africana Publishing Corporation, 1970.

Widstrand, Carl G., and Yash P. Ghai, eds. *African Cooperatives and Efficiency.* Uppsala, Sweden: Scandinavian Institute of African Studies, 1972.

Williams, Thomas T. *Seminar on Cooperative Experience in Africa, Nairobi, 1977.* Baton Rouge, La.: Southern University and A and M College, 1977.

VII. D. 4. c. Cooperative Experience—Asia/Pacific

Annotated Bibliography of Literature Produced by the Cooperative Movements in South-East Asia. New Delhi: ICA, ROECSEA, 1964.

Asian and Pacific Regional Agricultural Credit Association. *Report on the First General Assembly of the Association and the 3rd Asian Conference on Agricultural Credit and Cooperatives, New Delhi, October, 1977.* Bangkok: FAO, 1978.

A Bibliography of Cooperation in the South Pacific. Noumea, New Caledonia: South Pacific Commission, 1953.

Campbell, W. H. *Practical Cooperation in Asia and Africa.* Cambridge, U.K.: Heffer and Sons, 1951.

Catalogue of the South Pacific Commission Library on Cooperation. Noumea, New Caledonia: South Pacific Commission, 1963.

Cooperative-Government Relationship: Report and Other Documentation on the Second ICA Asia-Pacific Conference of Ministers Responsible for Cooperative Development, Jakarta, February, 1992. New Delhi: ICA, ROAP, 1992.

Cooperative Legislation in Asia: A Study. New Delhi: ICA, ROAP, 1991.

Cooperative Movements in Afro-Asian Countries. New Delhi: Afro-Asian Rural Reconstruction Organization, 1969.

Cooperative Press in South-East Asia. New Delhi: ICA, ROECSEA, 1969.

Cooperative Trade Directory for South-East Asia. New Delhi: ICA, ROECSEA, 1967.

Cooperatives and the Socio-economic Problems of Asia. Kuala Lumpur: ICA, 1964.

Cooperatives as Institutions for Development of the Rural Poor. Dacca, Bangladesh: Center on Integrated Rural Development for Asia and the Pacific, Study Series No. 86, 1986.

The Development of the Cooperative Movement in Asia. Geneva: ILO, 1949.

Directory of Cooperative Organizations in South-East Asia. New Delhi: ICA, ROECSEA, 1966. (Issued periodically.)

Dwivedi, R. C., ed. *Asia in ICA: Participation of Asian Cooperatives in ICA Congresses, 1900–1988.* New Delhi: ICA, ROAP, 1989.

———, ed. *Cooperative Ministers Conference, Sydney, Australia, February, 1990: Report.* New Delhi: ICA, ROAP, 1990.

———, ed. *Role of Government in Promoting Cooperative Development in Asia: Report of the Asian Regional Consultation, Singapore, 1988.* New Delhi: ICA, ROAP, 1988.

Eisenberg, W. *Foreign Trade of Cooperatives Based in South and East Asia; Performance, Problems and Prospects.* London: ICA, 1966.

Fourth Technical Meeting on Cooperatives, Noumea, New Caledonia, March, 1973. Noumea: South Pacific Commission, 1973.

Gunawardana, H. P. Lionel. *ICA in South-East Asia: The First Decade.* New Delhi: ICA, ROECSEA, 1971.

Guyart, J. *Développement communautaire et coopération dans le Pacifique sud.* Paris: Centre de recherches coopératives, 1959.

Inayatullah. *Cooperatives and Development in Asia: A Study of Cooperatives in Fourteen Rural Communities in Iran, Pakistan and Ceylon.* Geneva: UNRISID, 1972.

————. *Cooperatives and Planned Change in Asian Rural Community.* Geneva: UNRISID, 1970.

International Cooperative Alliance. *Cooperative Leadership in South-East Asia.* New York: Asia Publishing House, 1963.

Jacobsen, B. *Survey of Potential Export Products from Cooperatives in Selected Asian Countries.* Geneva: International Trade Center, UNCTAD/GATT 1979.

Lamming, G. N. *Promotion of Small Farmers' Cooperatives in Asia.* Rome: FAO, Economic and Social Development Paper No. 14, 1980.

Ledesma, A. L., et al. *The Cooperative Experience in Asian Cultures—Workshop Report.* Philippines: Center for the Development of Human Resources in Rural Asia, 1983.

Madane, M. V. *Agricultural Cooperation in South-East Asia—A Review.* New Delhi: ICA, ROECSEA, 1972.

————. *International Cooperative Trade in South-East Asia.* New Delhi: ICA, ROECSEA, 1973.

Maslennikov, Vladimir P. *The Cooperative Movement in Asia and Africa: Problems and Prospects.* Moscow: Progress Publishers, 1990.

Münkner, Hans H. *Cooperatives for the Rich or for the Poor? With the Special Reference to Cooperative Development and Cooperative Law in Asia.* Marburg, Germany: Philipps-Universität, 1976.

Overholt, W. H. *Peasant Organization in South-East Asia.* Croton-on-Hudson, N.Y.: Hudson Institute, 1976.

Prakash, Daman, ed. *Needs and Capacities of Cooperative Organizations in Developing Countries of Asia: Regional Compendium.* New Delhi: ICA, ROAP, 1989.

Rana, J. M. *Forms of Government Aid and Cooperative Democracy in South-East Asia.* New Delhi: ICA, ROECSEA, 1974.

Recent Changes, Trends, and Developments of the Cooperative Movement in South-East Asia. New Delhi: ICA, ROECSEA, 1979.

Report of the Asian Top-Level Cooperative Leaders' Conference, Tokyo, 1973. New Delhi: ICA, ROECSEA, 1973.

Report of the Regional Seminar on the Organization and Functioning of Cooperative Unions in South-East Asia, Seoul, 1966. New Delhi: ICA, ROECSEA, 1966.

Schiller, O. *Entwicklungsphasen und Gegenwartsprobleme des Genossenschaftwesens in Südostasien.* Göttingen, Germany: Schwartz, 1964.

Selected Problems of Cooperative Development: International Seminar, April, 1975, Berastagi, Indonesia. Berastagi: Friedrich Ebert Foundation, 1975.

Selwyn-Clarke, Hilda. *New Hope in Asia: A Story of Cooperation.* Manchester: Coop Union, 1952.

Singh, Mohinder. *Cooperatives in Asia.* New York: Praeger, 1970.

Strategies for the Development of Consumer Cooperative Movements in Asia: Report of the Workshop held at Kuala Lumpur, Malaysia, December, 1988. New Delhi: ICA, ROAP, 1988.

Summary Reports on Some Topics Concerning the Development of Cooperation in South East Asia. Stockholm: KF, 1966.

Taimni, K. K. *Creating a Favourable Climate and Conditions for Cooperative Development in Asia.* Geneva: ILO, Enterprise and Cooperative Development Department, 1994.

Valko, Laszlo. *The Cooperative Law in Asia.* Pullman: Washington State University, 1969.

Venkatappiah, B. *Regional Report on Training Facilities for Personnel of Credit Cooperatives and Agricultural Banks (Nepal, Bangladesh, Sri Lanka and India).* Rome: FAO, 1979.

Weeraman, P. E. *The Effect of Cooperative Law on the Autonomy of Cooperatives in South-East Asia: Regional Paper III.* New Delhi: ICA, ROECSEA, 1974.

———. *The ICA in South East Asia.* New Delhi: ICA, ROECSEA, 1971.

VII. D. 4. d. Cooperative Experience—Caribbean

Caribbean Commission. *Cooperatives in the Caribbean.* Port-of-Spain, Trinidad: Kent House, 1954.

Cheesman, W. J. W. *Handbook for Cooperative Personnel in the Caribbean.* Port-of-Spain, Trinidad: FAO, 1956.

Cooperativismo Centroamericano en Cifras. San José, Costa Rica: ICA ROA, 1992.

Dierckxsenns, Wim, and Jorge V. Roldan. *Nuevas estrategias del cooperativismo regional para el siglo XXI.* San José, Costa Rica: CCC-CA, 1994.

Directorio regional de cooperativas: Organismos de integración y cooperativas, 1989–1990. San José, Costa Rica: CCC-CA, 1994.

Gretton, R. *The Role of the Cooperative Movement in Economic Development, with Special Reference to the Caribbean Area.* Rome: FAO, 1957.

ILO/DANIDA Caribbean Cooperative Development Project: Final Report. Geneva: ILO, 1979.

Kwayana, E. *Marketing by Public Enterprises and Cooperatives—the Place of Marketing Boards. Conference on Agricultural Marketing for English-speaking Countries of the Caribbean, St. Vincent, 1969.* Rome: FAO, 1969.

Perspectivas del cooperativismo para la década del 90. San José, Costa Rica: CCC-CA, 1990.

Realidad y retos del cooperativismo del Caribe y Centro América. San José, Costa Rica: CCC-CA, 1990.

Report of a Regional Conference of Ministers Responsible for Cooperative Development in the Caribbean. Tobago: ILO, 1974.

Report to the Federal Government of the West Indies on Cooperative Development in Dominica, Barbados, Grenada, St. Lucia and St. Kitts-Nevis-Anguilla. Geneva: ILO, 1961.

Technical Meeting on Cooperatives in the Caribbean, Port-of-Spain, Trinidad, 1951. Washington, D.C.: FAO, 1951.

Wasserstrom, R. *Grassroots Development in Latin America and the Caribbean: Oral Histories of Social Change.* New York: Praeger, 1985.

VII. D. 4. e. Cooperative Experience—Latin America

América Latina: sindicatos y cooperativas. Seminario Latinoamericano sobre Sindicatos y cooperativas en el desarrollo de América Latina, Santa Barbara, Costa Rica, 1970. San José, Costa Rica: Centro de Estudios Democráticos de América Latina, 1971.

Angueira Miranda, M. A. *Explorando el futuro: El movimiento, el método cooperativo y sus posibilidades.* Buenos Aires: Intercoop, 1975.

Benecke, Dieter W. *Sinopsis del movimiento cooperativo en America Latina.* Bogota: Universidad Santo Tomás de Aquino, 1976.

Berthelot, J. *Communautés andines et développement coopératif.* Paris: Collège coopératif, 1975.

Cardoso, M. *Bases para el derecho cooperativo americano.* Washington, D.C.: Unión Panamericana, 1950.

Carrol, T. F. *Rural Cooperation in Latin America.* Geneva: UNRISID, 1968.

Chávez Nuñez, Fernando. *Análisis comparativo de la legislación cooperativa de Centroamérica y Panamá.* Washington, D.C.: Unión Panamericana, 1966.

———. *El cooperativismo agrario en América Latina.* Washington, D.C.: Unión Panamericana, 1962.

———. *Estudio comparativo de la legislación cooperativa de América.* Washington, D.C.: Unión Panamericana, 1957.

———. *La legislación cooperativa en América.* Washington, D.C.: Unión Panamericana, 1947.

Checchi and Company. *Cooperatives in Economic Growth: A Proposed Inter-American Cooperative Finance System.* Washington, D.C.: Checchi, 1963.

Coady, M. M. *Las cooperativas como método de desarrollo de regiones y comunidades.* Washington, D.C.: Unión Panamericana, 1964.

The Cooperative Movement in the Americas, an International Symposium. Montreal: ILO, 1943. (Also in Spanish.)

Cooperatives. Washington, D.C.: Pan American Union, [n.d.] (periodical).

Cooperativismo latinoamericano: Antecedentes y perspectivas. Santiago: Naciones Unidas, Comision Economica para América Latina y el Caribe, 1989.

Cooperativismo latinoamericano en cifras. Bogata: ICA, ROAM, 1990.

Cooperativismo latinoamericano en cifras. Bogata: OCA, 1995.

Cooperativismo y desarrollo rural: La experiencia latinoamericana. Quito: Ediciones de la Pontifica Universidad Católica del Ecuador, 1985.

Cooperativismo y las cooperativas en América Latina. San José, Costa Rica: OIT, Oficina area en San José, 1975.

Cooperativismo y sindicalismo: protagonistas del cambio social. San José, Costa Rica: CCC-CA, 1991.

Cooperativistas de caficultores latinoamericanos. La Catalina, Costa Rica: Biblioteca del CEDAL, 1971.

Desarrollo del movimiento cooperativo en América. Washington, D.C.: Unión Panamericana, 1954.

Desroche, Henri. *Problèmes coopératifs sud-américains.* Paris: Centre de recherches coopératives, 1964.

Development of the Cooperative Movement in America. Washington, D.C.: Pan American Union, 1953. (Also in Spanish.)

Dierckxsenns, Wim, and Jorge V. Roldan. *Nuevas estrategias del cooperativismo regional para el siglo XXI.* San José, Costa Rica: CCC-CA, 1994.

Directorio regional de cooperativas: Organismos de integración y cooperativas, 1889–1990. San José, Costa Rica: CCC-CA, 1994.

Domínguez Vial, Vicente. *Leyes de cooperativas: Ensayo de legislación comparada en países de Latinoamérica.* La Paz: Universidad Católica Boliviana, Departamento de Estudios Cooperativos, 1978.

Fabra Rivas, Antonio. *La cooperación, su porvenir está en las Américas.* Bogota: Editorial Optima, 1941.

———. *The Cooperative Movement in Latin America: Its Significance in Hemisphere Solidarity.* Albuquerque: University of New Mexico Press, 1943.

———. *Hacia un nuevo orden economico: Reflexiones dedicadas a la juventud iberoamericana.* Medellín, Colombia: Imprenta de la Universidad de Antioquia, 1943.

Fals Borda, O. *Cooperatives and Rural Development in Latin America.* Geneva: UNRISID, 1971.

Final Act: Second Inter-American Conference on Cooperatives, Santiago, Chile, May 1974. Santiago and Washington, D.C.: Organization of American States, 1974.

La formation coopérative en Amérique latine. Geneva: BIT, 1977.

Garcia, A. *Cooperativas agrarias en el desarrollo de América Latina.* Bogota: Ediciones Colatina, 1976.

———. *Las cooperativas en las reformas agrarias de la América Latina.* Lima: ISI, 1969.

———. *Régimen cooperativo y economía latinoamericana.* Bogota: Editorial Espiral, 1946.

Genossenschaften in der Entwicklungspolitik. Ein Ost- und West-Systemvergleich für Lateinamerika. Bonn: Friedrich-Naumann-Stiftung, 1982.

Genossenschaftswesen in Lateinamerika (Kurzbibliographie). Hamburg: Institut für Iberoamerika-Kunde, 1981.

Grosfeld, Jan. *Les coopératives et les changements agraires en Amérique latine.* Paris: Institut national de la recherche agronomique, 1978.

Hirschman, A. O. *Getting Ahead Collectively: Grassroots Experiences in Latin America.* New York: Pergamon Press, 1984.

Informe final del Seminario Interamericano de Cooperativas Agropecuarias y de Consumo. Bogota: Editorial Linotypie Bolívar, 1969.

Landsberger, H. *Latin America Peasant Movements.* Ithaca, N.Y.: Cornell University Press, 1969.

Manual de cooperativismo. Mexico City: Inter-American Regional Organization of Workers of the ICFTU. 1964.

Montolio, José M. *Legislación cooperativa en América Latina: Situación, derecho comparado y proceso de armonización.* Madrid: Ministero de Trabajo y Seguridad Social, 1990.

Morris, A. C. *A Study of the Cooperative Organizations in Selected Countries in South America.* Pullman: Washington State University, 1962.

Organización de los Estados Americanos. *Colonización y cooperativas.* Washington, D.C.: Unión Panamericana, 1964.

Ortiz Villacis, M. *Aspectos del problema agrario latinoamericano y la organización cooperativa.* Quito: Casa de la Cultura Ecuatoriana, 1968.

Perspectivas del cooperativismo para la decada del 90. San José, Costa Rica: CCC-CA, 1990.

Powel, J. *Agricultural Cooperatives in Latin America.* Washington, D.C.: Pan American Union, 1942.

The Program of Possible and Potential Activities by Credit Cooperatives in Latin America. Bonn: Friedrich Ebert Foundation, 1968.

Realidad y retos del cooperativismo del Caribe y Centro América. San José, Costa Rica: CCC-CA, 1990.

Reconversión y competitividad cooperativa: productos de la conferencia regional de El Salvador. San José, Costa Rica: ACI ROAM, 1993.

Reflexión sobre el cooperativismo latinoamericano en el año 2000. VI Seminario Iberoamericano de Educación Cooperativa. Buenos Aires: Intercoop, 1984; Rosario, Argentina: Instituto de la Cooperación, Fundación Educacional, 1984.

Rodriguez Quesada, José R. *Nuevo enfoque sobre el cooperativismo latinoamericano.* San José, Costa Rica: Mg. Editores, 1994.

Rojas Coria, R. *El cooperativismo en América del Sur.* Mexico City: Confederación Nacional de Cooperativas, 1954.

Rojas Viquez, Marielos. *Proyecto de investigación: situación actual del cooperativismo en América Central.* San José, Costa Rica: Universidad de Costa Rica, 1989.

Rosa, A. R. *Despertando al Gigante.* Mexico City: Editorial La Prensa, 1971.

Ruiz Lujan, Samuel. *Tercera opción: cooperativismo auténtico, un desafío para desarrollo de los pueblos de América Latina.* Bogota: Ediciones Tercer Mundo, 1976.

San Martin G., Orlando, Wim Dierckxsens, and Jorge Vargas Roldan. *Cooperativismo centroamericano en cifras: Con énfasis en sector agropecuario.* San José, Costa Rica: CCC-CA, 1992.

Series on Cooperatives. Washington, D.C.: Pan American Union, 1936– .

Stavenhagen, R. *Agrarian Problems and Peasants' Movements in Latin America.* New York: Doubleday, 1970.

Steele, Pablo. *¿Quiénes son los dueños de América Latina? El cooperativismo, una opción de rescate.* Panama: Instituto Cooperativo Inter-americano, 1973.

A Survey of the Cooperative Movement in the American Republics. Washington, D.C.: Office of Inter-American Affairs, 1944.

III Encuentro del Comité Regional Bancario para América Latina de la Alianza Cooperativa Internacional. Buenos Aires: FEBANCOOP, 1992.

Tereshtenko, Valery. *Cooperation in Latin America: A Bibliographical Review of the Literature.* New York: WPA, 1942.

Texier, J. *La Coopération et les réformes agraires en Amérique latine.* Paris: Institut des études coopératives, 1966.

Wasserstrom, R. *Grassroots Development in Latin America and the Caribbean: Oral Histories of Social Change.* New York: Praeger, 1985.

Whyte, W. F. *Working with Small Farmers and Agricultural Cooperatives in Latin America.* Tokyo: Food and Agriculture Policy Research Center, 1985.

Yuri Izquierdo, M. *Cooperativas agricolas y pecuarias.* Washington, D.C.: Unión Panamericana, 1956.

Zambrano, Miguel A. *El cooperativismo y el problema indígena.* Washington, D.C.: Unión Panamericana, 1951.

VII. D. 4. f. Cooperative Experience—Near East and North Africa

Abeidat, A. "The Concept of Cooperation in Islam and Arab Society." *Journal of Rural Cooperation* 3 (1, 1975): 3–12.

"Agricultural Cooperative Development in the Middle East." In *Year Book of Agricultural Cooperation,* ed. Kenneth J. McCready. Oxford: Blackwell, 1972, 1–12.

Atlas de la mutualité agricole en Afrique du nord, assurances, crédit, coopération, 1907–1947. Algiers: Caisse centrale de réassurance des mutuelles agricoles de l'Afrique du nord, 1947.

"Cooperative Legislation—Present Trends in Several Near and Middle Eastern Countries." In *Cooperative Information,* ILO, Geneva (2, 1968): 1–21.

Cooperative Organization. Regional Conference for the Near and Middle East of the ILO, Teheran, 1951. Geneva: ILO, 1950.

Idris, M. *The Mediterranean Cooperative Movements and Social-Economic Development in the Region.* Giza, Egypt: Central Agricultural Cooperative Union, 1985.

Imam, A. *El Taawan-wa mayadin el tanneya el ektemayea (Cooperative Principles, Objectives, Situation).* Cairo: Maktaba Ein Shams, 1970 (Arabic).

Klower, G. G. "Arabischer Sozialismus, Genossenschaften und Islam." *Internationales Afrikaforum* 14 (2, 1978): 152–162.

Labor Survey of North Africa. Geneva: ILO, 1960.

North African Workshop on Cooperatives and Small Farmers. Washington, D.C.: ACDI, 1977.

Paris, O. *A Study of the Working of Cooperatives in Cyprus, Palestine and Egypt.* Valletta, Malta: Department of Agriculture, 1946.

Plum, W. *Sozialer Wandel in Maghreb: Voraussetzungen und Erfahrungen der genossenschaftlichen Entwicklung.* Hanover: Friedrich-Ebert-Stiftung, 1967.

Report of the FAO Seminar on Marketing Programs, Procedures, and Organizations in the Near East, Beirut, November, 1968. Rome: FAO, 1969.

Report on the Expert Consultation on Cooperatives and Other Farmers' Organizations in Agrarian Reform Areas in Africa and the Near East, Cairo, December, 1972. Rome: FAO, 1972.

A Review of Rural Cooperation in Developing Areas. Geneva: UNRISID, 1969.

Soliman, M. A. *The Role of Cooperatives in Agrarian Reform. A Regional Survey of Selected Countries of the Near East.* Rome: FAO, WCARRD Meeting Papers, 1977.

Treydte, K. P., and W. Ule, eds. *Agriculture in the Near East.* Bonn-Bad Godesberg: Verlag Neue Gesellschaft GmbH, 1973.

Verdier, J. M., P. Desanti, and J. Karila. *Structures, foncières et développement rural au Maghreb.* Paris: PUF, 1969.

VII. D. 5. Assistance to Cooperatives in Developing Countries

Amir, S. *Israel's Development Cooperation with Africa, Asia and Latin America.* New York, Praeger, 1974.

Belloncle, Guy. *Organisations internationales et promotion coopérative dans les pays en voie de développement.* Paris: BECC, [n.d.].

Campbell, Wallace J. "Opportunities for Cooperation Among U.S. Cooperatives and Those in Other Countries." In *American Cooperation, 1982,* 183–194. Washington, D.C.: AIC, 1982.

Campleman, G. *International Collaboration in Assistance to Fishermen's Cooperatives. International Conference on Investment in Fisheries.* Rome: FAO, 1969.

Chávez Nuñez, F. *Some Observations on External Assistance to the Latin American Cooperative Movement.* Washington, D.C.: Pan American Union, 1968.

Commitment to Development Through Cooperatives. A Progress Report of the Overseas Development Programs of the Cooperative League of the U.S.A. Washington, D.C.: CLUSA, 1974.

Coordination, Integration and Marketing: Some Experience of the Swedish Cooperative Movement and the Adaptation to Conditions in Asia; Reports Submitted to the 6th Seminar by Participants. Stockholm: SCC, 1968.

Current Assistance to Cooperatives in Developing Countries—1982–1983. Supplement 1—Agency Profiles. Rome: COPAC, 1984.

Digby, Margaret. "Aid for Cooperatives in Developing Countries. Report of the Third International Conference." In *Year Book of Agricultural Cooperation, 1971,* ed. Kenneth McCready. Oxford: Blackwell, 1971, 273–279.

Directory of Agencies Assisting Cooperatives in Developing Countries. Rome: COPAC, 1989. (Revised/reissued periodically.)

Douthit, D. *The Role of US Cooperatives in the Foreign Assistance Program.* Washington, D.C.: Advisory Committee on Overseas Cooperative Development, 1970.

Holmberg, A. "Nordic Assistance to the Cooperative Movement in East Africa." In *Year Book of Agricultural Cooperation, 1971,* ed. Kenneth McCready. Oxford: Blackwell, 1971, 118–123.

Howell, J. *UK Aid to Cooperatives in Developing Countries, 1977–1981. An Evaluation.* London: Overseas Development Administration, 1982.

International Financing of Cooperative Enterprise in Developing Countries: A Study Prepared by the International Cooperative Alliance in Collaboration with the ILO, FAO and COPAC. Geneva: ILO, 1974.

Kanel, Donald. *Some Observations Based on Issues Raised in the Nine Workshops on Cooperatives, Small Farmers and Development.* Madison: University of Wisconsin, Land Tenure Center Paper Number 123, 1982.

Krasheninnikov, A. I. "Centrosoyus and the Developing Countries." *Review of International Cooperation,* ICA, London, 65 (1, 1972): 21–23.

"Nordic Cooperative Projects in East Africa in the Years 1962–83." *Swedish Cooperative Center News,* Stockholm (1, 1983): 16.

Parnell, Edgar. *Movement-to-Movement Aid.* Rome: COPAC, 1983.

Problems Relating to the Establishment of Cooperative Movements in Non-Self Governing Territories and Government Actions for Their Solution. Geneva: ILO, 1951.

Rana, J. M. *Forms of Government Aid and Cooperative Democracy in South-East Asia.* New Delhi: ICA, ROECSEA, Cooperative Series No. 12, 1974.

Report on Swedish Cooperative Development Assistance 1975–76. Stockholm: SCC, 1977. (Report issued annually.)

Role of Rural Organizations in Planning and Implementing Development Programs. Paris: International Federation of Agricultural Producers, 1974.

Saxena, Suren K. *Organization of Technical Assistance (to Developing Country Cooperatives) in Cooperative Movements in Canada, Sweden and the United States—Some Lessons for Other Movements.* Rome: COPAC, Number 84/10, 1984.

Shaffer, J. R. "The Cooperative Development Activities of the United States Agency for International Development." In *Yearbook of Agricultural Cooperation 1980,* ed. C. E. McKone and J. E. Bayley. Oxford: Blackwell, 1981, 43–61.

Shakya, S. R. *Forms of Government Aid and Cooperative Democracy. Background paper presented at the Asian Top Level Cooperative Leader's Conference, Tokyo, October, 1973.* New Delhi: ICA, ROECSEA, 1973.

Sprudzs, A. *Technical Assistance Delivery to Developing Cooperatives.* Ottawa: International Development Research Center, 1981.

Swedish Cooperative Technical Assistance to Developing Countries. Stockholm: KF, 1967.

Technical Assistance for Cooperatives in Developing Countries: Needs and Responses. Report of the 43rd International Cooperative Seminar, Dresden, September 1975. London: ICA, 1976.

Third International Conference on Aid for Cooperatives in Developing Countries, Loughborough, April, 1971. London: Overseas Development Administration, 1971.

"Towards Movement-to-Movement Cooperation." *Review of International Cooperation*, ICA, Geneva, 76 (1, 1983): 12–17.

Youngjohns, B. J. "British Government Assistance to Cooperatives in Developing Countries." In *Year Book of Agricultural Cooperation, 1970,* ed. Margaret Digby and Kenneth J. McCready. Oxford: Blackwell, 1970.

Zavidov, R. *L'expérience israélienne du développement des villages coopératifs dans les pays neufs.* Paris: Centre de recherches coopératives, 1974.

VIII. INTERNATIONAL COOPERATIVE ORGANIZATIONS

VIII. A. International Cooperative Alliance

Bottini, E. *Década del desarrollo cooperativo 1971–1980.* Buenos Aires: Consumo, 1973.

The Cooperative Development Decade 1971–1980. London: ICA, 1971.

Faucherre, H. *60 Jahre Internationaler Genossenschaftsbund, 1895–1955.* Basel: Buchdruckerei VSK, 1960.

International Cooperative Bulletin. (Periodical). London: ICA, 1907–1927. (Renamed Review of International Cooperation.)

International Cooperative Trade: Problems and Prospects. London: ICA, 1974.

Müller, Hans. *Geschichte der internationalen Genossenschafts-bewegung.* Halberstadt, Germany: H. Meyer, 1924.

———, ed. *Yearbook of International Cooperation.* London and Zurich: ICA, 1910– .

Report of the Congress. London and Geneva: ICA, various dates.

Review of International Cooperation (periodical). London and Geneva: ICA, 1928– present. (Continues *International Cooperative Bulletin.*)

Rhodes, Rita. *The International Cooperative Alliance During War and Peace 1910–1959.* Geneva: ICA, 1995.

Rhodes, R., and D. Mavrogiannis. *Thematic Guide to ICA Congresses 1895–1995.* Geneva: ICA, 1995.

Statistics of Affiliated Organizations. London and Geneva: ICA (issued annually).

Watkins, W. P. *The International Cooperative Alliance—1985–1970.* London: ICA, 1970.

———. *Die internationale Genossenschaftsbewegung.* Frankfurt: Deutsche Genossenschaftskasse, 1969.

Weeraman, P. E. *The ICA in South-East Asia.* New Delhi: ICA, ROECSEA, 1971.

Note: Numerous additional entries showing the International Cooperative Alliance (ICA) or its Regional Offices as author or publisher appear in the bibliography under a variety of subject headings.

VIII. B. International Raiffeisen Union

IRU-Courier. Bonn: International Raiffeisen Union. Published three times a year in English, French, Spanish and German.

Reports of the International Raiffeisen Cooperative Seminars. Issued periodically. The VIIIth Seminar was held in Budapest, Hungary, in October 1996.

VIII. C. World Council of Credit Unions

Davis, Robert W., and Alfredo Lanza, eds. *International Digest of Laws Governing Credit Unions: A Reference Guide to the Laws Under Which Credit Unions Are Organized and Operate in Various Countries and Jurisdictions Throughout the World.* Madison, Wis.: WOCCU, 1993.

Jerving, Jim. *The Central Finance Facility: A Guide to Development and Operations.* Madison, Wis.: WOCCU, 1987.

——— *Financial Management for Credit Union Managers and Directors.* Madison, Wis.: WOCCU, 1989; 2nd edition, 1994.

Tenenbaum, David. *Involving Credit Union Volunteers.* Madison, Wis.: WOCCU, 1988.

Note: Numerous additional entries showing the World Council of Credit Unions (WOCCU) as author or publisher appear in the bibliography under a variety of subject headings.

IX. THE UNITED NATIONS SYSTEM AND COOPERATIVES

IX. A. United Nations Secretary General's Reports

National Experience in Achieving Far-Reaching Social and Economic Changes for the Purpose of Social Progress. National Experience in Promoting the Cooperative Movement. Report of the Secretary General. New York: UN, General Assembly, 1983.

National Experience in Promoting the Cooperative Movement. Report of the Secretary General. New York: UN, ECOSOC, 1985.

The Role of the Cooperative Movement in the Achievement of the Goals and Objectives of the Second United Nations Development Decade—Report of the Secretary General. New York: UN, 1970.

IX. B. United Nations Secretariat

Cooperative Housing for Africa. Meeting on Technical and Social Problems of Urbanization, Addis Ababa, January, 1969. New York: UN, ECOSOC, 1969.

Louis, R. "United Nations General Assembly Resolution and the Future of Cooperatives." *Cooperative Information,* ILO, Geneva, 63 (1, 1977), 1–21.

Morsink, Hubert. "Technical Assistance to Cooperatives: The Revolution in Priorities as Seen by the United Nations."*Review of International Cooperation,* ICA, London, 68 (6, 1975), 190–196.

Mouton, G. *Crédit agricole et coopération en Haiti.* New York: UN, 1956.

Organización Naciones Unidas. *El progreso rural a través de las cooperativas.* Washington, D.C.: Departamento de Asuntos Económicos, 1953.

Promotion of the Cooperative Movement During the Second United Nations Development Decade. New York: UN, 1972.

Report of the Seminar on the Role of Government in Promoting the Cooperative Movement in Developing Countries, Moscow, May, 1987. Vienna: UN Office at Vienna, 1987.

Rural Housing, A Review of World Conditions. New York: UN, 1969.

Rural Progress Through Cooperatives: The Place of Cooperative Associations in Agricultural Development. New York: UN, Department of Economic Affairs, 1954.

IX. C. United Nations Regional Economic Commissions

IX. C. I. Economic Commission for Africa

The Cooperative Movement in Africa. New York: UN, Economic Commission for Africa, 1962.

Dadson, J. A. *Production Cooperatives and Rural Development in Ghana.* Addis Ababa: UN, Economic Commission for Africa, 1985.

Mascarenhas, O., and M. Mbilinyi. *Women and Development in Tanzania. An Annotated Bibliography.* Addis Ababa: UN, Economic Commission for Africa, African Training and Research Center for Women, 1980.

Opondo, Diane. *Women and Cooperatives: Egypt, the Libyan Arab Jamahiriya and the Sudan.* Addis Ababa: UN, Economic Commission for Africa, 1980.

Rapport du Séminaire sur la femme et les coopératives, Yaoundé, novembre, 1977. Addis Ababa: Nations unies, Commission économique pour l'Afrique, 1978.

Rapport du Séminaire sur la formation des femmes en matière de coopérative villageoise, Kabala, Mali, mai, 1980. Addis Ababa: Commission économique pour l'Afrique, 1981.

Report of the Workshop on the Participation of Women in Development Through Cooperatives With Special Emphasis on Handicrafts and Small-Scale Industries, Khartoum, October, 1979. Addis Ababa: UN, Economic Commission for Africa, 1980.

IX. C. 2. Economic Commission for Asia and the Pacific

Liang, C. C. *Mobilization of Rural Savings with Special Reference to the Far East.* New York: UN, Economic Commission for Asia, 1951.

Participation of Women in Dairy Development in South Asia. Bangkok: UN, Economic and Social Commission for Asia and the Pacific, 1981.

IX. C. 3. Economic Commission for Latin America and the Caribbean

Cooperativismo latinoamericano: Antecedentes y perspectivas. Santiago: Naciones Unidas, Comisión Económica para América Latina y el Caribe, 1989.

IX. D. Food and Agriculture Organization (FAO)

Gretton, R. *FAO and Cooperatives.* Rome: FAO, 1968.

Note: Numerous additional entries showing the Food and Agriculture Organization (FAO) as author or publisher appear in the bibliography under a variety of subject headings.

IX. E. International Labour Office (ILO)

Alcock, A. *History of the International Labour Organisation.* London: Macmillan, 1970.

Cardenas, G. "La OIT y la planeación del desarrollo en los países en vía de desarrollo." *Revista 1982,* No. 374: 301–319.

Cooperative Information. Geneva: ILO, 1924–1977. (Periodical, published in English, French and Spanish.)

"The Cooperative Movement and the ILO." *Cooperative Information 1969,* ILO, Geneva (3, 1969): 128.

ILO and UNDP Inter-regional Seminar on the Organization and Development of Work Cooperatives in the Field of Folk and Artistic Handicrafts and Cottage Industry, Poland, September, 1977. Geneva: ILO, 1978.

Ligue des nations. *Conférence des organisations coopératives dans le commerce international.* Geneva: BIT, 1926. (Also in English.)

Note: Numerous additional entries showing the International Labour Organisation (ILO) as author or publisher appear in the bibliography under a variety of subject headings.

IX. F. United Nations Center for Human Settlements (HABITAT)

Community-Based Finance Institutions: The Role of Cooperatives and Credit Unions in Mobilizing Finance for the Improvement of Low Income Human Settlements. Nairobi: HABITAT, 1984.

Community Credit Mechanisms: Training Module. Nairobi: HABITAT, 1989.

Cooperative Housing: Experiences of Mutual Self-Help. Nairobi: HABITAT, 1989.

Women of Kibwezi: A Case Study of the Kibwezi Women's Integrated Rural Development Program. Nairobi: HABITAT, 1990.

IX. G. United Nations Development Program (UNDP)

Cooperative Program Note: Rural Cooperatives—Some Lessons and Suggestions from a UNDP Evaluation Study. Rome: COPAC, 1983.

ILO and UNDP Inter-regional Seminar on the Organization and Development of Work Cooperatives in the Field of Folk and Artistic Handicrafts and Cottage Industry, Poland, September, 1977. Geneva: ILO, 1978.

IX. H. United Nations Educational, Scientific and Cultural Organization (UNESCO)

Ben David, J. *Agricultural Planning and Village Community in Israel.* Paris: UNESCO, 1964.

Colombain, Maurice. *Las cooperativas y la educación fundamental.* Paris: UNESCO, 1950.

———. *Les coopératives et l'éducation de base.* Paris: UNESCO, 1950.

Report of an International Conference of Cooperative Education Leaders (Co-sponsored by ICA and UNESCO). London: ICA, 1970.

Report on the Proceedings of the ICA/UNESCO Conference of African Cooperative Education Leaders. Moshi, Tanzania: ICA, ROECSA, 1973.

School Cooperatives. Paris: UNESCO, 1956.

IX. I. United Nations Fund for Women (UNIFEM)

Women in Cooperatives: Report of the Kenya NGO Sub-Committee Workshop held at the Cooperative College of Kenya, Nairobi, June 1984. Nairobi: Kenya NGO Organizing Committee, Forum '85 of the World Conference of the U.N. Decade for Women, 1985.

IX. J. United Nations Industrial Development Organization (UNIDO)

Nature and Role of Industrial Cooperatives in Industrial Development. Vienna: UNIDO, 1969.
Policies and Measures to Promote Industrial Cooperatives in Africa. New York: UNIDO, 1985.

IX. K. United Nations Conference on Trade and Development (UNCTAD)/General Agreement on Tariffs and Trade (GATT)

Jacobsen, B. *Survey of Potential Export Products from Cooperatives in Selected Asian Countries.* Geneva: International Trade Center, UNCTAD/GATT 1979.

About the Author

Jack Shaffer was born in Los Angeles, California, in 1925, into a family with three sisters and a brother. They were his introduction to the complexities of the concept of cooperation. He was a soldier (private first class) in World War II, trained as an infantryman. He learned the relationship of cooperation and authority, and saw in Europe what happens to a world that does not cooperate.

He graduated from the University of Southern California, where he majored in international relations and was introduced to political activism. At a revival meeting in the Baptist church he then attended (he is now Unitarian), he responded to a call to become a clergyman.

In seminary, at the Claremont School of Theology in California, he studied with two men who became his principal "gurus" and showed him how to integrate mind and action around the concepts of democracy and cooperation. In his preface, he dedicates this book to them.

His career after that was a mixture of accident and design. He became a member of the Centinella Valley, Hollywood and Green Belt consumer cooperatives (all now gone wherever old, failed cooperatives go). He organized and acted as advisor to Walden House, a men's residence cooperative, while working for ten years as Methodist chaplain at his alma mater. A loan from his credit union made possible a journey around the world and firsthand experience of want and need and refugee camps.

While serving as a Peace Corps director in Jamaica, he had an opportunity to work with a group of volunteers who struggled to help establish viable fishing cooperatives in difficult places. He saw how hard it is to institutionalize cooperation.

Periods of work at VISTA (Volunteers in Service to America) and Head Start and two unsuccessful campaigns to become a member of the United States Congress brought him to his formal career with cooperatives.

He worked as coordinator of cooperative development at the Agency for International Development in Washington, D.C., handling AID's relationships with the U.S. cooperative development organizations that help to establish and strengthen cooperatives in developing countries.

His cooperative work took on worldwide dimensions when he was selected in 1981 to be executive secretary of the Committee for the Promotion and Advancement of Cooperatives (COPAC), then based in Rome at FAO. COPAC works to promote and encourage support for cooperatives in the Third World. Much of this book, in fact, addresses issues and questions which brought about the creation of three United Nations agencies—FAO, ILO and the UN Secretariat—and four international nongovernmental organizations—ICA, IFAP, IFPAAW and WOCCU of COPAC.

Now retired, Jack Shaffer has written a book that summarizes much of what he has learned about the people, principles, politics and progress of the cooperative movement around the world. His judgment is that cooperatives are here to stay—and growing day by day. Someone, somewhere, at this very moment, is organizing one.